The Amazon

THE BRADT TRAVEL GUIDE

Roger Harris
Peter Hutchison

Bradt Publications, UK
The Globe Pequot Press Inc, USA

First published in 1998 by Bradt Publications

This second edition published in 2003 by Bradt Travel Guides Ltd,
19 High Street, Chalfont St Peter, Bucks SL9 9QE, England
Published in the USA by The Globe Pequot Press Inc, 246 Goose Lane,
PO Box 480, Guilford, Connecticut 06437-0480

ISBN 1 4162 070 X

British Library Cataloguing in Publication Data
A catalogue record for this book is available from the British Library

Maps Alan Whitaker
Photographs *Front cover* Cayman (Pete Oxford)
Text Roger Harris (RH), Peter Hutchison (PH), Pete Oxford (PO)
Illustrations Oliver Whalley

Typeset from the author's disc by Wakewing
Printed and bound in Italy by Legoprint SpA

About the Authors

Afflicted with an incurable travel bug acquired during his childhood upbringing in Africa, **Roger Harris** now regularly travels throughout South America – camera in one hand, notebook in the other – on his quest for ever more arcane knowledge. Throughout the book he draws on his degrees in biology and his experience leading dozens of natural history and photography tours to the Amazon and other parts of Latin America.

Peter Hutchison arrived in South America in 1993 after travelling through Central America. He lived and worked in Bolivia as a journalist in the mid-1990s and has since dwelled on an unhealthy obsession for Latin America, working as a journalist covering the region. In 2002 Peter received a Winston Churchill Memorial Trust Travelling Fellowship to lead an expedition to attempt the first descent of the River Parapeti in southeast Bolivia. The expedition down the Amazon's most southerly tributary was approved by the Royal Geographic Society.

THE BRADT STORY
Hilary Bradt

The first Bradt travel guide was written by Hilary and George Bradt in 1974 on a river barge floating down a tributary of the Amazon in Bolivia. From their base in Boston, Massachusetts, they went on to write and publish four other backpacking guides to the Americas and one to Africa.

In the 1980s Hilary continued to develop the Bradt list in England, and also established herself as a travel writer and tour leader. The company's publishing emphasis evolved towards broader-based guides to new destinations – usually the first to be published on those countries – complemented by hiking, rail and wildlife guides.

Since winning *The Sunday Times* Small Publisher of the Year Award in 1997, we have continued to fill the demand for detailed, well-written guides to unusual destinations, while maintaining the company's original ethos of low-impact travel.

Travel guides are by their nature continuously evolving. If you experience anything which you would like to share with us, or if you have any amendments to make to this guide, please write; all your letters are read and passed on to the author. Most importantly, do remember to travel with an open mind and to respect the customs of your hosts – it will add immeasurably to your enjoyment.

Contents

LIST OF MAPS

THE AMAZON BASIN

KEY TO STANDARD SYMBOLS

—·—·—	International boundary		🏰	Historic building
- - - - -	District boundary		✝	Church or cathedral
– – – –	National park boundary		♣	Buddhist temple
✈	Airport (international)		🏠	Buddhist monastery
✈	Airport (other)		⛩	Hindu temple
✈	Airstrip		☾	Mosque
🚁	Helicopter service		⚑	Golf course
▬▬	Railway		🏃	Stadium
··········	Footpath		▲	Summit
--🚢--	Car ferry		△	Boundary beacon
--⛴--	Passenger ferry		◉	Outpost
🅿	Petrol station or garage		⤬—⤬	Border post
🅿	Car park		⌂	Rock shelter
🚌	Bus station etc		□—○—□	Cable car, funicular
🚲	Cycle hire		══	Mountain pass
M	Underground station		○	Waterhole
⌂	Hotel, inn etc		☀	Scenic viewpoint
Å	Campsite		✿	Botanical site
♠	Hut		♤	Specific woodland feature
⚱	Wine bar		✲	Lighthouse
✗	Restaurant, café etc		⟋	Marsh
⊠	Post office		⚘	Mangrove
ℓ	Telephone		➤	Bird nesting site
ⓔ	Internet café		✦	Turtle nesting site
⊞	Hospital, clinic etc		∿∿	Coral reef
☖	Museum		➢	Beach
🐘	Zoo		⚶	Scuba diving
𝒊	Tourist information		🐟	Fishing sites
$	Bank			
⚑	Statue or monument			
∴	Archaeological or historic site			

Other map symbols are sometimes shown in separate key boxes with individual explanations for their meanings.

Acknowledgements

From Roger
First edition

I am deeply grateful to all involved in this project. In particular, I thank my family – Mum and Dad in England, my wife Sophie and my sister Jennifer – for their unwavering support.

Lots of people helped make this book possible, and I thank them all, in particular those named below. Any errors remaining are, of course, my own.

For information used in parts of Chapter Five, I thank scientists Ryan Hill and Tracy Munn in Ecuador who showed me hidden secrets of the rainforest I might never have discovered otherwise. I also thank Charlie Strader at Explorations Inc and Peter Jenson at Explorama Lodges in Peru, for their contributions to this project.

Ruth Anne Ronk helped in preparatory proofreading of the manuscript and assisted with the drafting of maps. Angelina Kuchar helped proofread early drafts.

In particular I am grateful to Peter Hutchison for his precise comments on the manuscript, and to Tricia Hayne at Bradt Publications, for overseeing the project from conception to completion.

Besides direct experience I have used notes taken from my conversations with native villagers, shamans, local and US naturalist-guides, and travel professionals here and in the Amazon. I especially thank staff and crew at Amazon Tours and Cruises in Iquitos for use of their facilities on many occasions. Naturalist-guide Daniel Rios in particular provided mountains of information during his shipboard lectures. I tip my cap to all those people with whom I have travelled in South America over the past six years, and who provided their experience, good humour and challenges to enrich my life and, I hope, the content of this book.

Second edition

Many friends helped with accommodation, facilities, and providing updated information. I am indebted to them all. In particular, I thank Peter Jenson of Explorama and Paul Wright of Amazon Tours and Cruises for use of their facilities, and insight into the ever-changing tourism scene around Iquitos. I am especially grateful to William W. Lamar of Green Tracks for correcting parts of *Chapter 5* – remaining errors are mine. George Dávila Flores of Muyuna Lodge kindly added to the table to identify animals by their nocturnal eyeshine.

From Peter

I now know that travel-guide writing is a labour of love and a workload that shouldn't be tolerated by one person without the generous help and support of an intricate network of friends and family.

In South America help came in different shapes and forms from Phil, Alice, Adrian and Alix and Hannah in Bolivia, Vitoria da Riva Carvalho in Alta Floresta,

Brazil, and Roberto Carlos Duorte Morinoni in Cacéres, also in Brazil. Thanks go to these and other friends in South America who helped prove that some journeys were worthwhile, others inadvisable and some just impossible or plain stupid, although you have a lot of fun finding out.

In England, my thanks go out to the many friends who have helped in too many ways to mention here. Special thanks go to my Mum for her keen eye and steady hand in drawing up some of the maps, to Kris and Jim for their continued and dependable support and to Tessa for her calming influence and love.

Long overdue thanks are due to Geoffrey Roy who helped in getting the right tone for the first edition – that gratitude still stands for this edition.

Specific thanks must go to co-author Roger, whose keen eye has weeded out errors that crept into the first edition. Also to Riaan Vorster for the first-hand and detailed information on Pico de Neblina. Thanks also to Hilary Bradt for her many contributions and comments and to Tricia Hayne for her continued support and patience.

Introduction

The Amazon is a river of superlatives. It carries far more water than any other river in the world, with around 16% of all river water passing through its 320km-wide delta, draining an area almost the size of Australia. The volume of sediment deposited by the river in the Atlantic is so great that it stains the sea for up to 300km from the shore. From its source 5,168m high in the Peruvian Andes – less than 200km from the Pacific Ocean – the main stream collects the waters from over 1,100 tributaries as it travels the 6,448km (4,007 miles) to the Atlantic – only the Nile is slightly longer at 6,670km (4,145 miles). Many of the Amazon's tributaries are amongst the world's largest rivers in their own right: the Negro and the Madeira rank as the fifth and sixth largest rivers in the world. Tributaries of the Amazon rise in Peru, Bolivia, Ecuador, Colombia, Venezuela and Brazil, draining 50% of the total area of South America.

For almost half its length the Amazon flows through the world's greatest rainforest, an area larger than the whole of western Europe. The river and the rainforest are inseparable. The Amazon rainforest is as diverse as the Amazon Basin is large, and vast areas remain unexplored and scientifically unresearched.

The Amazon is also home to some of the world's great unresolved myths and tales. From the first European encounters with this 'green hell', the Spanish conquistadors began promoting legends. The first journey downstream by a European, led by Orellana in 1542, recorded tales of warring female tribes that fought like the Amazons of Greek mythology. These female warriors were never found; neither was the tall race of white giants, nor the tribe with their feet facing the wrong way to deceive trackers. The search for the gilded city of El Dorado, meanwhile, continues to this day. With an area so vast and so densely covered in rainforest, who can say with confidence that it doesn't exist?

To travel the Amazon from source to delta is the dream of many: one of the world's great journeys. Others may prefer to strike out into the rainforest, or to explore countries on the outer edges of the Amazon Basin. Those in search of rainforests and wildlife should also consider visiting the pristine jungles of Guyana, French Guiana and Suriname, which, although they lie just beyond the watershed, offer some of the region's least disturbed and most inaccessible rainforest.

Whether you're travelling independently for months or booking a two-week trip to the Amazon it is essential to plan. Visiting the rainforest is exhilarating at any time, but if you want to explore the flooded forest you have to get the timing right (see *When to go*, page 30). Independent travel to the region is full of rewards but many of the lodges and riverboat trips get booked up, sometimes months in advance. Spend some time looking through the options in *Preparations and planning* (page 29) to minimise the possibility of disappointments once you arrive in the Amazon.

The deepest reaches of the Amazon are beyond all but the most adventurous traveller yet remain a source of fascination. For those wanting to break out on their own and explore the backwaters of some small tributary, we've given guidelines on expedition planning (page 69). If you want adventure but don't have the time or the inclination to go alone, rafting opportunities in Peru and Bolivia take you through some of the quietest parts of the river.

The *Natural History* section (page 99) provides an outline of flora and fauna that you might see on the river and in the rainforest, while the chapter on *Indigenous Tribes and Settlers* (page 161) looks at how mankind has adapted to life in the area. The country chapters, in addition to giving an overview of each country and the main gateway city for international arrivals, also provide pointers to the opportunities available in each country and how best to plan them.

Whatever style of trip you plan – whether a one-week riverboat trip or an extensive multi-country tour of the region – your experience will be unique. If you're lucky you may see some of Amazonia's elusive wildlife; more realistically you will come away with just some idea of the sheer scale of the Amazon and the region through which it flows. Whatever your reasons for choosing to visit there is certain to be an occasion when you stand in the rainforest or on your riverboat, mouth agape in disbelief. In Brazil they say 'Opa' – loosely translated as 'Wow!'

Part One

General Information

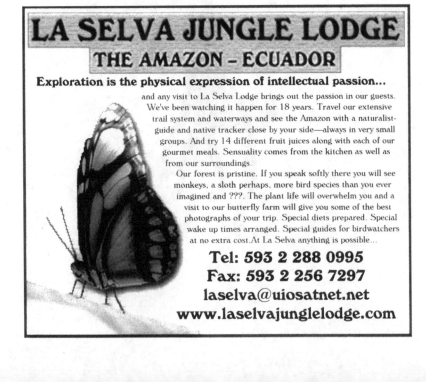

History and Background

THE AMAZON

From the air, the Amazon appears as a vast, uniform green carpet, embroidered here and there with sinuous, glinting ribbons. Once on the ground, though, you realise it is anything but uniform – this 'carpet' is the rainforest canopy, the crowns of millions of trees; the 'ribbons' are innumerable lakes and rivers reflecting the sunlight from their green, ochre and dark waters. Giant columns tower high above, draped with encircling vines. Mysterious squawks, chirps and buzzes break the silence. Warm, damp air envelops you with tropical scents of lilies, orchids, acacias and the musty smell of decaying vegetation... This is the Amazon, place of myth and legend – the Emerald Forest.

Even in our sophisticated jet-set age the Amazon remains a great unknown, inspiring poets, scientists and travellers. Much of it is physically unexplored. Most maps are compiled from satellite photos, and there are great gaps in our knowledge of the region's history; while there still – enticingly – exists the possibility of discovering lost cities and uncontacted tribes.

Biologists are scrambling right now to describe and catalogue its myriad life forms. The Amazon, upstream of Manaus, harbours the world's richest flora and fauna – most of which is yet to be scientifically described. These organisms may yield solutions to seemingly intractable problems of our modern world: food and energy shortages, and currently incurable diseases.

The river

The Amazon is a world of trees and water – life in an abundance unimaginable until seen first-hand and then overwhelming. This is by far the world's biggest river, running through the world's largest tropical rainforest. Even when you are there, its size is difficult to grasp: it is truly awesome!

The Amazon Basin is the earth's biggest freshwater ecosystem and reservoir for a fifth of our planet's fresh water. It drains an area of over seven million km^2, over half the South American continent and three-quarters the size of the continental United States. Its forests – home to the world's highest diversity of birds, insects and plants – comprise the largest remains of primary tropical woodland and half the world's rainforests.

At the river's mouth, water flows into the Atlantic at 160–200,000 cubic metres per second – a flow greater than the world's eight biggest rivers together, or ten times that of the Mississippi. This river could drain Lake Superior – North America's biggest lake – in under two years. As it approaches the ocean the river forms not one but several deltas, as a multitude of branches sprawl eastward and fan out to meet the sea. Along the tidal margins of the delta, only tough, salt-tolerant mangrove survives.

The Amazon River is 6,448km (4,007 miles) from source to mouth, second in length only to the Nile at 6,670km. During its journey it receives – directly or

THE SOURCE OF THE AMAZON

The location of the source of the Amazon has been debated by geographers for centuries. The quest has resulted in several competing claims, depening on how the "true" source is defined. In 2000 a National Geographic Expedition identified the source as a thin sheet of crystal water flowing down a rock wall on Nevado Mismo, a 5,597m mountain in Southern Peru. The team used Global Positioning System (GPS) technology to locate the most distant point in the drainage basin from which water runs year-around and the furthest point from which water could possibly flow into the ocean.

Competition to discover the Amazon's source is fierce. In 1996 an international team claimed it is an underground glacier near Arequipa. This gives rise to an icy creek, known as Apacheta Crevice, that lies at 5,168m on Volcán Chachani.

The definition of the source of a river is open to debate. Some geographers take it as the furthest point from the river's mouth and others the highest location (of the waters that feed it). An alternative view is that the true source is the river or lake that contributes the most water to the main river. For this reason Lake Lauricocha (4,838m) in Peru is cited in the Encyclopaedia Britannica as the source of the Amazon.

indirectly – water from over 15,000 tributaries, 12 of which are over 1,600km in length. The longest, the Madeira-Mamoré-Grande at a length of 3,200km, is the world's longest tributary and 14th longest river. In the flood season some two million kilometres of waterways are navigable.

Iquitos in Peru, a popular starting point for jungle trips, is 2,975km (1,849 miles) from the river's mouth as the parrot flies. For ships, the river's curves and meanders add almost 800km to the distance – a total 3,717km of navigable inland waterway, the longest stretch in the world. By comparison the Rhine, Europe's primary waterway, is just short of 900km.

At Iquitos the river is 7–9km wide during the wet season. Further downstream, in Brazil, the main stream is 65km wide in places. Unless you're in a plane you rarely get a sense of how broad the river really is, as midstream islands block the view of distant banks.

The depth of the Amazon varies dramatically with seasonal floods, its level rising and falling an average of 12m across the seasons. Despite that, the main stream is deep enough for ocean-going passenger liners and cargo ships to navigate year-round as far upstream as Iquitos, where the depth varies from 15 to 30m – but with shifting sand bars making navigation a nightmare. The deepest point of the Amazon at 62m is upstream of Santarém, at Obidos.

The rainforest
What is rainforest?

Tropical rainforests are found where temperatures and rainfall are high throughout the year. Such conditions occur only in equatorial regions in a belt 25° north and south of the Equator. All rainforests share similar features – a characteristic layered or stratified vegetation structure and high biodiversity.

Typically, annual rainfall ranges between 200cm (79in) and 1,000cm (394in). The latter extreme is not reached in the Amazon, where the average falls between 250 and 400cm. Temperatures rarely fall below 20°C (68°F), reaching a maximum

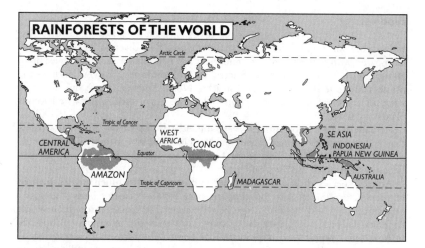

of 32°C (90°F). This is cooler than many people expect, but the high humidity makes the heat feel worse. Humidity is usually around 80%, though 90–95% is not uncommon.

Why is rainforest important?

Since rainforests were first explored scientifically in the 1800s, naturalists have been astounded at the diversity of plants and animals. The overwhelming numbers, variety of colour and form and intricacy of ecological relationships helped inspire the evolutionary theories of Darwin and Wallace (although only Wallace spent significant time in the Amazon). Rainforests occupy less than one tenth of the world's land area but are home to three-quarters of *known* species. As temperate fauna and flora have been researched in considerably more detail than their neotropical cousins, rainforest is clearly the most species-rich habitat on Earth.

Plants, fungi, insects and amphibians contain a host of potentially useful chemicals and genes awaiting discovery. Many plant species have genes resistant to disease or drought. Plants with powerful chemicals can provide pharmaceutical products. Agriculturists may find insect species that act as biological pest controls. Particularly in the brave new world of genetic engineering and biotechnology, a wealth of treasures is sure to come from the reservoir of genetic information stored in rainforests.

Besides lifetimes of work for naturalists, rainforest provides hundreds of economically valuable products: lumber, fibre, food, fuel and medicine. Multinational pharmaceutical and chemical companies apply massive efforts to looking for plants with 'miracle' compounds for use in medicine and industry, adding commercial weight to the importance of preserving whole ecosystems.

Many rainforest plants already have industrial uses. Numerous products are made from the rubber tree, *Hevea brasiliensis*. Aviation tyres are composed of 60% natural rubber as artificial rubber alone is too weak to withstand the extreme operating conditions. Other products made from 100% natural rubber include surgical gloves and condoms. Even your boat could be tree-powered: the *copaiba* tree of Brazil produces a sap that can be used directly as diesel fuel. Trees are harvested for fruits, and palms and brazil nuts, along with many lesser-known species, feed local people and make sustainable contributions to the local economy.

Biodiversity

Perhaps the most oft-cited reason to preserve rainforest is its high species diversity. Indeed, the Amazon rainforest has the world's highest diversity of plant species. Compared with temperate forests, rainforest has a far greater variety of trees: up to 300 species in a single hectare (2.5 acres) of Amazon forest, or over ten times the number found in the most diverse forests in North America. That's only the trees – the undergrowth also comprises hundreds of species of shrubs, vines, herbaceous plants and ferns.

Actually *on* the rainforest trees is yet another layer of diversity. Epiphytes (plants that grow on other plants) cluster on branches and tree trunks. They include unknown species of orchids, lilies, bromeliads, philodendrons, ferns, mosses, lichens and algae by the thousand.

Animal species diversity in lowland rainforest is also much higher than in temperate forest. The Amazon supports over 2,000 species of birds – almost a quarter of the world's total – compared with about 700 species throughout North America. Tropical rainforest also harbours more species of mammals (around 300 in Amazonia), reptiles and amphibians than comparable areas of temperate forest.

Insects epitomise the rainforest's species diversity. Of about one million known species, 90% are from the tropics. Scientists estimate that as many as 30 million species remain undiscovered. If true, this would mean that rainforests harbour 94% of all the earth's species, albeit mostly insects!

The Amazon is also unequalled in its aquatic diversity. The drainage contains over 2,000 fish species. Despite this being half of all known freshwater species, scientists believe that at least another thousand remain undiscovered. A single Amazon lake might have 200 species, a greater number than found throughout all of Europe.

Climate

The Amazon Basin does not have seasons as such. Apart from a few blips in the overall pattern, rainforest weather is remarkably constant; normally with fine balmy days, and an afternoon thunderstorm once or twice a week. Rain is possible, though unlikely, every day of your trip – so expect the unexpected!

The central Amazon Basin and the eastern slopes of the Andes have a tropical wet climate. The high precipitation in this zone results from low air pressure and wind convergence combined with intense surface heating and the air's high moisture content. Northeast Amazonia, as well as a vast area of southern Brazil and further south, experience both a wet and dry tropical climate, with a distinct dry season that lasts longer with increasing distance from the Equator.

AMAZON RAINFOREST – DISAPPEARING FAST

During the 1990s, the rate of destruction of the Amazon made world headlines as areas the size of European countries disappeared annually. Latest figures are encouraging. In 2001, 15,787 km² of Brazilian rainforest was destroyed – down from 18,226 km² the previous year. Officials said the reduction was achieved through increased monitoring and changes in land use. Conservationists counter that figures are massaged by the government to maintain a positive image. The point is not to get bogged down in the numbers – even though the 2001 figure is an improvement, it represents an area much bigger than the Amazon's largest nature reserve.

A COOL WIND

A severe El Niño effect hit South America in 1998; perhaps worse than that in 1982-83, previously the worst to date. Amazon wildlife is affected by such a dramatic change in climate. Some species, especially reptiles, undergo behavioural changes. As surface water temperatures drop, caiman are more likely to bask out in the open to warm themselves in the sun and anaconda emerge from the cooler waters, a quite unusual behaviour for this giant snake.

The winds can last for a couple of weeks or so – long enough to cool the surface of lakes and rivers. As the surface cools, the upper layer of cold water descends to the bottom stirring the rich organic ooze of decaying vegetation that traps large amounts of methane. The disturbed mud releases methane and other poisonous gases, creating an oxygen crisis. Desperate fish crowd close to the surface to gasp uncontaminated oxygen, dissolved in a thin layer where water meets air. Even so, vast numbers of fish and freshwater crustaceans suffocate and floodplains become feasting grounds for carrion feeders, especially vultures. This is just one consequence of a sudden temperature drop.

Temperatures

All rainforest climates are characteristically warm (but not excessively hot) with frequent rain. Around Iquitos, 3° south, temperature varies hardly at all. During the day it is 'shorts and T-shirt' weather, ranging from 24°C in the morning to 30°C in the afternoon. Occasionally temperatures may exceed 35°C, and at night fall to 21°C but rarely lower.

The overwhelming humidity is often an oppressive 80% or higher, inducing lethargy or sleep during the heat of the day.

Each year, the intensity of the cyclical weather system off the coast of Peru known as El Niño causes a cold southerly wind (*friagem* in Brazil or *surazo* in Bolivia) to blow from Patagonia. In certain years, daytime temperatures drop as low as 15°C.

Wind

High wind conditions in the Amazon are rare. Forest winds are light and at ground level are more or less non-existent as the forest canopy absorbs most wind energy. This is one reason why pollen and seeds of most Amazon plants are animal-dispersed; wind-dispersed pollen or seeds tend not to travel far. The strongest winds can occur in the middle of broad rivers and lakes, where there are sometimes severe gusts, especially during rainstorms. Windy conditions on a boat are not dangerous, the greatest concern being motion sickness.

Rainfall

A common assumption is that rainfall in the rainforest must be constant. In fact, it is intermittent though regular, occurring on average three or four times a week, often in the form of short and spectacular downpours. On the coast it can rain at any hour, day or night. Inland, early afternoon is most likely, although rain at night and in the early morning is possible. When it rains, water generally cascades from the heavens; in one hour two or three centimetres (around an inch) may fall. The high levels of precipitation in rainforest are the result of intense individual downpours rather than lighter rain over long periods. If it rains in the Amazon, you get wet; there's rarely the wimpish drizzle found in northern latitudes. In the upper Amazon, rainfall averages 305cm per year. This seems to have decreased in recent years. In particular 1994 was very dry, possibly because extensive deforestation disrupted local rainfall patterns.

Rainfall is predictably unpredictable. Around Iquitos, with the exception of May, every month recorded as the wettest one year has been recorded as the driest in another. July to November tends to be dry, while the wetter season is from February to April. In Bolivia the wet season runs from December to March. To the north in Venezuela, most rain falls between the months of June and October.

Thunderstorms

Tropical warmth and moisture create perfect conditions for spectacular thunderstorms. Huge cumulonimbus clouds bubble above the rainforest, stretching ever further into the sky above, fuelled by rising mists from rivers and vegetation. These formations may rise to 10,000m in a classic 'anvil' shape. These clouds harbour enormous potential energy, released as brilliant lightning displays and ear-splitting thunder.

Sunshine

As the Amazon is equatorial, days hardly vary from twelve hours in length. Of course the amount of sunshine depends on cloud cover, but there are usually nine to eleven hours of sunshine per day. Because the sun is directly overhead, it is more intense than in temperate latitudes. Take precautions to prevent sunburn, especially from reflected sunlight on water.

AMAZON HISTORY

Throughout Amazon history, extravagant wealth and sordid misery are dominant themes. Fortunes were found and lost; kingdoms were defeated; peoples were enslaved and freed. Deadly diseases, fearsome creatures, hostile Indians and rapacious settlers, all within the forest's immensity, set the stage for a fascinating and often turbulent history. Added to this, the overwhelming power of legends attracted conquistadors from halfway across the world in search of the gilded man of El Dorado, while explorers throughout the centuries have searched in vain for the women tribes of the Amazonas and numerous lost cities.

Origins of the Amazonians

Today the Amazon yields few of its past secrets. Unfortunately the heat, damp and acid rainforest soils conspire to decompose organic remains quickly before they can fossilise. Human fossils are virtually absent from the lowland regions, so we have practically no certain clues as to how and when people arrived in the area. Likewise, without animal fossils it is difficult to reconstruct ancient faunas and so we are denied the human picture in its ecological context.

Aboriginal peoples of the Americas are believed to have arrived on the continent around 13,000 years ago, during the two most recent ice ages. Migrating east and southwards, the hunter-gatherers made their way across the isthmus of Central America down to South America. This wave of migration gave rise to the Olmec, Maya and Aztec civilisations of Central America which flourished from 1400BC until the arrival of the Spanish conquistadors in the early 1500s. In the western coastal regions and highlands of South America the Chimú and Inca, along with many other cultures, left ample architectural and cultural artefacts for us to ponder. In the last twenty years, chance discoveries and finds of stone tools and ceramics have suggested that large populations were established on the flood plains near the

THE CHRONICLE OF AKAKOR

Tales of fabulous cities hidden in the Amazon permanently enhance the feeling of excitement and adventure that prevails throughout the region. While many lost cities have been found, the Chronicle of Akakor remains perhaps the most fantastic of all the legends.

The Chronicles are written in the tribal book of the Ugha Mongulala, a people 'chosen by the Gods' 15,000 years ago. Arriving in golden airships, white-skinned strangers civilised the tribe and built three great stone cities: Akanis, Akakor and Akahim. The legendary city of Akakor is on the Purus River, in a high mountain valley on the frontier between Brazil and Peru. The city-fortress was one of 26 stone cities stretching from Bolivia through to Venezuela, while another 13 underground cities were linked by an intricate system of tunnels and canals stretching right across South America.

The Chronicles record the existence of a large island to the west of South America, buried under an enormous tidal wave during the first great catastrophe, and predict cyclical devastations each lasting 6,000 years.

The recent discovery of pyramids on satellite images of the Madre de Dios regions correlates precisely with the location of the Lost City of Akakor. The pyramids remain unvisited and several attempts to reach the site have failed, resulting in fatal accidents. Lost cities must always, as everyone knows, be protected by a curse of death on those who enter!

current city of Manaus by 3000BC. Some authorities believe humans have been in the Amazon much longer than formerly thought. Recent work by archaeologist Anna Roosevelt of Chicago's Field Museum of Natural History indicates the interior Amazon Basin was extensively settled at least 10,900 years ago, much earlier than previously believed. David Childress, recounting *The Chronicle of Akakor*, describes advanced civilisations and lost cities in the Amazon dating back over 12,000 years ago!

The search for El Dorado continues today as several lost cities are still believed to exist, notably Akakor itself and the Lost Mines of Muribeca. Despite the scoffing of establishment archaeologists, in 1986 a lost city in Mato Grosso, Brazil, was actually discovered, visible in satellite photographs. Satellite images have also revealed what appear to be eight huge pyramids in the Madre de Dios region of Peru. But in both of these areas expeditions have so far failed to reach their destinations. Faced with such discoveries, established theories and ideas about the arrival and development of humankind in South America are continually being questioned.

A number of scholars believe the Chinese crossed the Pacific over 2,000 years ago and influenced the native cultures. Others think the pattern of migration went in the opposite direction, from South America. Best-known proponent of this theory is Thor Heyerdahl, whose Kon-Tiki expedition across the Pacific in the 1940s proved that a long journey across the ocean was possible with a simple craft made from locally available balsa wood. Still others, notably R Buckminster Fuller, cite evidence of Phoenician voyages to the South American coast around 200BC. We are unlikely ever to discover the whole picture and mysteries will remain.

The indigenous peoples of the Andean regions developed advanced architecture, mathematics, astronomy and agricultural systems unequalled for sophistication and productivity in contemporary South America. Megalithic works – Machu Picchu being the supreme accomplishment – and gold, pottery, textile and stone artefacts show the strength of the Inca and preceding cultures were primarily west of the Amazon.

In the Amazon itself, Inca presence was limited but significant. Well-established around the headwaters of the Putumayo near the Colombia-Ecuador border and along the Napo River, flowing from Ecuador to Peru, Inca outposts promoted trade in gold, pottery, agricultural produce and slaves. In recent decades the eastern slopes of the Andes have become a hot-spot for archaeologists keen to explore links between the high and lowland cultures of South America.

For thousands of years, tribes of the Amazon and the surrounding mountains co-existed as neighbours, albeit as rivals at one time, allies at another. Despite influences from the Inca many remote forest-dwelling tribes remained as hunter-gatherers, as a few do to this day.

In the late 15th century this balance was to be shattered in one swift event: the arrival of outsiders – the Europeans.

The Europeans arrive: paradise lost?

Apparently a shaman (a spiritual healer) prophesied the arrival of a white deity from the east, at the time that Columbus anchored off the shores of Cuba in 1492. If the conquistadors were considered to be gods, it is frightening to contemplate what the activities of evil forces would have entailed. The very first encounters between lowland Indians and Europeans were filled with curiosity from all sides, but the novelty soon wore off and the Europeans quickly demanded control of everything and everyone they encountered. The Indians did not realise the mistaken identity of these fair-skinned deities until it was too late.

The sea voyages of Pinzón, Ojeda and Vespucci had all travelled past the Amazon's mouth by 1500. On April 26 the Portuguese commander Pedro Álvares Cabral made the first landing on the eastern side of South America by a European and is now remembered as the founder of Brazil. But it was not until forty years later that the first Spanish conquistadors entered the Amazon heartland, opening the first chapter of the interior's written history.

Strangers in a strange land indeed, the new arrivals were men the like of whom had never been encountered by the Indians. The magic fire sticks that killed at great distance were a fearsome weapon and the Indians had never seen horses before. Armies thousands strong fell in battles against less than a hundred mounted Spanish soldiers under the command of Francisco Pizarro. The Spanish conquistadors were the strongest soldiers in the world at the time and, although the odds were stacked against them, the superior firepower of the Spanish made the defeat of the Indians inevitable.

Strength and fortuitous timing assisted greatly in the speedy dispatch of the Incas, who were still recovering from the division of near civil war in their empire. Restless and ready for action, once the battles with the Incas were over, the new Spanish governors turned their energies to in-fighting over new land rights. For war-hungry soldiers the prospect of peace time was uninspiring, and one suitable distraction was for energetic conquistadors to set off to explore new lands.

By 1540, having plundered the Inca Empire of its riches and claimed new lands for Spain, the Spanish turned their attentions further inland, while on South America's eastern coast the Portuguese had begun setting up colonies.

The attraction of the lowlands and the first descent

Gonzalo Pizarro, a younger brother and loyal supporter of Francisco throughout the conquest, had been appointed governor of Quito. With the coast to the west a certainty, the eternally curious Pizarro was drawn to the east, spurred on by rumours promising fantastic wealth. Indians spoke of the land of El Dorado where a gold-dusted king bathed in a sacred lake as his ancestors had done for generations. La Canela was another land filled with spices that were highly prized and valued back in Europe. Pizarro set about planning his trip from Quito.

With time on his hands, the similarly under-entertained conquistador Francisco de Orellana heard of Pizarro's plans in early 1541. Orellana had shown his drive and ambition when he left Spain for the New World at the age of just sixteen and was among the 168 conquistadors who fought under Francisco Pizarro during the conquest of the Incas. Pizarro was happy to have a man of Orellana's stature join the expedition.

Pizarro's expedition force left Quito at the end of February, 1541. The journey, which first had to cross the Andes to the east of Quito before forging a path through impenetrable jungle, was expected to be hard. Some 350 Spaniards, many on horse-back, were accompanied by 4,000 Indians acting as guides and porters. Hundreds of llamas carried supplies, 2,000 pigs formed a trotting foodstore, with just as many dogs to hunt Indians. Strength in numbers partly explains the large expeditionary force, but the scale suggests that Pizarro and his recruits believed their Amazon expedition was an opportunity to emulate the financial rewards of the Inca conquest. The departing procession must have been epic... and Orellana missed it by a few days! Assembling a small band of men and horses, he quickly set out to catch up with Pizarro. Both groups found the journey difficult although presumably Orellana had few problems following the detritus-strewn tracks of such a large expedition. When Orellana was finally reunited with the larger party, Pizarro quickly promoted this man of proven loyalty to second-in-command. Camping on the Upper Napo, near the modern-day town of Coca (Puerto Francisco de Orellana) in Ecuador, the group explored the area, hacking down jungle, making new paths and building bridges to cross rivers. By the end of 1541 dreams of El Dorado were fading. Most of the highland Indians had died, as had a number of Spaniards. Food was running low and the rains were getting heavier by the day. The search for wealth was replaced by the more basic need to survive.

A turning-point in the expedition was the decision to build a boat and use the rivers as highways. Despite the fact that every conquistador on the trip had reached the New World by sailing across the Atlantic, inspiration for the decision came from the efficient use of canoes by lowland Indians.

A vessel large enough to carry 60 men and supplies was built. Orellana was given command of the brigantine and, with 57 men and several canoes, set sail in search of food. This was close to Christmas in 1541. Pizarro and some 140 starving men were left on the banks of the river, watching their hopes for survival drift downstream with the current. Orellana never returned to them.

Orellana moved quickly: 'As the river flowed fast, we proceeded on at the rate of from twenty to twenty-five leagues [110–140km], for now the river was high [from the rains].' In early January 1542 his armada came across a village with food in abundance. As so often with the conquistadors, speed was the deciding factor in preventing a viable defence from being mounted. When the fleeing Indians returned to their village, Orellana's diplomatic skills, a basic grasp of the Indian language and a few traded items encouraged good relations. Attempts to send a canoe back to Pizarro failed. Whether Orellana had any intention of returning is debatable but he certainly did everything he could to clear his name for the sake of history. He stood down from his command to avoid any possible implications of treachery but was reinstated by the popular vote of his crew. The decision was made to continue with the voyage downstream, since enough was known about South America to assume that the river's mouth was somewhere on the Atlantic.

Back on the banks of the Napo River, Pizarro did not doubt Orellana's treachery. '[Orellana] displayed toward the whole expedition the greatest cruelty that ever faithless men have shown, aware that it was left unprovided with food and caught in a vast uninhabited region and among great rivers.'

After almost a month as overstaying guests, having stretched the hospitality of their hosts to the limit, Orellana's party set sail once more. Following the current they experienced few problems, apart from the temporary loss of two canoes that strayed too far ahead of the main group and got lost in a maze of streams and islands for a couple of days.

Approaching the confluence of the Napo with the Amazon, Orellana's band once more prepared themselves for conflict. According to the chronicler Friar Gaspar de Carvajal, as they neared one village scores of Indians climbed into canoes 'in the attitude of warriors'. Passing peacefully through the threat of war, diplomacy once more secured amicable relations. While Orellana and his two friars set about talking to the Indians of Christianity, the crew of professional soldiers began constructing a new and bigger boat in preparation for the sea voyage.

The stay at this cooperative village was made more memorable by the arrival of four white men described as being a span taller than the tallest Christian. Carvajal's records gave rise to the often-told legend of a race of white-skinned, fair-haired giants dressed with gold ornaments.

The vessel was completed in 35 days, and the two boats, several canoes and crew set sail on April 24. Two months of travel had passed and, although the Indians encountered so far had hardly volunteered food, acquiring it had not proved difficult. But Orellana's flotilla was about to enter the territory of the Machiparo who, according to Indians on the river, had 50,000 warriors.

For six weeks the Spaniards were hassled, cajoled, attacked and hijacked. After the warriors of Machiparo, the Indians of the Omagua guaranteed little rest for the tiring travellers. As word of the foreign intruders travelled downstream ahead of the Spaniards, the crew were welcomed by ever more inhospitable Indians and had to resort to increasingly aggressive ways of acquiring food.

Passing the confluence of the Madeira, downstream from what is now Manaus, the crew heard first mention of a tribe of women warriors. 'These women are very white and tall... and they are robust and go about naked, but with their privy parts covered, with their bows and arrows in their hands, doing as much fighting as ten Indian men,' wrote Carvajal.

The account of women in battle may well be true. But such a tribe was not seen after this journey and has not been since. As with the Greek legend of the Amazons, the existence of this fierce female tribe remains somewhere between the limits of geographical knowledge and the imagination. This reference of Carvajal's was to become the most memorable epitaph of this epic journey.

Seeing the ebb and flow of the ocean tide, the Spaniards carried out repair work on the vessels downstream of the Tapajós. On August 26 the two vessels sailed into the Atlantic, completing the first descent of the Amazon by Europeans.

Orellana will always be remembered for the first navigation of the Amazon, but in many ways history has not treated this accidental tourist too well. Orellana's emergence from the Amazon, eight months after his departure from the main group, coincided with Pizarro's return to Quito. Having retraced his route from the banks of the Napo, Pizarro, through pride and anger, paid much attention to blackening Orellana's name. A couple of years later Orellana tried to return to the river. With inadequate resources and funds, his second voyage up the Amazon resulted in his death in 1546. Although it was briefly called the Rio Orellana, the river became more commonly known as the River of the Amazons... a name far more fitting for a continent alive with fantastic legends.

Lope de Aguirre claims a new frontier of savagery

It took almost fifteen years for Orellana's accomplishment to be repeated and with certain parallels. Orellana had joined Pizarro's expedition and by luck reserved himself a place in history. Lope de Aguirre was recruited as just an ordinary member of the crew for the river's second descent but indisputably stole the fame. The expedition of Pedro de Ursúa flirted with disaster from the outset and most problems originated from one source – Lope de Aguirre.

Ursúa was the dashing, gallant, Spanish conquistador of history. Ambitious and young, he had already achieved numerous victories in battles throughout the New World. On arriving in Peru his energies obtained him a commission to follow in the footsteps of Orellana, conquer the lands of the Omagua and find, once and for all, that elusive city of gold.

With a motley crew of 300 Spaniards and 2,000 Indians, the trip left Lima in February of 1559 and crossed the Andes to Moyobamba. There they built two small ships, flatboats for transporting horses, twenty rafts and several canoes. By October 1560 the river journey had begun but not without warning signs of trouble ahead. Endless delays and frustrations had created a restlessness in camp; four men were sentenced to death for holding the second-in-command at gunpoint even before the river journey had started. Mutiny became increasingly likely and every man watched his back for fear of incriminations and false accusations.

A strong leader would have quashed the insurgents but Ursúa was too wrapped up in his own world, devoting his time to his beloved wife Doña Inez de Atienza. For some reason Ursúa had decided to travel with his love, an act hardly likely to endear him to his crew. And in truth history is not littered with characters who successfully led expeditions with their partners in tow.

Among the crew was the physically crippled and scarred Lope de Aguirre (The Wolf). Since arriving in the New World in 1534, Aguirre had successfully managed to avoid gaining wealth and acquiring honour. His career up to this point was a list of impressive failures, each one contributing to his growing feelings of bitterness and desire for revenge.

As the expedition literally drifted downstream, Aguirre saw the opportunity for long-sought leadership. Heading a band of men who favoured mutiny over loyalty he plotted against Ursúa and murdered him in his hammock with the agreement of second-in-command Fernando de Guzmán. All Ursúa's friends and sympathisers were similarly disposed of and the group began in earnest the search for El Dorado.

Guzmán became the expedition's official leader and was appointed Emperor of the Amazon. Aguirre modestly took the title of master of the camp. Having plotted against the authority of the King of Spain, the rebels now explored all kind of fantasies. Guzmán was crowned prince and king over the indeterminable territory. The search for gold was just one option, but why stop there? Aguirre suggested the regal forces return upstream to conquer Peru. As far from reality as they were from Spain, this notion slowly gained support. Dissenters, whether identified by rumour or fact, were immediately executed at Aguirre's whim. While the new leaders feasted like royalty, delusions of grandeur relegated the search for gold to a lower priority. Despite the lack of food, finances and weaponry, and with just over 200 men remaining, Guzmán and Aguirre planned an ambitious campaign for a second conquest of Peru.

Any glory that may have come from the journey down the Amazon was overshadowed by the omnipresent atmosphere of betrayal. Having played one rebellious group off against another, Aguirre finally tired of Guzmán and murdered the new king. Having dispatched all possible rivals he took complete command of the group. Travelling further downstream, Aguirre explored the Negro River seeking a shorter route to Peru. Whether he then continued to the mouth of the Amazon is unknown, but there is a slight possibility that Aguirre was the first European to use the Casiquiare Canal linking the Amazon and Orinoco watersheds.

The chronicles of the journey pay remarkably little attention to the region and its inhabitants, preferring instead to dwell on another first; an intimate demonstration of the phenomenon known as expedition madness. Clearly something had happened to the group. As Smith explains in *Explorers of the Amazon*, 'the expedition was not one of geography but of carnage, of Spaniards killing Spaniards'.

Aguirre's band arrived on the island of Margarita in July 1561. In a rage of anger spiked with paranoia he prepared to march on Peru, looting the city and enlarging the number of recruits to 150. Forces loyal to the Spanish crown finally halted the rebellion as Aguirre and his rebels marched through Venezuela en route to Peru. On the battlefield Aguirre's men were offered royal pardons in return for their surrender. When Aguirre himself was offered the chance to surrender he refused it, preferring to die a leader. He was killed in October 1561 with just one of his loyal soldiers by his side. Just before his death Aguirre penned a letter to King Philip of Spain. Aware of his treachery and somewhat proud of his actions he ventured to offer the king guidance, urging him 'never to send fleets to that cursed river'.

The upstream struggle

The above two voyages were downriver and Spanish. The more difficult journey upstream was completed in 1637–38 by the Portuguese veteran of the Amazon, Captain Pedro de Teixeira. His upriver journey explains, in part, why over three-quarters of the river, some 3,400km, lies within Brazilian territory.

The Portuguese had little interest in the portion of South America allotted to them in the Treaty of Tordesillas, which in 1494 divided the sub-continent between the Iberian powers with a straight line. They demonstrated very little concern over the encroachment when, following the tales of wealth and riches in the New World which were common in Europe by the 16th century, French, British, Irish and Dutch navigators were trying to gain footholds on the quieter eastern side of the continent. But as war spread across Europe, Spain wanted to ensure protection of her overseas territories and, forging Iberian alliance, Spain encouraged Portugal to remove foreigners from her part of South America. Fort Presépio was built in 1616, in the location where Belém now stands, and by the early 1630s the Portuguese had the eastern half of Amazonia to themselves. Previously unconcerned by the encroachment of other European nations, Portugal was now the sole beneficiary of the riches that flowed from the Amazon Basin.

But in 1637 the arrival of two Franciscan missionaries floating downstream into Fort Presépio unsettled the Portuguese. The missionaries were Spanish and had been working along the Napo River when illness forced them to abandon their village. The Amazon would never be free of foreign influence if Spanish missionaries could easily sail a small boat the length of the river, so the Portuguese felt compelled to travel upstream to prevent even greater numbers of Spaniards using the river freely as if it were open sea. Captain Teixeira left the port of Belém on October 28, 1637. Forty-seven canoes, powered by 1,200 Indians and Negroes, transported 70 Portuguese soldiers upstream. Even today planning a trip up the

Amazon from its mouth is hazardous, as several large tributaries can easily be mistaken for the main stream. Teixeira took with him one of the Spanish friars who may have been of some help; but, even so, moving the expedition forward must have been a massive task. After eight months of arduous travel, Teixeira reached the first Spanish settlement. One full year after leaving Fort Presépio, he arrived in the city of Quito.

Not surprisingly the Spaniards were as alarmed by the arrival of the Portuguese as the inhabitants of Fort Presépio had been one year earlier. They too wanted to find out how far the Portuguese had wandered west of the Tordesillas line so they sent the Jesuit priest Cristóbal de Acuña to join the Portuguese on their return journey with instructions to record all that he saw. Acuña's notes create a more detailed record of the region than those from the voyages of Orellana and Aguirre.

MAKING THE AMAZON PORTUGUESE

It's a common enough lesson learnt in schools that the Treaty of Tordesillas divided the South American continent between the imperial powers of Portugal and Spain. And so it did... to a degree. The treaty drew a line 370 leagues west of the Cape Verde group of islands – west of the line was Spanish territory, east was Portuguese.

So how did Portugal claim so much land to the west of this imaginary line?

Following the difficulties of Orellana's and Aguirre's descents of the great river, the Spanish were reluctant to mount further expeditions to the Amazon Basin.

The mouth of the river was a natural starting point for exploration to the hinterland. In the 17th and 18th century Portuguese expeditions down the main stream cleared vast areas of the Indian population while settlements of missionaries and gold prospectors had sprung up throughout the Amazon Basin.

The need to formalise boundaries became apparent as Brazil moved towards independence. On January 13, 1751, the Treaty of Madrid between King João of Portugal and King Ferdinand VI of Spain divided the South American continent between Portugal and Spain, marking out the international boundaries roughly as they stand today. Portugal's share was far greater than that allotted in the original Treaty of Tordesillas, and was due largely to the ease of navigation on the Amazon.

The treaty creating this new boundary recognised the difficulty of colonising the region, showing a remarkable openness and indifference to detail: 'without being bothered about a few leagues of deserted lands, in regions where each Crown will have such an over-abundance that they could not be inhabited for many centuries'.

The Indians encountered receive a generally better press, being credited with using the rainforest to ensure that 'these barbarians never know what hunger is'. He noted their skill in harvesting fruit and hunting game. When news got back, Europe was excited by reports of the electric eel, one hundred years before the discovery of electricity. Old myths were verified and new legends were born. The fierce female Amazons, Acuña was assured by local Indians, did exist but not on the Amazon main stream… they could be found living to the north in what is now Guyana. Acuña also wrote about tribes of dwarf Indians and yet another tribe with their feet back to front to deceive would-be trackers.

Teixeira's expedition returned to Fort Presépio on 12 December 1639 having been away for more than two years. Staking Spain's claim to the lion's share of the river, Acuña wrote to the Council of the Indies suggesting that Spain waste no time in establishing its right to the river so it could benefit from the river's riches and its value as a route to the Andes. But Teixeira's actions had established a presence on the river, founding Portuguese settlements as far upstream as possible and guaranteeing Portugal's claim to most of the river.

Missionaries followed the early explorers. Jesuits were first, followed by Franciscans and Capuchins. Each order set up settlements and brought Catholicism to the natives. Although many Europeans believed the Indians were savages without spirits, the missionaries were given control over their spiritual development. The Jesuits were the most active and numerous missionaries, encouraging Indians to descend into villages or *aldeias*, where they could live, work and receive religious instruction. Although the missions were a place of relative safety, missionaries often turned a blind eye to the slaving raids that permitted the collection of legitimate prisoners-of-war from inter-tribal conflicts.

With time the missionaries became increasingly powerful and vocally defended the Indians. Resentment over their pro-Indian stance led to the eviction of their leaders from Spanish and Portuguese territory in 1757. With the removal of the Jesuits, slow and steady colonisation of the area was the only European activity in the Amazon.

Explorer-scientists in search of knowledge

Following the intellectual enlightenment of the Renaissance, a new approach to scientific investigation reached its zenith during the Age of Reason in the mid-18th century. The Amazon was seen in a new light: the conquistador's green hell was replaced by the naturalist's green paradise. This change reflected a new awareness of the rainforest's immense botanical riches – an attitude that originated with the next group of people to discover the Amazon's wonders: the explorer-scientists.

Regarding the natural world, European views changed profoundly between the 16th and 19th centuries. Men became interested in knowledge for its own sake, while greater wealth and better technology gave them the means to pursue their goal to better understand the world around them. Attracted by reports of strange animals, plants and unknown tribes, they became seekers after knowledge. These men discovered riches in the Amazon Basin of far greater value than the gold and gems the conquistadors sought in vain.

Charles-Marie de la Condamine

Among the first and most influential of them was the Frenchman Charles-Marie de la Condamine who explored the main stream of the Amazon in 1743. Originally sent to South America to resolve an academic argument over the precise shape of the world, Condamine was eternally curious about this stimulating continent and seems to have been incapable of focusing on any one reason for his trip. If there

LOVE CONQUERS ALL

Travel arrangements in Amazonia don't always go according to plan. Jean Godin des Odonais, a member of Condamine's original expedition, decided that it was time to return to France having lived in Ecuador for several years. Leaving his pregnant wife Isabela in Riobamba in March of 1749, he promised to return when he was certain that passage down the Amazon River was possible and safe. Like his compatriot Condamine he was eternally curious.

After travelling as far as French Guiana he set about returning to collect his wife and family. But the return journey was out of the question. France and Portugal were not friends at the best of times and, without the backing of an official expedition, permission to travel the length of the Amazon was denied. For several years he wrote to friends in high places and government officials seeking permission to enter Brazil to collect his family. He even wrote to the French Foreign Minister advocating war against the Portuguese so France could claim the Amazon.

When a galliot, manned with 30 Portuguese oarsmen, arrived after 16 years of petitioning, Godin feared that his letter inciting war had fallen into foreign hands. Anxious for his own safety he entrusted his friend Tristan d'Oreasaval with funds to travel to Riobamba and return with the beloved Isabela; but d'Oreasaval failed to honour any of his commitments… apart from spending the money.

The vessel made it up the Amazon to Lagunas from where the crew travelled by foot to Quito. News reached Riobamba informing Isabela that transport awaited her in Lagunas. With all her children dead from malaria, yellow fever and dysentery she had nothing to lose.

A party of 41, of which 31 were Indian porters, left Riobamba in late 1769. Isabela's father went ahead to organise river travel and smooth out the journey not knowing that someone in the advance party carried smallpox. When his daughter arrived in Canelos 100km east of Riobamba the pre-arranged canoes were missing and half the villagers dead. The Indian porters then disappeared overnight suspecting the journey was doomed.

Using just one canoe and a raft, the remaining group headed downstream on the 200km journey to Andoas. Hitting a log they lost the raft but recovered their goods and decided to send an advance party ahead to fetch assistance. When help failed to return and with food supplies running low a second raft was built; once again to be smashed to pieces, this time losing all the supplies.

The rest of the group died from illness and no help came. Isabela set off alone through the jungle. After wandering for over a week she was found by Indians, who fed her and transported her downstream, so that she eventually arrived in Andoas two months after leaving Riobamba. In early 1770 she finally boarded the boat in Lagunas that was to take her to her husband.

From there it was plain sailing for Isabela, travelling 3,200km downstream before heading north at the Atlantic and to Cayenne where she was reunited with Godin in mid-1770 – 21 years after they had last seen each other.

was a way of deviating off a path he took it. Leaving Paris in 1735, the expedition that was originally meant to take just two years returned to Paris a decade later. The man's endless curiosity did much to fill his *Abridged Narrative of Travels Through the Interior of South America*, published in 1745. The book contained the first detailed report of a strange substance made from the sap of a rainforest tree. Along the Japurá River, Condamine observed Omagua Indians using the sap of a tree to make galoshes, rings and even syringes. Although others had seen this wondrous substance used to make bouncing balls and waterproof items, Condamine was the first to take it back to Europe.

Industrialising Europe and the United States soon found invaluable uses for rubber, a substance to which the Industrial Revolution owes much. Condamine also researched and confirmed the existence of a natural canal – the Casiquiare – connecting the Amazon and Orinoco river systems. His reports inspired a generation of scientists to carry on his work.

Alexander von Humboldt

One of the Amazon's greatest explorers was Baron Alexander von Humboldt (1769–1858), a well-to-do Prussian of noble birth. Beginning in 1799, he embarked on a four-year expedition to the Orinoco and the upper reaches of the northwest Amazon Basin. His high-level contacts assured him of every assistance from Spanish officials, giving him greater freedom to travel than Condamine had had some 60 years earlier.

Humboldt's inland expedition began in February of 1800. After seven weeks travelling the wide open expanses of the Venezuelan *llanos,* Humboldt and his companion Aimé Bonpland concentrated their efforts on the great River Orinoco. In particular Humboldt wanted to establish whether there really was a link between the Amazon Basin and the Orinoco.

Travelling up the Orinoco to the Atures rapids – where Puerto Ayacucho is today – Humboldt and his small party recorded suffering the vicious biting insects of the region. Visitors to the area today can still share in the misery of these minute yet ferocious flies known locally as *la plaga*. The suffering eased when the team reached the mission station of San Fernando where the acidic blackwaters of the Río Atabapo fail to support the insect larvae that flourish in the whitewaters of the Orinoco.

Travelling up ever smaller rivers, the canoe was pushed from the watershed of the Orinoco from the River Temi to enter the Amazon Basin on the River Guainía. Downstream Humboldt entered the Casiquiare; he measured the length of this remarkable natural canal and found it to be 322km. The canal, actually 354km in length, proved an arduous journey for Humboldt, with the return of insects reported by one missionary living in the area to be 'the most painful he had felt'.

The verification of the canal, a phenomenon subject to much disbelief in 18th-century Europe, was a considerable success for the Humboldt party but not the only one. His contribution to the field of botany alone ranks as a major scientific achievement, with a collection of over 12,000 plant specimens, most of which were new to science. Humboldt's scientific work was accurate, detailed and exhaustive. No topic was excluded. He wrote on botany, zoology, pharmacology and geology, creating what today is still considered a database of the region. But although Humboldt was a vital contributor to the increased awareness of rainforest, he never actually saw the Amazon River itself.

An explorer's paradise

Following in Humboldt's footsteps, botanists, zoologists and geographers from all over Europe and North America descended upon South America, and the Amazon

Basin in particular, to discover its hidden riches. These scientists unveiled a seemingly endless variety of plants and animals. Inspired Western naturalists from humbler backgrounds were to find new species and build their reputation on Amazon discoveries.

Naturalist Charles Darwin, famous for his theory of evolution, sailed past the river's mouth in 1834 on his famous round-the-world voyage in *HMS Beagle*. Alfred Wallace, Darwin's contemporary and co-discoverer of the principle of natural selection, spent four years in the Napo River area of present-day northeastern Peru – near Iquitos.

Wallace's friend, the botanist Richard Spruce, spent much longer in the area. For over fifteen years he collected, drew and noted thousands of Amazon plant species. During his time he fended off unfriendly Indians and recovered from tropical fevers. He is most remembered for obtaining quinine seeds for cultivation outside the Amazon, breaking the South American monopoly on the anti-malarial drug.

Henry Walter Bates, another of Wallace's companions, arrived in Brazil in May 1848. Bates' monumental collection involved the drawing and cataloguing of close to 15,000 insect specimens, more than half of them unknown to science. His lengthy research proved that some species of harmless insects actually mimic other more dangerous species. Now called Batesian mimicry in his honour, this strategy is recognised by biologists today as a fundamental process in the evolution of biodiversity. In 1863 Bates published *The Naturalist on the River Amazons* which is rightly regarded as the best contemporary account of Amazon natural history. The book made him famous and remains highly readable.

Bates' book stirred the imagination of stuffy Victorian England but life in the Amazon itself stayed much the same. However, change was not far off. The discoveries of La Condamine, Humboldt and the explorer-scientists coincided with the surging Industrial Revolution and its insatiable demand for raw materials. The Amazon, its inhabitants and its natural resources were about to play an essential role in the development of the modern world.

Early rainforest products

For centuries indigenous Indians have passed down their knowledge of herbal remedies, using the vast array of plants available in the rainforest. Of this diverse pharmacopoeia, the first of the Amazon's vegetal treasures to be discovered by the outside world was quinine. This bitter alkaloid obtained from the red bark tree (*Cascarilla roja, Cinchona* spp), native to Peru and Ecuador, was an effective treatment against malaria, the scourge of tropical latitudes worldwide. Malaria was the main disease preventing European incursion into lowland tropical areas throughout the world. With the discovery of quinine these areas became less dangerous. But production was limited to natural harvesting of the tree bark while the South American monopoly maintained high prices by strictly controlling exports.

Condamine had tried in 1736 to bring quinine to Europe but failed. The Englishman Richard Spruce finally succeeded in smuggling cinchona seeds from the Amazon in the late 1860s. Plantations were developed in British India and Ceylon (now Sri Lanka) and, with the monopoly broken, quinine dropped in price and became widely available.

Quinine contributed to colonial culture as well as to its medicine chest. The drug was prepared as a tonic and to offset its bitter taste colonials added it to gin, which was readily available and whose strong flavour of juniper berries effectively masked the bitterness of quinine. The gin and tonic cocktail became one of the world's first rainforest products and its popularity spread worldwide.

THE EXTRAVAGANCES OF MANAUS

Despite the recent growth in Manaus, the city feels as if it is past its prime. Walking around back streets you can still find the crumbling Edwardian buildings constructed in the city's heyday.

At the height of the rubber boom Manaus grew rapidly. With several major Amazon tributaries coming together close by, the city was a natural collection and distribution point for rubber going to Europe and the US. In 1880 production of 10,000 tons passed through the city's port creating revenues of £2,240,000. By 1910 the tonnage had risen to 44,000 and income to £63 million. Such vast amounts of money had to be spent and, with boats regularly making the journey to Europe with cargoes of rubber, what better way could there be to fill the holds on return journeys than with luxury items from Europe?

Cobblestones, marble slabs, tramways and telephone systems were all imported. The new rich of Manaus wanted to display their wealth to the world and expectations were high. Chandeliers, pianos, food, drink and jewellery all crossed the Atlantic and found their way to the heart of the Amazon.

The great symbol of Manaus' extravagance is the opera house which still looks out of place. Started as a modest project with funds of just £3,600, the eventual cost was close to half a million pounds. Everything used had to be the best, imported from Europe. When it was completed, a city with a population of just 30,000 had an opera house that could seat 1,600 people (larger than the current capacity). World-famous singers including Caruso, Pavlova and Bernhardt were invited to perform in this extravagant building but never did.

Numerous other products were, and still are, being discovered and exploited. During the 19th century harvested rainforest products included mahogany, teak and, for perfume, rosewood. Chocolate made from the fruit of the cacao tree (*Theobroma cacao*) became a popular drink among teetotallers, notably Quakers such as Cadbury.

The influx of settlers brought by new industries usually caused disastrous physical changes to the forest, the Amazon ecosystem and its inhabitants. But despite their value, neither quinine, rosewood nor lumber affected the Amazon as much as Condamine's strange latex.

The 19th-century rubber industry: boom and bust

The story of natural latex parallels quinine's. Like quinine, rubber was known to Indians and used long before Europeans arrived in the New World. Being of great value it was coveted by South American governments and private companies who strictly controlled exports.

The history of rubber in the Amazon is a savage tale. Voracious greed led to appalling abuses of wealth and power. In their lust for profit, powerful rubber barons, with fiefdoms the size of European countries, enslaved and decimated whole tribes.

The worst recorded atrocities were along the Putumayo River in Peru and Colombia, home to the Witoto Indians. The Putumayo was the personal kingdom of Julio César Arana and the indigenous people were his serfs. Arana was brutal and unforgiving to the local population. Plantation foremen with experience of slavery were hired from the West Indies to capture Indians, beating, torturing and starving them to death if they refused to work at tapping raw latex and preparing it for shipment.

Indians were literally worked to death – indentured to rubber barons living in extravagant luxury. Those who tried to run away, or failed to meet tapping quotas, were mercilessly punished. Torture was commonly used as an example to anyone who attempted not cooperating.

Indians who managed to survive the brutal treatment meted out on the plantations succumbed to an equally effective murderer – disease. Millions died from epidemics, against which they had no immunity, of the common cold, influenza, smallpox and venereal diseases introduced by gang foremen.

We have no real idea of the human cost of the rubber industry throughout the Amazon. Alain Gheerbrant calculates that for each ton of rubber exported, seven men, women and children died.

The Peruvian Amazon Rubber Company

Arana – and his company, the Peruvian Amazon Rubber Company – is singled out for particular vilification due to the wanderings of Walter Hardenberg. A young engineer from the US, Hardenberg and a friend were travelling from Ecuador to Bolivia where they hoped to work on the Madeira–Mamoré railway line. For adventure, they decided to travel by canoe down the Putumayo to take in the Amazon en route to Bolivia.

The excitement of adventure was quickly replaced by horror as Hardenberg encountered first hand the indentured labour, whippings, dismembering, murders, crucifixions and rape that were the everyday occurrences of Arana's company.

By 1905 the Peruvian Amazon Rubber Company's plantations had expanded to work a couple of hundred thousand square miles either side of the Putumayo as a result of border disputes between Colombia and Peru. In a territorial no-man's-land, Arana was free to use the population of 40,000 Witoto Indians without interference.

Hardenberg believed few people would tolerate knowing that Arana was treating Indians so badly but, with Manaus' luxuries founded on the wealth of the rubber boom, no-one was prepared to listen to such extravagant tales. Arana was a respected member of society in Manaus. Those who knew of his abuses were only too aware of the consequences of crossing someone who placed so little value on life itself.

Because the Peruvian Amazon Rubber Company listed on the London Stock Exchange, Hardenberg took his story to England. It was made public in 1909 and, despite attempts to buy him off, Hardenberg resolved to stop the slaughter. British authorities, recently shamed by similar atrocities in the Congo, did not want another international scandal.

Parliament sent a Mission of Inquiry to the Putumayo which returned with hard evidence of the atrocities. At the hearing in London Arana turned up in person to defend the family name, while Hardenberg countered with eyewitness accounts. In 1914 the Committee placed all the blame on Arana, conveniently absolving the company's British director of any responsibility. What punishment could be appropriate for such a crime? Even if the question had been asked, Arana had long since returned to South America and by now interest in the Amazon was fading fast... The rubber boom was over.

Beginning of the end

The Amazon rubber industry did not end, shame to say, because of admonitions against the brutality of the rubber barons. It was economic forces that dealt the final blow.

THE STORY OF RUBBER

In Europe and America, rubber was initially just a curiosity – slow to catch on. Condamine and other naturalists had noted that the Indians made several items from this strange product but initial interest failed to move beyond mere curiosity.

The Englishman Joseph Priestly found it erased pencil and coined the term rubber. In 1823, Charles Mackintosh rubberised cloth, making the first waterproof mackintoshes. But pure rubber becomes brittle at cold temperatures – a critical flaw in temperate climates – and the market for pencil erasers and raincoats was limited.

In 1839 Charles Goodyear made a discovery that solved the problem of brittleness. Vulcanisation, which introduces sulphur bonds between the rubber polymer chains, creates stronger bonds within the compound allowing the rubber to stay elastic at much lower temperatures than in the untreated product.

More and more uses for the wonder material were developed by new industries in Europe and North America. By 1850, when Spruce visited Manaus, the 'black gold' rush was on and trade was booming. The invention of the first pneumatic tyre in 1888 by John Dunlop was followed four years later with the creation of the first detachable pneumatic tyre by Edouard Michelin.

By the end of the 19th century, industry was mass-producing bicycles and automobiles. Demand for rubber in electrical products greatly increased as new technology took advantage of its insulating properties. The market mushroomed. In the 30 years from 1880 to 1910, rubber exports from the Amazon rose by a thousand tonnes a year to reach a peak of 44,000 tonnes in 1910.

Nature seemed to conspire on the side of the rubber barons as all attempts to grow the trees outside South America failed.

The Royal Botanical Gardens in Kew, London, were keen to plant the tree in other parts of the world to reduce dependency on South American suppliers. When officials at Kew came across the notes of the English adventurer Henry Wickham they quickly commissioned him to smuggle plants to London. In 1882 Wickham successfully smuggled 7,000 seeds and saplings of *Hevea brasiliensis* out of South America from Manaus. After a short time at London's Kew Gardens, specimens were despatched to British colonies and by 1889 the plant was being successfully cultivated outside South America. By the turn of the century huge rubber plantations with more efficient tapping techniques and greater economies of scale were providing large quantities of cheap latex in direct competition with the Amazon.

Meanwhile, in South America, yields fell due to over-tapping. The cost of tapping larger areas and the extravagances of the rubber barons conspired to push the price of Amazon rubber higher and higher.

In 1902 the first rubber from British Malaya reached the market priced at 2s. 8d. (then about US$0.43) a pound. In 1910, when exports from Manaus reached an all-time high, South American rubber was selling for 12s. 9d. (about US$2.55) a pound, almost six times the price of British rubber. Even though rubber from the Amazon was of better quality than the plantation product it could not compete in price. By 1912, although demand was still high, the boom was over. Rubber barons were selling off assets at a loss, financial empires collapsed and local economies followed. Visiting Iquitos in the 1920s F W Up de Graff noted that the population of Iquitos had shrunk to 'a handful of natives' from 20,000 or more at the rubber boom's height during the 1880s. The lords and ladies, riches and luxuries of Manaus drifted downstream back to Europe. Only the jungle remained, mute witness to the terrible human cost.

Indigenous history
Of an estimated seven million when Columbus arrived, fewer than one million Indians currently live in the Amazon Basin. Of their past little is known; the history of the Amazon tends to be the history of the white man's influence and incursion into the area. Indigenous Indians have consistently been considered last – if at all – when explorers or governments have contemplated expansion, usually with fatal results. Indigenous tribes continue to die from contact with new diseases and are still losing their rights to traditional lands. In Peru and Colombia, major remaining tribes include the Yagua, Witoto, Bora and Tikuna. In Ecuador, the Shuar (Jivaro) people are just coming to grips with the modern world. In Bolivia the Chimane, along with other indigenous groups, have only recently begun to fight for their rights. The Yanomami, who inhabit remote areas along the Venezuela–Brazil border, are one of the largest remaining indigenous groups.

What are the prospects for the Yanomami and others like them? Remnants of tribes not killed off by disease or conquistadors are having their culture and way of life wiped out just as effectively, by the destruction of their forest and rivers or, more insidiously, by the introduction of Western culture and material goods.

It is impossible to turn back the clock. So-called civilisation is reaching into the deepest, darkest corners of the Amazon. The best way of minimising the impact of unwanted outside influence is to extend to indigenous tribes the right to self-determination. With free choice and the protection of traditional land rights, remaining indigenous Indians will have the option to decide how much, if at all, they want to integrate with communities outside their own.

The 20th century
Upon the collapse of the rubber monopoly, many lowland towns became deserted. With Europe and the US preoccupied by two world wars, the Amazon was forgotten by outside influences. Military governments, without needing to seek the popular approval of democracies, ran the countries of South America like personal fiefdoms, with limited regard for the overall welfare of their citizens.

Once Europe had begun rebuilding after World War II, the newly created World Bank, formerly the International Bank for Reconstruction and Development, and the International Monetary Fund looked to help less developed countries with well-intentioned plans to relieve poverty and aid development.

The 1960s saw a wave of projects that pushed into the Amazon in the hope of opening up this new frontier. At a time when ecological awareness was in its infancy, the POLONORESTE project in the state of Rondônia, Brazil, was ploughing a road deep into the Amazon Basin. Retrospectively the colonisation project has widely been declared a failure. In many ways it was a disaster, certainly for the Indians living in the region and for the rainforest that used to grow there.

Almost every country with a share of Amazon territory began colonisation programmes that exerted pressure on the lowlands. The legacy is a continual, steady migration of people into the Amazon Basin. This encroachment of settlers, colonisers and ranchers is a major cause of deforestation. Commercial logging, mining and urbanization add to the problem. Potentially, mismanaged tourism could also create more harm than good.

CONSERVATION IN THE AMAZON
Endangered forests

Most people appreciate the rainforest's aesthetic value. Science too, recognises its worth: rainforests' economic and ecological importance have made them the focus of intense research efforts. Yet, our knowledge is far from complete and sadly may remain so as rainforest is burned, slashed, bulldozed and obliterated. Half the world's original rainforest is already gone and at the present rate of destruction it will disappear completely in 50 years. It is ironic that most deforestation has been during the past 25 years, just as we are beginning to see rainforests for what they are.

As you read this, the Amazon rainforest is being cut down or burned at a rate equal to 20 football fields a minute. Many species unknown to science are already extinct. Scientists estimate that deforestation wipes out 17,000 species of plants and animals per year – about 48 a day or two every hour – a mass extinction on a par with the end of the dinosaurs.

Unfortunately, investors obtain best returns when natural resources are converted to cash. It pays more to chop the forest down, invest the profits and collect interest than it does to use the rainforest sustainably – at least under present economic systems. Cost-benefit analyses of development projects consider the forest itself to be worthless, making ranching, mining and hydro-electric schemes seem profitable.

But when the forest is gone we will have lost a potential bonanza of biological wealth. Some 50,000 higher plant species from the Amazon are described scientifically. Only a tenth have been screened for useful drug or pesticide applications and thousands of species remain undiscovered.

Deforestation also affects climate, bringing into question our own long-term survival. Meteorologists tell us that local weather systems depend on forest cover to recycle water and maintain the hydrological cycle. Living rainforests consume vast quantities of carbon dioxide, the main greenhouse gas, helping to offset global

GLOBAL IMPORTANCE OF AMAZON RAINFOREST PRESERVATION
Oliver Whalley

Conservation of the Amazon rainforest, like conservation of any primary habitat today, is only a temporary measure unless the manmade causes of climatic change are addressed with the same urgency. The Amazon Basin contains by far the largest area of tropical rainforest left in the world, covering over six million km^2 (2.3 million miles^2). With more than 1,000 tributaries it must be considered a major arterial system, holding one-fifth of the world's freshwater. The forests generate and regulate this water, and are not, as many people believe, net producers of oxygen. Temperate forests and sea phytoplankton are net producers of oxygen, but tropical forests perform a vital role on the earth in the storage of carbon. Destruction of any forest releases carbon dioxide into the atmosphere, and so contributes further to global climatic change with all its harmful effects. A secondary effect of deforestation is the loss of the cloud cover, which together with the loss of the forest canopy leads to more of the suns rays reaching the earth's surface, so causing an unnatural heating effect. This extra heat with low moisture content for precipitation may instigate the type of drying out and desertification affecting areas of Africa and other parts of the world.

warming. Conversely burning rainforest is detrimental to the environment as it returns millions of tons of carbon a year back into the atmosphere, adding to the greenhouse effect with as-yet-unknown consequences for global weather patterns.

False economics of exploitation

As precious minerals and strategic metals become more and more scarce, we mine resources previously considered unprofitable; pushing into increasingly remote areas with drastic consequences for the rainforest and its inhabitants. Mismanaged industrial mega-projects have consistently failed to deliver the expected economic benefits. Henry Ford was unable to make money in the 1930s from his rubber plantation project in Fordlândia on the banks of the Tapajós south of Santarém. In the 1960s billionaire Daniel K Ludwig's paper mill at Jari near the mouth of the Amazon relied on unproven plantation species that were soon devastated by rainforest pests. More recently the US$1.5 billion bauxite processing plant at São Luís in Brazil, completed in 1984, uses virgin rainforest to create electricity from charcoal. Hydro-electric dams, notably at Carajás in Brazil, have been built with little attention to ecological impacts. Even conventional cost-benefit studies of these and similar projects show their astonishing expense and lack of profitability. If the actual value of destroyed rainforest is added, the losses become astronomical. Politics and business play a bigger role in these projects than economics or conservation.

Future prospects

Rainforest conservation requires attention to political, cultural and economic agendas. There are countless ways in which intact forest yields positive benefits. Local people can contribute their knowledge to research and ecotourism, improving their economic and political standing. Several programmes, involving both indigenous peoples and conservation organisations, already help native Indians to run jungle lodges and health programmes, market and distribute crops, and survey their own lands. New cultivation and logging methods offer practical ways to log and farm rainforest sustainably. Strip logging minimises erosion and maximises natural regeneration of cut areas. Farmers are encouraged to plant perennial shrubs and trees rather than such labour-intensive annual crops as manioc and maize.

Compared with traditional industries of lumber, mining, oil and fisheries, the alternatives provide more jobs, a healthier environment and, over the long term, greater wealth. Like those of most developing nations, the populations of Amazon countries are growing rapidly. Peru's rate of increase is around 1.8% per year, corresponding to the population doubling in 55 years. Other Amazon countries face similar or worse demographic problems and the demands on governments to provide for such an increase in numbers will place even more pressure on the Amazon lowlands. Just to maintain its present standards of living Peru must double its food supply, available housing, and the number of schools, hospitals and law enforcement facilities – all within 55 years.

Prospects might seem gloomy, but there is hope. Industries are becoming increasingly aware of the need for sound management of natural resources. In 1992 the Brazilian government stopped giving subsidies to lumber and mining corporations, and city dwellers were no longer eligible for grants to farm in the forest. Many believe Rio's 1994 Earth Summit was all politics and no action but at least it happened, which means issues are being addressed. Many governments of the Amazon now appreciate the immense wealth and value of intact rainforest.

The future for the Amazon's sustainable development is promising. Ecotourism is booming. Perhaps 150,000 visit the western Amazon region per year. There may be potential for at least five times that many. Locals are confident of better prospects. Supplies of oil, precious metals and gems are limited. Even lumber replaces itself only while there is a reasonably intact ecosystem. In theory tourism has the potential to last for ever – as long as rainforest exists, people will be drawn to experience it for themselves.

International reality

To blame the countries of South America alone for the destruction of the rainforest is naive. Every government in the world uses its natural resources to the maximum benefit of the country. And Amazonian countries are no different. Exploiting oil and gas reserves is as useful to Ecuador, Peru and Colombia as it is to the US and Europe. Similarly, now that the US and Europe have destroyed most of their natural forests, do these countries have any right to say that the Amazon should be protected as part of man's patrimony? It is one of the great ironies of history that the very nations who first set about clearing the rainforest of the Amazon now clamour for its protection.The only way vulnerable areas will avoid eventual destruction is by innovative incentives to encourage countries to leave rainforest standing instead of harvesting it for the quickest return. One promising system now working in several Latin American countries is the 'debt-for-nature swap' that allows a portion of the nation's debt to be written off in return for rainforest protection.

On a personal level it is worth asking yourself whether the people you meet in the Amazon Basin can make a living from the standing rainforest. If so, how? If not, what are the options open to them? You can join environmental groups who pressure politicians to tackle domestic environmental issues. Only when countries are serious about their own problems is it possible to believe that interference in the internal affairs of another is motivated by genuine concern. For more direct involvement, join international organisations who lobby governments and work to find ways of using the Amazon Basin's resources while leaving the forest standing. Some addresses follow.

In the US

Conservation International 2501 M St, NW, Suite 200, Washington DC, 20037; tel: 800 429 5660; email: membership@conservation.org; web: www.conservation.org

---

HELPING CONSERVE AMAZON RAINFOREST AT HOME
Oliver Whalley

Think 'globally and act locally' could be; 'to act locally is to act globally', this being a key to help conserve what is left of the Amazon rainforest. Every little bit helps, from recycling to just being informed.

- Campaign and support alternatives to fossil fuels and nuclear fuels.
- Steer clear of gold (especially when jungle produced).
- Steer clear of cocaine (millions of hectares of forest are lost for its production to supply the developed world's demand).
- Avoid buying tropical hardwood doors, furniture or plyboard (a lot of packing cases are made of tropical rainforest wood); there is no truly sustainable tropical hardwood harvested yet.
- Contribute to international and local environmental groups protecting the forest and Indians.

Rainforest Action Network 221 Pine St, Suite 500, San Francisco, CA 94104; tel: 415 398 4404; fax: 415 398 2732; email: rainforest@ran.org; web: www.ran.org
WorldWide Fund for Nature (WWF) 1250 24th St NW, Washington, DC 20037; tel: 202 293 4800; fax: 202 293 9211; web: www.wwf.org and www.panda.org

In the UK

Rainforest Concern 27 Lansdowne Crescent, London W11 2NS; tel: 020 7229 2093; fax: 020 7221 4094; email: info@rainforestconcern.org; web: www.rainforestconcern.org
Rainforest Foundation Suite A5, City Cloisters, 196 Old Street, London, EC1V 9FR; tel: 020 7251 6345; fax: 020 7251 4969; email: rainforestuk@rainforestuk.com; web: www.rainforestfoundationuk.org
Tourism Concern Stapleton House, 277-281 Holloway Road, London, N7 8HN; tel: 020 7753 3330; fax: 020 7753 3331; email: info@tourismconcern.org.uk: web: www.tourismconcern.org.uk
WorldWide Fund for Nature Panda House, Weyside Park, Godalming, Surrey, GU7 1XR; tel: 01483 426 444; fax: 01483 426 409; web: www.wwf.org and www.panda.org

MAJOR OVERLAND ROUTES IN THE AMAZON

Practical Information

PREPARATIONS AND PLANNING
Red tape

All travellers to South American countries need a **passport** valid for at least six months. **Visa** requirements for specific countries are given below with additional information provided in the individual country chapters.

VISA REQUIREMENTS OF AMAZON COUNTRIES

Country and visa	USA	UK	Can	Aus	NZ	SA	Fre	Ger	Neth	Jap
Bolivia 90-day	–	–	–	–	–	–	–	–	–	–
Brazil 90-day	+	–	+	+	+	–	–	–	–	+
Colombia 90-day	–	–	–	–	–	–	–	–	–	–
Ecuador 90-day	–	–	–	–	–	–	+	–	–	–
F Guiana 90-day	–	+	–	+	+	–	–	–	–	–
Guyana	–	–	–	–	–	–	–	–	–	–
Peru 90-day	–	–	–	–	+	–	–	–	–	–
Suriname 60-day	+	+	+	+	+	+	+	+	–	+
Venezuela 90-day	–	–	–	–	–	–	–	–	–	–

Visas required for entrance overland only.

('+' = required, '–' = not required)

If you are travelling overland and require a visa – which you have not yet got – to enter a neighbouring country, you will need to get it from the city nearest to the border. Few frontier towns have the authority to issue visas.

Regardless of nationality, visa requirements can change overnight so check directly with the embassy or consulate of countries you plan to visit. A good tour operator should be able to tell you if you need a visa. Alternatively a visa advisory service can arrange visas at reasonable prices if required. There may be delays so plan well ahead.

Zierer Visa Service tel: (USA) 800 843 9151; web: www.zvs.com.
MASTA (Medical Advisory Service for Travellers Abroad); Visa and Passport Information Line for up-to-the-minute advice; tel: (UK) 0906 8 224100 at 60p a minute; web: www.masta.org.

Entrance to a country is technically subject to you proving that you have a ticket for onward travel and sufficient funds to support yourself for the duration of your stay; in reality proof is rarely requested but be prepared.

Immunisations are recommended for travel to the Amazon and you should make an informed choice about taking malaria prevention. Brazil requires a yellow fever vaccination for travel in parts of Amazonia. Although it is very rare to be asked to show your immunisation certificate the situation would change immediately in the event of an outbreak. In the UK, MASTA also have a travellers' health line; tel: 0906 8 224100 at 60p a minute.

In South America you have to carry **identification** with you at all times. In most cases a photocopy of your passport is sufficient – with the exception of Venezuela where officials insist on seeing the real thing. Several countries have checkpoints along roads used to travel to the Amazon and you have to show your passport.

Money

Currencies for each country are dealt with in each country chapter. Below are a few general guidelines.

Without exception US dollars are the best currency to have when visiting South America. Travelling with a tour group, most of your main costs are prepaid but you will need currency to pay for drinks, meals, souvenirs, tips and airport taxes. Independent travellers may want the security of travellers' cheques – the most widely accepted being American Express.

Dollar bills, in tens, twenties and fifties, should not be damaged or even slightly torn as money-changers and exchange bureaux often refuse damaged notes. Travellers' cheques can be difficult or impossible to change in out-of-the-way places. Credit cards and automatic teller machines (ATMs) are increasingly common, allowing you to get cash out of hole-in-the-wall machines in some of the strangest places. A money belt or pouch is useful for keeping things safe and close to your body.

Insurance

Premiums and coverage levels vary dramatically between different insurance companies so it pays to shop around. In general if something is too precious to lose you probably shouldn't be taking it with you. If you have to spend all your trip in close proximity to your bags, worried that they might be stolen, your trip will hardly be the most relaxing.

Vital, however, is to get cover for emergency treatment and evacuation. Accidents do happen and the cost of emergency evacuation is horrendous. One story tells of an independent traveller who slipped when climbing off the back of a truck in Manu National Park, Peru. Returning home under her own steam with *two* broken legs was difficult enough; having to bear the financial cost as well would have added debt to injury.

When to go

Assuming a flexible schedule, the answer to this really depends on what you hope to get out of your trip.

For a lot of destinations, weather plays a decisive role. Not so with the Amazon. Much of the region shows no great difference in weather from month to month. Equatorial rainforest generally has no well-defined dry or rainy season. Some months are drier than others but you can expect rain any time. The wettest months south of the Equator are between November and April, while north of the Equator the heaviest rains fall between June and October. Humidity is high year-round and temperatures are warm but rarely unbearably hot. During the day, showers are most likely mid-afternoon.

Weather apart, what else can help you to time your visit? Perhaps most important is the dramatic annual change in river level. Every year around the same time the Amazon floods, and the river level rises and falls by as much as 12.5m in places. Floodwaters advance and then recede, creating flooded *várzea* forest with profound effects on the flora, fauna and human inhabitants. As you would expect, the contrast between highest and lowest river levels greatly alters the habitat. (See *Chapter 5* for greater detail on seasonal flooding.)

If your trip is to the flooded forest areas you have three choices of when to go. The 'seasons' are low water, high water and in between. In the central Amazon Basin, the lowest water period is from October to November. The level begins to rise between December and January, reaching high water during April and May. The converse is the case north of the Equator. After several weeks the floodwaters begin to recede. This timing varies slightly from year to year and recently the timing of the floods has become less predictable. Local people say that the rise and fall of the river is becoming more erratic than it used to be.

Low water

If aquatic life is your main interest, the low water period (July to February) is best. River channels are narrow and shallow, so fish, caiman and dolphins are more abundant – angling is also better. Land trails are drier at this time and insects tend to be less bothersome.

On the other hand at low water small channels get clogged with vegetation, restricting access to some wildlife areas. Your boat may run into submerged sandbanks, but this is more an occasional irritation than anything else.

Animals tend to disperse during low water, reducing the amount of wildlife you may see. However, isolated water bodies become more attractive to large animals and may be excellent sites to spot game. The time of lowest water, from October to November, is also usually the hottest time of year.

High water

For forest life, high water is best. Tree-dwelling animals have less space and become more crowded so you have a greater chance of seeing monkeys, sloths and birds. Also many inundated riverside plants flower at high water, notably acacias, cecropias and morning glory. River travel at high water along tree-lined tributaries brings you closer to the rainforest canopy.

During high water, land trails and footpaths may be cut short or totally inaccessible. For a deep forest expedition, camping out at this season ought to be avoided.

Aquatic life is more dispersed at this time, meaning that dolphins, caiman and piranha are locally less abundant. However, all these are encountered on the average trip, whatever the season.

As river levels rise, muddy banks erode and flooded meadows are flushed out. Debris floats downstream, often in spectacular log-jams.

In between

With all these possibilities it is hard to decide when to go. Picking a transitional time, say a month or two before high water, is a good compromise. Weather tends to be less cloudy at this time and it's not too warm. Fish are still moving upstream into newly flooded areas so plenty of aquatic life can usually be seen.

Where to go

The Amazon Basin is a big place. Choosing where to go is difficult but there are some general guidelines that might point you in the right direction. Get up-to-date country information such as travel warnings from the US State Department (web: travel.state.gov). Travelling around the countries in the order of the book chapters, consider the following:

Venezuela (*Chapter 7*, page 185)

This is arguably the most developed of Amazon countries. Tourism here is well established in general, so the fledgling industry developing in the rainforests of the Amazon and Orinoco Basins has a good understanding of the needs of the tourist. On the whole the rainforest has not suffered the large-scale logging experienced by many Amazon countries, so much of it remains undisturbed. Venezuela has a good selection of rainforest opportunities: secluded jungle lodges, floating hotels, river adventure trips and visits to several indigenous groups that have chosen to accommodate travellers. Throw in a bit of whitewater rafting and the all-round experience is complete. The normally flat relief of lowland rainforest is interrupted in Venezuela by the stunning flat-top mountains called *tepuis*. Unfortunately Venezuela is also one of the more expensive countries in the Amazon as all trips require a permit and have to be guided.

Colombia (*Chapter 8*, page 211)

This country gets a hard time internationally for being the cocaine production centre of the world. Travelling off the beaten track is generally discouraged for reasons of safety. Consequently the tourism industry in the Colombian Amazon is somewhat underdeveloped. Independent travellers may find visiting the Colombian Amazon rewarding but should be aware of the risks. Colombia's

WHERE TO WATCH BIRDS IN AMAZONIA

Nigel Wheatley, *author of 'Where to Watch Birds in South America'*

In birdwatching circles South America is known as 'the bird continent' with over 3,000 different species; almost one third of the world's birds, far more than on any other continent. Over 2,000 of them occur no where else. The reason for this incredible diversity lies with the continent's great variety of habitats, which range from the driest desert on earth (the Atacama) and the world's most extensive wetland (the Pantanal) to the luxuriant subtropical and temperate forests on the slopes of the Andes and vast swathes of lowland tropical rainforest. The latter is the most fruitful habitat of all, the richest on earth in fact, and most of it is confined to Amazonia.

The Amazonian forest is not all the same. There are numerous types of subtly different forests, according to local rainfall, relief and soils, and different birds have evolved in these different forest types; so, for example, a set of birds which inhabits one side of a ridge may be completely different from the set of birds present on the other side of the ridge. When one considers the size of the Amazon Basin (some six million km^2), it is easy to imagine how so many different birds evolved in the region.

World bird diversity reaches its peak in west Amazonia, in the eastern regions of Ecuador and Peru, where just 1km^2 supports as many as 300 different species! The world record for the most birds seen in a day, without the use of a light aircraft, is held by Manú Biosphere Reserve in south Peru. A mindboggling 331 different bird species were recorded in the Cocha Cashu area in September 1986. It is possible to get a taste of such terrific birdwatching by visiting the tented Manú Wildlife Centre, accessible by air, or by road and

Amazon gateway town of Leticia is one of the main towns on the Amazon River and in addition to being a main connection point for boats up and down the river, is also a good base for trips to nearby rainforest. Having said that it is probably best to include other countries in your Amazon visit. Colombia is one of the cheaper South American countries, but the distances involved can soon eat up your money especially if you have to take a few flights.

Ecuador (*Chapter 9*, page 237)

This beautifully compact country has just about got it all. With access to the lowlands possible by road and plane, Ecuador is popular with independent and group travellers alike. Several Amazon lodges can be accessed easily from the lowland towns of Coca, Tena and Misahualli. Adventure excursions into the rainforest are available and visits to indigenous groups open to travellers can also be arranged. For the truly adventurous, Ecuador is the place to follow in the canoe-wake of Orellana, Teixeira *et al*, and following the resolution of border disputes in 2000, it is now possible to travel into Ecuador from the Peruvian Amazon, and so replicate the great explorers' journeys. Ecuador is one of the cheapest countries for travel in South America. If you are looking for a multi-stop vacation, the unique Galápagos Islands will tempt any nature-lover.

Peru (*Chapter 10*, page 275)

Peru has a bit of everything. Iquitos in the northern lowlands is a focal point for Amazon visitors, with international flights direct from Miami making week-long visits to the Amazon a realistic possibility. A dozen jungle lodges, and two canopy

river from Cusco. Over 500 species have been recorded around here in a single year, and nearby is a riverbank macaw lick which is visited regularly by hundreds of parrots, including spectacular macaws.

Manú Wildlife Centre may claim to be the best for birds, at least in terms of variety, but there are plenty of other more comfortable, and consequently more expensive, forest lodges in west Amazonia and elsewhere across the region, where over 500 bird species have also been recorded. During the 1990s three or four new lodges and reserves opened each year and there are now far too many to list here. More details are in the chapters on individual countries.

It is important to remember that, even though the diversity of bird species is higher in Amazonia than anywhere else on earth, many of the individual species are very thin on the ground, and it is possible to walk for hours in the forests and end up seeing just a few birds. However, If you are fortunate enough to meet a feeding flock of birds then your list at the end of the day should be a lot longer, because these bird waves, as they are also known, may contain over 70 different individuals of 20 or so species. Either way, even veteran birdwatchers see many more birds with the help of experienced guides, and fortunately most lodges employ at least a few local people who are usually first-class bird finders.

Birdwatching novices need not fear being overawed. Such guides are used to showing newcomers the most spectacular species first. So even if you have just the slightest interest in birds it is worth visiting any one of the lodges and reserves mentioned in this book, or some of the many others, because a few days amongst the birdlife of Amazonia may well end up being the most pleasurable experience of your life!

walkways, are within a few hours of Iquitos. Tourist-standard riverboats travel the Amazonas (as the Amazon by Iquitos is named), stopping at villages and jungle trails en route, continuing downstream to Leticia on the border with Brazil and Colombia.

If you want to experience the epic length of the navigable Amazon from the confines of a gently swaying hammock, then Pucallpa in the central Amazon region is the starting point. For whitewater adventure kayaking near the headwaters of the Amazon high in the Peruvian Andes, use Cusco as a base. More sedate rafting through lowland tributaries can also be arranged from the Inca capital as can trips to the internationally famous Manú National Park and Tambopata clay-lick. Peru is still one of the cheapest countries in South America, although organised trips to the Amazon Basin can be quite pricey. If venturing as far south as Cusco then don't miss Machu Picchu, the lost city of the Incas.

Bolivia (Chapter 11, page 325)
This is the cheapest country to travel in, but the most expensive to reach, with the only direct flights coming from Miami. For a long time it was the independent traveller's paradise, but now trail-blazing tour operators are starting to put together trekking and rafting trips through the Bolivian lowlands in the northeast to Madidi and Manuripi Heath National Park, and west to Noel Kempff National Park. A floating hotel serves the central Amazon region near Trinidad. Connecting to the Amazon main stream along the Grande-Mamoré-Madeira river system it is possible to travel to the mouth of the Amazon, but river traffic is less common than in Peru and Brazil.

Brazil (Chapter 12, page 357)
This is, for many, the true home of the Amazon. Not surprisingly the opportunities are endless. Budget travel up and down the Amazon and its tributaries is easy, as an extensive network of passenger vessels travels to the border of most Amazon countries. Trips to secluded lodges and Amazon towns by boat or plane are easily arranged either from your home country or from Manaus, which has international air connections with Miami. Brazil is home to more indigenous groups than any other Amazon country, but travellers are not permitted to visit indigenous areas without difficult-to-arrange permission from the government agency FUNAI. Several poor roads stretch across the Brazilian Amazon providing insights into life in growing frontier cities and colonisation communities that are pushing deep into the rainforest. Brazil is an expensive country in which to travel, although since the devaluation of the currency in 1999, travellers have been getting better value for money.

Guyana, French Guiana and Suriname (Chapter 13, page 419)
These countries have, between them, some of the least spoilt rainforest wildlife on the continent. For years closed to travellers and external influence of any kind, the countries, although pricey to travel to and quite expensive once you arrive, offer some of the best chances for seeing wildlife in virtually untouched rainforest. Although even the most basic infrastructure for tourists is limited, new lodges and opportunities are being developed all the time.

GETTING THERE AND AWAY
By air
Countries within the Amazon Basin are served by numerous airlines and prices vary greatly. Limiting your route or the number of days you are available for travel is likely to increase the cost. If you have time, shop around or get in touch with a low-cost specialist travel agent. There are several that now specialise in travel to,

within and from South America. If you can leave at short notice then you may be able to pick up a bargain. There are a number of websites for companies which specialise in cheap flights. In the US, search the web for cheap tickets at www.cheapflights.com, www.orbitz.com, www.latindiscountair.com and lowestairfare.com. If you are new to air travel or want reassurance, www.airsafe.com features safety records by airline and aircraft type. Visit www.fearofflying.com for suggestions on how to overcome 'aerophobia'.

In the UK try www.opodo.co.uk, www.cheapflights.co.uk and www.airtickets.co.uk.

High season, when flights are more expensive, is between May and September, with a mini-peak close to Christmas.

Buying tickets in South America for travel back home is straightforward but discounted prices are rare. If you are uncertain when you expect to return it is possible to buy return tickets valid for up to a year. Open-jaw tickets are available for people who want to arrive in one country but leave from another.

More specific information for each country can be found in the relevant chapter.

From the USA

Most flights connect through Miami with most countries served by the US air carriers American Airlines and United Airlines. Most South America national airlines also have a connecting service. From Miami you can fly straight to the heart of the Amazon, with flights to Manaus with American Airlines.

Prices from the US vary considerably but you may pick up the occasional bargain. Shop around and you might get a bargain. **Around the World Travel** (tel: 1 800 748 8689; web: www.atwt.net) can help with flight details. Airline phone numbers and websites are:

American 800 433 7300; www.aa.com
Avianca 866 337 7342; www.avianca.com
Continental 800 231 0856; www.continental.com
Copa 800 359 2672; www.copaair.com
Iberia 800 231 0856; www.iberia.com
Japan Airlines 800 525 3663; www.japanair.com (US); www.jal-europe.com
KLM 800 374 7747; www.klm.com
LanChile 800 735 5526; www.lanchile.com
LanPeru 800 735 5590; www.lanperu.com
Lufthansa 800 645 3880; www.lufthansa.com
Varig 800 468 2744; www.varig.com

From Europe

A dozen or more airlines serve South America from Europe. Aerolineas Argentinas, Avianca, British Airways, KLM, LanChile, Iberia, Varig, AeroPerú, Viasa, American Airlines, United Airlines... the list goes on. Which you use depends on where you are leaving from. Each national airline leaves from, or ends up in, its own country with possible deviations en route. For example, flights with Iberia travel via Madrid, flights with KLM go via Amsterdam. There are direct flights to Brazil, Colombia and Venezuela from Europe. The only way of making Manaus your first port of call in the Amazon is by catching a connecting flight from Miami.

Use a specialist agency to help you get what you want. **Journey Latin America** (12 & 13 Heathfield Terrace, London, W4 4JE; tel: 020 8747 8315; fax: 020 8742 1312; email: flights@journeylatinamerica.co.uk; web:www.journeylatinamerica.co.uk) is an excellent source on flights, tours and travelling in South America. **Trailfinders**, with several offices throughout the UK (tel: 020 7938 3939), can offer a wide range of flights. **Bridge The World** (tel: 020 7911 0900; web: www.bridgetheworld.com) is also worth contacting, as is **Last Frontiers** (tel: 01296 653000; email: info@lastfrontiers.com). **Wexas** (tel: 020 7581 8761; email: americas@wexas.com) offers flights worldwide – but you must become a member, costing £48 for an individual.

Example budget fares from London covering low to high season averages are: Bogota £450 to £600; Caracas £470 to £600; Quito £580 to £670; Rio/São Paolo £370 to £550; La Paz £680 to £860; Lima £590 to £680, Cayenne £470 to £720 and Paramaribo £627 to £780 plus.

From Australia and New Zealand

Aerolineas Argentinas run a regular twice weekly service from Sydney (A$1099 return), and Auckland (NZ$1399 return) to Buenos Aires with good connections to Amazon countries. Qantas also provide a service to Santiago linking with LanChile to cover the rest of South America.

Airpasses

If you think you will be moving around a particular country, it is worth exploring the option of an airpass. Generally there are a minimum number of flights or 'legs' that are purchased as coupons for a set fee. There are usually some conditions in the fine print, a common one being that you cannot repeat any journeys. They are currently available for domestic flights within Colombia, Peru and Brazil, but this may change.

At the airport

At the **check-in** desk make absolutely sure your baggage is labelled correctly by the desk clerk. Luggage and passengers go on some pretty spectacular routes around South America and it's worth making sure you know where you and your luggage are next meant to meet. Even then, accidents can happen, so carry any essential toilet and medical items (particularly regular medication, if you take it) in your cabin bag, together with a spare set of basic clothing.

Passengers on all international flights from South American airports have to pay a **departure tax**. The tax varies between countries and changes without notice. Make sure you find out what the departure tax is before that last minute spending spree. Most countries also have a nominal airport tax ($3–5) for domestic flights. In the past some airports have required payment in US dollars but at present there are fewer restrictions on using local currency.

Overland
Border crossings in the Amazon Basin

The Amazon may be just one river, but that does not mean you can move about Amazonia without restrictions. International border crossings in South America range from barely noticeable frontier huts through to no-go internationally disputed territories where conflicts at times flare up. Sometimes you just have to follow the rules.

If you require a visa to enter a neighbouring country, you will need to get it from the city nearest to the border – be sure to check that this is possible. Few frontier towns have facilities with the authority to issue visas.

Venezuela has only one generally used crossing to **Brazil**, where buses leave from Sta Elena de Uairén (Venezuela) for Boa Vista and Manaus. A visa is required to enter Venezuela from Brazil. The triple-frontier between Venezuela, Colombia and Brazil is on the Río Negro at San Simón de Cocuy (Venezuela) and, if you do arrive at this point, there is no guarantee you will be able to cross into Brazil. If you do manage it, cargo boats can take you downstream to Manaus.

Crossing the border from Venezuela's state of Amazonas into **Colombia** is considerably more difficult and, even if possible, will require a great deal of smooth talking. There are several crossing points – Puerto Ayacucho, San Fernando de Atobapo, San Carlos de Río Negro – to Colombia, but no road connects the Colombian side with the rest of the country. Travel on the Colombian side of the border is considered by many to be hazardous.

Colombia's most commonly used frontier in the Amazon Basin is at Leticia, where border crossings to **Peru** and **Brazil** are largely a somewhat overcomplicated formality. Leticia has connections with the rest of Colombia by boat and plane. From Colombia it is possible to travel to **Ecuador** from the village of Puerto Asis, travelling to San Miguel before getting a boat upstream heading for Lago Agrio.

Crossing from **Ecuador** to **Peru** in the Amazon Basin is now possible following the 2000 resolution of long-standing border disputes. The easiest route for independent travellers to follow is along the Rio Napo (Orellana's route), although it's possible with careful planning to use other rivers.

In addition to the frontier with Colombia and Brazil on the Amazon main stream already mentioned, **Peru** has a couple of smaller frontier posts. An adventurous journey into **Brazil** can be organised from Pucallpa; it involves boat travel and a few days' walking in the jungle before you end up in Cruzeiro do Sul. Further south, having completed passport formalities in Puerto Maldonado, you can travel north to Iñapari and cross into Assis Brazil, or Bolpebra in **Bolivia.**

From the Bolivian side, crossing into **Peru** can be completed via Puerto Heath but questions will probably be asked as to why you are in a place that is so completely out of the way. Formalities can be completed in Cobija. Several crossing points into **Brazil** exist, including Cobija and Guayaramerín. Crossing is also possible at San Matías to the north of Santa Cruz which connects to Cáceres in Brazil by bus.

Overland crossings between **Guyana**, **Suriname** and **French Guiana** can all be completed using pedestrian ferries. The southern town of Lethem in **Guyana** is connected to **Brazil** by a road which carries regular buses from Boa Vista. Road connection from Lethem to the rest of the country is along a very poor road that is very often impassable. **French Guiana** has a border crossing with **Brazil** but there is no road on the Guiana side so you need a combination of canoes and walking.

TIME ZONES OF AMAZON COUNTRIES RELATIVE TO GMT

Country	Hours behind GMT	Country	Hours behind GMT
Bolivia	4	Guyana	4
Brazil	3 to 5	Peru	5
Colombia	5	Suriname	3
Ecuador	5	Venezuela	4
French Guiana	3		

Of the Amazon countries only Brazil has daylight saving time (equivalent to British Summer Time), but all states of the USA have it.

HOW TO GO

Some travellers have always been independent and wouldn't dream of changing. Others prefer the benefits of group travel. Opportunities for independent and group travel are endless in the Amazon. Some of the pointers below may help you decide which would be best for you.

If you want to take an organised trip with a group there are hundreds of tour operators offering trips to the Amazon. If you're travelling independently, even more possibilities arise. In either case, you can get a trip to suit almost any interest: a river cruise, a canoe or rafting trip, a small plane expedition and even jungle survival courses. There are trips focusing on wildlife photography, birdwatching, native traditional crafts and ethnobotany (the study of how people use plants for medicine, food, tools, etc). You can participate in scientific research on river dolphins or rainforest butterflies. Alternatively you can pursue spiritual development, accompanied by a psychic to get in touch with your 'spirit guide'. Other tours include visits to native shamans providing insight into native beliefs, some of which may actually involve 'trips' on hallucinogens used by the shamans.

Within each country chapter you will find information on tour operators who specialise in that country. First though, you need to have a good idea of the sort of trip you want.

Hard or soft adventure?

How much physical challenge do you want? Do you want to kick back and relax in a hammock, a beer in one hand and a good book in the other? Or maybe you crave the rush of whitewater rafting in the Amazon's headwaters? Could you rise to the ultimate challenge of a jungle survival course? In tour company jargon, do you want hard or soft adventure?

Soft adventure holidays appeal mostly to those seeking a relaxing time with little physical exertion. These are the most popular trips for group travel. Tourist riverboats are a comfortable way to visit remote areas, and several lodges, seemingly in the middle of nowhere, offer exceptional hospitality. Most tours of this type include walks along forest trails and canoe rides. Participants need be only moderately fit, though excursions are more enjoyable if you can at least walk a while without tiring. At a minimum you need at least to be able to clamber in and out of a boat and up steep and sometimes slippery steps, and to carry your own luggage.

Hard adventure appeals to the more active. These vacations involve considerable activity, from backpacking, trekking or hiking through to kayaking and river-rafting. Increasingly popular is the jungle survival course, during which participants live off the land. Most hard adventure trips involve a fair degree of exertion, some being very strenuous. Be sure to double-check with your tour operator on the activity levels and if necessary take up a fitness programme beforehand.

Here, there or everywhere?

Decide if you prefer to stay in one place to get to know it well or if you'd like to visit several places to get a broader perspective. If you travel independently you can visit more places than with a group, and in the order you choose, spending time where and when you want.

Group travel generally has a set itinerary. To avoid disappointments familiarise yourself with the trip itinerary to ensure it includes everything you expect. Ideally, time and money allowing, you would do everything. Whichever type of trip you opt for you must also select areas to visit. How do you decide?

This is where it is important to have as much information as you can lay your hands on about a prospective trip. Leafing through the pages of this book will help. For group travel, a good tour operator will provide enough details for you to make an informed decision.

Ask yourself what you would most like to see and do during your time in the Amazon. To a certain extent, the areas you visit will constrain your activities. Remote areas have fewer facilities but will offer a greater physical challenge for hard adventurers. Obviously, your own interests will be important. If possible talk to others who have taken the sort of trip you are interested in or, better still, who have travelled with the tour operator you are considering. A good company will provide ample pre-trip advice, such as wildlife information, packing lists, whether you need a visa, inoculation requirements and so on.

Independent or group travel?

Once you've decided on activity levels and where you want to go, the next choice is whether you travel independently or with a group. Each has its pros and cons.

Although a group obviously has greater overall environmental impact than one or two people, the impact per individual may be less. But then, in a group there is less room to apply one's individual ecophilosophy.

One of the main benefits of group travel is the ability to get to the place of interest with the minimum of fuss and hassle – ideal if you have a time constraint. Most group excursions are between one and three weeks long – though many are optionally longer – which is just about enough time to get out of work mode and relax.

If you decide to travel in a group, try to go with a small one, 15 people maximum, for several practical reasons. Smaller groups are better treated at hotels and restaurants. On wildlife excursions, a large group can crowd you out just as you are about to take that perfect shot – especially important for photographers and birdwatchers. But even small groups can be constraining and in too small a group it's hard to escape from someone you don't get on with.

Internet

The Internet is an excellent tool to help you explore possibilities, plan a trip and make reservations. Some airlines, hotels and tour operators provide discounts if you book online. The net is also the easiest way to get up-to-date country information. See *Appendix 3* for useful websites.

Several sites help you find tours or travel providers. Visit www.find-tour-operators.com to search from among over 1,000 tour operators by destination or interest. Interest categories include active, adventurous, family, history and culture, nature, wildlife, soft adventure and spiritual.

RELATIVE ADVANTAGES OF INDEPENDENT OR GROUP TRAVEL

	Independent	Group
Cost	+	–
Flexibility	+	–
Risk	+	–
Exertion	+	–
Variety	+	–
Impact	–	+

('+' = more, '–' = less)

GROUP TRAVEL: GREEN OR MEAN?

If you've decided to go for a group trip, your task now is to shop around for a suitable tour operator who runs your sort of trip – easier said than done. We provide tour operator information in each country chapter, with contact details. Get information from as many tour operators as you can, and compare. Cheapest is not necessarily best, as companies differ in their ecosensitivity. A lot of operators promote their trips as 'ecotourism' or 'green' tourism but check to see if this is just hype.

In the US, **The International Ecotourism Society** (PO Box 755, North Bennington, VT 05259, USA; tel: 802 651 9818; fax: 802 651 9819; email: ecomail@ecotourism.org; web: www.ecotourism.org) can supply a list of member tour operators; in the UK, contact **Green Globe 21** (7 St Stephens Court, St Stephens Road, Bournemouth BH2 6LA; tel: 01202 312001; fax: 01202 312002, email: info@greenglobe21.com; web: www.greenglobe21.com). If ecosensitivity concerns you, here are the sort of questions you can ask:

- What is the tour operator's environmental philosophy?
- Who will be leading the tour?
- Are excursions changed regularly to minimise ecological damage?
- How does the local economy benefit?
- Is the company dedicated to sustainable development of the tourism industry?
- How ecologically sound is the accommodation?

Tour operators in the US

Country chapters have information about tour operators providing trips to specific countries.

Adventures Abroad 1124 Fir Avenue, Blaine, WA 98230; tel: 800 665 3998; fax: 360 775 9926; email: sales@adventures-abroad.com; web: www.adventures-abroad.com. Small-group soft-adventure tours in most Amazon countries from one week to 40 days. Offices in UK, Canada and New Zealand.

Adventure Life Journeys 1655 S 3rd St West, Ste 1, Missoula, MT 59801; tel: 800 344 6118; fax: 406 541 2676; email: info@adventure-life.com; web: www.adventure-life.com. Lodge-based and camping/kayaking week long small-group tours in lowland forest of Ecuador, Peru and Bolivia.

Dreamweaver Travel 1185 River Drive, River Falls, WI 54022; tel: 715 425 1037; fax: 715 426 0829; email: dudley@dreamweavertravel.net; web: www.dreamweavertravel.net. Ecologically and culturally appropriate adventures to Brazil, Bolivia, Peru, Ecuador, and Guyana, including wildlife and birding tours to the Amazon.

Earthwatch Institute 3 Clock Tower Place, Ste 100, Box 75, Maynard, MA 01754; tel: 800 776 0188; fax: 978 461 2332: email: info@earthwatch.org; web: www.earthwatch.org. A non-profit organisation offering volunteers one- to three-week trips to assist researchers on scientific expeditions from archaeology to zoology. No special skills required. Also has offices in the UK, Australia, and Japan.

Earth River Expeditions 180 Towpath Rd, Accord, CA 12404; tel: 800 643 2784; fax: 845 626 4423; email: earthriv@ulster.net; web: www.earthriver.com. Whitewater rafting trips down the Upano (Ecuador) and other Amazon rivers.

Eco and Zegrahm Expeditions 192 Nickerson St #200, Seattle, WA 98109; tel: 800 628 8747; fax: 206 285 5037; email: zoe@zeco.com; web: www.zeco.com. High end group tours, including expedition cruises and land tours to various Amazon locations.

Far & Wide's Adventure Center 1311 63rd St, Ste 200, Emeryville, CA 94608; tel: 800 227 8747; fax: 510 654 4200; email: tripinfo@adventurecenter.com; web: www.adventurecenter.com. Affordable small group adventure tours from seven-day jungle adventures to eight-week overland expeditions.

Field Guides Inc 9433 Bee Cave Rd, Building 1, Ste 150, Austin, TX 78733; tel: 512 263 7295/800 728 4953; fax: 512 263 0117; email: fieldguides@fieldguides.com; web: www.fieldguides.com. Specialist birdwatching tours to South America since 1985 led by professional expert ornithologists.

Focus Tours 103 Moya Rd, Santa Fe, NM 87508; tel: 505 466 4688; fax: 505 466 4689; email: focustours@aol.com; web: www.focustours.com. Natural-history and educational tours including birdwatching with local naturalist-guides.

Forum International Travel 91 Gregory Lane #21, Pleasant Hill, CA 94523; tel: 800 252 4475; fax: 925 671 2993; email: fti@foruminternational.com web: www.foruminternational.com. Established 1965, originators of the ecotourism concept offering riverboat cruises to various Amazon countries.

GORPtravel 6707 Winchester Circle, Ste 101, Boulder, CO 80301; tel: 877 440 4677; fax: 303 635 0658; email: info@gorptravel.com; web: www.gorptravel.com. Wide range of tours in Peru, Brazil, Ecuador and Bolivia.

Green Tracks 10 Town Plaza, Ste 231, Durango, CO 81301; tel: 800 966 6539; fax: 970 884 6107; email: info@GreenTracks.com; web: www.greentracks.com. Nature trips ranging from relaxed riverboat trips to adventurous expeditions.

Holbrook Travel 3540 NW 13th St, Gainesville, FL 32609; tel: 800 451 7111; fax: 352 371 3710; email: Travel@holbrooktravel.com; web: www.holbrooktravel.com. Affordable custom-designed travel to lesser-known areas in Ecuador and Peru.

International Expeditions One Environs Park, Helena, AL 35080; tel: 800 633 4734; fax: 205 428 1714; email: nature@ietravel.com; web: www.internationalexpeditions.com. Luxury tourist riverboat cruises and walkway tour in the Peruvian Amazon.

Inti Travel and Tours Box 1586, Banff, Alberta, Canada, T1L 1B5; tel: 403 760 3565; fax: 403 760 3566; email: inti@agt.net; web: www.discoveramazonia.com. Comprehensive range of lodges, cruises and treks in Ecuador, Peru and Bolivia and Manaus, Brazil.

Journeys International 107 Aprill Drive, Ste 3, Ann Arbor, MI 48103; tel: 800 255 8735; fax: 734 665 2945; email: info@journeys-intl.com; web: www.journeys-intl.com. Selection of riverboat and lodge-based tours to Brazil and Peru.

Ladatco Tours 3006 Aviation Av, Ste 4C, Coconut Grove, FL 33133; tel: 800 327 6162; fax: 305-285-0504; email: tailor@ladatco.com; web: www.ladatco.com. Range of tours to the most sought after Amazon destinations in Brazil, Peru and Ecuador.

Latin America Reservation Center Inc PO Box 1435, Dundee, FL 33838; tel: 800 327 3573; fax: 863 439 2118; email: travel@larc1.com; web: www.larc1.com. Can organise arrangements for lodgings, air and land travel throughout South America.

Maupintour 10650 W Charleston Bd, Las Vegas, NV 89135; tel: 800 255 4266; fax: 702 260 3787; email: info@maupintour.com; web: www.maupintour.com. Group and individual tours throughout South America.

Nature Encounters, Ltd 2116 Arlington Av, Ste 310, Los Angeles, CA 90018; tel: 323 733 6622; email: info@nature-encounters.com; web: www.nature-encounters.com. General rainforest tours for groups and individuals.

Nature Expeditions International 7860 Peters Rd, Ste F-103, Plantation, FL 33324; tel: 954 693 8852/800 869 0639; fax: 954 693 8854; email: info@naturexp.com; web: www.naturexp.com. Founded in 1973, NEI operates upscale soft adventure, wildlife, cultural, and natural history tours led by local experts.

Neotropical Journeys 3920 SE 14th Terrace, Gainesville, FL 32641; tel: 352 376 7110/877 384 2589; email: info@njourneys.com; web: www.njourneys.com. Organise expert-guided

one- to three-week birding and nature tours to select destinations in Ecuador, Peru and Brazil.
Oceanic Society Fort Mason Center, San Francisco, CA 94123; tel: 800 326 7491; fax: 415
474 3395; email: office@oceanicsociety.org; web: www.oceanic-society.org. Natural history
expeditions to Peru, Suriname and Guyana accompanied by a university-level naturalist.
Small Ship Cruises email: Cruisesmallships@aol.com; web: www.smallshipcruises.com/
riveramazon.html. Internet-based referral service for small ship cruises: adventure, luxury,
freighters, riverboats and charters. Over twenty Amazon boats listed.
Sol International 13780 SW 56 St, Ste 107, Miami, FL 33175; tel: 800 765 5657; fax: 305
382 9284; email: info@solintl.com; web: www.solintl.com. South America specialists with
river cruises and lodge-based tours throughout the Amazon.
Southwind Adventures PO Box 621057, Littleton, CO 80162; tel: 800 377 9463; fax: 303
972 0708; email: info@southwindadventures.com; web: www.southwindadventures.com.
Tour operator specialising in South America, with general-interest tours to most countries.
Tara Tours 6595 NW 36th St, Ste 306, Miami, FL 33166; tel: 800 327 0080; email:
taratours@aol.com; web: www.taratours.com. Established US tour operator offering a
variety of tours in several Amazon countries.
Travel Innovations/Australian and Amazonian Adventures 2711 Market Garden,
Austin, TX 78745; tel: 800-232-56; fax: 512 442 8515; email:
jmc12@amazonadventures.com; web: www.amazonadventures.com. Moderate to
upmarket multi-activity adventures in Ecuador, Peru, Brazil and Venezuela.
Victor Emanuel Nature Tours (VENT) 2525 Wallingwood Dr, Ste 1003, Austin, TX
78746; tel: 512 328 5221/800 328 8368; fax: 512 328 2919; email: info@ventbird.com; web:
www.ventbird.com. Specialist birding tours with expert ornithologists to top nature
destinations.
Wilderness Travel 1102 Ninth St, Berkeley, CA 94710; tel: 800 368 2794; fax: 510 558
2489; email: info@wildernesstravel.com; web:www.wildernesstravel.com.

Tour operators in the UK
Amerindia Steeple Cottage, Easton, Winchester, Hants SO21 1EH; tel: 01962 779317; fax:
01962 779458; email: info@pkworldwide.com; web: www.pkworldwide.com or
www.quasarnautica.com. Has lodges in Ecuador.
Andean Trails The Clockhouse, Bonnington Mill Business Centre, 72 Newhaven Rd,
Edinburgh EH6 5QG, Scotland; tel: 0131 467 7086; email: info@andeantrails.co.uk; web:
www.andeantrails.co.uk. Tours mixing Amazon and Andes.
Condor Journeys and Adventures 2 Ferry Bank, Colintraive, Argyll PA22 3AR; tel:
01700 841318; fax: 01700 841398; email: danielle@condorjourneys-adventures.com; web:
www.condorjourneys-adventures.com. A variety of upmarket, budget and tailored
adventures in Brazil, Ecuador, Peru, Bolivia, Venezuela and Guyana.
Cox & Kings 10 Greencoat Place, London SW10 1PH; tel: 020 7873 5000; fax: 020 7630
6038; email: cox.kings@coxandkings.co.uk; web:www.coxandkings.co.uk. Organise several
all-inclusive trips throughout the Amazon region.
Discovery Initiatives The Travel House, 51 Castle St, Cirencester, Gloucestershire, GL7
1QD; tel: 01285 643333; fax: 01285 885888; email: enquiry@discoveryinitiatives.com; web:
www.discoveryinitiatives.com. Work with conservation organisations to ensure deep jungle
trips cause minimal damage. One of the few companies travelling to Guyana.
EarthWatch Institute 267 Banbury Rd, Oxford, OX2 7HT; tel: 01865 318838; fax: 01865
311383; email: info@earthwatch.org.uk; web: www.uk.earthwatch.org. Runs
environmental research trips to several locations in the region.
Footprint Adventures 5 Malham Dr, Lincoln, LN6 0XD; tel: 01522 804929; fax: 01522
804928; email: sales@footprint-adventures.co.uk; web: www.footprint-adventures.co.uk.
Specialist tour operator with a wide range of natural history, birding and special activity
tours to Ecuador, Brazil and Bolivia: 'totally committed to conservation'.

ECOTOURISM?
Oliver Whalley

Tourists on tours in lowland jungle, often having paid a lot of money, expect to see wildlife and, depending on the season, the region, their luck and their guide, they may see many animals or very few. Tropical forests offer many experiences but the pressure on tour operators to provide opportunities to see, photograph or video wild animals is great. In some areas this pressure has led to the retreat of wildlife and a decrease in numbers through disturbance, particularly of their feeding and breeding habits. In Manú National Park in Peru, research done by the Frankfurt Zoological Society and the Munich Wildlife Society found a drop in the number of giant otters, largely as a result of the presence of tour boats. Lactating mothers, stressed by the intrusions, failed to produce sufficient milk for their cubs, resulting in their death.

Tourists in South America can influence the way the landscape is used and conserved, especially in the Amazon region. To some indigenous people, they can be role models, coming from developed nations with their 'high' standard of living. This makes the behaviour of tourists all the more important. Yet demand by an increasing number of visitors for the hire of 4WD vehicles and high-powered motorboats has led in some cases to a degradation of the landscape and pollution of rivers. In the past 4WDs have been responsible for severe scarring, often lasting for decades, while wetter regions have been eroded in places not normally accessible to locals. High-powered outboard motors, on the other hand, generate noise disruption and pollution, causing problems to river animals such as Amazon dolphins, manatees and otters.

Many conservationists argue that tourism is bad for any sensitive ecosystem. However, most conservationists can also see that, apart from atmospheric pollution of the hundreds of thousands of ferrying aeroplanes, generally the effects of tourism are beneficial. The overriding positive effect, in the case of the Amazon, is that tourists want to see the high diversity of life that only comes in large areas of virgin rainforest. This means that in order to attract tourists governments and in turn locals must try to conserve the primary or undisturbed habitats.

Fred Olsen Cruises White House Rd, Ipswich, IP1 5LL; tel: 01473 742424; fax: 01473 292345; email: travel.direct@fredolsen.co.uk; web: www.fredolsencruises.co.uk. Have luxury cruises leaving from the UK for the Amazon.

Geodyssey 116 Tollington Park, London N4 3RB; tel: 020 7281 7788; fax: 020 7281 7878; email: info@geodyssey.co.uk; web: www.geodyssey.co.uk. Venezuela specialists.

Journey Latin America 12–13 Heathfield Terrace, Chiswick, London W4 4JE; tel: 020 8747 3108; fax: 020 8742 1312; email: sales@journeylatinamerica.co.uk; web: www.journeylatinamerica.co.uk. Organise several trips visiting the Amazon and excellent source of information on flights to South America.

Last Frontiers Fleet Marston Farm, Aylesbury, Buckinghamshire, HP18 0QT; tel: 01296 653000; fax: 01296 658651; email: info@lastfrontiers.com; web: www.lastfrontiers.com. Bespoke South America specialists who can arrange anything you can imagine.

Reef & Rainforest Tours #1 The Plains, Totnes, Devon, TQ9 5DR; tel: 01803 866965; fax: 01803 865916; email: mail@reefandrainforest.co.uk; web: www.reefandrainforest.co.uk. Organise trips to Brazil, Peru, Ecuador and Venezuela.

Scott Dunn Latin America 12 Noyna Rd, London SW17 7PH; tel: 020 8682 5030; web: www.scottdunn.com. Itineraries focusing on the Amazon and others regions of the sub-continent.

Tribes Travel 7 The Business Centre, Earl Soham, Woodbridge, Suffolk IP13 7SA; tel: 01728 685971; fax: 01728 685973; email: web@tribes.co.uk; web: www.tribes.co.uk. Culturally senstive tours in the Peruvian and Ecuadorean Amazon.

Trips Worldwide 14 Frederick Place, Clifton, Bristol BS8 1AS; tel: 0117 311 4400; fax: 0117 311 4401; web: www.tripsworldwide.co.uk. Tailor-made opportunities in the Amazon and throughout Latin America.

Wildlife Worldwide 162 Selsdon Rd, South Croydon, Surrey CR2 6PJ; tel: 020 8667 9158; fax: 020 8667 1960; email: sales@wildlifeworldwide.com; web: www.wildlifeworldwide.com. With good knowledge of tailor-made opportunities.

Wildwings 577-579 Fishponds Rd, Bristol, BS16 3AF; tel: 0117 965 8333; fax: 0117 937 5681; email: wildinfo@wildwings.co.uk; web: www.wildwings.co.uk. Reservation agents for a wide range of accommodations and tours in most South American countries.

World Aparts Travel 15 Clarence Parade, Cheltenham, Gloucs, GL50 3PA; tel: 01242 226578; fax: 01242 242007; email: info@worldsaparttravel.co.uk.

Worldwide Journeys 27 Vanston Place, London, SW6 1AZ; tel: 020 7386 4646; fax: 020 7381 0836; email: enquiry@worldwidejourneys.co.uk; web: www.worldwidejourneys.co.uk.

Several other agencies specialise in overland or adventure trips to South America which focus on one country or may involve travel across the Amazon Basin by boat. Most have international websites so you can book from anywhere in the world. They include:

Bukima Expeditions 29 Hamilton Rd, West Norwood, London, SE27 9RZ; tel 0870 7572230; fax: 0870 7572231; email: adventure@bukima.com; web: www.bukima.com. Overland safaris that dip into the Amazon.

Guerba Expeditions 40 Station Rd, Westbury, Wiltshire BA13 3JN; tel: 01373 826611; fax: 01373 858351. email: info@guerba.co.uk; web: www.guerba.com.

Kumuka Expeditions 40 Earls Court Rd, London W8 6EJ; tel: 0800 068 8855; fax: 020 7937 6664; email: enquiries@kumuka.com; web: www.kumuka.co.uk.

Travelbag Adventures 15 Turk St, Alton, Hants GU34 1AG; tel: 01420 541007; fax: 01420 541022; email: mail@travelbag-adventures.com; web: www.travelbag-adventures.com. For small group holidays off the beaten track.

Tucan c/o Adventure Bound, 19 Gloster Road, Martlesham Heath, Suffolk, IP5 3RB; tel: 020 8896 1600; london@tucantravel.com; web: www.tucantravel.com.

In Australia

Adventure Associates 197 Oxford Street Mall, Bondi Junction, Sydney NSW 2022; PO Box 612 Bondi Junction NSW 1355; tel: 6129 389 7466; fax: 6129 369 1853; web: www.adventureassociates.com. Australia's leading South America specialists, with a wide choice of tours in most Amazon countries.

At what price?

The price of a trip is usually the critical factor that decides whether it is booked or not. The lowest-priced trip is not necessarily the automatic choice. For a week-long package tour including airfare to and from Miami, lodge accommodation and all meals provided, you can expect to pay a minimum of US$2,000 (£1,380). Depending on where you are coming from airfares add upwards from US$400 (£275) to the cost of an Amazon trip. On a pre-paid tour budget U$100–250 per week for airport taxes, handicrafts, souvenirs, tips and bottled drinks.

Independent travel

If flexibility and lots of variety are important, you probably want to travel independently. By shopping around, the independent traveller can travel inexpensively. Bucket shops in the US and throughout Europe usually have good deals that will get you to South America for a reasonable price. From the United States, air courier travel brings the cost of flights to South America within reach of even the poorest student traveller but significant restrictions apply. In the US, contact the **Air Courier Association** (350 Indiana Street, Ste 300, Golden, CO 80401; tel: 800 282 1202; web: www.aircourier.org) or the **International Association of Air Travel Couriers** (PO Box 980, Keystone Heights, FL 32656; tel: 352 475 1584; fax: 352 475 5326; email: iaatc@courier.org; web: www.courier.org).

Independent travellers need to plan and research their trip in more detail than is necessary for group travel, especially if they have a limited amount of time and plan on visiting a particular site or area. Many tour operators will make arrangements for independent travellers, sometimes for no more than it would cost to book yourself. But with email, fax, telephone and international credit cards it is getting ever easier to reserve and pay for flights, hotels and jungle tours before leaving home.

One good compromise is to travel to the country on your own and then join a group on a pre-arranged date for a jungle trip. For those already in an Amazon country, local agencies operate a huge range of tours. Many of the better agencies are used by foreign-based tour operators and can work out cheaper if booked locally.

Independent travellers usually know what they want and are a pretty resourceful bunch. The Amazon is overflowing with opportunities for those with enough time. In general you'll have to do more of the groundwork and a cursory knowledge of Spanish and/or Portuguese is very useful, although not essential. Once you arrive, you are best off using the services of a local guide or someone who at least claims to know the area.

Passenger and cargo boats serve all of the major Amazon tributaries and most of the small ones. Swinging in a hammock while gazing into gallery forest is a strangely hypnotic experience.

Travelling on smaller rivers and using a canoe to explore the waterways gives a great feeling of independence and has the thrill of stumbling over the occasional new surprise. If you would like a degree of explanation or increased chances of seeing something in particular take a guide, or convince a local that he can do the job.

Moving off the water, walking in the rainforest is an exhilarating and stimulating experience. Even if you pay attention to where you're walking – which would mean you don't get to look at the rainforest – there is a very real likelihood of getting lost. This prospect, or even the thought of it, gives some people a real buzz. Fine, but for most sane people it's just plain scary.

One technique to avoid getting lost is to blaze a trail using a machete to chip away at tree bark, or break branches en route. For the experienced this may work, but even guides sometimes get lost using this method. If you're on your first trip into the jungle and trying this technique there'll be a few panicky moments before you're really confident. The purist ecotourist may baulk at this drastic method, so you're best off with a native guide who knows where he's going.

The financial realities are that independent travel in the Amazon is rarely cheaper than an organised tour. You can certainly travel through the region on a tight budget, but if you include any activities it is unlikely there will be much difference in cost by the time you get home. Going off foot-loose and fancy-free is all very exciting but it does tend to be the most expensive way, and perhaps riskier too.

Travelling with children

Children put a constraint on the type and length of vacation. The Amazon is great fun for youngsters of, say, ten and over, but any younger and they tend to be somewhat overwhelmed. An Amazon holiday with children may turn out well if the family stays at a good jungle lodge; tourist riverboats are also ideal for families.

US readers can get specialist travel equipment for children from **Tough Traveler**, 1012 State St, Schenectady, NY 12307, USA; tel: 800 468 6844/518 393 0168; fax: 518 377 5434, email: service@toughtraveler; web: www.toughtraveler.com. In the UK readers can contact **Nomad Travel Store** at 3-4 Wellington Terrace, Turnpike Lane, London N8 0PX; tel: 020 8889 7014; fax: 020 8889 9529; email: sales@ nomadtravel.co.uk, web: www.nomadtravel.co.uk.

For the truly adventurous

There are some fairly unique individuals who, like Orellana and other legendary travellers, just fancy the idea of exploring the Amazon or one of its tributaries with a canoe and a companion for months at a time. It's possible and people do, more often than not, come back alive… well, that's what John Harrison, author of *Up the Creek*, claims.

Expeditions into the Amazon represent serious adventure. Read the next chapter *Expedition Planning* for pointers on how to organise a bona fide expedition. Tanis Jordan and her husband Martin started travelling along Amazon tributaries back in the 1960s and their adventures can be read in more detail in *Out of Chingford*. John Harrison also covers a good deal of the realities of expeditioning in *Off the Map*.

Additional information

For practical travel hints the **South American Explorers** (126 Indian Creek Rd, Ithaca, New York, NY 14850, USA: tel: 607 277 0488; fax: 607 277 6122; email: explorer@saexplorers.org; web: www.saexplorers.org) is a mine of information, with current unbiased advice from all over South America on tour operators, hotels, security and travel problems. UK residents can join through Bradt Travel Guides; tel: 01494 873478, web: www.bradt-travelguides.com.

Staff can help with trip planning and assist members seeking travel companions or experts in a particular field. They can put you in touch with local rainforest conservation organisations who can update you on recent environmental issues or offer volunteer opportunities. To get all this you need to be a member which costs US$50 (US$80 for a couple) per year. Annual subscription buys the quarterly club magazine and use of the Quito and Lima clubhouses which are both packed with books, trip reports and other travellers. Club addresses are in the Ecuador and Peru chapters, pages 246 and 284.

Maps

Maps in this book give an approximate idea of a layout and geography. For adventure activities, high resolution, accurate maps of the Amazon are necessary, but hard to come by. The best practical sources are universities and government military institutions. Unless you've grown up in the Amazon, finding your way around the back-country with anything less than a 10m accurate GPS is virtually impossible, and then pretty pointless if you don't have a map. Hence for backpacking or hiking in the lowland Amazon, most travel will be along rivers and with a guide.

International Travel Map Productions (ITMB Publishing, 530 West Broadway, Vancouver BC, V5Z 1E9, Canada; tel: 604 879 3621; fax: 604 897 4521; email: order@itmb.com; web: www.itmb.com) publish an excellent map of the Amazon Basin (4th Edition) which has been used to produce some of the maps in this book.

General-interest maps of the Amazon Basin can be obtained (or ordered) from travel bookshops or mail order companies. In the USA high-quality scientific maps (eg: metallurgical, tectonic) as well as travel maps are available from **OMNI Resources** (1004 South Mebane Street, PO Box 2096, Burlington, NC 27216; tel: 336 227 8300; fax: 336 227 3748; email: custserv@omnimap.com; web: www.omnimap.com). In the UK **Stanfords** is the best travel bookshop and handles international mail order. Tel: 020 7836 1321; fax: 020 7836 0189; email: customer.services@stanfords.co.uk; web: www.stanfords.co.uk.

Guides

Seasoned travellers often baulk at the idea of using a guide. This phobia must be overcome for a trip to the jungle. A guide is essential for gaining some deeper understanding of the jungle. The naturalist-guide leads visitors along trails, takes them on canoe rides and helps them to spot wildlife. While it is possible to move around developed areas and between various Amazon towns independently, for any type of extended trip to remote areas a local or native guide is essential. The quality of guides can make or break the rainforest experience, so choose carefully.

Native local guides

Virtually everyone who visits remote areas of rainforest will be accompanied at some time or other by a local guide. The average local guide knows the area well, can identify most animals and some plants and can talk with the indigenous Indians in the area.

The experience and quality of local guides varies considerably. The best are highly knowledgeable and are able to talk at length on the ecology of rainforest species, scientific topics and native cultures. The worst guides – and they do exist! – drink on duty, promote their own business, speak little English, and have poor knowledge of wildlife and a nonchalant attitude to clients' well-being.

Independent travellers can ask others for recommendations. Group travellers should check suitability with tour operators.

University-trained guides and tour leaders

Owing to the lack of local guides with broad scientific knowledge, some travel companies offer group tours escorted by a qualified naturalist-guide. Some lodges and reserves may employ American or European researchers working on-site. They usually have expert knowledge in specific fields, such as ecology, ornithology or entomology.

As with local guides, the experience and background of biologist-guides or tour leaders is highly variable. The best are university-trained, have experience of travelling in the area and knowledge of tropical biology, and speak Spanish or Portuguese.

WHAT TO TAKE

What you stuff in your backpack or suitcase to take to the Amazon depends on what you'll be doing there, and where you'll be staying before and after. If you're travelling independently a daily set of clean clothes isn't that crucial. If you're on one of the luxury liners that cruises up the Amazon main stream then forgetting your tuxedo could be a real *faux pas*. A number of travel goods suppliers can provide virtually any product to suit your travel needs or imagination, including the tuxedo. We like **Magellan's** (110 W Sola Street, Santa Barbara, CA 93101; tel: 805 568 5400/800 9624943; fax: 805 568 5406; email: orders@magellans.com; web:

www.magellans.com) and **Travel Oasis** (PO Box 2191, St. Peters, MO 63376; tel: 877 894 1960; fax: 636 922 1979; email: information@traveloasis.com; web: www.traveloasis.com).

Packing

Before you even get out the bags, have an effective and efficient method of packing and aim to minimise what you pack. A traveller's rule of thumb is to pack what you think is essential and then halve it.

After this drastic measure, other methods reduce the load further still. Eliminate useless packaging, such as film boxes, by putting films in a water-tight container. Repackage items so you carry only as much as you need for the trip. For lotions and liquids, put the necessary amount in a small used container, such as a food jar, film canister, or pill bottle.

Clothing

Clothing should be lightweight and dry quickly. A pair of synthetic or cotton (some people are prone to heat rash wearing synthetics in a humid climate) athletics trousers is ideal. Light enough to stop you getting hot and sweaty and long enough to keep the insects off, they reduce the chances of scratches and infections when out on the jungle trail. They're easy to wash and dry very quickly.

Two or three lightweight cotton-mix shirts/blouses with long sleeves are ideal for your top half. Pull-over shirts minimise the risk of getting snagged in the jungle. Also take a few T-shirts or tops to wear when you're not on the move and a lightweight jumper to keep the occasionally chilly nights bearable.

A pair of shorts are good for the quieter, insect-less moments and some people actually prefer to trek in them.

In the rainforest you don't need expensive hiking or trekking boots. Running or tennis shoes or trainers with a lightweight sock are ideal. When you're not trekking or hiding every inch of your body from the insects, thongs or rubber sandals give your feet a breather and are good for tramping around boats, towns and villages.

Take a swimsuit or shorts if you like swimming, plus something to cover your shoulders in case of sunburn.

A lightweight, compact raincoat or poncho is good for the inevitable downpour and a broad-brimmed hat offers protection from the sun.

If you'll be passing through big cities you ought to take a smartish set of clothes for posher restaurants and hotels. A pair of casual trousers and a shirt – or separates and/or a dress, depending on your gender – along with a pair of clean shoes will get you into most restaurants. Check with your tour operator about the dress code in riverboats and lodges. In the Andean cities the altitude can make it quite chilly at night so you'll need to take a jacket or fleece if you're staying there.

For expedition clothing see also page 74.

Medical equipment

Medical essentials include anti-malarials (see pages 83–4) and of course insect repellent. The active ingredient in repellent is DEET which is highly toxic – a concentration of 30–50% should be adequate for use on the skin, but clothes may be impregnated with 100%. A natural option is citronella oil which achieves mixed results. More suggestions are in *Chapter 4*, page 83.

Hammocks and camping equipment

If you intend travelling on local riverboats a hammock is indispensable, so take yours if you have one. Otherwise, strong cotton hammocks are available for sale in

CHECKLIST
Clothes
Broad-brimmed hat; rain jacket; T-shirts or tank tops; shorts; long pants or trousers/skirt; long-sleeved shirt/blouse; sweater; socks; underwear; swimwear; set of 'smart' clothing.

Shoes
Deck/beach shoes or sandals or trainers; walking shoes or rubber boots.

Toiletries
Whatever you normally carry with you when travelling; plus a bar of biodegradable soap. Don't forget: shampoo, contraceptives, tampons, sanitary towels. If you use glasses or contact lenses, take spares.

Medical equipment (see also Chapter 4)
Malaria prophylaxis; anti-diarrhoea remedy; itch-ease; sunblock (SPF 15–30); moisturising cream; lipsalve; general painkillers; antibiotic ointment; a small first-aid kit; antihistamine cream or tablets; pre-sealed sterile towelettes; required prescription medicines.

Travel documents
Passport (with visa if required); tickets; travellers' cheques, credit card, cash; money/document pouch; photocopies of all important travel documents, kept in a different place.

Miscellaneous
Sunglasses; insect repellent (see page 83); torch/flashlight (for night excursions and badly lit lodges); strong one-litre water bottle; small backpack (for jungle excursions); large waterproof zip-lock bags (5 or 6); small towel (quick-drying); penknife; ear-plugs; cheap wristwatch; travel alarm clock; binoculars (vital to enjoy birdlife and wild animals); dictionary/phrasebook (see page 55); travel games (chess, checkers, Scrabble, backgammon, cards); ball of string (multiple uses...).

Photographic equipment (see also pages 51–3)
SLR camera with standard lens; zoom lens; wide angle lens; daylight (UV) filter; polarising filter; flash unit; spare batteries; film (as much as you think you will need for the trip); point-and-shoot camera (for back-up and spontaneous shots); camera bag (consider a PeliCase if conditions are likely to be rough); packet of silica crystals (to absorb moisture); ziplock bags (to keep used film in); lead bag (to protect fast film from airport X-rays); tripod or monopod and/or beanbag (to rest the camera on); cable shutter release.

most South American towns at incredibly low prices (usually under US$20). The lightweight hammocks available from survival shops tend to be uncomfortable and crucial pieces of string break fairly easily.

An outline of things to take if you plan on sleeping out is included in *Chapter 3*, page 69.

DON'T HAM IT IN THE HAMMOCK

Most lodges and tourist riverboats have spots where you can sling a hammock to relax and pass the time. Usually the hammock is already rigged up for you. On budget trips and when travelling by boat you will probably sleep several nights in a hammock. Having your hammock fall while you are asleep in it is one of the funniest things... about two days after it happened. There is a technique to putting it up and, if you're not sure how, ask crew members or lodge staff for a bit of advice. Basically you need a couple of pieces of string/rope to connect the end-loops of the hammock to a post or something. Ideally it should be hung level at hip height, without too much sag. On passenger boats hammocks may be stacked two or three high so you can't always achieve the ideal.

Once you have your hammock up, you need to master the art of getting in and out, and staying in it comfortably. Like eating with chopsticks, it is one of those things a lot easier to do than to explain! Similarly, everyone has their own technique and you will develop your own. Here is Roger's tried and tested method:

Getting in Pull the hammock together and press down in the middle, hike a leg over the hammock's lowest point, and stand astride. Stand on one leg, place the other in the hammock, sit down and spread the material to give enough room for your body. Once your weight is taken by the hammock bring the other leg in. Not very dignified, but this procedure is easier than it sounds. To save yourself backache, lie diagonally across the hammock which should just about have you sleeping level.

Getting out Sit up, put a leg down, bring the other leg across so you are sitting sideways on the hammock, and get up without putting any weight on the hammock.

Try it!

Luggage

This is a personal choice. Take a hard case if you plan to bring back fragile things. If you're on an adventure trip a duffel bag is best as it will stand up to a battering.

If you are hiking, doing significant amounts of walking, or will be carrying your own luggage for most of the time, take a rucksack.

More and more bags of all types are lockable. In reality your luggage is most vulnerable at the international airport either in your own country or in South America. If it can be locked this will deter the casual thief.

A small rucksack/daypack is ideal for keeping hold of important things like passports, tickets and so on, when logistics require you to be separated from your main luggage. In any case take a daypack for walks.

IN AMAZONIA
Hunting and shooting ... with binoculars and camera

To maximise your enjoyment of Amazon wildlife we provide some tips on the only way for visitors to hunt and shoot wildlife... with binoculars and a camera.

Viewing Amazon wildlife

Most large animals and birds you expect to see in the Amazon are rare, elusive and wary. To maximise the chances of spotting animals, remember the following:

- Be quiet! Most wild animals hear, see or smell us long before we are aware of their presence. Talk in low tones and step carefully.
- Be attentive! Many Amazon creatures are masters of disguise. Dense vegetation and low light in the forest make it hard to see well-camouflaged animals such as sloths and tree-snakes. Keep your eyes (and ears) wide open.
- Stay together! In the forest, many eyes are better than two, so in a group you are more likely to see interesting wildlife. People spread out across a distance scare away animals more than a compact group. Keep up with your guide who is more likely to spot animals.
- Look and listen closely! You may not see any big mammals or reptiles but the rainforest is a treasure chest of nature's smaller jewels. Observe closely a fallen rotting log, under leaf litter or among the leaves of a shrub and you are bound to find something.
- Avoid perfumes! Animals are often spooked by an unusual scent so wearing your favourite after-shave or cologne is only going to put more distance between you and what you have come to see.
- Early to rise! Makes you healthy, wealthy and wise… and you get to see more. Not only is it more peaceful, but birds and monkeys are more active around dawn, which is at sixish in the Amazon. Also, early morning light adds contrast and atmosphere to photographs.
- Wear 'quiet' clothes! Clothing subdued in colour, such as khaki, greens or browns, is less visible to animals. Primates and birds see colour, so bright blue, orange or yellow may frighten them off. (Avoid camouflage gear which will make locals wonder whether or not you are a soldier!)

Photography

Shooting the wildlife… with a camera. If you follow the above advice then with a bit of luck there will come the thrilling moment when you encounter a wild rainforest animal. You may well be happy with memories alone. But some people want to record the event and the most popular way is with a camera. However, to be pleased with results you should keep your expectations in proportion to your experience.

Nature photos matching magazine publishers' standards are taken after years of experience and are not likely on your first foray into the jungle. Professionals use expensive equipment, spending hundreds of arduous hours in blinds and tree-houses. Talent and imagination can make up for some of this, but most average photographers must practise and experiment for years. Whatever film or camera is used and whatever one's experience, it is almost impossible to capture the forest's grandeur on film. Bear this in mind and you'll be happier with your own initial efforts.

YOU NEED BINOCULARS

You may prefer to travel light but, whatever you do, don't forget your binoculars. There are times when, as you spend a quiet few moments resting away from other people, a solitary bird may accidentally wander within a few metres of you. These moments are unforgettable. But most birds, indeed most wildlife, that you see will be a considerable distance away – and hard to study with the naked eye.

Modern, compact binoculars are very light. Buying yourself a small, pre-Amazon adventure present (eg: 12x24) will bring the world of the rainforest considerably closer to you… literally.

In the jungle most wildlife is too far off or well-concealed for good pictures. Without a telephoto lens, a sloth, bird or monkey will appear as a blur or blob on most photos taken in the field. The least you need is a good camera (SLR) and zoom lens (minimum 70–210 mm). Unless you have a suitable lens and tripod (to steady the camera for the slow exposures needed with a long lens) and lots of time, the best way to use your film is to go for scenic views or close-ups of flowers and leaves. On the occasions when you do see some interesting wildlife, it is often better to enjoy the animals with binoculars rather than waste film.

As mentioned, good equipment, patience and lots of luck are needed for the best wildlife pictures. However, it is still possible to take pictures of animals with a point-and-shoot automatic camera if you can get really close. Mostly, these are invertebrates, some of which are exquisite and highly photogenic. Beetles, leaf insects and butterflies make good topics.

For close-ups you need a macro lens or extension tubes to magnify the subject, a flash to compensate for reduced light and a tripod when using slow shutter speeds.

Some amphibians also make beautiful subjects. Brightly coloured and relatively fearless, poison-dart frogs (eg: *Dendrobatidae*) can be approached quite closely. Unfortunately, their minute size makes it hard to get well-lit and composed photographs. Poison-dart frogs – or any amphibian to be on the safe side – should not be touched. They are easily damaged by handling and there exists a danger of poisoning from the highly toxic compounds secreted by their skin.

In addition to uncooperative wildlife, lighting conditions often conspire to frustrate the Amazon photographer. Darkness on the forest floor or glare from the river cause incorrectly exposed shots. To overcome exposure problems, automatic shutter-speed settings can be altered on most modern SLRs and combined with filters, flash and the right film speed. For the best natural light, dawn and dusk give ideal conditions. Close to the horizon, the low sun bathes the subject in a soft, golden glow and enhances contrast as it casts deep shadows.

Whether to shoot print or slide film depends on how the photos are to be used. If there is any prospect of the photographs being reproduced, slide film is a must. In South America, film bought in major cities is generally reliable, but check the expiry date. Whatever risk there is will be determined by the size, style and the location of the place you are buying it. Prices are sometimes (but not always) more expensive than in the US or Europe so the best bet is to take what you think you need. Some people would recommend as many as two rolls a day but keeping up that rate for three weeks or longer could be difficult.

Be selective with the film speed you use for specific shots. River and open village scenes with lots of light are best shot with ISO200 or ISO100. Slower film works fine, giving better definition and reproduction, but demands more light than fast film.

Under the canopy, a faster film is needed for low-light situations, so you might choose ISO400. For slower film, a flash is definitely needed for photography in the jungle as the forest floor is too dark for ordinary film. Try experimenting with superfast black-and-white film such as ISO1000 for interesting grainy effects.

With slow film or a telephoto or zoom lens more light is needed. Hence scenic shots will require longer exposures. To prevent blur with exposures longer than 1/60th second (1/125th with telephoto or 1/250th for action shots), you must use a tripod or other support, plus a cable release. A full-size tripod is bulky and heavy whereas a mini-tripod may be useful in some situations. A good alternative is a monopod, placed directly in the ground or leant against a tree. A beanbag is an even cheaper option and one you can make at home. It is placed on a wall or branch of a tree with the camera set on top.

An ultraviolet (UV) or daylight filter is useful to protect the lens, while a polarising filter greatly improves scenic shots. It reduces glare from the river, preventing over-exposure, and adds definition to clouds. The polarising filter gives a picture with contrast closer to what the eye perceives. Without the filter, many landscape shots turn out with the sky over-exposed or the river and forest under-exposed.

Annoying malfunctions can be avoided by caring for your camera equipment. Before departure, clean and check everything works correctly. If your camera is old, you might consider having it professionally overhauled or serviced before departure. Few things are as frustrating, and almost unresolvable, as your camera breaking down in the middle of the Amazon.

In the forest humidity can be a problem. Fungal growth on lenses may occur in very damp conditions. Put a sachet of silicon crystals beside the camera to absorb excessive moisture. With this precaution you're unlikely to experience any real difficulties.

Photography etiquette

It can be quite disconcerting, whoever or wherever you are, to have a camera stuffed in your face. When photographing local people, ask permission. To break the ice, let them look through the viewfinder first, and even take a picture of you. Children love the immediate results of Polaroid or the image preview available on most digital cameras.

Generally people do not mind being photographed and rarely ask to be paid. Courtesy dictates that you ask, and respect demands that you honour the person's wishes. Tour operators prefer you not to offer money simply for a photograph. To thank someone offer to send them a copy of the photograph, and of course remember to do so.

A walk in the dark: identifying wildlife at night

As you will hear from the cacophony of sound in the jungle at night, many Amazon animals are nocturnal. Most tours include a night walk or an excursion by boat. A powerful torch is useful and you really need your own; a head-mounted torch is ideal since it concentrates the beam at eye level and leaves your hands free. Animals are spotted mainly from eyeshine caused when a portion of their retina reflects back the light.

Night walks are the best opportunity to see cats. After dark they are most active and like to prowl along footpaths. They have a bright eyeshine which makes them easy to spot. To help you identify cats and other common nocturnal animals in the field, look over the summary (page 54) of animals most likely to be seen at night with descriptions of their eyeshine and preferred habitat.

Fishing in the Amazon: a different angle

Many visitors come to the Amazon expecting to fish and they are rarely disappointed. Virtually all organised tours include an excursion to fish for the infamous piranha with fishing tackle provided.

The tackle could not be simpler: a bamboo rod, line and hook. No weights, reel or floats. Even with this primitive set-up piranha fishing is often successful. Let your guide remove the hook. Local fishermen are often missing a piece of toe or finger because a piranha fancied a nibble.

Also caught with the bamboo rod are small catfish, called *squeakers* because they make a high-pitched sound out of water. More dangerous than they look, squeakers have a sharp, poisonous dorsal spine.

ANIMAL	EYESHINE	LOCATION
Mammals		
Brocket deer	brilliant yellow-white	swampy areas, riversides
Capybara	yellow to red (dim)	near water with aquatic plants
Jaguar	green-yellow	trails in wet forest areas
Kinkajou & olingo	bright orange	forest canopy
Margay	yellow	dense forest
Night monkey	reddish-orange	river edges, open areas
Ocelot	pale yellow	trails in forest and scrub
Opossums	yellow-orange, yellow	various habitats
Paca	bright yellow-orange	swamps, near rivers, occasionally forest
Peccary	reddish (dim)	wide range of habitats
Porcupine	faint dull red	secondary dense growth
Puma	pale yellow	widespread, many habitats
Rat	bright yellow	forest, inhabited areas
Tapir	yellow (dim)	water-edge forests
Birds		
Oilbird	bright red	near mountain caves
Owl	bright red	near mountain caves
Paraque	bright red	widespread along river edges, humid forests
Nightjar		forests
Others		
Caiman	red	water margins, floating meadows
Frogs	reddish	river edges, understorey, woody shrubs
Spider	pale green (small)	water margins, floating vegetation
Toads	green-yellow	river edges, open areas, trails, swamps
Tree boa	bright red-yellow	understorey, trees along river edges

Angling enthusiasts who want to do some serious sport fishing should take their own rod and tackle. The guide will provide chopped meat for bait and basic fishing equipment. With better equipment you can catch a greater variety of species, such as the larger catfish or better still the delicious *tilapia* (Cichlidae); the latter are highly valued as food. A large *oscar* is a real prize. Most treasured is the *tambaqui* which requires much practice and patience. Natives have the skill to mimic the splash of the falling nuts that are this species' sole food.

Most fish in the Amazon use smell or electric signals to detect food. Artificial lures for visually-oriented fish are usually unsuccessful, unless designed for certain species, such as peacock bass.

Most organised fishing tours in Brazil are organised from Manaus (book through **Rod and Reel Adventures** 2294 Oakmont Way, Eugene, OR 97401; tel: 800 356 6982; fax: 541 242 0742; email: info@rodreeladventures.com; web: www.rodreeladventures.com). Here the peacock bass (*Cichla ocellaris*) is large and abundant. This species is the most popular for sports fishing being aggressive and putting up a fierce fight. It needs specialised equipment such as heavy line, oversize topwater lures and stiff rods. Large fish, they average 2.7kg but specimens weighing 4.5–9.0kg are caught regularly. World record sizes (up to 12.3kg) are reported from the area. For week-long fishing cruises in Brazil, Peru or Venezuela, contact **Fishabout** (PO Box 1679, Los Gatos, CA 95031; tel: 800 409 2000; fax: 408 395 4676; email: trips@fishabout.com; web: www.fishabout.com).

THE PEOPLE
Languages and customs
Languages
You can travel anywhere in South America, or the world for that matter, without knowing the language. Getting from A to B is easy enough if that is all you want to do. But if you're curious enough about a country to go there, why not have a shot at its language?

Spanish is the *lingua franca* throughout South America except in Brazil (Portuguese), Guyana (English), Suriname (Dutch) and French Guiana (French). The type of Spanish spoken in South America is slightly different from European Spanish, but the differences are manageable.

In Brazil Portuguese is the official language but, as with Spanish, there are considerable differences from the mother-tongue in Portugal. Brazilians can usually understand Spanish if you speak it but understanding their reply to you is pretty difficult. Some people find making the leap between Spanish and Portuguese easy, others find it impossible.

With the expansion of tourism and industry in recent years, most guides in the Amazon's popular tourist areas speak some English.

The most widely spoken native language in the western Amazon is Quechua, for which bilingual dictionaries are available. Given the difficulty of pronouncing Quechua, with its many guttural rasps, the short-term visitor is easily deterred from further linguistic experiments.

In Amazonia, whichever country you are in, the language is generally used differently from in the more populated parts. The introduction of slang, slight changes in accent, developments in the concept of grammar and a host of other influences conspire to make it sound like a completely new language.

Just a few words and a natural ability to make a complete fool of yourself will get you far closer to people's hearts than linguistic perfection. And making a fool of yourself can lead to some fairly amusing situations, like going to the cinema for a haircut, going to a barbecue for a bus, or confusing your heart and a sausage.

Language dictionaries
Berlitz and Lonely Planet publish compact travellers' dictionaries specifically for Latin-American Spanish and Portuguese, with useful phrases and a phonetic pronunciation guide. Some of the basics are in *Appendix 2*, page 427.

Local customs and mannerisms
The *Latino* (a Spanish-speaking person from the Americas; feminine is *Latina*) is typically less reserved and more voluble than the American or North European. A

quick hug or *abrazo* is a normal gesture among men who know each other. A handshake is considered formal but suitable for most occasions, including greeting and parting. When men and women greet, they hug with a quick kiss on the cheek, or just hold hands and touch cheeks. For strangers, this is reduced to a shoulder grasp, leaning forward, first to the left, then the right.

Beckoning is opposite to the northern European gesture: Latinos typically beckon with one hand palm down, waving the fingers.

Contacts with local people

South Americans are a passionately laid-back people. The routine of life has created a culture that focuses on the importance of *mañana* with an impressive indifference to haste that frequently frustrates Westerners. Let's face it, rushing around while doing something rarely gets it done any quicker in reality. For the traveller on the receiving end this indifference can come across as a lack of concern. Lateness is almost institutionalised in South America and your visit will be far more enjoyable if you relax into that way of life. Buses and taxis don't go faster with stress, so if you have a plane to catch, leave slightly earlier.

Whether meeting people deep in the Amazon Basin or in a city, the conventional greeting is *buenas dias* – often shortened to just *buenas* – in all but Brazil where *bom dia* or *boa tarde* are used. In a social setting you will normally be introduced to everyone. For introductions and new acquaintants, men and women both greet with a handshake. The next step up, showing particular appreciation and strong friendship, is a rather intricate combination of handshake and pat on the back which stops just short of an all-out hug. Female friends greet with a kiss to each cheek, often accompanied in more formal settings by a small handshake. These gestures also cover separations.

Begging and trading goods

It's not uncommon for tourists in South America to be confronted with begging. Asking for sweets, food and presents in general may appear to be a natural response of villagers to a few seemingly wealthy gringos arriving in town. But as soon as you've been to somewhere truly out of the way, you'll realise it isn't.

Gift-giving by tourists, in whatever form, creates a dependency culture. Once established, the procedure is expected. It becomes a source of disappointment for locals – and a hassle for tourists – if gifts are not given. If you want to contribute to this impression of tourism, that is your choice. Simply saying 'no' usually stops the begging.

If the reason for giving gifts is to create temporary friendships, then with time on your hands and a creative mind you can devise plenty of ways of sharing experiences across cultures that don't relegate one half to the status of beggars.

If you do get to spend time with new 'friends', photographs of family and postcards of home are always interesting. A Polaroid camera's instant snapshot is a truly personal gift. If you want to help with cash, you can donate to local schools or hospitals or, back home, to conservation or health organisations who work locally.

Tipping

Tipping varies greatly across the region. Airport porters, hotel staff and restaurants all rely to a certain extent on the wage top-ups that come from tipping. Taxi drivers do not generally expect a tip although a few will probably do their best to encourage you. Agreeing on a price before you travel will reduce the chances of your bags being held to ransom.

Hospitality

If you are invited into someone's home you may be confronted with a banquet comprising the best the host can provide. If you feel guilty about not contributing to the feast remember your host expects nothing. With new friends, any hospitality you receive is freely given. There are ways of repaying generosity without giving money. You can send a gift from home, or take a photograph and mail it later.

Buying souvenirs

Shopping in South America is a lot of fun! The most popular souvenirs among Amazon visitors are native-made handicrafts. Wood carvings are widely available from city shops to remote forest villages. The commonest woods are mahogany, genipa or balsa.

Other local handicrafts include palm fibre baskets, mats and hats, woven goods, pottery and simple adornments made out of collected wild seeds, shells and insect parts. Animal teeth, feathers, claws and skin are sometimes used. On ecological, and in some cases legal, grounds, items incorporating animal parts or wood from rare or endangered trees should not be bought.

Except in town shops, bartering is commonplace but optional when purchasing souvenirs. If you like something and are happy to pay the asking price no one is likely to complain.

Other good buys are 'naive' paintings on postcards (Colombia) and woven goods (Peru and Ecuador). Gold and some gemstones, especially emeralds, sapphire and topaz, are good value (Colombia, Brazil). However, bear in mind mining operations cause significant habitat destuction. Basketry is of particularly fine quality in Venezuela. Textiles in Bolivia are probably the best on the continent although they are not widely available in the lowlands.

THE ANIMAL TRADE
Oliver Whalley

In the Amazon region many animals are exploited, often illegally. Live animals and animal parts are exported in large numbers but also supply local, mainly urban, demands and the tourist trade. The market for live animals is not always as pets or for zoos but often for scientific research; cruelly this includes various species of monkeys. Recently pharmaceutical companies have started collecting large numbers of animals, such as poison-arrow frogs, severely threatening their survival in certain areas.

As a traveller in the Amazon region you may see such animal abuse and exploitation; please report the sale of species, particularly protected endangered species, to conservation groups locally and at home and also to the local authorities.

Do not buy any of the following:

- Animal skins of any sort, part or whole
- Any animal parts, including parrot feathers, skulls (especially jaguar and caiman skulls, teeth and claws), toucan beaks, turtle shells, heads or fins
- Any insects, often sold mounted in glass cases. Particularly threatened by over-collection are species of very large or brightly coloured beetle such as the harlequin beetle or the hercules beetle, the large iridescent blue morpho and the large black and yellow/green papillon butterflies, and tarantula and other large spiders.

SLEEPING AND EATING
Accommodation

Finding a place to rest your head for the night in the Amazon, indeed throughout South America, is rarely a problem. As you'd expect from a continent of contrasts, the range covers the extremes. Major cities and large towns all have comfortable accommodation, with five-star standards occasionally found in the most out-of-the-way places. But comfort costs, and in some countries the best hotels will set you back over US$100 a night. Most towns have a number of mid-range hotels costing US$20–45. Although some of the luxury comforts may be lacking, it's unlikely that you'll notice if you're out and about exploring during the day.

The bottom end of the market is a delightful game of chance. While some are efficiently run small hotels that hold cherished reputations for friendliness and cleanliness, others cut costs in every way possible, cramming beds into the smallest of spaces. Genuine flea-pits are rare but the only way to avoid them is to have a look at the rooms first.

Away from towns, the priorities of the traveller take a back seat and hotels or *residencias* target locals passing through. Function takes priority over form. Small towns may have a variety of options, most of which will be acceptable to all but the pickiest of travellers. The very smallest settlements are likely to welcome you with little more than a wooden shack and something dubiously called a 'mattress', or even straw-stuffed flour sacks, with the river providing a rather handy all-in-one washroom-cum-bathroom.

Accommodation in the jungle varies greatly. The very best lodges offer excellent accommodation and food but most leave you wanting for some of the comforts of life. The best solution is to immerse yourself in the rainforest and avoid thinking about the largely irrelevant temporary discomforts.

The cheapest and arguably the best way to spend a night in the jungle is to sleep in a hammock inside a thatched hut, or under the stars during the dry season when insects are not too numerous. Although hammocks are comfortable if you are used to them, you might not want to spend every night in one, so check accommodations before booking a trip.

Youth hostels, or affiliated organisations, can be found in Brazil, Colombia and Peru, with an associate organisation in Ecuador. For the latest information contact **Hostelling International** (UK: International Youth Hostel Federation, 1st Floor, Fountain House, Parkway, Welwyn Garden City, Hertfordshire AL8 6JH; tel: 0870 770 8868; fax: 01707 323980; web: www.yha.org.uk; USA: 733 15th Street NW, Ste 840, Washington DC 20005; tel: 202 783 6161; fax: 202 783 6171; email: hostels@hiayh.org; web: www.hiayh.org).

Accommodation in this guide is divided between the top, middle and bottom end of the market relative to each country: twenty dollars spent on a hotel in Bolivia will get you far more than it would in Brazil. We avoid comparisons on price across countries, and in the country chapters instead focus on the relative comforts available.

In all but the very best hotels you should always ask to have a look at the rooms and the bathroom first. The vast majority of places are comfortable but there are a few that are so grubby that you'd be lucky to find any sleep, rest or comfort.

On a more personal level, plumbing can be quixotically erratic in the Amazon region and heated water is rare. Given the temperatures and humidity this is unlikely to cause a real problem. Where hot water is available, it is usually barely more than a trickle. The 'Frankenstein-switch' that will be somewhere close to the shower offers heated water should you feel like it. The system may look very low-tech and more than a little disconcerting to the non-electricians amongst us, but actual shocks are uncommon! Toilets throughout the region are not designed to flush paper, so use the basket next to the toilet.

Hotel and lodge rooms may have air conditioning – for which you pay more – but most rooms have at least a fan.. The best way of staying cool is to get up early, rest through the hottest part of the day, then get active again towards the end of the afternoon. It's what the locals do.

Food and drink: a taste of the Amazon

Food in Amazonia is varied and tasty, healthy but rarely 'haute cuisine'. Many foods in the Amazon are familiar – rice, bread and eggs are widely eaten, as well as most well-known vegetables, which are grown locally or imported from other parts of the country.

Tomatoes, lettuce, cabbage, potatoes and onions are all available. Restaurants and lodges which cater to international tourists serve wheat bread, invariably white; whole-wheat is non-existent in the Amazon. Meat served at tourist facilities is usually beef or pork. Vegetarians can ask tour operators to arrange non-meat dishes but make sure you point out that chicken is meat – many people in South America do not think so.

Breakfast tends to be something simple like eggs, bread and tea or coffee. A typical main meal served at jungle lodges and on tourist riverboats might include salad or soup to start, and a kind of beef and vegetable stir-fry, with corn tamales wrapped in banana leaves.

Certain foods are not found in the region. Virtually all the cattle in Amazonia are raised for beef, which, combined with the lack of refrigeration, means dairy produce is rarely available. Outside dairy-producing regions in the Andes foothills, cheese and fresh milk are scarce. Evaporated or powdered milk is normally used instead.

With wheat not being readily available, river people bake a flat loaf made from manioc flour. Try it if you get the chance although it is rather bland and rubbery. Local meats exclusive to rainforest areas include wild iguana, turtle, tapir and peccary. Due to hunting laws, with the exception of iguana these species are out-of-bounds for a law-abiding chef unless a tribal Indian. For poultry, locals occasionally keep curassows in captivity.

Not surprisingly the main source of animal protein in the region is fish, which is usually just filleted and fried. At restaurants and lodges it is sometimes cooked in batter which, along with manioc 'french fries', makes an acceptable 'fish and chips'. *Pirarucú* and *tambaqui* are the tastiest fish, and a *dorado* catfish or large silver dollar fish make a good meal. Piranha is high on the adventurous gourmet's list of 'must try' Amazon foods. Somewhat bony and oily, it can be made into a rich, brothy soup.

Local foods are generally inexpensive and nutritious. One of the best local dishes is fresh heart of palm salad. This excellent dish is often served for lunch or dinner at hotels and lodges. The raw ingredient is an ivory-coloured cylinder about a metre long, harvested from the heart or growing point of a *chonta* (*Euterpe* spp) or palm tree. In the case of *E. precatoria* this results in the death of the tree after 20–30 years. However, *E. oleracea* produces multiple stems and can be harvested sustainably.

Usually served on its own, the palm heart is shaved into thin ribbons. These are slightly crunchy, with a mild, delicate flavour. This dish is usually very safe as the vegetable is peeled and does not need to be washed.

You might want to try some of the jungle insects as food, including palm grubs – a traditional native Indian delicacy and a regional speciality. The grubs are beetle

MARVELLOUS MANIOC

Versatile, ubiquitous and easy to grow, manioc is the ultimate multi-purpose vegetable. With over 140 varieties under cultivation, manioc, or yucca as it is called within the Amazon (or cassava in Africa), is the principal ingredient in 14 foods and 13 beverages. Throughout Amazonia it is prepared into a ground course flour and sprinkled on virtually all food as *farinha*. This will test your dental fillings, and the taste benefit is negligible.

That manioc ever found its way to the Amazon table is surprising. Eaten as harvested, some types are highly toxic. Preparation requires two days of soaking before the root is pounded to a paste and dried.

Many indigenous groups believe the plant seeks the souls of children for nourishment, and needs to be carefully tended to keep the spirit of the plant under control. You may well doubt this, but if you dig up a manioc root following the death of a young child you will see red in the veins of the plant. What greater proof could you need?

larvae harvested from the heartwood of rotting palms. The creamy-white thumb-sized grubs are collected by locals, fried and eaten.

In the larger cities such as Iquitos and Manaus the urge for fast food and other Western-style cuisine can be satisfied. In most cases, it is convenient to dine at hotel restaurants. Here, the food is generally palatable but sometimes boring, so you might want to look elsewhere if time and budget allow.

Apart from fruit, few choices for dessert are found in the Amazon culinary repertoire. Ice-cream and slushy iced drinks are popular, and from street vendors you can buy pastries or sugared popcorn. You can also get sweet bread, cakes and cookies topped with powdered sugar, from most food stores and markets.

Eating out

Breakfast (*desayuno*) in restaurants or cafés tends to be a simple affair, as in the lodges; normally just bread and jam with coffee. A pre-set three-course lunch consisting of soup, a meat dish, and something for dessert is filling and enough to keep you going for the day. Available throughout South American countries, *almuerzos* can be found for as little as US$1 if you hunt around. Supper (*cena*) tends to be a lighter snack, and although pre-set meals can be found, it is less common and you probably have to find an eatery and choose from the menu. (Each country chapter has more specific details on eating out.)

Buying food

If you are camping, buying food is rarely a problem, although fresh vegetables can be difficult to find. Even the smallest towns will have a store of some sort selling a few tinned goods, pasta and rice. As the towns get bigger so does the choice.

The standard rules apply with all food you buy: peel it, boil it, cook it or forget it!

Drinks

Water is plentiful in most areas but remember to drink only purified, bottled water and never untreated tap or river water. If bottled water is not available, you will have to take water from a river or ask locals where they get their water. In either case, purify it if you are unsure of its quality.

Given the heat, it is important to drink more water than usual. At the better lodges and hotels drinking-water is available 24 hours a day. Fizzy drinks and beer are widely available. Alcohol dehydrates, so it is worth holding back a little if you have an active schedule.

Fruits of great variety, in some cases harvested from the forest, are used in beverages, for either a potent alcoholic brew or a refreshing soft drink. Numerous plant products are fermented, such as the ubiquitous manioc, which is made into *chicha* or *masato*, a drink of variable strength and appeal (see below).

Local beverages

The variety of beverages locally available in the Amazon is among the greatest anywhere in the world. Literally hundreds are made from unheard-of tropical fruits such as *naranjilla*, *guayaba*, *uvilla*, *obos*, *taxo*, and *morete* from the fruit of the moriche palm (*Mauritia* spp).

Guaraná is a widely consumed soft drink originating from tropical South America and made from juice of the *guaraná* or *cupana* (*Paullinia cupana*). Raspberry coloured, it is high in caffeine and locals swear it has magical and aphrodisiac properties. Whatever its powers, *guaraná* is a pleasant alternative to the ubiquitous Coke and Fanta.

Guanábana, also known as soursop or custard apple (*Annona* spp), makes a tasty beverage or can be eaten fresh or in ice-cream. It's about the size of a grapefruit, with a hard skin, and covered in blunt spines. The firm flesh is yellowish with a few large black seeds.

The oval dull-yellow **cupuasú** (*Theobroma grandiflorum*) fruit, about the size of an avocado, is a member of the cacao or chocolate tree family. A dozen large black seeds cluster inside. Its whitish creamy flesh is made into fruit juice. The drink has a distinct taste of citrus and locals drink it before a hunt or a day's fishing for its energising properties.

Locally known as **maracuya**, passion fruit or grenadilla (*Passiflora edulis*) is a popular fruit that mixes well with alcoholic drinks and is often used in ice-cream.

Tree tomato (*Cyphomandra hartwegii*), called **tomate de arbol**, grows on what looks like a giant tomato plant, and is a tangerine-sized tangy fruit. Not too dissimilar from the common garden tomato, the fruit is pale green with a lip-smacking flavour. It yields a tart, delicious juice, which tastes better with some honey or sugar.

Camu-camu's (*Myrciaria sp.*) plum-sized fruits are natural vitamin pills — each has ten times the vitamin C content of a lemon. They have a high caffeine content – several fruits keep you awake all night! The shrubby tree grows on riversides and lake edges, so it's easily harvested, but it is not cultivated.

Other Amazon drinks

Incakola is Peru's answer to Coca-Cola and in Peru is almost as popular.

Exclusively made by natives, *masato* is not, as yet, produced commercially… In fact, as the drink is normally only produced for special occasions, visitors can consider themselves most fortunate to be offered it. The gruel-like alcoholic brew is made from chewed manioc. Masato manufacture is the exclusive province of women who sit around, chewing and spitting wads of masticated manioc into a container. Saliva is the special ingredient supplying yeast to ferment the manioc's sugars. Water is also added and the mix is left to ferment for three to four days.

Drinking the soupy brew may take some courage. F W Up de Graaf, in a turn-of-the-century expedition to the River Napo, describes a friend who 'took exception to the *masata* [sic] prepared by an old hag who had but a few teeth left and did the work with her gums'.

Soaking the roots of various plants in rum (minus the spit) creates **root tonics**. The result is a pleasant tasting brew with punch. The tonic's potency depends on the number of different plants used in the infusion.

The wine available in most parts of the Amazon leaves a lot to be desired. On average, it is simply awful – vinegary and cloudy. Wine is available at tourist lodges and on riverboats but can be pricey (about US$10–15 a bottle) and can rarely be recommended, but you may get lucky. Try Tacama, grown in the Ica region of Peru. Beer, on the other hand, is the drink of the *latino* and is usually cheap, good and refreshing.

Coffee is widely grown in the Colombian and Brazilian highlands and rates among the world's best. Colombia and Brazil rank as the world's biggest coffee producers but both countries export most that they produce. Although good coffee can be bought in most towns in the Amazon, many lodges and hotels serve only instant coffee – decaf is unheard of. Tea is usually available.

TRANSPORT

If you're taking a group trip, most operators include transport within the cost of the trip, so logistics and cost of transport need not be a cause for concern. For independent travellers, moving around the region is rarely difficult... as long as comfort, cost and time are not an issue. But in reality there are usually limitations on at least one of these factors.

Buses

A limited road network serves the Amazon region from the more populated areas of each country. Brazil and Ecuador have an adequate network of roads within Amazonia itself. But while the system may look good on maps, the roads are often no more than well-travelled dirt tracks. In some cases, local weather conditions mean the tracks may have hardened to provide near smooth, almost dust-free roads down which buses and trucks thunder with little concern for passenger comfort. More common, though, is the creation of tyre-chewed mud-pools in the rainy season that dry and bake to create ornately rutted tracks in the dry season. Travelling along these roads is rarely comfortable and the buses on these routes are usually the more battered of a company's fleet. Bus companies may have plush air-conditioned buses in their fleet, as demonstrated in their adverts... they just don't send them into Amazonia. Check with the bus company when you buy your tickets if some degree of comfort is important.

Air conditioning is available on buses travelling from major cities in some countries, but as soon as you move into the less-populated areas the buses tend to become little more than travelling boxes with seats.

Systems of bus travel in the region and in connecting cities vary greatly. However, most towns and cities – except Lima – have a central *terminal* or *rodoviária* for long-distance buses. This terminal houses bus companies' ticket offices so here you get times and prices, and depart or arrive.

Depending on the bus, bags may be stored in luggage compartments under the bus or put in a rack on the roof. Although neither system is automatically safer, you may get a luggage receipt which at least gives you peace of mind. Staying outside with your luggage until it is stored in the luggage compartment or loaded onto the roof is the best way to stop someone walking off with it. If you are watchful and use common sense, bags are unlikely to go missing and padlocking bags will stop opportunistic pilfering.

All long-distance buses stop for food every few hours. The food available is usually authentic regional fare ranging from the acceptable to the inedible. This option is worth trying at least once. Alternatively take your own food to eat on the bus.

Unpredictable schedules and unreliable vehicles are accepted characteristics of travel in South America. Schedules are generally a rough estimate of when the bus leaves, but you can bet that the time you turn up late is the one occasion on which the bus leaves on time. Reliability also depends on where you are. In large towns, bus departures tend to be more reliable than in smaller ones. Some countries have more reliable bus systems than others.

Degree of confidence in bus travel also depends on the season. Sometimes roads are washed out in the wet season but when this happens buses tend to stop running the route. While you can rely on reaching your destination, don't place any great importance on the estimated time of arrival. Usually in the dry season a journey's duration is reasonably close to the scheduled time.

The merits of city buses depend on the city and are discussed in each chapter in more detail.

Taxis

Taxis are common throughout the Amazon region and can be found even in the smallest towns. Prices and quality vary greatly, from gas-guzzling air-conditioned US-made hand-me-downs through to battered early Japanese models on their last legs. Safety isn't normally a problem, but it has been known for the steering wheel to come off in a taxi driver's hand! 'I'll just fix that *Señor,* it won't be five minutes.' To avoid being swindled agree on a price before you start your journey.

In a few smaller towns, motorbikes can be hired to provide pillion rides across town but there are obvious restrictions and dangers for travelling with heavy luggage. Iquitos in Peru offers a quirky solution with converted motorbikes called *motocarros* working as motorised rickshaws ferrying people and goods around the city.

River travel

With the growth in road building and the increased use of air transport the amount of river traffic has declined in recent years. Tourist-standard riverboats operated specifically for foreign travellers are comfortably fitted out, providing good food and cabin arrangements as they follow a set itinerary.

Moving about on the river independently depends on the volume of traffic on a particular stretch of the river. This in turn depends on the number of people using a route and whether alternative modes of transport are available. If road transport is available for a particular route, river traffic is often minimal.

The busiest section of the river – between Iquitos and Manaus – is served by regular cargo boats that take several days for the journey. If you're in a hurry, express taxi boats will whisk you from Iquitos to Leticia on the border with Brazil in just a few hours. All major tributaries of the Amazon main stream have regular passenger services, while quieter rivers tend to have less traffic.

Travelling by riverboat is a joy for some, a painful memory for others. Riverboats make money in at least two ways: carrying cargo and carrying people. More people means more money. Most passengers sleep in a hammock and on medium- to larger-sized boats you will find yourself packed like sardines. If you didn't have any travelling companions when you started the journey you will have by the end. On smaller boats and tributaries you sleep on the cargo deck and tend to have more space.

Cabins, which cost slightly more than hammock space, are available on all but the smallest boats. The only clear benefit is a sense of privacy if you have the cabin to yourself, as the beds are often uncomfortable and the cabins cramped.

Food on riverboats lacks imagination, variety and taste, but what it lacks in stimulus for the primary senses it makes up for in challenges to the stomach, with serious stomach upsets a possibility. Drinking water is provided but there is no guarantee that it is any more hygienic than the food. Some foreign passengers prefer to take their own food and water. Most riverside towns and villages sell a variety of tinned goods and fresh fruit and bread that can be purchased as you travel.

Although it's a relatively relaxing way to travel and an ideal way to get a sense of the size of the Amazon, riverboat travel gives little feel for the jungle and is best used as a lazy means of getting from one place to another. When water levels are low, delays are commonplace as boats get stuck on shifting sandbanks. Ten days or more on a riverboat can start to test your sanity.

Hitching

It's popular to discourage hitching, but for some it is the best way to travel and in parts of the Amazon region it may be the only way. The basic rules of hitching hold true here and throughout South America: don't hitch alone, and don't hitch from

THE AMAZON: THE WAY IT WAS
Hilary Bradt

When I told this elderly woman I met at a San Francisco party in 1969 that I was going down the Amazon her face lit up. 'Oh, I've always wanted to go to Africa,' she said. For the last year I'd been wanting to make the trip – ever since I'd read a book about Indians with bones through their noses slipping silently through the jungle to hide stores of gold. I could hardly wait!

By the time I got to Pucallpa I'd been travelling alone for two months and realised that the gap between fact and travelogue was immense. But I owe it to *The Rivers Ran East* that I'd hung on to the ambition to boat it down as much of the river as possible. This meant, in those days, Pucallpa to Belém. My diary of the trip describes long days on the river and longer nights being bitten by mosquitoes (I proudly report the total count one morning: 116). There were no Indians with bones through their noses and no wildlife except what the crew caught and loaded on board for dinner.

I well remember the excitement and enjoyment of the first boat, from Pucallpa to Iquitos. We three gringos shared a cabin, with slatted bunk beds covered with dirty straw mattresses, but the boat was spacious enough to walk around on, and the food, rice and plantains, wasn't bad. It took five days to reach Iquitos, stopping at several Shipibo Indian villages. We reached the first one at dusk, and I recall the villagers running down the riverbank from their huts with goods for sale, followed by an enthusiastic cloud of mosquitoes. The Shipibos were selling their beautiful and distinctive pottery and live animals, including a charming (and sad) albino squirrel monkey. All that trip I was struggling with myself not to buy an animal companion. My diary records that I resisted a coati and a baby kinkajou, as well as parrots and macaws.

We stopped each night and anchored by a different village. Dawn would come like early morning on a farm: first the cocks would start crowing, then the pigs would want their breakfast and the ducks would get enthusiastic about their prospects of a swim. These animals were all part of the passengers' baggage. At one place about fifty turtles were brought on board and stored on their backs in the shower. Once I was woken to watch a display by the freshwater dolphins which were playing around the boat. Wonderful! The large cities where you clearly look out of place and perhaps rather vulnerable.

Petrol stations or checkpoints where cars and lorries are stopping are a good spot to look for a ride. If you find yourself at a checkpoint, the soldiers or police on duty are often quite helpful in trying to get you a lift.

In Andean countries people 'hitch' rides on the back of trucks. Cargo-carrying *camionetas* are often packed with people paying a small fee for the ride. It's a dusty, bouncy and often slow mode of travel, but as there is usually a link between speed of travel and appreciation of detail that isn't always a problem.

Hitching on the river is an Amazon variation on the theme which could get you to – and leave you in – the most inaccessible places. Asking around at ports should reveal whether there are boats travelling along certain rivers that look interesting. Get an idea of how long a journey is before you travel so you can buy enough food for the trip.

Internal flights

With so much of Amazonia inaccessible to all but river traffic, the use of the occasional internal flight can quickly get you to the heart of the region. Charter

captain told me that if a pregnant girl sees one of these river dolphins she will give birth to one (likewise if she sees a sloth; both offspring sound preferable to a human baby).

We waited ten days in Iquitos, lured by promises of a free ride on a luxury boat. When it didn't materialise we took El Socio, an overworked little craft hardly larger than a *pedalo* and towing two barges. It was loaded with oil-drums but just had room for us and five other passengers to sling our hammocks. The one loo was occupied by a hen, and drinking water was scooped from the river. The cook was enormous and bad tempered, and produced different versions of sludge at mealtimes. We had to provide our own crockery and utensils. We enjoyed El Socio; she was a companionable little vessel and being forced to spend your days and nights in a hammock (there was no room to walk around) wasn't so bad. The journey to Leticia, in Colombia, took three days.

Someone took us to an Indian village where they practise the hair-pulling ceremony at the onset of puberty. As far as I could gather, everyone gets roaring drunk and the women of the village pull the poor girl's hair out until she is completely bald. One rather sad-looking child had her head covered by a headscarf having recently been through the ceremony. In some villages she would have been deflowered at the same time. I was even more intrigued by a little girl clutching her favourite soft toy to her chest. It was a giant frog – or ex-giant frog – stuffed with kapok.

From Leticia we crossed the river to Benjamin Constant, in Brazil. Our last boat was the classic 'bird-cage' vessel, the sort that still plies the lower waters of the Amazon. The villages – small towns even – along the river became more interesting, with decaying signs of the rubber boom in some of their fine churches and other buildings. Things were always happening in the villages: women weaving palm thatch, pots being fashioned from the riverside mud mixed with powdered charcoal, a cow being butchered, a hen riding around on the back of a pig, and a parrot fluent in Portuguese swearing, laughing and coughing.

We reached Manaus on July 16. On July 20 at 4.30pm, all the church bells in town rang out. The Americans had landed on the moon. I told an old man about it. Oh no, he said, you can only go to the moon after you die. It's not for the living.

flight prices are rarely prohibitive and when you take into account the spectacular views from the air then the extra cost could be justified as an essential part of any trip. The largest settlements in all Amazon Basin countries get regular flights, often several times a week. Smaller towns throughout the region also have flights operated by the national military airline who, space allowing, may take passengers for a lower fare than commercial flights.

Where there are no regular flights you may have to get an air taxi which can be expensive. Prices are charged by the hour so it is most economic to make sure all the seats in the plane are filled. Depending on your destination, the air taxi may land on a highway or even on the river itself.

THE AMAZON FROM SOURCE TO MOUTH

It's a major ambition of many travellers to travel the full length of the Amazon from headwaters to delta. This may be to emulate the great explorers such as Orellana and Teixeira; or more recent celebrities like Joe Kane, author of *Running the Amazon* (Pan, 1997), who kayaked down the Amazon from its source to the mouth; or the late Jacques Cousteau. Or it may just be one of those things you want to do. Beyond the kudos of completing this epic trip, the journey confronts you with paradoxes and environmental problems which are both common to humanity and at the same time specific to the unique conditions prevalent in the Amazon.

If you want to follow the main stream by local riverboat for the longest distance, the starting point is Pucallpa in Peru, which is easy to reach by bus from Lima. The journey is often given the title of 'Most Boring Trip in South America' and for some such a title is apt and justified. It is true that a trip down the main stream will not provide the intimacy and excitement of a two-man canoe down some unexplored tributary, but there can be no better way of getting a real impression of the vastness of the river. Travelling by boat along a river without being able to see the banks is awe-inspiring: it is, after all, a river not an ocean. But there are moments when time can drag, so make sure you have plenty of books, entertainment and the energy to maintain an intensive Spanish- and Portuguese-language course for several weeks.

With planning and foresight it is possible to plan small excursions on your route downstream. Stopping off at any of the larger towns and cities along the river, and many of the smaller ones, you will be able to arrange a trip down some of the smaller tributaries and to less disturbed areas.

One of the best reasons for travelling this route is to get an idea of the working river. People travel vast distances to visit relatives, in search of work and for hospital treatment. Cargo is transported up and downstream along a seemingly chaotic distribution network, but all the time the river flows on.

Boats leave Pucallpa from La Hoyada docks for the 3–4 day journey to Iquitos. The journey itself is fairly straightforward and best achieved in a number of short legs, changing boats at Iquitos, Tabatinga/Leticia, Tefé (optional), Manaus and Santarém before arriving in Belém. The journey downstream will probably take around three weeks, or longer if you allow for sightseeing. Smaller boats tend to stop at smaller villages en route but also take a little longer. The cost will vary according to the type of boat and the time spent in cities but the bottom line is US$500 for transport, and another US$300 for food and spending money.

As a bare minimum you'll need a hammock, a sheet or sleeping bag and a small library of books. Spending in excess of three weeks in a hammock is not an exciting prospect for some and the journey by riverboat is certainly not comfortable. On some legs of the journey it will be possible to get cabin accommodation if you need

RUNNING THE AMAZON
Paul Cripps of Amazonas Explorer, Cusco

The first kayak descent of the Apurimac – the Amazon's longest tributary – is credited to a French couple, Michel Perrin and Teresa Gutierrez, who in 1953 attempted probably the hardest section of the river from below Puente Cunyac. Teresa was drowned after their wooden and canvas kayak turned over not far from their starting point.

More successful was a party led by J Calvin Giddings, whose book Demon River Apurimac is a gripping account of their epic attempts on two different sections of the river in the mid-1970s. Paddling long, fibre-glass kayaks they struggled through incredible hardships to conquer most of the upper canyons of the Apurimac.

Later in 1981 the Polish Expedition 'Canoandes 79' ran from even further up than the Giddings expedition. Finally, in the early 1980s, a Polish–South African–American team finally made a complete descent from source to sea. Two books have been written about this journey: *Running the Amazon* by Joe Kane, an interesting tale from the non-rafter's viewpoint, is probably most notable for his account of the internal conflicts that plagued the expedition, while a similar book by expedition leader François Odendaal sharply contradicts Joe Kane's account and really makes you wonder about the true story.

With the advent of the virtually indestructible plastic kayak, various expeditions have run many of the different sections of the river. Most of the first descents concentrated on the hardest section of the Rio Apurimac, the notorious Accobamba Abyss, where the sheer canyon walls rise thousands of metres above you, rockfalls are common in the afternoon and the rapids are all but unrunnable.

In 1997, an extraordinary South African appeared with tales of swimming the length of the Apurimac (including walking in from the Pacific) on a hydro-speed – a kind of surfboard. Fishing for food and carrying everything on his back (including a mobile satellite phone), he matter-of-factly told of getting stuck in whirlpools for up to half an hour, of having his helmet sucked off his head whilst travelling through a 40ft-long rock siphon and of having to cut off his fins to escape being sucked into an undercut. He was last heard of heading for the Atlantic with some 3,000 miles still to go. Having survived the worst of the rapids the Amazon could throw at him, his greatest threat in the lower stretches of the river will be the huge cargo ships – and boredom.

For information on rafting companies operating out of Cusco near the source of the Amazon, see page 315 in the Peru chapter.

a break from the hammock, but don't rely on it. Taking your own supplies of food – essential if you're a vegetarian – will add to the bland and unadventurous menu. Buying clean water or using purification tablets is also advisable. Don't stock up for the whole journey as you can easily buy extra supplies downriver in the larger towns.

Perhaps the most convenient way to travel the length of the Amazon is provided by a consortium of companies based in Peru and Brazil. You go from Chiclayo in Peru, over the Andes and along the Amazon from Yurimaguas, then to Iquitos, Leticia, Manaus and ending in Belém. The trip takes 25 days. It is possible to take only one or two segments but that would defeat the point of the trip! The basic option uses buses overland and hammock or dormitory accommodation on board ship, and costs US$730, or about US$30 per day. At US$2,912 for the entire trip, the 'deluxe' option uses private 4WDs for land portions and private cabins for river portions. Book through Amazon Tours and Cruises (page 280) or contact Swallows and Amazons in Manaus (page 388) or Amazon Tours in Santarem (page 402).

A more expensive, comfortable and convenient option is to book passage on one of the luxury passenger vessels that sail from Belém to Manaus or more rarely to Iquitos. Check out *Small ship cruises* (page 42) to get an idea of the options and prices.

Running the headwaters of the Amazon

Only seriously fit and experienced adventurers with adequate back-up should consider starting their trip at the Amazon's source in the Peruvian Andes (see box on page 67). This involves a major expedition, such as the one described in *Running the Amazon* (see *Further Reading*, page 457). However, the less intrepid (or masochistic...) can visit the Amazon's headwaters for some whitewater kayaking, and then pick the river up again at Pucallpa and continue downstream from there. Companies to contact for kayaking in the headwaters are listed in *Chapter 10, Peru*.

Mounting your own Expedition

Tanis Jordan

Tanis Jordan, with her husband Martin, has been making independent, self-financed expeditions since the late sixties. She has travelled extensively and made expeditions of several months' duration in Brazil, Venezuela, Peru, French Guiana, Guyana, Suriname and elsewhere. To date she has had two travel books and four children's books published. A Fellow of the Royal Geographic Society, she has lectured there on several occasions.

In the past decade Amazonia has opened up to travel. There is no shortage of companies that will take you there. You can rough it or smooth it, watch wildlife, visit Amerindian villages, go up mountains or down rivers; you name it, they arrange it. But perhaps that isn't what you want.

Picture this. Imagine waking at dawn, when it is just getting light. You are cosy in your sleeping bag as you peer out. Strange tree shapes appear and disappear as the morning mist swirls over the river and hangs in the trees. The occasional whistle of a tapir to its mate or the splash of fish jumping in the river disturbs the stillness. Then you hear the flap of wings and raucous cries as red and blue macaws fly across the river in twos and threes to their food trees. In the distance an eerie roar begins, coming closer and closer until it is deafeningly loud – then high in the treetops a troop of red howler monkeys appears, marking their territory.

You leave your hammock. The ground is damp and cool. You bang your shoes to remove scorpions, ants or cockroaches, fill the kettle from the river, then take your machete to chop driftwood and build a fire. After breakfast of coffee and oatmeal you wash the dishes in the river, while shoals of tiny coloured fish nibble at your hands. Checking that no unwanted 'guests' have dropped into the boat overnight, you break camp, load up, start the engine and chug off into the hot sunshine to the next set of rapids, with absolutely no idea who or what the day will bring.

This is what it's like to go it alone, to mount your own expedition to Amazonia. It will take endless planning and organisation, be tedious, frustrating and potentially dangerous; and when you do get there, jungle life is hard work. But the rewards are many. When at last you put your boat on the water and push off from the bank for the very first time, there is no other feeling quite like it, and one way or another it will change your life forever.

PLANNING AN EXPEDITION

The most important requirements for a successful trip are to have a purpose and a plan. Your expedition must have a definite goal otherwise you will just drift from place to place. Ask yourself why you want to mount your own expedition. If it's so that you are free to go where you want when you want, to stay away as long as you wish and to be in total control of your own destiny, then to achieve that much freedom you will need to finance it yourself. If you are sponsored, commissioned or under contract to carry out some sort of research you won't have complete choice in where you go and what you do.

Most expeditions use local guides, porters and boatmen. For a first-time independent jungle trip, travelling, camping and daily chores will take up most of your time and all your energy; you would need experience to be able to carry out project work as well. If you plan to write a book when you return home or make a film while you're there, then you will have to compromise your freedom. We've found that even the obligation of taking an occasional photograph gets in the way of just enjoying the moment. You may also spend days worrying that nothing exciting will happen to fill your book or film; and nights plagued with fearful dreams of what might.

Choosing your destination

Actually deciding where to go can be the hardest part of an expedition. Whether gazing at spaces on a map, picking up on a name or following in the footsteps of other explorers, you will probably have an incurable fascination about a place, region or subject.

For us it is usually an area of jungle or a river tributary as remote as possible and far away from towns and people. The more information you can gather about your destination the better equipped you will be to handle any unforeseen circumstances that arise – and arise they will. The most common form of transport for jungle expeditions is by boat, with forays of days or weeks spent exploring in the jungle. Buy the best maps and plan your route, then start doing the detective work. Contact embassies, ministries, tourist boards, but keep your enquiries brief and concise. Write letters, send faxes or search the web for any information about the river and the area. For most out-of-the-way places there is very little information available, but whatever you can get hold of will help you prepare. To make an expedition walking from A to B find out if there are rivers to cross and, if so, whether there are any settlements where someone can ferry you across. Once you reach B, is there any way of returning without retracing your journey? If it's a river trip can you find a boat there? If you want to use an outboard engine will fuel be available? For really remote areas we learned to take everything – on a five-month trip inside Manú National Park, Peru, we took ten five-gallon cans of gasoline in the back of a truck on a two-day journey across the Andes mountains, and one of us had to stay awake at all times to make sure nobody stole it.

Gaining permission

Whether or not you need a visa to enter the country itself, make thorough enquiries about requirements to enter the area you will visit. Some officials are sensitive if there is logging or mining activity. To travel in a national park, a protected area, or the home of indigenous tribal people may take six months or longer to gain permission. Be patient, polite and persistent and remember that some of the most interesting places cannot be visited on a whim. On the Trombetas river in Brazil we met a group of Spanish anthropology students who had decided to visit an Amerindian village high up in the Tumucumaque mountains. At great expense they hired a boat to bring them up the river to the highest navigable point and then a light aircraft to take them to their destination. Despite tearful begging and pleading, their plane was not allowed to land because they had not requested permission in advance. This aborted journey cost them thousands and could have ended differently if they had done some more research.

Some countries have limits on how many 'expeditions' are allowed in per year. I once telephoned an embassy in Britain to ask what permission was needed to make an expedition in its country to be told that 'absolutely no expeditions would be allowed in until further notice'! We quickly became two tourists on holiday.

When to go

Whether to go in the dry or rainy season is an important consideration. In the dry season the rivers will be low, sometimes so low that the riverbed is exposed, making river travel arduous. Hauling boats up rapids or unpacking the boat and carrying everything around the rapids overland (portaging) takes a lot of time and a phenomenal amount of energy. But in the dry season you will see lots more wildlife and camping is more pleasant because it's not raining all the time and more river bank and beaches are exposed. It's tempting to camp on those beautiful sand beaches but there is a very real danger of flash floods that arrive with no warning, often caused by rain far away in the mountains. Your pretty jungle stream may rise three metres in an hour and become a raging torrent or, worse, a wall of water may pour downstream engulfing all before it. In Peru we pitched our shelter on the edge of the jungle at least thirty metres from the river and tied the boat to an enormous fallen tree fifteen metres long. We were woken in the night by water swirling at our feet and both boat and tree had floated away. As a rule NEVER camp on beaches.

In the rainy season it rains nearly every day and river levels are high. Rivers will be flowing fast and the jungle may flood. Clothes that get wet take ages to dry, while mould grows on camera equipment and film.

But the rainy season does have its compensations, particularly if you are visiting a waterfall. All trips to Angel Falls in Venezuela, the highest waterfall in the world, are made in the rainy season. We travelled to it in the dry season when, to quote the late 'jungle Rudy' Truffino, 'in the rainy season it's the most impressive sight in the world, but in the dry season my dog can do better'.

Choosing your boat

Dugout canoes are the most common means of travel on Amazonian rivers. They are strong, and respond well under power, but they are heavy and sit low in the water. Sometimes the sides are built up with planks, which makes them more stable but even heavier. If you plan to paddle upriver or portage around rapids then you will need to be fairly strong. Dugout canoes are usually available in riverside towns and (sometimes) villages. Because they do not have fixed values, the price you pay depends on who's selling it, where you buy it, the country you are in and so on. The only useful tip is that you will probably get a better deal buying a secondhand canoe from a local person than a new one from an established river trader. If you are returning to your starting place an alternative may be to try and hire a canoe for your trip, the cost of which will vary greatly depending on availability and duration.

Fibreglass, plastic and aluminium canoes are light, fast and responsive under power. But they are not so readily available and are much more fragile than dugout canoes. Take this into consideration if your river is a rocky one. If you choose this type of boat you will probably have to take one from your home country. The alternative is to hire a boat and boatman, but it will be expensive and your expedition will be a different experience.

Inflatable boats are excellent, particularly for the novice. They rarely capsize even when punctured or full of water; they bounce off rocks, carry enormous weights and are repairable and comfortable to sit on day after day. But on fast water they slide, they spin, they are slow and almost impossible to paddle. However, for a first trip my choice would be an inflatable powered by an outboard engine light enough for one person to carry. We fold our inflatable as small as possible and carry it as ordinary luggage. It's easier to buy the engine out there.

If you opt for a canoe practise first, as a South American river is not the place to learn basic boating skills. Whatever your choice of craft, wear life jackets and tie everything in, including the engine. Tie heavy bags securely. If you don't and the

CANOEING

John Harrison

The advantages of paddling quietly along the Amazon rivers are many. The wildlife doesn't hear you coming and you can hear the rustles and calls that betray an animal's presence. You don't have to sit in a haze of petrol fumes, or be a slave to available fuel supplies. Being self-propelled gives a sense of satisfaction, and puts you on a shared level with the locals. There's no great haste, so why rush along pursued by the banshee wail of a two-stroke?

Admittedly it's quite hard work at first – but within a week you become fit enough to paddle six hours a day at a steady, economical rhythm. By the end of the trip you'll have a torso to die for, supported on a couple of spindly, atrophied legs.

My early canoeing in the Amazon was done in dug-outs or in canoes I made myself from locally obtained planks. Both craft are heavy and only suitable for rivers without rapids. Two people can barely lift them and some rapids require portages of several hundred metres.

In Brazilian Amazonia it's almost impossible to buy aluminium or fibreglass canoes. It's best to take alternatives from home that can be carried on aircraft as personal baggage. Never send canoes or anything else as unaccompanied freight to South America. You can waste half your holiday trying to get it out of customs.

Granta Canoes (Ramsey, Huntingdon, Cambridgeshire, UK; tel: 01487 813777) produce excellent plywood canoe kits for 5m, and 6m 'Canadian' canoes. Capable of carrying two people and 300kg, they can be supplied with a squared-off stern to take a small outboard motor if you must (at least then you have a craft that can be paddled easily when the fuel runs out). The only drawback is that assembly is completed using fibreglass which, because it can't be taken on airlines, has to be obtained in Amazonia. In Manaus, in 1987, I found

boat capsizes, the bags will hang down like anchors and make it very difficult to flip it back over. We learned this particular lesson when we capsized a fibreglass canoe on the Marowijne river in Suriname, couldn't right it, lost everything including the canoe and both nearly drowned.

When you leave the boat to spend time in the jungle, take the boat out of the water if possible and hide it in the jungle. Tie the painter – the rope on the front of the boat – high up a tree so that if the river rises and floods the bank the boat will float up. If it's not possible to take it out of the river then cover it with some greenery. If you plan to leave it in the river for some time, make sure you leave plenty of slack in the rope. If you don't and the river drops while you are away, you may come back and find your boat hanging in the air halfway up a tree. Don't forget to take a repair kit for your boat if appropriate.

If you plan something ambitious like crossing from one river to another, bear in mind that there is usually a hill or even a mountain range between river valleys or vast distances of jungle. Everything must be carried including the boat. If you are travelling upstream near the source, the going will become steeper, rockier and less navigable and you may even run out of river before you reach the source. This happened to us on the Mapuera River in Brazil when our river journey turned into a hiking trip.

What to take

It may be possible to buy most of the things you will need in larger towns, but if an item is essential take it with you. Where new roads have been built new only one factory that would sell me some of their stock – it wasn't sold in any stores. Availability may well have increased now. The Granta is easily repairable with fibreglass if damaged on the river.

Folding canoes and kayaks

There are several folding kayaks on the market, but they don't generally have enough carrying capacity for a long trip. The folding canoe that I use is the excellent Norwegian 'Ally'. It comes in various sizes but essentially will carry two people plus 300kg of gear. Not cheap – £1,000 (US$1,500) or so, but ideal for taking on planes and bringing home with you afterwards. **Bergans Fritid AS**, Industriveien, Box 293, N-3301 Hokksund, Norway; tel: 00 47 32 25 25 00; fax: 00 47 32 25 25 10; web: www.bergans.no. Tougher than it looks, if you do have an accident the Ally is repaired with stick-on patches.

Other folding canoes you may want to consider are: **Pakboats** PO Box 700, May St, Enfield, NH 03748; tel: 603 632 9500/888 863 9500; fax: 603 632 5611; email: info@pakboats.com; web: www.pakboats.com. **Feathercraft Folding Kayaks** 4-1244 Cartwright Street, Granville Island, Vancouver, BC, V6H 3R8, Canada; tel: 604 681 8437; fax: 604 681 7282; email: info@feathercraft.com; web: www.feathercraft.com. **Klepper Faltbootwerft** Klepperstrasse 18 M, D-83026, Rosenheim, Germany; tel: 08031 21670; fax 08031 216777; email: faltboote@klepper.de; web: www.klepper.com. **Nautiraid** Zone Industrielle, 53480 Vaiges, France; tel: 0243 902026; fax: 0243 905270; email: phguyot@nautiraid.com; web: www.nautiraid.com.

Paddles

Take a paddle from home – they're lightweight and built to last. The local ones are hewn from a piece of hardwood and are very heavy.

settlements will have sprung up, but don't rely on buying vital equipment there. In French Guiana we found a shack selling only Chanel perfume and ten-year-old French Cognac; nice, but not terribly useful. In Brazil, in what was marked on the map as a fair-sized town, we planned to buy wood to make a floor for our boat. It was impossible to find anything suitable. In desperation we searched close to the jungle's edge and found a washed-up packing case that was perfect.

Rucksacks and kit bags

Your choice of rucksack for an expedition is purely personal. There is a vast array available but still none that is completely waterproof and lightweight. Wrap everything in plastic first; self-seal bags are ideal for this. Take plenty of strong plastic bags. Don't have too many dangly straps or bits sticking out, as they will catch on bushes and trees and impede your progress through the jungle, as will rucksacks that protrude above your head.

Waterproof bags are available at camping shops but we make our own from the cloth that boat sails are made of. They are light, strong, waterproof and you can customise them to suit. If you need to travel on trucks or buses to reach your embarkation point it's a good idea to have bright-coloured bags that are easy to pick out. Our bright yellow kitbags travelled quite a few kilometres downriver on their own when we tipped that canoe on the Marowijne River. Eventually we found them washed up on rocks and our sleeping bags were still dry! Things wrapped in sealed plastic bags will usually float, which is another advantage. If you are planning a river/land expedition it might be worth looking at combination bags that convert to rucksacks. Anything too fiddly or complicated might not stand up to a lot of hard use, but a really strong, simple design could serve both purposes quite well.

Clothes

I have made many expeditions where the absence of biting insects meant that I spent all day in a bikini and the evenings in shorts and T-shirt. But in Manú National Park, Peru, we had to cover up from head to foot to avoid the night-time mosquitoes and day-time blackflies that never ceased their biting activities except for the two blessed 40-minute change-over periods at dawn and sunset. Upriver, near Tayakome, there were 24-hour mosquitoes and we had to walk up and down the beach eating our food.

If you have never been in the tropics you may not realise quite how hot it can feel. When you get off the air-conditioned plane it is like a hot, wet blanket enveloping you. There is no need to spend a lot of money on specialist clothing except for trousers. Trousers designed for travellers are light and strong, with lots of zip pockets, and they dry quickly. I prefer a polyester/cotton mix because it's strong and dries fast. I never wear heavy cotton in the jungle, as it holds the water, is slow to dry and tends to rot quicker than manmade fibres.

Take long-sleeved button-up shirts as protection against sun and insects, a warm sweater or sweatshirt for cooler nights and a hat with a brim or a peak – with a chin strap or you'll lose it – to protect you from the sun. We only wear simple no-frills tennis shoes (one pair lasts about two months) and have never worn jungle boots. If there are biting insects you will need to cover up. Wool socks are comfortable but manmade dry quicker. Make sure they are long enough to tuck your trousers into them. Put repellent on your socks and cuffs. A tropical rainstorm will drench you in seconds so a fully-waterproof poncho is more useful than a jacket.

Take two sets of clothing: one to wear during the day that will get wet and dirty, and a clean set to put on when you make camp. Keep the spare set dry at all times and never be tempted to put them on instead if your day set is wet and clammy. Dry clothes at the end of the day will keep you sane, and your body is less likely to develop fungal infections if you stay dry. The underwear you wear at home will be fine in the jungle. The way to keep clear of rashes, sores or fungi is to keep clean and dry and let the air get to your body as often as you can.

Sleeping equipment
Hammocks

Whether in the jungle or in a village hut, the most comfortable way to sleep is in a locally bought hammock of woven cotton. Before buying, check that the ropes and cords that gather the ends are strong, as these are usually the first to break. Keep your hammock dry as dampness will weaken it drastically. Hang your hammock high and tight as they drop at least a metre when you get in, and lie diagonally across it. Don't hang your hammock under dead branches – you don't want them crashing down on you in a storm. Likewise, amusing as it may sound, several fatalities have resulted when people sling hammocks between coconut palms. Check nothing worrisome is living in the trees above you; we slept without nets in Brazil and spent a night with large cockroaches dropping into our hammocks at regular intervals. In another camp we picked out dozens of pairs of eyes in the trees above and surrounding us. Investigation revealed them to be the eyes of huge black furry spiders.

Mosquito nets

With the ever-present danger of malaria, mosquito nets are very important. Hammock nets are available in most South American countries but I would recommend taking a tried and tested one. Several companies make purpose-built hammock nets available from good camping shops. Nets I've bought in Amazonia were either so flimsy that they split or so thick it was unbearably hot and like sleeping in a fog. Some had mesh so wide that while they kept out the mosquitoes, biting blackflies flitted joyfully through. The net must be large, loose and seal you in completely. Anywhere the net contacts your skin will be bitten. The slightest hole and mosquitoes will be queuing up to feast. Nets impregnated with repellent, usually permethrin, will prevent this but will need to be re-treated after about three months. The repellent loses its strength after a couple of washes so avoid washing nets unless essential. If you must wash them don't do it in the river as the repellent can harm fish and amphibians. Take plenty of rope for hanging the hammock and thin nylon cord for hanging the mosquito net high enough above the hammock to give you plenty of headroom. Some hammocks have a built-in mosquito net and waterproof covers. Personally I have never managed to get on with them but I know at least two jungle veterans who wouldn't use anything else. Depending on the length of your trip you can either take a large sheet of plastic to cover your hammock or make a proper shelter to take with you.

Take two large pieces of lightweight waterproof cloth (3m by 6m each), edged all round with Velcro so that they fit together to form a square or an L shape. Punch eyelets around the edges large enough to take rope. To hang the shelter, tie a rope at a high point between the two trees that support your hammock and drape the shelter over it. Tie the edges of the shelter securely to trees or bushes or it will take off in a tropical storm.

Tents

One disadvantage with a hammock as opposed to a tent is that when biting insects get the munchies you may have to retire under your net. Some things you can do in a tent are difficult in a hammock: read, write or eat by candlelight and seek protection from insect pests. In addition, if you are ill or the weather is bad it's more comfortable to spend time in one. You have privacy. The vast variety of tents available means that you can select one most suited to your needs. When we first travelled to South America the only tents available were windowless, net-less canvas heavyweights and we made our own. Now we use a one-touch Khyam Highlander, though for a long boat trip I would choose a three-man version of the same dome-type tent. Always secure the tent especially if you are leaving it for any time, as a tropical storm could blow it away, even in deep jungle. Bear in mind that tropical rain can devastate a single-skin tent and tropical heat can bake you in a double. Mosquito-net panels for ventilation are essential and a removable fly sheet advisable. Nights can be surprisingly cool in the highlands, so a sleeping bag is better than a blanket – synthetic filling dries more quickly than down.

Night comes quickly in the tropics: sunset around six and total darkness not too long afterwards. If you leave it too late to look for a place to camp you will find yourself working in the dark. It can take a couple of hours to make camp, light a fire and cook a meal.

Food

In more populated places along the rivers you will find trading posts and travelling shops on boats, but they may not have what you want and goods will probably be relatively expensive. One in Brazil sold only beer and biscuits. In villages where people grow their own food there may not be enough produce to sell. If you plan to be away from civilisation then take all you need with you. It is completely impracticable to live off the jungle: unless you are an authority on the subject or advised by a local you will probably poison yourself. As for 'eating what the monkeys eat' – if you are prepared to climb five metres or more up a tree every time you feel hungry you will have a very busy time.

The variety of dried food available means you can eat very well on long jungle trips. Lots of small packs are better than large ones as, once opened, the contents absorb moisture. Take oatmeal for breakfast: it's light, nutritious, filling and readily available. Rice, beans, pasta, coffee, salt, spices, soups, flour, dried milk and sugar will vary your basic diet. Take some luxuries for an occasional treat. Take vitamin supplements in case you can't obtain fresh fruit or vegetables. It's easy to dehydrate in the hot sun or if you lose fluids because of sickness, so sachets or tablets of rehydration mixture will be useful. We've never become ill or weak from eating this way for months at a time. Store supplies off the ground, as rodents can demolish plastic containers and devour the strangest things: on one occasion our whole supply of candles and a bar of carbolic soap.

Hunting

In a word – don't. If you can't get by in the jungle without killing wild animals, you shouldn't be there. Amazonian wildlife is under enough pressure without the added burden of being hunted. It's better to observe the wildlife than eat it. It's extremely dangerous and illegal to hunt while travelling through indigenous people's land. They do not take kindly to all the goldminers, loggers and prospectors who invade their territory and decimate their food supply by hunting and you will be regarded as no different. It's perfectly possible on a boat to carry all the food you will need for up to five months; we've done it on many occasions.

Water

'If you drink the water of the Tapanahoni river you will be sure to return to Suriname one day,' said the Bushnegro Granman as we bade him farewell. He was right and we did. We also picked up the 'Suriname shuffle' medically known as *giardiasis*, proving that water can be dangerous stuff. A reassuring fact is that we've only ever become ill when living in populated areas, never in quiet jungles far away from towns or villages. Always fill your water container upstream of any settlements. The most effective way to sterilise water is to boil it thoroughly. This is not always possible and water-sterilising tablets are the next best option. Double the dose when you think the water is very polluted. Chlorine-based tablets have less after-taste than iodine but take longer to become effective. Ones based on silver are tasteless but take two hours to work. Always leave the tablets for at least the required time and preferably longer.

Other equipment

In our experience gadgety tools don't stand up in the field; if you are going to need a tin opener then take a tin opener. Take a knife; it doesn't have to do everything, so the less complicated the better. Tweezers are useful for removing thorns and splinters. A compass is no good at all if you don't know how to use it; practise before you go. Lightweight torches designed for divers float beam up. A candle lantern when in-camp saves batteries. Take a sharpening stone for the machete you will buy out there, as metal files clog up and wear smooth quickly. Take a bit of rubber tyre; you can shave bits off to start campfires. Carry sun-block that you know is effective. If your nose is vulnerable take a zinc-based sun-block; the flesh-coloured ones won't make you look quite so ridiculous.

FISHING
John Harrison

With over 1,750 species – all the rivers of Europe hold only 150 – Amazonia has fish ranging from tiny blue aquarium specimens to monsters weighing 300kg or more.

While I wouldn't advise anyone to hunt to supplement their food supplies, I personally think fishing is acceptable, and a valuable source of protein. It's also great fun and a world away from the dull, damp activity pursued by bored individuals along the streams of England.

Methods

Fish can be caught by almost any method. The locals might fish very skilfully with a handline, but I think it's worth taking a rod and reel from home. A two-piece boat rod and a fixed-spool reel holding 15kg breaking-strain line is enough.

Depending upon what you're trying to catch, bait is a piece of meat, dead fish, or, in season, certain fruits and berries. It's wise to have a length of metal wire above the hook to prevent your catch biting through the nylon line. With the bait resting on the river bed you will generally catch one of the 500 species of catfish, piranha or traira – a mottled tube with big teeth and pink eyes that you'll recognise when you see it. Predators are caught with little live fish (caught first with a tiny hook and farinha bait), or metal lures that are drawn through the water to imitate small wounded fish. Buy lures that have detachable treble hooks, and take a lot of replacement hooks to replace the ones the piranhas have mauled. The advantage of spinning is that you don't need to carry a putrid piece of dead fish in the canoe to use as bait. The drawback is that a lure will only catch four or five species, but one, the tucunare or peacock bass, is one of the great sport fish and among the tastiest.

Almost everything you will catch is edible. Most fish get their revenge with a wealth of forked bones that seem designed to lodge in the throat, or be used to pin snakes to the ground. Eating a plate of fish stew in the flickering, feeble light of a camp fire is a challenge.

The best fishing spots are the eddies and patches of turbulence below a rapid or at the confluence of two rivers. The best time to fish is at night from a canoe. This is a magnificently spooky activity on a moonless night and it's best to keep a knife and torch handy. Not because caiman or anaconda might pluck you out of your seat (that's an improbable scenario that your imagination can't let go of), but because after a 15-minute tussle that has left your arms aching and towed the canoe a hundred metres, you will want to examine the fish as it rolls exhausted to the surface. Only then can you decide whether you really want that toothy great thing snapping and flapping around your bare feet in the dark.

Travelling companions

A common problem is the animosity that develops between members of even the least arduous expeditions. You are stuck with the same people for weeks, possibly months, and it's hard to believe the hostility that can build up. Your friends' endearing ways can become unbearable habits that you cannot stand. On an expedition in Brazil a normally charming man attempted to strangle and drown his best friend who had borrowed his toothpaste without asking. Competition can build up as to who can paddle faster, or go on longest without a break, turning an enjoyable trip into a contest of endurance. Some of our worst rows were over who was doing it wrong on rapids, and I know of two men who got on so badly they were reduced to writing derogatory observations and complaints about each other in their diaries and leaving them about to be read. It helps a lot if you genuinely like the people you intend to travel with, so that at least when things get a little touchy there's a chance you will sort the problems out.

Choosing your companion/s can be difficult. A combination of personal instinct and direct or indirect testing is an effective way of establishing someone's commitment to an expedition. If the expedition requires a particular skill then incorporating tests should highlight weaknesses in areas that need greater development. If an expedition has an academic angle, naturally that will need to be included in any selection process.

Hazards

A river expedition through uninhabited jungle can be an exhilarating experience. It can also be a nightmare. But it's said that 'adventure' begins when your plans go wrong – plans often do go wrong. It would not be fair to imply that everything on a river journey is absolutely safe. The river and the jungle demand respect and care should always be taken with both.

Man

When we started making expeditions in South America nearly 30 years ago the main human dangers were from the odd criminal, miners or gold prospectors (the mercury used in gold extraction affects the central nervous system and sends them mad). But there are new dangers now, in particular, the fact that crops of drug plants are often grown and processed in remote and inaccessible jungle areas, just the sort of places adventurous travellers like to visit. Also, if there is any kind of civil unrest in a country there are likely to be armed and potentially dangerous people in the most remote regions. It is unwise to make yourself look like a soldier or guerrilla by wearing camouflage clothing or army fatigues.

In the jungle
The small things (see also pages 93–4)

Scorpions, may crawl into places like shoes, bags or through open tent fronts. This is rectified by shaking out boots and bags, and keeping tents at least partially closed. Take care if you turn over logs or rocks where scorpions may live.

Ants usually pose few problems, unless you encounter a nest of tiny biting, stinging fire ants. The *tocandira*, a giant ant an inch long, is aggressive and known as 'ant 24' in Venezuela because its sting can produce pain and fever lasting up to 24 hours. It is quite easy to see and avoid (see page 146).

Black widow spiders are small – about 24mm or one inch – satiny black with hour-glass-shaped red markings on the underside of their abdomens. They have a habit of occupying dark, quiet places like sheds and outbuildings. Though the bite is painful it is rarely fatal. (See page 151 for information on the Brazilian wandering spider, considered among the world's most venomous spiders.)

Take care with **wasps and hornets**. They sometimes construct their nests low down, hidden on the backs of leaves where the unwary might walk into them. Some of these insects can inject extremely potent venom. I was stung by a black hornet, two inches long; the pain was tremendous but didn't last long, although it threw my body's defences into overdrive. If you should accidentally disturb a

IT'S NOT ALWAYS A BREEZE IN THE AMAZON

Amazing it is, but the South American rainforest is not always the paradise that people make it out to be. Trouble and strife can result in the most extreme reactions and disagreements between friends as this excerpt from Redmond O'Hanlon's adventures of travelling between the Orinoco and the Amazon in Venezuela, entitled *In Trouble Again*, points out:

'Why the hell should I put up with all this? That's what I want to know! You tell me! I can't stand it. Why should I? Why should I be stung by ants and wasps and hornets and bees all day? I've been thinking about it. It's nothing but rain and mosquitoes and the same bloody awful trees and endless rivers and disgusting food and being wet all the time. There's no comradeship. There's no wine and no women and no song and nowhere sensible to shit.'

'I'm sorry,' I said. 'You'll think differently in the morning.'

'No I bloody won't,' said Simon, his eyes white in the murk. 'Oh no I bloody well won't! I've been thinking about it for four weeks. It's not that I'm frightened. It's not really your fault. It's just that I can't bear to go back in there,' (he waved the bottle in the direction of the landing-stage and the uncut jungle) 'and why the hell should I?'

'Do you think you are so unstable already,' said Juan, in his most precise way, his beard outlined in the light of the kerosene lamp, pressed forward in interrogation, 'because of the sudden withdrawal of drugs and alcohol on this journey?'

'You stupid dago,' said Simon, exasperated, 'how the hell would I know?'

'Don't do it,' I said. 'You'll feel bad about it later. About deserting me.'

'Redmond,' said Simon, relaxing, 'I'll handle all that with the first pint of cognac.'

'Don't be silly. You'll never forgive yourself.'

'Oh yes I damn well will. I have already. Redmond – I've cried four times in my adult life. Once when my father died; once when my wife left me; once when Pinky my cat was run over in front of me; and every night when we were lost up that stinking pitsville of a swamp.'

'What about the Yanomami? What about your pictures?'

'I don't want to see the Yanomami. I can't stand all the poverty. These people are bad enough. They don't own anything. And anyway, my cameras are totally, but totally full of mould and gunge and parasites, and the odd fish too, I shouldn't wonder. It's the pits.'

Do you still want to go?

wasp's nest this advice given to us by a Guyanese 'porknocker' (gold prospector) may help. 'Drop everything, cover one eye with one hand, shut your mouth, run like hell to the nearest water and dive in!'

The bigger things

Large **mammals** are generally not dangerous in Amazonia (see *Chapter 5*).

In the water

In the river **stingrays** lie flat and still in shaded mud and sand shallows. Their sting is excruciatingly painful and can take months to heal. Shuffle your feet when you walk in the river and look carefully before you jump out of the boat. This may also prevent cuts from bottom-dwelling catfish with sharp spines.

MAKING IT HAPPEN
Peter Hutchison

For mere mortals interested in the Amazon, the idea of mounting an expedition down an unexplored river is the substance of dreams. But how do you turn a dream into a reality?

After years drifting through South America, gazing at maps and meddling with small journeys, I came across a report published in 1881 by the Royal Geographical Society in London that mentioned the River Parapeti in southeast Bolivia. There was, according to the report's author J B Minchin, some speculation as to the precise course of the river. A little more research revealed the river's route was still unknown.

As Tanis says at the start of this chapter, 'The most important requirements for a successful trip are to have a purpose and a plan.' I needed a plan.

The Parapeti has its source in the Andes, before flowing across the northern limits of the Chaco – a vast, dry plateau in the heart of South America. Minchin said the river flowed north through the wetlands of the Bañados del Izozog and linked with the Amazon Basin. Some, however, believed it flows east to Paraguay and the River Plate.

By the time the expedition set off in February 2002 after almost three years planning, we had a team of five – three Brits and two Izoceño Bolivians – and had worked with the local Izoceño group CABI (Capitania del Alto y Bajo Izozog), the Wildlife Conservation Society, an international NGO working to protect the 3.5 million hectares that make up the Kaa-Iya del Gran Chaco National Park, and countless other organisations.

We spent just under six weeks on the river. We nearly wrote off one of our Ally canoes on day one, our medic left the expedition after a couple of weeks,

Electric eels are related to catfish and can grow up to two metres long. A large specimen can render a human being unconscious with its shock. They are usually found in deep, slow moving waters.

Pity the poor **piranha** fish which has been given such a bad image by Hollywood. Yes, it can and does bite, but usually only when someone is trying to remove a fish hook from its mouth. However, in the dry season when the rivers dry up, leaving large pools cut off from the main body of water, piranha fish trapped there will be extremely hungry and you should exercise caution. In places where local people warn you about piranha fish, take their advice.

Amazon snakes

We have come across many snakes during our travels and, though neither of us has ever been bitten, we were always conscious that a snakebite would be a very serious problem. Because there is such conflicting advice about what to do in the unlikely event of snakebite I consulted internationally recognised herpetologist Mark O'Shea, who says:

> Snakes are often found near water, especially at dawn and dusk. They lack ears and rely on ground vibration. Despite popular local myths, most snakes don't chase people and would far rather save their venom for prey than bite you. If you want to look under logs, roll them toward you rather than away so a hidden snake can't strike at your legs. Wear boots and gloves while collecting firewood. If by some misfortune you do sustain a bite the most difficult advice to follow, but perhaps the most important, is

the spiders were unbearable and the mosquitoes monstrous. A worker at one of the isolated ranches we passed laughed at the insanity of the idea: 'Looking for an interesting way to die, huh?'

It was hard, the hardest thing any of the team had undertaken. And dangerous too. Amongst the madness were moments of magic: being woken one morning by a herd of peccary and splashed by the tail of a caiman, sheltering from the falling debris of a troop of monkeys feeding overhead or simply listening to the riotous bird calls of the morning chorus. For more information visit www.coursingtheparapeti.com.

The planning is a big part of any expedition, but it's definitely worth it. Another challenge is getting the funding. Again with a strong goal and a good plan you may be lucky to getting funding and sponsorship but it's tough. Team selection, day-to-day living are all part of the bigger picture and while there are some general rules the finer details depend on the expedition being undertaken.

We made every effort to minimise our impact and to share completely the work and experience with the local community. The world has moved on too far to justify inconsiderate travel just because you feel like an adventure.

Tanis and Martin Jordan have a lot to answer for. Back in the 1970s they wrote *South American River Trips* – that book in part inspired this guide. John Harrison too is a highly respected modern day Amazon expeditioner. Many people head out on South American river trips and with planning it could be you. A good starting place is the information in this chapter, then look on the internet at the Royal Geographic Society's Expedition Advisory Centre – www.rgs.org/eac

Just one word of caution – an important consideration is making sure you come back. Do the research, respect the environment and take care.

not to panic. Many bites can be from non-venomous snakes and even venomous snakes often inject no venom or sub-lethal doses.

As Mark O'Shea says, the DON'Ts are far more important than the DOs and his advice is:

- DON'T cut the bite with a knife or a razor, or apply a tourniquet, or give electric shock. Don't use ice or extreme heat or potassium permanganate, or alcohol.
- DON'T suck or use any sucking apparatus. It's instinctive to suck a bite but this isn't proven to do any good. Once the venom is in, it's in, and you can no more suck it out than you could suck out a tetanus serum that a doctor injects in your backside.
- DON'T give aspirin.
- DON'T mess with snakes.
- DON'T kill snakes unnecessarily; most snakes are harmless.

Venomous Amazonian snakes to be cautious about

Specifically, the banded **coral snakes** are related to cobras but they don't form hoods. Their venom contains neurotoxins which cause respiratory failure. They are usually red, black and yellow in bands while some are blue and black. Forget all the poetry used in North America – 'Red to yellow kill a fellow, red to black venom lack' – it doesn't apply to South American coral snakes. Fewer than one in a hundred venomous snakebites in Amazonian Brazil are caused by coral snakes. Coral snakes have great difficulty in biting through clothing but they have been known to come into sleeping bags on the ground. Bites are often on the fingertips or between the fingers and because the bite doesn't hurt, you may not even realise you have been bitten. Later symptoms are when the eyelids begin to droop and the tongue and the face muscles become paralysed. You can apply a pressure bandage as you would for an ankle sprain, so that you can still get a finger comfortably underneath. It's important not to cut off blood circulation. Don't use a tourniquet.

Pit vipers have heat-sensitive pits on their heads which are extremely accurate prey-locating receptors. Their venom attacks the blood and tissues, bites can bleed and there will be massive swelling, severe pain and discoloration. Keep the limb elevated but NEVER apply a pressure bandage because as the limb swells this will fast become a tourniquet.

In all cases of snakebite get the person to hospital as soon as possible. Don't waste time. If possible kill the snake and take it with you in a secure box for identification, but don't rush around in a panic trying to catch it. Record what it looks like (colours, patterns, length) time and location, but don't risk another bite. To measure swelling, put a tape measure around the victim's limb, mark the edges with a pen, remove the tape measure and continue to monitor the swelling this way. Reassure victims that they will be alright.

If all this seems rather alarming, remember that most people spend their entire life living in Amazonia without being bitten by a snake. Here are some snakebite statistics and the snake groups usually responsible:

- Fer de lance and relatives – 90% – all habitats
- Rattlesnake – 9% – prefer savannah but have been found near jungle edge
- Coral snakes – 0.9% – primarily forest
- Bushmaster – 0.1% – deep forest

Most non-venomous snakes will bite to defend themselves, and large species like boas and anacondas can inflict painful, bloody bites but they are harmless wounds. Wash with an antiseptic.

IS IT WORTH IT?

There will be days when it rains. Even in the jungle, it sometimes gets cold. In places the riverbank is slippery and you get covered in mud, the forest is murky and threatening, wet and clinging, all the trees seem thorny and there's nowhere to camp. You fantasise about the food you will eat when you get back to a town – how could there have been days at home when you didn't know what to eat, with everything in a supermarket to choose from? You miss newspapers, TV, the radio and your family and friends. You can't face another rapid, another uncomfortable night, another mosquito bite. Physically and mentally exhausted you wonder what you are doing there, and begin to feel miserable and just a bit frightened.

But if thoughts of snakes and spiders, rapids and roaches haven't put you off, then picture this. You pull your boat up the beach. In the cool jungle away from the hot sun you have your pick of trees from which to hang your hammock. You gather wood, light a fire and cook a meal. Later, sitting on the beach with a drink, you see the stars as never before. Caimans slip into the river with hardly a splash, a cacophony of frog voices fills the night and a deer barks. That night you are woken by a snuffling sound and a cough, then a sound just like somebody snoring, but you drift back to sleep. In the morning, all around your camp are huge paw prints, even between the hammocks hanging only a metre apart. A curious jaguar has visited in the night. It could come true, it happened to us and it could happen to you.

Health and Safety

Written in collaboration with Dr Jane Wilson-Howarth and Dr Felicity Nicholson

Most tropical diseases are rare, preventable and treatable. The scariest diseases are unlikely to trouble the short-term visitor if you follow a few standard hygiene practices. Far more likely are the usual travellers' woes.

HEALTH
Before you go
Malaria

Malaria is a serious, acute and chronic relapsing infection; symptoms include fever, chills, anaemia, and sometimes fatal complications. There is a risk travelling anywhere in the region. Because malarial mosquitoes cannot breed at cold temperatures, the risk is less the higher you go, and they and malaria are absent from areas above about 2,500m (8,250ft).

The disease is transmitted via the saliva of the female *Anopheles* mosquito. The microbe enters the bloodstream and infects the red blood cells. A blood sample usually diagnoses malaria infection.

Strains of malaria

Four strains of malaria commonly infect humans of which only two, *Plasmodium vivax* and *P falciparum*, are found in South America. *Falciparum* malaria is the commonest and most dangerous. The symptoms appear from one week to four months after exposure and consist of high fever, shivering, chills, profuse sweating and nausea. In severe cases, hallucinations, headache, numbness in the extremities, and/or diarrhoea and vomiting may also be experienced.

Given prompt treatment, adequate rest and good nursing care, most people (99%) recover from malaria. Following recovery *falciparum* malaria does not recur.

The *vivax* strain of malaria is less common than *falciparum*. Symptoms are similar to *falciparum* malaria, though usually less severe. If the patient is initially healthy the case may be no worse than a bad flu. Onset of the disease can occur any time from one week of being bitten. However, this type of malaria is resistant to therapy and can recur over a period of several years.

Prophylaxis and treatment

A number of effective drugs are available to treat malaria. Among the more important are Malarone, quinine and fansidar or quinine and doxycycline. These are active against malaria parasites in red blood cells. Many *falciparum* strains and some *vivax* strains are now resistant to anti-malarial drugs. The disease is spreading even faster where mosquitoes have evolved resistance to insecticides. Halfan may be offered but should not be used as it is considered to be dangerous. Likewise primaquine may be suggested but this is not suitable for everyone and again is best avoided.

The malaria found in the Amazon regions of the countries of tropical South America is predominantly *Plasmdium falciparum* and is largely resistant to chloroquine. Old-fashioned prophylactic drugs chloroquine and proguanil are considered to be last choice. More potent drugs such as mefloquine (Lariam), Malarone (proguanil and atovaquone) or even doxycycline are preferred. Each drug has its own particular set of advantages and disadvantages and advice should be sought from a reputable travel clinic.

If mefloquine (Lariam) is suggested, start this two-and-a-half weeks (three doses) before departure to check that it suits you; stop immediately if it seems to cause depression or anxiety, visual or hearing disturbances, severe headaches, fits or changes in heart rhythm. Side effects such as nightmares or dizziness are not medical reasons for stopping unless they are sufficiently debilitating or annoying. Anyone who is pregnant, who has suffered fits in the past, has been treated for depression or psychiatric problems, has diabetes controlled by oral therapy or who is epileptic (or who has suffered fits in the past) or has a close blood relative who is epileptic should avoid mefloquine.

Malarone (proguanil and atovaquone) is a new drug that is almost as effective as mefloquine. It has the advantage of having few side effects and need only be continued for one week after returning. However, it is expensive and because of this tends to be reserved for shorter trips. Malarone may not be suitable for everybody. It has recently acquired a licence for children over 11 – 39kg (after 40kg the dose is as for an adult).

The antibiotic doxycycline (100mg daily) is a viable alternative when either mefloquine or Malarone are not considered suitable. Like Malarone it can be started one day before arrival. It may also be used in travellers with epilepsy, unlike mefloquine, although certain anti-epileptic medication may make it less effective. Allergic skin reactions developing in sunlight can occur in about 3% of people. The drug should be stopped if this happens. Women using the oral contraceptive should use an additional method of protection for the first four weeks when using doxycycline. It is also unsuitable in pregnancy or for children under 12.

Chloroquine and proguanil are no longer considered to be very effective for this area. However, they may still be recommended if no other regime is suitable.

All prophylactic agents should be taken with or after the evening meal, washed down with plenty of fluid and, with the exception of Malarone (see above), continued for four weeks after leaving.

Travellers to remote parts would be wise to carry a course of treatment to cure malaria. Experts differ on the costs and benefits of self-treatment, but agree that it leads to people taking drugs they do not need; yet treatment may save your life. Discuss your trip with a specialist to determine your particular needs and risks, and be sure you understand when and how to take the cure. If you are somewhere remote in a malarial region you probably have to assume that any high fever (over 38°C) for more than a few hours is due to malaria (regardless of any other symptoms) and should seek treatment. Diagnosing malaria is not easy, which is why consulting a doctor is sensible: there are other dangerous causes of fever, which require different treatments. Presently Malarone, quinine and doxycycline or quinine and fansidar are the favoured regimes, but check for up-to-date advice on the current recommended treatment. And remember malaria may occur anything from seven days into the trip to up to one year after leaving a malarial area. There are now reputable, easy to use kits for testing for *falciparum* malaria (the most series form). A kit plus a thermometer would be useful for intrepid travellers.

Preventing mosquito bites

Malaria is not common in most parts of the Amazon. In addition to taking an appropriate course of prophylactics, the best prevention is to avoid bites from pestiferous carrier mosquitoes between dusk and dawn. At dusk, put on long clothes and apply insect repellent under the socks and to exposed areas of skin. Sleep under insecticide-impregnated mosquito nets. Clothes impregnated with mosquito repellent act as a buffer zone, while boats mid-river are too far for mosquitoes to fly and provide welcome relief. If necessary, burn mosquito coils at night.

Immunisations

It is wise to be up to date on immunisation from tetanus/diphtheria (tetanus is no longer available as a single vaccine in the UK), ten-yearly. You should also protect yourself against yellow fever (see *Yellow Fever*), typhoid and hepatitis A. Hepatitis A vaccine (Havrix Monodose or Avaxim) comprises two injections given a year apart. The course costs about £100, but protects for ten years. The vaccine can be used even close to the time of departure and has replaced the old-fashioned gamma globulin (see *Hepatitis* below). The newer typhoid vaccines (eg: Typhim Vi) last for three years and are about 85% effective. Immunisations against typhoid should be encouraged unless the traveller is leaving within a few days for a trip of a week or less when the vaccine would not be effective in time.

Further immunisations that should be considered include the following. Meningitis vaccine (A + C) is also recommended for people travelling to Rio, especially during the carnival time (see *Meningitis*).

Cholera vaccine is ineffective and no longer available in the UK. However, some border guards (most notably crossing between Bolivia and Peru) can demand a certificate as proof of immunisation. Exemption certificates are available from some GPs and all travel clinics. This is highly recommended otherwise you may not be allowed to enter the country, or worse still they may try to vaccinate you!

Vaccinations for rabies are advised for travellers visiting more remote areas (see *Rabies*).

Hepatitis B vaccination should be considered for longer trips (two months or more) or for those working with children or in situations where contact with blood is likely. Three injections are needed for the best protection and can be given over a four-week period if time is short. (Only Engerix B is licensed to date to use in this rapid schedule). Longer schedules give more sustained protection and are therefore preferred if time allows (see *Hepatitis* below).

A BCG vaccination against tuberculosis (TB) is also advised for trips of two months or more.

Ideally you should visit your doctor to discuss your requirements about eight weeks before travel.

Yellow fever

Transmitted via mosquitoes like malaria, yellow fever is much rarer. This acute infectious tropical disease is caused by a virus.

There are two types: urban or classical yellow fever, transmitted from person to person; and jungle yellow fever, transmitted from a mammalian host (usually a monkey) by mosquitoes to humans.

After an incubation period of several days the virus multiplies within the body. The initial attack includes headache, fever, nausea and vomiting. After two to three days the patient may begin to recover. If not, the disease enters a serious stage, marked by high fever, slow pulse rate and vomiting of blood. Death may follow within ten days after the first symptoms. Because the disease attacks liver cells, jaundice (bile pigment is deposited, turning skin and eyes yellow) is common, hence the disease's name.

Treatment relies on keeping the fever as low as possible and preventing dehydration. Convalescence can take a long time but recovery is complete and the patient acquires a life-long immunity. Mortality varies greatly according to the strain of virus and individual genetic resistance.

Yellow fever is completely preventable by immunisation, which is effective ten days after administration for ten years. The incidence of this disease is reportedly increasing, especially in the Manaus area, so we strongly advise you to get vaccinated.

Many countries require travellers who have visited an endemic zone to be immunised and to carry an international immunisation certificate at all times. Travellers on tourist riverboat day-trips from Peru into Leticia (Colombia) and Tabatinga (Brazil) do not need these certificates.

Hepatitis

This illness is basically inflammation (-*itis*) of the liver (*hepat-*). It is in fact a complex of acute viral and chronic diseases of differing rarity, severity and modes of transmission.

Hepatitis A and B are acute diseases caused by two different viruses, called A and B. These are the two commonest types of hepatitis.

Travellers are at greatest risk from hepatitis A. Though the least dangerous type of 'hep', recovery takes several weeks or months. It is usually contracted from contaminated food or water; immunisation against hepatitis A is recommended especially for those travelling rough. The virus inhabits the digestive tract, is passed on via faeces and is subsequently swallowed by the next victim. Hepatitis A appears within 20 to 40 days after exposure. Initial symptoms include upper stomach pains and mild fever, usually accompanied by chills and fatigue. Headache, muscle aches and appetite loss follow, and then later the classic symptoms of yellowish eye-whites and skin.

During this time the immune system produces antibodies against the virus. Treatment relies on rest and good care, as there is no cure. During recovery, the lost liver tissue regenerates and liver function returns. Once someone has caught hepatitis A they become immune to this type.

Hepatitis B has a longer incubation period than type A, taking 6 weeks to 6 months to show symptoms. It is transmitted via blood transfusion, contaminated hypodermic syringes, through dentistry, acupuncture, tattooing or sexually. This virus populates blood serum and semen. Unlike HIV, it can also be transmitted by saliva. Effective vaccination has been described above.

Meningitis

Can kill within hours of the first symptoms appearing. The telltale symptoms are a combination of a blinding headache (light sensitivity), a blotchy rash and a high fever. Immunisation protects against the most serious bacterial form of meningitis and the tetravalent vaccine A+C is recommended for people spending more than a day or two in Rio. Other forms of meningitis exist (usually viral) but there are no vaccines for these. A severe headache and fever should make you run to a doctor immediately. There are also other causes of headache and fever; one of these is typhoid, which occurs in travellers to Africa. Seek medical help if you are ill for more than a few days.

Tetanus

This is a disease caused by bacteria commonly found in soil and animal dung. Infection arises via a wound contaminated with dirt. Puncture wounds with little bleeding to flush out bacteria can result in tetanus. Symptoms consist of involuntary spasmodic contractions of various muscles, especially those of the neck and jaw (lockjaw).

Tetanus vaccination is effective and recommended for visitors on extended Amazon stays.

Rabies

Rabies is carried by all mammals (beware the village dogs and small monkeys that are used to being fed in the parks) and is passed on to man through a bite, scratch or a lick of an open wound. You must always assume any animal is rabid (unless personally known to you) and seek medical help as soon as possible. In the interim, scrub the wound with soap and bottled/boiled water then pour on a strong iodine or alcohol solution. This helps stop the rabies virus entering the body and will guard against wound infections including tetanus.

In South America rabies may also be transmitted through inhalation of bat droppings. Resist the temptation to visit local bat caves.

If you intend to have contact with animals and/or are likely to be more than 24 hours away from medical help, then pre-exposure vaccination is advised. Ideally three doses should be taken over four weeks. Contrary to popular belief these vaccinations are relatively painless!

If you are exposed as described, treatment should be given as soon as possible, but it is never too late to seek help as the incubation period for rabies can be very long.

Those who have not been immunised will need a full course of injections together with rabies immunoglobulin (RIG), but this product is expensive (around US$800) and may be hard to come by.

Tell the doctor if you have had pre-exposure vaccine, as this will change the treatment you receive. Remember if you contract rabies, mortality is 100%.

Dengue fever

This disease, like yellow fever, is transmitted by the *Aedes* mosquito. It may mimic malaria but there is no prophylactic medication available to deal with it. The mosquitoes that carry this virus bite during the daytime, so apply repellent if you see any mosquitoes around. Symptoms include strong headaches, rashes and excruciating joint and muscle pains and high fever. Dengue fever only lasts for a week or so and is not usually fatal. Complete rest and paracetamol are the usual treatment. Plenty of fluids also help. Some patients are given an intravenous drip to keep them from dehydrating. It is especially important to protect yourself if you have had dengue fever before. A second infection with a different strain can result in the potentially fatal dengue haemorrhagic fever.

There has been an upsurge in dengue throughout Central and South America, especially in Brazil. Use insect repellents during the day as well as at night.

Teeth

Get a dental check-up before travelling. You might want to take an emergency dental repair kit, available from camping stores and chemists. Anything you can do to avoid dental treatment in remote regions of South America is a wise precaution.

Travel clinics and health information

A full list of current travel clinic websites worldwide is available on www.istm.org/. For other journey preparation information, consult ftp://ftp.shoreland.com/pub/shorecg.rtf or www.tripprep.com.

USA

Centers for Disease Control 1600 Clifton Rd, Atlanta, GA 30333; tel: 877 FYI TRIP; 800 311 3435; web: www.cdc.gov/travel. Central source of travel information in USA. Publish *Health Information for International Travel*, available from the Division of Quarantine at above address.

Connaught Laboratories PO Box 187, Swiftwater, PA 18370; tel: 800 822 2463. Will send free list of specialist tropical-medicine physicians in your state.

IAMAT (International Association for Medical Assistance to Travelers) 736 Center St, Lewiston, NY 14092; tel: 716 754 4883; web: www.iamat.org. Non-profit organisation that provides lists of English-speaking doctors abroad.

UK

British Airways Travel Clinic and Immunisation Service There are two BA clinics in London. Appointments only at 111 Cheapside (tel: 020 7606 2977). Walk-in service Mon–Sat at 156 Regent St (tel: 020 7439 9584). For changes, look on the internet (web: www.britishairways.com/travelclinics). Inoculations and malaria prevention. Also health-related goods.

Fleet Street Travel Clinic 29 Fleet St, London EC4Y 1AA; tel: 020 7353 5678; web: www.fleetstreet.com. Injections, travel products and advice.

Hospital for Tropical Diseases Travel Clinic Mortimer Market Centre, 2nd Floor, Capper St (off Tottenham Ct Rd), London WC1E 6AU; tel: 020 7388 9600; web: www.thhtd.org. Consultations and advice. All necessary drugs and vaccines for travellers. Healthline (09061 337733) for country-specific information. Stocks nets, water-purification equipment and personal-protection measures.

MASTA, at the London School of Hygiene and Tropical Medicine in London, have premium line charged at 60p per minute. For a fee, they will provide individually tailored health brief, with up-to-date information on how to stay healthy, inoculations and what to bring.

MASTA Health Clinics Thirty or so clinics. To find nearest one, tel: 01276 685040.

NHS travel website, www.fitfortravel.scot.nhs.uk, provides country-by-country advice on immunisation and malaria, details of recent developments, and list of relevant health organisations.

Nomad Travel Store 3–4 Wellington Terrace, Turnpike Lane, London N8 0PX; tel: 020 8889 7014; fax: 020 8889 9528; email: sales@nomadtravel.co.uk; web: www.nomadtravel.co.uk. Sturdy travel gear and a medical clinic. Excellent one-stop shop.

Thames Medical 157 Waterloo Rd, London SE1 8US; tel: 020 7902 9000. One-stop travel health service. All profits go to affiliated company, InterHealth, which provides health care for overseas workers on Christian projects.

Trailfinders Immunisation Centre 194 Kensington High St, London W8 7RG; tel: 020 7938 3999.

Travelpharm The Travelpharm website, www.travelpharm.com, offers up-to-date guidance on travel-related health and has a range of medications available through their online mini-pharmacy.

Irish Republic

Tropical Medical Bureau Grafton Street Medical Centre, Grafton Buildings, 34 Grafton St, Dublin 2; tel: 1 671 9200. Useful website (www.tmb.ie)

Canada

IAMAT (International Association for Medical Assistance to Travellers) Suite 1, 1287 St Clair Av W, Toronto, Ontario M6E 1B8; tel: 416 652 0137; web: www.sentex.net/~iamat

TMVC (Travel Doctors Group) Sulphur Springs Rd, Ancaster, Ontario; tel: 905 648 1112; web: www.tmvc.com.au

Australia, New Zealand, Thailand

TMVC Tel: 1300 65 88 44; web: www.tmvc.com.au. 20 clinics in Australia, New Zealand and Thailand, including:
Auckland Canterbury Arcade, 170 Queen Street, Auckland City; tel: 373 3531
Brisbane Dr Deborah Mills, Qantas Domestic Building, 6th floor, 247
Adelaide St, Brisbane, QLD 4000; tel: 7 3221 9066; fax: 7 3321 7076
Melbourne Dr Sonny Lau, 393 Little Bourke St, 2nd floor, Melbourne, VIC
3000; tel: 3 9602 5788; fax: 3 9670 8394
Sydney Dr Mandy Hu, Dymocks Building, 7th Floor, 428 George St, Sydney, NSW2000;
tel: 2 221 7133; fax: 2 221 8401

South Africa

SAA-Netcare Travel Clinics PO Box 786692, Sandton 2146; fax: 011 883 6152; web:
www.travelclinic.co.za or www.malaria.co.za. Clinics throughout South Africa.
TMVC (Travel Doctor Group) 113 DF Malan Drive, Roosevelt Park, Johannesburg; tel:
011 888 7488; web: www.tmvc.com.au. Consult the website for details of clinics in South
Africa.

Switzerland

IAMAT (International Association for Medical Assistance to Travellers) 57 Voirets, 1212
Grand Lancy, Geneva; web: www.sentex.net/~iamat

Travel insurance

Anyone travelling to the Amazon should get adequate travel insurance. Full
coverage is best but if you need to save money the premium can be apportioned.
Emergency transport home and medical expenses are obviously more important
than baggage or trip cancellation coverage. Count on a minimum of US$2 million
worth of cover for medical emergency and evacuation.

Whether or not an emergency evacuation is possible depends on where you are
and also whether you are well enough to be evacuated.

Water sterilisation

Drinking clean water reduces the possibility of contracting several troublesome
diseases. Drink bottled water; it is available in all but the smallest towns and
villages and is reasonably priced. You should make sure the seal is not broken. Even
this regime isn't foolproof as studies in some countries have shown that mineral
water may be contaminated.

If you are worried, take along your own purification tablets, available from
camping stores and pharmacists. Chlorine-based purification tablets do not kill
amoebic cysts so you may want to take iodine. Tincture of iodine is widely
available throughout South America. Add two drops to one litre of water and leave
to stand for one hour. Alternatively you can buy iodine crystals or tablets from
camping shops back home. Read the label as instructions can vary.

If you are camping, carrying sufficient water is unrealistic so you will need to
boil the water or use iodine.

There are several water purification pumps available on the market. Make sure
the pump incorporates iodine in the system somewhere, as at present no pumps on
the market are capable of removing giardia.

First-aid kit

A kit should include: Band-aids (plasters) of various shapes and sizes; bandages;
absorbent pads; a good drying antiseptic such as iodine, or potassium

permanganate crystals to dissolve in water; antibiotic cream; soluble aspirin/paracetamol (as painkillers, for gargling and to reduce fever); and burn lotion.

Several companies market first-aid kits of various shapes and sizes. Purchase a basic first-aid kit packed small for travellers, or a larger 'expedition' size kit.

Remember that clinical thermometers (containing mercury) can't officially be carried on aircraft. Use a digital thermometer instead.

Minor ailments
Eating and drinking safely
Take scrupulous care over what you eat and drink. Basic precautions are:

- PEEL IT, BOIL IT, COOK IT OR FORGET IT!
- Eat only fruits and vegetables you have peeled yourself
- If you eat meat ensure it is hot, cooked through and fresh from the kitchen
- Order a la carte rather than eat from a buffet
- Do not drink unpurified water (never straight from taps or rivers)
- Do not use ice unless you know it was made from purified water

Avoid lettuce and beware of salads unless you know all vegetables were cleaned and soaked in iodine or potassium permanganate. Salad food at lodges and on tourist boats is treated to eliminate germs and parasites.

Traveller's diarrhoea
The trots, runs or Montezuma's Revenge — this is one of the commonest ailments to strike the Amazon visitor. The condition usually indicates contaminated food. The cause is often food prepared by someone with dirty hands or in unsanitary conditions.

On a week-long Amazon trip, diarrhoea may afflict one in a group of ten people. If you are in the region for longer you will probably experience 'a period of acclimatisation'. Even being careful one can be unlucky and come down with a tummy bug. In addition to diarrhoea, symptoms may include stomach cramps, nausea and fever.

Depending on the severity, dealing with diarrhoea is straightforward. As fluid loss is an inevitable consequence, it is important to replenish fluids, ideally with a rehydration salts mixture. These can be purchased ready-made in sachets, or made from a mixture of sugar (40g) and salt (3.5g), mixed in a litre of water. Milk, fatty foods and alcohol should be avoided, and rest certainly helps the healing process. Glucose tablets provide an instant source of energy – ideal if you are feeling run down due to diarrhoea.

When rest is not possible or when you have to travel, blockers such as Lomotil, Kaopectate or Imodium can be taken. They plug you up by paralysing the bowel but in overdose they paralyse the breathing muscles too. These drugs should be taken as a last resort, as they usually prolong the illness by keeping diarrhoea-causing bugs inside you.

Most cases of diarrhoea clear up in a day or two. Should the illness continue for more than a few days, see a doctor, as chronic symptoms indicate worse but treatable trouble. If it is impossible to see a doctor, a three-day course of antibiotics such as norfloxacin or ciprofloxacin may clear up the problem but self-diagnosis should be a last resort.

Independent travellers should carry a roll of toilet paper, as many public toilets (and some budget hotels and lodges) in Amazonia lack this rather essential item.

Altitude sickness

In general this only affects people arriving at altitudes above 3,000m directly from sea level. Visitors to La Paz (4,000m) in Bolivia should be aware of the risks; people travelling to Quito (2,820m) or Bogotá (2,650m) should also be aware, although the risk is reduced. Acetazolamide (Diamox) can be taken to speed up acclimatisation, but people with blood- or breathing-related illnesses should see a doctor before flying directly to La Paz.

Symptoms include breathlessness, insomnia, headache, appetite loss and possibly nausea. When arriving at altitude, make an effort to rest. The onset of altitude sickness can occur after a few hours even though you may be feeling fine initially.

Sunburn

Perhaps the commonest affliction of Amazon visitors. Use sunblock. SPF15–20 (SPF = Sun Protection Factor, eg: SPF15 offers 15 times your own skin's protection) is best. Fair-skinned people need a higher SPF than those with darker complexions. Severe sunburn may cause skin blisters that could lead to infection and it increases the chance of skin cancer. Wear sunblock whenever you go out in the sun.

Mild sunburn is at worst an inconvenience; but heatstroke can be a lot more serious. This is when the body temperature rises too high and, although it is often misleadingly called sunstroke, it need not be associated with too much sun. Initial symptoms are headache, faintness, dizziness and nausea. If heatstroke is suspected, move into a cool place and drink plenty of non-alcoholic fluids.

Dehydration

To compensate for perspiration, drink more water. Never rehydrate with alcohol. Drink before you feel thirsty (the first sign of dehydration).

Take a bit more salt on food than you normally would to help keep electrolyte levels in balance. If you are feeling low on energy due to dehydration, glucose-containing sports drinks help, although fruit juice or non-caffeinated soda are just as good.

Minor cuts and bruises

It is vital to treat even small cuts or insect bites immediately to prevent potentially dangerous infection. Wash any cuts with clean water, rinse and allow them to air-dry. Don't use antiseptic creams, as they are less effective in the tropics, and replace the dressing daily. A standard first-aid kit should be enough to cope with most minor emergencies.

Fungal infections

Bathing often and giving the body a chance to breathe are the best ways of avoiding infection. Symptoms include itchiness and flaking skin around the armpits, crotch and between the toes. Treatment requires a fungicidal cream and powder.

Motion sickness

Expedition cruise vessels entering the open ocean may hit a bad squall. Occasionally, when the water is rough, a ride in the *colectivo* motor boats can be a bit bouncy if they travel fast. Take motion sickness pills or use a hyoscine patch if you suffer from motion sickness; these need to be taken well before you feel the symptoms. Some motion sickness pills (eg: Dramamine) may cause drowsiness; others (eg: Stugeron) don't. Ginger is also claimed to be effective.

In a small plane there may be no flight crew aside from the pilot, so remember to take your own pills.

Bus rides will certainly be bumpy so, if you are a sufferer, be prepared.

More serious problems
Medical emergencies
Tourist lodges and riverboats usually have no staff nurse or doctor, but they do have two-way radio in case of emergency. In direst and potentially life-threatening situations not too far from a town or city, it may be possible for a helicopter or float-plane to evacuate a patient to a city within a couple of hours. Make sure you have insurance.

If you are travelling independently in the Amazon, unless you are close to one of the larger towns or cities you will probably be relying on your first-aid knowledge and initiative. If you have adventurous travel plans do your best to be prepared for any eventuality.

Sexually transmitted diseases and AIDS
The status of AIDS in the Amazon is poorly known. Its rate seems to remain low among rural populations but is rising around cities. Brazil's high rate of AIDS – well over one million – is mostly in coastal cities such as Rio de Janeiro and São Paulo. Only a handful of AIDS cases have been reported in the Amazon.

Using a condom protects against AIDS and other sexually transmitted diseases. Condoms, when available, can be bought from pharmacies but quality may be questionable. It is best to bring condoms from home so that you know they will fit; women may like to travel with a few femidoms.

If you are planning on having any injections or vaccinations in the Amazon consider taking a sterile needle pack to avoid the possibility of infection through shared needles.

Filth-to-mouth diseases
Giardiasis is a parasitic intestinal disorder commonly acquired from contaminated food or water. Associated with severe and intermittently persistent diarrhoea and eggy burps, this parasite can be quite insidious and may lie dormant for a considerable period before infection is apparent. If you believe you may have contracted *giardia* you need to see a doctor.

Prevention is by avoiding unhygienically prepared food or heavily contaminated water.

If a case of severe diarrhoea persists for more than a few days, coupled with stomach cramps and fever, **dysentery** could be the culprit. This waterborne disease has two forms – amoebic and bacterial – which show similar symptoms: severe inflammation of the mucus membrane of the large intestine, resulting in bloody evacuations. The bacterial form of dysentery responds well to ciprofloxacin (a 500mg tablet repeated 6–12 hours later) will usually do the trick. Clues that this may be the cause of the illness include fever, blood and/or slime in the stool. Any one of these symptoms is an indication to reach for the ciprofloxacin sooner rather than later. Amoebic dysentery or giardia is best treated with tinidazole (4 x 500mg tablets taken in one dose repeated seven days later if symptoms persist). Self-diagnosis and treatment of dysentery (or any serious disease) are not advisable if it is possible and practical to consult a doctor.

Cholera has a very bad reputation, but it tends to kill the ill, starving or debilitated. It is most often acquired through contaminated food or water. Any type of cholera-like watery diarrhoea requires lots of fluid replacement and a medical consultation if the illness seems bad. Most of the cure is through constantly drinking clean water with rehydration salts. Constipatives, to prevent diarrhoea, are dangerous. Another source of cholera is seafood contaminated by untreated sewage dumped into rivers or oceans. Hence, travellers to Peru are advised to avoid raw fish unless 100% certain it is uncontaminated.

Typhoid – also called enteric fever – is an acute, infectious fever, with symptoms of severe intestinal disturbances, pink spots on the chest and abdomen and physical exhaustion. Infection is usually through contaminated food. The newer typhoid vaccines are considered to be reasonably effective and should be encouraged. Typhoid is treated with antibiotics, rehydration, rest and a balanced diet.

The nasty side of nature

Chagas' disease, also called *trypanosomiasis*, is extremely rare in travellers. The disease is transmitted by an insect belonging to the same order as assassin bugs. The parasite is passed on when the bug takes a blood meal, typically on the face around the cheek. Rather than being transmitted by the bite itself, the parasite is ejected in the bug's faeces and deposited close to the wound. Scratching rubs the faeces into the wound, admitting the parasite into the bloodstream where it remains, often for many years, before symptoms become apparent.

The symptoms are acute and chronic. Initially, infection causes a flu-like fever, although there may be no symptoms at all. At this time the disease is treatable.

Avoid scratching bites, especially those not from mosquitoes, and wash them with alcohol or antiseptic. In the absence of any cure for this disease, prevention is the only medicine. Avoid sleeping on the floor of poor adobe huts.

Leishmaniasis is caused by sandflies (*Lutzomyia* sp) which transmit this parasite. Symptoms are chronic if untreated. Not usually a fatal disease, it can cause severe disfigurement by sores that refuse to heal, particularly around the face. Prevention is based on avoiding the sandflies, easiest achieved by liberal applications of insect repellent in areas where they are present. Additional protection is conferred by long trousers and a long-sleeved shirt. Although very unlikely to be caught on an average-length Amazon visit, *leishmaniasis* is a real risk for those staying in certain areas for more than a few weeks. Sleep under an insecticide-impregnated bed-net in high-risk areas.

Dengue fever is an increasingly common mosquito-borne disease that can be very debilitating, and potentially fatal. Flu-like symptoms include headache, fever, and pain in muscles and joints; hence it is also called 'break-bone fever'. There is no cure and no vaccine for dengue so avoid being bitten by the day-active *aedes* mosquito vector. Dengue is on the increase in the Amazon. Aspirin and related medications such as ibuprofen should not be taken if you think you have dengue.

On account of the diseases they transmit, **ticks** (*Acarina*), although tiny, are among the most dangerous arachnids. The **cattle tick** (*Margaropus annulatus*) and ticks of the genus *Ixodes* occur throughout the Americas and infect livestock and humans with a number of dangerous pathogens such as tick fever. Ticks are not common in forest. But in grassy open areas where cattle are present you should check your clothing and any exposed skin regularly for pests. Upon discovering a tick, remove it very gently to avoid infection. Slowly pull the tick out, making sure the tweezers are tight up against the skin, and it will hopefully come off in one piece. Insect repellent (applied to the tick) or a lighted cigarette also work well.

Rabies is an acute, ordinarily fatal, viral disease of the central nervous system (CNS). The disease is also called *lyssa* or *hydrophobia*. It is usually transmitted via domestic dogs, although wild carnivorous animals and bats frequently carry the disease. The active virus inhabits the salivary glands and is thus transmitted with a bite.

The virus propagates along nerve tissue near the wound and soon establishes itself in the CNS. After an incubation period of anything from ten days to several months (usually four to six weeks), the virus reaches the brain and full-blown symptoms develop.

Best of the available vaccines is the HDCV (Human Diploid Cell Vaccine), grown on human cells. Two injections are enough to immunise the patient, although four injections is a standard course. Initial HDCV treatment is followed with a series of vaccinations.

If you are bitten by any animal, treatment is simply to wash the wound immediately for five minutes and apply disinfectant. This removes infective saliva before too much virus has entered the blood, reducing the chances of contracting the disease. If rabies is properly treated prior to the onset of symptoms recovery should be complete. Without treatment, rabies is nearly always fatal once symptoms start.

Snakes

Twenty-three species of Amazon snakes are poisonous but most bites are not life-threatening. Even people with ophidophobia (fear of snakes) have no reason not to visit the Amazon – you are unlikely to even see one, and exceedingly unlucky to be bitten.

Snakes are abundant, but excellent camouflage and reclusive behaviour make them all but impossible to see under normal conditions. Most species are wary and quietly slither off as soon as they sense ground vibrations from human footsteps.

However, educate yourself as best you can regarding snakebite and focus attention on keeping the patient calm and rested. Identify the snake if possible and get medical professional help as soon as you can. Few cases of snakebite are life-threatening provided treatment is prompt. (For detailed advice, see pages 80–1.)

Keeping creepy-crawlies at bay (see also pages 78–9)

Insect repellent is necessary on jungle walks or night excursions by boat. Use products containing 30–50% DEET, though clothes may be impregnated with 100%; you can reduce the amount of repellent you need to apply by wearing long clothes. An alternative is repellent containing citronella oil. At some lodges liberal amounts of repellent may be needed when insects are abundant, especially in the rainy season.

If spending several days at a lodge, take mosquito coils, which can be bought from camping shops and are available in the larger lowland Amazon towns and cities. They are long-lasting, compact, economical and environmentally safe. (Pressurised aerosol repellents are banned from jet planes and not always ozone-friendly.) One coil lasts through the night.

Sandflies are especially bothersome pests with painful bite. This insect is often abundant around pasture or inhabited areas. It carries a parasitic disease, *leishmaniasis*, so wear long clothes and apply repellent to any bare skin whenever walking on land, especially where there are grassy areas grazed by animals or in forest.

The same regime should minimise attack by another 'no-see-um' pest of open pasture: **chiggers**. These burrow under the skin to appear as a tiny mole-like spot about the size of a pin-head. You can remove the creature with a pair of tweezers but make sure none of it is left behind. Applying ammonium hydroxide (Itch-ease®) reduces the itching. If the spot is not scratched it disappears without a trace. If not treated carefully, the bite may become seriously infected. **Botflies** also like to burrow into the skin. Several remedies are claimed to work, including smearing a petroleum jelly over the entrance hole to suffocate the creature out, or placing a piece of fresh meat over the wound in the assumption that a piece of juicy steak is more appealing than the inside of your arm! After treks it is worth doing a quick check over your body to remove uninvited freeloaders.

Any insect bite may become infected in the tropical warmth and humidity. If a wound reddens and weeps, clean thoroughly with a drying antiseptic and apply antibiotic powder or ointment immediately.

Although most **spiders** are harmless, some Amazon species are able to inject venom. A bite is most likely on a jungle walk or in bed (shake out the bedding and mattress). If a spider bite is not healing get professional medical attention. Dreaded 'tarantula' types of spider are very common in Amazonia but none is a threat.

Most **scorpions** can sting but inflict no harmful wound. A few are dangerous, but these species are rare and generally restricted to dry areas. To avoid being stung, simply don't put your hands and feet in dark nooks or areas.

On jungle walks, watch out especially for the huge bullet **ants**, an inch or more long. Insect repellent does not deter these gargantuan monsters, which wield an excruciating sting. The pain takes a while to subside and the area goes red and throbs for a day or so but no lasting damage arises. The same goes for bites from tree-dwelling ants, such as *azteca*, which inhabit Cecropia trees.

If you suffer from severe allergic reactions, consult your doctor for appropriate medication before visiting the Amazon.

When you get home
If for any reason you suspect you may have acquired a parasite or disease, go to your doctor.

SAFETY
Theft
The infamous government death squads, the activities of various drugs cartels – not limited, as some would have you believe, to Colombia – and the murder of street children have all made the international press. But keeping the threat in perspective can be an eye-opener. Peru's per capita murder rate is just one third of New York City's!

Travel in South America, and the Amazon in particular, is essentially safe. The reality is that most people do not experience problems first hand. If you are threatened with a weapon or outnumbered, the best advice is to co-operate.

If you do have any problems the worst you are likely to experience are petty crimes such as bag snatching, pick-pocketing and theft. It is most likely that any theft will occur near the airport, in the city, close to money-changing facilities or in any setting where the novelty of the situation may cause you to relax your natural levels of awareness. Here are a few tips to consider:

- Use a hotel safe for valuables when there is one. Although you may feel safer when close to your valuables they are more likely to be stolen from you when on your person.
- Take a small padlock or combination lock to secure the doors of cheaper hotels. You should also find a way of locking luggage to stop opportunistic thieves having a quick rummage through your bags.
- Leave all expensive jewellery and watches at home.
- Take a money belt, pouch or whatever you feel most comfortable with. It isn't the best idea to have all your money in one place whether that is your money belt or your pocket. Keeping a small amount of money close at hand for casual spending avoids digging away for your money belt in the middle of the street.

- Take copies of all-important travel documents, including passport, air tickets, travellers' cheques and credit cards. Keep them in a separate place from the originals. Note down ticket and travellers' cheque numbers along with serial numbers of any electronic or camera equipment.
- If you have a daypack to carry around your camera and other items, wear it on your front when in towns and cities. Hanging off the back it is an easy target for bag-slashers who are quite capable of cutting your bag, emptying it and disappearing without you noticing.
- Stay with crowds at night. Unless you know an area well you are more likely to become disorientated at night. Taking taxis at night instead of buses is preferred by some travellers.
- When using long-distance buses, check that your luggage is loaded before getting on the bus. Some companies provide luggage receipts.

If you have a problem you should report the theft to the police or a local authority who will provide you with the official bits of paper. The report is essential for any insurance claim.

A couple of things to watch out for...

Be wary of any sudden spurt of activity that criminals might use to distract you. Items dropped in your path, mud 'accidentally' thrown on to your clothes, babies being handed over... the list is growing and becoming more creative. While you are distracted, a member of the team sets about relieving you of any valuables.

Thieves in major South American cities have been known to impersonate police officers, accusing victims of drug possession and demanding an on-the-spot fine. Presumably similar types of crime occur throughout South America, but as yet no similar incidents have been reported outside major cities. Ask police for identification. If you are asked to go to the police station try, whenever possible, to go with a friend.

Drugs

Refuse any offer of drugs – it could be a set-up; sentences are long, jail conditions appalling and chances of help from your own country zero.

Drug use – or abuse – is not as widespread in South America as may be thought. Most cocaine produced is for use in the US and Europe. Drug use is illegal in all South American countries, and if you are found guilty of possessing drugs your embassy will do its bare minimum to support your case. To avoid problems, avoid drugs.

On occasion, in laid-back tourist hang-outs, travellers have been drugged and awoken to find all their personal belongings have disappeared, or worse. Don't accept medicine or drinks from anyone who is even remotely suspicious.

Drug production in South America is widespread. The coca leaf – a harmless plant, with medicinal and cultural uses – is the raw material for cocaine. Production of the leaf is not limited to Colombia. There is widespread cultivation in Peru and Bolivia – where growth of the plant is legal in certain locations – and there is no reason why it couldn't be grown in all other Amazon countries. Any 'traveller' wandering around likely production areas tends to be viewed with suspicion and may well be accused of being an undercover anti-narcotics agent. Whatever your claims for being in the area, they may be ignored. Fortunately most coca leaf production areas are well away from any tourist trails.

Terrorism in South America

Since the tragic events of September 11 2001, the world is a different place. Around the globe, security has stepped up to meet the greater likelihood of terrorist acts.

Among the Amazon countries, Colombia is the least safe (see *Chapter 9* for more information). Political upheaval in Venezuela during March 2002 led to violence in the streets, but tourists were not affected. Bolivia remains relatively peaceful. Ecuador remains among the most tourist-friendly destinations, although a kidnapping near Lago Agrio in mid-2000 resulted in an oil company executive's death. Travel in northern Ecuador is relatively safe but security along the Colombia border could deteriorate suddenly. In Peru, a bomb explosion in Lima in 2002 resurrected fears of the Shining Path — a group active in the 1980s. But this seems to have been an isolated incident. Robbery was the motive for yachtsman Sir Peter Blake's murder in Macapa, Brazil, near the mouth of the Amazon, in late 2001. Terrorists are politically motivated and tourists are not specifically targeted because in South America most conflicts are between political factions within a country and outside interference has been limited. The extremely rare occasions when tourists have been victims are more 'collateral damage' than active persecution.

In the wild
Close encounters of the wild kind
Most creatures are terrified of humans. As a rule, wild animals attack humans only if they are cornered or they think their young are threatened.

If you encounter a jaguar or other cat it is most likely to be on a trail at night. Should you feel threatened, make as much noise as possible. Do not run away, as the cat may sense fear and give chase, but such attacks are extremely rare.

Among the Amazon's crocodilians, only the black caiman grows big enough to pose a fatal danger to people. This reptile, up to 5.5m long, has largely disappeared from the Amazon, except in remote places. As with snakes, caiman are unlikely to attack unless their nest is threatened. Keep your distance from the water's edge in areas where large caiman are known to be present. Sandy banks during the nesting season (low water) should be approached carefully as nests are well camouflaged and the female may be out of sight but lurking near by.

Safe jungle walking
Forest trails and paths are usually safe and are well known by guides, but not all guides remember to give a safety talk. There are some simple precautions for safe jungle walking:

- Do not 'grab' at vegetation to steady yourself; many plants have thorns or spines or harbour hordes of aggressive stinging ants.
- Take care where you step on the trail; it is easy to slip on mud, trip on tree roots or end up standing in a column of army ants if you don't look where you are going. Staying on the trail helps you keep an eye out for potential hazards and minimises your impact on surrounding forest.
- Take plenty of water with you, and on longer walks, a small snack; it is easy to get dehydrated as the humidity, heat and exertion increase perspiration.
- Wear appropriate shoes for the walk; you do not need hiking boots. Some lodges and tour operators supply guests with rubber boots, which are ideal as they keep your feet dry. Old trainers or tennis shoes will get wet and dirty. The soles need grip for muddy paths.
- Wear appropriate clothes and apply insect repellent to exposed body parts before and during a jungle walk. Mosquitoes will attack any unprotected bits.
- Always take a waterproof. A sunny day can turn to a tropical deluge in minutes. A poncho is good as it also covers your daypack.

- On jungle walks at night take a torch. The light helps you see where you are going and illuminates nocturnal creatures. A climber's torch worn on your head is ideal for camping, but walking in the jungle at night it attracts insects to the light beam and thus to your face.

Safe swimming
Danger from piranha is much exaggerated, unless you are bleeding or have an open wound, so should not deter the prospective Amazon bather. Sting-rays, electric eels and the notorious *candiru* – which allegedly lodges itself in body orifices – can also be a risk to swimmers. However, these species are rare and do not pose a significant threat.

The two greatest risks of swimming are strong currents and water-borne microbial parasites. Ideally, the current should be a slow crawl, anything near walking pace means the current is too fast for swimming.

To avoid parasites, do not swim near villages and towns, particularly downstream. Most parasites are orally ingested so if the site is not ideal, avoid swallowing river water.

Boat safety
You are usually provided with a life-jacket, most often used as a cushion on long canoe rides. A few basic precautions if you're not used to boat travel are:

- When getting into a canoe, make sure only one person boards at a time, that they step into the middle of the canoe and are seated before the next person gets in.
- Once under way, never stand up. Always have your life-jacket to hand and wear it on open water or in rough weather.
- Only one person should get out at a time – and carefully, especially if you are disembarking on to a muddy riverbank or unsteady floating pier.
- When manoeuvring through overhanging vegetation along narrow streams, watch out for projecting branches which, besides poking you in the eye, are home to biting insects, notably ants which end up falling into the boat. Cecropia, common host plant for stinging ants, is a riverside-tree, so must be avoided on canoe rides to avert a serious and painful invasion.

FURTHER READING
Wilson-Howarth, Jane. *Bugs Bites & Bowels: Travel Health*. Cadogan Guides, London and Globe Pequot, Ct; 3rd edition, August 2002.
Wilson-Howarth, Jane and Matthew Ellis. *Your Child's Health Abroad: A Manual for Travelling Parents*, Bradt Publications and Globe Pequot (1998).

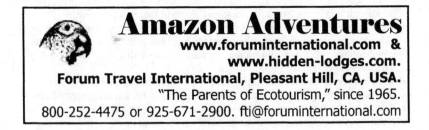

Natural History

'...the greatest evolutionary theatre in the world.'

Michael Goulding, *Amazon: the Flooded Forest*, Partridge Films, 1989

ORIGINS OF THE AMAZON RIVER BASIN

To get a full picture of how the Amazon ecosystem came into being let's look at its history. How were past conditions different? How did all the diversity come about? How long did it take?

Parts of the Amazon are ancient, hardly changed in 100 million years; as the rainforest's living fossils testify. We see evolution's fantastic tapestry, woven from billions of threads: plants, animals, decomposers and all their relationships. The origin of this complexity is in the forest's beginning.

When dinosaurs roamed the earth, over 220 million years ago, a huge river flowed west across what is now South America, into the Pacific. At that time, southern continents were joined, like pieces of a jigsaw, in a super-continent called Gondwanaland.

According to the theory of plate tectonics, continents and ocean floors form gigantic rocky rafts, or plates, that are moved by convection forces in the planet's interior. Sudden earthquakes and dramatic volcanic eruptions mark their boundaries as the plates bump and collide, sliding over, under or around each other. But the plates move extremely slowly. During our lifetime, a continent moves only three metres or so. Yet speed this up, and the landmasses wander and pirouette across the globe.

By about 150 million years ago, South America had become a huge island isolated from neighbouring landmasses. The continent's isolation had profound effects on its fauna. Primitive mammals, notably marsupials and edentates, proceeded to evolve in niches elsewhere occupied by more successful placental mammals. All the marsupials of the Americas are now extinct except opossums, while the last surviving edentates are sloths, armadillos and anteaters.

About 15 million years ago, tectonic movement caused huge eruptions and earthquakes all along the continent's west coast as the Pacific and South American Plates collided. Pushing against each other, the Pacific Plate was forced downwards while the South American Plate crumpled upwards. The Andes began to rise (and continue to do so) and during the Pliocene epoch – between 5.3 and 1.6 million years ago – blocked the westward-flowing river and so created a huge inland lake, the biggest ever. Marine animals were now trapped in a freshwater environment. Some adapted and remain to this day. Hence, the rivers are home to freshwater sting-rays and dolphins, and other animals normally found only in marine environments.

Around 5 million years ago, South America joined North America, forming the Panama Isthmus. Ocean currents changed and climate patterns altered. Placental mammals invaded southwards leading to the extinction of many of the previously isolated primitive mammals. Some 1.6 million years ago, tectonic movement tilted the entire South American Plate, and the river flowed east, in its present direction, into the Atlantic.

Over time the highlands on the basin's edges eroded. As sand and mud collected, the underlying rock sank under the weight and yet more silt piled on the deposits built up over millions of years when the area was an inland lake. Immensely deep alluvial deposits fill the vast network of ancient valleys that comprise the present-day river system – in the Amazon, you're on a pile of mud 4km deep.

The last great geological events to sculpt the lowland landscapes were the ice ages, the most recent of which ended 10,000 years ago. Sea level was 30m or more lower than today, causing the river to run much faster. Huge torrents cut deep channels in the mud, leaving hills and rises as the sea level dropped. Carved by primordial floods, the high banks your boat sails past are above today's highest flood levels. Beyond the reach of seasonal flooding, the forests on firm ground, or *terra firme* forests, are quite different from the *várzea* forest found in flooded areas.

Geography of the Amazon: flat, flooded and forested

With a shallow gradient along its course, gravity means that the Amazon barely flows. From Iquitos to the mouth, the river drops by a mere 70m, a gradient of 1 in 50,000… basically flat! The entire area's hydrology ultimately depends on snowfall in the Andes.

Sunlight warms lofty peaks. From on high, huge quantities of thawed snow rush downhill on a long journey to the sea causing the lowland river levels to rise dramatically. According to Michael Goulding, author of *Amazon: The Flooded Forest*, about 2% of the Amazon watershed is under water during seasonal floods. A small portion, but it adds habitat variety and hence species diversity.

Water is the forest's life-blood. Rivers annually deposit nutrient-laden silt to fertilise vast lowland areas. The enriched soils can support some agriculture and enhance the growth of natural vegetation. With every season's flood, the flow of the river changes. Where the flow is diverted, the river leaves behind oxbow lakes and newly formed land. New channels create 'edge' habitat essential for certain wildlife. Strong currents during annual floods or heavy rains scour weed-clogged streams and lakes. The river itself is a natural corridor along which animals migrate, be they fish, birds, or even small mammals that ride on floating rafts of dislodged vegetation.

Floods speed up erosion and deposition. Without large rocky areas, a lowland river's course is unstable. On the river's outside curve the current runs faster, eroding the bank and eating up to 30m of forest a year. Where the riverbank has collapsed trees lie askew in the river, a tangle of trunks and vines, ready to be swept away by the current. On the inside bend, the current slows, dropping silt, floating vegetation and anything else carried by the water. The inner banks grow, become exposed when waters recede, and new land is created. As the process of erosion and deposition continues, year on year, the meanders of the river make their way downstream, picking sediment up from the outside of one bend and depositing it on the inside of another, further downstream.

The process overall is a complex 'shifting mosaic' of innumerable islands, oxbow lakes, rivers, streams and sand bars – a wide variety of habitats for plants and animals. The constant change of occasional disturbance through seasonal flooding creates conditions that promote speciation.

Some 2,960km from north to south, the Amazon Basin's outer margins comprise montane forest to the west and dry grasslands to the north and south.

The vast, flat interior is mostly covered in dense tropical rainforest across which giant rivers gently wind thousands of miles.

Undiscovered until 1953, the source of the Amazon is high in the Peruvian Andes around 160km from the Pacific. (See box on page 4.) Waters gather and merge until they meet the westernmost major tributary, the Ucayali. About 100km west of Iquitos in Peru, this joins the main stream, now called the Solimões by Brazilians – and Amazonas by Peruvians. It is then another 3,720km from Iquitos to the mouth at Belém; the world's longest stretch of navigable river.

Soils of the Amazon River Basin

Amazon soils remain largely unsurveyed. But we can make some generalisations. Along lower floodplains so-called inceptisols dominate. These fertile alluvial soils are young, comprising primarily inorganic silt and freshly decayed humus. Regular input of fresh deposits from seasonal flooding supports intensive agriculture without the frequent manuring needed to cultivate soils of unflooded areas.

Older oxisols and utisols dominate the high ground and make up three quarters of the soils found in the region. Due to heavy rainfall, the mineral content of these soils has been washed out or leached, and they are subsequently of limited agricultural value. In extreme cases, when forest cover is removed and compacted, these soils are subject to laterisation, in which the sun bakes the surface into a brick-like substance. Good for making bumpy roads, but a poor basis for agriculture.

In rainforest, breakdown of vegetative matter is continual and the nutrient cycle is efficient, so there is never much time for soil to accumulate. Heavy rainfall leaches untrapped nutrients and concentrates certain elements, notably iron and aluminium. Although the lush vegetation of the rainforest creates the impression of mineral-rich soils, the success of the ecosystem relies on the efficient recycling of minerals close to the soil's surface.

Consequently the soils of the Amazon risk laterisation and toxification if not carefully managed. Recommended agricultural techniques are small-scale shifting cultivation and agroforestry (crops and trees grown together). Some experts believe oxisols are best utilised for sustainable timber sources and forest products.

Physical measurements of the Amazon River today

Over millions of years, geological and meteorological events laid the foundations for the Amazon's physical characteristics. Here we describe the present-day conditions as background to discussing an abundance and variety of life unequalled on earth.

Flow rate

The current speed depends on the combination of local terrain, flood conditions and recent rainfall. Gravity barely affects flow rate because the terrain is so flat and the current averages just 2–3km/h along the river's main stream. Similar speeds are measured for most lowland rivers. After heavy rains or during floods, flow rates rise to as high as 8-10km/h.

Depth

River depth varies greatly due to annual floods. Sand bars shift unpredictably making navigation a nightmare. Even so, the main stream is deep enough (undredged) for ocean-going luxury liners and cargo ships to sail year-round to Iquitos, where depth varies from 15m to 30m. The river's deepest point, 91m, is near Manaus, where the Rio Negro meets the main stream. The average depth from Iquitos to the mouth is 36m, according to Captain Todd's measurements made during the 1900 expedition in the gunboat *USS Wilmington*.

Seasonal floods

Due to cycles of snowfall and thaw in the Andes, river levels rise and fall on a seasonal basis throughout the lowlands. Around December, the river begins to rise until it peaks in April or May. At Iquitos, the highest water level is around 6–10m above the lowest and almost double this at Manaus. Peak levels downstream occur some weeks after as the bulge of floodwater takes time to make its way downriver. In June or July, the river subsides until October when it reaches its lowest levels. Then it starts to rise again. Recently the timing of annual floods has been more erratic than was historically the case.

Flooded-forest flora and fauna are adapted to yearly inundation. Trees stop photosynthesis. Acacia leaves droop, as though they are wilting. The high-water period is when many trees redirect energy stores to producing blooms and fruits. Rising waters reduce available habitat for arboreal animals. Local population density of animals increases along with the chance of a tree being visited by pollinating and fruit-dispersing animals.

Forest on land permanently above flood levels is called *terra firme* forest. It receives water only through rainfall and flowering seasons for its trees are less predictable.

Silt load

The amount of silt – called the silt load – carried by the Amazon varies enormously. Rivers are categorised by their colour, determined by the type and amount of silt. In the early 1980s, scientist Jacques Cousteau calculated that around 400 million tonnes of silt are discharged from the river's mouth every year. A giant fan-shaped mountain of mud extends 800km from the delta, descending 4,500m (14,764ft) to the floor of the ocean.

Geochemistry of Amazon rivers

The geochemical composition of a river depends on its origin and the types of habitat in its watershed. The types of suspended silt and detritus vary according to its course through the rainforest so the water colour tells you something about the river's chemistry. The Amazon's rivers and lakes are classified into three distinctly different types.

Whitewater

In this case, 'whitewater' has nothing to do with rafting down rapids. Most whitewater rivers (eg: Ucayali and Huallaga) rise in the Andes then flow east through the upper river basin. Heavy silt loads are fed by large quantities of loose rock eroded from the mountains. The Amazon main stream is classed as whitewater. Despite the name, these rivers are a pale murky yellow-brown, similar to *café au lait*. The water is close to neutral (pH7.0) and contains a high concentration of microbes and inorganic particles. The typical silt load of a whitewater river is 10–20mg/litre. When whitewater rivers flood each year, they renew soil fertility, replenish dried-out rivers and swamps and bring new life to the forest. The characteristic flora of forests flooded by these rivers is termed *várzea*.

Blackwater

Evidently named for its colour, the Rio Negro is the biggest tributary of the Amazon main stream and the biggest blackwater river. This type of river occurs

CLOUDFOREST
Oliver Whalley

The vast lowland rainforest of the Amazon Basin is swathed to the west by a band of higher, montane forests on the Andes. These cloudforests are often clothed in swirling mists and are an integral part of the region's ecosystem.

Up to an altitude of about 900m the rainforest is similar in appearance to, and generally considered to be, lowland rainforest; in the western Amazon this rises to about 1,700m. From this altitude the forest begins to change. From 900m to 2,000m, lower montane forest dominates before being replaced by upper montane forest between 2,000m and 3,200m. Subalpine or elfin forest reaches from 3,200m to 3,800m before the forests dwindle at the upper limit creating the tree or timber line. It is through the dense cloudforests that the headwaters of the Amazon seep and at times roar in cascading streams and towering waterfalls from the watersheds high in the Andes.

As altitude rises the forest canopy height drops considerably. In the low montane forest the height of trees is around 25m, whilst trees in hot lowlands reach 60m or more. In the tropics the temperature gradient is between 0.4–0.7°F (0.7–1.3°C) for each 100m rise. This change in temperature and air composition, combined with heavy rainfall, less evaporation, and higher winds, reduces metabolism and growth. The rate of decomposition and the release of nutrients is also slowed down.

There are other changes too; the number of insect species drops enormously and there is often a reduction in bird, amphibian and reptile biodiversity. Fruit eaters, scavengers and predators also decline rapidly with altitude. The number of species of omnivores stays approximately the same but there are large increases in the number of species of hummingbird and certain forms of plant life, especially epiphytes like mosses, ferns, lichens, bromeliads and orchids. In cloudforest epiphytes make up about 40% of the total plant biomass. Cloudforest trees are often completely covered in epiphytes, with as many as 50 different orchid species on a single tree.

High montane forest, although unsuitable for many mammals like monkeys, is home to endangered mammals like the spectacled bear and the very rare mountain tapir. The cloudforest is an essential part of the mountain ecosystem, the loss of which can create devastating changes. Approximately 95% of annual rainfall is retained temporarily in a complete cloudforest watershed. This water-retaining ability makes it essential for the regulation of water, especially during the drier seasons. It acts like a sponge, and so sustains both itself and forest below. As water can only trickle through, it prevents flash floods, severe erosion and landslides. With its thick complex of roots and humus it literally holds soils to the steep slopes thus preventing them slipping away under the assaults of pelting rain, high winds and the tremors or quakes of the growing Andes. These rare magical forests are not only fragile but irreplaceable.

over vast sandy areas common across northern Amazonia. Sandy soils lack the micro-organisms to break humus down into chemicals. (Humus is mostly decayed plant remains with few inorganic particles.) Heavy rain washes humic matter into rivers, staining water blackish or a very dark brown – like dark tea. The colour derives from dissolved plant compounds such as tannins, caffeines and phenols. The acidity of blackwater rivers (pH4–5) limits microbial activity and growth of aquatic flora and fauna, notably mosquito larvae. Their silt load (20–30mg/litre) is about twice that of whitewater rivers. The name *igapo* is given to flooded forest along blackwater rivers and lakes.

Clearwater

This third type of river has very low levels of humic matter, a tenth that of blackwater rivers. Most clearwater rivers rise in the Brazilian highlands (Xingu, Tapajós, Tocantins). Despite their often murky appearance, clearwater rivers have the least silt and humus because all the movable material in these mountains was eroded long ago. They vary from acidic to alkaline (pH4.5–7.8). Vegetation along clearwater rivers is of highly variable composition.

Meetings of the waters

The difference between river colours, most obvious where they meet, creates an impressive natural phenomenon. At the 'meeting of the waters', the two rivers maintain their independence, preferring to flow side-by-side yet sharing the same channel. To begin with the only mixing is along the meeting edge as the different current speeds create eddies and swirls to merge the waters of different densities. The most spectacular 'meeting of the waters' is close to Manaus where the Rio Negro, the largest blackwater river, flows into the main stream. More modest meetings of waters occur locally throughout the Amazon Basin and are fairly common.

Geology of the Amazon

Deep sediments cover most surface rock in the lowland floodplains. Significant rises begin only in the Andean foothills, around 300km west of Iquitos. From the east the broad basin stretches north to Venezuela and Colombia and south to the Andean foothills of Bolivia. Past the confluences of the Negro and Madeira with the main stream, the floodplain narrows like an hour-glass on its side until it is only 100km across. Constricting the plain are two massive ancient rock formations, the Guyana (or Orinoco) Shield to the north and the Brazilian Shield to the south. The floodplain widens again toward the mouth.

Surrounded by riches

As the rapacious Spaniards discovered, El Dorado is a myth. But throughout the highlands surrounding the Amazon Basin is wealth beyond even the greediest conquistador's imagining. In addition to gold and silver are such strategic metals as tungsten, molybdenum and uranium. Gemstones mined in the area include emeralds (for which Colombia is world famous), sapphires, topaz, tourmaline and the lesser-known tanzanite, citrine, rubellite, andalusite and heliodor. Semi-precious stones include amethyst, aquamarine, opal, lapis lazuli, agate, malachite and crystalline quartz.

The glamour of jewels need not outshine humbler minerals and ores that are of greater value to national economies. Peru is a major world producer of copper. Brazil has the world's biggest iron ore deposits, and important reserves of aluminium, tin and gypsum. Huge projects are under way, or planned, to mine and process ores for export. Ecuador's Oriente is oil-rich but exploitable metal reserves are lacking. Colombia's mineral wealth is concentrated in the highlands and few attempts at oil exploration have been conducted in its portion of Amazonia.

AMAZON FLORA: THE SECRET LIFE OF AMAZON PLANTS

Virtually all life depends on green plants. With their leaves plants harvest the energy in sunlight to power photosynthetic reactions. Inside leaf cells, molecular alchemical factories transform light, air, water and earth into living matter. Animals in turn depend on plants for energy from food and life-giving oxygen.

Warmth, strong light and lots of water speed up photosynthesis in rainforests making them extremely productive. One square metre produces up to 3.5kg of living material (dry weight) per year – the most of any ecosystem except coral reef. This figure – technically 3,500g/m²/year – is the ecosystem's productivity. Biomass is the total weight of living matter in a given area. In rainforest mean biomass is 45kg/m², the highest of any habitat. Tropical forests contribute 29% to the world's primary production, holding over half the world's biomass, despite covering less than 5% of its area.

Trees

Trees are the foundation of the rainforest as we experience it. Trunks, stems, branches, leaves, fruits and roots are micro-habitats for animals and smaller plants. On a broader scale, the rainforest absorbs and releases so much water, it determines the amount of rainfall – one reason to suspect deforestation as a cause of changes in weather patterns.

Rainforest trees need specific environmental conditions: year-round high temperatures and heavy rainfall. Floristic compositions of forests are based on terrain and the geochemistry of rivers. Of the three main biomes, *terra firme* has the

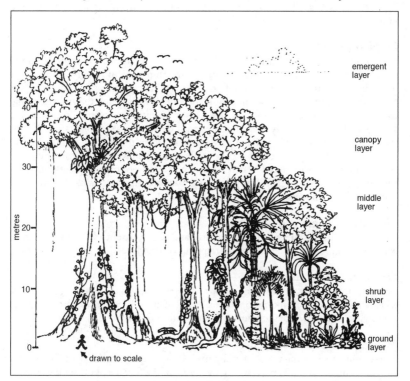

emergent layer

canopy layer

middle layer

shrub layer

ground layer

metres

drawn to scale

most species, although a layman would have trouble telling the difference from *várzea* or *igapo*. Scientists believe the biodiversity of *terra firme* is highest in northwestern Amazonia – the most species-rich region in the world.

Structure and function, diversity and design

When you walk through rainforest you feel overwhelmed by the abundance of plant life. At least 50,000 woody plants are recorded from the Amazon, around a fifth of all those known. Indeed, around Cuyabeno, Ecuador, *terra firme* rainforest harbours the world's greatest variety of trees, with over 100 species per 0.4ha – at least ten times the variety found in an equal area of temperate forest.

Most rainforest trees are broad-leafed evergreens that shed leaves continually, a few at a time. Groups not found in temperate forests, like palms and acacias, add to the variety. Yet the strikingly similar appearance of many rainforest trees hides their true diversity. Remember when you walk along forest trails away from rivers, you pass through *várzea* or *igapo* (floodplain forest) to *terra firme* (upland forest), but because of the trees' similarity the change seems imperceptible. Typical trees have straight trunks and smooth grey-to-brown bark splotched with moss and lichen. Leaf structure is also remarkably invariable – dark and narrow, with pointed 'drip-tips' and a waxy surface to help heavy rain run off easily, inhibiting colonisation by fungi and epiphytes.

Here and there, huge broad crowns of trees called 'emergents' rise above the canopy. Few have very thick trunks. Instead, to support themselves in thin soil too shallow for a tap root, forest giants have stabilising flared bases and buttress roots. Impressive root systems branch out for dozens of metres. Extensive roots also increase the area available for absorption of nutrients from the leaf litter on the rainforest floor.

Plenty amid starvation

Look under the mat of rainforest litter and you find bare clay. Termites, fungi, algae, insects and worms rapidly decompose the thin layer of rotting leaves. Dead vegetation decomposes 60 times faster than in temperate coniferous forests. Minerals and nutrients are so quickly incorporated into plants that most organic matter is locked up in living organisms. This is how infertile tropical soils support lush growth. So effectively does the forest absorb nutrients that plants use 98% of the phosphate dissolved in rain before the water reaches the forest floor. Innovative ways of maximising nutrient use have evolved. Certain kinds of symbiotic fungi (mycorrhizae) surround and penetrate epiphyte and tree roots to greatly increase the root absorption area. Nitrogen-fixing bacteria enable acacias to thrive in nitrogen-deficient soils.

Life in the forest's layers

Trees form the forest's vertical structure, and the apparent chaos of growth is actually organised in three or five overlapping vertical layers.

Emergent (or overstorey) layer

Forest giants tower above the canopy. Fig (*Ficus*), teak (*Tectona*), mahogany (*Swietiana*), kapok or silk-cotton (*Ceiba*) and many others reach 40m or more. Epiphytes cloak lower branches, and greatly add to floral diversity.

Middle (or closed-canopy) layer

These uniform-looking trees form the main canopy, growing 12–30m tall. This is the site of highest biodiversity, where over 90% of the forest's photosynthesis takes

CLASSIFICATION

Biologists have created a strict set of rules to identify organisms precisely. This is called classification or taxonomy and an understanding of its principles will help clarify the descriptions in this book.

The first division, called a kingdom, is very broadly defined, for instance, animal, plant or fungi. Each subsequent division then becomes more precisely defined, until the organism is identified: this is called the species. Here are two simplified examples from the Amazon region.

Southern two-toed sloth		Anaconda, or water boa	
Kingdom:	Animalia	Kingdom:	Animalia
Phylum:	Chordata	Phylum:	Chordata
Class:	Mammalia	Class:	Reptilia
Order:	Edentata	Order:	Squamata
Family:	Bradypodidae	Family:	Boidae
Subfamily:	Megalonychidae	Subfamily:	N/A
Genus:	*Choloepus*	Genus:	*Eunectes*
Species:	*didactylus*	Species:	*murinus*

Given in Latin, the universal language of biologists, only the genus (plural: genera) and species are quoted. This constitutes the 'scientific name' and is written in italics. The genus name always begins in upper case, while the species name is written entirely in lower case. If the genus is known, but not the species, it will be written thus: *Choloepus* sp, or if the description includes several members of the same genus (congeners), it will be written: *Choloepus* spp.

Some species are divided into subspecies or races. Often these groups have been separated for long periods, perhaps by geographical barriers, and evolution has changed, say, their colour. In this instance, the subspecies name is written after the species name.

place. Canopy trees have tall, narrow crowns, to efficiently occupy space between each other. Crowns of the same tree species at the same height never overlap or cover each other, an arrangement called 'crown shyness'.

Most amazing of all 'trees' is the strangler fig (*Ficus americana*). Seeds dropped by frugivorous birds germinate on a branch. From the seedling, shoots grow out and around the main trunk of a host tree. Ever-tightening, these tendrils encircle the trunk, cutting into the bark, and block vital cellular water channels. Doomed, the victim is eventually enshrouded under tightly woven roots and stems. After several years the host tree dies and decays leaving behind the shell of the living fig tree. This allows the fig to grow to canopy level much quicker than if it had to wait for the light and warmth created by a forest gap. According to Forsyth and Miyata, in *Tropical Nature*, the strangler fig is not all bad. Once grown, its maze of tangled roots and trunk crevices offer shelter for a wide variety of lizards and insects, especially the wasps *Polistes* and *Stelopolybia*. Indeed, the maligned strangler (subgenus *Urostigma*) is closely related to the common and popular houseplant, weeping fig (*F. benjamina*).

Tall palm and acacia crowns contribute to this level. Around 900 palm species are described from the lowland rainforest. The common stilt palm or *cashapona* (*Socratea exorrhiza*) has stilt roots to help support it in the thin soil. The moriche palm (*Mauritia flexuosa*), has among the largest leaves of any plant. It has so many uses that Alexander von Humboldt called it the 'Tree of Life'. The plant's fruits are edible, consumed fresh or as a juice, and the petiole is used to make mats and candles. Other palms important for income or subsistence include thatch palm (*Lepidocaryum tessmannii*), fibre palm or *chambira* (*Astrocaryum chambira*) and heart palm or *chonta* (*Euterpe* spp).

Understorey (or shrub layer)
At this level widely spaced treelets and shrubs reach upward from one to six metres. In forest undamaged by axe or saw, understorey plant growth is sparse. Small palms include the commercially valuable ivory palm (*Phytelephas macrocarpa*) and others with edible fruits (such as several *Astrocaryum* spp). Tree-ferns (*Cyathea* sp) and cycads (*Cycas circinalis*) also comprise this layer.

Ground level
In mature forest, dense closed canopy cuts off most light – up to 98% of it – so only shade-tolerant herbs, ferns, tree seedlings and fungi grow at ground level. Many herbs have long, narrow, often variegated leaves. Look for the beautifully variegated *Calathea* and *Caladium*, members of the arum family and popular as houseplants. Some terrestrial arums provide edible corms, notably arrowroot (*Maranta* spp), used in cooking as a natural thickener. The corm of the huge, pale green elephant's ear (*Xanthosoma* spp) is made into a taro-like flour.

Piper is a genus of low-growing shrubs with pointed, oval, shiny leaves with four parallel veins and swollen nodes (where the leaf meets the stem). It's among the most diverse plant genera, with over 1,000 species described, many from the Amazon. Mushrooms or *hongo* come in all shapes and sizes from classically-shaped *Agaricus* to jelly-like forms, of which tree-ear (*Auricularia* spp) is common. Selaginella and club-moss (*Lycopodium cernuum*) are abundant ground-dwelling mosses.

Forest edges and gaps
Where light is abundant, layered growth breaks down; creating 'edge habitat' – home to numerous specialised plants and animals.

Related to beans (family *Fabaceae*), acacias and mimosas are trees 4.5–30m tall, dominant along rivers and lake edges. Acacias often have elaborate red-orange flowers and many have large, attractive seed pods, like giant beans. The scarlet-flowered coral tree (*Erythrina* spp) has hard, red-and-black, poisonous seeds used in native handicrafts, such as necklaces, bracelets and earrings. A most unusual long, thin fruit is produced by the ice-cream bean tree (*Inga* spp), which grows to 15m or more. Break open the pod to find a delicious white flesh. It's light, almost fluffy, and edible fresh; or can be used as a flavouring in, you guessed it, ice-cream.

While you sip away at an orange juice and champagne Mimosa, a botanist will tell you there are hundreds of different kinds of mimosa endemic to the Amazon. Some species are small and shrubby, while others grow to sizeable trees up to 10m high. The globular yellow or creamy-white flower sprays produced by mimosas – the inspiration for the cocktail – are one way to tell a mimosa from the closely related acacias. Another distinction is that mimosas usually have delicate, feathery leaves. Their pods are generally small and fragile.

Retama (*Cassia* spp) is an unmistakable yellow-flowered legume with large oval leaflets, common along slow-moving whitewater rivers. Because legumes tend to have low levels of phytotoxins, many of these trees and shrubs are defended with large sharp thorns, home to their second line of defence: hordes of stinging ants. Another line of defence is exhibited by the so-called "sensitive plant" (*Mimosa pudica*) a small shrub with leaves that close when touched.

THE TREES THAT DEFIED TIME

A recent study has revealed that the trees of the Amazon are much older than anyone previously believed, with some growing for at least 1,400 years. Using carbon-dating techniques, a team from the University of California in Santa Barbara found that most of the trees felled in an area near Manaus were 500 to 600 years old, with a couple exceeding 1,000 years.

Scientists believe the discovery could have implications for forest management. Armed with this knowledge, loggers could leave the older slower-growing species behind to maintain the canopy, harvesting only the faster-growing ones.

Reaching heights of 20m, the cecropia or *cetico* (several species in Cecropiaceae) is one of the commonest trees of river edges. Easy to recognise, it has large five-lobed leaves, a greyish stem and a noticeable absence of epiphytes. It too gives food and shelter to aggressive stinging ants inside its stems.

Edge habitat is spectacular for sheer exuberance of growth and much closer to our idea of 'jungle'. Well-lit riverbanks are dominated by *Heliconia*, related to the banana and with similar leaves. The waxy red and yellow flowers are shaped so as to give rise to the popular name: crab-claws. Hummingbirds pollinate the flowers, tent-making bats use the leaves for shelter and antbirds forage among the stems. Such multiple roles make the plant essential to the river edge ecosystem.

Multiple roles for animal players

Animals inhabit ecological niches corresponding to the layered forest structure.

Life in emergent tree crowns consists mainly of birds and insects. Swifts and swallows race through the air in pursuit of insects straying too high above the canopy. Small primates are active at night, as raptors prey on them by day.

Site of highest biodiversity, the canopy harbours birds, mammals and reptiles. Tiny poison frogs inhabit tree-holes and bromeliad tanks. Plants provide food and shelter for animals who in turn help the plants to reproduce. Rodents, bats, hummingbirds and insects pollinate flowers. A unique characteristic of tropical trees is the production of tough blossoms directly from the trunk – *caulifory*. This aids pollination and seed dispersal as climbing mammals find it easier to reach the flowers and fruit.

In the canopy's shade, small arboreal carnivores such as the ocelot and margay prowl thick branches preying on sloths, monkeys and rodents. This habitat is ideal for tree-dwelling snakes hunting camouflaged tree frogs.

Ground-dwelling forest mammals have compact bodies to help them move through tangled undergrowth. Mice, shrews, tapir, deer and peccary are hunted by jaguar, puma and smaller cats on the forest floor. Anteaters feast on the abundant ants and termites while, in the soil and leaf litter, a host of invertebrates help fungi and microbes quickly decompose organic matter to provide vital nutrients to fast-growing vegetation.

Below the canopy, lianas, bark, branches, leaves of certain shrubs and tiny twigs are colonised by opportunistic shade-tolerant miniature ferns, along with mosses, lichens, algae and other simple plants. Within this mini-forest live detritus-feeding micro-animals: isopods, springtails, silverfish, millipedes and earth-dwelling oribatid mites. They break down a lot of dead plant matter and in turn are hunted by micro-predators: centipedes, hunting spiders, pseudoscorpions and predatory mites. Non-arthropod fauna are there too: tiny worms, nematodes and minute molluscs.

Epiphytes: living the high life

Among the treetops there is enough light to allow smaller plants to grow – ideal habitat for epiphytes (wrongly called 'air plants'). Incessantly reaching for light above gloomy lower layers, epiphytes perch on tree limbs but are not parasitic. Rooted in soil accumulated on branches or crevices, they take all their nutrients from rainwater, leaf litter, and dead microbes and insects. Epiphytes depend on their host tree to raise themselves to canopy height but do not directly harm it. Yet, they sometimes festoon boughs so heavily that their weight is up to one third of the tree's.

Although the 'high life' has its advantages, things are not that easy. Epiphytes must withstand the rigours of life in the treetops – the dangers of desiccation from winds and hot sun, and fierce competition for space among the branches.

Among the higher plants (ie: those having a vascular system with specialised water transport cells), the biggest epiphytes are bromeliads and arum lilies. In total some 28,000 higher plants are epiphytes including orchids, philodendrons, peperomias, forest cacti and ferns.

Smaller, more primitive inhabitants (lower, non-vascular plants) cram the remaining space. Velvet-green moss carpets every surface, and crusty lichens and primitive algae encrust branches and tree-trunks. Some of these, called epiphylls, live only on the leaves of bigger plants. Many lower plants can tolerate complete drying out.

Bromeliads: aerial aquariums

High in the branches of trees you notice the most conspicuous epiphytes: bromeliads. Often growing large enough to obscure the host tree's branches, bromeliads produce spear-like blossoms and some can be cultivated. Bromeliads are easy to recognise with leaves clearly arranged in a rosette. The bright green, waxy, strap-like leaves are often lined with thorns along the edges. Also called 'vase' plants, the Bromeliaceae family includes the pineapple. To mimic how rain falls in nature, gardeners pour water into the central vase-like water reservoir.

In the biggest specimens the vase holds as much as eight litres. This aerial mini-aquarium supports water ferns, algae and microscopic plants. They in turn are grazed by larvae of aquatic insects, food for small arboreal frogs who depend on bromeliads for a place to hide, mate and raise tadpoles. Sometimes you will find a poison-dart frog within a bromeliad.

Being epiphytes, bromeliads do not actually damage the host tree but the weight of many plants can indirectly cause damage. After heavy rain, water accumulates in the vases of huge bromeliads and the extra strain causes branches to break and even trees to fall.

Orchids: evolution's sculptures

Orchids or *orquídeas* are best known for their blooms. Their exquisite forms, colours and wonderful fragrance seemed mysterious to early botanists. Today we know their beauty results from intricate relationships with pollinating insects. The insect is often a small euglossine bee, but some orchids have intricate pollination relationships with wasps, beetles, butterflies, flies or even birds.

To prevent access by the wrong insect, flowers often have traps and passages. The insect must often negotiate a veritable obstacle course before it fertilises the flower. Each flower uses a unique method to attract the insect and to ensure pollen is placed on its body. Some orchids provide nectar or extra pollen to persuade their pollinators to make the effort, but the most interesting species, at least from an evolutionary view, offer no reward but rather trick the insect into pollination.

To be pollinated, orchids deceive the male insect. An orchid mimics the female bee in size, shape and colour pattern; even its perfume smells like her pheromone. So convincing is the deception, the male bee buzzes from flower to flower in futile attempts to mate. Over time orchids have evolved to mimic perfectly the female insect. In this way, tight bonds have evolved between orchids and insects.

With hot sun and drying winds, orchids are in constant danger of drying out so have unique structures called *pseudobulbs* to help them conserve water. In addition to these swollen leaf bases, their thick, waxy leaves minimise evaporative water loss. White, light-resistant roots affix the plant to branches and absorb nutrients from dripping rain. On a cellular and molecular level, orchids are rather like cacti. Like those of their prickly cousins, the leaf pores of orchids close during the day to reduce evaporation.

Visitors to the lowland rainforests often expect trees to be adorned with thousands of brightly coloured orchids. In reality, the flowers are not easily visible from the ground. Most rainforest orchids grow on branches in the middle and upper canopy, high up and hidden by dense vegetation. Only a few flower at any one time, so we see mostly leaves. The truth is that orchids are not very diverse in lowland rainforests. Only 125 kinds have been found around Iquitos. Orchids are most diverse in moist upland cloudforest which has ideal conditions for them.

From a conservation perspective, orchids are among the most threatened plants. Epiphyte species tend to be rare and orchids are no exception. Their beauty has meant that collectors have pushed populations to extinction. The problem has reduced slightly as the trade in wild botanicals is controlled but persistent habitat destruction continues to threaten orchids.

Commercially valuable ornamentals from Amazonia include *Cattleya, Laelia, Odontoglossum, Miltonia, Cymbidium, Oncidium, Epidendrum* and *Maxillaria*. An important non-ornamental is vanilla (*Vanilla planifolia*), cultivated for its aromatic pods.

Ferns: graceful simplicity

Some ferns grow as epiphytes, others are soil-bound at ground level and some are adaptable enough to not mind either spot. Familiar as house plants and cultivated by interior designers who love their graceful feather-like leaves, ferns do not have flowers.

Because their reproductive cells need free water during the crucial fertilisation phase, they are less restricted in moist tropical rainforests than in drier habitats.

Familiar to indoor gardeners is the terrestrial maidenhair fern (*Adiantum capillus-veneris*). Notable for its thin deltoid leaves and wiry black stems, it is used by natives for a variety of purposes including mosquito repellent. Bird's nest fern (*Aspelenium nidus*) has the form of a bromeliad but without the vase to hold water.

Tree-ferns (*Cyathea* spp) are puny compared with real trees. Their dignity arises instead from an immensely long lineage as 'living fossils', relics from the age of the dinosaurs. A botanical curiosity, they are more fern than tree, their crown of typically fern-like leaves supported by a tall, black stem about 3m high, thick as a man's wrist and covered in coarse black hairs. Over a thousand species are known from tropical areas around the world.

Other epiphytes

Other vascular epiphytic plants include philodendrons and monsteras, several of which are cultivated. You can recognise these plants by their heart-shaped, leathery leaves, climbing stems and long, stringy roots dangling down to the forest floor. Monsteras, also known as Swiss cheese plants because of the holes in their deeply divided leaves, have a dark and a light side. When growing on the forest floor, they grow toward darkest places, such as between the flat buttresses of tall rainforest giants which are ideal for providing support as the plant grows upwards. As they begin to grow up the trunk, their preference changes and instead they grow toward light.

Arum lilies are not climbers but they grow to huge sizes. Their shiny, dark-green, arrowhead-shaped leaves can grow to a length of 2m. The flowers are white or yellow, and unmistakable with a single petal or 'spathe' curved around the fleshy, finger-like head of pollen-bearing flowers. Arums (family Araceae) are a highly diverse and abundant group and many are raised as houseplants. Many arum lilies are epiphytic. However, because many tolerate low light, other species grow on forest floor where they are quite common, often being found along jungle trails.

Lianas and vines: living walkways

As we have seen, epiphytes live entirely *on* other plants. In contrast, ground-rooted vines and lianas get their nutrients from the thin forest soil. Rather than get to a high spot by chance distribution of seeds in the manner of epiphytes, lianas and vines germinate close by taller plants, choosing to grow up them.

These plants add much to the forest's botanical diversity and interest. They serve to physically connect trees, providing living walkways and highways for ants, caterpillars and arboreal mammals. You occasionally see a trail of leaf-cutter ants disappearing up a liana high into the canopy. On the other hand, their dense growth at forest edges impedes larger animals on the ground, including humans!

Lianas

Like ropes entangling the masts of some fantastic sailing ship, knotted stems straggle up thick trees and vanish high into the canopy. These are the stems of lianas, woody plants that grow up into the canopy but choose to cheat in the race for light. To avoid expending energy on growing a huge trunk of their own, lianas hitch a ride upwards on new trees growing in forest gaps or work their way up the trunks of existing trees. Large trees thus provide habitat for lianas and give them access to brighter levels. Lianas grow in all types of forest, living for over a hundred years in some cases, and develop intricate networks across the rainforest canopy. Woody lianas can reach a length of over 900m, trailing over acres of trees.

A liana can literally be the downfall of a tree as the weight of the plant, with its matrix of interconnections with other trees, spreads the stresses and strains of swaying action across several trees. When one tree falls, connections between lianas may also pull down others. In deep *terra firme* forest, some lianas grow to be as big as trees and are strong enough to support a person's weight; Tarzan swings on lianas, not vines.

Yet even he probably couldn't count all the types of liana. There are over 15,000 in the Amazon, many of which are distinguished only by flowers or leaves hidden from sight in the canopy. Some, including the water vines (*Doliocarpus* spp, *Pinzona coriacea*), contain water within their hollow stem. But drink with caution – a similar species is used in curare, a paste used for poison on the darts of blowpipes. Among the best-known lianas is *ayahuasca* (*Banisteriopsis* spp), also called spirit vine or vine of the soul and is widely used in religious ceremonies because of its powerful hallucinogenic properties.

Growth forms vary from slender stems to massive trunks in the shape of a simple cylinder or with helical twists, or two or three plaited together. Monkey ladder (*Bauhinia guianensis*), which grows in *várzea* forests, has a flattened wavy stem. A few lianas have protective thorns or spines, while others have hooks and suction cups on the end of long thin exploratory shoots to get a firm hold on nearby trunks and branches. Inevitably, some trees have evolved a defence. The smooth bark and frequent shedding of bark by such trees as *capirona* (*Calycophyllum* spp), *palo santo* or holy stick (*Bursera*) and *Terminalia* are believed to inhibit liana growth as well as epiphyte colonisation.

Vines

Some 90% of vines are tropical. In the Amazon these fast-growing plants are generally restricted to high, light areas around forest edges. They have thin, spindly, often thorny stems and most are short-lived. They drape trees and shrubs with a mass of green, enveloping riverbanks and forest glades. Missionaries believed the blooms of the passion vine symbolised Christ's Passion, confirming the Lord's blessing on their New World endeavours. One type of passiflora or *granadilla* (*P. edulis*) has edible fruits used to make a soft drink.

Cissus, with three-lobed leaves and sprawling tendrils, is a true vine (grape family, *Vitaceae*), but relatively poor in species. Morning glories (Convolvulaceae) grow fast, with papery, heart-shaped leaves. Delicate trumpet-shaped flowers open early in the day, attracting bees for a frenzy of nectar-feeding and pollination, but wither by the afternoon. It's all over in just one glorious morning. Of the many commercially important vines, one is the *camote* or sweet potato (*Ipomoea batatas*). Related to cleavers (family Rubiaceae), the *uña de gato* or cat's claw (*Uncaria* spp) shows promising medicinal properties. It, along with several other vines, is becoming rare around towns and cities due to over-collecting. Another important family of vines is the Cucurbitaceae or cucumbers. Amazon cucs don't give rise to anything like the familiar vegetables we see in our supermarkets, and wild cucumbers are small, bitter, and in some cases poisonous.

Floating meadows and water plants

Water plants form the floating meadows of the Amazon which provide food for fish, arthropods and the world's only herbivorous aquatic mammal, the manatee. Underwater roots shelter small fish, amphibians, crustaceans and molluscs. Above-water vegetation supports arthropods and other invertebrates, in turn sustenance for vertebrate predators.

Water plants quickly colonise oxbow lakes and slow-flowing rivers. This process is even faster if manatee are absent. Flood-tolerant *carricillo* (*Olyra latifolia*) cane first takes over, accompanied by forage grasses (*Paspalum* sp, *Eleusine indica*). If floods do not dislodge floating vegetation, it remains and eventually claims the waterway for the forest.

Only a handful of aquatic plant species are abundant, notably water hyacinth (*Eichhornia crasippes, E. azurea*) and water lettuce (*Pistia stratiotes*). The mosquito fern (*Azolla*) has pairs of simple leaves, only 1mm wide, the smallest leaves of any plant. In the main stream's lower reaches, water chestnut (*Montrichardia arborescens*) is common along sluggish *igapo* rivers. This arum, with typically arrowhead-shaped leaves, grows on a tall, stout stalk with a huge, edible, pineapple-like spadix.

Giant water lily

The Amazon or Victoria water lily (*Victoria amazonica*, previously named *V. regia*) is the mother of all water lilies. In permanent *várzea* swamp, the pads grow up to two metres across. Due to lower nutrient levels, lilies in blackwater lakes are only half the size.

The pad's underside and the stalk bristle with large spines to deter manatees and herbivorous fish. Its network of supporting ribs is said to have inspired the design of the Crystal Palace for London's Great Exhibition in 1851.

This water lily's sordid sex life involves bribery and kidnapping, perhaps justified as 'crimes of passion' as they ensure cross-fertilisation. White melon-sized flowers open in the evening, exuding a strong perfume. Nectar bribes scarab beetles to enter and feed within the flower. During the feast, pollen adheres to their bodies, sticky from the sweet nectar. With the beetles inside, the flower closes, kidnapping the beetle overnight.

Once pollinated, the flower turns purple and loses its scent. Next morning the flower opens again and the freed scarabs fly to white first-day flowers and continue the process of cross-pollination. Both organisms benefit. The beetle has a meal and secure home for the night and the lily gets pollinated.

Ecology of forest gaps and river edges

To understand rainforest biodiversity it is important to understand the significance of forest gaps and their role as one of the dominant evolution-promoting ecological phenomena. What is a forest gap? How are gaps made? How do competing plants fill gap space? What are the important evolutionary forces at work in gaps?

It seems esoteric, but gap ecology is useful to forestry managers. It provides models of how to reclaim damaged habitat using suitable plants, and offers guidance on how to optimise harvests of lumber or other forest products. During your visit to rainforest, look at gaps and forest edges in various states of disturbance and notice how they differ from mature forest. Nature repairs this natural and manmade damage with techniques evolved over aeons.

How gaps are made

When a large tree falls, it tears a hole in the surrounding forest. Dozens of other trees often fall along with it – dragged down by entwined lianas. Even without human interference, trees inevitably fall from old age, lightning, rotten branches and the domino effect of a downed tree.

When a gap is made, light increases dramatically. Shady areas with plants used to the dark forest floor are suddenly illuminated. Cool, damp conditions are replaced by a warmer, drier micro-climate. Decay of existing leaf litter speeds up and releases nutrients. Seeds germinate and dormant trees regenerate. Almost immediately, the forest begins to reclaim the open space. Taking place in an area previously occupied by other plant communities, this process is called 'secondary succession'.

How gaps are filled

With the increase in warmth and sunlight, dormant saplings spring to life. Without the light and warmth of forest gaps, seed energy raises baby trees only a short way. The energy required for them to attain canopy height depends on micro-climate change caused by forest openings.

Gaps create niches occupied by different plants. Early on, the gap is dominated by one or two types of short-lived trees. Vines, herbs, grasses and pioneer shrubs also colonise, their seeds rapidly introduced into the area by bats and birds.

After ten years or so this community is replaced by another distinctive tree flora of five to ten species. Their seeds, often brought in by rodents and squirrels, lie

SEED DISPERSAL

Forsyth and Miyata in *Tropical Nature: Life and Death in the Rainforests of Central and South America* unravel the complexities of seed dispersal ecology, pointing out that seed dispersal serves a number of functions; it allows the seedling to avoid competition with the parent and its other seeds; it moves the seed away from predators and disease that may be lurking near the adult plant; and, of course, dispersal can get the seed to a gap – optimum conditions for successful germination and growth.

As they do for pollination, many forest plants, especially with big seeds, rely on animals for seed dispersal. This is where fruits come in. Red fruits, which are often small-seeded, tend to attract birds, while mammals go for larger-seeded green or yellow fruits. By tempting highly mobile monkeys and birds to eat the seeds, the plants ensure maximum dispersal distance for their progeny. Better still, habitat preferences of many animals ensures seeds are more likely to be dropped in an environment similar to that which favoured the parent's growth.

A tree may depend on more than a few species for dispersal of its seeds. In western Ecuador, 23 bird species were counted eating fruits of a single *Castilla* tree. Animals disperse seeds for about half of all rainforest trees.

dormant in the litter until a gap appears. These trees are short and are unable to close the gap in the canopy. After two or three decades, they are outgrown by slower-growing but taller ones. Alive for 100 years or more, these eventually die. By this time more large trees have established themselves, with attendant lianas and epiphytes, to finally repair the gap created so long ago. Succession is complete and the gap becomes mature, high-diversity forest.

Old-growth rainforest was previously thought of as a balanced, steady-state ecosystem. A more accurate picture is provided by the shifting mosaic model, wherein the forest consists of various gaps of different size, stage of regeneration and species composition.

The road to recovery

If not disturbed too extensively, woodland recovers fully, although complete restoration takes time. Only specially adapted organisms can take advantage of changed conditions caused by gaps in the forest. Gap reclamation involves a 'competitive lottery' for space. The properties of a tree's seeds and an element of luck determine how and where it will end up. Small, widely distributed seeds (eg: wind or bird dispersed) are specialised to arrive quickly in large gaps, while large seeds (mammal dispersed) tend to be moved shorter distances and end up in smaller gaps, which are more common than big gaps. Variation of seed dispersal ability prevents overall dominance by just a few species. The 'lottery' winners are those to arrive first. But although they may be first off the line, it is the plants with the stamina to climb up to the canopy that are the eventual victors.

At any one time, new gaps cover about 2% of the tropical rainforest. Between 60 and 140 years pass before a falling tree opens up new space at a given spot, making rainforest a mosaic patchwork in various stages of regrowth. A patch's age determines its successional stage and species composition. Light-loving plants do well in the new gaps whereas gap-intolerant plants bide their time and do best in older gaps. Forests in various stages of succession constitute a quarter of lowland rainforest.

THE BIODIVERSITY CRISIS

National parks and reserves are often created to protect one or two especially glamorous species. We can sympathise with the plight of cute animals, beautiful birds or gorgeous flowers. Yet a different ethic is emerging. New ecologically sensitive areas are being set aside to preserve biodiversity – whole groups of species. But it can be hard to appreciate why we should care about trees, insects or obscure animals we will never see. But the rainforest has answers for current ills of the world and ones yet to emerge. Furthermore, as E O Wilson of Harvard University explains, loss of biodiversity is a crisis of unprecedented proportions and terrifying consequences:

Among the hundreds of experts on biodiversity I know, everyone, without exception, agrees that the world is in the early stages of a massive extinction of ecosystems and species. If not ameliorated in the next several decades, it will equal the last great natural spasm recorded by palaeontologists, which ended the Age of Reptiles 65 million years ago. Furthermore, the loss will not be replaced by evolution in any time that has meaning for existing humanity. In all five of the previous great extinction spasms, spread over the past 450 million years, it took evolution about 10 million years to make up the loss in full.

With each species lost or doomed to early extinction (now in the tens of thousands yearly), humanity is recklessly discarding priceless scientific information and other benefits that we are only beginning to appreciate. Of at least equal concern is the destabilisation of the biosphere. It is possible that when enough of the natural ecosystems are erased, the process might continue autonomously, triggering changes that will be catastrophic for *Homo sapiens*. We should be worried about these consequences.

A sobering thought indeed.

Reclaiming the beaches

Besides tree falls, water action intermittently disturbs the forest ecosystem. The various forces of water – rain, rivers, floods and erosion – all alter forest structure. Water creates unique habitats, adding to biodiversity. Waterbodies are reclaimed by the forest (see *Floating meadows*, page 113), beginning with primary succession, where colonisation begins on new land. A similar scenario occurs on the beaches. On bare beaches, fast-growing tessaria trees (*Tessaria integrifolia*) quickly create an even-aged stand about 6m high. A stout cane (*Cana*) then invades the tessaria within three to five years. The cane dominates for 15–20 years after which large, slow-growing trees take over, as for rainforest gaps.

People and diversity together

Many plants need forest gaps to survive but, in turn, a community of mammals, birds and insects are gap specialists and depend on the habitats. Native peoples have known this since pre-history, basing shifting agricultural methods on natural gap formation and succession. The light and warmth created by forest clearing favours the cultivation of legumes, rice, banana, plantain and manioc. Later, farmers plant fruit trees, shade-loving herbs and plants found only in natural gaps. These in turn attract such game animals as peccary and tapir. At a sustainable level, small gaps created by slash-and-burn shifting agriculture increase biodiversity, as much as, if not more than, the forest's natural gaps.

Mysteries of biodiversity

Tropical rainforests are dynamic ecosystems in a constant state of change over space and time. But it is the topography of an area combined with the interaction of plants and animals that promotes far greater biodiversity than in temperate forests. The absence of true seasons in the tropics allows continuous evolution that is interrupted by the changing seasons in temperate regions.

Any disturbance tending to isolate populations is likely to promote speciation and hence biodiversity. Millions of years ago, the continent's isolation set up initial conditions for South America's unique fauna to evolve. Plant isolation caused in part by seed dispersal and selective herbivory encourages faster evolution of new species than when plants are restricted to the same area and able to interbreed.

Intermittent disturbances in the rainforest canopy therefore increase the potential for diversity. In the Amazon, large and small-scale disturbances produce evolutionary hotspots. Forest gaps are 'islands' of unusual habitat that, being sparse in a mature forest, offer opportunities for genetic isolation. Given this set-up, forest openings and edges are ideal places to test new evolutionary combinations.

Biodiversity also arises through ecological specialisation. Most tropical organisms occupy narrow niches. For example, only one part of a tree may be a suitable micro-environment for a particular epiphyte species. Many animals can complete their entire life-cycle in the rainforest canopy, because a year-round supply of fruit allows monkeys, birds, bats and others, to keep to a wholly frugivorous diet. Where winters end the annual fruit supply, as they do in temperate zones, the year-round strictly frugivore niches are simply unavailable; which reduces the overall diversity of these areas.

The Amazon Basin's extensive river network also contributes to greater biodiversity by providing opportunities to isolate plant and animal populations. Rivers can stop migration and movement, prevent interbreeding and promote isolation. The ranges of several mammals and birds stop at wide rivers, creating isolated populations that can then evolve into new species. Small land animals on islands in the middle of rivers may be cut off from the main group. Those stranded on floating mats of vegetation can be transported far from their territory and so establish new colonies.

Life has invented wonderful ways to enhance its chances of successful reproduction. The techniques of water lilies and orchids demonstrate elaborate mechanisms that ensure cross-pollination. Such systems allow individual genes to combine with each other in novel ways. Animals use sex for the same purpose. Forsyth and Miyata suggest that the chief virtue of sex is the production of genetic diversity. New gene combinations provide raw material upon which natural selection acts. Cross-pollination promotes genetic diversity: essential for adaptation to changing conditions.

On the other hand, offspring of self-pollinated plants are clones, genetically identical to their parents and each other. A population of clones is more prone to extinction because it lacks the genetic variability necessary to adapt quickly. A varied population improves the chances of at least some individuals possessing traits that will help them to survive in a changed environment passing on successful genes to future generations. This principle is the core of evolutionary theory and explains, in part at least, the great biodiversity found in the Amazon.

ANIMALS OF THE EMERALD FOREST

Most of us have heard of the astounding biodiversity found in the world's tropical rainforests. Globally this habitat harbours at least 50% of all known animal species, a figure that would probably exceed 90% in the unlikely event that all the fauna were ever described.

Rainforest mammals

Walking through the rainforest it is so quiet that you wonder where the 200 kinds of mammals (excluding bats) you read about are. You see almost none, for several reasons. Most rainforest mammals are inconspicuous and hard to spot being small, well-camouflaged, shy and nocturnal. Populations are patchily distributed and you have to be in the right place at the right time. Even sizeable creatures can be overlooked because of dense vegetation. Around inhabited areas most mammals have been over-hunted. But animals there are, and with luck, patience and a good naturalist-guide you will probably spot at least four or five of those described here.

Canopy mammals

Canopy mammals interact broadly with their surrounding flora. Many pollinate flowers. Trees attract pollinators with large, strongly-perfumed, cauliflorous blooms coloured white for bats or rodents. Luscious fruit tempts monkeys who inadvertently disperse the seeds.

Sloths

Given the title of the world's slowest land animals, sloths barely manage 2m a minute, although when pushed they can race along branches at 4.5m a minute. Nature's couch-potatoes, they save energy and decline to move at all for much of the time. They are the world's laziest creatures, spending up to 80% of their lives asleep or dozing, suspended from the branches of trees. Like that of reptiles their body temperature varies with the environment. Minimal movement and a slow metabolism enables sloths to survive on a low-energy diet of leaves; clearly a highly successful strategy as they constitute two-thirds of all canopy mammal biomass.

Sloths must eat large quantities of leaves to meet their nutritional needs, but their peg-like teeth are poorly suited to the job – undigested leaves make up to a third of their body weight. They feed on relatively few trees because their digestive system can neutralise only a few toxic chemicals at a time. This may be why the non-poisonous cecropia is a favourite tree despite vicious stinging ants.

Easy prey for predators, sloths are well-camouflaged. Their grooved fur encourages algae growth creating a greenish hue. Opposite to that of other mammals, their fur grows up the back to help heavy rain run off the upside-down sloth. Several species live in the sloth's fur, including moths, spiders and several mites.

Sloths high in the canopy often suffer aerial assaults from eagles on the wing, while rainforest cats look out for sloths on the forest floor as they move to new feeding trees or while making their weekly trip to ground level to defecate. Although arboreal niche specialists, sloths are good swimmers and fearlessly paddle across rivers and ponds. Their first line of defence is to avoid being seen; their colour and ability to remain motionless for hours protect them from predators but also make

Hoffman's two-toed sloth

them hard to find on field trips. Still, sloths are the commonest large canopy mammal, so you should see at least one or two.

Of four types of Amazon sloth, visitors are most likely to see the **brown-throated three-toed sloth** (*Bradypus variegatus*). It is absent in eastern Amazonia, replaced by the very similar **pale-throated three-toed sloth** (*B. tridactylus*). Hoffman's two-toed sloth (*Choloepus hoffmanni*) has the smallest range, west of Iquitos to the Andes and the Napo. The **southern two-toed sloth** (*C. didactylus*) is the least known.

Sloths belong to the Xenarthra (also called Edentates), an order of primitive mammals which include anteaters and armadillos. Typified by primitive or absent teeth, these animals survived the Pliocene invasion of placental mammals some five million years ago.

Tamanduas

These edentates are small arboreal anteaters, specialist predators on ant and wasp nests. Related to the giant anteater, they share adaptations: powerful claws, long snouts and jaw-bones fused into a tube for the long, sticky tongue. Thick fur and small eyes and ears provide protection against aggressive stinging insects. Tamanduas are primarily arboreal and have

Southern tamandua

a coiling, prehensile tail, adapted for grasping. Only the **collared** or **southern tamandua** (*Tamandua tetradactyla*) is found in the Amazon, with a range that stretches as far south as the Argentine highlands.

Pygmy anteater

The smallest anteater is the **silky** or **pygmy anteater** (*Cyclopes didactylus*). No more than 20cm long and weighing 283g, it scores high on the cuteness quotient, with lustrous, silky, grey-gold fur. Despite a wide distribution in Amazonia, pygmy anteaters are rarely seen; they live solitary, mainly nocturnal lives out of sight in the canopy.

Primates

The expectation of seeing monkeys or *monos* swinging from the branches of every tree is quickly lowered on a walk in the rainforest. Monkeys are common but their activities rarely bring them within sight or sound of humans, unless at remote lodges or where they have become tame. In areas where they have been heavily hunted, they are extremely wary and disappear into the forest before you realise they were there. Elsewhere in the wild, monkeys may be as curious of you as you are of them. If your guide knows the correct call he may, with a bit of luck, attract a troop closer to your binoculars. However, you have to watch out because, following a territorial threat display, the creatures could defecate or pee on you – considered an honour by some! Three Amazon primates are officially endangered (CITES I) and the rest are threatened (CITES II).

The dominant primate family is the neotropical Cebidae. Characteristic of the cebid monkeys is a prehensile tail acting as a fifth limb. Marmosets and tamarins comprise the other important group. Some 30–35 lowland forest monkeys are known, with new ones still being discovered. The **Maués marmoset** (*Callithrix*

Squirrel monkey

mauesi) was discovered in 1993 in Brazil, the third new discovery in two years. By 1996 seven new species had been discovered in just five years.

The primate most often seen is the common **squirrel monkey** (*Saimiri sciureus*). Squirrel-sized and slender, it has a handsome coat coloured gold-green, and yellow-orange forelimbs. Though classified as a cebid, it lacks a prehensile tail. During the day, they roam in troops, on the look-out for fruiting trees. Often kept as pets, squirrel monkeys roam free at the zoo in Leticia where their antics provide amusing entertainment.

All six species of **saki monkey** are relatively rare. The **monk saki monkey** (*Pithecia monachus*) has a hairy crest above its naked face with the appearance of a monk's tonsure. It may be spotted in the wild because the long, fluffy, non-prehensile tail dangles down when it sits on a branch. The **equatorial saki monkey** (*P. aequatorialis*) has the narrowest range, along the western upper Napo River.

The large black **spider monkeys** (*Ateles* spp) have long, thin limbs and coarse fur. A punk hair-do doesn't hide their curiously human expression. To add grip, there is a patch of skin on the tail's underside. The black spider monkey (*A. paniscus*) is common where not hunted. Captured specimens are often kept as pets by locals.

Black spider monkey

The **woolly monkey** is superficially similar to the spider monkey, with a prehensile tail and skinny body but with thick, dense, dark-brown fur. The **common woolly monkey** (*Lagothrix lagothricha*) feeds in groups at middle to higher canopy levels. Tastiest of monkeys, this is the most intensively hunted primate and is rare or extinct in much of its former range west of the Río Negro.
Howler monkeys (*Alouatta* spp) often appear in nature films about the rainforest, and with good reason. Their impressive calls resound for great distances through the dense forest. Indeed, howler monkeys are, according to Guinness, the world's noisiest land creatures, audible for a distance up to 16km. The calls signal status and territory, allowing the howlers to communicate through dense vegetation where visual gestures would be useless. Howlers are sometimes heard during thunderstorms, adding their cacophony to the crescendo of thunder and hiss of pelting rain. The **red howler** (*A. seniculus*) is found only in northern and western Amazonia. East of the Purus River in Brazil is the **red-handed howler** (*A. belzbul*). Further south, the **black howler** (*A. caraya*) replaces it. Intensively hunted for meat, they are rarely sighted.

Attractive-looking, smallish, and grey-brown with a pale face and a prehensile tail, the **capuchin monkey** is the organ-grinder's monkey. Its hair resembles the cowl or *capuche* worn by monks. **Brown capuchins** (*Cebus apella*) are found throughout the Amazon Basin, except in Venezuela where they are replaced by the **wedge-capped 'weeping' capuchin** (*C. olivaceus*) also found in the Guyanas and northern Brazil. **White-fronted capuchin** (*C. albifrons*) range through central Brazil to the Andes. Capuchins are intelligent, noisy monkeys, foraging destructively in the mid to lower canopy for small animals as well as fruits and nuts.

Both the **black uakari** (*Cacajao melanocephalus*) and **red** or **white uakari** (*C. calvus*) are on their way to extinction in the wild. Quite large, with stumpy tails, uakaris are habitat specialists restricted to flooded forest, making them easy prey when hunting from boats. They are probably the primate species at greatest risk in South America (CITES I). Embarrassingly for the English, the red uakari's pink naked face and corpulent body inspired its nickname *mono Ingles*. It lives along the Javari River, north up to the main stream.

The **night or owl monkey** (*Aotus* spp) – the world's only truly nocturnal monkey – has nine recognised species at present. Grey-brown in colour with three black stripes down the face, the *douroucouli* is often kept as a pet. Night monkeys have enormous eyes to enhance night vision, and lack prehensile tails. They feed mostly on fruit, insects and nectar.

Marmosets and tamarins

The 14 Amazon marmoset and tamarin species, despite often being referred to as monkeys, are placed in a different family from true monkeys. They are small, with non-prehensile tails. Unlike monkeys, they have claws instead of fingernails.

The **pygmy marmoset** (*Cebuella pygmaea*) is tiny with a maximum body-length of only 15cm and weighing no more than 141g. Its tawny-yellow to reddish colour and mane around its face give rise to the local name *leoncito,* meaning little lion. Often kept as a pet, its nature is most un-leonine. It is quite common and found throughout western Amazonia. Too small to hunt, it prefers lowland flooded-forest areas and is potentially at risk as a result of deforestation.

The **saddle-back tamarin** (*Saguinus fuscicollis*) is the primate most likely to be seen in the wild after the squirrel monkey. So-called because of its large 'saddle' of dark red-brown fur on its shoulders, it has a black head and forelegs and a white muzzle.

Pygmy marmoset

Porcupines

Four types of these familiar rodents inhabit the rainforest canopy. All are in the same genus (*Coendou*). Typical characteristics include thick, sharp spines, long-clawed feet, tiny ears and a prehensile tail. Typical is the widespread **Brazilian porcupine** (*C. prehensilis*). Porcupines are not often spotted in the wild as they are quiet, slow-moving and nocturnal, preferring to spend the day curled up in a tree hole or an empty termite nest.

Squirrels

The six squirrel species are similar in appearance and difficult to tell apart. They resemble northern temperate squirrels, red to brown in colour with bushy tails, and feed primarily on nuts and seeds. Squirrels perform useful ecosystem functions. The southern Amazon **red squirrel** (*Sciurus spadiceus*) buries and gnaws large, hard nuts, continuing the reproductive cycle of nut-bearing trees, especially palms.

Racoon family

Here we briefly discuss lowland rainforest racoons along with the semi-terrestrial coati. (See also the crab-eating racoon, page 154.)

Although it suffers an identity crisis as a racoon, the **kinkajou** (*Potos flavus*) is the clear winner of the cutest rainforest animal contest. Thick golden fur, wide brown eyes and a docile manner endear it to all. Its diet is equally benign, consisting of fruit and a few insects. Uniquely in the family, the strictly arboreal kinkajou has a prehensile tail, helping it to find food among high canopy branches. About the size of large house cats, kinkajous are found in a wide range of forested habitats, even close to human settlements.

Kinkajou

With a similar niche and sometimes mistaken for a kinkajou, the **olingo** (*Bassaricyon gabbi*) is actually about three-quarters its size, brown, with a faintly banded non-prehensile tail. It is uncommon and restricted to western Amazonia; scientists believe the population may comprise several species.

More terrestrial than the olingo, the **coati** (*Nasua nasua*) accordingly demonstrates several more racoon-like characteristics, having a ringed, tapered tail and long low body. It takes a wide variety of food, from insects and small vertebrates to fruits, nuts and flowers, and is equally at home probing for food with its long snout under leaf litter or among canopy branches. Easily tamed, coatis are often kept as pets.

Coati

Bats

The bat or *murciélago* gets a hard time from many quarters, but these little winged mammals perform important ecological as well as mythical services. Bats are renowned as specialist predators of nocturnal flying insects and, with such an abundance of prey, tropical bats reach a high degree of diversity.

Depending on the exact boundaries and details of classification, 150–200 species are recorded from Amazonia: the most diverse bat fauna in the world and 40% of the region's total mammals. The majority are insectivorous. Notable are the **Vespertilionid** bats, found across the Americas, and the **spear-nosed bats** (*Phyllostominae*) who have complex ears and 'nose-leaves' to emit sound. Yet in this hotbed of evolution all these kinds of bats do not co-exist on one food source.

Best-known alternative niche occupants are **vampire bats** (*Desmodus* spp), inspiration for Hollywood horror movies. Of course, a diet of fresh mammal blood does not endear them to us, but vampire bats rarely attack humans – their usual victims are cattle or wild mammals. They do not suck blood. So gently do a vampire's sharp incisor – not canine – teeth cut a small flap of skin, it does not startle the prey. The bat then laps blood as it seeps from the wound, while anti-coagulant saliva prevents clotting.

The largest Amazon bat, the **greater bull-dog** or **fishing bat** (*Noctilio leporinus*), plucks fish from the water in the manner of an osprey. Besides piscivores, sanguivores and insectivores, there are frog-eating bats, bird-eating bats and even bat-eating bats.

Many are fruit- and nectar-feeders. Neotropical fruit bats belong to the order Microchiroptera. They evolved from insectivorous bats, rather than a separate ancestor as is believed to be the case with Old World megachiropterans. Frugivores disperse seeds and nectarivores pollinate many trees. Bat-pollinated flowers are often cauliflorous, large, white and heavily perfumed. Many bats leave their hiding-place just before or after dusk to forage overnight, spending the day roosting in well-hidden spots, including tree-holes, leaf-tents or caves.

Forest floor mammals

Porcupine, coati, tamanduas and related species cross easily from tree to forest floor. These medium-sized animals are equally at home among lofty branches or in shady undergrowth. Larger animals tend to stay on the ground, but not always. If scared, tapir charge headlong into water, whereas a jaguar or puma bolts into a tree.

The **giant anteater** (*Myrmecophaga tridactyla*) is the largest edentate and among the largest rainforest animals, up to 2.8m long and weighing 39kg. Strictly terrestrial, it searches the forest floor where ants and termites are most plentiful. Insects are no match for the anteater whose claws rip open nests in seconds, while tough hairy skin protects it against stings and bites. With a long snout and sticky tongue it probes for its abundant food. If you walk off a forest track a short way you often see holes where an anteater has dug through an ant's nest. Its powerful front legs also come in handy to defend itself and it can easily kill a dog. Rare in rainforest and locally extinct in many places, the giant anteater is threatened (CITES II). Anteaters are easiest to see in grassland savannah habitats.

Nine-banded armadillo

In the same order as sloths and anteaters, **armadillos** are well-known to US southerners, familiar with the nine-banded armadillo (*Dasypus novemcinctus*) whose range from South America to Texas makes it the most widespread armadillo. The largest is the **giant armadillo** (*Priodontes maximus*) at over 1.5m long from head to tail and up to 30kg in weight. Due to over-hunting the giant armadillo is extinct over much of its former range (CITES I). Armadillos are rarely seen, on account of their quiet, nocturnal and solitary habits. If you do see one it will more than likely be curled up in a tight ball to protect the vulnerable parts of its body. Broadly omnivorous, they feed on ants and other insects, various small animals, carrion, fungi and fruit.

Brazilian tapir

The biggest South American land mammal is the Brazilian **tapir** (*Tapirus terrestris*), about a metre high at the shoulder and weighing up to 250kg.

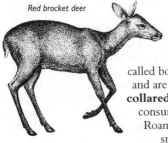
Red brocket deer

Tapir are related to horses but have an elongated, highly mobile snout, useful when searching out fruits, berries, tubers, fungi and herbs. Heavily hunted, tapir are rarely seen.

Peccaries or *sajino* (*Tayassu* spp), also called boars, are smaller than tapir, weigh around 30kg and are related to pigs. Commonest is the widespread **collared peccary** (*T. tajacu*) which is omnivorous and consumes any edible plant, small animals or carrion. Roaming in groups of ten or more, pungent cheesy smell reveals their presence long before sight or sound. Aggressive animals, they can inflict serious wounds with their 8cm-long tusks. Intensively hunted for meat, peccaries are listed as threatened (CITES II).

Red brocket deer (*Mazama americana*) venture into forest clearings or even to the edge of gardens and plantations. Although common and widespread, deer are shy and retiring (CITES III).

Carnivores

Carnivores are well represented, with the main terrestrial ones being cats or weasels. The dog family, with two rare and obscure species, is relatively insignificant.

The cat family (Felidae)

At the top of the food chain, wild cats are uncommon everywhere. Their conservation prospects are worsened by over-hunting. All South American felids are officially endangered (CITES I). Four are spotted cats; golden-yellow with black spots or stripes. Two others are uniform in colour.

For many, seeing a cat would be the ultimate highlight of a trip to the Amazon, but cats are extremely unlikely to be seen in the wild on an average-length visit. They are rare, wary of humans and usually nocturnal, but observe carefully and you can pick up evidence of activity. Look for tracks by muddy rivers or claw marks on a tree. Cats may be seen on trails at night or around water margins in remote areas. Local zoos sometimes display captured jaguars and smaller cats.

The **jaguar** (*Panthera onca*) is South America's biggest and best-known feline and its only 'big cat.' Extinct over much of its former range, it is thinly distributed but widespread across the neotropics. Jaguar, up to 1.8m in length and weighing up to 136kg, are the only predators big enough to tackle full-grown tapir, pouncing to break the spinal cord behind the neck. The name **jaguar** comes from the Indian word *yaguar* meaning 'he who kills with one leap'. Natives tell tales of titanic struggles between jaguars and anacondas, stories seemingly from the pages of an Edgar Rice Burroughs novel. The second largest rainforest cat, the **puma** (*F. concolor*), also known as the cougar or mountain lion, is the most widespread New World feline, with scattered populations throughout the New World.

The **ocelot** (*Felis pardalis*) looks like a miniature jaguar and grows to just

Jaguar

over one metre but with a less muscular build weighs comparably less at around 11kg. It ranges through the neotropics up into the southern US. The **margay** (*F. weidii*) looks similar to

Ocelot

the ocelot but is smaller and somewhat rarer. Both the ocelot and margay are nocturnal, so sightings are unusual. The **jaguarundi** (*Herpailurus yagouaroundi*), about the same size as a margay but without spots, is diurnal in nature. Interestingly, populations display a wide range of colour morphs: grey, red, tawny yellow, brown or even black.

Jaguarundi

These cats prey on rodents, small reptiles, birds and the occasional snake.

The elusive **oncilla** or **little spotted cat** (*F. tigrina*) is about the size and build of a house cat with markings similar to an ocelot: dark spots arranged in lines on a tawny coat. Its range is poorly known beyond coastal regions of Venezuela, the Guyanas and southern Brazil.

Dogs (Canidae)

The two wild rainforest canids are the **bush dog** (*Speothos venaticus*) and the **short-eared dog** (*Atelocynus microtis*). Both are small and racoon-like, but very little is known of their natural history with virtually all information coming from captive animals or dead specimens.

Weasels

These carnivores (*Mustelidae*) perform a vital role in the rainforest food chain, with each occupying a different ecological niche. The **grison** or **huron** (*Galictis vittata*), looks more like a skunk or a honey-badger than a weasel.

Tayra

It eats small animals and sometimes fruit. The **tayra** (*Eira barbara*) resembles the grison but is larger and darker, with longer legs and tail. A more generalist feeder on small vertebrates, insects and fruit, it occasionally climbs trees.

Capybara

Large rodents

On trails or canoe rides, a creature resembling an over-size guinea-pig on a diet is occasionally seen by a sharp-eyed observer. The animal is most likely a large rodent. Characteristically, species in this group are uniformly coloured, with a low stance, long legs and either a small or no tail.

The **capybara** (*Hydrochaeris hydrochaeris*), the world's largest rodent, weighs up to 113kg and can grow to 1.4m long. Tan to yellow-brown, it feeds on grass and leaves and has a squarish muzzle. Easily tamed by natives as pets, the capybara could soon be bred commercially in ranches as food as a sustainable rainforest industry, to the benefit of the ecosystem.

Agoutis (*Dasyprocta* spp), **paca** (*Agouti paca*) and **acouchys** (*Myoprocta* spp) are coloured orange-red to grey to black. Of these only the widespread paca has markings: rows of white spots. The **black agouti** (*D. fuliginosa*) is limited to western Amazonia, with the **red-rumped agouti** (*D. agouti*) prevalent only in Brazil and the Guyanas. Feeding on a variety of seeds and forage foods, agoutis use their sharp incisors to open the tough coconut-sized outer shell of the Brazil nut.

Opossums

Found only in the New World, opossums are the only marsupials outside Oceania. They are living survivors of the time before South America became an island continent; when South America, Africa and Australia were conjoined. While Australian marsupials have flourished, most South American marsupials went extinct when placental mammals invaded from North America. Only the opossums survived and they have diversified into a wide range of niches. There are at present 41 species of opossum. Amazon opossums, like most species, are nocturnal, sleeping by day and foraging at night.

Rainforest birds

In lowland Amazonia, there are at least 1,800–2,000 types of birds (excluding the 250 or so aquatic species; see page 134). Compare this with 500 species in all of Europe, an area half as big again as the Amazon Basin. The number increases seasonally with migrants from Patagonia or North America. Alarming declines in US songbirds, notably the **summer tanager** (*Piranga rubra*) and the **yellow-billed cuckoo** (*Coccyzus americanus*), are attributed partly to destruction of Latin American rainforests in which they overwinter.

Even non-ornithologists want to see toucans, macaws and parrots. However, these and most other birds are hidden until they fly out across a river or forest gap. There are a few birds that are easier to spot perching in the open, especially at water margins. These include hawks, kingfishers, orioles, flycatchers and anis. Small birds can be very hard to tell apart, even in the hand. Differences in song or behaviour are sometimes the only clues to identity.

Parrots and macaws

Endowed with a remarkable ability to mimic human speech, parrots are the quintessential tropical bird. Indeed Amazon parrots are common and diverse, with several dozen species. They use their powerful curved bill to break open hard nuts and seeds, notably those of the mucuja (*Acromia lasiospatha*) and tucumá palms (*Astrocaryum tucuma*). These are a favourite food of the **hyacinth macaw** (*Ara hyacinthus*) as described by the Victorian naturalist Bates in 1876. Found only in the lower Amazon Basin, this is still, as Bates puts it the 'finest and rarest species of the parrot family'. Words do not do justice to the shimmering purple-blue bird around 100cm in length, with a distinctive white eye-ring. It is very rare and at present considered endangered.

Other **macaws** are widely distributed and quite common. These are the largest parrots. With long tail-feathers, and nearly always in pairs, the fairly common **scarlet** or *guacamayo rojo* (*Ara macao*), **blue-and-yellow** (*A. ararauna*) and **red-and-green** (*A. chloroptera*) **macaw** are easily identified by their colouring.

Other parrots are smaller than macaws, have short tail-feathers, and prefer to fly in flocks. Common parrots include the **festive parrot** (*Amazona festiva*) and **mealy parrot** (*A. farinosa*). Along rivers in the evening you frequently see flocks of **canary-winged parakeets** (*Brotogeris versicolurus*) flying to their evening roost. **White-eyed parakeets** (*Aratinga leucophthalmus*) and **tui parakeets** (*B. sanctithomae*) feed on coral-tree blossoms and can often be found close to moriche palms. Most parrots are difficult, if not impossible, to distinguish in the field. They are usually flying overhead so you only see silhouettes and little colour; and most are greenish and similar in appearance. Differences are mostly in head-feather colours.

One of the best places to see parrots and macaws is at the famous clay-lick on the Tambopata River, Peru, where hundreds of parrots, mostly macaws, gather on clay walls along the riverbank. (See page 323.) The birds are present mostly from late July to late September. This cycle is believed to be based on seasonal availability of food plants and the birds' need to supplement minerals or perhaps detoxify the 'pre-season' unripe fruit which contains toxins. There are many less well-known clay-licks in Peru as well as on the upper Napo in Ecuador and one near Rurrenabaque in Bolivia.

Parrots and macaws, sometimes with clipped wings to prevent them flying away, are often kept as pets in hotels, lodges, or jungle villages.

Toucans

Their huge colourful bills have made toucans familiar rainforest icons often used to promote conservation or sales of rainforest products. Toucans have the biggest bills, relative to body size, of any bird, in some cases as long as the body itself. The bill is partially hollow, reinforced by an internal honeycomb structure, making it very light for its size.

Fruits are the toucans' main food and their long bill is ideal to reach figs and berries at the ends of thin branches. Distantly related to woodpeckers, toucans roost and nest in ready-made tree-holes. In addition to a diet of fruit, they prey on small animals and even eggs and nestlings of other birds.

One of the biggest is the **white-throated toucan** (*Ramphastos tucanus*), black with a white chest, yellow rump and blue ring of bare skin around the eye. As long as the body, the bill is black with a yellow ridge on top. This species' frog-like croak is the only way to avoid confusion with the nearly identical **yellow-ridged toucan** (*R. culminatus*) which has a polysyllabic yelp. A local guide should be able to point out the difference. Smaller toucans include the **chestnut-eared araçari** (*Pteroglossus torquatus*) and the beautiful **golden-collared toucanet** (*Selenidera reinwardtii*).

Hummingbirds

Considered by some pre-Columbian cultures as messengers to the 'gods' or spirits, hummingbirds are rarely seen for long. They are small and flit among vegetation, almost too fast for the eye to follow, and you will probably hear one before you see it. The humming is caused by the fastest wing-beat of any bird: up to 80 beats per second. Hummingbirds are beautiful and also ecologically essential to many trees, shrubs and epiphytes of which they are the primary pollinators. Hummingbirds are attracted to red, orange and yellow flowers such as crab's-claw (*Heliconia* spp) and *Aphelandra*.

Many hummingbirds are less than 8cm long and have a precarious existence. To remain alive, they need a meal every two hours. Only pure nectar has enough energy to maintain their fast metabolism. At night, they remain torpid until the morning. Their legs are virtually useless for walking, so they fly even the shortest distances. Woven from down, plant fibres, lichen, moss and even spider's silk, their nests are tiny, as small as 2.5cm across, and sometimes hung from the underside of a banana or heliconia leaf. Snug inside, the eggs are the size of peas.

Hummingbird diversity is highest in cloud and montane forest of the eastern Andes where, in Ecuador alone, over 100 hummingbird species are recorded. Contrary to what most people expect, lowland rainforest is relatively poor in hummingbirds. Still you may get lucky and hear one flit by or, if you're lucky, have one hover in front of you for a few precious seconds. Their charming names often refer to exquisite plumage; **glittering-throated emerald** (*Amazilia fimbriata*), **golden-tailed sapphire** (*Chrysuronia oenone*) and **black-eared fairy** (*Heliothryx aurita*) occur around Iquitos.

Raptors

The **harpy eagle** (*Harpia harpyja*) is the world's most powerful bird of prey. Adults stand a metre in height, with a wingspan of 1.8m, and have huge yellow talons. They are major predators of monkeys and sloths. Perhaps luckily for our furry friends this majestic eagle is rare, but is sometimes seen soaring above undisturbed old-growth canopy in search of prey.

Harpy eagle

Amazon raptors include other eagles, hawks, kites, falcons, vultures and owls. Commonest are the **yellow-headed caracara** (*Milvago chimachima*) which is a type of falcon, the **black-collared hawk** (*Busarellus nigricollis*) and the **roadside hawk** (*Buteo magnirostris*). In undisturbed swampy areas, the **slender-billed kite** (*Helicolestes hamatus*) perches high in a tree when not searching for freshwater snails.

The **black vulture** (*Coragyps atratus*) is abundant around settlements especially, not surprisingly, at rubbish tips. The biggest lowland scavenger, with a wingspan up to 2m, is the **king vulture** or *condor de la selva* (*Sarcoramphus papa*), the royal title confirmed by an appropriately grotesque crown of orange, yellow and purple wattles. Away from towns the most common vultures are the **turkey vulture** (*Cathartes aura*) and the **greater yellow-headed vulture** (*C. melambrotus*).

Hoatzin

The unmistakeable **hoatzin** or *shansho* (*Opisthocomus hoazin*) is a large, portly bird about the size of a turkey. Its head bears a prominent scruffy 'mohican' crest. Large blue eye-rings of bare skin add to its comic appearance.

They are poor flyers, as the pectoral muscles of the hoatzin are too small for sustained flight, limiting the seemingly clumsy bird to short, gliding flights. The reduced musculature makes room for the bird's oversized crop which stores its diet of 60% leaves. Gut bacteria ferment the material for up to four times longer than most birds. Fermentation by-products are believed responsible for the hoatzin's unpleasant smell, hence its rather unkind nickname, the 'stinkbird'.

Raptors and arboreal predators can make an easy meal of the weakly-flapping hoatzin, which therefore is quite wary, and often flies off as soon as it is disturbed. But when the prospect of mating comes along, hormones throw caution to the wind and shyness is reduced. Flocks of up to a dozen birds squawk clumsily among trees, especially along borders of permanent *varzea* swamp, cooperating in nesting with the mating pair assisted by a number of 'helpers'.

Hoatzin

The nest is built over water and, when threatened by a predator, the chick flings itself into the water below. It swims back to the nest tree where it uses its bill, feet and special wing-claws to climb back up. This latter unique and apparently primitive characteristic is believed to have evolved independently and is not evidence for the widespread belief that the hoatzin is related to the fossil bird *Archaeopteryx* – one of the first birds that evolved 120 million years ago – or is itself a 'living fossil.' Indeed egg protein analysis suggests it may be recently evolved from cuckoos. However, the bird is still weird enough to be classified in a family of its own, Opisthocomidae.

Where there's ideal habitat, hoatzins may be very common. In such cases, they form flocks of 25 or 30 and ignore benevolent human presence unless breeding.

Orioles

In the Icteridae family, which includes orioles and blackbirds, **oropendolas** are common riverside birds, coloured brownish with gold (*oro* in Spanish) on the tail feathers, with a loud burbling call. Their woven nests hang 2m or more, like large pendulous fruits, from the branches of trees. Most likely you will see the widespread **russet-backed oropendola** (*Psarocolius angustifrons*), common along *várzea* borders, or in *terra firme* forest the **olive oropendola** (*Gymnostinops yuracares*).

Caciques, with dark plumage and gold tail feathers, resemble the oropendola but are smaller. Their rumbustuous behaviour and loud calls that often imitate other birds make them hard not to notice. Caciques nest communally in riverside shrubs and trees, often around villages and jungle lodges, producing woven nests of compact globular form. Other birds in this family include true **orioles** (*Icterus* spp) and **yellow-hooded blackbird** (*Agelaius* sp). Cowbirds such as the **shiny cowbird** (*Molothrus bonariensis*) are common in ranches, cultivated and pasture areas. In the manner of cuckoos, these are brood parasites, and lay eggs of a size, shape and colour which mimic the unfortunate host's product.

Night birds

Several owls (Strigidae) are endemic to the Amazon. The **tropical screech owl** (*Otus choliba*) has a high-pitched whistle often heard just after nightfall or before dawn. The **ferruginous pygmy owl** (*Glaucidium brasilianum*) measures only 16cm high. Active day or night, it is sometimes seen perching on branches around tourist lodges. **Nighthawks** (Caprimulgidae) are often seen at dusk, flitting through the air catching insects on the wing. In poor light they are often mistaken for bats.

Similar to nighthawks but in a family of their own (Nyctibiidae), **potoos** (*Nyctibius* spp) hide during the day by mimicking a dead branch. Their grey splotched plumage and stiff, upright stance enhance the deception. **Nightjars** are also similar to nighthawks and have loud calls. These birds roost on riversides at night, and are easily picked out by their eye-shine reflected in torchlight. The **pauraque** (*Nyctidromus albicollis*) is the most widespread. The **sand-coloured nighthawk** (*Chordeiles rupestris*) is often seen at dusk around villages, towns and even airports.

The **oilbird** (*Steatornis caripensis*) looks a lot like a nighthawk, to which it is related. However, the oilbird can use echo-location to navigate and it nests solely in caves. Moreover it is the world's only nocturnal frugivorous bird and is placed in its own unique family.

Other forest birds

Numerous other forest birds inhabit the jungle. Of these, the following are the more commonly encountered.

The neotropical family of **antbirds** (Formicariidae) reaches its greatest diversity in Amazonia; a daunting array of 150 or more small birds of dull plumage that forage for prey flushed out by army-ant raids. Many resemble other birds, leading to the appropriately named antshrikes, antwrens and antpittas. In June 1998 a US team of ornithologists added to the diversity, finding a new species of antpitta in the cloudforests of Ecuador. A typical lowland species is the **ash-breasted antbird** (*Myrmoborus lugubris*). It has greyish underparts and black throat and cheeks. In open areas along the Amazon's main stream you may see it forage under heliconia plants. Among the commonest antwrens in the upper Amazon is the **white-flanked antwren** (*Myrmotherula axillaris*), which is black with white wing bars and makes a living gleaning the middle and lower canopy.

Barbets (Capitonidae) are most diverse in Africa and tropical Asia, but a few are neotropical residents. They are robust birds about the size of a starling, brightly coloured, usually with bars or spots on the chest and wings. Typical is the **black-spotted barbet** (*Capito niger*), replaced in *várzea* forest by the **scarlet-crowned barbet** (*C. aurovirens*).

The only Amazonian crow or corvid is the **violaceous jay** (*Cyanocorax violaceus*).

The diverse **cotinga** family (Cotingidae) of tree-dwelling birds has a broad range of habitats. Most are fruit eaters, but are highly variable in appearance and behaviour showing marked sexual dimorphism. Diverse in humid montane forests of Peru, Colombia and Ecuador, lowland species are numerous. Two attractive examples are the **purple-throated fruitcrow** (*Querula purpurata*), the female of which lacks the male's magenta throat fan, and the **plum-throated cotinga** (*Cotinga maynana*), the male of which is shiny turquoise while his mate is dull brown-and-grey. Both these species occur around fruiting trees. Another common cotinga is the **screaming piha** (*Lipaugus vociferans*). This bird's call is a quintessential sound of the Amazon – a very loud, three-syllable 'weet-wee-ooo,' with the last note trailing away. The **black-tailed tityra** (*Tityra cayana*) is commonest of its genus in lowland forest, especially around villages or tourist lodges, often with orioles. The strangest cotinga is the **umbrella bird** (*Cephalopterus ornatus*) named on account of its large parasol-like crest. This, along with a pair of dangling throat wattles, is used for courtship. The male's dating paraphernalia are considerably larger than the female's – another example of sexual dimorphism. As described by Bates, the wattles help amplify its 'singularly deep, loud, and long-sustained flute note'. The umbrella bird secretively lurks around its nest in riverside trees so although fairly common it is not often seen.

Cracids typically look like a cross between a turkey and a chicken. **Chacalacas** and **guans** are several species of similar-looking cracids that resemble a streamlined chicken and likewise readily become semi-domesticated, although in the wild they spend most of their time in trees. **Curassows** are pheasant-sized, dark-coloured, semi-arboreal forest birds, widely hunted for meat. The **wattled curassow** or *pauji* (*Crax globulosa*), has large, spherical yellow wattles. Curassows are intolerant of disturbed habitat, and their conservation status is causing concern.

Finches and **sparrows** are typical members of the order of perching birds (Passeriformes) and include one of the world's most widespread birds, the **house sparrow** (*Passer domesticus*). They are largely disregarded as boring and unimportant 'little brown birds'. Members of the family Fringillidae have thick, robust bills specialised to crack open hard seeds, especially grains. They are commonest in drier savannah-type habitat where grasses are more abundant. In the Amazon, there are a dozen or so common passerines plus a handful with spotty or patchy distributions.

Most likely to be seen in the field is the **red-capped cardinal** (*Paroaria gularis*). Its entire head and throat are scarlet, while the rest of the body is glossy blue-black above with white underparts. It's common along shrubby lakes and stream banks, in marshy areas with partially submerged branches on which to perch.

Cuckoos (Cuculidae) comprise 15–20 species, mostly cryptic and rarely seen, except for the uncuckoo-like **smooth-billed** (*Crotophaga ani*) and **greater** (*C. major*) **anis**. The greater ani is very common along vegetation-lined waterways. Anis are the size and build of a magpie but pure black. Unlike most cuckoos, anis are non-parasitic. Quite the opposite, they are social and gregarious, feed together and breed communally.

Perhaps the most species-rich Amazon family, there are at least 200 **flycatchers** (Tyrannidae) of diverse colour, occurring in every New World habitat from tropical lowlands up to the snowline. Many share the same technique to catch aerial insects: perching until one flies by, then sallying forth to catch it before returning to enjoy the meal. Others glean foliage or take fruit. The **fork-tailed flycatcher** (*Tyrannus savana*) is a common seasonal migrant that forms large flocks among stands of tall riverside grasses.

Flycatchers are commonly seen along rivers or the edges of large, open lakes. Many are attractive yellow-breasted birds with a prominent black eye-stripe. The **greater** (*Pitangus sulphuratus*) and **lesser** (*P. lictor*) **kiskadees** and **tropical kingbird** (*Tyrannus melancholicus*) are common along waterways. Birdwatchers will want to spot the distinctive **vermilion flycatcher** (*Pyrocephalus rubinus*).

Foliage-gleaners (Furnariidae) of the New World inhabit deep forest. Of about 70 species, 25 or so occur in lowland forest, many restricted in range. These small birds are also called ovenbirds, a collective name which includes foliage-gleaners, horneros and spinetails.

Despite the uniform appearance of these birds, they show a remarkable diversity of nest architecture from the dome-shaped mud nests of the horneros – hence the name ovenbirds – to the big tangled stick nests of spinetails and thornbirds. The nest of the **pale-legged hornero** (*Furnarius leucopus*) is smooth and oven-like with a side entrance that spirals inward. The structure is often seen at the cleft of a branch in a cercropia tree and may be mistaken at first for a small termite nest.

Diverse in the Old World, only four or five species of **gnatcatchers** and **gnatwrens** (Sylviidae) occur in the Amazon lowlands. All are insectivorous, as implied by the common name. Gnatcatchers are small, sprightly birds living in the middle- to upper-level canopy in lighter woodland. Gnatwrens, found in lower canopy, are wary and shy making identification somewhat more difficult.

Honeycreepers are related to tanagers and woodwarblers but placed in an artificial family (Coerebidae) which also includes **dacnis**. Some authors ally them to wood warblers. The most widespread species is **bananaquit** (*Coereba flaveola*).

They feed on flowers, being mostly nectivorous, but will take fruit and some invertebrates. Many honeycreepers pierce the flower's petals near the base with their bill to suck out nectar. This cheats the plant since it does not get the reward of pollination in return for its nectar. Strictly arboreal, honeycreepers have a deeply cleft tongue that is fringed or brush-tipped to help lap up nectar. Plumage varies from blue, purple, yellow and green, with considerable sexual dimorphism. The male **green honeycreeper** (*Chlorophanes spiza*) and **short-billed honeycreeper** (*Cyanerpes nitidus*) are both a dazzling purple with black wing coverts and throat.

The New World family of **jacamars** (Galbulidae) comprises several common kingfisher-like birds with small, compact bodies, lance-like bills and glossy green plumage. Jacamars catch insects on the wing like flycatchers. You might see the **white-eared jacamar** (*Galbalcyrhynchus leucotis*), perched among vegetation along a river or stream.

Manakins are a diverse group of small, highly mobile canopy birds (Pipridae) rarely seen from the ground. Manakins feed on fruits, berries and the occasional insect. Their breeding behaviour includes 'lek' formation where the male clears an area of rainforest floor to display his courtship dance. They are often black above with colourful head and throat, but females of most species are dull green. The **white-bearded manakin** (*Manacus manacus*) is found throughout lowland western Amazonia.

Motmots are small and chunky, their unusual tails ending in two racquet-shaped tufts. A scarlet breast and dark green wings characterise the **broad-billed** (*Electron platyrhynchum*), **rufous** (*Baryphthengus ruficapillus*) and **blue-crowned** (*Momotus momota*) **motmots**.

Among the most familiar birds, **pigeons** and **doves** (Columbidae) rarely get much attention. But in the wild, they're fruit-eating specialists playing critical roles in the ecology of many rainforest trees. About a dozen columbid species occur in lowland rainforest. Pigeons and doves typically fly fast and direct, manoeuvring with fan-shaped tails. They are robust in appearance except for their weak bills and small heads. Generally dull-coloured, grey or brown, pigeons and doves feed among trees or forage on the ground for fruits and the occasional insect.

Many rainforest species are shy and rarely perch in the open. The **plumbeous pigeon** (*Columba plumbea*) is occasionally seen, but it's more common in humid forest and on forest borders with advanced secondary growth. It is virtually identical to the **ruddy pigeon** (*C. subvinacea*) and impossible to distinguish in the field.

Terrestrial columbids include **ground-doves** and **quail-doves**, the latter being more terrestrial. The **ruddy ground-dove** (*Columbina talpacoti*) is associated with open areas and scrubland and is spreading in Amazonia, apparently because of deforestation.

Puffbirds (Bucconidae) have a tuft (the "puff") of bristles around the bill. This presumably helps to catch aerial insects. They are small-to-medium, robust birds with thick, slightly-hooked bills. Most are plain and drab in colour or have camouflaged or cryptic plumage. The **swallow-winged puffbird** (*Chelidoptera tenebrosa*) is sometimes seen in open *várzea* woodland. The **black-fronted nunbird** (*Monasa nigrifrons*) is often seen and unmistakable, as the only all-black bird with a scarlet bill.

Swallows and **martins** (Hirundinidae) are characterised by a streamlined shape, small head and beak, but large gaping mouth. In flight they can be recognised by deeply forked tails and swept-back, pointed wings. They resemble swifts in some respects but are less well adapted to aerial life. Swallows like to perch on branches, telephone wires and roofs. Most are gregarious and gather in groups or large flocks. Amazon species nest in cavities or holes and, unlike northerly species, tend to avoid using manmade structures.

Two notable species are **white-banded** (*Atticora fasciata*) and **white-winged** (*Tachycineta albiventer*) **swallows**. These are seasonally common, appearing in large numbers at certain times of year. At other times, they will be completely absent. The **brown-chested martin** (*Phaeoprogne tapera*) is quite common in areas with some vegetation, usually around water.

Swifts (Apodidae) are supreme aerial insectivores, spending almost their entire life on the wing. Agile and rapid fliers, they are perfectly adapted to life in the air. Unable to perch, swifts cling to vertical surfaces or hop around on small weak legs. Indeed, males of some species never return to earth, even mating on the wing. Only to raise young do females return to ground. Swifts rarely rest – it is believed that some species even sleep on the wing. Swifts differ from swallows in two main respects easily picked out in the field: swifts have a blunt, squarish tail and have more curved, scythe-shaped wings.

Apodids are often overlooked because of difficulty in field identification. Look for **white-collared swift** (*Streptoprocne zonaris*), a large species, 20cm long, with a notched tail. It's black except for a white collar around the neck. The **fork-tailed palm swift** (*Reinarda squamata*) has dingy brownish plumage but is gracefully built with a long tail, usually held closed in a point. This swift associates closely with *Mauritia* palms within which it roosts and nests. It is seen alone or in small groups, common over clearings and towns in forested areas.

Back down to earth, there are a dozen or so unusual ground-birds called **tinamous** (Tinamidae). Tinamous have rounded bodies, small heads and short tails. Being poor flyers they rely on dull brown-black plumage to avoid predators. Shy, furtive and hard to see, their loud calls are heard more often than the birds are seen. Most widespread are the **great** (*Tinamus major*), **little** (*Crypturellus soui*) and **undulated** (*C. undulatus*) **tinamous**. In a sex-reversal role, tinamou males incubate eggs and raise the young while females lay in several nests.

Tanagers are a diverse family (Thraupinae) of small birds akin to finches. Most of the 125 lowland species feed on fruit, making them important agents for seed dispersal. Perhaps the most beautiful is the **paradise tanager** (*Tangara chilensis*), with turquoise underparts, a scarlet rump and apple-green cheeks and crown. Among palm trees near clearings and villages look for **palm tanagers** (*Thraupis palmarum*), often found with **blue-grey tanagers** or *azulejo* (*T. episcopus*), the commonest type. The **magpie tanager** (*Cissopis leveriana*) looks just like its European namesake. Other family members include the more strictly frugivorous euphonias, a genus of some 15 species.

The New World family of a dozen or so species of **tapaculos** (Rhinocryptidae) is mostly confined to the southern half of South America. Tapaculos are terrestrial insectivores, in habit similar to antbirds but wren-like in appearance with a cocked tail. Only one species is known from the upper Amazon, the **rusty-belted tapaculos** (*Liosceles thoracius*). One of the largest, at 19cm long, it's dark rufous brown above, with flanks and abdomen heavily barred brown-and-white.

Familiar back-garden birds of almost cosmopolitan distribution, only a handful of **thrushes** (Turdidae) occur in the Amazon lowland rainforests. These birds are renowned for their fine songs. A thrush diet consists of fruits, seeds and insects, occasionally taken on the ground. Open cup nests in trees or bushes are typical. Shy inconspicuous birds, most thrushes remain out of sight, except for the **black-billed thrush** (*Turdus ignobilis*).

Trogons are easily identified, with multicoloured plumage and straight tails, barred black-and-white on the inside. The most famous of these beautiful birds (Trogonidae) are the quetzals. Lowland Amazonia is home to the **pavonine quetzal** (*Pharomachrus pavoninus*) and the **collared** (*Trogon collaris*), **black-tailed**

(*T. melanurus*) and **blue-crowned** (*T. curucui*) **trogons**. These birds are fruit- and insect-eaters, and take both foods on the wing, having weak feet. They nest in disused insect nests or woodpecker holes.

The **grey-winged trumpeter** (*Psophia crepitans*), lo and behold, has an extremely loud call, enabling this highly sociable bird to communicate through thick undergrowth. It prefers dense woodland where it forages on the ground for a variety of fruits and invertebrates. They are occasionally kept as pets, making useful alarm animals.

A handful of species of **vireos** and **greenlets** (Vireonidae) are found in Amazon rainforest. All are rarely seen. Primarily arboreal insectivores, some are also seasonally frugivorous. One species which might be seen in humid lowland forest is the **red-eyed vireo** (*Vireo olivaceus*) of small chunky build. It has rather plain plumage distinguished by a grey crown and white eye-stripe. All vireos are characterised by sluggish behaviour and dull plumage.

As the name implies, **woodcreepers** forage up and down trees. They use their specialised bills to prise out insects hidden in crevices. Hence the shape of the bill varies somewhat, ranging from short and wedge-shaped to long and sickle-shaped. Strong legs with angled toes similar to a woodpecker's help the woodcreeper grip tree-trunks. Like woodpeckers these birds have a stiffened tail with projecting spines that aid climbing. These poorly known arboreal insectivores and bark foragers are rarely seen, being cryptically coloured.

About 20 species are known from Amazonia. Common in disturbed areas is the **straight-billed woodcreeper** (*Xiphorynchus picus*), which is 20cm long with a straight, whitish bill. The song is a series of descending whistles. This species may be in pairs or in mixed flocks, and is seen climbing smaller branches in lower and mid-elevations of the canopy.

As might be expected from the world's biggest tropical forest, **woodpeckers** (Picidae) are highly diverse. They have long, sticky tongues to snare insects stuck in crevices. Some occasionally turn to fruit or specialise on tree-borne ant or termite colonies. With heavy, chisel-like bills, these birds are specialist excavators of old wood and their brains are thickly cushioned to prevent damage from the continuous pounding. Invariably, loud drumming first reveals their presence, but they prefer thick forest cover and are hard to glimpse, let alone identify. The **chestnut** (*Celeus elegans*) and the **lineated** (*Dryocopus lineatus*) **woodpeckers** may be spotted by a keen-eyed twitcher. Included in the family are the **piculets**, a group of hard-to-identify, cryptically coloured birds.

Small to tiny birds, **wrens** (Troglodytidae) are remarkable for their beautiful calls, trills, whistles and warbles: members of both sexes often sing duets. These chunky birds have small bills and cocked tails. Eight species are known from the upper Amazon but most are not often seen, though they may be heard.

Most likely to be spotted is the **black-capped donacobius** or mocking-thrush (*Donacobius atricapillus*) which is one of the biggest species in the family. It is 22cm long, and is a slim jay-like bird with a strong bill and long tail. Noisy, with a wide variety of cries and whistles, it has a distinctive yellow eye-stripe, chocolate-to-black on the side of the head and pale-yellow-to-buff underparts. It is common in marshy areas, around pools with vegetation, often seen low down or on the ground.

Aquatic birds

A world of rivers, streams, lakes and swamps, the Amazon is haven for some 250 or so species of aquatic and shore birds. Many are easy to identify, including herons or *garzas*, the most diverse group.

Most common are the **great** (*Casmerodius albus*) and **snowy** (*Egretta thula*) **egrets** and the **little blue heron** (*Florida caerulea*). Morning boat rides along quiet rivers and streams disturb the elegant **white-necked heron** (*Ardea cocoi*). It flies fruitlessly ahead of the boat, then tires and flops on to a branch. The compact, well-camouflaged **striated heron** (*Butorides striatus*) opts to stay perfectly still. Also striped is the rufescent **tiger heron** or *pumagarza* (*Tigrisoma lineatum*), sometimes flushed out by a passing boat.

At night look for **black-crowned night heron** (*Nycticorax nycticorax*). Also crepuscular is the **boat-billed heron** (*Cochlearius cochlearius*, family Cochleariidae) which indeed has a huge prow-shaped bill, ideal for foraging through water for shrimp, fish, insects and other small prey. The beautiful **zig-zag heron** (*Zebrilus undulatus*) is among the smallest Amazon herons and a special rarity birders often seek to tick off their list.

Of storks, the only common species is the **jabiru** (*Jabiru mycteria*), a tall, primitive-looking white bird with a huge black bill, with black skin covering the head and swollen neck. It prefers drier areas and is often seen flying in flocks above ranchland.

The **sunbittern** or *tanrilla* (*Eurypyga helias*), the only member of the Eurypygidae family, is a graceful waterbird sometimes spotted along the margins of shady streams and quiet lakes. Another species in its own family (Heliothornidae) is the **sungrebe** (*Heliornis fulica*), whose short legs and lobed toes suggest its ancestor was an evolutionary step towards web-footed ducks and geese.

Along muddy banks, **sandpipers**, **snipes** and **plovers** and other shorebirds forage for titbits left behind as the flood waters recede. **Ibises** and the diverse rail family (Rallidae) including **crakes**, **rails**, and **gallinules** are also present.

Around lakes several birds hunt for fish including the **osprey** (*Pandion haliaetus*), the **anhinga** or snake-bird (*Anhinga anhinga*) and the **olivaceous cormorant** (*Phalacrocorax olivaceus*).

Classic riverside birds, **kingfishers** are among the commonest birds of waterways and lake margins. They are stout, with short necks and long, pointed bills. Kingfishers perch on a branch waiting for a fish to swim by before plunging into the water after it.

The entire Amazon has only six species. Most common are the **ringed kingfisher** (*Ceryle torquata*), which grows to a length of 38cm, and the slightly smaller **Amazon kingfisher** (*Chloroceryle amazona*). These are found along the edges of wide deep rivers and open lakes. With luck, you will spot the **pygmy kingfisher** (*Chloroceryle aenea*) that is just 14cm in length. The **green** (*Chloroceryle americana*) and **green-and-rufous** (*Chloroceryle inda*) **kingfishers** are less often seen as they prefer small, shady streams with overhanging vegetation. Kingfishers nest in riverbank holes excavated by a burrowing catfish. When the waters recede after the flood season, the holes are exposed and make ideal burrows.

Amazon kingfisher

A common bird of undisturbed wetlands and backwaters, the lily-trotter or **wattled jacana** (*Jacana jacana*) is a chestnut-brown crow-size bird. With long, skinny legs, it looks like a moorhen on stilts. Common and often observed, the jacana is well-adapted to open, swampy habitat where its long, thin toes spread the weight to stop it sinking through floating vegetation.

Because of its unusual physical and behavioural traits, taxonomists place the jacana in its own family, Jacanidae. It has a polyandrous mating system; females mate with many males and maternal duties become the male jacana's responsibility. Males incubate eggs and tend to the young. Unlike most eggs, the jacana's float so they are easier to recover – the male's job – should an accident occur. When danger looms, the male runs away, skinny legs propelling him rapidly with the chicks tucked under his wings.

The **horned screamer** (*Anhima cornuta*) is another oddity in its own family (Anhimidae). It is a large goose-sized bird, greenish-black with a white belly, neck and shoulders, and with a prominent quill or "horn" projecting from the forehead. Its very loud call sounds a bit like 'Yoo-hoo!' Having trouble getting airborne, this mostly vegetarian bird makes a memorable sight as it flaps clumsily through trees and shrubs among vegetation-lined swamps, lagoons and lake margins. When alarmed they quickly try to move to higher branches before flying away on thermals in the manner of vultures.

Rainforest reptiles

Reptiles are successful due to their relative independence of open water. Waterproof skin and eggs enable them to colonise areas without free water. Many get all the water they need from their food. Reptiles slow metabolism reduces water and food requirements. Their distribution and activity are limited because they are 'cold-blooded'. But reptile blood is not cold and the animals behave in such a way as to regulate their body temperature. When they need to warm up they bask in the sun, and to cool down they seek shade; useful clues on when and where to look for them. Land reptiles are snakes, lizards and tortoises – all represented in the Amazon. Aquatic reptiles are covered later in the chapter.

Snakes

The most famous South American snake is the **anaconda** (*Eunectes murinus*), which was represented with excessive artistic license in a film of the same name. This huge non-venomous constrictor reaches up to 8m in length and, according to Guinness, is the world's heaviest snake weighing over 225kg. Bates measured a 5.7m specimen that he regarded as 'not very large', but reveals a typically Victorian attitude to the snake, remarking that 'the reptile has a most hideous appearance'. Although not poisonous, their bite can inflict a serious wound. They kill prey by constricting it within powerful coils, so tight that blood flow ceases and the heart stops. The process is swift and the victim is quickly despatched whole.

Among the most beautiful and common constrictors is the **rainbow boa** or *boa arco iris* (*Epicrates cenchria*). Between 1.5m and 2m long, and orange brown with black-purple circles along its back, its iridescent skin shimmers and reflects all colours of the spectrum. The **emerald treeboa** (*Corallus caninus*) is blue-green or red-orange with green flecks that appear with maturity. This species is nocturnal, hunting small mammals, birds and lizards near water. On its upper jaw are several heat-sensing pits enabling it to hunt warm-blooded prey at night. The pits, called labial thermoreceptors, are possessed by several types of snakes. The emerald treeboa is *ovoviviparous*; like other boas it does not lay its eggs, but carries them internally until they hatch so the female gives birth to live young.

The **boa constrictor** (*Boa constrictor*) is a big snake, though never over 4m. It is diurnal and hunts mostly large rodents. The subtle shades of dark greens and browns blend together creating a diamond pattern across the upper parts of the snake's body. The ovoviviparous females have been known to give birth to as many as 80 young but 20 is average.

ANACONDAS DON'T EAT PEOPLE ... AS A RULE!

Your Indian naturalist-guide will tell you that anacondas do not eat people. You will be surprised therefore when you're in a remote Amazon town gazing at a photo or a postcard that contradicts your guide's reassurances. As in photography shops everywhere copies of the best pictures are displayed in the shop. Some are made into postcards.

The 12m dead anaconda straddles the back of a truck surrounded by people. It is a poorly composed photograph, but there is a pronounced bulge halfway down the serpent's body. According to the back of the postcard an Indian who had been missing for three days was found inside the snake. What a way to go!

The **garden (Amazon) treeboa** (*C. hortulanus*) is totally arboreal and has a prehensile tail able to curl tightly around branches. Individuals come in a wide variety of colours from orange to grey. Females are ovoviviparous. It is noted for its irritability.

Venomous snakes are in fact mostly harmless to humans and in rainforests do not generally pose a threat. In Amazonia, 23 snakes are considered poisonous including pit vipers, colubrids and coralsnakes. Only five or six are dangerous. **Pit vipers** (Viperidae) have a notorious reputation. These snakes have pits in their snouts helping them detect body heat emitted by prey. The **fer-de-lance** or *jergon* (*Bothrops atrox*) averages 1m and is responsible for most attacks, but very few are fatal. These snakes, light brown with darker diamond patterning, are most active around twilight and just after dark. Fer-de-lance are common especially along trails, around riverbanks, cultivated areas and near human dwellings. More dangerous than the fer-de-lance is the much rarer **bushmaster** (*Lachesis muta*), the world's largest pit viper and Amazonia's biggest poisonous snake growing to over 3m. Other vipers include the **speckled forest pitviper** (*Bothriopsis taeniata*), a striking species with bold black and gold markings. This snake is nocturnal. Another nocturnal species is the **two-striped forest pitviper** (*Bothriopsis bilineatus*) marked by two bright ventral lines. This snake is ovoviviparous, producing six to eight young per litter, and is highly venomous.

Colubridae are the most diverse snake family, with about 50 genera in South America which are mostly harmless. Canopy-dwellers include the extremely slender vine snakes (*Oxybelis, Leptodeira*). The slow-moving but beautifully patterned **dipsas** is just fast enough to outrun its main food staple of snails. **Green tree-snakes** (*Leptophis*) are less slim but swift-moving. When threatened, non-venomous **Xenodon** displays alarmingly and strikes vigorously with loud hisses; but if molested ceases action and plays dead. **Spindle snakes** (*Atractus*) are well-adapted to burrow in the forest floor.

Colubrid ground-dwellers include the **indigo snake** (*Drymarchon corais*) and **false coralsnakes** (*Erythrolamprus*). The latter mimic the poisonous coral snake but are impossible to tell apart unless examined in the hand, as the only clear difference is the fangs in the back of their mouth.

True **coral snakes**, numbering over 70 species, are South America's only representatives of the family Elapidae which in the Old World includes cobras, kraits and mambas. Growing to a maximum 1.2m, coralsnakes have powerful venom. They may be active day or night and are most likely to be found under logs and rocks. Owing to their secretive habits, coralsnakes are rarely encountered. The most likely bite candidates are herpetologists and perhaps small children who play with a specimen out of curiosity. Although statistically uncommon, bites can be very serious and have caused death. Coloration is highly variable between species. The most familiar coralsnake is red, yellow/white, and black, but they can be uniformly black or red, or red and yellow, bi-colored black and white, or red and white. Some (*Leptomicrurus*) are not even ringed but rather blotched ventrally. *Micrurus langsdorffi* occurs in the Iquitos region in three distinct color morphs: red-yellow-white, tan-white-pink and maroon-white.

Iguanas and other lizards

The prehistoric-looking **green iguana** (*Iguana iguana*) often basks on a tree branch overhanging a river and dives in at any hint of danger. Their long toes and nails grasp branches to help them stay aloft. Individuals grow large, over 1.8m long, of which more than half is the tail. The green iguana is also known as the 'chicken of the forest'. Tests show that meat yields from forest-raised animals exceed those from cattle raised on an equivalent parcel of land. No doubt idealistic, the hope is for iguana to replace beef and so eliminate one cause of deforestation.

Most lizards are small and furtive. Geckos (Gekkonidae), generally nocturnal, are often seen prowling around lights on walls and ceilings of hotels and lodges. Quite cute-looking and with friendly faces, they cling to the wall munching their way through any insect that comes too close. They range in size from 5cm to 15cm.

A large lizard inhabiting most types of forest, especially during the dry season, is the **black-and-gold tegu** (*Tupinambis teguixin*). This large, robust lizard has shiny grey-green scales and forages noisily among leaf litter for a variety of invertebrate prey, fruits, caiman eggs or anything else it can eat. The largest lizard is the **caiman lizard** (*Dracaena guianensis*) which looks like a caiman and is almost as big, reaching 1.5m. It looks rather like the iguana, though flatter and without the dorsal crest. This species is common but very shy and hence rarely seen.

Smaller lizards include **ameivas** (*Teiidae*), beautifully mottled in a wide range of colours. The diminutive **anoles** (*Anolis* spp) are slender, fast moving insect-eaters. Uniform pale green or brown, they are able to change colour slightly, so are sometimes incorrectly called chameleons. Males contend for territory or females with jerky push-ups while thrusting out their colourful dewlap.

Tortoises

These familiar inhabitants of drier climes are poorly represented. The **yellow-footed tortoise** (*Geochelone denticulata*) is found in rainforest throughout northern Amazonia. Breeding males fight in ponderous competitions for females who lay 15–20 eggs. The tortoise's carapace, up to 45cm long, is sometimes seen discarded by a dwelling, the animal being a popular delicacy.

Rainforest amphibians

People are rarely ambivalent towards amphibians. To many they are sluggish and slimy, on top of which many Amazon amphibians have the liability of being poisonous. Others admire them because most are active, beautiful and, on the whole, harmless. Indeed they eat bothersome insects such as flies and mosquitoes.

Amphibians were the first vertebrates to live on land and still need water to reproduce. To overcome this limitation they evolved ingenious strategies and fill a myriad of ecological niches. Today amphibians are the most diverse and abundant terrestrial vertebrates and are at peak biodiversity in the lowland tropical rainforests.

PRECIOUS POISONS

Poison frogs are perfect examples of why we must preserve biodiversity. Only recently have scientists recognised that frog-skin toxins yield biochemicals potentially useful in medicine and industry. Amphibians' damp skins produce agents to inhibit fungal colonies and are under close scrutiny as sources of new fungicides. Furthermore, frogs and toads yield neurotoxins produced as a defence against predators. The Ecuadorian *D. tricolor* exudes an analgesic 200 times as powerful as morphine yet non-addictive. Chemicals found in amphibian skin secretions are often unknown to science and undoubtedly many are yet to be discovered.

But time is running out. Several factors exacerbate frogs' vulnerability to extinction. Their reproductive success depends on water availability. Permeable amphibian skins readily absorb environmental pollutants and have little protection against the sun's ultraviolet radiation. Small frogs tend to have very limited ranges. Hence habitat loss, low rainfall, rising pollution and loss of the ozone layer could all damage frog populations. Reports of worldwide declines in amphibian populations worry ecologists who think they represent an early warning of ecosystem malfunction.

Poison-dart or poison-arrow frogs

So-called poison-dart frogs, properly called poison frogs, of the families Dendrobatidae and Phyllobatidae, are exquisitely coloured to warn predators of their highly poisonous skin. *Dendrobates tinctorius* of eastern Amazonia is shiny black, mottled with yellow stripes, *D. azureus* is iridescent turquoise, splotched with irregular black spots, and the Peruvian *D. fantasticus* is orange-gold decorated with black filigree. Among the commonest species inhabiting the forest floor is the **strawberry poison dart frog** (*D. reticulatus*) with scarlet head and torso but mottled cobalt hind legs. Compared with families of frogs in temperate climates, poison frogs are highly diverse. However, not all species are poisonous. Of 135 known types only 55 are toxic. Toxicity is diet-dependent – captive animals lose their poison after being kept on non-natural food. Many are tiny, from just 1.5cm to 7.5cm long, ranking among the smallest terrestrial vertebrates.

Dendrobatids and their relatives are hardly ever seen, being arboreal and so small. Many live out their complete life-cycle in the canopy, and complete their life cycle in pools of water in bromeliads or tree-holes. Looking in fallen or cultivated bromeliads may reveal a frog living inside. A few live closer to the ground or breed among leaf litter.

These frogs care for their young rather than abandon them to chance it in a pool of water as do most amphibians. From two to 20 eggs are laid. In some species of dentrobatids the fertilised eggs are attached to the male's back where they hatch before he releases them in a suitable bromeliad plant or tree-hole. Females of some species lay a sterile egg in the water to sustain the tadpoles while they adjust to their new home. Other species make sure that each tadpole is placed in a separate plant increasing the chances against their all being taken by one predator.

While Shakespeare's witches used frog skin in a prophecy-inducing brew, it is widely held that native Indians use frog poison on tips of arrows or blow-gun darts. However, this technique is rarely if ever used – curare preparation relies primarily on plant derivatives. The Indians appreciate that use of these toxins can be highly dangerous. Indeed, these are among the most poisonous of vertebrate animals. For example, *D. tinctorius* yields a poison of which one ten thousandth of a gram is sufficient to kill a man. Just handling the **golden-yellow Colombian** *Phyllobates terribilis* could be lethal.

Treefrogs

Chemical 'warfare' is not the only way to escape predators. Treefrogs use other strategies. Many blend in superbly with vegetation, or mimic natural objects. Hylids have feet with sucker pads for acrobatic climbing. *Hyla riveroi* found in the western Amazon and the widespread *H. granosa* are, like all hylid frogs, entirely insectivorous.

To avoid unnecessary competition, different frogs are very fussy about their preferred habitat. A niche might be ephemeral pools on the forest floor or among reeds of waterside vegetation.

The 24 neotropical **glass frogs** (*Hyalinobatrachium*, *Cochranella*, *Centrolene*) eschew most of their colour. Typically, the colours of the plant they rest on go right through the transparent skin and muscles that reveal the heart, digestive system and bones of the frog.

Other frogs

Large frogs do not usually have toxic skin secretions so rely on camouflage to hide from predators. Many are also nocturnal so, if frogs are your thing, you will have to go out at night to find them on floating vegetation or on a riverbank. You might discover the **Amazonian horned frog** (*Ceratophrys cornuta*), about 10cm long. Going down in scale, some horned frogs are not much more than 2.5cm long.

You may not find one on your trip but you do not have to go far to hear them. Frog and toad voices are a distinctive part of the rainforest chorus. Come dusk, croaks, whistles, trills, burps and grunts prove the abundance of frogs of all sizes as they prepare for amorous encounters of the night. Expandable throat pouches greatly amplify their calls. The male call attracts the female who chooses the one with the best-sounding croak. Different call types ensure species remain separate, so a skilled listener can tell frogs apart by call alone.

Usually insectivorous, adult frogs and toads are voracious and will eat practically any moving thing they can swallow – even each other. Some mimic other frogs' calls so when a curious female arrives she is promptly eaten!

A strong contender for the title of Weirdest Amphibian is the **Suriname toad** (*Pipa pipa*), shaped like a pancake with legs. Coloured black-brown it blends in perfectly with dark mud. Its 'fingers' have filaments at the end, greatly adding to tactile sensitivity. This adaptation allows it to find food in soft mud or the murkiest water. Its breeding method is equally bizarre. The female's skin grows over the eggs so each rests in a little water-filled pocket of its own. The young emerge as mini-adults, without gills or a tail, as they pass the entire tadpole stage within the female.

Other large toads include **narrow-mouth toads** (Microhylidae) and **true toads** (Bufonidae). One species of **leaf-frog** (*Phyllomedusa* spp), inhabits the forest floor, where a wide triangular head and cryptic camouflage blend in perfectly with dried leaves.

Native to Latin America the **cane toad** (*Bufo marinus*), growing to around 12cm, is now established in the US and Australia and is a serious pest in places. It preys on birds, reptiles and even small mammals. Being so large it could be considered a worthwhile meal itself but has powerful skin toxins for protection.

Caecilians

Their name sounds as if they come from a certain Mediterranean island, but caecilians are only found in tropical South America. Up to five species may co-exist together in rainforest. They are mysterious worm-like amphibians, with a worm-like lifestyle burrowing through leaf litter in damp, shady forests. But they do not eat earth and instead search for standard amphibian fare: insects, spiders and other small creatures. Some species are aquatic. Caecilians vary in length from 10cm to 150cm and are coloured blackish to pinkish tan. Unlike other amphibians, their fertilisation and embryonic development take place within the female. These are the only viviparous amphibians. Even more bizarre, embryos eat the oviduct wall for nourishment.

Salamanders

Half of the world's 400 salamander species are from New World rainforests, Most are in one genus, *Bolitoglossa*. They're quite common. If you look in damp leaf litter or tree holes, one or two may turn up.

Rainforest insects and other invertebrates

Let's face it, most people dislike creepy-crawlies. Many find insects and spiders repulsive, scary, or simply uninteresting.

A visit to the rainforest could change that. The beauty of invertebrates – creatures without a backbone – comes in many guises. We can easily appreciate the exquisite colour and form of butterflies and moths. But there is a more subtle beauty in the inter-relationships between insects and other rainforest organisms. The interdependence of rainforest inhabitants lies in their ecological roles as symbionts, predators, prey, herbivores, parasites, mutualists, commensalists or any number of these together. Insects invariably play a crucial role somewhere in this web of interdependency.

Arthropod diversity is at least ten times that of all other groups combined. Recent estimates, based on studies of rainforest canopies, suggest 30 million insect species. Just the insects comprise 34 orders compared with 16 orders of mammals. There are 20 families of flies (order Diptera), compared with seven families in the order Primates. Our knowledge of rocks on the moon is more complete than of forest insects. Whatever we feel about insects, without them life on land would quickly collapse down to a few simple plants and microbes and the rainforest would not function or even exist.

Incessantly active, countless tiny hexapods sustain our world unthanked. Forest insects recycle nutrients, maintain soil structure and fertility, pollinate plants, disperse seeds, control populations of other organisms and are a major food source for birds, mammals, reptiles, amphibians, other insects... even carnivorous plants. Tight, mutually beneficial interactions are common among rainforest organisms, but especially between plants and insects. Indeed, some plant-insect relationships such as those between orchids and bees, are almost unbelievably elaborate.

Beetles

The famous English biologist J B S Haldane remarked 'God must have been inordinately fond of beetles', with good reason as beetles are the most diverse group of terrestrial animals. Far too many Amazon beetles exist for a systematic treatment here. That would require several books, and this has not been attempted. Of the 1.75 million animal species so far described, some 60% are insects and a third of these are beetles, about 350,000 species. Of these at least half are tropical. On a single tropical tree entomologist Terry Erwin found 1,500 beetle species, 163 of which specialised on that tree alone. Such discoveries are the basis of seemingly extravagant claims that rainforest holds 95% of the world's species.

Despite the wide range of shapes and sizes among beetle species, they all have a single pair of membranous wings covered by a pair of hard chitinous plates called elytra. This gives the order its name *Coleoptera,* meaning sheath-wing. The tough elytra are moulded by evolution into a wide variety of forms to exploit an equally varied range of niches.

Among the most exquisite specimens is the **golden tortoise beetle** (Chrysomelidae). This looks like a living Egyptian scarab, carved in gold, under a curious transparent tortoise-shaped carapace. Chrysomelids, or **leaf beetles**, are among the most diverse beetle families. Many feed on live plant material and some are pests, though others have been employed to control weeds and others to pollinate flowers.

In the same superfamily as chrysomelids are the **long-horned beetles** (Cerambicidae). Among the longest insects, these giants of the beetle world include *Titanus giganteus* which is up to 20cm long and comes from northern Amazonia.

Although the golden tortoise beetle may look like a jewel scarab, real scarabs are usually quite plain, though some are pretty. This family, the Scarabidae, consume dung and are important recyclers of nutrients. Large scarabs tend to be black or dark brown, smaller ones vary from green to orange or blue. They all share the dungball-rolling ability and powerful limbs to push the precious cargo around. This is buried in a suitable spot where the female scarab lays her eggs, from one or two to a couple of dozen, depending on the species. But not all scarabs have scatalogical tendencies; one species (*Cyclocephala* spp) pollinates the giant water lily. Scarabidae includes among the largest Amazon beetles. The **rhinoceros beetles** (*Megasoma actaeon, M. elephas, M. anubis*) are large, robust beetles up to 12cm long. You may see the males' impressive antler used in handicrafts. A related giant is the **Hercules beetle** (*Dynastes hercules*), up to 17cm, whose modified head and thorax forms an appendage, as long as the body, that is used in male contests over females.

Fire-flies, also called lightning bugs, are neither flies nor bugs but beetles (Lampyridae) responsible for spectacular displays along river edges and lowland areas at certain times of year. The light is generated by a non-heat-producing enzyme reaction. Each species has its own identification code of short and long flashes, used to attract mates. Iridescent **click beetles** (Elateridae) are also bioluminescent.

Another important beetle family is **coccinellids** or ladybirds. Coccinellid adults and larvae are important predators of aphids which are voracious pests.

Weevils are notable pests of stored grains but wild species abound. Indeed, the weevils (Curculionidae), numbering some 60,000 described species, have more species than any other beetle family, about a fifth of the entire order of Coleoptera. Weevil lifestyles vary widely. In nature, they use their snout to bore into plant leaves, stems, seeds and roots for feeding or oviposition. These beetles look like miniature tanks, armed with a large nozzle-like proboscis, antenna and a set of jaws attached to its end, and a rounded carapace lined with small longitudinal pits. The **palm weevil** (*Rhynchophorus palmarum*) lays its eggs in fallen euterpe and bactris palms. The thumb-size grubs are harvested by Indians for a handy, nutritious snack, called *suri*.

Among the most beautiful insects are the woodboring beetles (Buprestidae). Serious pests of wooden buildings, in nature their feeding habits help speed up decomposition of dead wood. Popular with collectors, buprestids are also called

jewel beetles because of their dazzling iridescence. Natives use metallic green elytra from a buprestid, *Euchroma gigantea*, for necklaces and other adornments.

The **ground beetles** (Carabidae) are a cosmopolitan group of small to medium-sized, shiny black, fast-moving predators of other insects and small invertebrates. Despite the name, many carabids are found in trees.

The **rove beetles** (Staphylinidae) can be recognised by their foreshortened elytra which leave the posterior abdomen exposed. This seems no hindrance to success as they are very diverse, ranging in size from tiny (under 5mm) to over 2.5cm. Some are black and dull, others may be iridescent green or blue. Aggressive predators of other insects, rove beetles are creatures of dark, damp crevices and corners, living among leaf litter, under rocks and logs and along muddy waterways. **Darkling beetles** (Tenebrionidae) are found worldwide and eat dead or dry vegetation.

Wasps

Wasps can be nasty stinging pests spoiling a summer's day, but they are just one of a group of insects, including ants and bees, or Hymenoptera, the second most diverse insect order (*circa* 100,000 described species).

It's hard to generalise about such a diverse group. Wasps vary greatly in size from the tiny to the worryingly large. Among the biggest wasps is the **tarantula hawk** or, in Brazil, the **devil's horse** (*Pepsis* spp), which up to 10cm in length is largest of the spider wasps (Pompilidae). Despite its fearsome appearance it is harmless, and lacks a sting. It is a parasite of tarantulas, laying its eggs in the victim.

Some wasp species build large intricate nests, others build simple ones and many build none at all. A few wasp species are solitary, such as **potter wasps**. Most are communal, living in hives of from five or ten individuals to many tens of thousands. Although hive wasps operate a caste system incorporating a queen, workers and so on, each species has its own unique life history. Some live by scavenging, others live by robbing ants or other insects of larvae. Minute non-communal parasitic wasps, able to fit in this printed 'o', lay their eggs in a caterpillar which then produces dozens more tiny wasps instead of a moth or a butterfly. Before they emerge from the caterpillar, the tiny maggots are in turn parasitised by an even smaller wasp – a hyperparasite.

Another highly specialised group of tiny wasps (Cynipidae) – gall wasps – lay their eggs in tree branches and, by some unknown chemical means, force the tree to produce a spongy amorphous tissue called a gall. Safely within this chamber the wasp maggot will develop into an adult to continue the cycle. That is if it escapes predators or parasites, at least one of which may well be another wasp.

Some wasps have coevolved, creating fascinating relationships. Fig trees (*Ficus* spp), fairly common in the rainforest, display a remarkable symbiotic relationship with **fig wasps** that are about the size of a match-head.

Inside the hard and gourd-like fig are minute, composite flowers which are female, male or sterile. Despite having male and female flowers side-by-side pollination cannot occur because the female flowers mature earlier than the males. A few of the flowers are sterile and are used by the previous generation of female fig wasps to lay eggs in. The male wasps hatch first and inseminate the still unborn female wasps. As the females hatch at precisely the same time that the male flowers reach maturity, they exit the flower laden with pollen in search of another fig. Searching for a sterile flower in which to lay her eggs, the female deposits her precious pollen cargo on female flowers. After laying her eggs the female fig wasp dies, at least if she isn't finished off first by one of the parasitic male fig wasps

JAWS

Matthew Parris, author of 'Inca Cola'

Many have walked down the Mapiri Trail from Sorata to Mapiri in the foothills of the Bolivian Andes, but nobody who has ever recorded the trip has made the journey up. We decided to try this. We left Mapiri with the fat restaurateur who runs the chicken shack on the corner running after us shouting 'You're going to die! You're going to die!'

It was incredibly hot. You toil up the road towards San Juan until you reach a hairpin bend. Just before this the path departs, to the right. At first you are walking up and down hilly, cultivated land, crossing streams.

Then you begin to climb. Our backpacks were loaded with a week's provisions and it was the end of a long, wearisome afternoon. We decided to camp in a clearing burned for agriculture: open and flat, with excellent views up towards the Andes and down over the rainforest. I pitched my tent, threw off my sweaty clothes, slung my underpants – red, pretty cool – over a singed bush outside, unrolled my sleeping bag, climbed in and passed out.

In the small hours I awoke, disturbed by what sounded like something grinding its teeth under my ear: a very faint gr-gr noise, just by my right ear, which would stop whenever I moved my head. I poked around but could find nothing. Could it be from under the groundsheet? I drifted back to sleep.

The dawn was clear and fresh. I leaped naked from my tent. One does find – does one not? – that under these extreme conditions one can get two days out of a pair of underpants, not to say four. But where were they?

Hanging from the bush was a sort of rag, full of holes and as woebegone as a discarded washing-up cloth. Moving across the ground beneath was a line of leaf-cutter ants, each waving a small red flag. They had also eaten a corner of Keith's towel and half of Tim's cap.

'Ah,' said Louis, who keeps the Residencial Sorata, when we limped in seven days later, 'the tent-eating ants. You passed through their kingdom, at the bottom of the trail. You were lucky. Others have lost the groundsheets to their tents.'

I checked mine. There was one small, neat hole, just beneath where my right ear would have been positioned. Obviously this leafcutter ant had made a start, then opted for my underpants in preference. These had been, after all, Calvin Klein. Cutting edge.

---

roaming around inside the fig looking for partners to mate with.

Each fig tree relies on just one species of wasp to do the pollinating. According to tropical biologists Forsyth and Miyata, around 900 kinds of neotropical fig tree are known, so there must be at least 900 fig wasps to go with each tree species.

Ants

A dominant aspect of ant biology is that no species directly consumes conventional plant matter such as leaves and stems. Ants are secondary consumers and rely on other organisms to convert plant matter into edible fare. There are at least three different ways to do this. Some live in a plant utilising specialist cells to provide food. Others consume the waste products of herbivorous insects, and others eat a primary consumer, usually herbivorous insects or another organism able to break down the plant into edible matter. In many cases, social organisation of the ants facilitates their exploitation of a food source.

With these strategies and endless variations, and well-adapted to darkness and high humidity, ants so successfully exploit forest production they are the most abundant rainforest insect. Indeed, they comprise up to a tenth of total animal biomass. Ants are very species-rich in tropical rainforest. In the lowland rainforest of Peru, scientists counted 30 to 40 species per hectare. In Tambopata Reserve, a single leguminous tree yielded 43 ant species. The entire Amazon fauna could number as many as 2–3,000 species. Ants are the dominant insects, and indeed, are second to none.

A fascinating symbiosis involves the common riverside **cecropia tree** (see *Forest edges and gaps*, page 114) and **ants**, typically *Azteca* or *Pseudomyrmex* spp, which are particularly aggressive and defend the tree accordingly. The cecropia's hollow stem serves as army barracks, mess and headquarters. The interior is furnished with automatic, inexhaustible food dispensers in the form of special glands which exude nectar. Modified leaf structures provide protein-rich rations in little ant-sized packets. The tough dry stem makes an ideal nesting place and the ants depend entirely on cecropia, the only place they survive.

In return, stinging ants fearlessly defend the host tree from hungry caterpillars, beetles, leaf-cutter ants and mammals. Workers snip away at every sprouting epiphyte or entwining vine tendril. Tap the trunk and hordes of small, reddish-brown ants gather around your finger and immediately start stinging. Only the sloth and a few insect-eating birds find the tree approachable. Some woodpeckers and antbirds feast on arboreal ants, so you often see several perched on a single tree at one time.

Such symbioses are common. Another tree, the **tangarana** (*Triplaris surinamensis*), recognisable from its smooth brown bark and racemes of pink flowers, also harbours stinging ants. These pour out of small holes in the bark whenever the tree is disturbed.

Ant dairy farmers
Rather than protect plants in benign symbiosis, many kinds of ants contribute to their demise. For example, **honey ants** (subfamilies Camponotinae and Dolichoderinae), the **Argentine ant** (*Iridomyrmex humilis*) and the **fire ant** (*Solenopsis saevissima*), tend plant-sucking hemipterans, mostly aphids and scale insects. These pests literally drain a tree's resources. When ants are about, they get especially abundant, clumped around a young shoot like a bunch of grapes. Like miniature dairy farmers, the ants milk their charges as they collect honeydew sugars excreted by plant-suckers. As a farmer defends his livestock from wild beasts, so ants defend their charges from ladybird larvae and adults, hoverfly larvae, parasitoid wasps and flies. Some ants even go as far to build protective covers as 'barns' for their valuable livestock. The ants effectively help the pests destroy the plant. Plants with aphids protected by ants suffer much more from the ravages of herbivorous insects than plants without aphid-tending ants.

Agricultural ants: farming for fungi
They can defoliate a whole shrub in a few days, but **leaf-cutter ants** (*Atta cephalotes*) are strictly speaking not herbivorous. Worker ants harvest leaves, cut them piece by piece into neat shapes, then carry these back to cavernous underground nests.

But why do the ants work so hard? They cannot actually eat the leaf pieces because they lack the enzymes to break down plant toxins and the cellulose in leaf cell walls. Instead, they use leaf pieces as a compost for a fungus (*Leucoprinus* spp). The fungal mycelia feed every ant in the colony and are incessantly tended by workers. Leaf-cutter ant nests go deep beneath the soil, to where conditions are ideal for fungal growth. Nests stretch over distances of 50m, and last up to 20 years or more, housing as many as eight million ants. The fungus grows only in the ant nest and the ants depend entirely on the fungus. Their activities have a major impact on the forest by defoliating whole trees and creating forest gaps, sometimes extending for several metres around their nests.

Ant armies on the march

Other conspicuous rainforest ants include army ants (*Eciton, Labidus* and other genera). The nest-raiding activities of *Eciton rapax, E. legionis* and the two commonest species *E. hamata* and *E. drepanophora*, are described by the Victorian naturalist H W Bates. He tells of 'eager freebooters' who plunder other ant nests for eggs and larvae. Bates also discusses a dwarf species (*E. praedator*), who move in 'dense phalanxes', rather than in the long columns of other ecitons. Huge colonies of up to a million individuals form bivouacs in tree-holes and hollow trunks. Tens of thousands of worker ants hook limbs together to form the living walls of a nest. Within, the queen and her progeny are dutifully tended.

At daybreak, the horde decamps and workers and soldiers sally forth in dawn raids, fanning out from the tree trunks and consuming all edible prey in their path. One entomologist describes army ant raids as 'an attack of 50,000 miniature wolves'. The flurry of activity caused by insects trying to escape the raiders draws insectivorous birds, like the antbirds, and parasitoid flies to the scene.

The glossy black **bullet ant** (*Dinoponera grandis)* is the world's largest ant – up to 3cm long. Its excruciating sting is presumably the origin of its name. It's also called the **24-hour ant**, from the time taken for the pain to subside (though it's given numerous unprintable names by people who get stung!). There are dozens of related species, such as *Paraponera clavata* found in the lowland rainforest of Ecuador. Bates describes *D. grandis,* as having a sting 'not so severe as in many of the smaller kinds'. These ants are solitary by day, presumably scouting out their territory for prey opportunities, and at night, they gather in small bands of a dozen or less and sortie out to collect the booty. Ants such as **carpenter ants** (*Camponotus*) and the lesser-known genera, *Solenopsis, Monacis* and *Paratrechina*, are semi-nomadic, setting up camp for a while before moving on.

Ants are ubiquitous in the rainforest and in many ways crucial to its ecology. The sooty antbird (*Myrmeciza fortis*) and many other niche specialists follow army ants to glean insects trying to escape the horde. Old ant nests provide nest sites for birds and arboreal animals.

Insect architects

Some insect constructions, particularly nests of social insects, rival human buildings in complexity. Ants, bees, wasps and termites are renowned for architectural skills. All social insects have a caste system delegating work in the nest to queens, workers, soldiers or drones. Each individual is efficiently communicated its task from chemical signals which emanate from the queen.

Wasps build combs similar to those of bees but of chewed wood-pulp paper. A common wasp (*Chartergus* spp) builds finger-shaped nests 2m long. Others, notably the **potter wasp** (*Polybia* spp), use clay to build compact globular nests. *P. emaciata* from Colombia moulds a spherical clay nest about 10cm in diameter which, being covered in a cement of clay and sand, is virtually impenetrable, except via a small entrance or flight hole. Another species of the upper Amazon,

P. singularis, has rectangular clay nests 30 x 15cm or larger, distinctive on account of the long slit-like flight hole. English naturalist H W Bates described several species of potter wasps. *Trypoloxon aurifrons* and *T. albitarse* are big black wasps that build little pot-like structures much like those of **mason wasps**.

From Santarém in Brazil, Bates collected *Pelopaeus fistularis*, a 'large black and yellow wasp with a remarkably long and narrow waist'. He goes on to describe how this solitary species builds its 50mm long pouch-shaped nest, containing a single large grub. These wasps paralyse other insects, then leave them in the nest as fresh baby-food for the larvae. Other kinds of wasps, including the **sand wasp** (*Bembex* spp), anaesthetise prey for their young, placing it in a tunnel dug in soft dry ground wherein its offspring – usually only one per nest – is ensconced. Bates mentions *B. ciliata*, a small pale green wasp, and a solitary species that excavates its nest 'with wonderful rapidity' throwing sand from 'out beneath their bodies…in continuous streams'.

Stingless bees (Meliponinae) build combs in nooks and crannies of trees such as the strangler fig. Others use silk from their own larvae to weave nests from folded leaves.

And precious dwellings should be protected. Certain tree-dwelling ants have a caste of 'doorkeeper' ants. These stalwarts block the entrance hole with square-shaped heads employed for no other task. Some ants live on the outside of trees. Often seen on canoe rides, triangular mud nests are shaped around the underside of branches so rain does not enter and they point down to help the water flow off.

Termites (Isoptera) are not ants but they *are* master builders. In dry areas, their 3m-tall mud mounds are equipped with a queen's chamber, living quarters, nurseries, gardens, defensive walls, waste disposal and air-conditioning. In flooded forest, termites build their ball-shaped nest up a tree trunk; lower down it could be washed away by floods. These nests employ delicate free-form architecture to maximise available space, minimise weight and maintain structural strength. Related to cockroaches, termites lack tannin in their chitinous shell so they are easily damaged by light. To avoid sunburn, they remain in the nest. To move afield, they construct long mud tunnels, sometimes tens of metres up a tree-trunk.

Butterflies and moths

Among rainforest butterflies and moths, several evolutionary strategies are more or less in play continually (see box, page 148). We do not know precisely the number of species recorded from the lowland Amazon, let alone the true number. Accurate measures may never be possible. Lepidoptera is perhaps the best-known invertebrate group, with about 112,000 species worldwide, of which some 4,000 butterflies have been described from Peru alone.

The world's largest moth is the splendid **white witch** or **birdwing moth** (*Thysania agrippina*) with a wingspan up to 30cm. Occurring throughout much of the Americas and Europe, **hawkmoths** are very large and resemble a hummingbird in form and size, so closely in fact that Bates 'several times… shot by mistake a hawkmoth instead of a bird'. The biggest hawkmoths are sometimes called **hummingbird moths** as they 'hum' due to rapid wingbeats while hovering. They hover while feeding on flowers during nocturnal forays. Indeed this is the nocturnal equivalent of the hummingbird's ecological niche, and flowers are usually white and pungent to attract the moth.

Pierid butterflies are a family in which most species appear to have only four legs compared with the normal six of virtually every insect. In fact the forelegs are held close to the body and only the two pairs of rear legs are used to stand.

THE ETERNAL ARMS RACE – BUTTERFLIES, MOTHS AND THEIR ENEMIES

Stories of fairies and angels could have been born of the most beautiful insects: butterflies and moths (Lepidoptera). Behind the myth and beauty lies a biology marvellous and near-miraculous but at the same time somewhat sinister. Lepidoptera metamorphose from larva to pupa to adult, so the first phase of life is spent as a caterpillar. Its sole purpose is to accumulate enough food and energy to complete pupation, making it little more than an 'eating machine'.

Caterpillars generally feed only on one or two plant species. They specialise because most rainforest plants produce toxic, sticky or indigestible substances which deter herbivorous insects. So as not to starve, the caterpillar has counter-measures – an array of toxin-neutralising enzymes. But these are expensive on energy so the caterpillar can make only limited quantities. It just can't make enough enzymes to neutralise the defences of more than a few different plants. As one plant evolves greater defences, the caterpillar must produce more and more enzymes to deal with it. Inevitably, the caterpillar evolves to become increasingly specialised to feed from one or two plants, creating a natural arms race between the plant and caterpillar. Such runaway coevolution is believed to be an important speciation-promoting mechanism. In terms of diversity, Lepidoptera rank about equal with Hymenoptera, with about 100,000 described species worldwide.

As the caterpillar munches away out in the open, it cannot help leaving evidence of its activities. These eventually catch the watchful eye of a bird or predator. Now begins the second arms race, as the caterpillar tries to avoid becoming a meal itself. Two basic strategies are used.

Lying is one strategy, more properly called mimicry: relying on deceiving a curious predator. Mimicking species copy a particular natural object. Many look like twigs. Other species mimic eyes, or other parts of bigger animals. One species of moth caterpillar resembles the whole head of a snake complete with wiggling tongue-like appendage. Another looks exactly like a bird dropping. To

Rainforest savants are familiar with **morpho butterflies**, distinguished by their large size and wings of iridescent blue, which may be 15–20cm across. But despite being obvious in flight the resting morpho is cryptic, showing only the underside of its wings, and almost indistinguishable on the trunk of a tree. These magnificent creatures seem barely able to fly under their own impressive size and weight; their looping flight path appears both laborious and strained. Typical upper Amazon species include *M. achilles*, *M. negro* and *M. didius*. These butterflies are highly diverse with over 80 species of morpho within the subfamily *Morphinae*. Another subfamily (Brassolinae) includes *Caligo* spp which has superb eye spots – perfect replicas of owl eyes – while the rest of the wings and body complete the deception, mimicking the bird's 'ears' and beak.

In the Nymphalidae family, along with morphos, is the beautiful Heliconiinae subfamily, or **longwings**, which have a convoluted evolutionary interaction with their passiflora vine host plant. Cyanide compounds produced by passifloras put off most insect herbivores but not the heliconiids. Female longwings lay eggs on the leaves of the vines, which try to prevent this by producing, direct from the leaf, tiny protuberances that look like eggs. Fooled into thinking that these are real eggs, the female wrongly decides the plant is already taken. She moves on and the plant has saved itself from an army of hungry caterpillars.

get a meal their predators must become better and better at spotting deception. To avoid detection the caterpillar must become more and more like the object it mimics –epitomising the art of camouflage in the eternal battle between hunter and hunted.

Some caterpillar species opt for a second strategy by using poison and bright warning colours to defend themselves, often acquiring their toxins from the host plant. Rather than starve, predators evolve ways to deal with poisons so, in turn, the caterpillar becomes ever more poisonous. This chemical warfare arms race spirals as each species stakes its survival on the next generation improving on the last. Although a natural laboratory of chemical experiments, little research is devoted to insect pharmacopoeias.

Out in the open, butterflies and moths are again targets. Now we have aerial warfare. Mimicry, such as spots like a bird's eye, is a common defence. Caligo spp have owl's eyes emblazoned on their wings' underside and the hairy thorax mimics the owl's beak. A particular form of mimicry is when a non-poisonous butterfly has almost the exact appearance of another related but genuinely toxic species. First discovered among Amazonian insects by Bates, Batesian mimicry is particularly widespread among butterflies and moths. Müllerian mimicry is when a series of toxic species hedge their bets by all looking similar, so a predator gets the idea "something that looks like this tastes bad."

Moths have also entered the 'arms race'. Bats emit clicks to detect their environment at night and hunt aerial insects. Some poisonous moths emit a warning click to announce their unpalatability. How do non-poisonous moths protect themselves? When tiny hairs on the moth detect air vibrated by the bat's click, the moth instantly drops from the sky, beyond the bat's flight path. You can probably guess the scenario as the bat's sonar gets better and better. It's one explanation for why bats have such huge ears.

Who knows the end result of these life-and-death struggles? One thing is certain. As long as plants and caterpillars, butterflies, moths and their predators exist, nature's 'arms race' will continue.

But of course, there is strong selection for females who are not easily deceived and, when they can tell the difference, plonk, down go the eggs. Selection favours the plant that produces a more realistic fake egg, and the butterfly evolves to get better at detecting the fake and we have another evolutionary arms race. Some passion vines produce nectar to attract ants and wasps that attack butterfly eggs and caterpillars.

Many heliconiids are highly poisonous, 'a flying cyanide capsule', in the words of butterfly expert Diane Murawski (1993). Exactly how they acquire the poison is unknown, but it is believed to depend on toxins produced by the host plant, ingested by the caterpillar or butterfly, and sequestered for later use.

Now it gets really interesting. Different species of poisonous heliconiids have evolved to mimic each other, sharing similar wing patterns. In the Amazon of southern Colombia and western Brazil, two different species, *Heliconius erato* and *H. melpomene*, each have a race (or subspecies) that share virtually identical wing patterns. Hence the two races *H. e. reductimacula* and *H. m. vicinus* look the same. Müllerian mimicry was first discovered in the late 19th century by the German naturalist Fritz Müller.

One or two tastes of either of these two poisonous species and predators associate the 'search image' used to recognise food with poison; subsequently all butterflies which share the pattern will benefit from being off the menu. Thus, natural selection favours similar-looking individuals whether or not they're different species.

Trays of mounted insects are sold by hawkers who hang around tour operator offices and airports. Some insects – notably morphos – and large beetles like Cerambycidae and Lucanidae species, especially the hercules and rhinoceros beetles are at risk or threatened from over-collection, so don't buy them.

Other insects

Although most of us see **cockroaches** as revolting, they do have a certain academic appeal. Cockroaches have a most distinguished lineage having existed on the planet for some 300 million years. Cosmopolitan pests, they are persistent and hardy, able to survive considerable maltreatment, as anyone who has tried to kill one knows. Aside from various species found around huts, homes and hotels, guests would probably not want to encounter the world's largest cockroach, *Megaloblatta longipennis*, recorded from Colombia at 9.68cm long and 4.50cm across. Unsuprisingly, this fact is never cited in tour operator brochures.

John Kricher in *A Neotropical Companion* stretches out an olive branch to the beleaguered cockroach saying: 'They do not bite or sting, nor do they carry vile diseases. So relax and enjoy them. You might as well. In the Neotropics, at least, they are always close by.'

It is said some people have been driven mad by the ever-present electronic rasping of **cicadas**, with the appearance of huge flies. Our intrepid reporter Bates thought they had a 'harsh jarring tone… a long and loud note resembling the steam whistle of a locomotive'. Like the rest of their order (Hemiptera), cicadas possess a sharp, hypodermic proboscis to suck plant fluids. They are diverse, varying in size from about 10 to 50mm, and sound out different songs according to species to mark territory and attract mates. Assassin bugs (one of which causes Chagas' Disease) use the implement to suck animal fluids, usually from other insects.

Most hemipterans are less than 10mm long but you can see them if you examine closely a green stem or leaf. Here you will also find **aphids**, and **greenfly** and **plant-lice**, **leaf-hoppers**, which jump as you go to touch them, **scale insects**, which look like tiny shields and **mealy bugs**, which are fluffy or spiky, covered with a whitish woolly substance. Most sedentary plant-suckers produce some type of defensive chemical as a defence against predators and parasites.

Suddenly, a twig moves without a breeze, and you look closely to notice it is a 15cm long **stick insect**, to which are related **leaf-insects** (*Phasmida*), another twist in evolution's game of hide and seek. **Mantids** are voracious predators of other insects and mimic leaves, sticks or even flowers to ambush prospective prey as well as hide from their own predators.

Flies (Diptera) appear mostly around your food or rubbish pits, but less-obvious parasitoid flies attack pest insects like leaf-cutter ants. **Blowflies** hasten the decomposition of dead animals and **fruit-flies** help break down rotting flowers, fruit and fungi. **Mosquitoes** are probably the most troublesome members of this order.

Grasshoppers, **katydids** and **crickets** (Orthoptera) are abundant and highly diverse. These plant eaters do not swarm locust-like but whole fields can be stripped overnight to satisfy their voracious appetites. Katydids are nocturnal and have long, whisker-like antennae. Most are cryptically camouflaged. Go on a walk after dark to look for them, of which an incredible number emerge as night descends.

Here we have touched on the best-known insect groups: social insects, butterflies, beetles. But these are the tip of the iceberg, with dozens of other insect orders. Mostly these are inhabitants of places biologists have difficulty reaching; for example, the high canopy, or the middle of swamps, or dark, dank places. The true diversity of these cryptobugs is anyone's guess. One could start looking at tiny soil insects such as **springtails** or **thrips**, or look for bigger ones: **earwigs** or **mayflies**, or **scorpionflies**. These are just a few orders of insects that have yet really to come under the scrutiny of tropical entomologists, whose task to catalogue and name but a fraction will surely occupy many, many years.

Spiders: a real web sight

The Amazon endlessly fascinates arachnophiles – those select few who admire spiders. Admittedly we do not all share a love for them but we ought to respect these eight-legged arthropods. Spiders are major predators of pest insects and are an important food source for many birds.

On jungle walks or canoe rides, everyone notices huge, funnel-shaped webs, up to a metre across. The finely meshed traps are woven by communal spiders, thankfully much smaller than the web size implies! Huge stretches of nature's finest cloth, tattered here and there, hang down and around trees at forest edges. The webs are shaped to catch prey dropped from the canopy. Collectively, dozens of tiny spiders dash out, inject the victim, then suck out its juices.

Communal spiders would not get the prize for the most beautiful webs. This is awarded to the **orb-weaving spiders**, like those you see in your house and garden. But the rainforest, in characteristic profligacy, harbours orb-weavers much bigger and more striking. The elegant **golden orbweaver** (*Nephila clavipes*) with an elongated black and silver body and long black legs, spins a giant web of strong gold silk that stretches across forest gaps and trails. (Don't walk into one, it is a most disconcerting sensation!) These catch large insects and the biggest, up to 2.5m across, can snare small birds and bats.

Big, robust and hairy, **tarantulas** fit our preconception of a rainforest spider. They do not spin a web but actively hunt for prey in swamp vegetation or other damp habitats. Mostly harmless, tarantulas are more fearsome in appearance than in actual bite. Take care though; they should not be handled because their hairs irritate skin. Amazon species include the world's biggest spider, *Theraphosa leblondii*, weighing 120g and with a legspan of 28cm. Recent work has shown tarantulas are major predators of tree-frogs, but the **Peruvian pinktoe** (*Avicularia urticans*) preys on moths. A number of tarantulas, the so-called **bird-eating spiders** (Avicularinae), also prey on tiny birds, stalking nests or by ambush. Scholars at first dismissed early reports (Bates *et al*) of spiders big enough to eat birds as clearly the stuff of legend. These species (*Avicularia avicularia*) are, in Bates' words 'large and hairy' with 'coarse grey reddish hairs'. His Victorian distaste shows through in his description of the spider's kill, in which one of the birds killed 'lay underneath the body of the spider... and was smeared with the filthy liquor or saliva exuded by the monster'. Whatever Bates' feelings, these are impressive creatures.

Some small spiders are dangerous. These have cytolytic venom that dissolves cells. This causes cells to break down and die, hindering the healing process. Untreated, the wound spreads and ulcerates. A few spiders are life-threatening, but only two or three species out of tens of thousands. One of these species is considered the world's most venomous spider: the **Brazilian wandering spider** (*Phoneutria fera*), which lives in the thatch or walls of jungle huts.

A group of spiders not commonly known to bite people are the **hunting** or **wolf spiders**. These occur throughout the world and hunt by ambush or chance encounters. The **funnel spiders** (Depleuridae) produce neatly spun funnel-shaped webs between clumps of grass, against tree trunks or among leaf litter.

These are the spiders' lairs. Here they wait patiently for feckless insects to wander by. Then, almost too fast to see, the spider leaps out, grabs the prey, injects it with venom and drags it back into the funnel, all in one swift, smooth move.

Other arachnids

Despite its large size, about 10–15cm long, and terrifying appearance, the **tailless whip scorpion** (Amblypygidae) is all bluff. The beast is harmless and lacks a sting. Fearsome in looks and reputation is the **scorpion**, an arachnid of which dozens of species are known from South America. They are generally animals of drier climates, but many are rainforest inhabitants. (See page 93.)

Millipedes and centipedes

These arthropods (Myriapoda) look like armoured caterpillars. **Millipedes** are usually round in cross-section, shaped like a cylinder. In contrast, a common rainforest species (*Barydesmus* spp), greyish and up to 13cm long, is flattened, with horizontal projections from each segment. Millipedes have two pairs of legs per segment of which there may be as many as 60. They feed on dead vegetation. If threatened they eject an unpleasant-smelling fluid and roll up but they are harmless.

Centipedes (*Scolopendra* spp) are flattened in cross-section and have only one pair of legs per segment. They prey on small insects and other invertebrates. Most are harmless but some species have a venomous and painful bite.

WATERWORLD

The Amazon is so big that early explorers thought it was actually a giant lake. Now we know it's the world's biggest river with the most diverse freshwater fauna on the planet. There are at least 2,000 fish species with perhaps a thousand more to be described. By comparison, about 150 fish species are known from all of Europe's rivers.

Aquatic mammals
Freshwater dolphins

Although Amazon dolphins do not take as much interest in people as their open-water relatives, they occasionally tolerate humans and often allow people close. To this day, these fun-loving creatures thrive in the Amazon, largely left alone by man who generally has taboos against hunting or eating dolphin. However, fishermen occasionally do kill them by accident or deliberately when dolphins become entangled in nets.

Worldwide, there are five freshwater cetaceans of which the Amazon has two, found in most lowland rainforest rivers and lakes. They are smaller than their marine relatives, but are still formidable predators. River dolphins prefer clearwater rivers, but they also roam blackwater rivers, being least common in murky whitewater rivers. Size, colour and behaviour distinguish the two.

Natives call the **pink dolphin** (*Inia geoffrensis*) *bôto* or *bufeo colorado*. About 2.4m long and weighing around 160kg, it has a low dorsal ridge in place of a fin. The pink dolphin swims slowly while flat triangular pectoral fins guide it along the river bottom where it does most of its feeding, using

Pink river dolphin

RIVERINE ROMEOS

Like their ocean-dwelling cousins, Amazon dolphins are widely revered and respected. Because indigenous beliefs confer magical powers on the freshwater dolphins, they are not hunted and populations remain viable.

One such myth is that the dolphins temporarily leave the river while transformed into handsome men. Free to roam beyond the river they seduce young girls and then return to the river rather than face the responsibility of fatherhood. On this basis, freshwater dolphins are often blamed for unwanted pregnancies.

sonar to search for fish, crabs and turtles. According to experts, the dolphin stuns prey with sound bursts from the 'melon' organ in its bulging forehead. Pink dolphins are active day and night, and you will often see a bachelor male, or sometimes a family pod of three or four, swim by. When they leap, their body does not clear the water, giving the impression that they are less agile than their saltwater relatives.

Locally called *tucuxi*, the **grey dolphin** (*Sotalia fluviatilis*) is about 1.5m long and weighs 53kg. Tucuxis are pinkish when young and turn dark grey to black with adulthood, which can create a little confusion if you're trying to work out which Amazon dolphin you have seen. Greys are shaped more like a marine dolphin, with a curved dorsal fin and small pectoral fins. When they jump, their bodies clear the water, reminiscent of marine park performances. Grey dolphin feed mainly on fast-swimming fish close to the surface, reducing competition for feeding between the two species. Found throughout the Amazon and in the lower reaches of the Orinoco, grey dolphins also venture along the Atlantic coast of South America.

Manatee

Once forgotten by all except lonely sailors who mistook them for mermaids, recent attention to its imminent extinction has put the unphotogenic manatee in the limelight. As most Florida residents know, these huge, gentle herbivores are in a highly precarious situation.

There are two species (*Sirenia*) in tropical America. The **West Indian manatee** (*Trichechus manatus*) is found in coastal waters from southern Florida to the mouth of the Amazon, while the strictly freshwater **Amazon manatee** (*Trichechus inunguis*) is found only in the river basin.

Weighing up to 500kg and 2.7m long, the manatee is the largest Amazon mammal, and wins no beauty contests. Its squarish, whiskered muzzle bears nostrils at the top to allow breathing while the barrel-shaped body and head remain mostly submerged. A powerful paddle-like tail moves it ponderously through the water. Manatees are purely vegetarian and consume over 45kg a day of water weeds. In the absence of manatee grazing, water weeds quickly clog rivers and streams.

Unlike the dolphin, no taboos protect the manatee. Docile, slow-moving and conspicuously swimming just under the surface, it is easy hunting. To make it even easier, floating dung leaves a convenient trail. When hunted the peacefully munching beast is harpooned from a boat. Panicked and hurt, it swims off with the harpoonist hanging on. The huge bulk of the manatee has strength to tow its burden for an hour or more. As the manatee tires, the hunter closes in and stuffs the nostrils with wooden plugs. Suffocation is slow but certain. Packed in old petrol cans, manatee meat keeps for years, preserved in its own oil. Most is sold at market. A high price is a strong incentive to hunt, an opportunity a poor *rivereño* cannot afford to pass up.

The long-term outlook for wild manatees is not positive and both species are endangered (CITES I). Despite this, their hunting remains virtually uncontrolled.

Otters

The **southern river otter** (*Lutra longicaudis*) is dark brown above, with creamy-coloured underparts. It feeds on fish and crustaceans in clear rivers and fast streams, and can be found throughout the Amazon and Orinoco Basin. The **Brazilian** or **giant otter** (*Pteronura brasiliensis*) is the world's

Giant otter

largest freshwater otter, up to 34kg and 1.9m long. Highly social and gregarious, their loud playful antics do little to disguise their whereabouts from hunters. Formerly common and widespread, both species are endangered (CITES I) as a result of hunting for their pelts and their supposed competition for fishing stocks.

Crab-eating racoon

The only aquatic member of its family, the **crab-eating racoon** (*Procyon cancrivorus*) resembles its North American relative with a black mask over the eyes, ringed tail and similar body proportions. With a quite different lifestyle, the crab-eater is specialised to prey on crabs and other aquatic animals including fish, molluscs and amphibians.

Water opossum

One of 40 or so opossum species, the **water opossum** or **yapok** (*Chironectes minimus*) is the only one to have an aquatic lifestyle, feeding on fish, crabs and insects. Curiously it has exceptionally fast gestation: 12–13 days, the shortest of any mammal, of course facilitated by marsupial biology which produces young born at an earlier stage than placental mammals.

Aquatic reptiles

Tropical freshwater is ideal for aquatic reptiles. The two main groups are crocodilians and turtles. Their Amazon representatives are unique and mostly endemic species, evolved from ancestors isolated when South America became an island continent.

Caiman

Among the most impressive Amazon reptiles are **caiman**, the South American crocodilians. The four species differ in size, enabling them to use different ecological resources and so co-exist in the same habitat. All caiman eat fish, but turtles, frogs, other reptiles and anything else that gets in the way are also suitable prey. Throughout the Amazon, populations are under severe pressure due to hunting.

The largest is the **black caiman** (*Melanosuchus niger*), an awesome creature at its full-grown length of 6.1m. Bates was impressed with the 'cunning, cowardice and ferocity of this reptile…' but admiration was not among his feelings as he considered 'the enormous gape of their mouths…' believing 'the uncouth shape of their bodies makes a picture of unsurpassable ugliness'. This seems somewhat unenlightened in our conservation-minded age, but it shows how much our attitudes differ from those of the first naturalists to explore the Amazon.

On night boat rides you will probably see the red eyeshine of the **common** or **spectacled caiman** (*Caiman crocodilus*). They grow up to 2.5m, but the majority are considerably smaller. If you manage to see one close up, you will see that the bony ridges above the eyes convey a bespectacled appearance. These caiman are found throughout the Amazon and Orinoco Basins. They lay communally on the same beach. Caiman lay 30 to 60 eggs at a time – food to attract many predators. Egg mortality is high (50–80%) and even after hatching, juveniles have a slim chance of making it to adulthood. Wading birds and especially tegu lizards take their toll, with perhaps just one or two individuals in a clutch surviving to adulthood. Two species of **dwarf caiman** (*Paleosuchus* spp) are widespread in Amazonia.

River turtles

An abundance of ideal habitats and food makes the Amazon perfect for *tortugas*. The 13 Amazon species of river turtle are all side-necked turtles, so-called because they retract their head sideways into the shell. This primitive group's fossils date back to the Cretaceous period over 140 million years ago. Up until recently, river turtles were abundant. Traditionally, Indian tribes kept turtles and farmed them for their oil, eggs and meat. Their abundance was still notable when Bates travelled the Amazon:

> Cardozo... could not turn the [turtles] on their backs fast enough so that a great many clambered out and got free again. However, three boatloads, or about eighty [turtles] were secured... When the canoes had been twice filled, we desisted...

As Bates discovered, turtle is 'a most appetising dish', a fact that has led to their downfall. Turtles still occur in many parts of the Amazon, but are rare in most places. Even where common, they tend to be shy and you'll catch but a glimpse of a trio lined up on a rock or branch before they see you and quietly slip into the water.

Your best bet to see turtles in the wild is in remote, protected areas, with lots of lakes and rivers. Where left alone, they may even come to tolerate human presence, allowing you close enough to take a good photograph. At La Selva Lodge in Ecuador turtles regularly bask on branches protruding from the nearby lake.

Largest representative is the **giant river turtle** (*Podocnemis expansa*), over 0.9m long and weighing 75kg. This species has potential to be farmed for meat, eggs and shell – projected meat yields far exceed those of conventional cattle ranching. Sadly, these marvellous prehistoric creatures continue to be over-exploited in the wild. Each of the four *Podocnemis* turtles are listed as threatened (CITES II).

The bizarre-looking **matamata** (*Chelys fimbriata*) has a neck longer than its backbone. The snout is long and tube-like to act as a snorkel. Its carapace has pointed peaks on the top – camouflage to hide it among floating leaves in wait of prey. It feeds on fish by opening its wide mouth suddenly to draw in small fish like a vacuum cleaner. Related species include *charapita de aguajal* (*Batrachemys raniceps*), a small, nocturnal piscivorous turtle, and the **twistneck turtle** or *asna charapa* (*Platemys platycephala*).

Fabulous fishes

Over 2,000 endemic Amazon fish species have been catalogued – making the Amazon Basin the most diverse freshwater fauna in the world – and scientists estimate as many as two thousand more remain to be described.

From relatively few ancestors Amazon fishes evolved and diversified into a multitude of niches in a process called *adaptive radiation*. Around 80% are characins, the largest family of neotropical freshwater fish. To these belong such groups as catfish, lungfish, gaudy aquarium fishes and the less alluring but more famous piranha.

Characins
Piranha
If we were to believe B-movies, we would think there is only one type of Amazon fish, the deadly and vicious piranha. In fact some 25 species of piranha lurk in lowland rivers: a few are specialist carnivores, one type feeds exclusively on fish fins and some are even vegetarian. Piranha attacks have injured people, but records show not one fatality. Nevertheless, piranhas partly deserve their reputation as aggressive, ferocious fish – proven by the number of fishermen in the Amazon missing toes and fingers.

Red-bellied piranha

The most famous piranha is the **red-bellied** or *paña roja* (*Pygocentrus nattereri*), which ranks as the world's most dangerous freshwater fish. Its best-known attribute is extremely sharp teeth, serrated and triangular, just like a shark's, but no more than 6mm long. Red-bellied piranhas grow to 20–23cm and are diamond-shaped with a silvery back and an orange-red underside. Very easy to catch with a piece of raw meat, and with seemingly hundreds of tiny bones, piranha are an acquired taste – locals consider them delicious and eat them often. **White piranha** or *pana blanca* (*Serrasalmus rhombeus*) lack the red belly.

In blackwater lakes some piranha attain impressive size. The biggest species, the **black piranha** (*S. manueli*) reaches almost half a meter. Luckily these are not flesh-eaters, but instead patiently wait for fallen fruits. Indeed, most species feed only on floating fruits, berries or insects.

Piranha detect the splash of potential food as it falls into a stream or lake and smell it in the water. They attack prey only if it is bleeding and moving erratically. The famous flesh-stripping abilities depend on fish numbers, carcass size and season. Low water-levels are likely to reduce food availability and increase competition. Indeed, tourists fishing for piranha invariably catch more in the low water season than those fishing during high water.

Electric eel
Unlike the piranha, a number of documented cases report fatalities caused by the infamous **electric eel** (*Electrophorus electricus*). This 'stunning' fish discharges a shock of up to 1,000 volts to knock out or kill prey; also an effective defence against predators. The current is usually between 0.5 and 0.75 amperes, non-lethal for humans, but powerful enough to cause temporary paralysis. As most encounters are in water, the immobilised victim is drowned rather than electrocuted. Rarely encountered, the fish is a bottom-dweller in sluggish channels and streams, although surfacing every now and then to breathe air, or rather absorb it through specialised buccal filaments.

Able to move backwards is the **knife fish** (*Gymnotus* sp), a relative of the electric eel and an electro-navigator but lacking a significant current.

Parasitic catfishes: leech-fishes, water vampires and living arrows
The notorious candiru family (Trichomycteridae) are small, scaleless fish. A few species are free-living but others have various obnoxious lifestyles. Some attach

themselves to other fish, using spines on their gill openings, and rasp away at scales and flesh like fishy leeches. Half a dozen or more wriggling, slimy appendages infest an afflicted fish. Another candiru lives in the gill filaments of larger fish, vampirically feeding off the blood supply.

Most notorious of this group is *Vandellia cirrhosa*. This extremely thin fish normally dwells within another fish's waste tract but is believed to wriggle up urogenital and, some say, other orifices of human swimmers. Apparently attracted by the warmth of the urine, it zooms inside the body opening, whereupon its sharp spines project into the tender flesh. Stuck like a living arrow, the fish is only removable by surgery. In areas where vandellia are present natives wear protective garments and menstruating women do not swim as they believe blood attracts the fish. Attacks are virtually unheard of but just to be safe, wear a bathing suit and don't pee in the water while swimming.

Fruit-eating fish
Flooded forests are important habitat for fruit-eating fish. **Tambaqui** (*Colossoma macropomum*) is said to be the best-flavoured of fishes and has been over-fished, especially around Manaus. This and other frugivorous fish disperse the seeds of numerous tree species, but we can only guess at the consequences of their loss. Efforts are underway in Iquitos to investigate this species' suitability for aquaculture – a development sure to relieve pressure on wild populations.

Other catfishes: giant fish, fish of gold and talking fish
Catfish make up the majority of neotropical characins. Most of the hundred or more species are bottom-feeders, and use their long whiskers (barbels) to search the river mud for worms, crustaceans and snails.

The largest catfish, and one of Amazonia's biggest fish with a scientific name to match, is *Brachyplatystoma filamentosum*. Individuals grow up to 3m long. Good to eat and a popular catch their huge jaws can easily wound the careless fisherman. But size is no indication of danger where catfish are concerned. Small **squeakers** referred to as *cunchi* include *Pimelodella cristata*, *Pimelodus pictus*, and *P. maculatus*. These squeak when caught and possess long, toxic spines on the dorsal and pectoral fins.

Not all Amazon fish are horrible nasty creatures. The **dorado** (*B. flavicans*) is a common catfish, reaching a metre in length, coloured pale gold along its flanks with a silvery back. It is a staple food fish for people along the river, and often served at tourist lodges and riverboats. Species in the Doradidae family have fat bodies and four to six barbels. The **talking catfish** (*Acanthodorus spinosissimus*) makes grunting sounds in and out of water. Aquarium species include the **arch-backed catfish** (*Corydroras* sp) and the **hassar** (*Callichthyes*).

In fish markets you may see the **suckermouth catfish** or *carachama* of which the commonest is *Pterygoplichthys marmoratus*, dark brown and up to 30cm long. Its heavy scales bear ornate horns and each pectoral fin has a long curved, toothed bony projection. Also popular with fishermen is the thorny catfish (*Megalodorus uranoscopus*). The fish probably uses them as anti-predator defence; locals use them in handicrafts. Other heavily armoured catfish include *Plecostomus,* a popular aquarium species.

Living gems of murky *igapo* waters, **jewel tetras** (*Hyphassobrycon* spp) are among the most sought-after aquarium fish. Under lights these tiny specimens glow brilliant primary colours, giving rise to names like **cardinal tetra**, **neon tetra** and **glo-lite tetra**.

Shaped like a miniature barracuda, the **dog fish** (*Rhaphidon vulpinus*), 30–45cm long, is coloured silvery-yellow and possesses two long canine-like teeth. It uses these weapons to stab prey, typically other fish, up to half its size. Unrelated to small sharks of the same name found only in oceans, dog fish are often seen in a fisherman's catch or on sale at city fish markets.

Flying hatchet fish (*Carnegiella*) use their pectoral fins as wings to propel them through the air. This seems to be a defence against predatory fish but they will often fly high and far enough to land in a speeding canoe. Others behave equally strangely. The more sedate **headstanders** (*Abramites*) spend the majority of their lives with their tail up in the air, whereas **pencil fish** (*Poecilobrycon*) live mostly head-up.

Bony-tongued fish

Bony-tongued fish (Osteoglossidae), with fossils dating back to the Cretaceous era, are South America's most primitive piscines, now represented by relatively few species. Their diagnostic feature is a hard, stiff, bony tongue, stiff scales and dorsal and anal fins continuing almost to the tail.

Arapaima: armour-plated lung-fish

The Amazon boasts one of the world's largest freshwater fish, called **paiche** in Peru or **pirarucú** in Brazil (*Arapaima gigas*). Shaped like a huge pike they are predators of other fish. Specimens up to 4.6m long and weighing 250kg were known but this fish's huge size and tasty flesh have led to its demise. Most caught today are usually less than 2.5m and weigh no more than 90kg.

Their greenish-bronze scales turn white when removed. As big as your palm and hard as plastic, they evolved as armour plating against caiman or dolphin attack, and are ideal for decoration or jewellery. They also make a good nail file. Natives use arapaima's rough bony tongue as coarse-grade sandpaper.

A type of lung-fish, arapaima can breathe air if necessary. When water warms up, oxygen levels drop, which forces the fish to gulp air which is absorbed through a modified air bladder. Other lungfish use this ability to crawl across land when waters recede. Arapaima aestivate – they relinquish the fish lifestyle and hibernate through warm, dry periods. They burrow deep in mud, curl into a ball and stay cocooned until the water returns.

Arowana: mouth-breeding water monkeys

Many rainforest fish consume insect prey and hunt among the tendrils and roots of floating vegetation or rely on insects floating on the water's surface. The **water monkey**, locally called the *arowana* or *arauana* (*Osteoglossum bicirrhosum*), depends not on a chance meal to fall from overhanging vegetation: it jumps. Up to a metre long, it leaps a full body length out of the water to gulp unsuspecting meals perched on a leaf or branch. Given the opportunity it will catch small reptiles, birds or even baby sloths.

The arowana is a mouth brooder. After the eggs hatch, the male scoops the tiny larvae into his mouth to protect them. When the yolk-sac is consumed he releases fry for sporadic feeding and guides them back to safety by waving barbels on his lower jaw, a successful strategy to protect the young against natural predators. Human fishermen, who

Arowana

capture fry for sale to foreign aquaria, catch and behead breeding males for their conveniently packaged young. Predictably, arowana are a threatened species in the wild.

Cichlids

Cichlidae is an important family of tropical freshwater fish with some 150 species described from the Amazon. Many are commercially important either as food or sport fish, or for the aquarium trade.

Of greatest economic importance is the **peacock bass** (*Cichla ocellaris*), the biggest neotropical cichlid. Found in blackwater rivers, it grows to a length of 1m weighing up to 30kg, and is golden-yellow with black dorsal bars and a prominent eye-spot on the tail. Experiments show the eyespot redirects a predator's attack towards the tail where damage is less likely than an assault on the head. Other cichlids with eye-spots are **acarahuasú** (*Astronotus ocellatus*) and **tucunaré** or **oscar** (*C. monoculus, C. temensis*). Bates encountered the *tucunaré* along the Tapajós River. He notes it is 'a most delicious fish… esteemed by natives'.

Discus fish (*Symphysodon* spp) have a round, compressed body. Their attractive markings make them popular with aquarium hobbyists. Two species are found in tributaries of the main stream that provide parental care for their young by producing a mucus exuding through the skin on which the young feed.

Other Amazon fishes

The **leaf fish** (*Monocirrhus polyacanthus*) mimics a dead leaf floating on water. Drifting around, pointing downward, it preys on other fish as they swim by oblivious to the danger. A transparent tail and pectoral fins allow it to move without being detected.

Four-eyed
fish eye

Common in quiet streams with overhanging vegetation, the **four-eyed fish** (*Anableps*) is uniquely equipped to spot danger in or out of the water. Each eye is divided in two so one half is above water with the other half below.

Tiny **killifish** (*Cyprinodontei*) spend most of their lives as tough, drought-resistant eggs in shallow, ephemeral ponds. Some killifish have adapted to hatch, grow, mate, lay eggs and die in places where water persists for a mere two or three weeks. (And you think your life is hectic?)

Sting rays or **dasytid rays**, notably of the strictly freshwater genus *Potamotrygon*, are the only freshwater cartilaginous fishes (although sharks roam upriver from the ocean). The 'sting' is a venomous barbed fin at the base of the tail. Rays are bottom-dwellers, resting half-covered in sand on the beds of shallow rivers.

Aquatic arthropods

Tropical rivers, streams and lakes are among the least biologically explored habitats. Ecologists lament how few land arthropods are studied relative to their diversity, but forget there is a community of largely unknown species among the weeds and floating meadows. Who knows how many species are to be found? Lift up a mat of floating vegetation and you see water snails, diving beetles, water boatmen, aquatic stages of flying insects, paleomonid shrimp and other crustaceans.

Indigenous Tribes and Settlers

The Amazon is commonly referred to as one of the last frontiers of humanity, but the notion of an empty area devoid of people is a myth. True, the Amazon Basin is not packed with people, but neither is it empty. More than 20 million people live within its 7.3 million km² watershed. Indigenous tribes, rubber tappers, gold prospectors, cattle ranchers and forestry workers have made the headlines from time to time. But in the cities, life continues pretty much the same as in any city of the world.

Every person living in the Amazon Basin arrived there through migration, the majority of them in their own lifetimes. A consistent factor of these migrations is the adaptation of each group, within the limits of technologies and vision, to the environment. Some seem to manage a little better than others.

ORIGINS

Experts generally agree that the original inhabitants of South America arrived from Asia via North and Central America, crossing the Bering Strait during the last ice age, around 22,000 years ago. As they migrated further south, tribal groups adapted their lifestyles to the wide variety of environments encountered. The first arrivals to the Amazon Basin reached the open plains and southern regions 12,000 years ago, having followed the line of the Andes southwards before heading east through modern-day Bolivia. Stone projectile points excavated near Monte Alegre, Brazil, indicate Amazonian populations were established at least 11,000 years ago.

Archaeology is difficult in the Amazon Basin. Organic remains rot quickly in the warm, wet climate and fieldwork, often in remote areas, is difficult to support and sustain over long periods of time. Piecing together fragments found so far, by 10,000BC communities were well-established along the Amazon main stream when the core languages of the region began to fragment and diversify. The warlike Tupi pushed north from their Paraguayan homelands to contest the central plains of Brazil. Preferring a quiet life, the Gê-speaking Indians dispersed from the central plains and moved west towards the heart of the Amazon, allowing the Tupi to occupy territory as far north as the Amazon main stream. By the time the Gê moved into the Amazon, Carib and Arawak tribes had long since settled in the region from their Caribbean homelands having followed the coastline of South America to the river's mouth. Warfare and consequent migration resulted in distribution of groups throughout the Basin.

But in this huge and complex area little is certain. An alternative route for migration to the Basin, and one that is more widely accepted, is the Andean route. According to this theory, Arawak tribes went overland, migrating from their Central American homelands through what are now Colombia and Venezuela. Other groups migrated from Ecuador down the Napo River and other tributaries into the Amazon Basin.

It is easy to see how migration was the dominant vehicle for change. Using the rivers as highways, even today village communities and families can collect their belongings and rapidly move from one location to another. With different Indian tribes advancing and retreating, groups readily fragmentated and dispersed.

Although migratory patterns are uncertain, the existence of trade and warfare between the Indians of the Amazon and those of the mountains is beyond dispute. The eastern slopes of the Andes in Ecuador, Peru and Bolivia are littered with strategically located forts and trading posts. The oral history of the Incas mentions raiding parties by jungle Indians. The eastern quarter of the Inca Empire was called *Antisuyo* and its inhabitants were known as *Antis*; from where the Andes mountain range gets its name. The rainforest lowlands, even for the Incas, were considered impenetrable, so it was to the jungle that the last Inca fled when seeking protection from the invading Spanish.

When the Portuguese arrived the indigenous population of the Brazilian Amazon was between 1.5 and 7 million. Today across all Amazon countries the figure is below one million. Of the 2,000 different indigenous tribes that existed at the time, fewer than 400 remain.

Languages

The dominant languages of the Amazon Basin are Spanish and, in Brazil, Portuguese. Brought in by conquering European powers these languages are by far the most widespread.

In the Andes, Quechua was the *lingua franca* of the Inca Empire. As a result, even today Quechua is the dominant language among many people living in western Amazonia.

The number of indigenous languages in the Amazon reflects the diversity of ethnic groups. There are at least 170 known languages or dialects. The majority of dialects spoken by Brazilian Indians derive from one of four languages: Gê, Tupi, Carib and Arawak. The development of language families reflects the movements of respective groups. Gê- and Tupi-speaking Indians arrived from the south of Brazil and fought for domination of the coastal regions. The Tupi expanded faster than other tribes and pushed the less warlike Gê-speaking tribes further inland. The diversity of languages was increased further by Carib-speaking tribes, linguistically related to the original inhabitants of the Caribbean, and the arrival of Arawak tribes from Central and North America. While most indigenous languages are based on one or a combination of these four languages, in a few rare cases the language bears no relation to these core groups.

BELIEFS AND CUSTOMS

Many Indians are animists, believing that all living things possess a spirit. A complex hierarchy of spirits governs the natural world so hunting certain animals is taboo. Songs, chants and dances keep evil forces at bay and offer protection on hunting trips and safe passage when travelling.

Upsetting the balance can arouse vengeful spirits, who make themselves known in several ways. Dreams are an important medium of communication with the spirit world. They offer insight on an illness or prospects for a hunting expedition. Illness is usually blamed on malevolent spirits and may be caused by annoying the spirits, or a curse. Either way, healing comes with special songs, dances and herbal concoctions are administered by the tribe's shaman (spiritual healer).

Shamans can see the invisible magic darts that cause pain, curses and illness, a skill enhanced by the use of hallucinogens. Experience and strength determine a shaman's ability to defend his people against the darts of vengeful shamans from neighbouring villages. He spends his life building up an armoury of magic darts, each one equipped with special powers to deal with specific situations.

The effect of order and responsibility in the spirit world is reflected in daily life. Social interaction is highly ordered, relying heavily on ritual. Domestic life too is structured, with responsibilities clearly divided between the sexes. Men hunt, fish and build new homes; women tend the garden, prepare food, look after the children and manage the house.

In such a carefully ordered world, stepping over the line that constitutes responsible and acceptable behaviour demands revenge, usually resulting in raiding parties and death. As a result many Indian tribes have been described as aggressive and warlike. At a cursory level there often appears to be an excess of violence, but it is rarely violence for its own sake. A system of honour prevails and, when placed in context, there are usually complex and justified reasons for the warlike behaviour.

Life and death

Indians have a wide range of myths and legends to explain their place in the universe. The creation myths of different tribes usually reflect some part of the natural environment, if not from the area currently occupied then from a region lived in by earlier generations. Belief in the existence of an afterlife is common, but judgement on whether it is paradise varies greatly.

After giving birth women commonly have to observe taboos on eating certain foods. Furthermore, birth is often without the degree of care to which we are accustomed. Frequently, after the woman bears the infant, she immediately returns to her daily chores. For their part, the men protect the 'empty soul' from evil spirits, requiring their complete attention for several days.

Although young girls have a degree of sexual freedom, villages would not support an illegitimate child.

Infanticide was once widespread especially of female babies, if several same-sex babies were born concurrently, if twins were born or if a baby was handicapped.

Death too requires a flexible outlook to understand of some apparently bizarre practices. The Yanomami of Brazil and Venezuela cremate their dead, consuming the ashes several months later and thus enabling the dead to continue their lives through the living. The Achuar of Ecuador bury their dead but dispel the spirit of the dead from their world and their memories. The French anthropologist Philippe Descola explains that this 'reflects the notion that the living cannot be truly living if the dead are not truly dead'. For other groups the spirit travels to a village in the sky where the spirits of all the dead live. The journey confronts the spirit with dangers so he is buried with his bow and arrow.

But once the celestial village has been reached, the spirit requires no further nourishment or assistance. The rivers and forests, without fish or game, are there for nothing more than the memory of the soul as it dances to the rhythm of eternity.

INDIGENOUS TRIBES TODAY

Tribal peoples living in the Amazon today are descendants of the original inhabitants. Present population is just a fraction of the number before Europeans arrived, although some tribes are increasing (see Box *Indigenous populations today*). The degree of assimilation into the dominant culture varies widely. Some tribes have disappeared completely while a few remain virtually unchanged.

Societal structure

The Yanomami are arguably the best-known Amazon tribe that remain unassimilated. Numbering around 20,000, they live in an area bridging the borders

INDIGENOUS POPULATIONS TODAY

It is impossible to obtain universally agreed figures on how many indigenous groups live in the Amazon and the size of their populations. Organisations and governments have different definitions of what constitutes an ethnic group, based on linguistic or cultural differences. Some authors divide ethnic groups into smaller groups. National census figures are unreliable, and in some countries do not even require statement of ethnic group. When population figures are compiled they are usually best 'guestimates'.

A widely agreed figure puts the Indian population at just under 700 thousand. Current populations vary dramatically in size ranging from less than a hundred to over 40,000.

The largest ethnic groups in the Amazon are:

Ethnic group	Population	Location
Chiquitano	40,000	Bolivia
Kampa	31,919	Peru, Brazil
Mojeño	30,000	Bolivia
Achuar/Shuar	30,000	Peru/Ecuador
Tukano	27,000	Colombia, Brazil
Tikuna	25,637	Brazil, Colombia, Peru
Arguarana	25,000	Peru
Shipibo	20,000	Peru
Yanomami	19,727	Brazil, Venezuela
Makuxi/Makushi	15,132	Brazil, Guyana
Wapishana	13,467	Brazil, Guyana

Although disease, encroachment of tribal lands and violence against Indian groups has been highlighted in recent years, comparison of figures between 1970 and 1990 show that Indian populations have, as a general trend, increased over the last twenty years. Explaining the increase is difficult. Significant improvements in health services are rare and inconsistent across the region and environmental conditions tend to have deteriorated. One suggestion is that groups have now acquired resistance to imported disease.

The number of populations that are disappearing is relatively small – some 6% of the total. Some of these groups, such as the Pakaguara of Bolivia, will soon disappear.

This information has been taken from an EC-funded report looking at the state of indigenous populations living in rainforest areas. Data on population statistics for Amazonian Indian tribes varies widely.

of Brazil and Venezuela. They inhabit highland *terra firme* forest, living communally in *shabonos* – large huts inhabited by several extended families.

Life of the Yanomami is based on individual independence, rights and obligations. A careful balance between these three core values sustains a society that speaks out against wrong and promotes sharing. Such egalitarianism requires no central leadership so the authority of chiefs is resorted to only in times of conflict. When disagreements rise to unacceptable levels, defending self-respect is essential and may escalate, leading to permanent division of the community.

This social structure recurs in various guises throughout the Amazon. Yanomami society, which has been well-researched, offers a point of comparison to the varied lifestyles of other tribes.

Amazon tribes can broadly be divided into those like the Yanomami, who occupy *terra firme* rainforest above the floodplain, and those who live alongside the river in flooded forest (*várzea* or *igapo*).

Agricultural practices

Tribes in *terra firme* forest rely primarily on slash-and-burn agriculture for most of their food. Small plots, about half a hectare in size, are cleared with axes and machetes. Brush is then burned *in situ*. Large trees are chopped up for use as firewood. Fertilised by the ash, the garden is planted with the first round of crops. To ensure a constant food supply, crops that mature at different speeds are planted. Maize is ready to harvest in four months. Sweet potatoes, manioc, bananas and plantains are ready within a year. Palms take three years or more to become productive.

Plots are typically planted with one staple crop across 80% of the garden. Manioc is by far the most popular. Some tribes, such as the Yanomami and the Shipobo of Peru, prefer plantains. A few (including the Araweté of Brazil and the Amawaka of Peru/Brazil) choose maize.

The gardens need constant attention to keep weeds at bay and to prevent reclaiming by the forest and its malevolent spirits. After a few years, the soil's productivity falls and the community moves on. Heavy rain leaches and erodes the plot after clearing but left untended the forest soon returns. The plot regains the appearance of primary rainforest within 50 years but takes several hundred years to reach its original diversity.

After villagers leave the plot to be reclaimed by the forest, they return occasionally to harvest long-term crops. A community typically works a young plot, a mature plot and an old plot. In addition to cultivation, foraging for seasonal fruits, hunting and fishing provides food.

Agriculture is also extensively practised in *várzea* areas. Rice, beans, peppers and cocoa are planted in such a way to maximise benefits from the annual floods. Varieties of manioc mature in six months rather than twelve to optimise the shorter growing season forced by annual flooding.

The benefit of seasonal floods is annual renewal of soil fertility. Readily available fish, caiman, turtles, and birds, and hunting of mammals visiting the water's edge, reduces the reliance on cultivated food and increases the time between moves to new areas.

Before the Europeans arrived, *várzea* communities living close to the Amazon main stream raised fish and turtles in pens. Social interactions were dominated by seasonal flooding. Conflict was highest during annual floods when food stocks were low and warring parties would often raid neighbouring villages for food. In times of plenty, *várzea* habitat was capable of supporting large populations.

Indian tribes in the Amazon today rely on a mix of agriculture, hunting and fishing. A drop in wildlife populations has increased the importance of agriculture in recent years so that hunting and fishing in general can provide no more than half the dietary needs of a tribe.

Social groups

Social structure among Amazon tribes varies greatly with some sharing common features. The Yanomami live in communal structures called *yanos* or *shabonos* that are home to the whole village of between 25 and several hundred people. Several families live within each dwelling and social interaction is an essential part of life. The huge 'o' shaped houses, thatched with palm leaves, enclose a wide open space. The space is reserved for dancing and ceremonies, with festivals often lasting for days. Festivals are essential to maintaining a sense of community.

Other tribes choose smaller structures. The Achuar of Ecuador use individual family dwellings and the head of the house takes two or three wives with other men occasionally living in the house.

Social groups vary from settled villages with large numbers of people and elaborate dwellings, to nomads living in bands of 30 to 40 and moving every few days without the need for permanent houses.

Dwellings built with forest products provide shelter from heavy rains, hot sun and seasonal floods. Tall, straight tree-trunks are ideal for sides of buildings, and stilts raise houses above the flood level.

As many as 20 different tree species are used to construct a traditional house, without using a single nail. Leaves of the thatch palm or *irapay* (*Lepidocaryum tessmannii*) provide palm fronds for roofing. Split down the middle rib they are doubled over and then laid pointing downwards on parallel roof beams.

Simple housing suits the subsistence life led by most forest dwellers. People usually move to a different place long before their organic house becomes affected by termites and fungi. More often a settlement is vacated due to floods or declines in the yields of crops and game. When it is time to move, the old house is left behind and another constructed in a new site from nearby materials. A palm-thatch stilt house may last up to ten years before returning to the forest whence it came.

Living off the land

Indigenous groups live in apparent harmony with the surrounding habitat. Hunting and foraging upset the ecological balance of the rainforest, but the smaller population size has a reduced impact on the rainforest from which it is easier to recover.

Hunting

The work of men, hunting is carried out primarily with a bow and arrow. The bows are made from the strong, flexible wood of palms, with bowstrings fashioned from braided palm fibres. Arrows are made from cane, found in the wild or grown in the garden, fletched with primary feathers of birds. Bows and arrows are generally used to shoot terrestrial game, such as rodents, deer, tapir and peccary, and arboreal game including monkeys and birds. They have even been adapted for the water species including fish, turtles and caiman.

Blowpipes are used throughout the Amazon and are particularly common in the western Amazon although guns are slowly, but increasingly, being used. Over nine different species of plant are used in the construction of blowpipes. The darts are made from slivers of wood of the inayuga palm (*Maximiliana venatorum*). Down from kapok (*Ceiba* spp) pods is wrapped around the base to create an airtight seal. Bags for carrying the curare-tipped darts are made from fibre palm (*Astrocaryum chambira*) and chonta (*Euterpe* spp).

Hunting itself is carried out in a number of ways. Men may go on short solitary hunting expeditions. Dawn or dusk, when birds and animals are most active, are the favoured times for the hunt. Silent stalking or mimicking bird or monkey calls are advanced techniques used by skilful hunters.

Hunting expeditions that last several hours or even days require careful planning and support. As most Indian groups live communally, hunting doubles up as an opportunity to spend time with a partner. The pair follow the sounds,

CURARE

The Indian hunter needs years of experience to learn how to use the blowpipe as a highly efficient method of killing birds and mammals. But the tiny darts shot out of the blowpipe's barrel seem incapable of killing. The blowpipe's efficacy lies in the curare that is smeared on the dart's tip.

The dart is honed to a fine point that readily pierces the skin. Upon entering the bloodstream, highly bioactive ingredients in the curare relax muscles and induce death by preventing the heart and lungs from working. The immobilised animal falls from the rainforest canopy enabling the hunter easily to retrieve his prize – wasteful hunting is sure to annoy vengeful spirits.

Exact numbers are unknown, but at least a couple of hundred plant toxins are used in the various forms of curare used throughout the Amazon. Colombian Indians use at least 75 plant species in preparing curare. The plants' bark and wood, notably from the liana Strychnos toxifera, are boiled down to a viscous resin. The poison is most potent when it is slightly bitter – Indians assess the quality by directly tasting the product.

Western doctors have used the muscle relaxing properties of curare derivatives in a number of ways: for surgical operations and to relieve paralysis, multiple sclerosis, lockjaw, epilepsy and Parkinson's disease.

tracks and droppings of animals. With experience comes the ability to differentiate between animal spoors, and close examination reveals how recently the animal was in the area, also whether it was feeding or just passing through. Guans and curassow, along with macaws, parrots, toucans and doves, are common prey and monkeys are widely hunted. Peccary and tapir are the most sought after terrestrial animals.

The introduction of hunting dogs has added a new dimension, enabling a hunting couple to tackle larger prey that previously required hunting in large groups. In some groups the breeding and care of hunting dogs is the women's responsibility, with the performance of a woman's pack directly reflecting her status. Women are responsible for butchering the larger animals making it easier to carry the meat home in simple baskets made *in situ* from forest plants.

Prior to the arrival of missionaries, most cultures were polygamous. An invitation to go hunting showed favour to a chosen wife creating an opportunity for intimacy away from the communal home.

Groups of hunters normally participate in hunts for peccary and other herd animals. With team work the herd can be trapped, increasing the chance of killing several animals. Danger from the aggressive peccaries is also less for people within a group than for the solitary hunter.

Fishing

The most widespread means of catching fish is with nets, although poisons are also used. The roots of the *barbasco* (*Lonchocarpus*) plant are pounded into a thick, white liquid. The fluid is then released into a river that has been blocked off downstream. Stupefied, but not dead, the fish are picked out of the water as they float towards the barrage. The mild toxin in *barbasco* only temporarily affects the fish so causes no permanent damage to fish that are not caught and, importantly, is not toxic to people.

The use of ichthyotoxic plants is widespread throughout the Amazon but especially in the smaller rivers of the Andean foothills. Fishing expeditions are most

HEAD-HUNTERS

Head-hunters are as much part of Amazon lore as giant snakes and vicious piranhas. The practice has long been banned in Peru and Ecuador, where it was formerly practised by the Achuar/Shuar tribal groups. These inhabitants of the upper Marañon watershed were the most feared head-hunters although other tribes performed the rite.

Headhunting was widely written about but little understood. When discovered, the ritual was taken out of context by sensationalist film-makers who portrayed frenzied savages immobilising victims with deadly blow darts, and viciously slicing off heads to shrink at weird cannibal rites. All of this is pure fiction.

In fact, the reason for headhunting revolves around the spirit world. Indians believe the soul resides within the head which is beautiful and revered. The body is merely a vessel for the head. To own an enemy's head is therefore to possess his soul and use its power… if you know how.

In 1960, Jack Walker went to the headwaters of the Santiago and Pastaza rivers in Ecuador to live for some two years in an Achuar village, where he underwent the rituals to become a fully-fledged Achuar warrior. His accounts give one perspective on their rituals, taboos and sacred procedures.

First, blow darts are for hunting game and not to be used on humans, as the enemy must be nobly killed with hand weapons. The shrinking process is straightforward, requiring the removal of all fat and muscle from the head by boiling. What remains of the head is filled with hot sand which begins to contract and harden as water is removed from the tissues. The victor must conduct interminable magical rites to control the victim's soul resident in the head. The eyes and mouth are sewn shut to imprison the soul in the head, as it would otherwise haunt the possessor's dreams. Long periods of celibacy and isolation are also necessary.

Three years of incantations, rituals and potion-making must pass before the head is fully empowered as a magic fetish.

Complexity and risk in headhunting rituals deterred tribes from actively seeking victims, and taboos affect whose head can actually be chosen to make into a trophy. A head can only be taken as an act of revenge and, although the subject must be a member of a local tribe, the individual cannot be personally known.

A person whose relative dies by weapon or witchcraft is justified in seeking vengeance and only the murderer's head can be taken and shrunk. Thus, headhunting was a ritual which served as a social control, apparently rare even before it was actively suppressed.

common at times of low water. Virtually all Indian groups that have fish in their diet use poisons. Several are adept users of harpoons or bow and arrow, especially in sluggish rivers where low oxygen levels force fish to the surface to gulp air.

Gathering

The impression that the jungle is a Garden of Eden with fruits hanging from the boughs of every tree is common – but wrong. Wandering through the forest will not produce impressive yields of fruit. But gathering is a crucial activity for Indian societies. In addition to seasonal plant foods, wild honey and eggs, edible insects such as palm grubs are harvested, as well as shellfish. Plants for medicine and poisons for hunting are also collected. Indeed, Indians use forest products for virtually all their daily needs: weapons, the structure and roof of dwellings, rafts and boats, basket-making materials, dyes, fibres, handles for tools and clay for pots.

Clothing

Religious zealots in Amazonia saw the absence of clothes as savagery rather than innocence. For many Indian groups, with limited or reduced contact with the outside world, clothing is replaced by adornments made from bird feathers, palm and grass fibres.

Certain types of cloth are also used for ceremonies or dances. The Bora of Peru wear skirts made of bark cloth which comes from a fig tree called *chuchuara* (*Ficus yoponensis*). Yagua on the other hand, wear 'grass skirts' and other accoutrements made from chambira palm leaves, shredded into long fibres.

Some *várzea* communities encountered by the early Spanish and Portuguese, in particular those of the Omagua upriver from the main stream's confluence with the Rio Negro, were reported to grow cotton and were recognised for their weaving skills.

Dyes are used for painting cloth and baskets, as well as body decorations used at festivals. Juice pressed from the fruit of the genipa tree makes a deep blue-black colour, while orange-red colours come most often from urucum seeds (*Bixa orellana*) which provide annatto used as food colouring in Western foods such as margarine and cheese.

Feathers from brightly coloured birds, including macaws and toucans, are used to create dramatic head-dresses bound together using plant fibres and beeswax.

Flutes fashioned from bamboo or from the hollow leg-bones of animals provide music for ceremonies. The maraca is made from a small gourd filled with seeds or pebbles, and wooden drums are widespread.

Material wealth

Recent anthropological studies have contributed to the view of Indian as materially poor, but rich in ingenuity. Hence, from rainforest materials a basket can hastily be assembled if the hunting trip turns out to be successful. With the bare minimum of material goods, Indian groups exist comfortably at subsistence level working for about three or four hours a day.

Further reading

Our generalisation of indigenous tribes belies the subtlety and complexity of Indian life in the Amazon. For a deeper understanding of Indian culture consult the books that report details of individual Indian groups. Several give considerable insight and are good reading for an Amazon trip. (See *Appendix 3*.)

WAVES OF SETTLERS

The first European forays to Brazil were by the Portuguese along the southeast Atlantic coast close to Illhéus and present-day Salvador. This is where the earliest colonisation began, around 1530, because ocean currents and trade winds made approaching the mouth of the Amazon directly from Europe difficult. As pressure on these lands grew, colonists pushed north closer to the mouth.

Early encounters with Indians relied on bartering metal tools and beads in return for precious *pau do brasil* or brazilwood, used to produce valuable reddish dyes for sale in Europe. As Indian communities were decimated by contact with European diseases, the need for more 'workers' to clear land and work on farms became apparent. With time the barter system was replaced by slavery.

THE INDIAN PHARMACY

The potential of the rainforest as a medical pharmacy seems infinite. Whether you choose to believe in or try any of the medical concoctions available depends on your outlook and condition at the time. Use of ichthyotoxic plants for fishing and the removal of toxins from manioc are just two examples that show sophisticated knowledge accumulated over generations.

Indigenous remedies tackle a wide range of maladies including bug bites, back pain, diarrhoea, intestinal parasites – and many more. Given that quinine, until recently the primary defence against malaria, comes from the Amazon, it is reasonable to assume that other medicinal breakthroughs are waiting to be made, research and funding permitting. Ethnobotanists are certain of the need to explore the rainforests and the minds of the shamans to garner what information remains.

One of the more widely known products of the rainforest is hallucinatory drugs. In some tribes only shaman or elders consume the sacred drug. In most, only men are permitted to partake. Used for ritual purposes the hallucinogen induces vivid hallucinations which assist in experiencing the spirit world. The shaman communicates with spirits to prophesy or divine, protecting the tribe against sickness, making hunters alert and discovering the identity of enemies.

There are several different plant genera recognised as having hallucinogenic properties. The best known is *ayahuasca* or the vine of the soul (*Banisteriopsis caapi*), common in the western Amazon. Pieces of stem are cut up, ground and boiled as the main ingredient of the powerful brew used by the shaman to reach a state of altered consciousness.

Ayahuasca frees the soul from corporeal confinement, to wander and return at will. Ingestion of the brew causes nausea and vomiting. With intoxication

---

With the arrival and settling of the Spanish on the western coast of South America from the 1540s, exploration had focused on the search for El Dorado. The explorers didn't know whether El Dorado even existed, but the huge quantities of gold taken from the Incas was insufficient to quench the lust of the conquistadors.

Early forays into the Amazon did little to dispel the rumours of El Dorado. During the first descent of the river by Orellana the expedition encountered tribes who told tales of great cities laden with gold. Whether the Indian yarns were based on fact or simply a way to ensure the quick movement downstream was not important; they simply added fuel to the fire.

Orellana's descent took place in 1542, several years after the Portuguese of the eastern coast had fully embraced slavery of the indigenous peoples for agricultural production. Among large indigenous populations along the main stream, rumours of increasingly unwelcome visitors from foreign lands spread up and down the river, its tributaries and inland to smaller settlements.

While El Dorado and women tribes lived on only in the deepest recesses of the European mind, the heavily populated banks of the rivers were to produce a new wealth to fund Portuguese expansion through Brazil. The labour of the Indians and the fruits of their land were essential to the success of European colonisation, as sure as if the blood of the Indians had been gold itself.

Sickness and disease

Early chroniclers were surprised at large numbers of Indians and villages found along the Amazon River and wondered how the land was capable of supporting so comes power of prophecy, divination, sorcery and healing. Frequently, the shaman will see overpowering visions, including attacks from huge snakes and jaguars, which humble him as a mere man.

From ayahuasca, chemists have isolated several active compounds called indoles, resembling LSD in their molecular structure – scientific confirmation of the powerful hallucinogenic properties of this plant. Due to the large number of tribes that use hallucinogenic drugs, the vine is known by many other names including *natema* among the Ecuadorean Shuar and *yajé* by the Desana of Colombia.

In the western Amazon and upper Orinoco, another vine, *Virola elongata*, along with several other virola species, is widely used to make a snuff. Bark-scrapings are collected, boiled, simmered and refined into a fine powder. It is administered by blowing a charge down a pipe into the nostril – and the symptoms look bad. It induces heavy production of tears and mucus. In Amazonian Peru and Colombia it is used by the Bora and Witoto for similar purposes to ayahuasca. A related plant processed into *yoppo* snuff is used by the Yanomami and Amerindians of the Caribbean.

The Amazon lowlands provide another plant called *ipadu* (*Erythroxylum coca var ipadu*) which is the raw material for cocaine. While cocaine is seen as a problem internationally, in South America coca has a wide range of medicinal and cultural properties. The leaf of the plant is chewed or taken as a brew which releases the alkaloids in it. Nutritionally, chewing coca provides a range of vitamins and minerals, and is used to reduce fatigue and counteract altitude sickness. Chewing coca or drinking the brew is not the same as taking cocaine as there is only a tiny quantity of active alkaloids in the coca leaf.

many people. They theorised that the tribes were so hostile they killed enough of each other to prevent overpopulation.

From the moment the Europeans arrived, indigenous populations were affected by imported illnesses. When the Europeans stepped ashore they brought with them smallpox, influenza and a range of other Eurasian and African diseases to which the Indians had no natural immunity. While the Jesuit priests proclaimed the maladies were punishment for lack of faith, the Indians were in no doubt that the Europeans had brought these evils with them.

This pattern of illness continues today. As the population of the Amazon grows Indians are increasingly likely to come into contact with fatal diseases. When contact is made, the consequences are dramatic. Recent incursions by gold prospectors into Yanomami territory introduced smallpox and measles, and caused a dramatic rise in malaria cases, resulting in thousands of deaths.

Protection of indigenous tribes

Today the legal status of lowland Indians and the protection of their lands varies greatly across the region. Countries such as Colombia and Ecuador offer a degree of protection to Amazon Indians under the umbrella of active indigenous organisations.

In Peru, with the highest proportion of the Amazon Basin comprising its national territory, the need to demarcate indigenous lands is recognised but carried out by government officials. There is no consultation with indigenous tribes.

Bolivian indigenous rights have been subject to an attitude of *laissez faire* until 1997 when Marches for Dignity put them on the political agenda.

FROM NOBLE SAVAGES TO SLAVES

The first encounters of the Europeans with the Indians of the New World fostered the image of the noble savage: a people who ran naked in the world, living without greed and without reference to poverty. Indian tribes willingly helped the Portuguese harvest the precious pau do Brasil in return for simple iron tools. But this utopian image, created by 18th-century philosophers, became fashionable after it was too late for the Indians.

At the time of their arrival, the Portuguese entered an area recently conquered by an aggressive tribe called the Tupi. Fighting was a way of avenging past wrongdoings and of kidnapping enemy tribes. The wars achieved a degree of territorial balance and fighting kept population levels down to numbers the land could easily support.

The outcomes of tribal wars were an abhorrence to the European mind. The spoils of war involved the ritual killing of prisoners by their captors. Once killed, the victims would be eaten, as would any creature of the rainforest. The eating of a prisoner was an intolerable insult against the defeated tribe and demanded revenge, continuing the cycle of war. Although cyclical aggression and cannibalism were not uncommon throughout the Amazon, the Portuguese based their opinions on the particularly aggressive Tupi.

As demand for wood rose, so the Indians were less inclined to travel further into the forest to collect it. The need for workers became even more apparent when Portuguese settlers began growing sugarcane. Planting and harvesting sugar required labour and, to justify enslavement, the Portuguese believed they would eliminate cannibalism by putting prisoners-of-war to work on plantations. Metal tools were no longer traded for work or wood, but for prisoners who became slaves.

As labour demands rose, the Portuguese incited inter-village rivalry, thus ensuring a steady supply of prisoners-of-war. Before long, whole villages were forced to accept 'protection' against imminent attack in return for working for Europeans.

For the Indians, however, the reality was different, as the French Capuchin missionary Yves d'Évreux noted in a conversation with an Indian. This extract is taken from John Hemming's *Red Gold: The Conquest of the Brazilian Indians*: 'When you are dead you no longer feel a thing. Whether they eat you or not is all the same to a dead man. But I should be angry to die in bed, and not in the manner of great men, surrounded by dances and drinking and swearing vengeances on those who would eat me before I died.'

And so begins the tragic enslavement of the Amazon Indian, based on the practice of a few Indian communities' ritual eating of human flesh.

In Brazil, recognition of territorial rights provides a degree of federal protection. However, obtaining recognition requires a lengthy and tiresome procedure which, without government support, is difficult to obtain. Of the 87 million hectares claimed as indigenous territories, just 17 million have been recognised.

Historically Brazil has recognised the need to address indigenous issues for some time, with the formation of the Indians' Protection Department back in 1910. This was replaced by the National Indian Foundation, FUNAI, the government agency responsible for Brazil's Indians. Although the recent work carried out by the employees of FUNAI is widely seen as good and well-intentioned, the attachment to government prevents the organisation acting in a truly independent way. The lack of funding has resulted in inefficiency and corruption, doing little to promote confidence in FUNAI as the real guardian of indigenous peoples.

A new law in 1996 changed the legal position of the Indian lands. Any person or organisation who could prove they had a legal claim to indigenous lands could claim their part of the reserve. Objections from international and indigenous groups failed to change government policy.

The Amazon frontier

Missionaries soon followed the Amazon's Portuguese colonisers who had built forts to defend the waterway. Jesuits, from the Society of Jesus, formed in 1534, were intelligent and ambitious young men dedicated to spreading Catholicism. Soon after they arrived in 1549, Jesuits established control over selected Indian villages or *aldeias*. By the time they were expelled from South America over two hundred years later, the Jesuits had over 60 *aldeias* along the Amazon comprising thousands of Indians.

Charged with the Indians' welfare, the Jesuits encouraged them to move to the missions to live and work. Indian labour helped sustain mission communities that accumulated wealth through large herds of cattle – in contrast to the failure of colonists farming the Amazon's poor soils. While the Jesuits were the best European friends the Indians had, it wasn't beyond them to occasionally turn a blind eye. In raids *bandeirantes* kidnapped Indians to work for new settlers. Condoned by government officials and with Jesuits on hand as witnesses, raids were supposed to take only bonded captives – prisoners-of-war from inter-tribal conflict. But *bandeirantes* would execute uncooperative Indians to intimidate others to say they were bonded captives which would keep them alive as slaves for the immediate future at least. By the late 1750s, the Portuguese economy was beginning to falter. The Jesuits, wealthy and powerful from the labour and conversion of countless Indians, were suitable scapegoats to take the blame for the shortcomings of settlers. The removal of the Jesuits, it was argued, would make Indians available as labour for all colonisers.

When the Jesuits were expelled from Portuguese territories in 1757, the final hindrance to full exploration of the Amazon was removed, along with the notion of fair treatment of the indigenous Indians.

The first settlers

With the removal of religious pontificators, the colonisation of the Portuguese territory continued unobstructed.

By the 1750s land-hungry plantations using Indian labour had begun to encroach on the Amazon Basin. Rice plantations in the lower Amazon made Portugal self-sufficient in this staple crop. Cocoa became a fashionable drink in Europe, making it an important crop. As epidemics decimated local Indian populations, slavers pushed along and away from the main stream to find much needed labour for the harvesting of wild cocoa from the forest and later on plantations.

Sugar and cattle were produced on ranches, with the enforced assistance of Indian peoples and slaves from Africa. The success of plantations encouraged colonists to look for suitable sites, and they spread rapidly along the rivers of the Amazon. By the 1770s colonisers had reached, and attempted to establish villages on, the grassy savannahs near the headwaters of the Rio Branco, northwest of Manaus.

In the mid-1840s the wave of enlightened thinking that gripped Europe nearly saw the introduction of legislation to protect the Indians and their right to tribal lands. But by now the march of colonising settlers was too strong.

At this time the seeds of current problems were sown. The idea of the 'noble savage' living in a primitive Utopia had little effect on the rainforest reality. Brutal frontiersmen bent on personal gain and satisfaction were outside the control of any law. As is the case today, any legislation designed to protect the rights of individuals required adequate resources to enforce it.

Legal protection for the Indians was tabled but never implemented. Western economies were rapidly industrialising and needed one Amazon product in particular to ensure continued growth – rubber.

Rubber goes boom

By the 1850s, as the boom in rubber hit Amazonia, the high ideals of protection for the Indians of Brazil were promptly forgotten in a quest for wealth. Europeans migrated to the region rapidly, to benefit from the rich pickings of the rubber industry. However, Indian communities were not forthcoming in working for the rubber barons. Rubber tappers or *seringueiros* migrated from the coastal areas to take advantage of the booming work opportunities.

When rubber prices crashed, most non-Indians involved in the industry left the Amazon. Hemming concludes 'the rubber boom was not as catastrophic to the native population as might have been expected... Ecologically, rubber tapping caused almost no damage'. However, when the rubber barons deserted the Amazon in droves, many of the *seringueiros* remained stuck in conditions of debt bondage where they continued to toil with minimal reward.

Interest in rubber waned as profits fell and investment moved to the south of Brazil. Production briefly increased to supply the Allies in World War II, but by the 1960s the few remaining estate bosses gave up their Amazon holdings. Debt bondage was removed so rubber tappers now owned their stand of trees. New freedoms brought new opportunities. In addition to the regular visits to the rubber stands, nuts, fish, hides and a range of products could all be harvested from the rainforest. A new type of Amazon settler, with a new set of territorial land rights, had been created.

Recognising the land rights of rubber tappers

In the 1970s governments began to modernise Amazonia in attempts to integrate it into national economies. In Brazil, generous financial incentives subsidised ranching and settlement in southern Amazonia.

As cattle ranchers occupied more land they encountered rubber tappers, now the rightful owners of the land. But the tappers' prospects were not good, given the settlers' long history of ignoring land rights. Resistance in the form of *empates* or stand-offs, organised by newly-formed unions, raised temperatures in the conflict zones. In 1988 ranchers murdered Francisco Alves 'Chico' Mendes, leader of the Xapuri Rural Workers' Union. This focused world attention on the rubber tappers' plight.

Chico Mendes' death was at a time when international protests against the rapacious destruction of the Amazon rainforest were at an all-time high. The murder globally publicised the value of protected extractive reserves proposed by rubber tappers' unions, resulting in their official recognition.

By 1990 four extractive reserves covering two million hectares and providing an income to around 23,000 Brazilians had been recognised. These areas are: the Juruá valley in northern Acre; the Chico Mendes Reserve in southern Acre; Rio Ouro Preto in Rondônia; and Rio Cajarí in Amapá, north of the Amazon's mouth.

MAKUXI OF AMAZONIA TODAY – LIFE, DEATH AND MYTH

'The white man built roads, houses, farms and opened the way to disease, poverty and death.' So said Waldir Tobias, a Makuxi Indian of Raposa-Serra do Sol, Brazil.

The Makuxi are a hunting and farming people who live in a hilly region known as the Guyana Shield, near Mount Roraima on the border between Brazil and Guyana. There are an estimated 16,000 Makuxi, with the majority living in Brazil and the rest in Guyana. In Brazil, they are concentrated in the Raposa-Serra do Sol Indigenous Area in the border state of Roraima, north of the Amazon rainforests. Theirs is a spectacularly beautiful land of mountains, tropical forest and savannah, where they raise cattle.

Makuxi believe that they, and the neighbouring Ingariko people, are descended from the brothers Macunaima and Anique, the children of the sun. Macunaima and Anique discovered a tree known as Waxaca, the Tree of Life, which is the origin of all the plants and wild fruits on which the Indians' lives depend. The brothers left behind them some good legacies, including the gift of fire, but they also created disease and the hardships of nature. The Makuxi believe that stkaton, the life principle, governs everything and comes from the sun.

Raposa-Serra do Sol has two distinct seasons; winter, with heavy rainfall from May to September, and a long dry summer between November and March. In summer, the Indians plan hunting and fishing expeditions and visit friends and relatives in neighbouring villages – such visits are not possible in the rainy season. Fishing is a favourite Makuxi activity, both as a pastime and as an essential source of food, but it is often made difficult by the drying-up of rivers and streams.

Makuxi villages are linked together by a complex network of paths and tracks. They range in size from settlements of two houses to large communities with clusters of houses built around central courtyards. These communities are based on ties of marriage and family. Makuxi extended families hunt together, but the planting of crops for personal use is done by individual households. Houses are built and repaired during the dry season, when the Indians have easier access to wood and clay for the walls and can gather palm leaves for the roofs.

When Makuxi marry, they live in the wife's family's village and submit to the authority of their fathers-in-law. A young husband has to provide his father-in-law with game and carry out domestic services like house maintenance. When the couple have children, they can move to their own plot of land. The father-in-law is the most important figure in the Makuxi kinship groups. When he dies the group often dissolves, and married men return to their original villages, taking their wives and children with them.

Since their 'discovery' by European invaders, and their colonisation by the Portuguese in the 18th century, the Makuxi have experienced land theft, murder, torture and slavery. Today, they are still fighting for recognition of their most basic human rights. Although the indigenous area is officially demarcated, neither the federal nor the state authorities of Brazil make any attempt to stop the advance of ranchers and gold prospectors.

THE EXPERIENCE OF AN AMAZON SETTLER

Some agricultural settlers in the Amazon have flourished in their new lands. A more common scenario is illustrated by the International Amazon Cooperation Treaty's review of abandoned plots within settlements of Brazil's POLONORESTE's (Northwest Region Integrated Development Progamme) large-scale colonisation project in Rondônia, in Brazil's southern Amazon.

Attracted by government publicity seeking to encourage settlement of rural communities in the Amazon, settlers are told the land is fertile. If they move to Rondônia the colonisation programme will provide 30 or more hectares of land, with technical assistance and credit to hand.

Settlers often arrive in the Amazon accompanied by a wife and several small children with neither money nor family goods. Untrained and normally illiterate they settle on the land.

The land assigned to them by the colonisation agency has been carved from jungle, located beside a path barely wide enough for a cart. There is no water at the site, so it must be brought long distances until a well is dug. The settler-turned-farmer naturally builds his first hut close to the road.

Clearing the jungle is tiring and exhaustive work. In addition to this, to support a period with no income, the family will have to look for income from wherever it is available. If the season is right, felled trees can be burnt and the first crops of rice, corn and beans are planted. In between seasonal work and the demands of farming, if the opportunity arises a small house can be built from wooden planks, with palm thatch for a roof.

In the background, all the hopes for prosperity are slowly fading. The promised health clinic and school have closed or, worse still, never opened. The family is probably suffering from a variety of intestinal parasites. It is also possible, indeed highly likely, that the settler and some of his family have contracted malaria, greatly reducing their ability to work. And the farmer can consider himself extremely lucky if no member of his family suffered a serious accident felling trees.

If the first crop was good, it is possible, if the marketing centre is operational and the freight costs are not too high, that produce over and above subsistence requirements can be sold to prepare for the second crop. More than likely, however, is the reality that through planting at the wrong time of year, poor crop maintenance and lack of help, the crop is poor.

The optimistic words of agricultural technicians seem ill-founded as the high returns offered by permanent crops such as coffee and cacao are barely worth it, given the time requirements. The rosy picture of agroforestry in harmony with nature is blocked by the presence of too many obstacles.

Large-scale colonisation projects

In recent decades government programmes have worked hard to integrate the Amazon regions into their national economies. From a national perspective this is sound policy. Three-quarters of Bolivia and Peru lie within the Amazon Basin. Nearly 60% of Brazil is within the Amazon, while for Ecuador the figure is just under 50%. As such a large part of a nation's resource, it is understandable that governments have encouraged economic growth in the Amazon lowlands.

The result has been massive immigration. Manaus and Belém on the Amazon main stream in Brazil have more than one million inhabitants each, while Porto Velho in the southern Amazon has nearly half a million. Iquitos in Peru, even without outside road connections, has 600,000 inhabitants, and to the south Pucallpa has grown dramatically following improvements to the road from Lima in the last decade. Santa Cruz in Bolivia is mushrooming, currently with around 600,000 inhabitants; it is expected to be Bolivia's largest city early in the 21st century. The momentum for growth has taken the Amazon's population up to 20 million and shows no sign of stopping.

People move into the Amazon for a number of reasons. Many want to work in the burgeoning cities. Others believe they will make a fortune farming, ranching or prospecting for gold. The vast majority of these migrants are first-generation. When travelling around the Amazon Basin, particularly away from the rivers, it is quite difficult to find someone of working age who was born in the area. As families grow the pressure on land is certain to increase.

Road-building greatly speeds colonisation. Road-building itself causes relatively little damage – rainforest has reclaimed underused parts of the Transamazonica Highway in Brazil. But in most places, after roads are built, colonists soon follow. Once sufficient numbers settle along a highway, the roads are improved – raising the rate of immigration. In southern Brazil the road between Cuiabá and Porto Velho was asphalted in the mid-1980s. Heading west the road steadily deteriorates but buses, lorries and a few shaky cars transport people and supplies to new settlements springing up along the road. Previously rainforest, vast tracts of land alongside the road are now completely cleared.

The history of colonisation globally has gone hand in hand with the destruction of forested lands. In the USA colonisation destroyed 95% of natural forests before any were protected.

Farming and settling – clearing the forests

Currently some 20% of the Amazon population are farmers or *campesinos*. Most are poor farmers working small plots of land. Although land is promised through government programmes *campesinos* often have no legal right to the land they farm. Where possible, they seek seasonal work on larger farms. A large number of small farmers move spontaneously, settling haphazardly along new highways.

Medium- and large-scale plots are also widespread and commonly used for grazing. With the use of fertilisers and more advanced technologies these can be productive year-round operations. Agriculture and livestock production is extensive but yields are low. As with many colonisation projects, applying temperate-climate agricultural methods to the rainforest rarely works.

In the 1970s, the Brazilian government used subsidies to encourage the creation of large-scale ranches in excess of 20,000ha. Although no longer actively encouraged, the subsidies still cost the Brazilian treasury over US$2.5 billion annually. Yet meat output from the ranches is just 9% of what was projected.

Although such projects are clearly failures, their effects extend far beyond the loss of rainforest. Failed rural projects increase migration to urban areas and increase pressure on the stretched services of cities like Manaus. Also, when agricultural prices fall illegal drug production is relatively more profitable.

Urban settlers

Between fifty and sixty percent of people in the Amazon Basin live in cities. Many of the large population centres – Manaus, Belém, Iquitos and Porto Velho – are relatively old, established during the colonial era or more recently in the years of the rubber boom.

These, along with others, like Pucallpa in Peru, Riberalta in Bolivia and most lowland towns in Ecuador, have grown rapidly following colonisation and road-building programmes. Mining, primarily for gold, fuels urban growth. Once mining camps are established new towns mushroom around them.

The population of the principal cities is a mosaic of races of different origins who migrated there for a number of reasons. Local migration occurs as a result of failed colonisation projects, while others move from areas of poverty believing the rapid growth of lowland cities is proof of better opportunities. A walk around any Amazon city quickly proves that without a lot of luck finding work, the reality is very different.

Some cities have experienced a fifty-fold increase in population since 1940, becoming important commercial and communication centres in their own right. Rapid growth has led to a proliferation of slums in urban areas with the predictable consequences of insecurity and poverty. The population increase places untenable demands on water, sewage, rubbish and electricity services. Such conditions favour disease and epidemics of cholera, hepatitis and dengue fever break out from time to time.

Miners – still seeking El Dorado

The Amazon's mineral resources are relatively unexplored and undeveloped. Easy pickings have lured swarms of *garimpeiros* or gold prospectors. Between one and two million are searching for gold or gemstones throughout the Brazilian Amazon. They operate 25,000 pieces of equipment. Some 30,000 prospect for gold in Peru's Madre de Dios region. Although the miner's life is hard, the attraction of striking gold is irresistible compared with the grim prospects elsewhere.

Travelling around the Amazon you find that most medium-sized towns have shops buying and selling gold. A friendly conversation on a bus, truck or boat heading towards one of these towns may reveal that despite the poverty-stricken appearance of the man sitting next to you, he actually has a small fold of paper holding gold dust, or a small ingot worth several thousand dollars in his pocket. He is unable to pay the bus fare in cash, so the bus driver makes a detour, stopping at a shop so the gold can be sold and the fare paid.

About a third of the Amazon Basin's population is directly or indirectly employed in gold mining. In addition to prospectors, construction, maintenance services, logistical support, transportation and prostitution employ vast numbers. In the Brazilian Amazon gold mining is the most important economic and social activity.

Territory invasion

This huge population of prospectors has taken over large areas of indigenous territory. In the 1980s 40,000 *garimpeiros* invaded Yanomami land, making world headlines. Outbreaks of malaria, other diseases, and violence soon followed. In response the Yanomami Park was created. Uninvited visitors are restricted but violations still occur. *Garimpeiros* are periodically expelled when international pressure is sufficiently vocal. But the reality is that permanently keeping the prospectors out is impossible.

In 1993, 70 Yanomami were murdered by *garimpeiros* in what became known as the Haximu Massacre. In recent years more than 1,500 Yanomami have died from malaria, tuberculosis, influenza and other diseases. Pollution from mining has also reduced food supplies to the hunter-gatherer community. As recently as 1997, new camps of miners had entered the park, many of them crossing into Venezuela.

Habitat destruction

Besides effects on indigenous people, the environmental effects of mining are catastrophic. The techniques used to extract gold by small-scale operations can have disastrous consequences. The extraction of two grams of gold requires the removal of one cubic metre of sediment. Dredges excavate the riverbed and the banks, disrupting river flow and altering the watershed. As the dredges work an area, oil pollution from machinery escapes and pollutes the river system far beyond the immediate area of operation. Around 7,000 dredges dump five million litres of oil every year into the River Madeira in southern Brazil – and this is just one tributary of the Amazon!

River sediment is processed close to mining areas where miners use mercury to separate out fine gold particles. They burn the gold-mercury amalgam to recover the metal and release mercury vapour. The miner often inhales the vapour and may suffer severe nerve damage. What isn't inhaled or spilled directly in the river escapes into the atmosphere and eventually returns to the ground in rain. Mercury released into the environment contaminates soil and water, and is absorbed by animals, working its way up the food chain – ultimately to people.

A new type of prospector

While many rivers in the Amazon have some *garimpeiros* dredging and sifting through sediments, most gold deposits remain out of reach of the small operator. This explains why prospectors push ever further into new lands. In many regions, however, the heyday of the small-scale *garimpeiros* has passed. On the River Tapajós in the state of Pará, state records show small prospector production falling rapidly – large companies dominate new production. The state government is marketing the mineral wealth of the state in the hope that the concessions sold to large multinational companies like Rio Tinto Zinc, Placer Dome and Anglo-American will eventually provide much-needed royalties for the state's economy.

When large mining companies move to the Amazon, a new spate of migration will begin, placing even greater pressure on the region's resources.

Mega-mines

One example of how large mining companies operate is the Grand Carajás mega-mine – the world's largest mining complex. Located in eastern Brazil, southwest of Marabá on the Tocantins River, it was built to extract the estimated 18 billion tonnes of iron ore reserves.The project's level of success depends on whom you ask. Around 15,000 direct jobs have been created since the project's inception in the 1970s. It has required the development of a rail network, hydro-electric dams and agro-livestock enterprises in an area equal in size to France and Britain combined.

For the rainforest the project has been a disaster, as land has been cleared to make way for the mega-mine and associated services. Entrance to Carajás itself is heavily controlled but the effect on the region is clear. The nearby town of Marabá has boomed from just 10,000 people in the 1970s to over 200,000 and is still growing. Power to support the region's growth comes from the massive Tucuruí hydro-electric dam which creates 8,000MW annually, a project that in itself supports a town of 65,000. The creation of the 12km-long dam flooded 2,360km^2 of rainforest.

DANGER ... TOURISTS!

All too often a visit to Indian villages results in awkwardness. Asking if you can take photographs leads to feelings of embarrassment by those on both sides of the camera. It is a difficult situation: one that demands stepping outside the singular goal of getting good shots from your holiday.

Tourism need not be a destructive force for tribal peoples but unfortunately it is: if it violates their rights it should be opposed. Tourism must be subject to the decisions made by the tribal peoples themselves. Here are a few guidelines issued by Survival International:

- Do be respectful. Tourist companies should insist their staff and clients behave respectfully towards tribal peoples. (In practice, many tourists who visit tribal areas simply have their false stereotypes reinforced.)
- Don't demean, degrade, insult or patronise. All tourism and advertising which treats tribal peoples in an insulting, degrading or patronising manner (for example references to 'stone-age cultures', 'untouched by time', etc) should be opposed. They are demeaning and wrong.
- Do ask permission. The lands lived in or used by tribes should not be entered without the free and informed consent of the tribal peoples themselves. Obtaining this consent can be lengthy; it requires money, respect, tact and honesty. Bribery should never be used.
- Do pay properly. Tribespeople should be properly recompensed for their services and the use of their territory. Payment should be agreed in advance with their legitimate representatives. Where profits arise from using tribal areas, this should be properly explained to the tribes who may want a share. Anyone who is not able to accept tribal peoples' own terms for payment should not be there.
- Do recognise land rights. Tribal peoples' ownership of the lands they use and occupy is recognised in international law. This should be acknowledged irrespective of whether the national government applies the law or not (governments are amongst the principal violators of tribal rights). When in tribal lands, tourists should behave as they would on private property.
- Don't bring in disease. Care must be taken in areas where tribal peoples' immunity to outside diseases may be poor. Some contagious diseases which affect tourists only mildly – colds and influenza, for example – can kill tribespeople.

Survival International, 6 Charterhouse Buildings, London, EC1M 7ET; tel: 020 7687 8700; fax: 020 7687 8701; email: info@surival-international.org; web: www.survival-international.org

At the outset of the project, about 22,000 people were removed from their homes without discussion or compensation. Today, a vast area of habitat continues to be destroyed.

Oil and gas prospectors

Oil and its extraction are increasingly important to the region. Most operations are in the western Amazon and cause particular concern amongst environmentalists. Oil companies in Ecuador are regularly criticised for their disregard of environmental laws governing drilling and storage facilities. Exploration is also

Left Red and green macaws, *Ara chloroptera*, on salt lick, Madre de Dios River, Peru (PO)

Above White-throated or Cuvier's toucan, *Ramphastos tucanus* (PO)

Below Tiny hawk, *Accipiter superciliosus*, Yasuni National Park, Ecuador (PO)

Above left Hoatzin, *Opisthocomus hoazin*, Manú National Park, Peru (PO)

Left Mealy (*Amazona farinosa*), yellow-crowned (*A ochrocephla*) and blue-headed (*Pionus menstruus*) parrots and dusky-headed parakeets (*Aratinga weddellii*) on salt lick, River Napo, Ecuador (PO)

Top left Leaf frog, *Agalygnis craspedopus* (PO)

Above Amazon horned frog,
Ceratophrys cornuta (PO)

Below Glass frog, *Centrolenelid sp* (PO)

Top right Double-striped forest pit viper, *Bothriopsis bilineatus*, eating mouse (PO)

Above Emerald tree boa, *Corallus coniuis* (PO)

Below left Black caiman, *Melanosuchus niger* (PO)

Below Iguanid lizard, *Enyaloides laticeps* (PO)

stepping up in Colombia and Peru, with Bolivia only just beginning to explore opportunities in the lowlands.

The Camisea Gas Field in the southern lowlands of Peru exemplifies the problems of lowland development. It is among the world's largest gas fields, and the Peruvian government is keen to exploit the estimated 11 trillion cubic feet of gas reserves. This would require an investment of US$2.8 billion from an international consortium including Citigroup, Plus Petrol and Hunt Oil and others. Unfortunately the gas field lies in a very ecologically sensitive area. A Smithsonian Institute study recognises the area 'to be in nearly pristine condition, showing no evidence of human activity'. The proposed pipelines cut through the Vilcabamba region that 'contains a biological and cultural richness perhaps unparalleled anywhere else in the world,' according to Conservation International, Global Environment Facility and the World Bank. The project also infringes on the traditional lands of 7,000 indigenous Indians most of whom depend on the rainforest for subsistence and choose voluntary isolation. Early encounters during feasibility studies with indigenous groups in the area caused whooping cough and influenza epidemics that killed off almost 50% of the population. Despite the withdrawal of the original consortium, the project is scheduled to go ahead at the end of 2003.

Part Two

Countries of the Amazon

Venezuela

Venezuela promises lofty Andean peaks and crisp, clean
Caribbean beaches in abundance for the vertically and
horizontally inclined. For those seeking jungle tours, Venezuela
is a place of extremes and unique opportunities. The truly
adventurous can spend two weeks paddling in the canoe strokes of
the great Prussian explorer Baron Alexander von Humboldt, while
more genteel options include treks of just a few days that give a
flavour of the jungle.

Venezuela was introduced to written history in 1498 when
Christopher Columbus landed on the Península de Paría close to Trinidad. The
name, Venezuela, literally translated as Little Venice, was inspired by sightings of
Indian communities living in huts on stilts in Lake Maracaibo.

FACTS AND FIGURES
Geography

Venezuela's geographical variety offers the visitor a wide range of experiences. The
north has idyllic Caribbean coastline with a large number of developed and
undeveloped beaches. Along the coast the humid tropical warmth of the east
contrasts with the dry deserts found in the west.

Lake Maracaibo, towards the border with Colombia, with an area of
21,470km² (8,286 miles²), is the largest lake in South America. The highest
peaks of the Cordillera de Marina reach an altitude of 5,007m. The flat
expansive *llanos*, found to the south of the Cordillera and north of the River

---

BASIC FACTS
Official name República Bolivariana de Venezuela
Area 912,050km² (352,144 miles²)
Population 24,169,744 (2000)
Capital Caracas
Largest city (population) Caracas (3,672,779)
Main Amazon city Puerto Ayacucho
Official language Spanish
Date of independence 5 July 1830
Major industries Oil and derivatives, manufacturing and mining
GDP per capita US$8,000
Currency Bolívar (US$1=Bs1,348; £1=Bs2,083)
Major attractions Isla Margarita; the Gran Sabana; Angel Falls.
National holidays Carnival (Monday and Tuesday before Lent), Easter,
Apr 19, May, Jun 24, Jul 5, Jul 24, Oct 12, Dec 25

Orinoco, make up a vast low-lying savannah scattered with ranches. The life of the *ranchero* is dictated by extremes: widespread flooding in May contrasts with the dry season between December and April that leaves riverbeds dry and livestock parched.

To the south of the Orinoco lie the Guyana Highlands, the remains of a sedimentary layer which was first laid down around 1.7 billion years ago and has experienced extensive erosion. Vertically-sided *tepuis* (flat-topped mountains) rise abruptly to an altitude of 3,000m, their summits hosts to hundreds of endemic plants including numerous insectivorous species.

Angel Falls cascades for almost one vertical kilometre off the side of Auyán *tepui*, and Mount Roraima, on the disputed border with Guyana to the east, was the inspiration for Arthur Conan Doyle's *The Lost World*.

The Guyana Highlands drop away to the southwest giving way to flat tropical lowland and the state of Amazonas, comprising almost a fifth of Venezuela's national territory, where occasional *tepuis* break the green carpet of tropical forest. The highest, with an altitude of 3,014m (9,888ft), is Pico da Neblina on the border with Brazil, just a degree north of the Equator.

Rivers

In Venezuela the Amazon plays second fiddle to the Orinoco. Virtually all the country's rivers drain into the Orinoco and out to the Atlantic.

The Orinoco flows along a giant fishhook-shaped channel for over 2,100km. From its headwaters in the Sierra Parama on the Brazilian border, the river is forced to travel in a westerly direction round the immovable Guyana Highlands, before turning back on itself to head northeast through the heart of the country.

Such a prominent artery has proved vital to the economic development of the Venezuelan heartland. The Orinoco is navigable by ocean-going ships for 240km upstream and river steamers for 1,100km. A series of rapids prevents navigation beyond Puerto Ayacucho, the state capital of Amazonas.

Prior to the road link with the north of Venezuela, Puerto Ayacucho was just a transit point where cargo was unloaded and taken by land to the port of Samariapo, 63km upstream beyond the rapids. From Samariapo hundreds of smaller boats ferry cargo to communities upstream.

The Amazon Basin proper constitutes a very small part of Venezuelan territory – just over a quarter of the territory of the state of Amazonas. The small part that is an Amazon tributary comes courtesy of the natural Casiquiare Canal which diverts one third of the Orinoco's headwaters south to join the Río Negro.

Climate

Temperatures in Venezuela are fairly constant, allowing for geographical differences. The dry season runs roughly from December to April, with the wet season taking up the remainder of the year.

An important climatic determinant is local topography, in particular the altitude. The Andean hills around Mérida have comfortable day temperatures of around 20°C, while the night can bring a slight chill. Coastal regions are comfortably warm with temperature increasing as you travel further west. Maracaibo can be uncomfortably hot, at over 30°C.

To the south the Guyana Highlands and the state of Amazonas experience rain that is sudden and often accompanied by powerful lightning storms. Temperatures on the Gran Sabana are around the mid-20s°C. Amazonas is around the high 20s, but this can be oppressive when humidity rises.

Flora and fauna

The easiest place to see large animals in the wild is the *llanos*. The flat, open and normally dry savannahs concentrate animals around water channels. Capybara, armadillos, tapirs, caiman and jaguar are found in the region. Piranha are abundant and freshwater dolphins are often seen.

Venezuela is home to over 1,300 bird species (some 44% of South America's avifauna). Many of the cloud and lowland tropical forests in the hills of the north are within the protected boundaries of national parks.

In Amazonas attractions for birdwatchers include the Cock-of-the-Rock, Amazonian umbrella bird, kingfishers, macaws, toucans and parrots. Over 670 bird species have been recorded in Amazonas, over half Venezuela's known species.

Over 30,000 species of insect have been recorded including 1,200 species of butterfly. Best known is the iridescent blue morpho with a wingspan up to 15cm. According to locals, tarantulas used to be very common throughout the area but numbers are reduced somewhat by the Piaroa Indians, who see the spiders as both a food delicacy and a protective spirit.

Aquatic animals are also in abundance with a thousand or more species of fish. Freshwater turtles include the curiously horned *matamata,* and freshwater dolphins, caiman and snakes can all be seen in the region. Over 190 mammal species have been recorded including nine species of primate, along with tapirs, peccaries and jaguars.

Land use

Venezuela's dependence on oil has discouraged development of a viable agricultural sector. Although a variety of products are produced throughout the country about 60% of food is imported.

Tropical forest regions produce orchids, wild rubber and timber while on the *llanos* to the north the beef and dairy industry is being developed. The hilly and mountainous regions to the north produce a wide range of agricultural products including staple foods and cash crops such as cocoa, coffee and bananas.

The people
Population

Over 90% of Venezuelans lives in urban areas. Population is growing by 2.6% annually and just under half the population is under 20. The average Venezuelan woman has 3.6 children. Population density varies greatly, peaking at 1,090 per km^2 in Caracas and falling to below five per km^2 in the states of Amazonas, Bolívar, Apure and Delta Amacuro.

Over two-thirds of the population are of mixed Indian-European descent known as *mestizos*; one-fifth are Europeans; 9% are blacks; and indigenous Indians make up 2%. Of the indigenous Indians, 29 groups total around 200,000, with 21 distinct indigenous languages. The main groups of the south include the Yanomami, Piaroa and Pemón, located in the southern states of Amazonas and Bolívar.

Languages

Spanish is the official language of Venezuela. Many indigenous languages are disappearing as acculturation introduces Spanish into groups that are numerically strong but linguistically vulnerable.

Education

In the 1970s and 1980s state-funded institutions had hoped to put Venezuelan universities among the best in the world. The worsening economy of the 1990s forced funding cut backs and put an end to that dream.

Education is free and compulsory between the ages of five and 13, with secondary education lasting an additional four years. There are 11 state universities in the country and 13 private higher educational institutions.

Culture

Whether monuments of past optimism or inspiration for future hopes and dreams, the towering modern architecture of Caracas is certainly impressive. The clean-cut lines and extensive use of mirrored glass create an air of prosperity, but the push for modernisation did much to destroy the city's colonial heritage.

Art is appropriately contemporary. The success of kinetic artist Jesús Soto in recent decades has done much to promote Venezuela on the international scene. Several modern sculptures are dotted about the public places of Caracas, particularly in Sabana Grande.

When South America caught the soccer bug, Venezuela was in close association with the US so baseball is the national sport.

The drive to modernise in the northern economic heartland has protected southern lowland tribes from the colonisation that plagues indigenous people in other Amazon countries. Consequently the region's indigenous culture and welfare are not prominent in the national consciousness. Compared to Indians in neighbouring countries, the lack of interference allows some tribes to preserve their way of life and maintain a strong identity.

A brief history

Pre-conquest

Pre-Hispanic populations were primarily located in three areas. The coastal regions were occupied by fishing cultures who also practised shifting agriculture, while the *llanos* were home to groups of hunter-gatherers. As with much of South America, in Venezuela the Andes range was the cradle for more developed cultures. The Timote-Cuica used terracing to increase agricultural productivity on the sloping terrain.

Smaller groups living in the lowland areas to the south included the Yanomami, Piaroa and several other groups, along with the Pemón Indians of the Guayana Highlands. Most of these groups have only recently experienced large-scale influences on lifestyles maintained for thousands of years.

Post-conquest

Columbus' arrival in 1498 marked the European discovery of Venezuela. The country lacked the mineral wealth and large indigenous populations to work on plantations. Consequently the Spanish exploited the local tribes considerably less than elsewhere in the New World.

The first permanent Spanish settlement was Nueva Cádiz on the island of Cubagua, close to Isla Margarita, where local Indians were forced to dive for pearls from the rich oyster beds in the coastal waters.

Colonisation continued at a steady pace, with Europeans creating a number of coastal towns.

Independence

The general state of calm in Venezuela was eaten away as careless orders from Spain increasingly frustrated the colonists. The hunger for independence rooted in Venezuela that swept the continent in the late 18th century created the stage for one of South America's great men, Símon Bolívar. This legendary figure, born in 1783, travelled to France and the USA at the turn of the century, experiencing at first hand the euphoric feelings that came with liberation and independence.

Peaceful attempts to bring about independence failed. Bolívar's army achieved independence for Colombia in 1819, securing Venezuela's liberation within two years.

In 1830 *El Libertador*, as Bolívar became known, was exiled to France. Yet, before boarding the ship he became ill with tuberculosis and died in his homeland.

The 20th century

Venezuela's economic boom began in the 1920s when oil was discovered below Lake Maracaibo. From the mid-1920s until World War II, Venezuela was the world's largest exporter of oil. General Juan Vicente Gómez seized power in 1908 and governed during the oil boom. When he died in 1935 he was one of the richest men in the country, having diverted some of the profits from oil and thereby setting a precedent for rulers that lasted for much of the 20th century.

Little wealth from the oil boom filtered down to improve the general standard of living. Demanding accountability from its leaders, Venezuela experienced an eight-month period of democracy in 1947 before the military regime of General Marco Pérez Jiménez marked a period of oil-funded public investment. Jiménez's regime commissioned the first skyscraper erected in Caracas, setting the tone for the architecturally impressive urban development that dominates the city today. Economic incompetence, corruption and repression forced the regime to stand down in 1958.

The return to democracy under a new political system favoured cooperation rather than adversarial power-broking. After joing the OPEC oil cartel in 1960, Venezuela oil revenues dramatically increased. The Arab-Israeli War of 1973 boosted oil prices so in that year Venezuelan income rose by 40% and government revenues by 170%.

Taking advantage of the new wealth, government spending skyrocketed. The oil industry was nationalised. Venezuelans were encouraged to share in the high life. Imports of foreign goods rose dramatically. What the government could not afford to pay for immediately would be paid back from future revenue. This approach dramatically increased government borrowing and the national debt rose to over US£30 billion.

As oil income fell, many Venezuelans could not give up its benefits. Inflation increased. By the end of the 1980s a sense of foreboding gripped the country.

Austerity measures aimed at restructuring the economy were introduced by President Carlos Andrés Pérez but the public demonstrated their objection to the reforms with streets riots in 1989. Sections of the military shared their dissatisfaction with the state of the country. Venezuela teetered on the edge of a new military regime as two attempted coups in 1992 – one by Colonel Hugo Chávez – saw war planes flying between the skyscrapers of Caracas.

Economic chaos hit the country in 1993 when Pérez was impeached for playing the currency market for personal gain. His replacement Raul Caldera oversaw the near complete collapse of the banking sector in 1994 when 13 major banks went to the wall. In 1995 he declared a 'state of economic emergency' until stability was restored.

Attempts to remove structural economic weaknesses in the late 1990s were largely ineffective and the economy continued to limp along. Hugo Chávez was elected president in 1998 on a wave of support for reform. Little was left untouched as Chávez set out to change the constitution, the name of the country to the Bolivarian Republic of Venezuela and the presidential term from five to six years with the opportunity for re-election.

Chávez also set to reform the economy with changes in appointment to the state-owned oil company, and increased government powers to expropriate unproductive land. The resulting power clash led to general strikes in early 2002, and protest rallies which resulted in 10 deaths and over 100 injuries. Chávez stood down on April 12 in expectation of charges resulting from the violence only to return three days later to resume control from the interim government.

After an extended general strike that continued into 2003, pressure on Chavéz is expected to add to the aura of uncertainty for the country's future.

Practicalities
Money
The bolívar continues in a state of flux. Currency controls imposed in the mid-1990s have been removed but the weakness of the bolívar continues to limit Venezuela's ability to pay off its national debt. If you are in Venezuela for several weeks, change your money slowly as the falling exchange rate will almost certainly work in your favour. Although there are no currency restrictions at present, check for the latest information before travelling.

Credit cards are the most convenient way to carry your money. Changing travellers' cheques and cash is straightforward in *casas de cambio* throughout Caracas. To use a bank, usually the only option outside the major cities, you will have to stand in long queues. Credit cards are widely accepted in the better hotels and shops and can be used for cash advances. ATM machines are widespread, but don't rely solely on your cards, lest you end up somewhere without a machine. Branches of Banco de Venezuela usually have cash dispensing machines, even in out-of-the-way Puerto Ayacucho.

The cost of living in Venezuela makes the country very affordable. Budget travellers can get by on US$25 a day, rising to US$50 per day and above when taking excursions. From that figure the sky's the limit with no shortage of first-class hotels and travel operators that provide high-end tours with excellent standards.

Accommodation
Hotel pricing in Venezuela definitely favours group travel. A *simple* (single room) for one person is usually available only in the cheapest hotels and is rarely cheaper than a *doble* (two single beds) or *matrimonio* (one large bed).

Safety
The proximity of the Venezuelan Amazon to troubled areas in Colombia has led governments to recommend travellers avoid the area. In reality the risks are not apparent. The impact has limited tourism in the area compared with other Amazon countries. On the positive side that means areas are still well off the beaten track.

Troubles within Venezuela are likely to flare from time to time. Common sense suggests you avoid public demonstrations. There is no reason for tourists to be targeted, but being in the wrong place at the wrong time is never good.

Highlights
In the rainforest, standard tours are limited, but only your imagination restricts tailor-made travel. The rainy season in Puerto Ayacucho is from June to October.

All jungle trips go through Puerto Ayacucho, from where you can spend a couple of weeks relaxing in one of the top quality jungle lodges, venturing out to the rainforest for the occasional foray. Several tour operators arrange boat trips lasting three or four days to the region south of Puerto Ayacucho, taking in visits to Indian villages, treks through the rainforest and trips to Cerro Autana.

The truly adventurous can explore the Humboldt Route for ten days or so, taking in the Casiquiare Canal and Venezuela's part of the Amazon Basin proper.

Judging by the bite-covered bodies of returning travellers, the insects are as vicious as Humboldt recorded back in 1800.

If you have a day or two in Puerto Ayacucho, consider a half-day whitewater rafting trip down the Atures rapids on the Orinoco.

Venezuela offers among the most luxurious rainforest travel experience. For the truly extravagant, helicopter and light-aircraft tours will take you to any part of the lowlands, giving aerial tours of Cerro Autana and flying close to Pico da Neblina.

In Amazonas, technically you need a permit for travel south of La Esmeralda. Depending on your ability to look harmless and sweet-talk you may be able to travel to San Fernando de Atabapo and beyond without one.

To see animals outside Amazonas, spend a few days in one of the *hacienda* ranches on the *llanos* that are set up to cater for tourists. For trips to Angel Falls, travel to the nearest town of Canaima can be easily arranged from Caracas or Ciudad Bolívar.

On the coast, the beach town of Choroní in Henri Pittier National Park is a quiet alternative to the more commercial resorts of Puerto La Cruz and Isla Margarita to the east, where you can sunbathe, windsurf, scuba dive and dance throughout the night.

Tour operators
Several agencies operate in Puerto Ayacucho for those wanting to turn up and book on the spot. Details are in the Puerto Ayacucho section on page 199. If you'd prefer to book internationally here is a selection of agencies handling travel to and in Venezuela:

In Venezuela
Auyantepuy Travel Agency Calle Bolivar Edificio Roque Center #6, Ciudad Bolivar; tel: 285 632 0748; fax: 285 632 8702; email: travel@auyantepuyonline.com; web: www.auyantepuyonline.com. Many years experience in the Venezuelan tourism industry, with packages for Amazonas.

Cacao Amazonas in Puerto Ayacucho; tel/fax: 0248 521 3964; email: wildnatureexp@hotmail.com; web: www. www.amazonasvenezuela.com. Excellent array of day and multi-day tours in the state of Amazonas, focusing on nature and ethnology, including the Ruta Humbolt and trips to Cerro Autana.

Eco Voyager Los Chaguaramos, Av Stadium con Alma Mater, Edif Irma #52; tel/fax: 212 662 6282; tel: 212 762 1571; fax: 212 762 4967; also in the US tel: 800 326 7088; email: info@ecovoyager.com; web: www.ecovoyager.com. Have trips to jungle lodges in Amazonas.

Il Delfino Tours PO Box 61800, Caracas; tel: 212 267 5175; fax: 212 265 6021; email: info@delfinotours.com; web: www.delfinotours.com. A new arrival to the tourism market, developing a good reputation for reliable service and high standards.

Orinoco Tours Edif Galerias Bolivar, Piso 7, Ofic. 75-A, Boulevard Sabana Grande, Caracas; tel: 212 761 8431; fax: 212 761 6801; email: info@orinocotours.com; web: www.orinocotours.com. A few metres from Gran Café, between Sabana Grande and Plaza Venezuela metro stations. Tours covering the entire country including Amazonas, Cerro Autana and the Caura River.

Sonderman Air Safaris offer one of Venezuela's premier travel opportunities. Bob Sonderman is an experienced bush pilot and with your own pilot you can travel to the most remote corners of the country. Organised through Last Frontiers (see below).

Tobogan Tours Av 23 de Enero #24, Puerto Ayacucho; tel: 0248 521 4865; fax: 0248 521 4553. One of the few agencies in Puerto Ayacucho geared up to take international bookings. They can arrange trips throughout the state and to surrounding jungle lodges.

In the US
Field Guides Inc 9433 Bee Cave Rd, Building 1, Suite 150, Austin, TX 78733; tel: 800 728 4953; fax: 512 263 0117; email: fieldguides@fieldguides.com; web: www.fieldguides.com Organise specialist birding trips to lodges deep in Amazonas.
Lost World Adventures 112 Church St, Decatur, GA 30030; tel: 800 999 0558; fax: 404 377 1902; email: info@lostworldadventures.com, www.lostworldadventures.com.

In the UK
Geodyssey 116 Tollington Park, London N4 3RB; tel: 020 7281 7788; fax: 020 7281 7878; email: info@geodyssey.co.uk; web: www.geodyssey.co.uk. Venezuela specialists covering everywhere from Amazonas to the Caribbean.
Last Frontiers Fleet Marston Farm, Aylesbury, Bucks HP18 0QT; tel: 01296 653000; fax: 01296 658651; email: info@lastfrontiers.com; web: www.lastfrontiers.com. Tailor made South America specialists who can arrange anything you can imagine, with a strong track record on Venezuela.

GETTING THERE AND AWAY
By air
Venezuela is the easiest, though not the cheapest, South American country to travel to, from both the US and most of Europe.

From the US
Flights are channelled through Miami which is just four hours from Caracas, although there are services from several other US cities. Prices change and strong competition on this route means good bargains can be found. Return tickets from Miami are currently around US$200.

From Europe
Competition here is also hotting up. British Airways offers a direct service from London. Other airlines include KLM, Iberia, Lufthansa, Air France, Air Portugal and Alitalia. For the best and latest flight deals contact a specialist tour operator such as Journey Latin America. Prices from London start at around £470 return.

Overland
Entering the state of Amazonas directly from Colombia is technically possible through Puerto Carreño, arriving in the small town of Burro. On the border further south, immigration offices can be found at crossings between Guaviare in Colombia and San Fernando de Atabapo; also between the Colombian town of San Felipe and its Venezuelan neighbour San Carlos de Rio Negro. At both points there are no road links to the rest of Colombia which makes travelling further a tough proposition – but your mere presence will create a fair amount of interest and curiosity. Obtaining the necessary stamps and permission could depend on the mood of the officials. Other crossing points from Colombia are between Maicao and Paraguachón, north of Maracaibo; at San Antonio del Táchira in the mountains; and a little further south where the Venezuelan town of El Amparo de Apure and the Colombian town of Arauca sit either side of the Brazo Guárico.

Entering southwestern Venezuela from Brazil is possible, but again is subject to the suspicions of officials. The crossing point is San Simón de Cocuy, connected to Puerto Ayacucho by a weekly flight. Entering Venezuela on this route requires a visa which can be obtained in Manaus. Officials may also want to see a permit for travelling in the restricted region. The more widely used overland frontier with Brazil is in the far southeast of Venezuela near Santa Elena de Uairén. A good road links the town with Boa Vista in Brazil and beyond. For those entering Venezuela, roads lead north to Ciudad Bolívar, from where you can get a bus to Puerto Ayacucho.

There are no border crossings between Venezuela and Guyana.

Customs and immigration

There are currently no visa requirements for US or European nationals entering Venezuela by air. However, if you wish to enter Venezuela overland you do need a visa, which you should obtain from a Venezuelan consulate either in the neighbouring country or in your home country.

Security

When travelling in Venezuela you should always carry your passport with you. Spot checks are common and authorities insist on seeing the real thing. It is not uncommon for police to arrange impromptu spot checks in the street or in bus stations, especially in areas close to any of Venezuela's borders.

Getting around

Travel in Venezuela is very easy. Roads are good and internal flights serve most towns. Puerto Ayacucho has road connections with major cities in Venezuela but for the sake of speed consider taking a plane.

By bus

Hundreds of intercity buses criss-cross the country. The air-conditioned buses leave on time, arrive on time, and usually show a video. Air-conditioning is a definite bonus and a break from the stickiness of travel in humid climes, but take extra clothing in case you feel cold.

If you are at all curious about the difference, travelling by the only slightly cheaper buses ventilated with windows will help you decide.

Venezuelan bus travel has an element of security not shared with some of its South American neighbours… a luggage ticket. Bus stations are busy, frantic places where luggage can easily go missing. If you put your bags in the 'hold', you will get a receipt that is checked when you collect them.

Travelling to Puerto Ayacucho is easy. Long-distance buses make the journey from central Caracas (US$12), Ciudad Bolívar (US$9), Valencia (US$12) and Maracay (US$11). Should you find yourself in the *llanos* you can catch a bus from San Fernando de Apure (US$6).

Hitching

The adventurous and curious could hitch from Caracas down to Puerto Ayacucho, but finding a good starting point would be difficult. It's probably better to start from a smaller city. Hitching is a great way to meet people you wouldn't otherwise come across. The usual commonsense rules apply: there is safety in numbers, and women travellers do run an extra risk, especially if travelling alone.

By air

Internal flights in Venezuela are convenient and reasonably affordable. All major cities and towns are served by regular scheduled flights. Several companies provide internal flights from Caracas to Puerto Ayacucho. Santa Barbara Airlines run a regular service from Caracas costing around US$65 one way. Tickets can be bought from the domestic terminal, next to the international airport near Caracas, or from travel agents in town.

Once you're in small towns there are usually air taxis that can take you to smaller towns. In Puerto Ayacucho, flights can be arranged with Aguaysa near the Plaza de los Indios. They also have some charter flights to small settlements in the region. Air taxi services can be found at the airport.

COMMUNICATIONS

For a country displaying all the visual signals of a modern economy, Venezuela's prosperity is severely restricted by its poor communication networks.

Mail

Postal services are run by Ipostel and are infamously slow and expensive. Three weeks is the minimum time for a postcard to reach the US or Europe. Parcel post is expensive. Not surprisingly, private courier companies offering alternative services have sprouted up.

Telephones and fax

The CANTV-operated telephone system is good… when it works. Telephones use magnetic *tarjetas* ranging in value up to Bs5,000. Cards are sold by vendors close to phone boxes, in hotels and at news-stands. International calls can be made direct from call boxes. The main problem is finding a telephone that works. Not surprisingly, mobile telephones are becoming extremely popular.

Both the terrestrial and mobile systems are overstretched and tempers fray when numbers alter monthly as digits are added and codes are changed. If you are having problems contacting a company in Venezuela check with international operators for changes to the network. If you are in the country, hotel staff may be able to help.

Fax machines are widespread in the better hotels and in the regional offices of CANTV. Fax services through private companies are widely available.

The international country code for Venezuela is 58.

Internet

A system that has proved a lifeline for many other isolated countries was slow to take off in Venezuela. But internet use is growing steadily with internet services in large and small towns.

Television and radio

Venezuelan television is dominated by *telenovelas,* movies and baseball. The five channels coming out of Caracas cannot all be received countrywide. Satellite has added to the appetite for more of the standard fare. News on television is notable by its absence.

As on radio in so many countries, a few popular tunes are played endlessly.

Newspapers

Several newspapers are available throughout the country, with *El Universal* and *El Nacional* being the main ones from Caracas. *The Daily Journal* is an English-language daily available in Caracas, with good coverage on Venezuelan and international issues.

CARACAS

Caracas is a vibrant, modern city nestling in a valley 900m above sea level. The altitude makes for fairly comfortable temperatures hovering in the low 20s Celsius despite being only 11° north of the Equator. The view of the coast just 35km away is blocked by the deep-green hills of El Avila National Park which loom over the city, rising to 2,765m. To the south, lower and slightly less steep hills are laden with shanty towns which cling precariously to the unstable slopes.

The city sprawls along a valley stretching east-west. The city centre's shiny façade of impressive skyscrapers, highways and urban designs in many ways masks the city's chaos. But despite urban planners' attempts to design out poverty, slums lurk in spaces around the old Nuevo Circo Bus Terminal.

The main areas of interest to the tourist are **Central Caracas** and **Sabana Grande**, a few kilometres to the east.

Central Caracas is home to the remaining colonial heritage of the city. The focus is Plaza Bolívar – a feature repeated in every Venezuelan town or city – where there are several museums, some interesting architecture and significant places of history. Accommodation in the city centre tends to be rather shabby and the streets can be eerily empty at night and weekends.

In contrast Sabana Grande is a lively district packed with restaurants, several good hotels and plenty of things to do at night. The central boulevard has several *al fresco* restaurants ideal for people-watching and letting the world pass you by.

Caracas has a reputation as a dangerous city and, if what the residents say is true, this is justified. Stay in the more popular areas to avoid problems. Walking around on your own, particularly at night in quiet areas, should be avoided. Take precautions to avoid attracting attention, and if you are not sure of your bearings take a taxi.

At the airport
Símon Bolívar International Airport is 35km outside Caracas near the Caribbean coastal town of Maiquetía. A bus service leaving from outside the terminal building and serving the city centre costs US$2. When returning to the airport the bus leaves from a rather eerie lay-by under Avenida Bolívar close to the Museo de los Niños. Very few people in the street know the service exists and even fewer can give instructions on how to find it. The evening service stops 'when there are no more passengers' so arrive early if your plane travels late at night.

Alternatively take a taxi to or from the city. This costs around US$18 and has the added benefit of getting you direct to your hotel.

The airport departure tax changes often. It is currently US$22. If short of cash there are ATMs upstairs in the terminal building.

City transport
Taxis and buses can take you all over the city and both are fairly cheap, but the streets are usually close to gridlock. Clean, quiet and efficient, the Metro passes within walking distance of most places of interest in Caracas and is worth using even if just for the few stops between Sabana Grande and Central Caracas.

Metro La Hoyada is closest to the central district of town, Metro Sabana Grande closest to most hotels in Sabana Grande. Metro Bellas Artes is the stop closest to the airport bus service.

Where to stay
The most convenient place to stay is Sabana Grande. The atmosphere is pleasant and any trips to Central Caracas are just a few stops away on the Metro.

First class
Caracas Hilton tel: 212 503 5000; fax: 212 503 5003; web: www.hilton.com. In the heart of Caracas, midway between Sabana Grande and Central Caracas. A mere US$150 a night… but they can arrange specials if you are planning to stay for a few days!

Key

Places of interest

1 Government Palace
2 Casa Amarilla
3 Casa Natal del Libertador Símon Bolívar and Museo Bolívariano
4 Museo de Arte Contemporáneo
5 Museo de Ciencias Naturales
6 Galeria de Arte Nacional
7 Centro Artesanal Los Guajiro

Middle range

Hotel Kursaal Avenida Casanova esq Calle El Colegio; tel: 212 762 2922; fax: 212 762 5715. Just off the main Boulevard de Sabana Grande, this is a clean and tidy 3-star hotel three blocks south of Metro Sabana Grande. US$36 for a double.

Hotel Luna Calle El Colegio; tel: 212 762 5851; fax: 212 762 5850. A 3-star hotel just round the corner from the Kursaal but with a friendlier atmosphere. US$27 for a double.

Hotel Galeria Av Sur Las Acacias. The best hotel on a street packed with possibilities. US$26 for a double.

Hotel Las Americas Calle Los Cerritos, south of Sabana Grande in Bello Monte; tel: 212 9517133; fax: 212 951 1717; email: americas@cantv.net; web: www.hotellasamericas.com.ve. Tower block hotel. Popular spot with good bar, restaurant and roof-top pool.

Budget

Budget travellers will find plenty of cheap hotels down Av Sur Las Acacias in Sabana Grande. **Nuestro Hotel** on Calle El Colegio opposite Hotel Luna is one of the friendliest budget places in the area. The really cheap hotels are found further west one block south of the Nuevo Circo Bus Terminal. It's not a safe part of town so take care walking about at night. If you want to be in Central Caracas, the old part of town, there are a few good hotels. These two are reasonable.

Hotel Tiuna Av Urdaneta esq La Pelota (near McDonalds). Basic, but cheap, friendly and helpful. US$12 for a double.

Hotel Metropol Av Fuerzes Armadas between Plaza Lopez and Socorro. An alternative if the Tiuna is full. US$16 for a double.

Where to eat

Breakfast is one meal Caraqueños have down to an art form. *Pastelerías* serve pastries and cakes with a small cup of potent coffee. The early morning rush can be amusing. Um and errr for too long and you'll be lost in a flurry of activity.

Arepas are small fried cornmeal rolls filled with vegetables or meat and great for snacking throughout the day. Lunch or *almuerzo* is usually a set menu served with soup, a main course and dessert. Eating out in the evening tends to have fewer set menu options.

CARACAS: CENTRE

Facilities
(8) Hotel Metropol
(9) Hotel Tiuna
(10) Hotel Luna
(11) Hotel Kursaal
(12) Rest Chez Wong
(13) Rest El Rugantino
(14) Rest Al Vecchio Mulino
(15) Banco Mercantil
(16) Las Novedades, newsagents
(17) Hotel El Condor
(18) Banco Orinoco

Metro stations
(19) Metro Silencio
(20) Metro Capitolio
(21) Metro La Hoyada
(22) Metro Carabobo
(23) Metro Bellas Artes
(24) Metro Colegio Ingenieros
(25) Metro Plaza Venezuela
(26) Metro Sabana Grande
(27) Metro Chacaíto

Around Sabana Grande there are plenty of eating options. Al fresco restaurants fill the main boulevard between Metro Plaza Venezuelana and Metro Sabana Grande. One street north, the Avenida Francisco Solano, is packed with more atmospheric restaurants costing from US$15. **Restaurant Al Vecchio Mulino** is an Italian restaurant decorated with a windmill that stands out. Others along the same street include **El Rugantino** and **Chez Wong** on the other side of the street. There are too many to list. Take a walk and make your choice.

Finding food in the centre can be a bit of a chore in the daytime. There are several *pastelerías*, pizza places and *tasca* bars along Avenida Urdaneta. Juice bars serve tasty *batidos* refreshments to keep tired feet on the go for the afternoon bout of sightseeing. The choice of fruits is bewildering.

A must for an evening meal in Central Caracas is **El Coyuco** which is usually filled with Caraqueños... always a good sign. Their speciality is grilled meat brought to the table on your own personal charcoal grill. Wash it down with an ice-cold *Polarcita* beer and you're halfway Venezuelan!

What to see

Many tourists go to Caracas because they have to rather than for any wish to explore the city, but there are plenty of things to see that encapsulate Venezuela, ancient and modern, perfectly.

Essentially within a few blocks lies what remains of the colonial heritage of Caracas. **Plaza Bolívar** is a shaded plaza with a statue of Venezuela's national hero Símon Bolívar on horseback. The hustle and bustle of the city seems quite forgotten in this peaceful and quiet small square. Bordering the plaza are several buildings of interest including the **Casa Amarilla**, currently the foreign ministry, which was the house of the nation's president before Miraflores Palace was constructed. You can also see **Caracas Cathedral**, and the **Museo Sacro** displaying a collection of 17th-century artworks.

Two blocks east is the uninspiring Plaza El Venezolano. Facing the plaza on Calle San Jacinto is **Casa Natal del Libertador Símon Bolívar**, where the legendary figure was born on July 24 1783. The restored house is home to several paintings and items paying tribute to the man and his life. Next door the **Museo Bolívariano** also houses memorabilia in homage to the great liberator.

Several blocks north of Plaza Bolívar is the **National Pantheon** in which rest Bolívar's ashes. As precious as the man's memory is to the nation, the building is in a pretty sorry state and is surely due for refurbishment once the government's finances improve.

A visit to **Parque Central** takes you from the ancient to the modern. A city within a city, seven skyscrapers are filled with homes, offices, shops and museums. Within, people quietly move around like rabbits in a huge concrete warren. The complex was part of Venezuela's vision for a brave new world. Several museums are in Parque Central including the **Museo de los Niños** (Children's Museum) and the **Museo de Arte Contemporáneo** (Contemporary Art Museum), which includes significant collections from international artists including Picasso.

Slightly north of Parque Central and close to the Caracas Hilton is the **Complejo Cultural Teresa Carreño**, a modern performing arts centre. Its neighbours include the **Museo de Ciencias Naturales** (Natural History Museum) with a changing selection of exhibits, and the **Galeria de Arte Nacional** (National Art Museum).

Shopping
Central Artesanal los Guajiro is a small craft market selling hammocks, clothes and other items in Sabana Grande, close to Metro Chacaíto. For the best shopping, you're better off going to El Hatillo (see below).

Excursions from Caracas
El Hatillo
El Hatillo is a suburb of Caracas some 13km south of the city. Regular city buses leave from Av Humboldt close to Metro Chacaíto in Sabana Grande. Quaint streets lined with pastel colonial buildings and street cafés give a cosmopolitan feel to the atmosphere. El Hatillo is very calming: a welcome break from the chaos of Caracas.

The main reason to visit El Hatillo is for shopping. There is no shortage of places selling all things Venezuelan – traditional and contemporary, old and new. Everything is within two blocks of the main plaza.

For excellent handicrafts and service seek out **Hannsi** at Calle Bolívar #12; tel: 963 7184, email: hannsi@directnet.com.ve; web: www.hannsi.com.ve. The shop sells crafts from throughout Venezuela including those from the Indian tribes of Amazonas. There are Yanomami baskets with characteristic geometric designs, and straw-fringed masks of the Piaroa that pay tribute to the tarantula; blowpipes, carvings, hammocks and even dug-out canoes are also sold.

Larger items can be shipped home, and Hannsi takes credit cards. It's the kind of place where vacation budgets go seriously awry.

Leaving town
Buses to Puerto Ayacucho – and most other places in Venezuela – leave from the Nuevo Circo Terminal on Av Lecuna. The nearest metro stop is La Hoyada. Internal flights depart from the domestic airport next door to the international airport.

Buses for eastern destinations leave from Terminal de Oriente, 8km out of town. A local bus takes passengers from Metro Petare to the terminal.

PUERTO AYACUCHO: GATEWAY TO THE VENEZUELAN AMAZON

Officially founded on December 9, 1924, Puerto Ayacucho is the Venezuelan Amazon's administrative and distribution centre – a role that naturally stimulated growth. A Salesian missionary living in the region since 1932 remembers when Puerto Ayacucho was a tiny hamlet of just 200 people. Today the Amazonas state capital is a dusty town of 60,000 and not especially lovable. The heart of the town centre is a long way from the Orinoco River, and the lack of chaotic riverside activity distinguishes it from most lowland settlements. But there is a wide range of services and it's a convenient base from which to explore the rainforest about 80km south.

Puerto Ayacucho owes its existence to the Orinoco. Boats travel here unhindered from the Orinoco Delta, 900km downstream. But beyond Puerto Ayacucho the Atures and Maipures rapids make the river unnavigable for 60km. All river cargo must be unloaded, moved overland upstream to Samariapo above the rapids, and then reloaded to continue the journey as far as 1,160km upstream. When roads reached Puerto Ayacucho, they removed the town's *raison d'être*. As so often with Amazon towns, the road changed it forever. Puerto Ayacucho is still a river port but depends little on the river. Today, the town relies on road and air connections to fulfill its function as the main distribution centre for the state of Amazonas.

The central part of the town is very compact – nowhere is more than ten minutes' walk away – making it very easy to get around. The town centres on Plaza Bolívar from where the statue of Simón Bolívar watches over the comings and goings of visitors to the government buildings, the faithful and sinners to the Salesian Mission, and students to the library and school.

The average temperature is 27°C and, although more than 900km away from the Atlantic, the town is just 110m above sea level. Rainfall here is almost 2,200mm annually with the rainy season from June to October. The area in the immediate vicinity of Puerto Ayacucho is plains savannah covered with grasses and giant-leafed moriche palms. The rocky terrain around the town limits soil production and a number of crystal clear rivers flow through the region.

Getting there

Puerto Ayacucho airport is 5km south of the town. Taxis make the journey for around US$5. The small bus terminal is a few kilometres east of town. Local buses marked *Centro* regularly run the route from the main road outside the terminal, taxis charge US$0.50 for the trip.

Where to stay

There is a surprising number of hotels in Puerto Ayacucho providing for all but the most luxurious tastes.

Middle range

Hotel Orinoco at the bottom of Av Orinoco near the port; tel: 0248 414 6562. Comfortable and quiet. A fair hotel that has seen better days. *Dobles* start at US$14 with AC and TV.

Hotel Apure Avenida Orinoco on the way out to the airport; tel: 0248 521 0516. A well-kept hotel that caters for organised tours. Quite a way from the centre of town. *Dobles* with AC and TV are US$20. Probably the best comfortable hotel in town, although there is no restaurant.

Hotel Restaurant 'Mi Jardin' Av Orinoco close to Hotel Apure; tel: 0248 521-4647. Good hotel with restaurant and a patio garden. *Dobles* with AC and TV are US$23.

PUERTO AYACUCHO

Budget

Residencia Siapa Calle Carabobo (no sign); tel: 0248 521-0138. Comfortable and friendly. Very popular with visiting Venezuelans. *Dobles* with AC and TV are US$12.
Residencial Internacional Av Aguerrevere 18, tel: 0248 521-0242. The budget travellers' favourite. The rooms aren't much, but it is a good place to meet up with other travellers. *Simples* are US$6, *dobles* US$8 and *triples* US$14.

Out of town

An alternative option is to stay at one of the many jungle-style lodges in the area using them as a base for trips to the jungle. Most can be booked internationally or from Caracas. **Aguas Bravas** (tel/fax: 0248 521 1529; email: aguasbravas@cantv.net, or **Tobogan Tours** (Av 23 de Enero #24, Puerto Ayacucho; tel: 0248 521 4865; fax: 0248 521 4553) can advise on availability if you are in the area.

Just out of Puerto Ayacucho is the popular resort of **Campamento Tucán** also called **Campamento Genesis** (tel/fax: 0248 521 0409). Set amongst trees with spotless rooms, a pool and a thatched dining room based on the traditional thatched round-houses of the Piaroa Indians, this is a relaxing retreat: an ideal way to start and finish trips to the rainforest. Prices from US$80pp.

Further south is **Campamento Las Garzitas**, tel: 0248 521 4958, overlooking the rapids of the Orinoco. At US$40 it's slightly cheaper than other lodges and can help arrange tailored trips throughout the region. If you call in advance they will arrange transfers from the airport. They share an office in Puerto Ayacucho with Siapa Amazonas Expeditions on Plaza de los Indios.

Nearby is the new **Orinoquia Lodge** on the banks of the Orinoco, with headquarters in Caracas (tel: 0212 977 1234; fax: 0212 977 0110; email: cacaotravel@cantv.net; web: www.orinoquialodge.com). Ten very comfortable *churuatas* (thatched bungalows) are in a riverfront setting. Double and triple rooms all have private bathrooms. Prices start at US$42pp for bed, breakfast and supper. A wide range of packages and multi-day tours available, including trips to Cerro Autana, along the rivers Cuao and Sipapo and the Ruta Humbolt. Contact Cacao Travel for prices (see page 191).

Camturama Resort, tel: 048 210266, is the largest resort. It features air-conditioned chalet-style rooms, a large restaurant, bar area and disco. On the banks of the Orinoco, day fishing and birding trips can be arranged, along with jungle excursions. Prices from US$85pp including meals. Enquiries and bookings can be made in Caracas (tel: 212 941 8813; fax: 212 943 5160).

Where to eat

El Capi on Calle Evelio Roa is a small restaurant on a covered terrace. It is an awe-inspiring experience to relax on a terrace while a powerful tropical rainstorm does its best to wash the town downriver. **Tasca Restaurant Rio Negro** on Av Rio Negro, close to the plaza, is an intimate little place. The early evening is quiet and relaxed; later at night live entertainment keeps going till the early hours.

Restaurant El Angoleño is a restaurant and bar a couple of blocks north of the plaza. From El Capi, head down Calle Evelio Roa and it is on the left at the end. There is no sign to guide you so you may have to ask. The food is good and covers a wide range of fish and meat dishes and the service is very friendly.

For snacks, **Le Petit Café** on Av Orinoco sells very tasty *arepas* with a wide selection of fillings. There are several bakeries/juice bars in town, the best of which is on the corner of Av Bolívar and Av Orinoco.

Money

Banco Union and Banco de Venezuela, both on Av Orinoco, change cash and travellers' cheques. If you want to avoid queuing use their ATM machines that take Visa and MasterCard. Most of the tour agencies accept travellers' cheques.

What to see

Mercado Indigena (Indian market) is on Plaza de los Indios one block south of Plaza Bolívar, selling a wide range of items from the area. You can pick up Piaroa, Guahibo and Yanomami crafts. The distinctive red-and-brown basketry of the Yanomami is finely crafted. There are several different sizes of *guatura* or *wii* for sale. This device is a flexible tube, woven out of palm fibres, that works like a giant finger trap – the simple children's toy. The Indians use it to squeeze toxic juices out of soaked, mashed manioc.

Opposite the market is the **Museo Etnológico del Amazonas**, open Tuesday to Saturday all day, and in the morning on Sundays. It's a small museum but packed with information about the Indian tribes of the region. There are several rooms with models and artefacts reflecting the main indigenous cultures of the region including the Piaroa, Guajibo, Yanomami, Arawak and Ye'kwana Indians. On Plaza Bolívar itself is the Salesian Mission and the library, with displays and videos about the region.

Not too far from the centre of town is **Cerro Perico**, a small hill with a viewing post at the summit which gives an excellent view of the surrounding area and the Orinoco. To get there follow Av Aguerrevere west looking to the left until you see the hill. The road meanders round the hill and becomes a path towards the top. The impressive view is best at sunrise or sunset.

On the road out to the airport is the rather eccentric **Casa de La Piedra** (House of the Stone). It is not in itself remarkable, but the building, constructed in the 1960s, sits atop a massive boulder balancing precariously 10m above the ground. The house is currently being renovated and, if funds don't run out first, the plan is to use the building as a hotel or hostel.

Tour operators
In Puerto Ayacucho the tour agencies seem to start up and go bust daily. Most of them can help with almost any enquiry or request. It is worth comparing a couple of agencies for price and level of service. Here are a few of the recommended agencies in Puerto Ayacucho in addition to **Aguas Bravas** and **Tobogan Tours** mentioned on page 200 and those at the beginning of the chapter (page 191).

Amazonia, Av. Río Negro 33-A, Plaza de Los Indios; tel/fax: 0248 521 4926; email: amazonia-c.a.@gmx.net; web: www.amazonia-venezuela.net. Adventurous travel opportunities including to Yanomami communities and a 20-day Ruta Humboldt.
Turismo 'Yutaje' Monte Bello 31; tel: 0248 521 0604. This established agency is trying to stimulate interest in sustainable ecotourism in the Venezuelan rainforest.
Cruising Tours Tel/fax: 0248 521 0443. A couple of blocks north of the plaza, this new agency is building a solid reputation.

Indigenous groups of Amazonas State
In 1992, government figures put Amazonas' indigenous population at 43,366, with 17 different ethnic groups. The largest populations are Ye'kuana (4,000), Yaruro (4,859), Curripaco (2,623), Piaroa (8,030) and Yanomami (over 10,000). Each ethnic group has its own language and set of beliefs, usually based around complex relationships with spirits of the forest.

The Yanomami inhabit an area of forests and mountain valleys that cross the Venezuelan-Brazilian border, straddling the headwaters of the Orinoco in Venezuela and several tributaries feeding into the lower section of the Río Negro in Brazil. Yanomami live in communal houses called *shabonos* that house as many as 400 people. The dwellings are oval, and have steep walls to protect an inner open area.

The Yanomami are semi-nomadic. They grow manioc, bananas and other crops tended in gardens close to the *shabono*. They hunt with bows and arrows tipped with *curare* – a natural poison made from forest plants that attacks the nervous system. The Yanomami decorate their faces with wooden plugs and their bodies with red paint made from vegetable dyes of *onoto* seed. They also use a hallucinogenic snuff called *yoppo*.

The Piaroa, like the Yanomami, are semi-nomadic, clearing land for settled agriculture before moving on after four years or so. The land is cleared by burning

NO WAY TO DECIDE...

Beata Pawlikowska, a radio personality with the Polish radio broadcaster Vheadline/VENews.

It's easy – you get on a plane and fly to Caracas. Then you go by bus as far south as it can take you. Finally, you go to a local travel agency and say that you want to go and see the Yanomami Indians. You pay a substantial sum of money, get on a boat and after a few days you arrive at a Yanomami village.

You see slim dark-skinned people, barely dressed, men with scars on their heads, women with wooden sticks put in their cheeks and chins. You see the shack-like *shabono* houses, thatched with palm leaves. You see the bows and arrows, naked children grimy with soil, and you think: 'Oh my goodness! They are so poor, dirty, lazy and primitive!'

But stop and consider this:

Some civilisations focus on changing the environment around them so that it serves all their needs. Other civilisations make the effort to adapt themselves to the existing conditions.

There is no way to decide which is better: people who burn and cut the forest to build a city with shops, streets, concrete houses and an airport; or people who make the jungle their home.

Once you are born in either of these civilisations, you will never be able to comprehend the nature of the other.

and then cultivated as a garden or *kanuku* to produce around 50 different types of vegetable, mainly bitter manioc, corn and sweet potato. For fishing they use poisons and for hunting rely on blowpipes and curare-tipped darts – a product for which the Piaroa were once famous within the Amazon. Their spiritual leaders or shamans have a good reputation amongst indigenous groups and use hallucinogenic substances in rituals and healing. Circular communal houses or *churuatas* built from hardwoods and thatched with palm fronds reflect the status of the chief and accommodate up to 100 people.

Excursions near Puerto Ayacucho

El Tobogán de la Selva, 30km south of Puerto Ayacucho, is a huge rock escarpment with a river running down its face. Erosion has created a natural waterslide almost 100m in length – it's great fun if you can handle a few bumps and bruises. Towards the top of the slide are a couple of natural jacuzzis that look just like shallow puddles but are actually several feet deep, and at the summit is a natural diving pool. There are shelters with barbecue racks and picnic tables, but the place does get crowded at weekends and holidays. Camping is allowed but there is no food for sale close to the area.

El Tobogán is not served by any public transport. To get there hitch a ride south to the turn-off at Kilometre 30 and then walk or hitch the remaining 6km. There is an hourly jeep that travels south down to Samariapo from Av Orinoco (near Banco Venezuela) which stops at the turn-off. Alternatively trips can be arranged through agencies or with a taxi. Hitching is easiest at weekends and, with due care, a good way to make new Venezuelan friends.

On the way to El Tobogán is **Piedra de la Tortuga**, a couple of rocks that from the right perspective, look like a giant tortoise. It's about 8km out of town. From the wrong perspective, however, they appear to be a couple of rocks...

About 17km south of town you can also see **Cerro Pintado**, home to

PUERTO AYACUCHO AREA

Villacoa

Puerto
Páez

Meta

Burro

PUERTO
CARREÑO

Orinoco

Chiripue

Raudal Tabaje

Raudal Borje

Parguasa

Pozones

COLOMBIA

Pozo Azul

Orinoco

C E R R O
G U A N A Y

Casuarito

PUERTO
AYACUCHO

AMAZONAS

Gavilán

Raudal Atures

Caño Santo

Yutajé

Raudal Garcitas

▲ Cerro Pintado

STATE

Coromoto

San Juan de Manapiare

Raudals
Maipures

El Tobogán

Marieta

Morrocoy

Samariapo

Cuao

Camani

Venado

Maco

I. Ratón

Morganito

Santa Rosa

Cerro Autana
▲ 1208m

San Vicente

Parú

Autana

San Pedro

Sipapo

N

Guayapo

Bradt

Caño Mure

Caño Plojo

Ventuari

Marueta

San Fernando
de Atabapo

Carmelitas

Orinoco

Yapacana
National
Park

C E R R O
Y A P A C A N A

Sta Bárbara

Orinoco

0 ————————— 50 km

Atabapo

0 ————————— 40 miles

Tamatama,
Casiquiare Canal

prehistoric petroglyphs. It is best to visit the site with a guide as some of the images can be difficult to see.

A swimming hole called **Pozo Azul** is 30km north of town. The water appears bluish and if you go midweek you may have the place to yourself. There is regular traffic on this route so catching a ride is fairly easy.

Aguas Bravas offer half-day trips down the Atures rapids, US$35 per person. Traditionally rafts are powered by oars but Aguas Bravas use outboards to make the trip less strenuous. In the dry season (December to April), stops are made at Sardinata Island to see the petroglyphs. Trips are tailored to each group's preferred level of excitement and all equipment and training is provided.

Jungle tours

The strong competition between agencies in Puerto Ayacucho is great news for travellers visiting the area. There are several itineraries to choose from. For something more adventurous – such as a canoe trip down a remote tributary – agencies in Puerto Ayacucho will gladly help. A few moments pondering over a map of Venezuela produces endless exciting possibilities. The downside of competition is that tour operators cut corners and the environment can suffer so remember to wear your ecotourist hat.

Travel in the region is restricted and only allowed with a permit. Travel down to San Fernando de Atabapo by boat and further south to Maroa and San Carlos de Río Negro by light aircraft is permitted. Any travel south and west of this route without a permit is beyond official protection.

A couple of days

The simplest option is a short two-day, one-night trek in the jungle. Most of these stay fairly close to Puerto Ayacucho and don't actually get into lowland rainforest but reports are generally good. Trips include visits to Piaroa communities to experience the culture at first hand, including the use of blowpipes, medicinal plants and various natural materials. These 'anthropological tours' start at around US$40 per person per day. As with most of the jungle tours, the night is spent in a hammock which may be on a river beach if local guides think the river is safe. Mosquito nets are generally provided but check first.

Four days to a week

An especially rewarding trip is 80km south of Puerto Ayacucho to Cerro Autana, called Wahari Kuawai by the Piaroa. The sheer cliffs of this tepui jut out 1,200m above the surrounding uniformly flat rainforest – a profoundly striking visual feature. A three- or four-day trip takes you in a *bongo* up the Orinoco, Sipapo and Autana rivers. Originally the name for the traditional dugout canoe used by people above the rapids, 'bongo' means almost anything that travels on the water. Accommodation is in hammocks with local Piaroa communities. The trips include visits to nearby waterfalls and walks in the jungle looking for tarantulas; increasingly difficult as they are not only revered by the Piaroa as protectors of the rainforest but also eaten as delicacies.

Trip prices start at US$40 per person per day.

The geology of Cerro Autana is complex and recent aerial expeditions have discovered a horizontal cave passing through the *tepui* from one side to the other, impossible to see from the ground. Air taxis and helicopters can be hired from Puerto Ayacucho for a flying tour.

One extended alternative is travel by boat to San Juan de Manapiare. It is five or six days upstream, depending on how many smaller tributaries you explore along the way, but the main route follows the course of the Orinoco before heading north up the Ventuari. Flights from San Juan de Manapiare to Puerto Ayacucho are around US$60 one way. Prices for the expedition are about US$80pp per day.

Over a week

A more adventurous option is to follow the *Ruta Humboldt*; retracing the journey of Baron von Humboldt in the early 19th century when he made the crossing between the Amazon Basin and the Orinoco River by way of the Brazo Casiquiare. This natural canal diverts up to one third of the Orinoco River's volume down the 354km-long canal from Tamatama, flowing on to join the River Negro, one of the Amazon's major tributaries. The waterway is unique in that it connects two major watersheds and defies accepted rules of hydrology by flowing in both directions – depending on the local conditions.

It's a fantastic journey and *enjoyed* by the most hardy of fools. The region is pristine rainforest and the insects do their best to keep people away – a couple of hundred bites wouldn't be uncommon. Fortunately if you are travelling by motorised boat the insects can't keep up.

Heading upstream from Puerto Ayacucho, the canoe travels to San Fernando de Atabapo and beyond, following the Temi River to Yavita. A road link crosses to Maroa on the Guainía River which flows down to meet the Casiquiare when both rivers merge to become the Río Negro. Heading up the Casiquiare against the current, the route rejoins the Orinoco before heading back down to Puerto Ayacucho.

You need to take food for the journey, supplementing it with fish caught while travelling and supplies brought on the expedition. En route you can stay with Piaroa, Yanomami and several other indigenous communities.

In total the journey takes at least eight days or maybe longer. Several smaller tributaries are also worth exploring if you can tolerate making innumerable blood sacrifices to the local biting insects. Animal life goes beyond insects, with dolphins, giant otters, jaguar and tapir all found in the area. There are also hundreds of butterflies, birds and other rainforest wildlife to see on the smaller tributaries. Prices start from around US$100 per day.

Ruta Humboldt and cruising in style

The Ruta Humboldt is hard or soft adventure travel, depending on your budget and stamina. The trip is best organised through one of the operators in Puerto Ayacucho or Caracas. The journey begins in Puerto Ayacucho and takes in Autana *tepui* and several small Indian villages and communities en route to the mission outpost of La Esmeralda, before turning round and heading down the Casiquiare. Stopping to explore tributaries and lakes, and with time for fishing and swimming, the trip follows the Casiquiare downstream before flying you back to Puerto Ayacucho from the town of San Carlos de Río Negro.

The trip takes at least 15 days and can include trips to the triple frontier where Venezuela, Colombia and Brazil meet, and to Piedra del Cocuy. This National Monument rises 400m above rainforest and gives a fantastic view of the rainforest lowlands.

A second comfortable option for cruising the waterways of the Orinoco and the Amazon is to board the ***Capitán Barata***. This Brazilian-registered floating hotel is reached from Puerto Ayacucho on a charter flight to Tamatama. Cruising along the Casiquiare, the *Barata* stops to explore smaller tributaries and for treks in the rainforest. Some trips stop off at San Carlos de Río Negro from where you can return to Puerto Ayacucho. Trips also travel further south, visiting Piedra del Cocuy and connecting with a dug-out canoe for the eight-hour trip to São Gabriel de Cachoeira in Brazil. After another four days of local excursions in the Brazilian rainforest, flying to Manaus provides a stunning aerial view of the heart of the rainforest before you catch a flight back to Caracas. Ask at main tour operators for latest contact details.

Lodges near San Juan de Manapiare

Jungle lodges close to San Juan de Manapiare are targeting the comfortable end of the market. The lodges are all in the middle of the rainforest; ideal places for combining true relaxation with the occasional burst of, albeit mild, energy.

Campamento Camani is on the banks of the Ventuari south of San Juan de Manapiare and claims to be 'the cure against civilisation'. Surrounded by rainforest, the lodge is perfectly located for treks into the jungle. Excursions include boat trips to the Caño de Piedra and Tecuna waterfalls, along with shorter walks to indigenous communities and sites of special natural interest. Fishing can also be arranged. The luxury *churuatas* have hot water and electricity and the international menu is beautifully presented. There is also a swimming pool. The lodge costs US$140 per person per night, plus charter flight to the airstrip. The journey from Caracas takes two hours and requires a minimum of six people for the charter flight. From Puerto Ayacucho it is 50 minutes. Details from Tobogan Tours in Puerto Ayacucho (see pages 191 and 200) or Eco Voyager in Caracas (page 191).

AUTANA – THE TREE OF LIFE

The local Indian legend tells of a giant tree that offered all the fruits of the world to the people of the earth. Nobody had to work to get the benefits. The fruits of the giant tree were within hand's reach.

But one day ambitious men possessed the people and decided to cut the tree down to get all the fruits. The fallen tree couldn't give any more food to the people and its trunk remains in the earth as a symbol of the dangers of ambition.

Today all that remains of the tree is the *tepui* Autana, indeed reminiscent of a giant stump.

Nearby is **Junglaven**, which is slightly less comfortable but gets rave reviews nevertheless. The area is perfect for birdwatching and the owner has compiled a bird list that now includes over 420 species. The camp also offers excellent sports fishing for peacock bass, payara, catfish and pacú between November and May. There are ten *churuata* cabins each with private bathroom and shower. Birding and general trips are US$120pp per night, fishing trips are US$250pp. Flights can be organised from Caracas or from Puerto Ayacucho. Details in Caracas on: tel/fax: 212 991 8478; fax: 212 991 5083. Field Guides in the US (see page 192) has trips to Junglaven for 12 days from US$2,750 (land only).

North of San Juan de Manapiare is **Yutajé Camp**. Set up in 1967 for private guests, the camp is now open to visitors. The accommodation is simple and the rainforest remains unspoilt – home to large numbers of birds along with giant otters and river dolphins. Trips can be made to the nearby Yutajé Falls which cascade off the southern rim of the Guyana Shield. Four-day packages to the camp, based on five passengers and including the flight from Caracas, cost US$480. Book through Eco Voyager (page 191) whose flights depart every Sunday.

If a small plane trip over the rainforest is too scary or expensive consider **Caura Lodge** on the Caura River. The lodge is a colonial house close to the rainforest with sleeping options of hammocks and mosquito net in one of the *churatas* or a double room indoors. It's reported to be a good spot for birdwatching and fishing. Trips by land, boat or plane can be organised through Orinoco Tours in Caracas.

Independent travel
Non-boat trips

For those wanting the freedom of independent travel without restrictions the options are rather limited, and there is always the chance of being turned back by one of the many checkpoints. On the other hand, it can be a liberating experience to travel on your own, or even without a guidebook!

The most straightforward destination is San Juan de Manapiare. Its population of 1,200 lives in temperatures in the high 20s Celsius. The region produces the majority of Amazonas' agricultural produce. San Juan de Manapiare is surrounded to the east, north and west by the most westerly outcrops of the Guyana Shield. Although only 140m above sea level, it is some 1,400km to the Orinoco Delta. The combination of rainforest lowlands with the steep mountains rising to over 2,400m make this an ideal place for guided treks. Salto Yutajé is one of the many waterfalls in the area worth exploring. Flights for San Juan de Manapiare leave several times a week from Puerto Ayacucho and cost US$60 one way.

For the really adventurous, Cruising Tours in Puerto Ayacucho (see page 202) organise treks on foot or horseback between Puerto Ayacucho and San Juan de

Manapiare, or north to the town of Guaniamo. Both trips involve trekking over parts of the Guyana Shield. Prices vary depending on the number in the group.

South towards Brazil

Several communities live along the road that connects Puerto Ayacucho with Samariapo upstream of the Maipures and Atures rapids. None offers hotels or services but they could be good places to stop if you are camping through the region.

At Samariapo there is little more than a few huts, selling soft drinks and meals. Any other produce you can see is probably in transit. There is no accommodation. The biting insects are vicious, making it uncomfortable to stand still, which is another excellent reason for moving on.

Boats regularly travel to the small community on the unfortunately named Island of Rats (Isla Ratón). There is a mission and small school on the island but not much else. The island is close to the Sipapo River which goes towards Cerro Autana and it may be possible to catch a ride with a small supply boat.

Upstream you come to San Fernando de Atabapo, a small town with a couple of hotels. The last surviving communities of Piapoco and Piunave Indians live nearby. Just in front of the town is a clearly defined meeting of the waters where the blackwaters of the Atabapo River meet the brown-coloured waters of the Guaviare flowing in from Colombia. Transport from Puerto Ayacucho with Camani Transportes near the electricity generator cost US$5.

Maroa, founded in 1760 by Chief Maruwa, is an island settlement that acts as a transit point between San Fernando de Atabapo and San Carlos de Río Negro. It is possible to get to Maroa by boat, pushing up to Yavita, then making the land crossing over the watershed between the Orinoco and the Amazon to the town.

San Carlos de Río Negro is a small town downriver from Maroa with a square, church, a small hotel and not much else. Founded in 1759 by Colonel Solanos this is the oldest town in the region, and is the closest to the outlet of the Casiquiare Canal. The area is home to the Baré Indians.

The triple frontier with Colombia and Brazil is further south in Cocuy.

San Fernando de Atabapo, Maroa and San Carlos de Río Negro are all served by regular flights with Aguaysa from Puerto Ayacucho. There is a landing strip just north of the frontier in the town of Santa Lucía.

NATIONAL PARKS AND WILDLIFE RESERVES

Venezuela has a vast range of habitats, protected by 42 national parks. In addition to parks there are 41 natural monuments, including Cerro Autana and Piedra del Cocuy, nine forest reserves, including the Sipapo reserve south of Puerto Ayacucho, and five wildlife reserves.

Within Amazonas there are four national parks, all of which require permits to visit.

Yapacana National Park

Created in 1978, this park covers 320,000ha close to the merging of the Orinoco and the Río Ventuari. The park includes extensive savannah and the region is believed to have among the higest levels of biodiversity in Venezuela.

Duida-Marahuaca National Park

This 210,000ha park touches La Esmeralda to the south, and stretches north to include the peaks of Duida (2,232m) and Marahuaca (2,890m), western outcrops of the Guyana Shield. The park has a series of cylindrical mountains similar to *tepuis,* and there is a wide diversity of flora and fauna in the region.

Mount Neblina National Park

On the southernmost tip of Amazonas State, this park of 1,360,000ha encompasses craggy landscapes, deep rich valleys and views of Pico da Neblina.

Parima-Tapirapecó National Park

(also called the Alto Orinoco-Casiquiare Biosphere Reserve)

Formed in 1991, this national park protects 3,420,000ha of jungle and savannah encompassing the headwaters of the Orinoco River. In addition to protecting a wide range of flora and fauna, about which very little is known, the boundaries form part of the territory of the Yanomami Indian communities. There are strict controls on entry to the park.

Giant otter

Colombia

8

Although named after the 'discoverer' of the Americas, Colombia was never visited by Christopher Columbus. Presumably he had no idea what he was missing, for even today Colombia compels the attention of the curious traveller. It is the land of emeralds and legends of El Dorado. From snow-capped volcanoes and sunny beaches to the vast tropical woodlands, Colombia – more than most countries – merits the tour brochure's description, 'a land of contrasts'.

FACTS AND FIGURES
Geography

Colombia is South America's fourth biggest country, just over twice the size of France. Neighbouring countries include Peru and Ecuador to the south, Venezuela to the north and east, and Brazil in the southeast. Colombia's shortest frontier is with Panama, where South and Central America meet. The Isthmus of Panama splits Colombia's 2,890km (1,800 mile) coastline between the Pacific to the south and to the north the Gulf of Darien in the southern Caribbean.

Inland from the coast, the terrain graduates, by fine degrees, up through every major biome, from tropical rainforest to temperate woodland to alpine.

Colombia's interior is divided by several mountain ranges or *cordilleras*. From the south, the northern Andes spread out into three diverging ranges that separate western Colombia from the eastern lowlands. From the border with Ecuador, the Cordillera Occidental continues north toward Panama. Cordillera Central heads

BASIC FACTS
Official name República del Colombia
Area 1,141,748km2 (440,831 miles²)
Population 42.1 million (2000 est)
Capital Bogotá
Largest city (population) Bogotá (4.5 million)
Main Amazon city Leticia
Official language Spanish
Date of independence 1819 (Spain)
Major industries coffee, oil and natural gas, cotton, sugar, mining
GDP per capita US$6,200
Currency peso (US$1 = 2,350 pesos; UK£1 = 3,525 pesos)
Major attractions Cartagena Old Town, emerald mines
National holidays January 1, March 19, May 1, July 20, August 7 & 15, December 8 & 25

COLOMBIA

CARIBBEAN SEA

CARIBBEAN SEA

CARACAS

Riohacha
Santa Marta
Paraguachón
CARTAGENA
Cristóbal Colón 5775m
Valledupar
Lago Maracaibo

PANAMA

VENEZUELA

CUCUTA
SAN CRISTOBAL
Arauca
Puerto Carreno

PACIFIC OCEAN

MEDELLIN

PUERTO AYACUCHO

Boyaca

BOGOTA

Vichada

Nevada de Huila 5750m
CALI
Neiva

Uva
Guaviare

Popayán
San José del Guaviare
Inírida
Guainía
Isana

San Agustín
San Vicente del Caguán
Calamar

PASTO
Florencia
MOCOA
WATERSHED
MITU

Barra
Pto Asis
Chiribiquete NP
Vaupés
Apaporis

Quito
La Paya NP
La Tagua

BRAZIL

Negro

ECUADOR
Pto. Leguizamo
Aracuara
Caquetá
Cahuinari NP
Japurá

Carapaná

Arica
Içá
Amazon

PERU

Amacayacu NP

IQUITOS
Amazon
LETICIA
BRAZIL
TABATINGA
Benjamin Constant

N

Bradt

0 — 150km
0 — 150 miles

north-northeast, toward the Caribbean. Longest of the ranges, Cordillera Oriental veers northeast toward Venezuela.

To the north of Cordillera Oriental a separate geological formation, Cordillera de Mérida, rises on the Colombia-Venezuela border. A low series of hills and valleys to the southeast of Cordillera Oriental form a large plateau. The southern part of this formation, is encompassed by the department of Amazonas – the northernmost extent of the Amazon watershed in Colombia. The country occupies about 6% of the watershed's total area. The northern part of this plateau, the *llanos* (or Orinoquia), gives rise to numerous tributaries of the Orinoco River that flows through Venezuela.

Rivers

Colombia's natural waterways reflect its complex topography and comprise no less than five major watersheds.

In northwest Colombia, the Magdalena begins between the Cordilleras Central and Oriental, flowing northwest into the Caribbean. The Río Cauca flows along the central valley between the Cordilleras Central and Occidental and into the lower reaches of Río Magdalena. West of Cordillera Occidental the Artaro heads north, parallel to the coast, into the Gulf of Darien by the Panama border.

Colombia's other major rivers originate in the Cordillera Oriental. High in the southern half of this range are sources for several major tributaries of the upper Amazon, which flow eastwards in the river basin. In southeast Colombia, the Putumayo forms the southern border with Peru. This is the Colombian Amazon's most used river as it is the region's second longest and navigable for most of its 1,800km length.

Rivers rising in the northern half of Cordillera Central are claimed by the Orinoco flowing through neighbouring Venezuela.

Climate

Colombia's climate is as variable as its habitats, from alpine to dry savannah to tropical rainforest.

In the Amazon lowlands, annual temperatures average 23°C while rainfall is around 2,500mm and tends to be heaviest in late December to January. Beginning in July or August and lasting anywhere from two to eight weeks, the *veranillo* is a short period of lower precipitation during which temperatures can get very warm. The upper Magdalena Valley, Atlantic lowlands and *llanos* region share a tropical savannah climate of alternating wet and dry seasons. The dry season is from November to April. Weather in the mountains depends on elevation. Temperatures drop about 0.6°C for every 100m of ascent.

Flora and fauna

Ever since the early 1800s when Alexander von Humboldt first described Colombia's wildlife, naturalists have been impressed by its variety and abundance. Varied climate, soil and topography support an extraordinary diversity of plant and animal communities. Mangrove swamps dominate tidal zones, La Guajira is desert scrub, while the Atlantic Lowlands and eastern *llanos* support savannah grasslands and gallery forest. Montane ecosystems are found among Andean slopes and valleys, while the Choco region and Amazonas are primarily tropical rainforest.

For the visitor, there is the usual panoply of tropical South American animals. Colombia's birdlife comprises some 1,500 species (about one sixth of the world's total) over a third of which are found in lowland Amazonia. Dozens of North American songbirds and flycatchers overwinter in Colombia but most species are endemic. About two hundred mammal species are known, and the same number of reptiles. Aquatic life is rich, except for the overfished and polluted Magdalena and Cauca.

Mountain habitats support a different variety of animals, although some of the larger mammals range from low to high elevations. Montane vegetation of *páramo* regions is a highly diverse alpine flora, including a large number of endemic species.

Conservation efforts in Colombia are highlighted by the national parks and extensive investment in biopharmacology and ecotourism. However, pollution and deforestation are taking their toll outside protected areas. Illicit cocaine labs, well-hidden in remote forest, utilise toluene, benzene and other solvents and reagents. Used chemicals are dumped into a river.

Legal extractive operations have also disrupted local ecosystems, mostly along the flanks of the Andes. Colombia's diversity of plants and animals is poorly known. In 1995, a 75m-high tree (*Pseudomonotes tropenbosii*) was found in the Colombian rainforest by two graduate students. Though not new to science, the species was previously known only from Africa. Scientists concluded the tree must have evolved before South America and Africa separated – it is a living fossil.

Land use

About a third of Colombia's land area is permanent pastureland, while 5% is suitable for crops and about half the country is forested. Most arable land is scattered among the high valleys of the Magdalena and Cauca rivers. A significant proportion of Colombia's land remains uncultivated due to poor soils or unsuitable weather or terrain. The Amazon lowland soils are lateritic and clayey, except in fluvial plains, where regular deposits of silt maintain soil fertility. However, Amazonia's sparse population limits agricultural activity.

The people
Population and ethnic groups

South America's third most populous country, Colombia has the second highest population density, around 30 people per km². Most people (65%) live in upland cities, notably Bogotá, which has some 15–20% of the country's population. This is a reversal from the case just 20 years ago when the majority of the population was rural.

Originally, some 75 tribes inhabited Colombia. But today, pure-blood Indians are a mere one-fiftieth of the population – the smallest share for any Andean country. Some 80% of the population is *mestizo*, 12% white of Spanish descent, 5% black and a small percentage Asian.

Languages

Castilian Spanish is the official language but over 180 indigenous dialects and languages are spoken. Major linguistic groups include Arawak, Chibcha, Tupi-Guaraní and Yurumanguí. There are around 50 tribes in the Amazon region. The largest groups are Tikuna and Witoto living near to Leticia. In isolated hinterlands to the north are less well-known tribes including Makuna, Yukuna, Barasana and Desana, while Ingara and Cofan live in the Ecuador border region.

Education

Schooling is a high priority for Colombians, both officially and among the people. Virtually all children attend kindergarten, primary school and secondary school. At 87%, the adult literacy rate is among the highest in South America. Public universities include the National University of Colombia (founded in 1867), the Central University and the Women's National University. Most universities are in Bogotá.

Culture

Understanding the principle that to conquer a people you must control their culture, the colonials assaulted pre-Columbian secular and religious arts, suppressing weaving, basketry, ceramics and musical crafts. In 1583, Chibcha – the mostly widely spoken language – was banned but traditional arts revived during the early 20th century.

Bogotá is the country's cultural capital, Cali, Medellín, Manizales, Cartagena and Tunja are also important art centres. The arts are well-funded and the Banco de República is renowned for contributions to museums, art galleries and the performing arts. The country's literary heritage is reflected in the achievements of Gabriel García Márquez, awarded the 1982 Nobel Prize for Literature. His award-winning novel, *One Hundred Years of Solitude,* tells the story of family life in a small jungle settlement.

A brief history
Prehistory

Colombia's uplands were inhabited at least 2,000 years ago, probably much earlier. These inhabitants were predecessors of the Chibcha and other tribes who settled the area.

Indigenous peoples developed an advanced culture, in the absence of any outside influence. Because they used wood for building, little evidence of their achievements remains. Unlike Central America and other Andean countries, Colombia was considered to be devoid of large stone structures. This changed in 1976 with the discovery on Colombia's Caribbean coast of a 600ha 'lost city', built around AD900 by the Tairona, an advanced offshoot of the Chibcha tribal group.

Conquest

During 1500–01, Rodrigo de Bastidas sailed along the northern coast of Colombia and the Gulf of Darien and in 1525 founded Santa Marta on the north coast, the first European settlement in South America.

Cartagena, a major outpost of the Spanish empire, was founded by Pedro de Heredia in 1533, and by the mid-1500s all major coastal cities along with connecting roads had been established. Bogotá, the first major upland city, was founded in 1538 by Gonzalo Jiménez de Quesada.

At the time the Spanish arrived, several tribes inhabited what is today Andean Colombia but did not have the resources to resist the invasion. Due to disease and the Spaniards' bad treatment of the Indians, Colombia's population declined precipitously. During the early 18th century this trend reversed. Mining, agriculture and textile industries were established and slaves were imported to meet the labour demand.

Independence

In 1794, Antonio Nariño led the call for independence, publishing a Spanish version of Thomas Paine's *Declaration of the Rights of Man*. Spain was hard-pressed to maintain control. In 1808 when Napoleon Bonaparte replaced Spain's King Ferdinand VII with his son, Joseph, the colonialists refused to recognise the new monarch and Colombian towns began to declare independence. By 1810, several parts of Colombia had seceded from the Spanish Empire. Colombia achieved full independence from Spain in August 1819, after the Battle of Boyacá in which Venezuelan Simón Bolívar was hero of the day.

Post-independence

Despite Nariño's ideals, upheaval plagued post-independence Colombia. By 1840 civil war broke out, followed by counter-revolutions, dictatorships and mass repression. The 1886 constitution declared Colombia a republic, and set up the country's political system. Two major political parties, Liberals and Conservatives, were established, but did nothing to ameliorate the situation. In 1899, the so-called 'Thousand Days War' erupted and dragged on until 1903. An average of 100 people a day died.

The 20th century

After the turn of the century, Colombia's political scene remained stable until 1948, when disagreements again erupted into open hostility, ceasing only when the Liberals and Conservatives united to defeat the dictator Gustavo Rojas Pinilla from 1957–74. In 1974 Colombia resumed its traditional two-party system.

Despite Liberal-Conservative rule during the second half of the 20th century, Colombia's politics have been dominated by military juntas and their main funding source, the *narcotraficante* (cocaine barons). Adding to the violence are the left-wing insurgence groups, notably the FARC (Colombian Revolutionary Armed Forces) and the National Liberation Army.

In late 1992 a state of emergency was declared, renewed in February 1993 and again in May, a total of 180 days in under a year. The army claimed to have killed or captured over 1,200 rebels. In August 1995 a National Conciliation Committee

COCAINE, COLOMBIA AND THE WORLD

Despite being an admirably democratic and free society, Colombia's constantly changing government destabilises the country and has helped cocaine attain high importance in the country's politics and economy – a touchy subject but essential to understanding Colombia's recent turbulent history.

Cocaine is the mainstay of Colombia's illicit exports. This provides great wealth for giant underground corporations who are wealthier and better equipped than the government. Police, judges, lawyers, politicians and businessmen are bribed or threatened – many lawmen have lost their lives – and the cartels retain their power. With so much money at stake, someone always pops up to replace captured or killed drug lords. When the head of the Medellín cartel, Pablo Escobar, was killed by police in 1993, the rival Cali cartel quickly stepped in to take Escobar's business.

One approach to this persistent problem would be to eliminate the huge profits – and thus the incentive for organised crime to produce and sell drugs (some experts advocate legalisation as the only way to achieve this). However, locals point out that the responsibility for the present situation lies as much with those countries where cocaine is consumed as with those where it is produced. Families growing coca are generally growing the crop that gives them the best return for their work. As long as coca can be grown in the labyrinthine hills and valleys of the rugged Andes, as long as people will pay lots of money for tiny amounts and as long as there are crooks to exploit the system, the drug trade will continue.

was established to examine proposals for peace between various factions. For several years, President Ernesto Samper maintained a firm rule, and the country prospered for the most part. However, his tenure was marred by allegations of corruption and enrichment through the drug trade. Clinton's August 2000 visit was followed by the announcement of a joint US-Colombia initiative, dubbed Plan Colombia. This US$7.5 billion proposal aimed to eradicate drug output, strengthen democracy and foster peace. President Andrés Pastrana pledged US$4 billion and called on the international community to provide US$3.5 billion. However, because the guerrillas are so involved with the cocaine industry, the plan holds little hope for peace. Critics claim the military-dominated Plan undermines democracy, boosts the guerrilla movement, spreads narcotics production and further destabilises the region. Indeed, by October 2001 talks between the government and rebel groups stalemated and the situation resumed its downward spiral.

In February 2002, presidential candidate Ingrid Betancourt was abducted while in FARC territory. Later that month Pastrana finally ended the three-year peace negotiations; headlines simply stated, 'It's Over.' The immediate reason for ending the much-criticised peace process was the hijacking of a civilian airliner in southern Colombia and the kidnapping of a senator who was on board. Up until then the government and insurgents had been locked over the administration's demand for a rebel withdrawal from demilitarised zones.

March 2002 legislative elections were relatively calm, with the Liberal Party winning a majority of seats in both houses. Leading up to the May 2002 presidential elections, insurgent and paramilitary groups intimidated voters in various municipalities, creating tension and undermining the democratic process, according to politicians. Current president Alvaro Uribe has pledged a hard-line approach to rebels, who responded with a series of deadly bomb attacks in Bogotá during his inauguration in August 2002. He had survived a bomb attack on April 14 2002 that killed three people and injured more than 20. Five assassination attempts in a year also failed. Whether he survives the presidency remains to be seen.

Government

The 1886 constitution declared Colombia a republic and vested power in executive, legislative and judicial branches of government. The president is elected for a single four-year term. All citizens over 18 are eligible to vote. Guaranteed civil rights include the right to strike, to assemble, to petition and to exercise freedom of speech. Colombia's portions of Amazonia comprise five departments (of the country's total 32): Amazonas, Putumayo, Caquetá, Vaupés and Guaviare.

Economy

Analysts predict modest growth over the next several years. This is an improvement on the severe 1999 recession when GDP fell by about 4%. However, widespread prosperity remains elusive. Over 60% of the population live below the poverty line because of the extreme inequality of income distribution exacerbated by high unemployment – 20% in 2000. Two main exports, oil and coffee, are declining in their contribution to earnings. As investor confidence depends on public security, peace negotiations are important to economic performance.

Colombia possesses every major natural resource in abundance: metals and gems, coal, rivers for hydro-electric power, freshwater and marine fisheries, oil reserves, forest for plant products, and coastline for maritime trade and recreation.

Private enterprise is more important than the public sector. Agriculture and manufacturing each contribute about a fifth of GDP. Coffee is the mainstay of

Colombia's legal agricultural exports, with about 15% of arable land devoted to its cultivation. Flowers are widely grown in highland greenhouses. Exports of cannabis and coca products are estimated at twice the value of coffee. Gemstones are economically important, especially emeralds, of which half the world's total comes from Colombia.

Practicalities
Money
Colombian currency is the peso, with US$1=2,350 pesos (compared with 1,100 pesos to US$1 in 1998). US dollars are widely accepted but you get a better price paying with pesos.

Get only as many pesos as you think you need for your trip. Most banks will not exchange cash dollars for pesos, but they will cash travellers' cheques or give advances on Visa or MasterCard. Credit cards tend to get a better exchange rate than cash. As a rule of thumb, use a credit card or travellers' cheques for hotels, tours and large expenses, and carry small dollar bills and pesos for souvenirs and emergencies. Credit cards can be used for cash advances from ATMs but avoid making withdrawals in secluded locations.

Colombia has two exchange rates: the official rate and the 'free market' rate. The official, lower rate is what you get for cash (when accepted) or travellers' cheques at banks. You get the better free-market rate for cash from *casas de cambio*, which is 100% legal, although travellers' cheques are not always accepted.

Highlights
Colombia offers idyllic tropical beaches, high mountain ranges, rainforest and native tribes. It is perhaps the source of the legend of El Dorado – the 16th century Spanish observed Muisca Indians conducting a ceremony where a gold-covered 'king' bathed in the waters of Lake Guatavita.

Because of the Colombian Amazon's underdeveloped infrastructure, travel there can be a challenge. It is for independent travellers who can handle the absence of tourist facilities. First-time visitors to the area, particularly non-Spanish speakers, are better off taking a package tour. There are two points from which to start. The most popular is Leticia, reached by air from Bogotá, or by ship from Iquitos or Manaus. Starting from the Andean foothills, Florencia or Mocoa offer an alternative route and can be readily reached by bus from Bogotá. Due to security concerns, travel overland to the east of this area is not recommended.

Security
Colombia has the sad distinction of being the least safe country in South America. Although Colombia's murder rate (annual deaths per capita) is nine to ten times higher than the US average most violence is due to the on-going forty-year-old civil war between the government and rebel forces. Kidnappings and murder of foreigners does occur. Robbery is common. At the time of writing (mid-2002) due to security problems travel to regions east of the Andes, aside from the Leticia area, is unadvisable. Although towns and cities tend to be safer than rural areas rebel incursions into urban areas have increased recently.

While some argue the world's best coffee is grown in Colombia the country is more famous for its illegal product, cocaine (see box). The coca plant does not grow well in lowland rainforest but the dense cover is ideal to hide clandestine processing facilities. Both military and rebels are active in these areas which should be avoided by inexperienced travellers. Check news updates regularly (eg: websites in *Appendix 3*) for travel warnings.

Tour operators

Few US or UK tour operators offer organised tours to the Colombian Amazon but several companies in Bogotá and Leticia can organise trips.

Tierra Mar Aire (TMA) in Bogotá have offices at the Hotel Tequendama and on Carrera 7, No 35-20; tel: 1 288 2088; fax: 1 288 5558; email: tma0020@colomsat.net.co
Viajes Chapinero Av 7, #124-15; tel: 1 612 7716; fax: 1 215 9099; email: chapiner@cable.net.co
Eco-Guías Cra 3 #18-56, Oficina 201; tel: 1 334 8042; fax: 1 284 8991; email: info@ecoguias.com; web: www.ecoguias.com. Anglo-Colombian tour operator offering all-round travel service, including a four-day tour to a private nature reserve near Leticia. Widely recommended.

For a list of more tour operators in Bogotá, try the WebColombia site (www.webcolombia.com). In Leticia **Anaconda Tours**, **Amaturs** and **Amazon Explorers**, all close to the Hotel Anaconda, can help to arrange trips to nearby areas.

GETTING THERE AND AWAY
By air

Non-stop flights to Bogotá depart from Miami (from US$500 return, with American Airlines) and several other US cities, including New York. From the UK there is a daily service with British Airways, and several airlines from Europe have direct services including Avianca, Air France, Iberia, Alitalia and Lufthansa. Prices from London start at £450 in the low season. The **Avianca Airpass** makes internal flights much cheaper.

From Ecuador, Avianca has daily flights from Quito to Bogotá (US$168).

Overland

Travelling overland? Some say don't, others say no problem. You can travel safely by road, but the experience is likely to be a bit nerve-racking. Get all the up-to-date information you can. South American Explorer's (page 46) has reports from travellers who've been in the area. Another useful source of current information is at www.colombiaupdate.com.

From Venezuela there's a road to Maicao north from Maracaibo. In the mountains you can cross to Cucuta from San Antonio del Táchira or further from El Amparo de Apure to Arauca. Puerto Carreño on the Río Meta is accessible from El Burro, north of Puerto Ayacucho.

Leticia, accessible only via the Amazon River, is on the border with Brazil and Peru. It is also possible to cross from Lago Agrio in the lowland regions of Ecuador to Puerto Asís.

The Pan-American Highway links the southern Colombian highlands with Ecuador. Research safety issues before crossing from Ecuador.

Customs and immigration

Colombian entry procedures are fairly relaxed. Visas are not needed by citizens of most countries. DAS (Departamento Administrativo de Seguridad) is in charge of immigration affairs. Day-visitors to Leticia on tourist boats from Peru and Brazil do not need to complete border formalities.

Airport departure tax in Colombia must be paid for in hard currency. It is US$17 if you stay under 60 days, US$30 for longer.

Getting around

Colombia's transportation system ranges from relatively efficient, in large cities, to primitive or non-existent in remote rural areas. In many cases the only feasible way to reach remote areas is by air. Hitching in Colombia is not recommended.

By bus

Surfaced roads between major cities are in good-to-fair condition, but minor roads connecting remote jungle towns are unsurfaced and vary from bad to terrible. Major towns in the western highlands are served by comfortable buses. Around one sixth of the roads are paved, and the condition of the remainder depends on a subtle interplay between the depredations of the elements and the occasional efforts of road repair crews. Travelling by bus carries risks due to the theft (high risk), violence (lower), and kidnapping (even lower). If you do travel by bus, refuse food or candy, be wary and keep a low profile.

By air

The national airline is Avianca, South America's oldest, founded in 1919. Several other domestic airlines are in operation including ACES, SAM, Aires and the military airline Satena. There is one flight a day (Avianca) from Bogotá to Leticia (US$100). Several local carriers offer scheduled or charter flights between Bogotá and Leticia. It is possible to get on a cargo or military flight. Domestic air travel is fairly expensive so most independent travellers may choose to move around the country via bus. However it is presently safer to travel by air. Avianca's airpass has five flights including Leticia for US$300-330 (low/high season).

Bogotá's Avianca office is at Carrera 7 #16-36; tel: 1 266 9700. SAM's offices are at Carrera 10, #27-91; tel: 1 266 9600. Satena have flights to the remoter parts of Colombia which can be booked at their office at Ave 19, #13A-18; tel: 1 283 5557. Airline offices close at weekends. Your best strategy is to have all your flights and travel arrangements organised even before leaving for Colombia. Whenever you travel by air, be sure to secure checked baggage to prevent casual pilfering.

By river

Lowland rivers remain important conduits for people and goods. For transport the rivers are most important in the eastern lowlands. The Putumayo, Caquetá and Vaupés rivers conveniently connect up with the Amazon's main stream giving access to Brazil and eventually the Atlantic.

COMMUNICATIONS
Mail

Mail is reliable and efficient in Colombia, especially compared with Peru or Brazil. Adpostal runs the service and rates are reasonable. Within the Americas a postcard costs US$0.50 and a letter just US$1, taking about a week. Packages cost about US$12 per kilo. To all these prices, add about 15–20% for destinations outside the Americas. Surface mail is the cheapest way to send large packages but it takes five times longer.

Telephone, fax and email services

Telephone and fax services are available at most hotels, while email is used by most tour operators and travel agents. To phone outside Colombia it is cheapest to use the public phones of the state telephone service Telecom. These are found throughout the large cities, but don't expect every phone to work...most don't. Head for the nearest Telecom offices to make things easier. Here you can buy telephone cards for public phones.

The international country code for Colombia is 57.

Internet services in Colombia are available in larger towns. In Bogotá, there are several to choose from.

Copix Net Calle Cedritos 140, #20–50, Local 12, Centro Comercial, "La puerta Del Sol"; tel: 1 216 9889; email: lav@usa.net; web: www.angelfire.com/biz/copix. Open 09.00–21.00. US$1.80 per hour.
Cybertown Calle 81, #11–16; tel: 1 616 3444; email: cybertw1@cable.net.co; web: www.piedemont.com/cybertown.html. Open 10.00. US$2.00 per hour. Newest Internet café.
Virtualia Estudio-café Carrera 7, #44–29; tel: 1 288 2886; email: virtual@cable.net.co; web: www.tecnopia.com. Open 09.00–21.00. US$2.00 per hour.

Television and radio
Easier to control than print media, Colombia's broadcasts reflect a stricter degree of control than is exerted over newspapers and periodicals. Regarding government, television and radio strive for a balance between patriotic support and guarded criticism. Programmes are professionally produced, although the domestic productions are a stale fare of soap operas and chat shows.

Newspapers
All Colombia's major newspapers and magazines are in Spanish, but English and US newspapers are available in larger cities.

Colombia's press freedom has historically depended on the government in power. However, freedom of expression is generally respected, a privilege that extends to the press. At present it is free to criticise the government – and does. Widely circulated Bogotá newspapers are *El Tiempo* and *El Espectador,* both considered supporters of the Liberal Party. *El Pais* is another important newspaper.

BOGOTÁ
After losing four-fifths of his men in the gruelling journey along the Magdalena River, in 1537 Gonzalo Jiménez de Queseda reached the mountain valley that was to become the site of Bogotá. Today it has a multiple personality, with modern Bogotá contrasted against the poorest parts of the city.

In a bowl among the Andes mountains, Bogotá (elevation 2,652m) is one of South America's great cities. Packed with six million people, it is also becoming one of South America's worst cities. Drugs, violence and pollution are major problems facing this sprawling conurbation.

As Bogotá is at such a high altitude, its climate is mild and cool, but the equatorial location (4.36° north, 74.05° west) keeps temperatures within narrow limits around 14°C. Bogotá is relatively dry compared with other parts of Colombia and has annual rainfall around 1,100mm.

At the airport
El Dorado International Airport is 12km from town, about 20 minutes ride. There is no good bus system so take a taxi (US$5, US$7 after dark). Ask a policeman to note your taxi's registration number. He will give you a piece of paper stating the fare. A reliable taxi driver should have no problem with this. Do not take unregistered taxis or use porters not in uniform.

To get to the airport is easier. Your hotel can book a taxi or you can take a bus. Marked 'Aeropuerto', these depart regularly from Avenida 19 between Carreras 3 and 10.

City transport
Public transport is good enough to get around on your own and very inexpensive. However, take the utmost care before jumping in a taxi or *colectivo* (a communal taxi with set routes like a bus), especially on your own.

BOGOTA: CENTRE

Make sure your taxi is registered and agree on the cost beforehand. The police are helpful in ensuring you are not over-charged.

Frequent and reliable buses are the cheapest way of getting around. Pick up buses at the red and yellow signs (marked 'Paradero') or else flag them down as you would a taxi.

Security

Stay aware of surroundings and people. There are several no-go areas in the city. Beware of the area near the railway station, especially between Carreras 15 to 17 and Calles 15 to 18. Never take out money or passports on the street. Keep valuables and money at the hotel. If someone in uniform asks to see documents politely refuse and say you will be happy to go to the police station and show any papers there. If the request is from a uniformed official and is for a legitimate reason (eg: at a roadblock), common-sense dictates compliance.

Bogotá's western side is more industrial and rougher than the eastern half and, in the main sightseeing area, Montserrate is unsafe any time except weekends. Daylight muggings are frequent here. Other dangerous areas are in the southwest, older part of the city (west of Carrera 13 and south of Calle 12). The oldest part of the city around the Candelaria district has numerous buildings from the colonial era, a number of which are museums. The new part of the city, Centro Internacional to the north, is relatively safe.

Where to stay

Hotels in Bogotá range from expansive and expensive (US$100+ per night) to dirty and dirt-cheap (US$10 and under). To remain in the safety zone, stay in the northern part of the city. Book in advance if at all possible, so that you have somewhere to go and someone is expecting you. For a listing of 50 or so hotels in Bogota visit the Hotel Association of Colombia website (www.cotelco.org).

First class

Bogotá Royal Ave 100, #8-01; tel: 1 218 3261. The poshest hotel and said to be among the best hotels in South America. From US$145pp per night.

Charleston Hotel Carrera 13, #85-46; tel: 1 218 0590. From US$105. More centrally located than the Bogotá Royal.

Tequendama Carrera 10, #26-21; tel: 1 286 8111; fax: 1 282 2860. From US$150. One of Bogotá's oldest hotels. Now belongs to the Intercontinental chain. Rooms have great views across the city, and it has a very good restaurant.

Cosmos 100 Calle 100, #21-A41; tel: 1 257 4000; fax: 1 635 4935. From US$100. This has the best views and among the friendliest staff.

Von Humboldt Grand Hotel Calle 74 #13-27; tel: 1 317 0566; fax: 1 317 1817. For the price (from US$75), offers excellent service and full range of facilities. Well-located within easy reach of the business district and half an hour from the airport.

Middle range

Las Terrazas Calle 54, #32-16; tel: 1 255 5966; fax: 1 255 6834. In the city centre but worth considering for the value and views of the city. The restaurant serves local and international dishes.

San Diego Hotel corner of Carrera 13 and Calle 24; tel: 1 284 2100. From US$20, this hotel is centrally located, near Parque Independencia and close to the Natural History Museum.

Hotel Casa Santa Monica Carrera 3 # 24 11; tel: 1 336 8080; fax: 1 336 3601; email: hcsantamonica@thefamtrip.com. Centrally located in attractive garden setting with easy access to historical sites. Prices from US$50–60.

Budget

Here are a few of the many budget hotels to choose from.

Internacional Hotel Carrera 5, #14-15; tel: 1 341 8731. Rather shabby, but clean rooms have private bathrooms and hot water. Well-located in the Candelaria district, and offers a lot for the price (from US$15).
Hosteria Hametayel Carrera 4 #11-78; tel: 1 341 6479. In Candelaria district from about US$6.
Virgen del Camino Calle 18A, #14-33; tel: 1 282 4450. In a quiet safe area, with pleasant helpful staff.
International Youth Hostel Association members can stay at the **youth hostel** (Carrera 7 #6-10; tel: 1 280 3202; fax: 1 280 3460; email: fcaj-hostelling@navegante.com.co; web: www.hostelslatinamerica.org/colombia.htm) for about US$6.

Where to eat

International food is served at the excellent **Refugio Alpino** (Calle 23 #7-49), and **La Fragata** at the World Trade Center (Calle 100 #8A-55 12th floor; tel: 1 616 7461) has good seafood, but neither restaurant is cheap. **Carbon de Palo** (Calle 106 No A-60A; tel: 1 214 5482) is famous for grilled meat. It's frequented by locals. Meals begin at about US$20 a head. **Casa Medina** (Carrera 7 #69A-22; tel: 1 217 0288) is one of Bogotá's premier restaurants. French cuisine is served in surroundings of Old World charm. **Romana** (Av. Jiménez #6-65, tel: 1 334 8135), serves cheese and bread with hot chocolate for about US$5. For lunch, the pasta dishes are popular. It's closed Sundays. At **El Patio** (Carrera 4A #27-86; tel: 1 282 6141) you'll see local characters coming in to enjoy the food (especially salads), from US$7 a head.

Chinese restaurants are inexpensive– try **Bambú**, Carrera 7 and Calle 62. Some fast-food restaurants offer take-away service, but when in Colombia, why not do what the Colombians do… and eat *al fresco*. Wander along Carrera 15 where there are several options.

Govinda's (Carrera 8, #20-56) is an international chain serving tasty, healthy vegetarian food at an unbeatable price. **Acuarius** is a small chain with several restaurants that specialise in vegetarian food. Try the one near Plaza Bolívar (Carrera 8, #11-19). At **Vega** (Calle 59 #10-59) dishes are delicious and generous. The menu includes plantains, beans, brown rice, manioc, salads, and fruit desserts.

Most restaurants are closed Sunday evenings.

What to see

As Colombia's cultural centre Bogotá offers much to the visitor. Historic buildings, art galleries and museums offer examples of Colombia's past achievements and unique artistic heritage.

Museums

Bogotá's museums are among South America's best. Most are either free or charge a small admission fee, usually under US$1. Museums are closed on Monday. Here is a selection of some of the best:

Museo del Oro (Gold Museum) at Parque de Santander, Calle 16 and Carrera 6-A, houses the world's largest collection of worked gold, with over 30,000 pieces. Open Tue–Fri 9.00–17.00; Sat 09.00–13.00; Sun and holidays 9.00–12.00.
Museo de Arte Colonial (Museum of Colonial Art) at Carrera 6, #9-77. An impressive collection of Creole religious sculpture and painting housed in a building that exemplifies colonial architecture. Open Tue–Sat 10.00–13.00; Sun 10.00–17.00.

Museo de Historia Natural (Natural History Museum) at Parque de la Independencia, Planeterio Distrital. For wildlife enthusiasts, this is a 'must'. Although some of the stuffed animals need patchwork, they give a good idea of the country's biodiversity. Open Tue–Fri: 9.00–18.00; Sat and Sun: 10.00–18.00.

Corporación de Araracuara at Calle 20, #5-44. This organisation holds the best sources of information on the Colombian Amazon. The library comprises several thousand books, journals and articles on natural history, tribes and history.

Cathedrals and churches

Bogotá's religious buildings come in an impressive range of styles. Most notable is **La Catedral**, completed in 1807 and with strong classical influences. You can see a banner carried by de Quesada on his campaign against the indigenous people. La Catedral is located in the district of the same name on Calle 10 between Carreras 6 and 7. Behind it on the same block is the **Chapel of El Sagrario** dating from the late 1600s.

Other things to see in Bogotá

For views of the city, make your way to the top of **Montserrate** on the east side. This area is only safe at weekends and especially dangerous after dark. Do not walk as muggings are very common. Instead use the funicular railway or cable car (both US$2.50). You can see a small selection of Colombia's plant life at the botanical gardens on Calle 57 (free admission)

Shopping

The best places for folk art and handicrafts is at **Artesanias de Colombia** in the San Diego Church (Carrera 10, #26-50). Next to the Church of the Waters (Iglesia d'Aguas) is **Almacén Las Aguas** with well-priced handicrafts. Less expensive still are street markets, such as the one on Carrera 15, and on Carrera 7 opposite the Tequendama. If you are off into the jungle you can pick up most of your supplies in Bogotá. The best place to get a hammock is at **Pasaje Rivas** (Carrera 10, #10-54).

Leaving town

Long-distance buses depart from the terminal at Av Boyacá west of the city centre. This area is not safe so time your arrival and departure for daylight hours. Numerous buses run up and down Av Boyacá, but you should get a taxi. It's relatively safe from your hotel or the airport and costs about US$6.

You can take a bus as far as Florencia, a 12-hour journey (cost US$25, one way). A recommended bus company is Coomotor, with offices both in Florencia and at the terminal in Bogotá. Bus is a cost-effective way of seeing the country and meeting Colombians.

THE COLOMBIAN AMAZON

Although Colombia's Amazonian territory is small compared with that of Brazil or Peru, it covers a third of the country. Amazonas is Colombia's largest province. Covering some 110,000km², it's four-fifths the size of England. About 95% of this region is uninhabited and rarely visited. The total population is about half a million, most of whom live along the Andean foothills in the provinces of Caquetá and Putumayo far to the west.

Half of Amazonas state's 60,000 people live in Leticia. Due to the heavy traffic on the main stream and the Putumayo, the town is the commercial centre of southeastern Colombia. The peculiarly wedge-shaped boundary, established in 1922, covers just 130km or so of the Amazon River (Solimões). Nevertheless,

Colombia is proud of its small foothold on the world's biggest river, and indeed seems to value its rainforest.

On the Putumayo and other Amazon tributaries, water levels rise as much as 7m during flood season. River levels fall from August to January, then rise rapidly from April to June and peak mid- to late-July. A minor rise is usually experienced during October or November.

Leticia: Gateway to the Amazon

Originally in Peru, Leticia was founded as San Antonio in 1867. The town was jump-started into industrialisation by the 19th-century rubber boom. Now with around 30,000 inhabitants, Leticia is Colombia's largest settlement east of the Andes and the second largest, after Iquitos, in lowland Amazonia west of Brazil. Below the fourth parallel, it is also Colombia's southernmost town.

The nearest international airport is Iquitos in Peru, just over 400km from Leticia as the parrot flies. By river, the distance is about 560km. The town marks the turn-around for regularly scheduled tourist riverboats. Thanks to its airport and its reputation as Colombia's centre for Amazon tours it has grown fast.

Tabatinga, just inside Brazil, is Leticia's poor relative. Because of the lack of border formalities, it is difficult to tell when you have gone from one town to the other; or from one country to another. This area is a free-trade zone with the nickname Tres Fronteras ('Three Frontiers') because the boundaries of Colombia, Peru and Brazil meet here.

Getting there

Leticia, stuck in Colombia's most distant corner, is difficult to reach from within the country, so most people arrive here by riverboat via the main stream.

For those who want to travel by air, Leticia is served by an airport, but then you miss the experience of river travel.

By boat

To reach Leticia by boat from within Colombia you have to travel from Puerto Asís, close to the border with Ecuador, and take a boat down the Putumayo (see Puerto Asís, page 233).

Internationally by riverboat, it takes seven days to reach Leticia from Manaus (Brazil), or three days downstream from Iquitos (Peru). If approaching Leticia from Manaus, you will arrive at Tabatinga after transfer through the town of Benjamin Constant, 34km south of Leticia. If travelling on a local riverboat, you complete Brazilian exit formalities at Benjamin Constant (sometimes at Tabatinga), then register with Colombian immigration in Leticia (see next section). If travelling from Peru you complete exit formalities at Santa Rosa.

By expedition or cruise ships, the voyage from Manaus to Leticia takes four days, or two from Iquitos, and the crew usually take care of the paperwork.

By road

Leticia is not connected by road to any other city save a few outlying towns. Because of poor maintenance, road transport is unreliable and possibly hazardous, especially during the flood season. Leticia is a long way from anywhere and to reach it overland is a major expedition.

Getting around

Local taxis are good for one or two trips. For city tours VW minibuses are used by tour operators to take up to seven passengers.

For independent travellers, the local taxi system suffices to get around town. You can rent a motorcycle or car if you are going to stay a while. In any case you can walk to most places provided it's not in the heat of the day.

Where to stay

Like everything else in Leticia, accommodation is expensive by Amazon standards, though you could hunt out a cheap *residencia* for under US$10. There are about a dozen hotels to choose from.

For most travellers and tour operators the usual choice is the **Hotel Anaconda** on Carrera 11 #7-34; tel: 098592 7119; fax: 098592 7005; email: hotelanaconda@hotelanaconda.com.co; web: www.hotelanaconda.com.co). It has above-average facilities, including a swimming pool, restaurant and bar. Sadly, the reception staff and waiters win no awards for friendliness. Per person it costs US$53 (twin) or US$90 (single) per night for air-conditioned rooms, but no hot water. It is conveniently located, with a tour agency, bank and post office nearby and a small shopping mall next to the lobby. More affordable hotels offer fewer facilities. Check out **Hotel Yurupary** (Calle 8 #7-26 tel: 098592 4743; fax: 098592 7983) or **Hostal Amazonas** (Carrera 6 #11-84 tel: 098592 5536; fax: 098592 5534).

For the budget traveller the comfortable and friendly **Residencias Fernando**

is on Carrera 9, between Calle 8 and 9 (US$46 double, US$33 single per night).
Also worth a try is **Residencias Internacional** on the road to Tabatinga.

Where to eat

The Hotel Anaconda has a restaurant. Elsewhere in town several bars and
restaurants serve inexpensive meals or snacks. Fresh fruit and vegetables can be
bought in markets or stores around town.

There are lots of restaurants along Av da Amizade (main road to Tabatinga market)
serving reasonable food at a fair price. But check what locals pay before you order.
Often the prices increase the moment a hungry gringo walks through the door!

In Leticia

Varying from bustling jungle town in the cool of morning to lazy backwater during
a heat-drenched siesta, Leticia's beauty is in the eye of the beholder. It's clean
compared with most Amazon towns cobbled together with breeze-blocks and
concrete, or wood, nails and plastic – not smart, but friendly enough. This is a
working town, somewhat indifferent to tourists, perhaps sensing that they are
temporary like previous Amazon economic booms.

Strolling along cracked pavements or half-surfaced streets are tradesmen,
fishermen and the occasional sailor. Filling the grid of streets, oriented north-
south along Carrera 11 and the airport road, nondescript flat-topped blocks of
variously coloured and windowed concrete house the shopkeepers, restaurateurs,
tour agents and hoteliers of most interest to the traveller.

Apart from the standard city tour, which takes in the museum, zoo, fish market
and border crossing, there is not much to entertain outsiders.

Along the lower part of Calle 8 near the riverfront small stores house money-
changers. They change dollars, pesos, and Peruvian or Brazilian money. Rates are
reasonable. The occupants are honest and there's not much difference between
them. They may refuse to change travellers' cheques or amounts under US$10. If
you need to change travellers' cheques, banking hours (and times for the post
office and museums) are from 08.00 to 12.00 with a long siesta until 14.00, after
which places stay open until 18.00.

The Hotel Anaconda overlooks Parque Orellana with a bust of the park's
namesake Francisco Orellana, the first full-length Amazon voyager. A corner of
the park has a concrete map of Colombia, where you can stand on Leticia.

Left out of the Anaconda is the unfortunately named Amaturs tour company.
On the corner is El Toro bar, like a Wild West saloon complete with swing doors.
Sip the local lager, Antarctica, served as cold as its name suggests, while you sit
outside and watch life go by.

What to see

Along the airport road, about 1.5km from the Anaconda, is the **Jardín Botánico
Zoológico** (Botanical and Zoological Garden), right next to the airport.
Fortunately, there are few flights and the inconvenience seems not to bother the
animals.

Jet noise apart, the zoo is worth a brief visit if you have time to spend in town.
A friendly tapir roams freely. More dangerous animals are caged, notably a jaguar
and ocelots. Other mammals you can see here include peccary, kinkajou, coati and
sometimes a capybara or agouti.

Reptiles include the spectacled caiman, matamata turtle and a couple of
medium-sized anaconda. Several huge black caiman up to 5.5m long are fed
around mid-morning – a popular event with local school groups.

Above left Katydid, *Tetigonidae*, resembling a dead leaf (PO)

Above Butterfly, *Dryas iulia* (PO)

Left Owl butterfly, *Caligo eurilochus* (PO)

Above Broad-winged katydid, *Tetigonidae*. Note resemblance to species top left. (PO)

Below Spider (PO)

Above Giant otters, *Pteronura brasiliensis* (PO)

Above right Pygmy marmoset monkey, *Cebuella pygmaea* (PO)

Below Brown-throated three-toed sloth, *Bradypus variegatus* (PO)

Right Ocelot kitten, *Felis pardalis* (PO)

Below Baby tapir, *Tapirus terrestris* (RH)

COLOMBIAN COFFEE

On the lower part of Calle 8 toward the riverfront (turn right as you leave the Hotel Anaconda) are small stalls selling everything from fake designer watchers and shoes to haircuts. The best deal here is the famous Colombian coffee. You can buy ground or whole beans. The best brand is Sello Rojo ('Red Seal'), at about 5,200 pesos per kilo. Other brands are cheaper but not as good. Whole bean is scarcer than ground coffee which is available only in one consistency – very fine – suitable only for espresso or filter machines.

On display in a couple of pools are a small pirarucu and several armoured catfish. There are some birds, such as harpy eagle, curassows and guans. There is considerable turnover of the zoo animals. Keepers say that the animals are returned to the forest every six months. Draw your own conclusions, but in any case, don't rely on the above list to know exactly what animals are on display.

The 'gardens' include a small selection of local plants; nothing more than in nearby parks and gardens, mostly acacia trees, palms and lilies.

The **Museo del Hombre Amazonico** (Museum of Amazon Man), funded by the Banco de Colombia, is on Carrera 11. The museum consists of one room which houses a small but well-displayed collection of post-Columbian Indian artefacts. Overall they give a good sense of how indigenous people use rainforest materials to survive day-to-day.

For those more interested in local culture than animal rights, Leticia's **cockfight ring** on Avenida Internacional holds matches Sunday evening. Huge amounts are bet and emotions run high. These performances are not for the squeamish, as blood is usually drawn and contests frequently end in the death of the losing cock.

Shopping

Next to the Anaconda Hotel lobby is a small arcade with souvenir and jewellery shops, where you can buy a T-shirt claiming 'I survived the Amazon', a giant carved balsa parrot, precious stones or painted postcards.

Nearby on the same block as the hotel are several curio stores. These are Aladdin's caves for the souvenir hunter – packed from floor to ceiling with masks, carvings, palm-fibre baskets and hammocks, seed necklaces and less desirable items like caiman skulls and mounted piranha.

Whether or not souvenirs are on your shopping list, visit the **Amazonas** curio shop around the corner (turn right) from the Anaconda on Calle 8. Beyond shelves piled high with carved animals, bark cloth paintings, toy blowguns and preserved piranhas, behind a curtain towards the back of the store is a small 'museum' with dozens of exhibits, in varying states of preservation. One wall is adorned with wasps' nests and on shelves opposite are fossils, birds' nests and animal parts, including skulls, claws, shells and skins. A glass cabinet holds dozens of pieces of native pottery, some of it 'pre-Columbian'.

Shops along Calle 9 adjacent to the Museum of Amazon Man sell strong cotton hammocks, which are more comfortable than the native ones and cheaper from US$15.

If you are travelling up to the highlands and need some warm clothes, goods from the Andes area are worth considering: sweaters, gloves and hats will keep out mountain chill. In the central commercial area several shops sell a wide range of leather goods of excellent quality. Most popular items are jackets and duffel bags.

Further information

For travel advice and suggestions on accommodation, the staff are helpful at the regional tourist office on Carrera 11, #11–35 (tel: 09819 27505).

If you are entering or leaving the country you will need to visit the various immigration authorities for exit and entry stamps (or visas if necessary):

Colombian Immigration (DAS) Office Calle 9, Mon–Sat 07.00–12.00 and 14.00–18.00.
Brazilian Consulate Calle 13, Mon–Fri 08.00–14.00.
Peruvian Consulate Carrera 11, Mon–Fri 08.30–14.30.

To enter the national parks in the region, you need an entry permit (US$1) from the Colombian National Parks Authority (UAESPN Cra 10 #20-30 4th floor; tel: 243 1634; fax: 2434174; email: amazonia@col1.telecom.com.co).

Choosing a jungle tour

As most travellers visit Leticia for the jungle, the primary objective is to find a good tour operator with reliable guides and decent prices. This is easier said than done, especially if you have been spoilt for choice in Manaus, Iquitos or Quito. Tours from Leticia are costlier and the options are fewer compared with more popular tourist spots. It's difficult to organise tours from Leticia before you get there. Tour operators in Bogotá can make arrangements. In Leticia there are a handful of tour operators and freelance jungle guides.

In the offices next to the Hotel Anaconda are three tour operators: **Anaconda Tours**, **Amaturs** and **Amazon Explorers**. These companies specialise in day trips to Monkey Island, city tours and bookings.

There are a few freelance guides operating in the area who can guide more adventurous deep forest trips. For up-to-date recommendations on freelance guides, ask around at hotels as well as the aforementioned local tour operators.

If you are in Leticia, ask at the Hotel Anaconda for **Luiz Valera**. He's a white-haired but fit-looking gentleman of short height, stocky build and amiable character. Besides leading city tours for local tour operators, he arranges and leads expeditions into less travelled parts of the interior.

Sr Valera once trained Colombian air-force officers in jungle survival and now offers trips by covered canoe deep into remote tributaries to encounter tribes rarely contacted by the outside world. He takes the minimum of supplies and relies on the jungle and river to provide food for the party. The charge is reasonable: US$60–100 per day, depending on group size. On his trips sightings of large land mammals, manatee, black caiman, anaconda or giant otters are possible. If Luis is not around, then **Amazon Jungle Trips** (Av Internacional, #6-24; tel: 9819 27377), on the Tabatinga road, is recommended.

When booking follow the advice given in *Chapter 2*. Stipulate what you expect, where you want to go and what type of accommodation you want. These trips are only for the adventurous, willing to put up with discomfort and privation. You travel by *colectivo* (motorised covered canoe) and paddled canoe, and you might have to trek miles through jungle and sleep in a hammock or temporary forest camp. Expect heat, sweat, effort, thirst and hunger. The reward is to merge into wilderness, one step closer to the mystery that is the Amazon.

Amacayacú National Park

In the wedge of rainforest reaching down to the Amazon River, Amacayacú is the only national park in the Amazon Basin to include a portion of the main stream. This was the first national park in the Colombian Amazon. Established in 1975, its

BUYING EMERALDS

Colombia is the emerald centre of the world, producing the finest gems and in greater quantity than any other country. Anyone can afford a low-grade emerald as a unique souvenir. But how do you know if you're buying the real thing?

It is better to buy a small fine stone, rather than a large one of dubious quality. The finest emeralds are sea-green and flawless. Black spots or 'gardens' are normal in all but the very best stones. Flaws, specks or opacity indicate authenticity.

Beware of apparent bargains. A perfect-looking dark green stone for less than US$1,000/carat (1 carat = 2 grams) may be glass or a low-quality emerald artificially darkened. They have a bluish hue and return to their original colour after a few weeks. The fakes are very difficult to spot and when they fade it's too late to return and get a refund.

Agata in the small arcade adjacent to the Anaconda lobby, is run by Sr and Sra Almir and Gloria Da Silva. These people are reliable and offer certificates of authenticity, but their prices are relatively high.

Rodrigo Valderrama is a roving gem dealer, who sets up shop by the Hotel Anaconda swimming pool shops. Recognised by his withered right arm and somewhat shifty countenance, he seems reliable and entertains reasonable offers.

A flawed but genuine emerald is within most budgets. Souvenir-quality half-carat emeralds cost US$20–50. The novice buyer should stick to the low end of the price scale. Among the most valuable gems, emeralds sometimes cost more than diamonds. A top-notch one-carat emerald can easily dent your wallet by US$2,000–3,000, even in Colombia. Perfect specimens cost as much as US$15,000/carat. Be as sure as possible that you know what you are buying and if you are paying by credit card, check the receipt. It is easy to be ripped off. With few exceptions, it is better to pay a little more for a certified gem from a store, rather than pay less for something dubious from someone you'll never see again.

1,700km² encompasses much of the watershed of the Río Amacayacú, which joins the Amazon River about 65km west of Leticia.

Within the park are typical tropical flora and fauna. Plants include teak, mahogany, capirona, acacias and uncounted herbaceous plants and epiphytes. Mammals include jaguar, anteater, armadillo, sloth, tapir and peccary, with pink dolphin and manatee along remote tributaries. Reptiles include anaconda, caiman, river turtles and the green iguana. Some 500 birds are known from the park, a third of Colombia's total.

A few areas can be visited on foot but access is reduced at high water; as elsewhere in the Amazon, you generally travel around by canoe. To explore the area on foot, the best time to go is at low water from August to January.

The Ticuna tribe lives in the park, mostly around San Martín. This three-hour walk from Puerto Nariño may be difficult or impossible at high water between February and June.

At the visitors' centre you can hire a guide to take you along the well-marked trails into the forest. A guide is essential to point out all the birds, plants, animals and organic minutiae you may otherwise miss.

To visit from Peru you must first clear Colombian immigration authorities in Leticia.

To get there, take a two-hour river taxi from Leticia to Puerto Nariño (Expreso Amazonas, US$10 one way), the closest village to the park. If you organise your own transport for a small group, *colectivos* can be hired for US$100 per day. Trips to the park have to be booked and paid for in Leticia at the UAESPN offices.

Tour agencies in Leticia can arrange for tours to the park, or freelance guides will offer less expensive trips. In either case check what's included. Whether you choose this option depends on your confidence level, as it's straightforward to book through the UAESPN offices in either Leticia or Bogotá.

Tourist facilities include a visitors' centre with lodging for 40 people (about US$15pp), a museum and a research centre. There are four canopy platforms from which to observe flora and fauna.

Palmari Nature Reserve

Located about three hours by motor launch from Leticia this private nature reserve protects an area of virgin rainforest near the confluence of the Javari and Palmari rivers in Brazilian territory. Accommodations within the reserve are at a basic lodge on the banks of the Javari River. Rooms have private bathrooms and beds with mosquito nets. Lighting is with gas lanterns. You can relax in a hammock in the common area. Activities include nature trails, caiman spotting and piranha fishing. Nearby indigenous groups include Yagua and Mayorana. At the village of Palmari you can observe rubber-tapping techniques. The reserve is in Brazil so you need your passport. Check *Chapter 2* for Brazil visa requirements. Book through Eco-Guías (page 219).

Other Amazon towns

Other towns smaller than Leticia have fewer facilities and are far from the Amazon main stream and hence not so popular for jungle trips. This section includes towns and villages likely to be visited when approaching Leticia from the Colombian highlands. These towns are well-served by domestic air carriers, with reasonable fares. Bus links provide overland access, but the local buses, colourfully painted *chivas,* are slow, unreliable and often crowded. If you're not in a hurry, they're the best way to get around on the cheap.

Florencia

This is the biggest town in the Colombian Amazon, with a population of around 100,000. Founded at the beginning of the 20th century, by Italian missionaries from Florence, the town is less inspiring than its namesake, with little to commend it to the tourist. It suffers acutely from water shortages and power cuts. The main reason to travel here is en route to Leticia or Mitú on the border with Brazil. The surrounding rainforest has been degraded and the pristine forest east of Florencia is inaccessible to the average traveller. If you intend going further east, you are better off heading down the Caquetá from the nearby village of Curillo; or instead go south to Puerto Asís, for a trip down the Putumayo to **La Paya National Park** (near Puerto Leguízamo).

The tourist office (Instituto de Cultura y Turismo, Calle 15, #10-11), open weekdays 07.00–12.00 and 14.00–18.00, will help you organise accommodation, tours and so on. The best hotel in town is the **Hotel Plaza** next to the Banco de República. If it is full try the **Hotel Metropol** at Carrera 11, #16-52; or **Hotel Chairá** on the corner of Calle 16 and Carrera 13. These have private bathrooms and fans...when there's electricity. Low-budget travellers should try the **Hotel Central** at Carrera 11, #15-26, near the central park. The accommodation near the bus station is even cheaper but not very pleasant. Other hotels in Florencia: **Caqueta Real Calle** 18 #9-49; tel: 8351040; fax: 8351079; **Cesar Palace** Carrera

11 #16-52; tel: 8 355352; fax: 8 355351; **Guaycaba** Calle 14 #13-31; tel: 88352226; fax: 8358787; **Kamani** Calle 16 #12-27 tel: 8 435410; fax: 8435683.

The **Ethnographical Museum** (Museo Etnográfico) has a collection of tools, weapons and crafts used the Witoto and Coreguajes tribes. It is next to the cathedral and opens weekdays 08.00–12.00 and 14.00–17.00.

Florencia is served by several flights daily from Bogotá (US$85 one way) and three or four flights a week to Puerto Asís (US$35). To get to the airport on the La Montañita road take any bus heading out that way or a taxi (US$3 from the centre). For travel overland, the Bogotá buses, costing US$15 one way, depart from Carrera 10. These are comfortable and air-conditioned – a civilised enough way to travel the 12 hours on appalling roads to Bogotá.

Excursions from Florencia

For destinations within the Colombian Amazon, there are several buses daily to **Getucha**, for around US$6, taking five or six hours. For the same price you can get a *chiva* to **Curillo**, from where you can take a boat down the Río Caquetá. Further downstream is **La Tagua**, south of **La Paya National Park**. Further down the Caquetá is **Araracuara**, from where you can take a trip into Colombia's remotest lowland rainforest national park. Below Araracuara the Caquetá is unnavigable due to rapids. From here you may be able to get transport into Brazil, but this territory is inaccessible for the inexperienced or budget traveller.

An easier trip is to go by road from **La Tagua** to **Puerto Leguízamo** on the Putumayo and then south to **Arica**, and into Brazil.

Puerto Asís

A few miles north of the Ecuadorian border, this ramshackle town is the biggest port on the Putumayo, but offers little by way of amenities or entertainment. The main reason to be here is en route between Lago Agrio in Ecuador or Mocoa, or to take a trip down the Putumayo River.

Founded in 1912, Puerto Asís (population around 20,000) has rapidly outgrown its original infrastructure. The area is pervaded with drug-related activity and can be dangerous for tourists. Leave extra time to get through police checks, which are thorough. Puerto Asís is useful as a point from which to launch off into the jungle by boat, although there are not many options. If wildlife and nature are your interest, then take the trip to La Tagua for **La Paya National Park**. If you are travelling to Leticia, you have a long journey, some tough negotiating and considerable expense. It is cheaper to fly to Leticia if you are simply trying to get there.

There are lots of hotels, mostly of low standard. Two of the better ones are **Hotel Camba Huasi** at Carrera 22 between Calles 10 and 11, and **Hotel Continental** on Calle 12.

The airport is within walking distance of town, if you have little or no luggage, and served by several flights daily to/from Bogotá (US$100–120). There are three flights a week to Florencia (US$35) and connections with most Amazon towns with airports. If you aren't up to the potentially risky overland journey to Ecuador, Aires has a cheap quick flight three times weekly to Lago Agrio (US$15, one way).

By bus you can get to Puerto Asís from Ecuador (about six hours, US$6.50) via San Miguel on the Colombia-Ecuador border. This route is rarely used by foreigners so take care. Bus connections to the highlands leave daily for Pasto (US$12) going through Mocoa.

If you are looking for a boat you may have to wait a couple of days. To take a boat from Puerto Asís to Leticia is an adventure but trying to book passage can be an ordeal. There are no scheduled passenger services and making arrangements before you arrive is impossible. Two places to check for arrivals and departures are at Transportes Fluviales del Amazonas on Carrera 20 and Calle 10 or the Oficina de la Inspección Fluvial at the Alcadia Municipal building on the Central Plaza. There are two port areas. One is on the riverfront in Puerto Asís and the other, the Port of Hong Kong (!), is 2.5km to the west along Calle 12. The latter serves larger ships and the military but both have vessels departing for Leticia.

You will probably end up on a cargo boat as military vessels leave only once or twice a month, so a hammock is essential. Negotiate the fare with the captain, and be sure to check if it includes food, although you might want to consider taking your own if you have the equipment to prepare it. Expect to pay US$100–150 for the ten-day trip downstream and make sure you get a receipt or ticket when you hand over your cash.

Mocoa

This town is capital of Putumayo province, but such status confers no additional reason to stop here. The town centre is small, as the majority of the 15,000 population live in outlying homesteads. Although friendly to strangers, the inhabitants couldn't care less about tourism, as theirs is a market town and centre of distribution for local farm and forest products. As the surrounding country is heavily altered by agricultural activity, nature seekers will find little to please. In reality visitors to Mocoa are usually transiting between Puerto Asís and towns further north. A beautiful drive to Pasto through the pass to the west gives access to the good roads through central Colombia and up to Bogotá. The town has few amenities, a handful of hotels and several places to eat. If you are heading for Ecuador through Puerto Asís or San Miguel you need to get your passport stamped at the DAS office in the town centre. Buses to nearby towns are frequent, with three or four a day making the trip to Puerto Asís for under US$5.

Curillo

This small town on the banks of the Caquetá is a speck among the vastness of trees and rivers. It's mostly a through-town, with most visitors on their way to or from Mocoa or Florencia. This is the only other place beside Getucha to look for a boat down the Caquetá to La Tagua, but if you want to go elsewhere you have to make your own arrangements with a local boat owner. If you're thinking of heading to Mitú it will be a challenge. If cost is a factor you're better off flying from Bogotá, as boat passage is expensive at US$75 or more per day. If you want to get to Brazil, travelling the Putumayo from Puerto Asís is a cheaper option.

Mitú

Capital of Vaupés province with a population of 5,500, this small town in lowland rainforest was established to consolidate Colombia's claim over one of the remotest parts of the Amazon. You go there to take a boat to Brazil down the Río Vaupés, or perhaps for the challenging journey to Puerto Inirida, a distant outpost in the northern Guainia region close to the Venezuelan border. Flights to Bogotá are relatively inexpensive (US$78 one-way), and offer the only realistic opportunity to visit this back of beyond. As a rule of thumb, Colombian Amazon settlements such as Mitú are so remote or hard to reach as to be cost-ineffective in terms of dollars spent for wilderness experienced. Unless you are on a special project, working as a doctor, biologist, missionary or prospector, there's not much reason to visit Mitú.

NATIONAL PARKS AND WILDLIFE RESERVES

Relatively conservation-conscious, Colombia was the first and only country to establish a national park along its portion of the Amazon River. Management of the national park system is with the Ministry of the Environment through UAESPN (Unidad Administrativa Especial del Sistema de Parques Nacional), or Unidad Administrativa for short. Colombia's total number of national parks is 33, including three in the Amazon. Altogether, including protected reserves, about 8% of the country is set aside for conservation. In Colombia, which values its relatively small portion of rainforest highly, sale of wild-captured game and under-sized fish is illegal and laws are strictly enforced. However, there is little money for patrolling parks and the small number of staff are insufficient to manage a combined area bigger than Wales. Information on Amacayacú National Park and La Paya National Park are in the sections on Leticia (page 230) and Florencia (page 232) respectively.

Cahuinari National Park
The second and newer of Amazonas' two national parks, Cahuinari is even more remote and unspoilt than Amacayacú. It covers 5,750km² (2,220 miles²) of tropical lowland rainforest along the middle reaches of the Río Caquetá. The park can be reached via Puerto Guzman (catch a boat) down the Río Caquetá to Araracuara. From Araracuara you can hire a guide to take you to the park. Alternatively, you start in Manaus, and take a boat up the Japura River to the border to La Pedrera, where the river now becomes the Caquetá. Before you set off, obtain a permit to enter the park in Bogotá or Leticia. Within the park there are no tourist facilities so you and your guide will need camping equipment and food.

Chiribiquete National Park
Colombia's biggest national park, protects 12,800km² of moist tropical rainforest between the Yari River and its major tributary the Apaporis. Extensive flooded forest is included within the boundaries. As well as the largest protected area, this is also the most inaccessible. The park has no infrastructure within its boundaries and there is no recognised way of getting there.

La Paya National Park
Covering some 4,220km², La Paya was established in 1994 to protect an area of the Putumayo and Caquetá rivers, adjacent to the Ecuador border. Aside from Amacayacú this is the only national park that is accessible to the average traveller. The best way to reach it is by boat from Puerto Asís to Puerto Leguízamo or taking the short road trip to La Tagua. Both work well as a base for day trips into the park. The park has no permanent tourist facilities so you have either to content yourself with day trips or take camping equipment.

Monkey Island
This is the only private reserve in Colombia's lowland Amazonia. Along with the Anaconda Hotel and other establishments, the reserve was set up in the 1970s by Mike Tsalakis, an American businessman. In 1987 he was sentenced to a long term in a US jail for cocaine smuggling. Today managed by the Hotel Anaconda, the reserve remains open to the public. Tour operators in Leticia can arrange guided day trips there, costing around US$20.

About 10km long and 2km wide, Monkey Island is located about 40km west of Leticia, and is home to a variety of monkey and marmoset species. The monkeys were brought in when the reserve was set up. Most were yellow-footed titis and now their descendants populate, indeed over-run, the island. Plans are afoot – not a yellow foot – to reopen the island's single lodge, but exactly when this will happen is anyone's guess.

Ecuador

Divided between the northern and southern hemispheres by the equator which passes just north of Quito, Ecuador justifies its name perfectly. Excluding the Guyanas, Ecuador has the smallest area of lowland Amazon and is the fourth smallest country in South America. Despite being not much bigger than Britain its variety of life represents one of the planet's greatest stores of biodiversity. In mountainous cloudforest and undisturbed lowland rainforest, the species diversity of plants, birds, mammals, amphibians and insects is among the world's highest.

FACTS AND FIGURES
Geography

As with Peru and Colombia, Ecuador's territory includes the Pacific *costa* to the west and the Amazonian *Oriente* to the east. These two regions are separated by the Andean *sierra* region bisected by a high central valley where Quito lies.

Among Ecuador's Andean peaks is Cotopaxi at 5,897m, the world's highest active volcano. At Cayembe, northeast of Quito, the equator reaches its highest elevation around the globe (5,800m). Numerous peaks of 5–6,000m form two parallel chains running from the country's north to the south. The eastern one, being of lower elevation, forms the Amazon Basin's westernmost rim.

Comprising about half of Ecuador's land area, lowland rainforest has a

---

BASIC FACTS
Official name República del Ecuador
Area 284,000km² (110,000 miles²)
Population 13 million (2000 est)
Capital Quito (1.3 million)
Largest city (population) Guayaquil (1.5 million)
Main Amazon city Coca/Puerto Francisco de Orellana
Official language Spanish
Date of independence August 10 1830
Major industries petroleum, agriculture, wood products, tourism, fisheries, textiles and beverages
GDP per capita US$2,900
Currency US dollar
Major attractions Galápagos Islands, Otavalo Market, Podocarpus National Park
National holidays Jan 1, Jan 6, Carnival (week before Lent in March or April), May 1, May 24, Aug 10, Oct 12, Nov 1, Dec 24, Dec 25

disproportionate share of natural resources, and oil extraction in the Oriente is causing major problems for local indigenous people.

The Galápagos Islands are a group of volcanic islands, 1,000km off the coast, famous for their unique wildlife.

Rivers

The Ecuadorian Amazon is dominated by the Napo-Aguarico watershed. Except for the Río Guayas that flows through Guayaquil, virtually all Ecuador's major lowland rivers head in the same direction: east, then southeast before joining the Amazon main stream. Most important from a commercial standpoint is the Río Napo, which crosses the Ecuador-Peru frontier at Nova Rocafuerte to enter the Amazon main stream just below Iquitos. To the south is the Río Zamora Valley in what was the disputed border region between Peru and Ecuador.

Strategically important, the Putumayo forms the Colombia-Ecuador border east of the Andes to Peru.

Climate

Ecuador is equatorial and relatively small so latitude and season have little effect on climatic variation, making topography the dominant factor.

Oriente temperatures range between 18–25°C. Maximum rainfall is between April and July, peaking in June, while it is driest in January and February. The lowlands are the wettest region of Ecuador with annual rainfall of 3,000–6,100mm.

Coastal regions are 25–30°C with highest temperatures between December and May. Despite the humidity the coastal region is quite dry; Guayaquil gets annual precipitation of 1,000mm.

A temperate zone between 750–2,000m results in the central valley having weather likened to perpetual spring. Upland Ecuador is driest between June and September. Annual rainfall is 1,000–2,000mm.

Flora and fauna

Ecuador's mainland wildlife comprises typical Andean and neotropical flora and fauna. The Galápagos Islands comprises a unique ecosystem of plants and animals adapted to life on the remote, oceanic islands.

Ecuador's lowland rainforest wildlife consists of all major Amazon fauna featured in *Chapter 5* and lots, lots more. Ecuador has dozens of endemic bird and amphibian species and thousands of insects.

Land use

In the highland sierra, farming, llama herding and handicrafts are major rural occupations. The range of crops includes some 300 varieties of potatoes. Lowland areas are planted with cash crops, notably bananas and oil palm.

There is little heavy industry in Quito so its rival and the country's biggest city, Guayaquil, is the industrial centre. On the coast, extensive areas are devoted to export-based shrimp farms for which ecologically important mangrove swamps are cleared. Ecuador has a thriving tourism industry and is increasingly concerned with conservation. Some 40% of Ecuador remains forested, mostly in the Amazon lowlands, and is now increasingly protected.

The people
Population and ethnic groups

South America's seventh most populous country, Ecuador has the continent's highest population density at 44 people per km². Half the population is in towns and cities, with Quito and Guayaquil home to one fifth of the whole population. Population density in the Oriente is lower than average for the whole country and vast tracts of lowland rainforest remain virtually empty.

Ethnic composition is poorly known. The majority are of *mestizo* – of mixed Indian and Spanish descent. Most Caucasians (10% of the population) are pure-blood descendants of Spaniards who arrived during the 16th to early 19th centuries.

EL NIÑO

Long-term weather patterns dominate the country's climate from time to time. Most notable is El Niño, a climatic anomaly with a five- to eleven-year cycle, seven on average. One of the most serious El Niño events was in 1982–83, during which heavy rainfall and subsequent floods caused widespread damage. Wildlife was hard hit, especially on the coast and in the Galápagos Islands. Weather in the Amazon Basin is also altered during El Niño events. Temperatures drop to 15°C or even lower and rainfall decreases as cool, dry northerly winds blow from frigid Patagonian plateaux.

Meteorologists say the El Niño of 1998–99 was even worse than that of 1982–83. In just one week, the death toll from El Niño-related causes was 600.

Languages

Spanish is the official language and spoken by almost everyone. Survival Spanish should be enough for most situations, but unless you are fluent you need to acquire an ear for regional accents. English is quite common in popular tourist areas like Quito and at the better Amazon lodges.

Ecuador's linguistic heritage comes from numerous aboriginal native tribes. The *lingua franca* among Indians is Quechua, spoken by most tribes. The main linguistic group in the Ecuadorian Amazon is the Achuar (Jivaro) complex.

Tribes of Amazonia

Ninety per cent of the Amazon population is either Indian (comprising 50%) – mostly Quechua-speaking – or *mestizo* (40%), who together number about half a million, 4% of Ecuador's population.

The largest single group is the Achuar or Shuar – disparagingly called Jivaro, meaning savages – who live in deep forest in remote southeast Ecuador between the Santiago and Corrientes rivers. They were the last major indigenous group in the Ecuadorian Amazon to remain isolated until the discovery of oil in the 1970s. The Achuar have the dubious honour of having practised headhunting.

Education

Standards in city schools and universities are among the highest in South America. Spanish is the language of instruction, though classes are also held in Quechua, and English is widely taught as a second language. For children between ages 6 to 14, education is free and compulsory. The country's largest university, the Central University of Ecuador in Quito, is one of South America's oldest, established in 1586.

In the Oriente, isolated schools teach local children the three Rs, but little more. Teachers try hard but school supplies are meagre and travel conditions make regular attendance difficult. During the 1997–98 El Niño, schools had to extend the rainy season holiday by two whole months.

Religion

Roman Catholicism is practised by 93% of the population. Other Christians include Protestant, Baptist and Mormon. Most Indian groups originally had nature-based beliefs but are now nominally Catholic.

A brief history
Pre-conquest

Little is known of Ecuador's earliest inhabitants. By 5,000 years ago, diverse tribes of sedentary agricultural Indians occupied most of the country. Of these, the Caras came to dominate, establishing their capital at Quito. The Caras were conquered in the late 15th century by the Incas and Quito became the main city of the empire's northern half. Upon Huayna Capac's death the empire was divided between his two sons. Atahualpa took command of Quito. The division created weaknesses readily exploited by the Spaniards when they arrived in 1532.

Conquest

In 1534 conquistador Sebastián de Benalcázar, Francisco Pizarro's lieutentant, battled his way into Quito, only to find it razed to the ground by the retreating Inca. Using the Spanish grid system, he mapped out a new city that survives mostly intact to this day. In 1539, Pizarro replaced Benalcázar with his brother Gonzalo. Gonzalo left Quito in 1541 with Francisco Orellana to explore the Napo. Leaving his commander behind, Orellana drifted downstream to the Amazon's mouth, the first white man to travel the full length of the river.

THE 'NOBLE SAVAGE'
Hilary Bradt

An honest look at Indian culture can prove disappointing to some. The 'Noble Savage' is demystified and sometimes emerges as being more pragmatic and less spiritual than many writers would have us believe. During a story-telling session round the fire over which half a peccary carcass was being smoked, Randy Borman (see page 263) gave an example of how myths about Indians come about:

> An old man from the village was stopped in Lago Agrio by one of those smart, intelligent army officers on assignment in the jungle and waiting to return to Quito with some good stories. 'Tell me about jaguar-hunting,' he said. The old man was instantly on his guard, knowing that the army was actively involved in the campaign to stop the trade in jaguar pelts. So he answered to save his own skin: that they never killed jaguar except in self-defence, that if they had to kill one they would apologise to it 'because we are brothers', that the spirits of dead Cofans go into jaguars ... and so on.
>
> The Indian went back to his village and said: 'You should have heard the stories I told that army officer!' Everyone laughed. The army officer went back to Quito and said: 'You should have heard the stories I learned from an old Indian shaman!' Everyone listened. He wrote up the stories – with embellishments – and they were published. Generations from now, when the Indians have lost their culture, they will read these stories and assume it is their lost inheritance. After all, it's happened in North America!

It is worth adding that many tribes still respect the jaguar and sincerely believe that they are 'brothers'.

Colonialism

As in Peru and other Spanish possessions, wealth relied on Indians working on vast estates. Spain ruled Ecuador as part of the Viceroy of Peru until 1740, when it became part of the Viceroyalty of Granada. In 1809, rebellion shook the country as dissatisfaction spread among working classes, voiced most clearly by an emerging Creole middle class. Independence was declared, but the leaders were executed and the uprising was crushed.

Independence

At the Battle of Pichincha in 1822, Antonio José de Sucre, helped by Simón Bolívar, defeated the Spanish and Ecuador became part of Gran Colombia. In 1830 Ecuador seceded and adopted its own constitution. In the same year, Ecuador and Peru signed a treaty establishing international boundaries between their Amazon possessions.

Post-independence years were marked by infighting among various families and factions. Civil disorder was widespread and governance next to impossible for succeeding regimes. Focus of the struggle for power was rivalry between Quito and Guayaquil.

The 20th century

Increasingly authoritarian administrations dominated by the military governed the country until the mid-20th century. In 1941 a politically and economically weak Ecuador was invaded by Peru along the eastern frontier. The 1942 Río de Janeiro

Protocol resolved that conflict but Ecuador disputed lost territory, unresolved until a treaty signed in 1998.

After World War II democratic governments were undermined by economic difficulties and political instability.

The 1970s economic boom from petroleum profits was temporary as lasting benefits were offset by severe inflation. During the 1980s the economy suffered under massive external debt, exacerbated by low oil prices and high inflation.

Natural disasters compounded economic difficulties. The 1982–83 El Niño resulted in extensive flooding. In 1987 a powerful earthquake caused much loss of life and extensive damage. Then, in March 1993, the country suffered its worst-ever catastrophe when a huge landslide dammed the Paute River, burying hundreds and cutting off communication between Guayaquil and Quito. Thousands were made homeless and the cost of damage was put at over US$100 million.

From 1997 to mid-2000, the country went through considerable political upheaval and six presidents. President Bucaram and his high opinion of himself acutely embarrassed the country. Several appearances on TV chat shows exacerbated his notoriety and he was deposed in February 1997 on grounds of mental incompetence after holding power for six months. Rosalia Arteaga replaced him but lasted only three days. Congress then elected Fabian Alarcon as interim president. He ruled until the election in 1998 of Jamil Mahauad, an Ecuadorean of Lebanese descent. Despite his confidence that 'Ecuador is like the Titanic but we won't sink!' on January 21 2000 he was forced to resign following military objections and widespread protests by Indians. The current president (mid-2002) Gustavo Noboa pledged to continue with Mahauad's plans to 'dollarize' the economy. Despite this policy's relative success, most Ecuadoreans believe Noboa won't be re-elected to a second term in 2004.

Heavy rainfall in April to June of both 2001 and 2002 caused severe flooding and widespread damage throughout the country. The high cost of these disasters further dampens hopes for economic improvement.

Government
Ecuador is governed by a representative democracy elected for a four-year term. All citizens over 18 years of age are required by law to vote. Ecuador has many political parties and it is rare for any one to win a controlling majority, with the result that the ruling government is composed of coalitions. The country is divided into 21 provinces, each subdivided into cantons and parishes.

Money
The US dollar is Ecuador's official currency. Due to severe economic problems the Ecuadorian currency, the sucre, depreciated 70% during 1999. To avoid complete disaster, President Noboa signed a decree pegging the currency to the US dollar in April 2000. The sucre is no longer used. Ecuadorean coins are the same size and weight as US coins.

Take US$100 or so in small bills (ones, fives, and tens) for tips and minor expenses. If your tour is prepaid you'll need money for souvenirs, tips and bar bills – figure on about US$10–25 per day while in the jungle. Cash enough travellers' cheques in Quito before leaving as commissions are high outside the capital. ATMs do not allow you to withdraw over US$100 at a time.

Highlights
Ecuador's natural and cultural resources present ample opportunities for all travellers. Wildlife is abundant in rainforest, coastal and montane biomes while the Galápagos Islands are renowned for unique birds and reptiles.

Tourist facilities are widely available and of good quality. Compared with neighbouring countries, Ecuador's Amazon region is well-developed for commercial travel. Independent travellers will appreciate the public transport system. Buses are relatively safe and reliable, frequent and inexpensive. Air travel is inexpensive and efficient. Numerous tour operators provide competitive packages to the many excellent lodges.

Yet much of Ecuador's lowland rainforest remains undiscovered by the travel industry and offers among the best nature experiences in the Amazon.

Jungle tours

Dozens of tour operators sell jungle trips to suit every pocket and schedule.

For wildlife, go to the remotest areas. For botanising and birding, the best place is undisturbed parts of the lower Andean foothills, such as the upper Aguarico and Napo watersheds. Where lowland and highland habitats merge, Amazon (indeed global) biodiversity reaches its zenith.

Many tours include visits to indigenous communities – sure to interest those wanting a cultural component to their rainforest experience. These may include observations of shamanism, herbalism and the daily life of a rainforest tribe.

Several lodges recently opened in the Ecuadorian Amazon have made outstanding attempts to fulfil the ideals of ecotourism. Major lodges have their own programmes – a convenient all-inclusive package. Alternatively you can easily arrange your own transport, lodgings and meals.

The best lodges work out at over US$100 a day. Most people who stay at these places are with tour groups. With airfare to and from Quito included, a three-day stay at Ecuador's best jungle lodges will cost US$500–750.

With planning and negotiating, you could do something similar for US$150. Take a bus and camp in the native-style *cabañas* (raised thatched huts without walls) or sometimes in a tent. On a basic trip you won't get gourmet food or the most educated guide, but you might get the best experience of your life.

Tour operators

Hundreds of tour operators offer trips to Ecuador's Amazon. You can do a lot of homework researching trips online. For a list of Quito tour operators visit www.goecuador.com. This list includes the more established companies.

In Ecuador (Quito)

Andisimo Av 9 de Octubre #479 and Roca; PO Box 17079736, Quito; tel/fax: 2 250 8347; email: tours@andisimo.com; web: www.andisimo.com. Tailor made programmes for groups and individuals to Cuyabeno, Rio Pañayacu, Lagarto Cocha, Cononaco and Yasuni National Park. Outdoor equipment sale and rental.

Campus Trekking Vargas 99 and Calderón, Conocoto (just outside Quito); tel: 2 234 0601; fax: 2 234 5290; email: campus@pi.pro.ec; web: www.campustrekking.com. Tailor-made tours: trekking, mountaineering and cultural. Eight-day expedition to the Huaorani territory.

Columbus Travel Leonidas Plaza 353 and Roca; tel: 2 223 6688; fax: 2 250 4977; email: bolivar@accessinter.net; web: www.columbusecuador.com. Dedicated to sustainable tourism with tours to top lodges.

Emerald Forest Joaquín Pinto E4-244 and Av Amazonas; tel: 2 254 1278; fax: 2 254 1543; email: emerald@ecuanex.net.ec; web: www.emeraldexpeditions.com. Legendary guide Luis García runs trips in the Misahuallí-Coca area. Pañacocha Lodge and ten-day trips down the Tiputini, Cononaco and Curaray rivers.

Equateur Voyages Passion Gran Colombia 1138 and Yahuachi (inside the Auberge Inn Hostal); PO Box 17079763, Quito; tel/fax: 2 254 3803; email: info@equateur-voyages.com;

web: www.equateur-voyages.com. Programmes include Shiripuno, Cononaco or Cuyabeno and the Huaorani Reserve.

Fundacion SELVA Vida Sin Fronteras Pasaje 'A' # 1 and Rocafuerte, Urb. Mosquera; PO Box 17079107, Quito; tel/fax: 2 289 2247; email: selvaeco@andinanet.net; web: www.selvaeco.org. Non-government organization, concerned with social, economic and political development and habitat protection. Their Amazon Jungle Resort and Ecological Reserve is on the banks of the Aguarico River.

Islazul Viajes La Isla N26-46 and Mosquera Narvaez; tel: 2 222 4393; fax: 2 223 0194; email: islazul@ecuador-travel.net; web: www.ecuador-travel.net/amazon.htm. Tours to Yuturi and Cuyabeno. Camping trip to the Tiputini River. Two-week trip from Misahualli to Iquitos in Peru.

Jarna Travel Tomás Bermur N39-337 and Urrutia; PO Box 17171763, Quito; tel/fax: 2 246 2213; email: service@jarnatravel.com; web: www.jarnatravel.com. Tours near Misahualli and into Cuyabeno. Bookings for El Jardín Alemán and numerous small hotels throughout Ecuador.

Jatun Sacha Foundation Eugenio de Santillán N34-248 and Maurián; PO Box 1712867, Quito; tel: 2 243 2240; fax: 2 245 3583; email: jatunsacha@jatunsacha.org; web: www.jatunsacha.org. Bookings for Cabañas Aliñahui on the Napo River. In the US: **Health and Habitat** 76 Lee Street, Mill Valley, CA 94941; tel: 415 383 6130; fax: 415 381 9214; web: www.healthandhabitat.org.

Julio Verne Travel Calle 5 de Junio 21-46 and 10 de Agosto, Riobamba; tel/fax: 3 963436; email: julioverne@andinanet.net; web: www.julioverne-travel.com. Treks from Puyo and expeditions in remoter areas. Five-day jungle survival camping expedition.

Kapok Expeditions Pinto E4-225 and Amazonas; tel/fax: 2 556 348; email: kapok@kapokexpeditions.com; web: www.kapokexpeditions.com. Ecotours to Cuyabeno Reserve and Lagartococha. Camping trip to Yasuni. Cultural trips to the Cofan Indians in Zabalo.

Kempery Joaquin Pinto 539 and Amazonas; tel: 2 222 6583; fax: 2 222 6715; email: kempery@kempery.com; web: www.kempery.com. Programmes available for Rio Cononaco, Bataburo Lodge and Cuyabeno Wildlife Reserve.

Klein Tours Eloy Alfaro N34-151 and Catalina Aldaz; tel: 2 226 7000; in the US tel: 888 505 5346; fax: 2 244 2389; email: ecuador@kleintours.com.ec; web: www.kleintours.com. With 20 years of experience, one of Ecuador's leading tour operators offers three days in the Upper Napo from Misahualli, four days to Limoncocha and Cuyabeno, or four days at Kapawi Lodge.

Latin Tour Edificio Blanquius Av Almagro 1219 and la Niña; tel: 2 250 8800; fax: 2 256 8657; email: latintour@galapagos-tours.com; web: www.galapagos-tours.com. Tours to Yasuni. Also to Bataburo Lodge and Tapir Lodge.

Magic Globe Manuel Lasso 178 and Mariana de Jesus; tel: 2 553944; fax: 2 546132; email: emilia@magicglobe.com; web: www.magicglobe.com; in the UK at 335 Eccleston Sq, London, SW1V 1EB; tel: 0870 0110270; 020 7976 5455; email: ccuzme@magicglobe.com; US tel: 888 822 8006; email: info@magicglobe.com.

Metropolitan Touring Av Republica Del Salvador N36-84; PO Box 17171649, Quito; tel: 2 298 8200; fax: 2 246 3681; email: avinueza@metropolitan-touring.com; web: www.metropolitan-touring.com. Ecuador's biggest tour operator. Tours to most major jungle lodges.

Native Life Foch E4-167 and Av Amazonas; PO Box 1703504, Quito; tel: 2 255 0836; fax: 2 222 9077; email: natlife@ecnet.ec; web: www.native-life.com. Tours from their base in the southern Cuyabeno Reserve. Widely recommended.

Neotropic Turis Amazonas N24-03 and Wilson; tel: 2 252 1212; fax: 2 554 902; email: info@neotropicturis.com; web: www.neotropicturis.com. Owners of Cuyabeno Lodge. Discounts to university students. Once-in-a-lifetime trip: eight-day, 500-mile journey

AMAZON AND GALÁPAGOS?

A dilemma for travellers is whether a Galápagos Islands trip should include the Amazon at the beginning or the end. Trying to 'do' the Galápagos and Amazon in one trip is possibly doing too much and dilutes the experience of both. These two places are among the world's greatest natural treasures. Much better to spend two weeks (or more) in the Amazon region and save visiting the Galápagos for another year (or vice versa).

However, time and money are limited. If you must combine the two, visit the Galápagos after the Amazon. You'll have earned the rest! Barry Boyce's *A Traveler's Guide to the Galápagos Islands* (available from Galápagos Travel) is highly recommended; also *Galápagos Wildlife* (Bradt Publications).

from Quito to the Marañon and Amazon River in Peru to Iquitos.

Nomadtrek Av Amazonas N22-29 & Carrión 2nd floor; tel: 2 290 6036; fax: 2 254 6376; email: nomadtre@uio.satnet.net; web: www.nomadtrek.com.ec. Caving trips to see the 'Oil Birds Cave' near Miasal. Also have trips to Yasuni and Tapir Lodge.

Safari Tours Calama 380 and J L Mera; tel: 2 255 2505; in the US tel: 800 434 8182; fax: 2 222 3381; email: admin@safari.com.ec; web: www.safari.com.ec. Mountain biking, trekking, rafting and climbing. Also 4WD safaris to remote areas and bookings for jungle lodges. Represent Amarongachi Tours in Tena.

Salsa Reisen Joaquín Pinto 356 and Juan León Mera, second floor; tel: 2 250 0536; fax: 2 254 9358; email: salsa@interactive.net.ec; web: www.salsatravel.com. Itineraries to parts of Ecuador not covered by other tour operators. Outstanding ascent of Volcan Reventador with camping in the Cayembe-Coca Reserve.

Sangay Touring Amazonas 1188 and Cordero; tel: 2 255 0176; fax: 2 256 0426; email: info@sangay.com; web: www.sangay.com. British-owned travel and adventure specialist. Bookings for most first class lodges.

SunWind Travel Chimborazo 111, Cumbayá; PO Box 17078981, Quito; tel: 2 289 0418; fax: 2 255 9714; email: land@sunwindtravel.com; web: www.sunwindtravel.com. Trips to Kapawi and Sacha, river-rafting along rivers in the Napo region, and Tapir Lodge in Cuyabeno.

Surtrek Av Amazonas 897 and Wilson; tel: 2 223 1534; fax: 2 256 1132; email: surtrek@surtrek.com; web: www.surtrek.com. Organises tribal visits and run two eco-lodges: Las Cascadas and Isla Amazonica Eco-Jungle-Lodge.

Tropic Ecological Adventures Av República E7-320 and Diego de Almagro, Edif. Taurus, Dpto. 1-A; tel: 2 223 4594; fax: 2 256 0756; email: tropic@uio.satnet.net; web: www.tropiceco.com. Award-winning tours with indigenous tribes including to the Cofan, with Randy Borman (see page 263), and most lodges.

Turisaven Lerida 381 and Pontevedra; PO Box 1703850, Quito; tel/fax: 2 250 2234; email: turisavn@ecuanex.net.ec; web: www.turisaven.com. 'Beyond Expectations' arrangements to luxury lodges including La Selva, Yachana and Yuturi. Manage El Cipres hostel in Quito.

Turisvision Calle Ultimas Noticias N37-97 and Espectador; PO Box 1717512; tel: 2 224 6756; fax: 2 224 5741; email: info@turisvision.com; web: www.turisvision.com. Bookings for jungle lodges. Escorted tours and security arrangements for VIP visits. Represented in the US by Latin America Reservation Center (page 41).

Zenith Travel JL Mera 453 and Roca, Edif. Chiriboga Ste 202; tel: 2 252 9993; fax: 2 290 5595; email: zenithtravel@andinanet.net; web: www.zenithecuador.com. First gay-owned travel agency in Ecuador, and a member of the International Gay and Lesbian Travel

Association (IGLTA), in business 15 years. Trips to Yuturi, La Selva and Yarina and arrangements throughout Ecuador and Peru.

In the US
DeRiemer Adventure Kayaking PO Box 559, Lotus, CA 95651; tel/fax: 530 295 0830; email: info@adventurekayaking.com; web: www.adventurekayaking.com. Lodge-based kayak adventures from expert to beginner, include Papallacta, Quijos, Oyacachi, Cosanga and Tena Valley.
Pachamama Alliance Presidio Bldg #1007, Ste 215, San Francisco, CA 94129; tel: 415 561 4522; fax: 415 561 4521; email: trips@pachamama.org; web: www. pachamama.org. Represents indigenous people.
ROW Expeditions PO Box 579, Coeur d'Alene, ID 83816; tel: 800 451 6034/208 765 0841; fax: 208 667 6506; email: rowinc@aol.com; web: www.rowinc.com. River-rafting expeditions down the Río Upano from Macas (Sep to Mar only).

In the UK
Tribes 12 The Business Centre, Earl Soham, Woodbridge, Suffolk IP13 7SA; tel: 01728 685971; fax: 01728 685973; email: bram@tribes.co.uk; web: www.tribes.co.uk.
Worldwide Journeys 27 Vanston Place, London, SW6 1AZ; tel: 020 7386 4646; fax: 020 7381 0836; email: enquiry@worldwidejourneys.co.uk; web: www.worldwidejourneys.co.uk.

To include the Galápagos on your itinerary most Ecuadorian tour operators can make arrangements. Research this carefully to get the trip you want. To book a tour before you are in the country, try the following.

Galápagos Travel 783 Río del Mar Bd, Ste 47, Aptos, CA 95003, USA; tel: 800 969 9014; fax: 831 689 9192; email: info@galapagostravel.com; web: www.galapagostravel.com.
Galápagos Adventure Tours 79 Maltings Place, 169 Tower Bridge Rd, London, SE1 3LJ; tel: 020 7407 1478; fax: 020 7407 0397; email: info@galapagos.co.uk; web: www.galapagos.co.uk.

Both specialise in the Galápagos but can organise jungle extensions as well.

GETTING THERE AND AWAY
Weather need not be a consideration as there is not much difference year-round. To keep away from the tourist crowds and if finances are tight, avoid the high seasons (June to August, and December).

By air
Mariscal Sucre International Airport is 10km north of the central commercial district in downtown Quito, somewhat confusingly called Mariscal Sucre as well. Departure tax is US$25 on international flights.

From the US
International flights arrive in Quito and Guayaquil. Quito is the better arrival point for visitors to the Amazon and has direct flights by American Airlines and LanChile from Miami. American also fly direct from New York, while Continental has daily flights from Houston.

From Europe
British Airways flies from London into Miami for connections with American Airlines direct to Quito. Flights from Frankfurt, Amsterdam, Paris and Madrid include a layover, usually in Miami.

By boat

Reaching the Ecuadorian Amazon by riverboat from Iquitos is possible although at present there are no scheduled departures. Islazul Viajes and Neotropic Turis run trips from Ecuador into Iquitos and may be able to provide transport in the opposite direction. This trip on local riverboats is offered by Dreamweaver Travel (page 40) for US$2,250 (excluding air). *Jungle Discovery I* is a new 28-passenger tourist riverboat. Double cabins have private showers with hot water. The owners plan cruises from Coca down the Rio Napo to Iquitos. For information contact Kempery in Quito (page 244).

Overland

The Pan-American Highway runs from the northern frontier with Colombia and continues south to Peru. Both frontiers are served by international buses and large numbers of private vehicles make the crossing.

It is possible to cross between Lago Agrio and Puerto Asís in Colombia. Note the warnings on travel into Colombia before attempting this. Several tour operators suspended operations in this area following incursions by Colombian rebels. There are two main crossings from southern Ecuador into Peru. Buses go from Loja to Macará and from here into the Peruvian town of Sullana. The other crossing is along the coast, at Huaquillas, reached from Machala.

Customs and immigration

A **passport** is required. Upon entry you get a 60-day **visitor's permit**. Ask for a 90-day **visa** if you wish to stay longer. To stay over the allotted time get an extension from the Ecuadorian Immigration Authority who have offices in Quito at Amazonas 2639.

Getting around
By bus

Ecuador has a good public transport system. Prices are low and the better buses come equipped with air-conditioning, reclining seats, onboard toilets and TV.

Buses to the Amazon Basin from Quito leave from Terminal Terrestre in the south of the city. Beware of pickpockets and minimise signs of wealth. Be vigilant on public transport especially in Quito and watch out for petty thieves at the Terminal Terrestre and on the long-distance buses. Direct buses are available to most Amazon towns. Trans Esmeraldas and Transporte Baños are two of the better companies.

By air

From Quito destinations for Amazon travellers include Tena, Coca, Lago Agrio or Shell-Mera near to Puyo on TAME. Main offices are at Av Amazonas 1354 (tel: 2 509382) and Colon 1001 (tel: 2 509382), with several other offices around town.

ICARO serves Coca, Lago Agrio, Shell Mera and Loja in the Oriente, and other cities throughout Ecuador. Contact them at Palora #124 and Av Amazonas; tel: 1 800 883567; fax: 2 243 9867; email: customer.service@icaro.com.ec; web: www.icaro.com.ec.

By boat

Transport to and from popular tourist facilities is usually via motorised *colectivo* or small motorboats. With increasing wealth due to oil and tourism, conventional motorboats are common on the Napo, and the tourism industry now makes extensive use of Ecuador's rivers.

Maps

Outside the country, it's easiest to order maps online (see page 46). In Ecuador, the best place to get maps is at the Military Geographical Institute (IGM) in Quito (Calle Paz and Miño; tel: 2 522 066) who have a variety of maps at different scales.

COMMUNICATIONS
Mail

Post from Ecuador takes up to three weeks and on the whole is reliable and relatively inexpensive. A postcard within the Americas costs about US$0.45, or further afield US$0.55. The main post office is on Av Colon. International courier companies offer a more reliable service for packages.

Telephone and fax

Phone and fax are widely available and public telephones are in the commercial areas of all cities and large towns. Many public phones now only take pre-paid 'smart' cards. The cheapest place to make international calls is at a branch of the state-owned telephone company EMETEL. There is one at the airport. The main office is on the corner of Colon and Av 10 de Agosto.

The international code for Ecuador is 593.

Internet

Most tour operators in Ecuador now use email. This is the most efficient way to book jungle trips with Ecuadorean agencies. Many larger tour operators and lodges now have websites so you can check facilities and prices from home.

There are a couple of dozen internet cafés in Quito. Most have several computers (PC), printer, scanner, international fax and phone facilities. Ones that stand out are:

El Choque Calama 317 and Victoria (corner); tel: 2 546 086; fax: 2 545 500; email: elchoque@latinmail.com. Open 8.00-24.00. Snacks, fruit juices and full bar. Free salsa lessons at 20.00 every Wednesday!

Monkey online Corner of JL Mera and Jorge Washington; tel: 2 500 979; email: info@altesa.net; web: www.altesa.net/monkeyonline; Open 9.00-24.00. Costs US$5 per hour.

Papayanet JL Mera 413; email: papayanet@papayanet.com.ec; web: www.papayanet.com.ec. Most popular, open 9.00-24.00. Snacks and juice bar.

Television and radio

Ecuadorean broadcast media consists of several state-run and private stations. Programming is predominantly current affairs. Sports are also popular, mainly soccer. Occasional educational programmes are shown, while evening slots are occupied with game shows or music videos. Most larger hotels have satellite TV.

Newspapers

All widely circulated newspapers and weeklies are in Spanish. Quito newspapers include *Hoy, El Comercio* and *El Tiempo*. *Hoy* prints daily weather reports and TAME airline schedules with internal flights from Quito to Amazon towns.

US and European newspapers are not widely available but may be stocked at airports and larger hotels.

South American Explorers

All of the above in one place... SAE members can receive mail, phone calls, faxes and email at the Quito clubhouse (Jorge Washington 311 and Leonidas Plaza;

tel/fax: 2 222 5228; email: quitoclub@saexplorers.org; web: www.saexplorers.org).
If you're not a member join when you arrive (see page 46).

QUITO

Close to the Equator and nestled 2,820m (9,300ft) up in a high central Andean
valley, Quito's climate is an 'eternal spring' with average daytime temperatures of
15°C. The city is surrounded by lofty snow-capped mountains including the active
volcano Pichincha (4,760m). Ecuador's second biggest city, with 1.4 million
inhabitants, Quito seems more dignified than similarly-sized South American
cities.

Quito has historic relevance to the Amazon as the departure point for the first-
ever full-length Amazon voyage, by conquistador Francisco de Orellana.
Geography and growth have divided Quito into two cities, New and Old. The Old
City, to the south, filled with colonial buildings, was declared a World Heritage
Site by UNESCO in 1978 and is governed by strict building regulations.

Today, the Old City looks much as it did when Orellana departed on that cold
morning in 1541, less than half a century after Columbus first reached the
Americas. Red-tiled roofs atop whitewashed stucco buildings stretch into the
distance, punctuated here and there by cathedral spires and curly wisps of smoke
rising into the bright sky.

Orientation is along a north–south axis constrained by the narrow valley. Within
this groove Quito is easy to navigate. The airport is to the north in the New City,
the long-distance bus station – Terminal Terrestre – is south in the Old City and
the hotel and commercial area is roughly in the middle. A variety of online
resources (see *Appendix 3*) enable you to research more about the city and simplify
your visit if looking for accommodation, tours or other facilities.

At the airport

There are plenty of yellow taxis clustered outside the airport. The 25-minute ride
to your hotel in the New City costs US$4–6. Alternatively catch a bus from across
the airport into town for about US$1 to the city's main commercial area on Av
Amazonas.

WARNING Quito's elevation may cause altitude sickness. These range from mild
headache to nausea and dizziness. Sleeping may also be difficult. Minimise
exertion, especially for the first day or two, and keep alert for symptoms. (See
Chapter 4, page 89.)

The main tourist area around Av Amazonas has become less safe recently.
During the day it seems fine, but after dark tourists have been mugged. Take a taxi
and stay with a group if possible.

City transport

The cheapest way to get around is by bus – no more than US$0.50 for a trip within
the city. The buses follow set routes advertised on plaques in the front window.
The conductors yell out their destinations, you can yell back and, if they go where
you're going, the bus stops and you get the ride.

Tram (*El Trole*) run along the north–south axis making an easy connection
between the Old and New cities. The standard fare is US$0.25. The stop nearest
to the centre of the Old City is Santo Domingo.

Taxis should not cost more than US$8 for even the longest journeys. If you take
a taxi, make sure the meter is working, and if there is no meter agree on a price
beforehand.

QUITO: MAIN AVENUES

Mariscal Sucre Airport

Calderón, Otavalo (N Ecuador)

Pululahua Geobotanical Reserve, Mitad del Mundo 40km

NUEVA VIA ORIENTAL

AV EL INCA

AV DE LA PALMERAS

AV DE LA PRENSA

AV EL INCA

AV LOS SHYRIS

AV DE LOS GRENADOS

N

Bradt

AV MARISCAL JOSE DE SUCRE

Tramway terminus

ASCARAY

AV GASPAR DE VILLAROEL

Puerto Camaron

AV GRAL ELOY ALFARO

AV NACIONES UNIDAS

Sushi Itto

AV 6 DE DICIEMBRE

AV 10 DE AGOSTO

AV AMAZONAS

AV LOS SHYRIS

Parque Carolina

AV AMERICA

Science & Natural History Museum

AV DE LA REPUBLICA

Immigration office

Tourist information

AV DE ALMAGRO

La Ronda

AV GRAL ELOY ALFARO

Tramway System

CORONA

AV AMERICA

AV FRANCISCO DE ORELLANA

UK Embassy

Post office

AV 10 DE AGOSTO

CRISTOBAL COLON

AV AMAZONAS

AV 6 DE DICIEMBRE

AV 12 DE OCTUBRE

AV PATRIA

Parque El Ejido

see page 242

Instituto Geográfico Militar

Casa de Cultura Ecuadoriana

Old City, Terminal Terrestre

0 — 1km
0 — 1 mile

Where to stay

Quito has hundreds of hotels, *hostales*, *residencias* and *apartmentes* to choose from. They are loosely concentrated around Mariscal Sucre in the New City, with quite a number in the Old City. If new to Quito base yourself in the New City – it is safer and easier to get around. A number of hotels offer discounts of 10% or more for booking online with a credit card. Check online for lists of Quito hotels at www.metrocityguide.com and www.quito-hotels.com. This list is a selection of what's available.

First class

Hotel Alameda Real corner of Amazonas and Roca; tel: 2 562 345; fax: 2 565 759. One of the city's top hotels with rooms from US$79pp.

Colon Hilton Internacional Amazonas and Patria; tel: 2 560 666; fax: 2 563 903; web: www.hilton.com. As you would expect for a Hilton, it has everything. Used by upmarket tour operators. From US$95pp for a double.

Hotel Sebastián Almagro 822 and Cordero; tel: 2 222 400; fax: 2 222 500; email: hsebast1@hsebastian.com.ec. Most eco-conscious of the luxury hotels. Laundry is washed environmentally and organic fruits and vegetables are used in the restaurant – a great hotel for the price, from US$60pp single, US$70pp double.

Middle range

Café Cultura Robles and Reina Victoria; tel: 2 558 889; fax: 2 224 271; email: info@cafecultura.com; web: www.cafecultura.com. A converted colonial house with 26 spacious rooms. Neo-traditional décor. Ground floor café serves fresh bread and homemade jam, and tasty lunches and dinners. Single $49pp, double $59pp. One of the world's 50 best budget hotels according to UK newspaper *The Independent*.

Madison Hotel Roca 518 and Reina Victoria; tel: 2 508 617. An antidote to busy, anonymous five-star hotels: gourmet dining, cable TV, gaming and saloon-style bar. Rooms from US$45.

Budget

El Cafécito Luis Cordero 1124 and Victoria; tel: 2 223 4862; email: cafecito@ecuadorexplorer.com; web: www.cafecito.net. Convenient location, cheap and cheerful, very popular with backpackers. Restaurant has great desserts. From US$6 per night in shared rooms, US$9 single, US$14 double room.

Casa Helbling General Veintimilla 531 and 6 de Diciembre; tel: 2 256 5740; fax: 02 250 0952; email: casahelbling@accessinter.net; web www.casahelbling.de/enindex.htm. Single room rate is US$10 or US$14 with private bath, doubles are US$7pp and US$8pp respectively. Clean and secure. Helpful staff. Mail, email, faxes and phone services. Cooked breakfast is about US$3, or use the self-catering kitchen. Small library with guidebooks, maps and dictionaries. Do-it-yourself laundry costs about $4 a load.

Magic Bean Foch 681 and JL Mera; tel: 2 256 6181; email: magic@ecuadorexplorer.com; web: www.ecuadorexplorer.com/magic/home. Fashionable hotel/restaurant with dormitory (US$7 per night) and private rooms (US$22 single, US$26 double). Prices include continental breakfast.

Villa Nancy Carrion 335 and 6 de Diciembre; tel: 2 563 084; fax: 2 549 657; email: villa_nancy@yahoo.com; web www.villanancy.com. In a quiet area a few minutes' walk from Av Amazonas. Clean and safe. US$18 for a single, US$20 for a double. Price includes breakfast, airport transfer and tax.

La Posada del Maple Juan Rodríguez 148, near Av 6 de Diciembre; tel: 2 237 375; email: admin@posadadelmaple.com; web: www.posadadelmaple.com. Casual friendly atmosphere. Self-catering. Small but clean rooms from US$13, including breakfast.

International Youth Hostel/Centro Hostelling International Pinto 325 and Victoria;

tel: 2 543 995; fax: 2 508 221; email: booking@iyhf.org; web: www.hostelling-ecuador.org. Basic but welcoming. Restaurant, café and laundry, luggage storage, fax, post and email. From US$9.

Staying in the Old City

The Old City is less safe than the New City. Although incidents are mostly limited to petty theft and bag-snatching, be on your guard. Romantics will enjoy the **Teatro Internacional**. Near the theatre at Guayaquil 1317 and Esmeraldas; tel: 2 216 195. Another mid-range hotel in the same area is the **Real Audencia**, Bolívar 220; tel: 2 512 711, while budget travellers should enjoy the **Grand** at Rocafuerte 1001; tel: 2 210 192.

Where to eat

For the gourmet or glutton, trencherman or connoisseur, there's no shortage of opportunities to guzzle and quaff in Quito. Some restaurants do not accept credit cards even though they have the sticker in their window. Before ordering ask if the 22% restaurant tax is included in the price.

For speciality Ecuadorian food try *llapingachos*, a type of cheese and potato rissole with hot peanut sauce. *Empañadas* are pasties filled with potato and meat, sold by street vendors and posh restaurants alike. *Humitas* are made from mashed maize with seasoning, wrapped in maize leaves and steamed. A traditional highland dish is *cuy*, roast guinea-pig. *Ceviche* is a popular seafood dish and fresh.

La Ronda (Bello Horizonte 400 and Almagro; tel: 254 0459) excels in traditional Ecuadorian dishes. House specials include a seafood casserole and roast pork with llapingachos. Folk musicians accompany your meal. Ask for a table on the interior balcony. Credit cards accepted. The best *ceviche* is at a restaurant of the same name, **Ceviche** (1232 JL Mera; tel: 252 6380). For a variety of seafood dishes, focusing on shrimps, try **Puerto Camaron** (6 de Diciembre 5052 and Granaderos; tel: 225 0213). **Meson Español** (Carrion 974; tel: 222 5585) serves Ecuadorian and Spanish meals. **La Querencia** (Eloy Alfaro 2530; tel: 246 1664) is renowned for traditional dishes, a quiet atmosphere and friendly service. The cognac-flambéed lobster is a speciality. It's good value, from US$20–25 a head.

Good French food can be found at **La Marmite** (287 Mariano Aguilera; tel: 223 7751). Italian food at **El Hornero** (854 Amazonas and Veintemilla) is recommended. For a less expensive Italian meal try **Spaghetteria Romulo y Remo** (JL Mera 1012 y Foch). **Il Grillo** (Baquirizo and Almagro; tel: 222 5531) is relatively new, and popular among locals. Sushi lovers should visit **Sushi Itto** in the Quicentro Shopping Center (corner of Av Naciones Unidades and Seis de Diciembre; tel; 227 2665; web: www.sushi-itto.com). **Magic Bean** (Foch 681 and JL Mera) serves great coffee (the 'bean'). With its American-style breakfast, pizza for lunch and kebabs for dinner, you could eat three meals a day here. The atmosphere is casual and with luck you may be serenaded by a roaming musician (tips expected). Expect to spend US$10–20 for a full meal.

The **British Council** (1534 Amazonas) does vegetarian food. **Superpapa's** (JL Mera 741 and Veintimilla) serves inexpensive meals based around the potato (the 'papa') alongside continental or American/English breakfasts.

The **Victoria** (Victoria 530 and Roca) is a British-style pub with pub-grub and English beer. Several other restaurants cater to a more exotic palate including a number of Indian restaurants such as the **Taj Mahal** (San Ignacio 953 and Gonzáles Suárez; tel: 222 5126). Chinese food is very popular; try **Pekin** (197 Bello Horizonte).

QUITO: CENTRE

What to see

A city tour will ensure you see the best of the city. Most places of historical interest are in the Old City. A half-day itinerary costs US$35–50 per person (excluding lunch). Visit **Calle de Morales** for examples of early colonial architecture. This is one of Quito's oldest streets, with some buildings dating back to the 17th century.

Plaza de Independencia is a welcome space among the Old City's cobbled streets. Surrounding the plaza architecturally accomplished buildings including the Palacio Municipal (City Hall), Palacio Arzobispal (Archbishop's Palace), Palacio de Gobierno (Presidential Palace) and the Cathedral. From the Plaza, you can see Panecillo Hill and Quito's most visible and famous landmark, **Virgen de Quito**, which represents the Virgin of the Americas. Crowned with a circlet of twelve stars, the figure restrains a chained dragon under foot. The hill presents a panorama of Quito and on clear days across to Cotopaxi. It's best from the statue itself, which is hollow and accessible for about US$1.

It's safest to visit by taxi or with organised tours as it's unsafe to walk to the top of Panecillo Hill.

Museums

Quito boasts dozens of fine museums. Most are in the New City and focus on the history and culture of Ecuador. Admission fees are very reasonable. The best and most relevant to visitors to the Amazon are:

Museo Amazónico (Amazon Museum) at 12 de Octubre 1430 and Wilson. Displays of Indian cultural life with the Achuar well-represented and some flora and fauna exhibits. Open Mon–Fri 11.30–12.30 and 13.00–17.00; Sat 11.30–12.30.

Casa de Cultura Ecuatoriana (House of Ecuadorian Culture) at 12 de Octubre and Patria. On the east half of Parque El Ejido, this is Quito's flagship museum. It comprises five museums in one, covering archaeology, ethnology, art, musical instruments, and religious and colonial art. Open Tue–Fri 10.00–18.00; Sat 10.00–14.00.

Museo de Sciencas y Historia Naturales (Science and Natural History Museum) at Rumipamba 341 and Shyris. Within La Carolina Park, this small but informative museum has sections on Ecuador's geology, geography and biota. Open Mon–Fri 08.30–13.00, 14.00–16.00; Sat 09.00–13.00; Sun 09.30–14.30. US$1 admission.

Vivarium/Gustavo Orcés Fundación Herpetológica (Herpetological Foundation) at Casa de Ajedrez in Parque Carolina. Email: fherpeto@pi.pro.ec. A collection of live snakes with specimens from the Oriente along with caiman, turtles and poison-dart frogs. Worth a visit. Open Tues–Sat 09.00–13.00 and 14.30–16.00; Sun 11.00–18.00. US$1 admission.

Shopping

The city is choc-a-bloc with shops, stalls and kiosks selling clothing, handicrafts, curios, antiques, leather goods, coins, semi-precious stones and all manner of knick-knacks and bric-a-brac. Go to Parque El Ejido on the weekend for all the above, paintings, and woollen goods from Otavalo.

Shopping in the Old City is best around Avenida 24 de Mayo.

Additional information

Several city guides include lists of hotels, restaurants and interesting visitor sites. (See *Appendix 3* for online guides.) CETUR (Corporación Ecuatoriana de Turismo; Victoria 514 and Roca; tel: 2 527 002) has an excellent tourist map of Ecuador. The Military Geographical Institute (Calle Paz and Miño; tel: 2 522 066; fax: 2 569 097; email: igm@uio.satnet.net; web: www.igm.gov.ec) also has various maps.

Purchase national park permits from offices in towns near the parks or from INEFAN (Instituto Ecuatoriano Forestal y de Areas Naturales y Vida Silvestre) at the Ministerio de Agricultura y Ganadería, 8th floor Amazonas and Eloy Alfaro; tel: 2 541 955; fax: 2 564 037.

Excursions from Quito

Leap from the southern to the northern hemisphere at **La Mitad del Mundo** (The Centre of the World) where a marked line divides the world in two. Located 25km north of Quito a day trip to the monument costs US$15–25. Alternatively catch a bus to the monument from Av America in the Old City, cost about US$0.50.

Otavalo, some 100km north of Quito, is probably South America's most famous arts and crafts market, hence its popularity with tourists. Local people wear characteristic felt hats. The women dress in long purple dresses and gold bead necklaces, whereas the men wear dapper black suits. The costumes set them apart from non-Otavaleños. Most activity revolves around Plaza de Ponchos between Av Sucre and Jaramillo.

Many products flow from the Otavalo area to other parts of Ecuador, South America and indeed the world. Woven goods, many made from alpaca, are high quality and excellent value. Bargaining is the order of the day. After arts and crafts, immerse yourself in local life at the animal market (early to mid-morning), west on Av Calderón in Barrio San Juan, or the produce market (morning to early afternoon) at the west end of J Montalvo, at 31 de Octubre.

Tour operators in Quito have day trips costing from US$45; a bus from Quito is about US$2.

Jungle tours

Options for lodges, camps, huts, tours, expeditions, guides, etc are mind-boggling. If you are researching at home and booking in advance spend time on the internet to get as much information as possible. If you are in Quito the best strategy is to visit tour operators listed on pages 243–5 – most are in Mariscal Sucre – collect brochures and then look online for reports and reviews. The SAE clubhouse has member reports – mostly oriented to budget travellers. Your basic options are to stay in a lodge or with an indigenous community, or to take a forest trip (camping, huts, etc). Remoter locations have more wildlife and less forest degradation, but tend to be more expensive. Have a clear idea of your budget and what you want, and do the research.

THE ECUADORIAN AMAZON

No settlement in the Ecuadorian Amazon has a population over 30,000. Most jungle towns were established in the 1970s and have grown since on account of nearby oil or gold exploration.

These rough and ready hamlets are not geared to tourists and share common characteristics: small, enclosed by jungle and hard to reach, and when you get there dusty streets, poverty-stricken inhabitants and in some cases lack of basic amenities. Ecuador's oil riches have come at a high environmental cost. Travellers must endure oil-boom towns of stunning ugliness, pervasive pollution and faulty infrastructure; luckily these tend to be only stopover points between jungle visits. It seems that oil wealth never gets back to its place of origin.

Coca (Puerto Francisco de Orellana)

If any town in the Ecuadorian Amazon is a 'must' on the Amazon tourist's itinerary it is Coca, officially Puerto Francisco de Orellana. Though other towns are bigger, Coca is nearest to primary rainforest and the region's best lodges. On the upper Napo, some 1,000km upstream from where the river joins the Amazon proper, the town is unimpressive. Built for oilworkers and hewn from the jungle, it consists of cheap concrete buildings bounded by unpaved streets of potholes and puddles, and sidewalks of rubble and rubbish.

Its importance is based on the oil pipeline and drilling, the amount of tourism generated by nearby lodges, and its function as a military base. Oil industry activity in the area has has already degraded the upper Napo on account of oil spills around its watershed.

Fortunately, expanses of pristine rainforest beyond the town quickly help you put the experience of Coca behind you.

Getting there

It's a half-hour flight direct from Quito into Coca with Icaro who have three morning flights daily (except Sundays). The flight is US$56 one way but often full so book in advance. The Icaro office in Coca is at Hotel La Misión near the water front (tel/fax: 6 880546).

By bus from Quito the 12-hour journey (US$10) involves a long but spectacular drive over the Andes via Baeza and passing through Lago Agrio. Buses also connect to Tena to the south.

If you take the bus, stop overnight at San Rafael Falls on the Río Reventador, Ecuador's biggest waterfall at 150m high, about an hour past Baeza. Ask the bus driver to stop at the 'Cascada de San Rafael.' There's a little hut there where, on your way back, you can wait to flag down a passing bus. If you want to stay the night San Rafael Lodge consists of prefabricated buildings built for workers on the nearby oil pipeline. Rooms are comfortable ($35pp if booked in Quito, less if you just turn up) and there is a simple restaurant. Don't let the pipeline put you off. Slivers of waterfalls cascade off thousand foot cliffs and the forest is unspoiled, the pipeline aside. Nearby looms the 3,485m Volcan Reventador, said to be Ecuador's most unpredictable volcano.

At the margin of upland cloudforest and the lowlands, biodiversity here is very high. Along the easy trail to the falls you may see cock-of-the-rock, one of the area's most colorful birds. At the foot of the falls (you must have a guide – this part of the trail is very difficult) are weird sculptures formed by mineralised water coating rocks and branches.

Salsa Reisen's camping trip of five to eight days takes you into the wilder parts of the Coca-Cayambe Reserve around Volcán Reventador. German travel guide author Volker Feser leads this trip – US$100 per day. Check to see what equipment you need to take. Book through his company in Quito (page 245).

Where to stay and eat

Most accommodation in Coca consists of *residencias*, but the best hotels are within the average budget. **La Misión** (tel: 06 880260), has rooms overlooking the riverfront, a pool and a basement nightclub. US$20 for a room with AC.

Hotel Auca is halfway along the main street on Napo and García Moreno (tel: 06 880600). It's a good place to meet fellow travellers for a jungle trip. For US$15 per night, **Hostería Amazonas** (Espejo and 12 de Febrero; tel: 06 880444, or in Quito; tel: 02 244 1533) is on the riverfront and away from the centre of town.

The cheapest places to eat are dubious from a health standpoint… what you save on meals you might end up spending on medicine. The restaurants in the **Auca** and **La Misión** hotels at US$3–5 for a main meal are quite good. **Papa Dan's,** run by a couple of Americans, serves cocktails from US$2, beer and the best burgers in town.

Additional information

Tour agencies pop up then disappear almost daily it seems. You will be able to get a good deal but be sure you are getting what you pay for. These smaller tour operators are less accountable than those in Quito, and consequently have lower standards of business. Once you're in the forest a lodge can turn into a hut or a hut into a tent.

Manatee Amazon Explorer

The three-deck *Manatee Amazon Explorer* has 13 double cabins with air conditioning and hot water. Facilities include dining room, bar and lounge area, and laundry service. The crew of 11 includes English-speaking naturalist guides. From Coca the boat heads down the Napo to Yasuni National Park. You can book on the *Manatee* through Metropolitan Touring in Quito (page 244), from US$461pp sharing for four days. In the US, Big Five (1551 SE Palm Court, Stuart, FL 34994; tel: 800 244 3483; fax: 772 287 5990; email: info@bigfive.com; web: www.bigfive.com) organise tours on the *Manatee* from US$745pp.

Jungle lodges near Coca
La Selva Lodge

La selva means 'the forest' – an appropriate name for this lodge, established in 1986. From Coca, a three hour motorised canoe trip takes you down the Napo to a walkway on the north bank. It's a kilometre walk to Garzacocha Lake. A 20-minute paddled canoe ride across the lake takes you to the lodge.

The lodge's guides lead you along the trails extending several kilometres into the rainforest. Itineraries combine guided walks, canoe rides and birding.

The most popular trail is a moderate hike to a 40m-high wooden tower. From here you get a parrot's-eye view of unbroken canopy.

The Amazon Light Brigade is a separate programme from the lodge. It's a point-to-point trek for eight guests. On this trip, you stay in cabañas at Sloth Camp, near Mandicocha Lake. The itinerary features moderate to difficult trails and walking for up to eight hours at a stretch, so a good level of fitness is needed.

A 'must see' is the parrots' clay lick, on a high bank of the Río Napo – where thousands of parrots flock for the nutrients they crave. It's best in the early morning.

Studies at the research station focus on tropical butterflies. Visitors are allowed access to the flight area which houses pierid and heliconid species.

Guests at the lodge stay in one of 16 double cabins built in Indian style. The dining room and bar overlook the lake, its tea-dark waters fringed by unbroken vegetation. Buffet meals cater admirably to the Western palate. Vegetarian meals are available if advance notice is given. La Selva is even luxurious by Amazon standards.

Prices start from around US$575 for a four-day programme, including transport to and from Coca. The 'full package' includes two nights at Hotel Colon in Quito for US$985. The seven-day Light Brigade programme costs US$1,640 including transfers and hotel in Quito.

You can book a stay at La Selva through any of several US tour operators, or in the UK through Journey Latin America (see page 43). Most Quito tour operators will make reservations for you, or you can book direct at La Selva's office at 6 de Diciembre 2816 and Paúl Rivet; PO Box 171235, Quito; tel: 2 255 0995; fax: 2 256 7297; email: laselva@uio.satnet.net; web: www.laselvajunglelodge.com.

Sacha Lodge
Eighty-five kilometres down the Napo from Coca, Sacha Lodge is a luxury facility set within 1,500ha of pristine lowland rainforest comprising flooded forest and *terra firme* habitat. Birdlife is currently recorded at over 500 species. A raised lookout above the main bar and lounge offers a scenic view and excellent birdwatching opportunities.

Within the lodge grounds a platform overlooks the surrounding forest, and a trail behind the lodge leads to Sacha's 43m tree tower. A recent addition is a 300-metre long canopy walkway. Approximately 35 metres above the ground, the walkway is suspended from metal towers. Sacha Lodge is home to one of the largest butterfly farms in Ecuador. Designed as a live exhibition conservatory, the Butterfly House now successfully breeds 40 local butterfly species. Guests are shown how these insects are bred and raised. Book through Explorer Tours (Victoria 1235 and Lizardo García, Quito; tel: 02 250 8871; fax: 02 222 2531; email: beniet@uio.satnet.net; web: www.explore-net.net/explorer) or most major tour operators in Quito (pages 243–5). Field Guides (see page 41) offer trips catering for birdwatchers. Other companies include Latin American Reservation Center, Australian and Amazonian Adventures, Ladatco or Forum Travel (see pages 41–2). In the UK Condor Journeys and Wildwings (pages 42 and 44) take bookings. Cost is from US$560pp for three nights.

Yuturi Ecotourist Complex and Reserve
Some 180km (106 miles) east of Coca, this comprises about 2,000ha of fluvial lagoons among primary rainforest with typical lowland fauna.

Four- or five-day programmes feature guided jungle hikes and canoe rides, day and night, as well as early morning birdwatching and visits to the local Samona indigenous communities, followed by a trip to Monkey Island. A night hike follows a trail around Parahuaco Lake. 'Yuturi' refers to the giant ants found in the area.

The complex consists of 15 cabins and a restaurant. Cabins, with mosquito-netted beds and shaded veranda with space for a hammock, face on to a large lawn area. Food is simple but tasty and well-prepared.

All-inclusive prices from Coca are US$400pp for three nights. Yuturi Tur (Av Amazonas 24-236 and Av Colón; tel: 2 504 037; fax: 2 503 225; email: yuturi1@ yuturi.com.ec; web: www.yuturilodge.com) in Quito manages the facility, and other companies take bookings. In the US, Forum Travel, Inti Travel, Neotropical Journeys, Magic Globe and Kon-Tiki Travel have tours here (pages 41–2).

Pañacocha Lodge
On the banks of the Pañayacu River, five hours from Coca by boat, is Pañacocha Lodge. The cabañas are on the shores of a large outlet that drains Pañacocha Lake into the Napo. Accommodation is three thatched cabañas with double rooms for a total 24 guests. Two of the cabins have private bathrooms. Food includes both international and local dishes.

Four- to seven-day trips with English-speaking naturalist-guides cost US$60-65pp per day from Coca. Book through Emerald Forest Expeditions in Quito (page 243).

Yarina Lodge
About an hour east of Coca down the Napo River, this lodge is situated on a bluff overlooking the forest and the Manduro River. Built 1998 in the traditional style, it offers a good level of service and is more affordable than luxury lodges in the area. It is set in a 450ha reserve. Prices begin at US$320pp for three nights. Book direct with Yuturi Tur (see above) who manage the lodge, or through most Quito tour operators.

Sani Lodge
This Quechua-owned facility is on an oxbow lake between Cuyabeno Reserve and Yasuní National Park. Accommodation for 16 is in eight, private, thatch-roofed cabañas, each with a modern bathroom including hot shower and screened windows. Electric lights run from solar energy; oil lamps are also provided. Facilities include a bar, lounge, and dining room overlooking the lagoon. Meals are made with fresh, local ingredients with an international style including vegetarian, chicken and fish. Breakfast is fresh bread and local fruits with a selection of exotic juices. Tours here include jungle hikes, canoe rides, piranha fishing and night excursions to look for caiman. Rates at the lodge begin from US$295 for a three-night stay. Sani Lodge can be booked direct online or through their Quito office (email: info@sanilodge.com; web: www.sanilodge.com).

Bataburo Lodge
Located 90km from Coca on the Tiguino River in the heart of Huaorani territory, this lodge is a joint project of tour operator Kempery and the Huaorani indigenous organisation (ONHAE). The 24 cabins have double rooms with shared bathrooms (two cabins have private bathroom), mosquito nets and 110V electricity. The main cabin is both bar and dining room, and has hammock space. Meals are local and international in style. Near the lodge is a 40m-high observation tower. For more information visit www.bataburo.com. Prices begin from US$235pp for three nights. Book in Quito through Kempery or Latin Tour (page 244).

Amazon Jungle Resort Village

This comfortable lodge is on the banks of the Aguarico River, in a 100ha private reserve bordering the Cuyabeno National Reserve. From Lago Agrio, it is 90 minutes by car, or two hours by canoe. A total of 24 cabins in seven bungalows house 40 guests. Spacious, charmingly decorated rooms have private bathrooms, hot water and sculptured stone bathtubs. The cabins are situated so as to make the most of the surroundings. Creatively presented meals comprise local and international dishes: 'a very good kitchen is guaranteed'.

Rates begin at US$290pp (minimum three people) including transfers to and from Lago Agrio. Fundacion SELVA, as a non-profit organization, (page 244) directs proceeds derived from ecological tourism to sustain development projects and to support philanthropic projects in three indigenous communities.

Baumenos Huaorani Community

Within Yasuni National Park, the Baumenos Huaorani Reserve allows the Huaorani people relative independence from industrial and urban development. To get there you travel two and a half hours by road from Coca to the Shiripuno River. Then you take a four-day journey downriver to the community, also called 'Sandoval.'

Their way of life is little changed. Comprising about 1,500 people, the tribe's language is Wao Terero. Some tribal elders dress in the traditional *komi*, a type of loincloth that some wear under western style shorts.

Men hunt with curare-tipped darts and blowgun and fish with harpoons. they also hunt, clear forest for gardens, make weapons and protect the family. Women cultivate crops, cook food, raise children and make items used in daily life.

At the village accommodation is in tents, with visits to the community during the day. Food is local, comprising rice, fish, soup, vegetables, and fruit prepared by the team. There's a chance to taste traditional beverages including *chicha* (manioc beer). Lighting is by gas lamp. Washing is in the river. For this trip you need to be in good physical condition and have an adventurous outlook.

Several tour operators offer trips to the Huarorani. Equateur Voyages Passion (page 243) offer eight-day programmes from US$400pp (4 people minimum).

Nova Rocafuerte

On the banks of the Napo River, Nova Rocafuerte is Ecuador's frontier town on the Peru border. From Coca you can take a local riverboat to Nova Rocafuerte – a day's journey (about US$25). If crossing into Peru you will need to stop off at the border post for customs formalities. Islazul Viajes (page 244) in Quito offers a 15-day expedition beginning in Misahualli that takes you virtually the full length down the Napo. The trip includes stops for swimming in hot springs, exploring caves, birdwatching and meeting indigenous tribes. Accommodation is in small lodges and tents. For a group of five, the price is US$850pp.

Lago Agrio (Nueva Loja)

Capital of Sucumbios Province, Ecuador's northernmost Amazon territory, Lago Agrio is among lowland rainforest, with the foothills of the Andes to the west and the Colombian frontier 20km to the north.

Lago Agrio is the oil capital of the Ecuadorian Amazon, with 20,000 inhabitants and growing fast. The town itself has a languid energy; everyone seems hot yet anxious, on their way to someplace else. With income from oil and tourism, the place prospers, but little development seems planned in any way. On the outskirts are storage tanks, minor refineries and well-sites with burn-offs around the clock. Scattered debris sticks to the oiled road, mixing in after heavy rain to create a greyish porridge-like sludge. No amount of rain washes away the pervasic aura of dirt. Lago Agrio is not a place you want to stay in for long.

Despite the grime and tackiness, lots of tourists come here as it is the gateway for trips to indigenous communities at Dureno and to the Cuyabeno Reserve along the Aguarico River, and lodges and cabins near the reserve.

Getting there

From Quito by bus, Lago Agrio is a slow but interesting eight- to nine-hour journey (US$5–10) from Quito's Terminal Terrestre. It is three hours from Coca (about 75km, US$4) or nine from Tena (US$8).

TAME have one or two flights a day twice a week (except Sunday) to Lago Agrio (US$48 one way). Icaro's main office is at the airport, with two flights per day. Cost is US$53 one way.

Where to stay

Most hotels are along Av Quito, the main road through town where the long-distance buses stop and where you'll find the post office. Phone services are at the EMETEL office (18 de Noviembre and Orellana), about 500m from Av Quito.

Even the best hotels seem beat-up and grungy from the outside, as paint peels in no time and even concrete rots. Better hotels include the **Araza** (Av Quito 604; tel: 06 830223) and **El Cofán** (12 de Febrero and Quito; tel: 06 830009). The latter is most popular with tour groups and is generally considered the best hotel in town. Rooms with private bath, hot water and fans are US$24 (single) and US$42 (double).

Lago Agrio has several economy establishments including the **Hotel Lago Imperial** (Av Quito; tel: 06 830 453; fax: 06 830 460) with nice clean rooms for US$11–18, and the **Machala 2** (Av Colombia 122; tel: 06 830 073) which is safe, welcoming and clean for US$10.

Piraña Tour (Casa de la Cultura, Colombia and 18 de Noviembre, Lago Agrio; tel: 06 830624; fax: 06 831311; email: cce-ns@ecuanex.net.ec) is a Secoya community where you can stay in cabins. They also offer an eight-day canoe trip to Rio Lagartococha on the Peruvian border. In Quito, contact Tropic Ecological Adventures (page 245). **SionaTour** (12 de Febrero 267 and 10 de Agosto, Lago Agrio; tel: 06 831875; fax: 06 830232) represents the Siona organization ONISE. Tours include the Siona communities of Orahueaya, Biana and Puerto Bolivar.

Jungle lodges near Lago Agrio

Grand Cuyabeno Lake Lodge

This lodge has an itinerary leaving Quito for Lago Agrio on a 10.30 flight with TAME. A bus ride from Lago Agrio takes you to the Cuyabeno River followed by a two-hour motorised canoe ride through to the lodge, on an island within the Grand Cuyabeno Lake. You work your way through a maze of channels. Here in these backwaters is the most abundant and varied wildlife.

Thatched, raised cabins are built of wood from outside the reserve. The lodge has solar energy for communications, and oil and gas lamps.

Programmes are well-priced, from US$50 to US$70 per day. There is a US$20 park entrance fee for admission to the reserve. Book through Neotropic Turis in Quito (page 244). They can also arrange private transportation to Lago Agrio where you will be met by lodge staff.

Excursions include Dureno to meet Cofan Indians and to the Siona at Eno and the Secoya at Katecilla. Other itineraries include the Quihuaro, Curaray and Cononaco rivers, comprising visits to native tribes who have had very little contact with outsiders.

Tapir Lodge

Built in 1999, Tapir Lodge is within the Cuyabeno Reserve, and has no electric lights or noisy generator; instead it composts organic material, and ships out recycling. It comprises two thatched bungalows and a multistorey tower. The tower must be one of the highest habitable buildings built in the indigenous style. You wake up 13m in the trees, at eye level with the branches.

The tower has four double suites each with private bathrooms, hot water, and balcony with hammocks.

The bungalows have four double rooms built following Indian methods. One bungalow has private bathrooms.

Every bed has a mosquito net and cabins are screened to keep out insects. Facilities include a hammock area, bar, gift shop and book exchange. It's operated by Nomadtrek (page 245), or you can book from the Tapir Lodge website (web: www.tapirlodge.com). A number of Quito tour operators take bookings. Packages start from US$420 for three nights.

Paradise Huts Lodge

Head from Lago Agrio 70km down the Rio Aguarico and you come the Paradise Huts Lodge, on the banks of the river just outside the Cuyabeno National Reserve. The lodge is within a 110ha private reserve adjacent to Cuyabeno. More 'paradise' than 'hut' this lodge offers an affordable alternative to more luxurious facilities. Six bungalows each have three double rooms with private bathrooms. Prices begin at US$275 for four days. Book through Sangay Touring, Islazul Viajes or other tour operators in Quito (pages 244–5) or Forum Travel in the US (page 41).

Nativo Lodge

This facility in a 300ha private reserve adjacent to the southern Cuyabeno National Reserve is reached by motorised and paddled canoe along the Aguarico River and surrounding tributaries. The seven-day 'deep jungle' adventure in the Cuyabeno is based at the lodge. You camp for successive nights and spend four days exploring this utterly unspoiled area before you make your way back to civilisation. Made with local materials the lodge comprises nine four-bed cabins, with private shower and toilet. All-inclusive prices from US$220pp for five days to US$420pp for the eight-day deep jungle expedition. Book through Native Life in Quito (page 244).

Dureno and Sabalo

Along a rough road 21km east of Lago Agrio, Dureno is the central town for Cofan Indians. In town there are a few basic *residencias*. Guides are available for about US$20–35 a day. Take a hammock and/or sleeping bag, cooking equipment and food, and be prepared for primitive conditions.

About 130km from Dureno, down the Aguarico, is the Cofan village of Sabalo. Tribal chief is American Randy Borman, protagonist in the book *Amazon Stranger* by Mike Tidwell. Read the book to get some idea of the environmental cost of Amazon's black gold. Borman and his people literally risked their lives to halt illegal oil exploration. Due to his efforts, and other groups, the upper Cuyabeno appears safe from further drilling. (See box on page 263.)

A number of Quito tour operators run jungle trips to Sabalo and Dureno. Tropic Ecological Adventures (page 245) are the representatives in Quito. In the US, Wilderness Travel (page 42) have occasional departures to Sabalo, led by Mr Borman (enquire for prices). Proceeds from these trips go directly to the Cofan.

Tena

At the confluence of the Pano and Tena rivers, on a clear day you can see Volcán Sumaco 50km to the northeast. Besides the scenery, Tena is distinguished by its heritage, stretching back to 1560. Established by the Spaniards as a remote trading post for trading goods from the rainforest, Tena's isolation made it vulnerable. Sacked several times by forest Indians, its biggest upset came in 1578 when an Indian tribe rebelled against the colonials and stormed the fledgling town, though the uprising was swiftly quelled.

Today Tena (population 15,000) is capital of Napo province. Main activities are farming and tourism. Oil is also important. Although it's not a bad base for jungle trips, the main reason to go to Tena is to get to Misahuallí, a stepping-stone to the jungle, where most tour agencies in this area base their operations.

The town has banks, an EMETEL phone office and post office. For information in Tena try the CETUR office on Bolívar.

Getting there

By air, flights from Quito land at the nearest airstrip in Shell-Mera, from where you catch a bus to Tena.

By bus the most direct route from Quito passes through Baeza, and turns south at the Lago Agrio turn-off. A dozen buses (Pelileo, Baños or Amazonas) make the run each day, from Terminal Terrestre (US$5). Buses also travel from Baños (two hours), Ambato (six hours) and Riobamba (six hours; US$5) to the west. In the Oriente there are regular connections with Coca (six hours; US$6.75) and Lago Agrio (one a day; 10 hours; US$9). Local buses to Misahuallí leave hourly.

Where to stay and eat

Los Yutzos (Augusto Rueda 190; tel/fax: 06 886717; email: losyutzos@andinanet.net web: www.geocities.com/losyutzos/main.html) overlooks the Río Pano. Rooms (US$8–35) have private bathroom and hot water, telephone, TV, airconditioning and a refrigerator. The owners offer kayaking, whitewater rafting and jungle trips, from US$150 for two days. Many of Tena's hotels are along 15 de Noviembre in the east of town across the footbridge from the main plaza, or along Olmeda. In the mid-range, **Media Noche** (15 de Noviembre 1125; tel: 06 886490) is near the long-distance bus terminal and has rooms from US$15. **Hostal Traveler's Lodging** (15 de Noviembre 438; tel: 06 886372), on the riverfront, is clean and modern, and is run by the reputable tour operator Amarongachi Tours. Its best rooms sport private bathrooms with hot showers. Dormitory accommodation is also available (US$7–15).

Alternatively, try the **Villa Belén** on Jumandy (tel: 06 886228; US$8) or **Enmita** (Bolívar 447 and Montalvo; tel: 06 886253; US$4), which is simple but well kept and has a café.

Most of the hotels have places to eat and there are some acceptable restaurants.

Excursions from Tena

Tour operators in Quito and Tena will happily offer suggestions, but among the more interesting options is to stay at one of the indigenous communities in the vicinity. One of the most popular is **Capirona**. Most of the communities run jungle tours and take you to places and give insights not on the itinerary of larger tour operators.

Jungle trips, including village stays, are sold by **Amarongachi Tours** (15 de Noviembre 438; PO Box 154, Tena; tel/fax: 06 886372; email: amarongachitours@

RANDY BORMAN
Hilary Bradt

Randy Borman was born and raised with the Cofan Indians of Ecuador. His parents were missionaries from the Wycliffe Bible Translation Society in the United States, sent to Dureno in the 1950s, shortly before Randy was born. There they began the laborious process of learning the Cofan language. Unlike most missionaries who maintain a Western lifestyle, the Bormans lived like the Cofans and their children grew up with all the skills of their playmates. By the time he was five, Randy was competent with the blowgun (a skill he was to use effectively in his college days in America, supplementing his frugal diet with squirrel meat) and as a teenager he wrestled with alligators and anacondas. He also learned how to use forest products for medicine, food and shelter. In this respect he is completely Indian. But as a jungle guide, he is all-American, understanding the different culture and needs of visiting tourists. In his words, 'What I want to emphasise is that this is the real thing. We show visitors what the Indian way of life is all about. Of course we have to make some concessions to comfort and hygiene, but I'd never want to promote the sanitised "Jungle Lodge" type of experience. I'm not putting it down – this type of comfortable accommodation is just right for most tourists – but I do feel that we can offer something unique.'

Randy's tours last from five to seven days. During the tour, visitors stay in a 'camp', reached in six hours by motorised canoe. Here they learn about Cofan culture. Another full day downriver is where Randy has established a small Cofan community, away from the increasing spread of Westernisation, where he hopes to maintain the traditional Cofan lifestyle – but using some benefits of civilisation – for as long as possible.

Randy may be contacted at Casilla 6089, Quito, Ecuador; tel/fax: 02 243 7844.

yahoo.com). Their tours last from one day to a week including the Jatun-Yacu and Anzu rivers and stays at their own jungle cabins for US$40pp per day. In Quito book through Safari Tours (page 245). A reliable alternative is **Ecoselva Travel Agency** (PO Box 2-52, Tena; tel: 06 890019; email: ecoselva@yahoo.es; web: www.soft.net.uk/rainforest/main/page11.html) run by Pepe Tapia Gonzalez, an English-speaking licensed guide. He leads one- to ten-day tours from US$20pp per day. **Huacamayos** is a network of eleven Quichua communities in upland forest in the Huacamayos Cordillera near Tena. Contact Benito Nantipa in Tena (Union Huacamayos, c/o FION, Calle Augusto Rueda 242, Tena; tel: 06 288826; in Quito tel: 02 466 6223). A short bus ride from Tena are the Jumandy Caves, once off-limits as tribespeople held strong beliefs against exploring them. The caves have vampire bats among their more familiar inhabitants, but look also for bizarre troglodytic insects. The interior features extensive stalactite formations. A swimming complex complete with restaurant is nearby.

Misahuallí

In the south of Napo province, this town (pronounced Mi-sah-oo-ah-yee) is at the confluence of the Napo and Misahuallí rivers. Its importance as an access point for the Napo River has declined in recent years and the town's economy is based almost entirely on tourism.

Although small, Misahuallí (population 4,000) is important for jungle trips. Birds and butterflies are plentiful and diverse, but little unspoilt habitat is found near the town. Close to the town centre, **Misahualli Butterfly Gardens** is filled with tropical flowers and butterflies and open to visitors. It's on G Rivadeneyra Street, 200m from the main park on the road to Pununo.

Getting there
First travel to Tena, by bus or plane, and then on by bus to Misahuallí (see *Tena*, page 262), in total taking seven to eight hours from Quito or five from Baños.

Where to stay and eat
In town, there are plenty of choices for accommodation. Several of the hotels offer a room rate or accommodation packages which include excursions. **Hostal Dayuma** (Calle Principale; tel: 06 584 964) has first-class, by Amazon standards, lodgings in relative comfort for US$20. **Albergue Español** (Juana Arteaga; tel: 06 890127; fax: 06 890004; email: alb_esp@uio.satnet.net; web: www.albergueespanol.com) is among the best lodges in town, and costs from US$20pp. Favourites include **El Paisano** (near the military guardpost) from US$4 and **Fifty** (near the plaza) for US$2.50. Both have good restaurants, with vegetarian meals for under US$3. **Hotel Shaw**, next to the Ecoselva Travel Agency (page 263) on J A Santander Street, is another option.

Accommodation in the jungle nearby
There are a number of pleasant jungle lodges in the area. None is in pristine forest, but offer accommodation with comfort. **Misahuallí Jungle Hotel** (Frente Puerto Misahuallí; tel: 06 520043; fax: 06 454146; web: www.misahuallijungle.com) has riverfront cabins with electric light and private bath with hot water. Facilities include a swimming pool, restaurant and bar, satellite TV, games room and a small library. Cost is from US$24 per night. Book through Miltour in Quito (Dávalos 251 and Páez; tel: 02 520043; fax: 02 504872; email: miltour@accessinter.net; web: www.misahuallijungle.com) who can also arrange tours.

Medium-priced establishments (US$15–25) include: **Jungle Lodge El Jardin**

LIVING WITH AN INDIGENOUS COMMUNITY
Numerous opportunities exist for the student, researcher or traveller to stay with a family in an indigenous community. Programmes vary in cost, facilities and guides. Most community-run lodges have volunteer programmes that include discounted room and board.

There are many volunteer opportunities with indigenous communities near Tena.

RICANCIE (Av 15 de Noviembre 772, Tena; tel/fax: 06 887953; email: ricancie@ecuanex.net.ec; web: www.ricancie.nativeweb.org) represents nearby Quichua communities and operates three- to six-day programmes. Prices average US$40 per day depending on group size. Enquire in the UK at Condor Journeys (page 42).

Familia Cerda at 9 de Octubre 356 in Tena is an indigenous family whose tours vary in length. Trips stay at Cabañas Sacharicsina with bedding provided. The guides speak German and some English. Visit the South American Explorers (page 248) website or clubhouse in Quito for a wide range of opinions on most volunteer opportunities.

(on the Minas road; tel: 06 522927); the **Dayuma Lodge** (tel: 06 584965) not to be confused with the hotel; the **Jungle Lodge Albergue** (tel: 06 553857) and **Txalaparta** (tel: 06 545131).

A couple of moderate-level trails along the Río Latas, about 7.5km west of Misahuallí, take you through dense jungle and swampy areas for about 5km to waterfalls with swimming holes. To get to the trail, catch a bus from Misahuallí to the third bridge out of town and then head upriver.

English-speaking guide Luis García specialises in tours from Misahuallí down to Pañacocha (see *Coca*, page 255). He charges US$80 per day including meals and all services and should be advance-booked through Emerald Forest in Quito (page 243).

Jungle lodges near Misahuallí
Cabañas Aliñahui/Butterfly Lodge and Jatun Sacha Biological Station

Jatun Sacha Biological Station is on a 2,000ha site, bought in April 1994 with voluntary donations. The lodge's purchases of endangered cloudforest has added 4,000ha to the areas protected. Proceeds are returned to the community for rainforest purchase and protection, ethnobotanical research, training of naturalist-guides, school programmes and field studies for Ecuadorian biology students.

The research station and cabins are about 10km downriver from Misahuallí on the upper Napo. The station has publications and courses on Amazon ecology. It supports a number of science projects aimed at pure research and applied methods to secure local people's future. Medicinal plants are cultivated at the Conservation Center for Amazonian Plants. Activities include guided night and day walks, canoe trips, and opportunities for birding, botany, photography, swimming and gold-panning. Visits to indigenous communities can be arranged by prior reservation. Education programmes are presented by lodge staff, local shamans, herbalists and visiting scientists. English- and German-speaking guides are available.

The open-air dining room has well-prepared food with international and Ecuadorean dishes. Cabañas Aliñahui accommodates up to 45 guests in 26 rooms. These are in eight wooden cabins built with simple modern materials but in traditional form.

A three-day stay starts at US$115. Each night at the lodge without excursions costs US$25 plus tax in shared rooms with three meals a day. Volunteer work for a minimum one-month commitment costs US$300 fee plus US$30 application fee. Take the bus to Tena from the terminal and from there take either the Santa Rosa or Ahuano bus to Jatun Sacha. Have the driver tell you when you are there. Alternatively use the US$75 door-to-door service from Quito. Although more expensive than a bus you have a knowledgeable driver-guide to make the journey more interesting. Book direct in Quito (Mosquera Narváez 668 and Ruiz de Castilla; PO Box 17 11 6353, Quito; tel: 02 222 7094; fax: 02 222 7095; email: alinahui@interactive.net.ec; web: www.ecuadorexplorer.com/alinahui/index.html), through the Jatun Sacha Foundation (page 244) or any major tour operator.

Yachana Lodge

This lodge is in the village of Mondaña, two hours by motorised canoe down the Napo from Misahuallí. The lodge is run by the locally controlled FUNEDESIN Foundation. The foundation helps 30 indigenous communities develop workable solutions to the dilemmas presented by rainforest preservation and the realities of daily life for the local people.

Situated in 350ha of mixed primary rainforest, secondary forest and agricultural land, the lodge offers plain but clean rooms lit by hurricane lamps. The dining area, part of the two-storey central building, contains several tables with simple wooden benches. A hammock hangs outside each cabin.

Programmes include exploring 12km of trails into surrounding greenery and canoe rides with visits to an indigenous community. There's a tour of a nearby coffee plantation, where you watch beans roasting in a clay bowl over an open fire, and a visit to some beehives.

Yachana's prices begin at US$225pp for four days in the low season. Make reservations through the Quito office (Baquedano 385 and JL Mera; PO Box 171785, Quito; tel/fax: 2 256 6035; email: info@yachana.com; web: www.yachana.com) or at most Quito tour operators. In the US, book through Inti Travel or the Latin American Reservation Center (page 41).

Casa Del Suizo

This modern tourist complex is near the town of Ahuano, half an hour from Tena. Situated above the banks of the Napo River, in a 300ha private reserve, the hotel accommodates 145 guests in luxurious cabins. Facilities include two swimming pools, one for kids and the other for adults, a bar and restaurant. Per night rate is US$70pp. They are managed by the Sacha Lodge company (see www. casadelsuizo.com). You can book through them and most Quito tour operators or from the US through Latin American Reservation Center, Travel Innovations (pages 41–2) or in the UK through Condor Journeys and Adventures.

El Jardín Alémán

Opened in 1996, El Jardín Alémán ('The German Garden') is 2km from Misahuallí by road. The main reserve is 120ha, and the lodge protects another 110ha along the river. This will suit those who want a short tour. Built in 1995, it has comfortable, clean rooms (double or triple) with private bathroom, hot water, electricity, and a balcony. So you don't feel too far from civilisation, 'spacious and excellent installations offer every comfort' with laundry, satellite television, lounge with a pool table, and a large jacuzzi. The gardens are home to various animals.

Their Psychologist-guided Self Awareness Course offers 'freedom in the abandonment' and to 'waken the senses to develop harmony with the cosmos'. Alternatively, attend a 'cleaning ceremony' conducted by the resident shaman.

Rates start from US$40pp per night. Bookings are direct (email: eljardinaleman@onlinehome.de; web: www.eljardinaleman.com; tel/fax: 06 890122), or through Jarnatravel (page 244), or most Quito tour operators.

Isla Amazonica Lodge

On the shores of the Napo River, this lodge offers private cabins with electricity and hot water. Amenities include a restaurant, cafeteria, bar and tropical garden. The lodge is set in the Cotococha private reserve which protects 250ha of primary forest. Surtrek (page 245) offer a six-day kayaking and rafting trip based here for US$360pp (add US$145 single supplement) with private transport to and from Quito.

Baños

Literally on the edge of the Amazon Basin at 1,800m, this attractive town is a stopping point for many visitors on their way to the Oriente. Above the mosquito line and below the snow line, this is pretty close to Shangri-La. Billed as a 'mountain spa' this town of 20,000 inhabitants has hot springs, luxuriant greenery, spectacular landscape and what seems to be permanently perfect weather. Hence it swarms with tourists and Quiteños looking for a getaway. In 1999, the town was evacuated due to an imminent eruption from the nearby volcano Tungurahua;

though it did not materialise, it still may at any time, so check the situation before planning a visit here. If you come through Baños it's worth stopping a night or two.

For accommodation, one of the best is **Palace Hotel** (Montalvo 20-03; tel: 02 740470; fax: 02 740291; in Quito book with Jarna Travel), only five minutes from the hot springs. Each of the 29 rooms has private bath. Luxuries include a swimming pool, steambath, jacuzzi and fitness centre. Rates start from US$24 for a single room and US$29 double. Another option is **Hotel Sangay** (Plazoleta Isidro Ayora 101; tel: 03 740490; fax 03 740056), at the foot of the Baños waterfalls. Facilities include swimming pool, squash and tennis courts, sauna and Turkish bath. Prices start at US$27 for a single cabin. Book in advance through Sangay Touring (page 245). **Hostal Isla de Baños** (T Halflants and Montalvo; tel: 02 740 609) is US$15 per night.

In Baños, there's lots to do: cycling, horse-riding, or river-rafting. If you want to take a jungle tour it's a good place to find partners for a group.

Tsantsa Tours (Oriente and Eloy Alfaro; PO Box 18-02-1930; tel: 03 740957; fax: 03 740717) has trips at US$50 per day run by an English-speaking Shuar guide. They run several tours from Baños, starting at US$45 per person per day (including meals) for a group of four with reductions for larger groups. In the same price range, **Rainforestur** (Ambato and Maldonado; tel: 02 740423; fax: 02 740743; Quito office: Amazonas 420; tel/fax: 02 223 9822; email: rainfor@interactive.net.ec; web: www.ecuador-paginaamarilla.com/rainforestur/) can arrange tours to lowland Amazonia. Research Baños tour operators to avoid 'cowboy' or 'fly-by-night' outfits. Check guides have an official licence (Operación Turística).

Puyo

Largest town in the Oriente and capital of Pastaza Province, Puyo grew around missionary settlements to its present-day population of around 25,000. This uninspiring town functions as an oil storage depot, tourist gateway town and trading centre for Indians. The town lies east of the Andes, by a tributary of the Pastaza River which joins the Marañon, some 500km west of Iquitos (in Peru).

There's not much to do in Puyo, unless you're into oil or religion. It has banking facilities, a phone company office and a post office, all within easy walk of the town centre.

Getting there
You can fly to nearby Shell-Mera (US$141 round-trip) and take the bus (30 minutes, US$0.25). Buses link Puyo to major cities including Baños (two hours; US$1.75) and Quito (eight hours; US$8), and to several destinations in the Oriente including Tena to the north and Macas to the south. The Terminal Terrestre is in the southwest of town on the road to Baños.

Where to stay and eat
Hostería Turingia (C Marin 294, at Villamil and Orellana; tel: 03 885180; fax: 03 885384) is considered the best with small chalets set in an attractive garden; from US$20. **Hosteria Safari** (tel: 03 885465, fax: 03 823588), about 6.5km along the Tena road, has a pool, sauna, hydromassage and ice bath! Rooms have private bath and hot water. Prices start at US$25. **El Araucano** (C Marin 576; tel: 03 883834; fax: 03 885227) is well managed and charges US$12 per night. **Hotel Chasi** (9 de Octubre; tel: 03 883059) has rooms at the same price.

For refuelling, your favourite pitstop will be the **Europa Internacional** (9 de Octubre and Orellana; tel: 03 885407), which besides its fine restaurant has nice rooms. The **Rincón Ambateño** (along 29 de Julio) has airs and graces and okay food.

You can cool off with a swim in the Río Puyo close to the bridge, about 1.7km out of town. Visit the nearby **botanical gardens** (Parque Pedagogico Ethnobotanico; tel: 03 883 001), to look over their collection of herbal plants used by shamans. A nice day trip is to the **Tropical Forest Reserve** (Reserva de Bosque Tropical), about 16km along the Macas road. Lovely trails and a waterfall make for a relaxing but rewarding day. It is possible to stay at simple shelters within the reserve, for just over US$1 per day. Take your own food, cooking equipment and sleeping bag, but you don't need a tent.

On **Julio Verne's** short treks you stay in basic huts from US$50 for a one-day trip. Their five-day expedition includes a small plane flight over the forest to stay with the Huaorani tribe in traditional huts (US$550pp).

Atacapi Tours (27 Febrero and Sucre, Pastaza; tel/fax: 03 883875; email: papangu@ecua.net.ec) is run by a local indigenous organization. In Quito contact Tropic Ecological Adventures (page 245) for more information. **Ikiamp Ecological Reserve** (Contact Pascual Kunchikuy: Casilla 16-01-703, Shell, Pastaza; tel: 03 883332; email: ikiamp21@hotmail.com) is a rainforest tourism and conservation project in a Shiwiar community.

Excursions from Puyo
Fátima Experimental Station is a small ecological reserve just 15 minutes from Puyo. Take a bus from the centre of town or hire a pick-up for a couple of dollars. The station is home to semi-captive rescued animals. Some of the species found here are on the endangered species list. Basic lodging is available.

Learn about Indian cultures at the **Center for Indian Communities** located in Union Base, outside Puyo. You can observe craftsmen working on balsa wood carvings, paintings, and other handicrafts.

Plantations of the **Sangay Tea Company** at Zulay Hacienda are a half-hour bus ride from Puyo. **Hospital Voz Andes**, an hour away, is a jungle hospital managed by foreign doctors who provide medical care to local Indians.

The **Guasaloma-Cavernas de Anzu Nature Reserve** protects a large cavern complex.

Cueva de los Tayos is another natural cavern with hot springs. The cave's distinctive structure has led to speculation that extra-terrestrials built the caverns! Visit the **Cascada Safari** at the confluence of the Indillan and Puyo rivers for weird rock formations.

Jungle lodges near Puyo
Kapawi Lodge and Ecological Reserve
This 'eco-lodge' is recognised worldwide as a model system by which local people benefit while preserving their lands. Begun in 1993, the project is a cooperative venture involving FINAE (Federation of Achuar Nationals) and Canodros, a private corporation. The aim of the venture is to benefit the Indians and, by 2011, all the facilities will be owned by the Achuar themselves.

Their booklet has checklists of mammals and some birds and information on the Achuar people, with helpful notes on Achuar etiquette; for example, 'The Achuar are very jealous. If you are a man, you should never look directly at a woman's face.' This is useful as the naturalist guides are Achuar.

Programmes include short hikes or longer treks to visit Achuar communities. Canoe trips include overnight stays in tents. Camping trips last several days, with porters carrying food and camping supplies.

Kapawi's 20 double cabins each have private bathroom and showers with sun-heated water. Native-style buildings are constructed to satisfy the ecotourist – 'not a single nail was used' claims the company. Seventy-two solar panels, each supplying 75 watts, meet 80% of required power.

Two central cabins make up the reception area and bar, and a library. Guest cabins along the shore each have a clear view of the lake. Food is international and Ecuadorean, plus the usual array of tropical fruit juices.

On a tributary of the Pastaza, the lodge can be reached only by air. A private plane from Quito to Kapawi (1 hour) leaves three days a week. After landing you have an hour and a half canoe ride to the lodge.

Five days cost US$640pp (double occupancy). Quito transport adds another US$150. Book Kapawi through the office in Guayaquil (tel: 04 251 4750; fax: 04 228 7651; email: kapawi@canodros.com; web: www.canodros.com). Most tour operators in Quito offer the same programmes. ROW Expeditions combines a visit here with river rafting. Other contacts include Adventure Associates (Australia), Inti Travel (Canada) and in the US, Victor Emanuel Nature Tours, Ladatco, Big Five or Travel Innovations (pages 41–4). Taratours offer a 20-day Galapagos-Kapawi combination from US$4,993.

Las Cascadas

This lodge is 40km east of Puyo, five hours' drive from Quito. Nearby a 25m waterfall tumbles into a swimming hole amid pristine rainforest. The habitat supports a high diversity of lowland and montane wildlife. Hummingbirds and butterflies abound and with luck you'll see small monkeys. Orchids and bromeliads are diverse. Las Cascadas offers five double bedrooms with private bath and hot showers. Surtrek's five-day tour costs US$325pp from Quito (page 245).

Macas

In the province of Morona Santiago, Macas (population 10,000) is a centre for oil development, with tourism steadily increasing. Founded as a mission station in 1590, the town's religious tradition continued with the completion of a cathedral in 1992. This town has striking views with Volcán Sangay, still active, smoking in the distance.

At 1,000m altitude in the Upano River valley, Macas' climate is typified by balmy days and cool nights. Most travellers come for the rafting down the nearby Upano River. This tour may include a visit to caves and a 25m waterfall. ROW (page 246) and Earth River Expeditions (page 40) specialise in rafting tours in this area.

Getting there and away

Unless you fly from Quito (TAME, twice a week; US$131 return) getting to Macas is not so pleasant. The bus to Macas from Puyo is a bouncing six-hour ride (US$5).

Where to stay and eat

There are a few decent *hostales* and *residencias*. All are comparable and under US$20. **Peñon de Oriente** (Domingo Comín 837 and Amazonas; tel: 07 700124; fax: 07 700450; US$5–10) is popular. Most expensive in town is **Esmeraldas** (Cuenca 6-12 and Soasti; tel: 07 700160), which is worth the US$6 per night.

Eateries in Macas include a Chinese restaurant (near the Peñon). A couple of cafés, both on Amazonas, the **El Jardin** and **Eros**, serve meals under US$3.

Cross-country

From Macas, Neotropic Turis (page 244) offer a river expedition all the way to Iquitos, Peru. You go down the Morona and Marañon rivers through the Pongo of Manseriche, arguably Peru's most scenic rapids. You travel several days from there through the Pacaya-Samiria Reserve (See *Chapter 10, Peru*). A minimum of ten people are required for this trip. The US$720pp price includes air from Quito, plus one night each in Quito and Iquitos.

Sucúa

On the banks of the Río Puni, Sucúa is the main base to visit remote tribes of Achuar Indians. This small town can be reached from Quito by air or, for the more adventurous (or less hurried), by bus from Quito travelling through Macas. For accommodation try **Hostal Karina** near the plaza.

Not far from Sucúa, about a one-hour (3.5km) walk, is the Río Upano. In the US ROW Expeditions (page 246) sell rafting trips down the river and the ride is a spectacular contrast of habitats as you descend from whitewater Class III and IV rapids (V is the roughest) to the placid curves typical of lowland rivers.

Loja

Largest city in southern Ecuador, Loja (population 150,000) has a mild climate, being at an elevation of 2,063m. No buildings remain from its founding in 1548 due to being demolished by two major earthquakes that flattened Loja. It was the original source of quinine into the European pharmacopoeia and the first town in Ecuador to have electricity.

Tourism is expanding now the Ecuador-Peru border is open. Native Life (page 244) has a 21-day birding tour that includes Loja and Zamora. Most people visit here on their way to **Podocarpus National Park**. Get permits to the park at the INEFAN office (Miguel Riofrio and Bolivar). Other visitors stop off here on their way to or from Peru. You can get a visa if needed from the Peruvian Consulate (Sucre 10-56 and Azuay).

There are daily buses from Quito (US$25), a scenic but long 14-hour ride. Loja's airport is at the town of Catamayo, 30km away, from where you take a bus (US$3) to Loja. TAME (24 de Mayo and Av Orillas de Zamora) have an early morning flight daily (except Sundays) for US$42 one-way. Icaro (José Antonio Eguiguren and Olmedo; tel/fax: 07 578416) have one or two afternoon flights daily (except Mondays and Saturdays) for US$55 one-way.

Quito flights may be cancelled at short notice, so check with the airline offices before leaving for Catamayo.

Most hotels are in the town centre between Av Iberoamerica and Olmedo. The **Grand Hotel** (Iberoamerica and Rocafuerte) is among the best, with rooms from US$35pp. There's a wide choice of cheaper accommodation, and numerous small restaurants. During mid-August the Fiesta de la Virgen del Cisne is a three-day religious procession that attracts thousands of visitors. Check well in advance for room availability.

NATIONAL PARKS AND WILDLIFE RESERVES

Ecuador's exemplary system of nature reserves and parks includes 25 areas administered by the government agency INEFAN. Nine are national parks, five of which are in the Amazon watershed.

In all, the protected areas cover a fifth of the country. Supplementing government conservation efforts, private organisations run a number of small biological reserves, some in the lowland Oriente.

To get into national parks and reserves in Ecuador you have to get permits (US$20) in advance from INEFAN at their offices in towns throughout the Oriente or in Quito. The agency's offices also have more detailed information about facilities within the parks.

Cuyabeno Faunistic Reserve
Established to preserve one of the world's biodiversity hotspots, Cuyabeno holds the world record for plant diversity, with 277 tree species recorded in just one hectare. Some 1,275 bird species include toucans, parrots and macaws along with over a hundred hummingbird species and many more. Within the boundaries are significant portions of the watershed of the Aguarico River, a major tributary of the Napo.

Protecting 242,162ha of lowland tropical rainforest in the Sucumbios Province of northeastern Ecuador, the reserve is reached from Lago Agrio where the local INEFAN office can give you information. Accommodations near the reserve are at Paradise Huts, whereas Tapir Lodge (page 261) is within the reserve itself.

Cayambe-Coca Ecological Reserve
Covering a rectangle approximately 83km by 62km, this is Ecuador's second largest protected area. The reserve straddles the Cordillera Oriental. Protected habitat includes tropical rainforest on the easternmost flank of the park up to sub-tropical forest, cloudforest and *paramo*.

Visits to Cayambe-Coca Reserve can be arranged through Quito tour operators. Information is available from INEFAN in Quito and Lago Agrio. **Oyacachi** is a Quechua community in the reserve. They offer single or multi-day guided hikes in rugged mountains and cloudforest. Enquire through Ecociencia (PO Box 1712257, Quito; tel: 02 245 1338; fax: 02 224 9334; web: www.ecociencia.org). Salsa Reisen offers four- to eight-day camping trips in the reserve (page 245).

Yasuni National Park
Between the middle Napo and upper Curary rivers, and accessed via Coca, this is Ecuador's largest protected area. Covering 970,512ha, Yasuni protects an area of typical tropical lowland rainforest flora with riparian vegetation, *várzea* and *terra firme* forest. Over 700 woody species have been so far identified. Animal life comprises some 200 types of mammals and 500 of birds.

Numerous endemic species are found in this biodiversity hotspot, which scientists say was a Pleistocene refuge. Within the park is the Huaorani (Waorani) Indian Reserve. The Indians live a traditional lifestyle with little or no impact from the outside. There are a few lodges on the edge of the park, and basic camping facilities are available. **Apturc/Pavacachi** is a Shuar/Quichua programme with cultural tours, jungle walks and canoe trips. Enquire with Tropic Ecological Adventures (page 245).

Sadly the future of this park is in doubt. In 1991, Conoco was awarded concessions within the park boundaries and drilling activity continues.

Limoncocha Biological Reserve
This reserve protects a small area along the middle Napo River. About 370km from Quito, it is reached via Coca and a 45km boat ride down the Napo. It's 5,300ha protects Limoncocha Lagoon, within a unique natural area with 347 recorded bird species. Surrounded by *várzea* forest, the lake is lined with semi-aquatic and aquatic plants. Microscopic phytoplankton in the lake's water give it an odd lemon-green colour.

Sumaco National Park
In Napo province to the north of Tena, Ecuador's newest national park was established in 1992 to protect a unique ecosystem of lowland rainforest. The region encompasses Volcán Sumaco, which rises 3,732m like a giant pimple from an ocean of green. In the upper Napo watershed, the park covers 205,250ha of mixed forest, rivers and abundant of wildlife.

To get there you travel to Baeza, then take the southern fork to Tena and drive 30km south to the Coca turn-off. Head east along here for 21km to Huamaní, a small village where you can hire a guide.

Sangay National Park

Declared a UNESCO World Heritage Site in 1984, this park protects the habitat surrounding Volcán Sangay, Ecuador's second highest active volcano. The volcano's 5,230m peak is often cloaked in clouds. On the slopes of the volcano are representative habitats of all the major biomes, from tropical rainforest to alpine.

The best way to get here is via Macas. You can access the southeast of the park from Macas. Take the road to the village of 9 de Octubre and the park entrance.

Podocarpus National Park

Named after a species of indigenous pine, Podocarpus National Park (established 1982) is the southernmost of Ecuador's national parks and the hardest to reach. Covering 146,280ha, at elevations over 3,000m, the park protects extensive cloudforest and diverse wildlife.

The INEFAN office in Loja issues permits only for day trips. From Loja you can travel to Vilcabamba or Zamora. Vilcabamba appeals to mystics and ageing hippies, being in the so-called Valley of Longevity, home to supposedly long-lived inhabitants (a scientific survey negated the claims). It has a perfect climate, is quiet, scenic and provides easy access to the park. From Loja's main bus terminal minibuses (Vilcaturis) run to Vilcabamba (US$1). It's quicker but more expensive (about US$2) to take a shared taxi from Loja's southern terminal (Co-op 18 de Mayo). Vehicles serving Vilcabamba are paid commission by a couple of hotels so be insistent about your hotel of choice. Visit www.vilcabamba.org for a map and information on the options. The small zoo, **Area Nacional de Recreación Yamburaro** (US$1), has a modest collection of rather sad animals and an orchid house with over 300 species of orchids. The aim is to breed new varieties for sale to international markets. Proceeds will be used to help preserve local habitat and provide a sustainable source of income for local people. It's a short walk from the central plaza.

The **Hidden Garden** is a small hotel just off the main square. Clean and comfortable rooms face onto a garden courtyard. Amenities include shared showers and a swimming pool, and a self-catering kitchen with necessary utensils. Cost is US$10 per night.

Cabañas Rio Yambala (tel: 07 580299; email: rio_yambala@yahoo.com; web: www.vilcabamba.cwc.net) is 5km east of town (take a taxi from the town centre). Thatched wood cabins or adobe cottages are clean and comfortable with hot showers and balconies with hammocks. In the vicinity are opportunities for hiking and birding, and marked trails lead to swimming holes and waterfalls. Dinner, bed and breakfast is from US$10–14pp.

Cabañas Rio Yambala own and manage **Las Palmas** – a private reserve bordering the park – about 15km from Vilcabamba and accessible only by horse or foot (4/5 hours). A simple refuge within the reserve is ideal to explore the park. You can visit Las Palmas on a do-it-yourself hike for US$8 per night at the refuge. Prices for fully-guided hiking trips begin at US$50 for two days, and for horse trekking from US$60.

You can book a birding trip to Podocarpus through Field Guides (page 41), Magic Globe in the US, or in Quito through several tour operators.

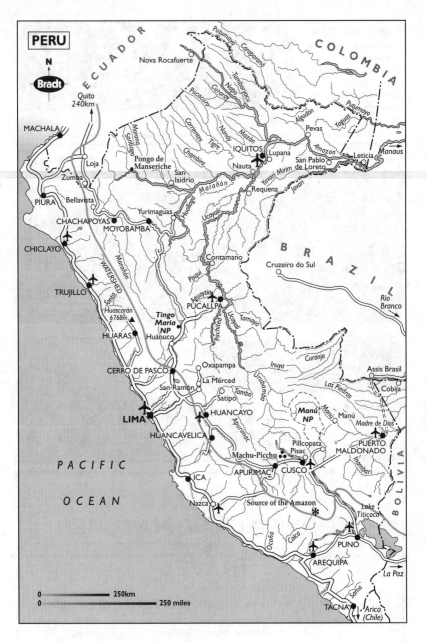

Peru

10

The name 'Peru' conjures images of a remote, far-off land, but Peru is today one of South America's most popular travel destinations. Yet, despite its popularity, Peru rarely seems overcrowded with tourists, except perhaps at the best-known places like Machu Picchu.

FACTS AND FIGURES
Geography

Peru is a big country, the third largest in South America, covering 1,285,216km² (496,225 miles²) – more than twice the size of Great Britain. It has frontiers with five countries. To the east is Brazil, while Peru's southeastern border with Bolivia rises from the Amazon Basin to cross Lake Titicaca.

The district of Loreto covers most territory in the Amazon Basin. Its total area is 348,177km², over a quarter Peru's total. Loreto is the biggest department of Peru, with Iquitos as the regional capital. In 1980, Loreto was re-zoned, creating the new department of Ucayali to the south, with Pucallpa as the administrative capital.

Rivers

Peru's main rivers are in the east, flowing into the Amazon Basin. Most important is the Ucayali-Amazon system, rising in the Andes near Arequipa. Formed by the confluence of the Apurímac and Urubamba rivers in east-central Peru, the Ucayali

---

BASIC FACTS
Official name República del Perú
Area 1,285,216km² (496,225 miles²)
Population 25.7 million (1997 est)
Capital Lima
Largest city (population) Lima (7.2 million)
Main Amazon city Iquitos
Official language(s) Spanish, Quechua
Date of independence July 28 1821
Major industries petroleum oil, fisheries, lumber, agriculture, mining, tourism
GDP per capita US$2,100
Currency nuevo sol (US$=S/3.28: £1=S/4.95)
Major attractions Machu Picchu, Nazca Lines, Sipán
National holidays Jan 1, Jun 24 & 29, Jul 28 & 29, Aug 30, Oct 8, Nov 1, Dec 8, Dec 25

meanders north before heading northeast into the densely forested eastern floodplains. After some 1,500km it joins the Marañón, 90km southwest of Iquitos.

Forming part of the Peru–Brazil border, the Río Javari flows northeast for 870km joining the Amazon near Benjamin Constant, Brazil.

The Río Marañón's source lies above Lake Lauricocha, near the town of Huanaco in central Peru, some 250km northeast of Lima. Also, here in the windswept Andes, merely 150km from Peru's Pacific coast, the Amazon's source flows northwest across high plateaux some 3,500m in altitude and joins the Marañón before it carves a deep canyon through the lower Andean ranges. Some 1,416km in total length, it passes through a series of falls and rapids before plunging to the floodplains.

A major tributary is the Huallaga River which joins the Marañón as it winds eastward before it meets the Ucayali. A major river in itself, the Ucayali follows a course that joins it to the Huallaga-Urubamba system. The Huallaga River reaches high into the central Andes, to a point once considered a source of the Amazon. Lacking this distinction, but nevertheless a magnificent river, the Urubamba originates near Cusco.

East of the Urubamba's headwaters, the Madre de Dios flows eastwards across the Bolivian border, eventually joining the Madeira, an Amazon tributary that enters the main stream 100km east of Manaus.

The 885km Napo River is among the best known of Peru's rivers. It was first explored by Orellana in 1541. Originating high in the Ecuadorian Andes, it drops eastwards toward the Peruvian border, turning south before joining the Amazon some 80km downstream from Iquitos. It is mostly navigable and used for transport.

The Putumayo River flows through densely forested lowlands, forming the frontier between Colombia and Peru.

Climate

Peru's variety of climate zones are defined by three geographical areas: narrow, dry coastal plain to the west; cool arid highlands of the Andes; and moist tropical lowland rainforest occupying the east.

The coast is a cool desert, with temperatures of 19–22°C. Rainfall is very low; however, humid winter fog (*garúa*) from March to October provides some moisture. In the mountains temperatures range between 1–14°C but vary greatly. Rainfall is heaviest in the eastern forests at between 1,900–3,200mm per year.

On an irregular cycle of five to seven years, Peru's climate suffers an about-turn, caused by the poorly understood El Niño phenomenon. Typically, the coastal areas are deluged with rain, while lowland forests experience plunging temperatures, and prolonged drought afflicts the southern highlands. Severe El Niños cause extensive ecological and economic damage. Bird and fish populations are particularly affected. The El Niño event of 1997–98 was the strongest ever recorded, causing heavy flooding in Peru and several other South American countries.

Flora and fauna

At the last count, Peru's diverse habitats support a total of 361 mammal species. Carnivores include the jaguar, puma, ocelot, margay and the spectacled bear. Primate diversity is among the world's highest. Peru is home to 1,800 bird species, about one-fifth of the world's total. Hummingbird diversity reaches its highest in the eastern Andean cloudforests.

The rainforests have an exceedingly rich invertebrate fauna. Peru has more butterfly species than any other country, with around 4,000 species, and at least 20,000 moths. Peru's flora is astounding with at least 1,300 orchids.

Previous page Cofan Indian in traditional dress, Ecuador (PO)

Above Riverboat hammocks (PH)

Right Large riverboat on the Rio Madeira, Brazil (PH)

Above Quichua Indian making canoe, Ecuador (PO)

Left Quichua Indians in motorised canoe, River Napo, Ecuador (PO)

Land use

Owing to unfavourable climate, unsuitable terrain or poor soils, only 3% of land is considered arable. Tropical forest is subject to the traditional 'slash-and-burn' technique. Main crops are manioc, bananas, maize and beans. The land is beginning to feel the impact of growing populations and industrial activity but, even today, forest still covers over half the country, most of it pristine rainforest in the Peruvian Amazon.

Along rivers and floodplains fertile soils offer better conditions for settled agriculture. In areas above floodplains, traditional slash-and-burn methods are used. On a small scale this need not damage the forest as a whole, but ever larger areas are being cleared to provide for growing populations.

Large-scale lumber and mining operations have caused localised environmental damage, but not on the scale seen in parts of Brazil.

The people
Population and ethnic groups

With 24 million people, Peru's population density is fairly low – 18 people per km². Loreto's population is around 700,000 – a density about one tenth that of the country as a whole. Over one fifth of Peru's inhabitants lives in the capital, Lima – South America's fifth most populous city. Most of Peru's population is urban following large-scale migration to cities during the 1950s.

Native Indians comprise about half the population. As well as Witoto Indians, visitors are likely to encounter the Bora and Yagua along the main stream around Iquitos. Matses and Marubo Indians live along the upper Río Javari and remain largely unassimilated. In the uplands, despite considerable Western influence, Shipobo continue their way of life in many ways unchanged.

Catholicism is the main religion, practised by nearly everyone. In remote areas, the Christian rites are overlain with remnants of tribal religions.

Languages

Spanish is the dominant language throughout Peru. Quechua is the second language with Aymara still spoken in isolated pockets. Witoto is the most widely spoken Amazon Indian language but over 300 other languages and dialects are found in Peru's lowland rainforests.

Education

The country has a strong emphasis on learning and supports more than 30 universities nationwide, including one in Iquitos. Lima boasts South America's oldest university, the National University in Lima (founded in 1551). Schooling is compulsory where practicable and for children aged 6–15 no fees are charged.

Culture

Western art flourishes alongside pre-Columbian creations of pottery, weaving and metalwork. Peru's Chavin, Chimu, Moche and Inca cultures produced exquisite works in gold, and highly expressive pottery. Modern-day folk arts are continued by rainforest Indians, whose basketwork and pottery are of excellent quality.

Soccer is the national sport and is played with rare devotion and enthusiasm. World Cup matches are followed avidly countrywide, more so when Peru's team is playing. Every village and town has a soccer pitch, with matches played on Sundays.

A brief history
Pre-history
Archaeological finds date human habitation of coastal areas of Peru to at least 12,000 and possibly even 20,000 years ago. These populations were primarily hunter-gatherers but soon developed sophisticated civilisations with advanced agriculture and architecture.

By 1,000BC, several advanced civilisations had developed along the central and northern coastal valleys near present-day Chiclayo and Trujillo. Other significant peoples were the Nazca, Tiahuanaco, Chavín and Chimú. Little is known about the settlement of the Amazon Basin due to the lack of archaeological evidence.

In the coastal and mountain areas, the Inca Empire consolidated and unified the region. By the time the Spaniards arrived in the early 1500s, their empire included all of present-day Peru, Bolivia and Ecuador, and large parts of northern Argentina and Chile. The population of the Inca Empire was perhaps 12 million.

In 2002, in a Lima shanty town, archaeologists discovered one of Peru's largest pre-Columbian cemeteries, covering eight hectares. Over 2,200 mummy bundles (layers of cloth encasing a body and personal effects) have been examined.

The conquest
The strategic importance and purported wealth of Inca strongholds at Cusco and Lima resulted in aggressive incursions by the Spaniards. Betrayal, murder and pillage were all in a day's work for the conquistador, firm in the belief it was God's will they dispose of non-Christian Indians.

Setting up base in San Miguel on Peru's northern coast, Pizarro crossed the Andes to meet the Inca emperor Atahualpa, recently victorious in a civil war against his half-brother Huascar. Pizarro and Atahualpa met in Cajamarca.

Pizarro, with 150 men against 30,000, arrested Atahualpa who had refused fealty to the Spanish crown and the Bible. After getting a room full of gold as ransom, Pizarro promptly executed Atahualpa for the murder of his brother Huascar and installed Huascar's brother, Manco Capac, as puppet ruler. By late 1533 the conquistadors occupied the Inca capital of Cusco.

Colonialism
Manco Capac proved less pliable than the Spanish expected and in 1536 led an Indian rebellion which inevitably was mercilessly crushed. The Spaniards squabbled over the spoils of war, leading to the execution of several conquistadors.

The Spanish attempted to introduce the *encomienda* system to placate the warring conquistadors, but nearly a decade passed before calm prevailed. The 1568–81 administration of Viceroy Francisco de Toledo established a system to allow local chiefs to rule over traditional lands in return for tribute and free labour.

Independence
Nationalism and notions of freedom from imperialist powers were born early in Peru's colonial era. After several uprisings, in which numerous natives were slaughtered in brutal reprisals, José de San Martin, helped by Simón Bolívar, led a final revolt and in July 1821 Peru declared independence from Spain.

The 20th century
In 1922, Peru's claim to the Putumayo region was put to rest as it ceded the curious wedge-shaped portion that gives Colombia access to the Amazon River. Peru made no such concession to Ecuador and in 1942 the Rio de Janeiro Treaty established

the present-day border, the southern portion of which was not ratified and remained disputed until a 1998 treaty signed in Brasilia.

The 1933 constitution granted power to the president and congress but military juntas ruled the country for three decades. In 1963, Fernando Belaúnde was freely elected but was overthrown by an army coup in 1968. Military rule lasted until 1980 when the army returned Peru to its civilians, but the military had set in motion economic problems that worsened soon after Belaúnde's re-election.

The situation reached its lowest point during the office of Alan García, president from 1985 to 1990. The economic and social disaster engendered by García's socialist experiment eventually forced Peru to default on its massive foreign debt. The World Bank froze aid to Peru and imposed international boycotts on goods and arms. Sanctions devastated the economy. Inflation spiralled sky-high, peaking at 2,600% per annum in 1989. Unemployment afflicted two-thirds of the working population in some cities and crime shot up. Travel and foreign investment plummeted.

Under such awful conditions a number of revolutionary organisations emerged, mostly bent on violent overthrow of the regime. Best known of these is Sendero Luminoso (Shining Path).

In 1991 Alberto Fujimori was democratically elected with a top priority to eliminate the Shining Path. He took emergency powers in April 1992, dissolved Congress, suspended the constitution and restricted civil liberties. In late 1992, the rebel leader, Abimael Guzmán, was caught and sentenced to life imprisonment. Guerrilla activity significantly declined and ceased to be a threat to daily life. A national referendum approved a new constitution in October 1993 which promotes free enterprise and democracy.

Fujimori turned the economy around. Unlike previous leaders, he did not neglect the Amazon. His government provided every village with a motorised boat – improving local trade and communications. Cocaine trafficking, once a serious problem, was heavily suppressed. Conservation laws were strictly enforced, allowing the return of wildlife, and tourism reached all-time highs.

Peru hit the international headlines in December 1996 when a faction of the Tupac Amaru Revolutionary Movement took control of the Japanese ambassador's residence and held hostages, demanding the release of political prisoners. The episode ended violently in April 1997 when special forces stormed the building, killing all the guerrillas and saving all but one of the hostages.

By the late 1990s Fujimori's presidency encountered significant problems. Popular support fell due to increasing authoritarianism and an economic slump. In spring 2000, he won re-election to a third term amid accusations of electoral fraud. Following international pressure, corruption scandals and a government declaration that he was unfit to govern, Fujimori resigned. While on a trip to Asia he returned to Japan claiming citizenship by ancestral privilege.

A caretaker government supervised new elections in spring 2001. Alejandro Toledo became new head of government – a demanding task given high unemployment and foreign debt, and the impact of global recession on exports and tourism.

Government

Peru's constitutional government has an elected president who is also head of state and commander of the military. Presidential decrees and draft bills are reviewed by a cabinet and prime minister appointed by the president.

Money

Peru's monetary unit is the nuevo sol. The currency has remained relatively stable since introduction in 1992.

US dollars are widely accepted but you need to change money once you are in the country. Take plenty of small-denomination dollar bills for tips and buying handicrafts.

Take another US$200 in US$10 and US$20 bills if you are a keen souvenir-hunter. Travellers' cheques are difficult to change but many stores accept credit cards.

Businesses do not accept notes with even the tiniest tear, so make sure all the dollar bills you take are in good condition.

Highlights

Jungle lodges, taking trips on tourist riverboats and guided jungle tours are the best ways to make the most of birding and nature opportunities in ease and comfort in the rainforest.

For those who just want to 'do the Amazon' and travel to interesting parts of the Amazon Basin, Peru has three basic options available.

From Iquitos, for an easy tour of the area, take the round-trip down the main stream to Leticia, and perhaps visit the famous canopy walkway or lodges in the area. Another route takes you southwest from Iquitos, up the Ucayali to Pucallpa and then to Lima by plane or bus. Various tour operators offer trips lasting several days up remote tributaries in the area south of Iquitos, to the Pacaya-Samiria Reserve, Peru's only officially protected area in the Amazon lowlands. From Lima or Machu Picchu/Cusco, the nearest place to visit the Amazon is Manú National Park and Bahuaja-Sonene National Park/Tambopata Reserve. Rolling hills divided by snaking river valleys comprise habitat quite distinct from the lowland rainforest.

Besides the rainforest areas covered in this guide, visitors come to experience the rich pre-Columbian history west of the Andes. You could spend several months in Peru and still feel as if you've left important bits out.

Tour operators

Research travel opportunities and their promoters carefully. Some lodges and boats are booked well in advance. Most tour operators make reservations or organise tailored trips. Many tour operators in *Chapter 2* (pages 40–4) have trips to the Peruvian Amazon.

In the US

Amazonia Expeditions 10305 Riverburn Drive, Tampa, FL 33647; tel: 800 262 9669; fax: 813 907 8475; email: Paul.Beaver@gte.net; web: www.perujungle.com. Natural history tours to Tamshiyacu-Tahuayo Reserve and the Tahuayo Lodge.

Amazon Forays PO Box 126, East Haddam, CT 06423; tel: 860 873 8286; web: www.amazonforays.com. Amazon herbal medicine tours led by US artists, musicians and scientists. Healing ceremonies with local shamans. 'The Wild Mushroom Traveling Road Show!' led by professional mycologist.

Amazon Tours & Cruises 275 Fontainebleau Blvd Ste 173 Miami, FL 33172; tel: 800 423 2791; fax: 305 227 1880; email: info@amazontours.net; web: www.amazontours.net. In Iquitos: Requena 336; tel: 094 23 3931; fax: 094 23 1265. Own and operate fleet of tourist riverboats and expedition boats. Highly recommended.

Explorations 27655 Kent Rd, Bonita Springs, FL 34135; tel: 800 446 9660; fax: 239 992 7666; email: info@ExplorationsInc.com; web: www.Explorationsinc.com. Since 1992, a leading speciality tour operator of group and independent programmes. Small group tours escorted by top USA biologists and educators expert in biodiversity, culture, photography and ornithology. Highly recommended.

Margarita Tours PO Box 2513, Ft Lauderdale, FL 33303; tel: 954 764 8274; fax: 954 767 9567; email: margaritatours@aol.com; web: www.amazon-ecotours.com. Tours out of Iquitos since 1983. Small group expeditions based from riverboats or field stations. Kayaking, birdwatching, sport-fishing; tropical fish, reptile and amphibian expeditions; nature photography; medical and civic service expeditions; high school, university-level, and teacher expeditions. Family and small group charters. All accompanied by an expert. Proceeds help fund Project Amazonas (web: www.projectamazonas.com).

National Wildlife Expeditions 11100 Wildlife Center Drive, Reston, VA 20190; tel: 800 606 9563; fax: 703 438 6042; email: expeditions@nwf.org; web: www.nwf.org. National US conservation organisation organises tours for riverboat cruises from Iquitos.

Rainforest Health Project PO Box 624, Deer River, MN 56636; tel: 800 870 8325; fax: 877 737 6219; email: rhp@pobox.com; web: www.rainforesthealth.org. Non-profit international relief organisation provides medical assistance to bring basic health to local people.

SACA Tours 44 Pond Street, Nahant, MA 01908; tel: 800 707 5275; fax: 781 581 3714; email: info@saca.com; web: www.saca.com. US representatives for Explorama.

Special Interest Tours and Travel 10220 N 27th Street, Phoenix, AZ 85028; tel: 800 525 6772; fax: 602 493 3630; email: questions@gosafari.com; web: www.gosafari.com. River cruise and canopy walkway in the Peruvian Amazon.

Tropical Nature Travel 14503 NW 146th Avenue, Alachua, FL 33616; tel: 888 287 7186; fax: 386 462 4579; email: liz@tropicalnaturetravel.com; web: www.tropicalnaturetravel.com. Operate several lodges in and around the Tambopata and Manú protected areas.

World Class Travel 808 NW 13th Street, Gainesville, FL 32601; tel: 800 771 3100; fax: 352 371 7660; email: info@peruperu.com; web: www.peruperu.com. Booking service for jungle lodges, expeditions and educational tours.

In the UK

Peruvian Secrets Bryn Chwilog, Talwrn, Llangefni, Anglesey; tel: 01248 751 005; email: info@peruviansecrets.co.uk; web: www.peruviansecrets.co.uk. Fully escorted tours and custom itineraries. Educational groups with Tambopata Research Centre. Canoe trips to Pacaya-Samiria Reserve. Work with Wasai for specialist groups and difficult-to-reach places.

In Peru

Most of the tour operators listed below are based either in Lima or Cusco. Most Cusco tour operators offer only Manú or Tambopata. Most Lima tour operators can organise trips to either lowland rainforest (Iquitos lodges or riverboat cruises) or Manú and Tambopata.

Amazonas Explorer PO Box 722, Cusco, Peru; tel/fax: 084 236826; email: info@amazonas-explorer.com; web: www.amazonas-explorer.com; UK tel/fax: 01437 891743. Specialising in environmentally safety-conscious expeditions with inflatable kayaks. Trips include Amazon source and rafting the Apurimac; Tambopata and Cotahuasi Rivers in Peru and Río Tuichi in Bolivia.

Abacus Travel Av Pardo 1040, Miraflores; tel: 01 444 3031; fax: 01 242 1273; email: info@travel-peru.net; web: www.travel-peru.net. Wide range of tours throughout the Peruvian Amazon.

Atalaya Calle Arequipa #242, Cusco; tel: 084 228327; fax: 084 221826; email: atalayan@terra.com.pe; web: www.atalayaperu.com. Economical tours in Manú and Tambopata. Continuously improving the ecotourism approach, eg: negotiating with companies for ecological hygiene products (toiletries shampoo, insect repellent) to offer clients at no additional cost.

Chancas Expeditions Jiron Rioja 357, Tarapoto; tel: 094 52 2616; email: chancas@terra.com.pe; web: www.geocities.com/amazonrainforest. Canoe and camping trips into the Pacaya-Samiria Reserve.

Class Adventure Travel Grimaldo del Solar 463 Miraflores; tel: 01 444 2220; fax: 01 241 8908; email: info@cat-travel.com; web: www.cat-travel.com. Dutch-owned tour operator, with tours to Tambopata, Manú and the Iquitos area. Emphasis on efficiency, reliability and safety. Widely recommended.

El Tigre Journeys Calle Nanay #145, Iquitos; tel/fax 094 223595; US: PO Box 1704, Boulder, CO 80306; tel/fax: 303 442 8090; email: eltigrejourneys@bigfoot.com; web: www.biopark.org/peru.html. Educational tourism organisation with conservation, cultural and educational programmes near Iquitos. Ecology and culture workshop at Amazon Camp for teachers, school classes, youth organizations and families.

Explorama Lodges Av La Marina #340, PO Box 446, Iquitos, Loreto, Peru; tel: 094 25 2530; fax: 094 25 2533; email: amazon@explorama.com; web: www.explorama.com. In business 40 years, own and manage the various Explorama Lodges around Iquitos. Highly recommended. (See SACA Tours in US.)

Jungle Expeditions Calle Pevas 199, Iquitos; tel: 094 261582; fax: 094 260721; email: junglex@junglex.com; web: www.junglex.com. Owns and manages fleet of upmarket tourist riverboats out of Iquitos.

Lama Tours & Education Flora Tristan C-201, Arequipa; tel/fax: 054 251123; email: info@theperuspecialist.com; web: www.theperuspecialist.com. Four- to six-day tours, including Manú, Tambopata and Iquitos, including Muyuna Lodge. Birdwatching with Dutch and English speaking guide; 24-hour online help service available.

Machete Tours Calle Teqsecocha 161, Cusco; tel: 084 224829; email: info@machetetours.com; web: www.machetetours.com. Birdwatching and survival expeditions led by local guides.

Manú Expeditions Av Pardo 895; PO Box 606, Cusco; tel: 084 226671; fax: 084 236706; email: Adventure@manuexpeditions.com; web: www.manuexpeditions.com. Co-own and manage Manú Wildlife Center Lodge, a safari camp concession in the Manú Biosphere Reserve. 'Pioneer rainforest eco-tour operators in Peru' with fixed-departure general interest or birdwatching trips. Owned and run by Barry Walker, British Consul in Cusco. Quality trips with 20 years' experience. Weekly fixed departures and custom trips for private parties.

Manu Nature Tours Av Pardo 1046, Cusco; tel: 084 252721; fax: 084 234793; email: mnt@amauta.rcp.net.pe or manu@amauta.rcp.net.pe; web: www.manuperu.com. In business since 1985, own and operate Manú Lodge and Cloud Forest Lodge.

Manu Safaris/Explorandes San Fernando 320, Miraflores, Lima; tel: 01 445 0532; fax: 01 445 4686; email: postmaster@explorandes.com; web: www.explorandes.com. Three to five day programmes in Manú at their lodge on the Madre de Dios River. River rafting on the Tambopata River.

Mayuc Portal Confiturís 211. Plaza de Armas, Cusco; PO Box 422; tel/fax: 084 232666; chando@mayuc.com. Tambopata, Manú and adventure tours to other Andean countries.

Peru Traces 1167 Pardo Av, Ste 302, Miraflores; tel: 01 242 9408; fax: 01 242 9387; email: info@perutraces.com; web: www.perutraces.com. Booking and service agents for most lodges including Heliconia Amazon Lodge and Tambo Amazonico, and tourist riverboats.

Peruvian Safaris Alcanfores #459, Miraflores, PO Box 10088; tel: 01 447 8888; fax: 01 241 8427; email: safaris@amauta.rcp.net.pe; web: www.peruviansafaris.com. Since 1976 owner/ operator of Explorer's Inn in the Tambopata-Candamo Reserved Zone. Well-known supporters of research and educational outreach, conservation and support of sustainable tourism.

Rainforest Expeditions Av Aramburu 166, Dep 4b, Miraflores, Lima 18; tel: 511 421 8347; fax: 511 421 8183; email: rforest@perunature.com; Cusco: Portal de Carnes 236; tel: 084 246243; email: cusco@rainforest.com.pe; US: 98 Creekside Unit B, PO Box 2937, Frisco, CO 80443; tel: 877 905 3782; fax: 970 668 0549; email: mc@andeanrain.com; web:

www.perunature.com. Award-winning Peruvian ecotourism company combines tourism with philanthropy. Tours to Posada Amazonas and Tambopata Reseach Center.
Silvana Tours Av 28 de Julio 660-11, Miraflores; tel: 01 242 8202; fax: 01 446 8750; email: silvanatours@silvanatours.com.pe; web: silvanatours.com.pe. Established Peruvian tour operator with scheduled departures on four- to six-day tours to Pacaya-Samiria and Manú.
Wasai Las Higueras 257, La Molina; tel/fax: 01 436 8792; email: wasai@wasai.com; web: www.wasai.com. Own Wasai Maldonado Lodge in Puerto Maldonado, Wasai Tambopata Lodge and Peru Wildlife Center. Offices in Cuzco and Puerto Maldonado.

GETTING THERE AND AWAY

Many towns in the Peruvian Amazon are quite isolated from the outside world. No railroads or highways connect most settlements or villages in the region. Indeed, Iquitos, a city of 600,000, is accessible only by ship or aeroplane. Iquitos and several other towns have airports or at least a landing strip. Float planes are used to get to remote outposts or for small group transfers to lodges or small towns.

By air
From the US

Most visitors to Peru fly in from Miami, a route served by several US and South American airlines. Other US cities also have direct flights, considerably more expensive. Daily flights direct to Lima with American Airlines come from Miami (US$575-600) and Dallas (US$1200). Peru carrier Aerocontinente has six flights weekly from Miami (US$530), whereas COPA's daily flight offers the best price (US$515). Continental flies daily from Houston, Delta has a daily flight from Atlanta, and LanChile have a daily flight from New York.

There are ongoing permanent discussions about direct Iquitos-Miami flights. Ask your local agent. Aerocontinente has a direct flight (US$425).

It is important to keep US$20–50 in hard currency to pay airport departure taxes. The international departure tax is US$25 payable in sols or dollars. Departure tax for internal flights is US$4. If you are visiting several different places the costs do mount up.

From Europe

Cities with direct flights to Lima include Amsterdam (KLM) and Madrid (Iberia). Flights from London with American Airlines or other European cities and airlines are routed to Lima through Miami. Prices start from £590 return in the low season.

Overland
By road

Connections with neighbouring countries are in the highlands. To the north the frontier with Ecuador is served by regular buses. To the south the options divide, take you south into the arid deserts of northern Chile or east to Bolivia crossing the frontier near to Lake Titicaca.

Land crossings to Brazil and Bolivia are possible from Puerto Maldonado in southern Peru or from Pucallpa in central Peru. Both are considered arduous or adventurous depending on your perspective.

By boat

By boat the main route to Iquitos is from Brazil. You sail westwards, upstream from Manaus or Belém at the river's mouth. The long local riverboat journey from Manaus requires the traveller to have a suitable budget, strong constitution and a flexible schedule.

It is the cheapest option but rough conditions and safety and health worries discourage most travellers. You provide your own hammock and manoeuvre around sleeping people, dogs and chickens, doing your best to dodge the swinging bunches of bananas. Meals may be included in the price, but even if they are you need to take your own food to supplement the basic fare. Using local cargo riverboats may be faster and better for getting from A to B but they leave no time for sightseeing beyond brief stops at a few ports and villages. Short village-hopping journeys can be quite expensive.

A trip from Manaus to Iquitos on local river transport takes a minimum of ten days. Progress depends on local schedules, flood conditions and the vessel's reliability and crew. The only certainty is that it takes less time to go downstream, with the current in your favour, than upstream.

Top-end option for cruising the Amazon is on a luxury liner or 'expedition' ship. Mostly these sail up to Manaus, but during high water season may travel up to Iquitos.

A popular compromise between local banana boats and luxury liners is a tourist standard riverboat. These natural history-oriented trips run from Iquitos to Leticia or Manaus. Down the Amazon main stream, the voyage takes three days to Leticia and eight to Manaus. Tourist riverboats have a naturalist-guide aboard and make stops along remote pristine tributaries for birding and hiking, and may stop at night for night hikes or canoe rides.

Since the border dispute was resolved, you can travel downriver from Ecuador into Peru. A handful of Ecuadorian companies have tours to Iquitos from various towns in Ecuador. Alternatively, independent travellers can find boats from Coca to Nova Rocafuerte and then down the Napo River to Iquitos. See *Chapter 9: Ecuador* (page 247) for a detailed description.

Customs and immigration

You need a **passport** valid for six months. US citizens and nationals of European Union countries do not need a visa to travel to Peru unless staying for more than 60 days. When entering Peru you fill in an immigration form; you should keep the copy of this with your passport as you need it to get out of the country.

Getting around
By bus

Long-distance buses are cheap and reliable, but bus stations are infested with casual thieves so you should buy your tickets in advance, without the distraction of bags and backpacks. Avoid long-distance buses at night as thieves sometimes target these. There is no central long-distance terminal in Lima so you have to find the company's terminal and office. Ormeño is the biggest bus company (Carlos Zavala Iquitos 177; tel: 01 275679), with routes to major cities along the coast. TEPSA (Paseo de la República 129; tel: 01 731233) is the best company in Lima but also the most expensive. It has fewer routes than Ormeño and costs more, but you'll appreciate the extra comfort. There is no way to get to the Iquitos area of the Amazon by bus. However, you can start a trip in Pucallpa on the upper Marañón, accessible on the Empresa Transmar and Transportes León de Huánaco bus companies, both on 1500 block of Plaza 28 de Julio (US$35 one way).

By air

From Lima daily flights direct to Iquitos are offered by Aerocontinente (morning flight), Aviandina (afternoon) or TANSPeru. Cost is US$75 one way. Get a window seat so you can enjoy views of the snow-capped Andes.

To get to Manú or Bahuaja/Tambopata in southern Peru fly from Lima to Puerto Maldonado (US$104 one way). If these flights are full, or cancelled due to bad weather, fly to Cusco (US$104 one way) and complete the remainder of the journey with an eight-hour bus ride. Aerocontinente is slightly cheaper than Aviandina or LanPeru.

If you are travelling to two or more cities in Peru, the LanPeru airpass offers substantial savings. It includes five flights for US$390-431 (low/high season). A single flight airpass is US$86-91 and you can additional coupons for US$78–86. To buy an airpass you need an international return ticket and must use coupons within three months.

By boat
One option to reach the main stream is by river-raft down rapids of the Apurimac River, a tributary of the Ucayali, on waters that originate from the Amazon's source high in the Peruvian Andes. The ride starts on a series of rapids and proceeds through lowland forest, joining the Ucayali and ending up in Iquitos. Several tour operators offer this as a package tour, including Inti Travel, Travel Innovations (pages 41–2) and, in Peru, Mayuc or Amazonas Explorer (pages 281–2).

The rapidly growing capital of Ucayali department, Pucallpa, is a good point to join the main stream if you want to complete a full-length navigation of the Amazon (see page 66). No tourist boats serve Pucallpa so you will have to catch a cargo boat, hang your hammock and relax in style.

COMMUNICATIONS
Mail
Postal services in Peru are slow, inefficient and expensive. It will cost a dollar to send a postcard back home, more for a letter. Make sure you have local currency, as post offices do not accept dollars or travellers' cheques. Letters and postcards often go astray. There are many reports of incoming and outgoing packages being lost or opened.

Phone, fax and email
Most city hotels have phones but international calls can be expensive. To get the best rate go to the Telecom offices, present in all cities and most towns and villages. Most public telephones take phonecards bought from Telecom offices.

The international country code for Peru is 51.

Fax machines are available at most hotels and tour operator offices, but charges may be high (up to US$5 per page). Most tour operators have email facilities so you can book online. The number of internet cafés in Lima and other Peru cities has exploded. Costs are around US$1. per hour. In Lima try **Cabinas Dragonfans** (Calle Tarata 230, Miraflores; tel: 01 421 1462; fax: 01 421 1462; email: cabinas@dragonfans.com; web: www.dragonfans.com), Lima's biggest internet facility. It's open 24 hours, for US$1.50 per hour.

Television and radio
Public television and radio emit a stale supply of government-run programming – mostly upbeat news and current affairs with some sports, mostly soccer. Picture quality is correspondingly bad. The best TV – programming and reception – is on cable or satellite, increasingly available in even the smaller hotels.

Newspapers
The country's main papers are all produced in Lima, the most prestigious of which is *El Tiempo* with right-wing views. Also published in Lima is *El Libro*, said to cater

for a more centrist viewpoint. A number of regional newspapers are published for local consumption and focus largely on rural concerns. For the best unbiased news, reviews and commentary, the magazine *Caretas* is really on the ball.

LIMA

Lima is dusty, badly polluted, overpopulated and full of life… just as you'd expect from a South American city. From afar, gleaming office blocks declare the city's commercial prowess. Closer up, in the old plazas, you see a heritage of rich colonial architecture. Yet away from the centre small children and their families pick their way through piles of garbage, scraping together a living from the rubbish of over six million people. Lima has some plush districts, but outside the centre it seems to be one huge shanty town.

Proximity to the ocean and the influence of the cool current makes winters (May to October) cool and humid, with *garúa* or sea fog blanketing the city most mornings. Exacerbated by pollution this leads to the uniform white sky that hangs over Lima for most of the day. During summer, days are sunnier. Rain is infrequent and Lima ranks among the world's driest capitals. Temperatures average 18°C (65°F) year-round.

Tourist and commercial activity centres on the Miraflores and San Isidro districts. On the coast, in the southeast of the city, Miraflores is a 30-minute taxi ride from the airport. It has a better selection of hotels and restaurants than the city centre and is relatively safe. San Isidro is just north of Miraflores, between it and the city centre. It is quieter and more exclusive than Miraflores and the city's best (and most expensive) hotels are here.

You can get a map of Miraflores and San Isidro and other information on Lima over the internet at www.peru-hotels.terramagica.com and other websites (see *Appendix 3*), or free of charge from your hotel.

At the airport

The Jorge Chávez International Airport (web: www.corpac.gob.pe) is 12km from the centre of town, 16km from Miraflores. There are minibuses to town from the street outside, but unless you're confident where you are going it is probably best to get an official taxi, which costs US$20-25. Taxis do not have meters so agree in advance on a price. For US$5 there is an airport shuttle-bus to your hotel.

The airport has a three banks, ATMs, money exchange, telephones and a few cafés, shops and restaurants. There is also a tourist booth to help with reservations.

International airlines in Lima

American Canaval and Moreyra 380, 1st floor, San Isidro; tel: 442 8595
Continental Av Víctor Andrés Belaunde 147, Vía Principal, 110 edif. Real Cinco Oficina 101–201, San Isidro; tel: 221 4340
Delta Centro Empresarial Camino Real, Víctor Andrés Belaunde 147; Vía Principal 155 Torre Real Tres, Oficina 701, San Isidro; tel: 440 4328
KLM Av José Pardo 805, 6th floor, Miraflores; tel: 242 1241
Taca tel: 213 7000; web: www.taca.com

City transport

Within Lima, use the minibuses to get around if you are on a tight budget and have little or no luggage. During rush hour they are overcrowded and uncomfortable. Local buses have signs indicating their destination and, although there is a system of bus stops, you don't need to use them; just flag the bus down. Within the city, a bus trip costs US$0.25–1.00 depending on how far you go.

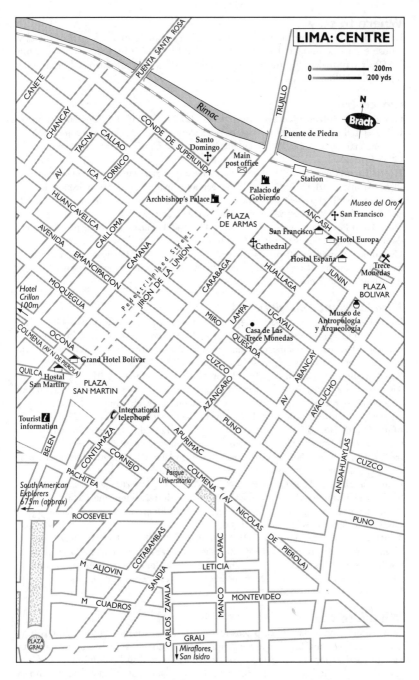

Taxis are numerous, cheap and the easiest way to get around. They have a small sticker on the windscreen. Unlicensed taxis are half the price of licensed cabs which are yellow and blue. As usual, agree the fare before you start the journey.

Where to stay

Lima has lots of accommodation. Choose a secure place in a safe part of the city. Those on a low budget should set aside US$15 per day food and lodging while US$25 a day makes life more comfortable and luxuries affordable. For five-star hotels, US$100 per day is a starting point.

City centre

Grand Hotel Bolívar Plaza San Martín; tel: 01 427 2305; fax: 01 428 7674. History buffs will revel in this resplendent fossil's air of faded glory. Rooms are clean and comfortable, with airconditioning, cable TV and antique bathroom fittings. Rates are US$60pp single, US$30pp double.

Hostal España Azangaro 105, close to the Convento de San Francisco (4 blocks from Plaza Mayor); tel: 01 428 5546. Popular budget hostal makes a good base to explore Lima and meet other backpackers. Eccentric décor including a roof garden inhabited by tortoises and caged birds. Dorms US$3, single US$6, double US$9.

Hostal San Francsico Ancash 340; tel: 51 1 428 3640. Popular with young people and a great place to meet fellow travellers. US$10/20.

Hostal San Martín Av Nicolas Pierola 882 Piso 2; tel: 01 428 5337. Rooms have private bath with hot water. Rates are US$35/46, including breakfast. Bookings through www.hostelworld.com.

Miraflores and San Isidro

Hotel Las Americas Av Benavides #415, Miraflores; tel: 01 241 2820; fax: 01 444 1137; email: postmaster@americas.com.pe; web: www.hoteleslasamericas.com. All 151 rooms have cable TV, airconditioning, direct international dialling, data P/C connections, safe, and minibar. Every conceivable amenity. Rates begin at US$180pp (single or double).

San Antonio Abad Ramón Ribeyro 301, San Antonio, Miraflores; tel: 01 447 6766; fax: 01 446 4208; email: hotelsanantonioabad@mail.com; web: www.hotelsanantonioabad.com. All 25 rooms have private bathroom and hot water. Rooms have telephone, cable TV, and security box. Widely recommended. Rates including breakfast and taxes are US$45/55.

Malka Youth Hostel Los Lirios 165 (Av Javier Prado Este cdra. 4), San Isidro; tel: 01 442 0162; fax: 01 222 5589; email: alberguemalka@hotmail.com. Climbers will enjoy spectacular mountain photos and the small climbing wall in the backyard. Rooms have four to six beds. Dormitory rooms US$6. Widely recommended.

Mami Panchita Av Federico Gallesi 198, San Miguel; tel: 51 1 263 7203; fax: 51 1 263 0749; email: raymi_travels@perusat.net.pe; web: www.bed42.com/mamipanchita/. Two single rooms (US$15pp), and seven doubles (US$25) with private bathroom. In-house travel agency specialises in domestic flights.

Youth Hostel Av Casimiro Ulloa 328, Miraflores; tel: 01 446 5488; fax: 01 444 8187; email: hostell@terra.com.pe; web: www.limahostell.com.pe/indexi.html. Cheapest place to stay in Miraflores and ideal place to get travel information or meet companions. Members pay US$10 for a dormitory bed. Non-members can stay for a couple of dollars extra. Private double room is US$25.

Where to eat

Lima offers a wide variety of places to eat out. Most tourist-standard hotels have acceptable food but, for a change, sample some of the local dishes or try a unique variation on a more familiar food. Restaurants are listed in *El Tiempo* and *El Libro,* the latter of which gives ratings, but ask locals and you might find a culinary treasure.

   La Costa Verde (Barranquito Beach in Miraflores; tel: 01 477 2424) is set in pleasant tropical gardens and serves the best lobster in Lima. **La Rosa Náutica**

(Espigón 4, Costa Verde; tel: 01 447 0057) ranks as a landmark. The food is considered gourmet (but receives mixed reports): US$25-30 from the fixed menu, US$50 à la carte. It's worth a visit for the atmosphere in the Victorian-style building at the end of a pier with views of the Pacific Ocean. Sushi fans must visit **Matsuei** (Manuel Bañon 260; tel: 01 422 4323) in San Isidro, Lima's best Japanese restaurant. For local dishes, try **Manos Morenos** (Av Conquistadores 887) is highly recommended for *criollo* food. For international food, locals recommend **Carlin** in Miraflores (Av La Paz 646; tel: 01 444 4134). It is invariably busy and rather expensive.

Las Trece Monedas (Ancash 536, tel: 01 427 6547) is set in a historic colonial mansion and is popular for formal dining. For a quieter pace try **Chifa Lung Fung** (Av Rep Panama 3165; tel: 01 441 8817). This San Isidro restaurant has tranquil interior gardens and some of the best – and most expensive – Chinese food in Lima. Vegetarians may be familiar with the global chain **Govinda's** (Schell 634, Miraflores; tel: 01 442 871; open 10.00–20.00) run by Hare Krishnas. Their Indian and Peruvian dishes are delicious and inexpensive. **Natur** (Moquegua 132; tel: 01 278 281) serves a Peruvian and international menu with organic foods, soy dishes and fruit juices (open 08.30–21:00). **Vrinda Café** (Av Javier Prado 185) serves fruit with live yogurt – very soothing for an upset stomach.

For ceviche, try the excellent but expensive **Al Fresco** in San Isidro, Miraflores or the old town.

Additional information in Lima

If you spend any time in Lima, or South America, it pays handsomely to join **South American Explorers** (SAE). They are in Miraflores at Calle Piura 135 (tel: 01 445 3306; email: limaclub@saexplorers.org). Members can get up-to-date information on travel conditions in the Amazon and throughout South America. Open Mon–Fri 09.30–17.00 (See page 46.) Their Cusco clubhouse is at Choquechaca 188 #4 (tel: 084 245 284; email: Cuscoclub@saexplorers.org). Another useful resource is the **British Council** (Torre Parque Mar, Floor 22, Av Jose Larco 1301, Miraflores; tel: 01 617 3060; fax: 01 617 3065; email: postmaster@britishcouncil.org.pe; web: www.britcoun.org/peru). The internet is an increasingly valuable resource of information on every aspect of travel. Refer to our list of websites in *Appendix 3* to get started.

What to see

To orient yourself in Lima's historic district, start from the huge Plaza Mayor (previously Plaza de Armas). It's well-served by buses, every taxi-driver knows where it is and it's popular with the local citizens. A few homeless people live around the square. The plaza's centre features a huge intricately cast bronze fountain dating from 1650. The plaza is bordered by several important buildings. The **Palacio de Gobierno**, built in the 1920s, is Peru's seat of government. Rebuilt in the same period, the **Archbishop's Palace** with wooden balconies ranks as an impressive example of period architecture. **Lima Cathedral** is the city's oldest colonial building dating from 1555. Holding the remains of Lima's founder, Francisco Pizarro, the cathedral is on the southeastern side of Plaza Mayor, and is open 10.00–13.00 and 14.00–17.00.

Most historically significant of Lima's churches is **San Francisco**, the most intact to date from early colonial times. On the corner of Lampa and Ancash, the building itself is a beautiful mix of styles. For the morbidly inclined the catacombs hold some 70,000 bodies. Hours are 10.00–12.45 and 15.00–17.30 daily, admission US$3.50. On the first block of Camaná **Santo Domingo** was constructed on land

Pizarro granted to his friar in 1535. Work began five years later but was not completed until 1599. Now resplendent within, redecorated in the 17th and 18th centuries, this church's two towers have resisted earthquakes for some 400 years. It opens 08.00-13.00 and 16.00–18.00, admission US$0.50.

Museums

For the capital of a country of such impressive cultural and natural resources, Lima is endowed with a suitable number and variety of museums. Most museums open 09.00–17.00 Tue–Sat. Admission charges range from nothing to a few dollars.

Museo de Antropología y Arqueología (Museum of Anthropology and Archaeology), Plaza Bolívar in Pueblo Libre. Ancient Peruvian cultures including the Moche, Chimú and Inca are represented with over 80,000 artefacts including fabric, jewels and gold. Excellent! Opens 10.00.

Museo del Oro (Gold Museum), Av de Molina 1110. One of South America's most impressive collections of pre-Columbian goldwork and jewellery, yet still privately owned. Most metalwork pre-dates the Inca. If you only have time to see one museum in Lima this is the best option. It's difficult to reach without patience and an understanding of Lima's bus system, so take a taxi. Opens 12.00, admission US$6.

Museo de Historia Natural (Museum of Natural History), Av Arenales 1250, Aptdo 14-034, at the University of San Marcos (Universidad Nacional Mayor de San Marcos). An especially impressive insect collection although the mammal and bird specimens are somewhat moth-eaten. Closes 15.30 (13.00 on Sat).

Museo Amano, off Av Santa Cruz, Miraflores. Focused on textiles and culture.

Parque las Leyendas

On the road to Callao (catch bus #75 from Jirón Azangaro), this is Lima's zoo, with fauna from Peru's three major habitat types: tropical forest, arid coast and cold highlands.

Shopping

In Miraflores, on Av Petit Thouars at the top of Larco there are a couple of *artesanias* co-ops, selling crafts and clothing from around the country. In San Isidro there is a similar set-up at Jorge Basadre 610. Woollen and leather goods are excellent value and high quality, as is handmade silver jewellery.

Several markets in central Lima offer a wider selection and cheaper prices than Miraflores souvenir shops, but you'll have to search hard to match the store quality.

THE PERUVIAN AMAZON

For visitors to the Amazon Basin the city of Iquitos in the northwest of the country's Amazon gives you direct access to the great river. Several jungle lodges with trails and a canopy walkway are within easy access of Iquitos. Tourist riverboats travel the main channel upstream and downstream from Iquitos.

Cargo boats from Pucallpa in the central Amazon stop at Iquitos on their way to the triple frontier with Colombia and Brazil and further downstream to Manaus. In southeastern Peru, Manú National Park and the Tambopata National Reserve/Bahuaja National Park system protect the world's highest biodiversity.

Iquitos: gateway to the jungle

Most people have never heard of Iquitos despite its being a major port, the fourth largest city in Peru and the third largest on the Amazon after Belém and Manaus.

Named after a local Indian tribe, Iquitos is brash and noisy but, like a root from some parasitic jungle plant, it grows on you. The only large town for hundreds of miles, it is an important commercial centre and retains a cosmopolitan feel from its large influx of foreign visitors and status as a busy port. This is the starting point for thousands of visitors every year on rainforest tours.

Hotels are pleasant, and shopping for souvenirs, food and travel supplies is inexpensive. Iquitos has an international airport and dock facilities. The sprawl covers most of a large rise at the confluence of the Amazon and Nanay rivers. To the west is a large island (Padre Isla) about 16km long and 8km wide, in the main stream of the Amazon River.

Iquitos is the world's largest city inaccessible by road – the only way in and out is by air or ship – and the world's most inland river port and naval base. Ships must sail upstream from the mouth of the Amazon for 3,701km (2,300 miles) to reach the city. Yet this is only just over halfway along the river's length with another 2,848km to the Amazon's source. Despite its location Iquitos is only 115m above sea level.

Founded as the Jesuit mission of Santa Maria de Iquitos in the 1750s, the town remained a remote backwater trading post. During the rubber boom it grew rapidly from the 1880s to the early 1890s when huge fortunes were made almost overnight. Many of the city's buildings reflect the prosperity of the past, with fine tile and iron work imported from Europe

The discovery of oil has led the latest boom which, combined with ecotourism, has seen the city's population rise rapidly to 600,000 compared with 250,000 in the 1970s.

Iquitos' other economic activities include small ship-building, fisheries and lumber. Most important of the exported woods are mahogany and Spanish cedar. Jute is exported for use in fibre products. Fish exports include varieties for fish markets in Lima and dozens of species coveted by aquarists the world over. Worth several million dollars annually, natural rubber is still exported from Iquitos.

Getting around

In Iquitos there are taxis and buses some of which look as if they were rescued from a junkyard! There are also three-wheeled motorised rickshaws, or *motocarros*. Basically small Japanese motorcycles with two-wheel cabs on the back, *motocarros* are the best option for speedy cheap travel around the city but not recommended for long distances or for those carrying a lot of luggage. Breakdowns are frequent so be sure to choose a relatively new vehicle (don't worry, there are plenty to choose from!).

Agree on a price before you get in. The usual cost is one sol (about US$0.40) for a ride in the city, or four to five solés for an hour's ride around the city.

Inadequate spending on roads, local drivers' etiquette and the natural elements conspire to make the trip a fairground ride – you weave here and there, bone-jarringly bouncing in your seat, deafened by shouts and blasts on the horn exchanged between irate drivers. It's fun!

Licensed taxis operate from Empresa de Transportes (Napo 127; tel: 094 243131) just off Plaza de Armas.

If you must contact the outside world, there are several internet cafés. Most are open from early to late and cost US$1–2 per hour:

Cabina de Internet Manguare Prospero 249; tel: 094 242148; email: webmaster@manguare.com.pe.
El Cyber Fitzcarraldo 120; tel: 094 223608; email: elcyber@iquitos.net; web: www.iquitos.net. El Cyber claims 'Faster connection in the best place of the city ...fasten seat belts.'

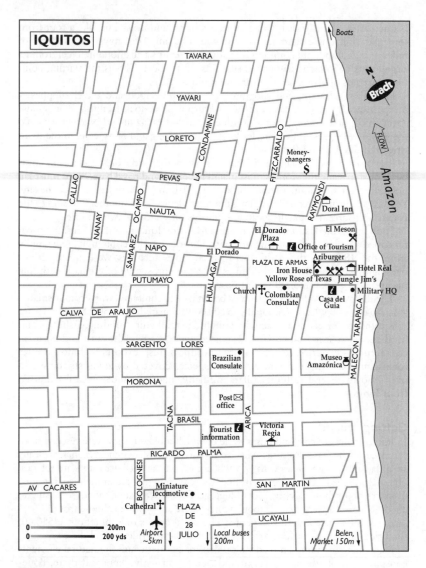

Where to stay

Most people stay in Iquitos just a night or two, in transit to one of the many jungle lodges or riverboats in the area. Conditions are simple compared with those of modern Western hotels, but acceptable in most places, considering that you are in the middle of the Amazon jungle, hundreds of miles from the nearest Hilton or Sheraton.

Hotel El Dorado Napo 362 and Arica; tel: 094 237 326; email: dorado@amazon-travel.com; web: www.amazon-travel.com/hdorado.htm. Quiet but convenient location. Rooms have airconditioning, hot water and cable TV. Amenities include a restaurant and indoor swimming pool. Price US$80 single, US$120 double.

El Dorado Plaza Hotel Napo 258-266; tel: 094 222 555; fax: 094 224 304; email: haguilar@eldoradoplazahotel.com; web: www.eldoradoplazahotel.com. Located on the

Plaza de Armas, this is Iquitos' only five star hotel. The 65 rooms include AC, minibar, telephone (with voice-mail), digital safe and cable TV, and endless hot water. Full amenities and even a hairdresser on call to redo your perm after your jungle tour. Single or double for US$143.

Doral Inn Raymondi 220; tel/fax: 094 241 970. New hotel near Plaza de Armas, a block from the waterfront. Rooms are small but clean and comfortable: private bathroom, hot shower, airconditioning and cable TV. US$10 single room without AC, US$20 with AC, including breakfast.

Hotel Réal Malécon Tarapaca; tel: 094 231 011. In the best location in town – right on the river front – the rather dilapidated building is a colonial relic, with expansive hallways and wide staircases. Staff speak little or no English. Street noise can be irritating so get a room on the other side. Rooms are basic but clean and comfortable. A double is US$60, a single US$50, including continental breakfast.

Rio Grande Hotel Aguirre 793; tel: 094 243 530; fax: 094 243 527; email: contactanos@riograndehotel.com; web: www.riograndehotel.com. Located on 28 de Julio Plaza near the centre. Rooms have private bathrooms and airconditioning. Rates are US$80 for a single room, US$100 for a double.

Hotel Victoria Regia Ricardo Palma 252; tel/fax: 094 231 983; email: info@victoriaregiahotel.com; web: www.victoriaregiahotel.com. Rooms are small but there is a restaurant and an indoor swimming pool. Quiet, with courteous, English-speaking staff. Rate for a double room is US$60 and a single is US$40. Prices include breakfast and airport transfers.

Where to eat

El Meson (Malecon Maldonado 153; tel: 231 197), on the riverfront has a quiet atmosphere and attentive service. Avoid the caiman and turtle (both very rare locally); better options are the fish and manioc (yucca) dishes. A meal costs US$5–10 but there is no charge for the *ambienta distinguido*.

For the best value in town, with cheap and excellent lunch menus, scout the area down Ricardo Palmo, about four blocks from Prospero. A number of small restaurants including **El Callefan** and **La Paulina**, serve fish, yucca and chonta (palm hearts) for less than US$3.

Ask around for the **Regal Restaurant** (Putumayo 182A; tel: 222732; fax: 223607), in the Iron House. If you're homesick go upstairs (round the corner to the right) and there's as authentic a British pub as you are likely to find in the Amazon, complete with dartboard and pool table. Try fish 'n' chips while enjoying the view of Plaza de Armas below. **Jungle Jim's** (Putumayo 168; tel: 235294) is a bar and restaurant with 'typical' English dishes, open 24 hours. Try the bangers and mash! It's worth spending an hour here just to see who drops in... **Yellow Rose of Texas** (Putumayo 180; tel: 241010) serves Tex-mex style barbecue and chili and Louisiana cajun in an American south atmosphere, down to the cowgirl waitresses. On the same theme, **Ariburger**, also called 'Gringolandia', is a burger joint on the edge of Plaza de Armas, popular with locals and gringos alike. They'll change dollars. There is a Chinese restaurant nearby (Napo 159; tel: 241386). Bread, canned foods, vegetables and fish can be bought at markets and supermarkets on every other street corner throughout Iquitos.

Nightlife

Iquitos' tourism boom has resulted in numerous nightclubs and dance halls. Most clubs feature a wide variety of music including the local chicha or technocumbia, merengue, Colombian vallenato, Brazilian toada as well as pop and salsa.

What to see

The **waterfront** (Boulevard Malecon) and **Belen market** are ideal for observing local life. Along the waterfront, overlooking the Nanay River, Malecon Tarapa Boulevard is frequented by locals looking to relax away from the city bustle. On weekend evenings it's packed with families, onlookers, street performers, and vendors of plastic toys, handicrafts, and snacks. Kids ride around in miniature *motocarros*, Indians perform racy dances with snakes, and mimes and magicians practise their craft.

Also on the Boulevard, housed in the former Loreto State Government Building dating from 1863, the **Museo Amazónico** is worth an hour and the US$1 admission fee. The main attraction is 50 plaster statues cast from living Indians. The haunting life-size sculptures are authentic down to the most intimate detail. Also featured are pottery displays, various photos of Iquitos, a portrait of Julio César Arana (notorious for his treatment of Indian rubber tappers) and military memorabilia.

Nearby is the regional **military headquarters**, housed in a 1912 building that is arguably the city's finest example of early-20th-century, rubber-boom architecture. Particularly notable are the wrought-iron balustrades outside each balcony and the fine blue and pink tiles.

At the **market**, just about everything is sold from fluorescent pink plastic shoes and bootleg tapes or CDs to unidentifiable animal parts awaiting the pot. The market can be exhausting. It is crowded, noisy, smelly and dirty, but to see how local people live, this is the best one or two hours you can spend.

Near to the market is the Floating City or **Ciudad Flotante** of several thousand shacks, hovels and huts that float, rising and falling with the river. From the market a long flight of crumbling concrete stairs leads down to the shanty town. It's safe during the day but muggers prowl the area at night.

Close by the waterfront is the Plaza de Armas. On one corner of the square is **La Casa Fierro** (the Iron House), a two-storey edifice with iron panels painted silver-grey, designed by Gustav Eiffel and imported to the city during rubber-boom days. A wealthy rubber baron bought it after the Paris Exposition of 1889 and had it shipped in pieces. It was destined for Pucallpa but the river dropped and the vessel reached no further than Iquitos and, as they say, the rest is history. The Iron House is a nice spot for views of the plaza The present owner, Phillip Duffy, is the **British Honorary Consul** (Putumayo 182A; tel: 094 222 732; fax: 094 223 607) and can help UK nationals who have lost passports or other significant problems.

In a quirk of fate so typical of the Amazon, Iquitos' largest building is unnamed and incomplete and has been mostly derelict since its beginning. The huge concrete edifice looms over Plaza de Armas, and dominates the city's skyline. Originally built by cocaine dealers in the 1970s as an apartment and hotel complex, money ran out after the main shell was completed. Later plans were to convert the building to a hospital, hence the current sign: 'More health for more Peruvians'. These were abandoned after the design was found unsuitable. Today it is occupied by a few squatters and is used for telecom and cellular antennas. One TV station has a control room two-thirds of the way up and Social Security uses a couple of the lower floors. Sporadic rumours circulate of buyers who are turning it into a five-star hotel. Locals say it is collapsing. The roof swimming pool is ideal for breeding millions of mosquitoes but otherwise it remains only a monument to yet another faded dream.

Visit the **Santa Fe Aquarium** at Calle Abtao 1474 (tel: 094 263 349; fax: 094 266289; email: acuariosantafe@hotmail.com) to see dozens of different kinds of

Amazon fish. You get an idea of the amazing variety of fish inhabiting the waters of the region. The **miniature locomotive** in Plaza de 28 Julio was once used to haul raw rubber to the river where it could be floated to market for sale. In contrast, the same square has a modern church, with geometric architecture and a bold mosaic. An appropriate last spot to visit in Iquitos is the **city cemetery** for the colourful and eccentric tombstones and mausoleums.

Shopping

There is some good shopping in Iquitos besides jungle souvenirs which you can buy or barter for at Indian villages. If you leave souvenir buying until towards the end of your trip you'll have a better idea of what you want. Tonics prepared from plant roots infused in rum, are *siete rais* (seven roots) and *viente-un rais* (twenty-one roots). The numbers signify how many different plants are used to make the brew. Vendors in Belen market claim the tonics have aphrodisiac or healing properties. In any case they make a fine aperitif or nightcap, a great party drink or an exotic flavouring for desserts and cakes. A large bottle of *seite rais* is US$5–7, a small bottle US$3–5.

These local herbalists know the properties of hundreds or thousands of plants. They have a remedy for practically anything, from a sore throat or upset tummy (*yerba luisa*, lemon grass) to skin tumours (*uña de gato,* cat's claw)!

Some of the old skills are alive and well, including pottery. Observe the age-old 'coil-method' in action – nothing to do with contraception – at Indiana, a village half an hour by boat downriver from Iquitos. At Padre Cocha on the Nanay River, the potters mix clay with charcoal to create distinctively dark pieces. Delicate, intricately painted Shipobo Indian pottery is not widely available outside Iquitos, unless one travels to Pucallpa. This is the centre of the Shipobo tribe who make the best pottery in the region, known for compelling mystical designs. Shipobo women hang around Plaza de Armas selling embroidered cloths with similar designs for US15–20.

Shipobo pieces such as plates, bowls and vases can be bought in Iquitos souvenir stores for US$5–20. Larger pieces are available for US$100 or more.

If you can't wait to see your holiday snaps, or you need that hard-to-find camera battery, go to **Foto Aspinwall** (Próspero 271; tel: 233022; email: easpinwall@amontes.com). They're a Kodak dealer and recommended by the Iquitos Office of Tourism.

WARNING Those seeking a special kind of 'trip' might be offered potions claimed to be ayahuasca. This powerful hallucinogen is not a recreational drug. Entheogenic (the proper term) drugs are important and interesting, but potentially dangerous. Ideally, they are taken as is part of a larger cultural whole... not likely with the average tourist. In the *Amazonian Ethnobotanical Dictionary* Jim Duke warns 'a few cases have been mental one-way trips. Beware!' Reports of charlatans abound. Ask yourself, why is it necessary for participants to rub their naked bodies with cow dung? Some ayahuasqueros seem contemptuous of New Age, patchouli-reeking yuppies. We do not endorse self-diagnosis and medication. For those genuinely seeking an alternative path to personal growth and healing, we recommend Amazon Forays (page 280) or El Tigre Journeys (page 282).

Excursions from Iquitos

Some 15km outside Iquitos is a small zoo, **Quistacocha Park**, with a variety of local wildlife in various conditions of health, mostly bad. A tour of the zoo can be arranged with local tour operators for US$40. Alternatively, catch a bus (US$2) from Abato between Aguirre and Grau. Of course, you forfeit the services of a guide who expounds on the animals, life in Iquitos, Peruvian politics, dreams of the US and so on.

A half day at **Pilpintuwasi Butterfly Farm** introduces you to some of the region's butterfly species. The aim is to sell live pupa to butterfly houses in the US and Europe. At the entrance a pair of macaws greets visitors with loud caws of 'Ola!' The owner gives a brief orientation, followed by a tour of the flight area, a screened area with a variety of plants including heliconia, costus and others. Butterflies include morphos, caligo, heliconius and swallowtails. In the pupa room eggs are hatched and raised until they metamorphose into pupae whereupon they are transferred to the flight area. The owner is lobbying the Peruvian government to ease restrictions on the export of live pupa. Pilpintuwasi has a few rescued animals including a jaguar, a tapir, some agoutis and a couple of tortoises. The easiest way to get here is on an organised tour. To save a few pennies you can get a *colectivo* from Masusa or Bellavista dock for about US$2 and then pay the entrance fee, US$5.

River transport
Given the near complete absence of ground transport in the jungle, to move beyond the city one must use rivers, which in the Amazon serve as highways.

Local riverboats
The 'banana' boats that run between Leticia and Iquitos and to various other cities are sometimes the only option to get from one city to another. Local riverboats are the cheapest way to travel on the river but often break down, are usually overloaded and very occasionally sink.

If you are undeterred, a local riverboat costs US$20 from Iquitos to Santa Rosa/Leticia, meals included. The week-long passage to Pucallpa costs about US$30. Food aboard the local vessels is rarely inspiring so take your own if you'd prefer, in which case ask for a discount off the ticket price. If you have to eat their fare, take along extra food in case you are served up something really unpalatable. Buy canned goods and bread, crackers, fruit and sweets at small villages and towns en route.

You'll need a hammock, which you can buy in Iquitos (or Leticia). Take the upper deck to get the best sleep. Even then, you may end up being squeezed between other hammocks, so try to get an outside spot, which is cooler. Some boats have cabins that tend to be hot and cramped. Keep an eye on your belongings. Some boats have locked storage, so you don't have to stand guard all day. Book passage on a local riverboat from **Puerto Masusa**, along Av Marina in the north of town. The dilapidated official noticeboard may or may not be accurate so check with tied-up boats that have blackboards with scrawled departure information. You can sleep aboard while waiting to depart, perhaps an hour or a day later than scheduled.

On riverboats you do not take any nature excursions, the object being simply to get from A to B. However, most vessels make frequent stops and, if you're not in a hurry, these are a great chance to see how local people live. Also, as you are not with a big group, locals are less intimidated and more inclined to chat.

Small local boats and canoes
Locals use small longboats, or *colectivos*, in the same way we use cars. *Colectivos* serve as private transport or river-taxis. These are long wooden canoes, 6–12m long,

fitted with a palm thatch roof and small outboard motor called a *peke peke*. They are loaded with vast quantities of bananas or firewood, bicycles and chickens – or even another canoe stacked on top. When the thing is fully loaded, the water-line can be within a hand's-breadth of its gunwales.

With the exception of tour company *colectivos* (which lack the chickens and intimate waterline), this mode of locomotion is not recommended. Only the young, adventurous and budget-minded should consider it. If you do, head down to the Masusa dock area in Iquitos and ask around.

Express taxi-boats

For rapid transit between cities there is a fleet of express taxi-boats. These dash from Iquitos to Leticia in under a day. However, speed and not comfort is emphasised. Seating only is provided, with little room for luggage and a small toilet. Taking around twelve hours, the trip costs about US$50.

Expresso Turística Loreto in Iquitos (Loreto 151, Raymondi 384; tel: 238652) or Leticia (Avenida Marechal Mattel) is one of the better companies.

Jungle tours

If you arrive in Iquitos without a pre-booked tour, plan on a couple of days to organise a jungle trip. Lodges range from simple to comfortable. Tourist riverboats are the best way to travel along the river. Before you sign anything, visit various companies. Ignore hyperbole and beware potential rip-offs. Most tours include jungle walks, canoe trips, piranha fishing and night-time excursions to look for caiman. Downriver trips include some of the jungle towns mentioned below. You'll need to be resourceful to use local riverboats to go town hopping, but in any case, it's certainly worthwhile to visit the smaller towns for an insight into the typical life of Amazon people.

If you do not have a pre-arranged tour, visit the **Iquitos Office of Tourism** (airport, and Napo 226; tel: 235621). 'See us first' is their motto and it's a good idea to make sure you get what you want. The office is staffed with English and Spanish speakers. It attempted to improve the tourism industry by requiring guides and tour operators to be licensed. Most local companies and guides are happy to comply. IOT maintains a folder of comments on various tour operators and guides – good and bad. Although they do not recommend specific lodges or tour operators, their information can help you decide from among the numerous options. All services are free of charge. Office hours are from 08.00 to 20.00, Monday through Friday and during weekends from 09.00 to 13.00.

The City of Iquitos set up **La Casa del Guia** (Putumayo 163; tel: 094 241386) in an effort to control the burgeoning number of unlicensed guides. In reality most independent guides (not employed by a lodge or tour company) dislike the idea of licensing. Initially around 60, the La Casa del Guia's membership has dropped because members received no tangible benefit. Thus the guides have no incentive to behave ethically. Indeed, IOT cites numerous complaints against La Casa del Guia members.

A typical ploy is for the 'guide' to point a prospect to a particular tour operator's office. The company pays the guide commission if you book a tour or lodge with them. Although not illegal, the practice is reprehensible because the guide pressures you into buying a tour before you've shopped around. It also increases overhead for lodge and tour operators.

Some guides (who may or may not be licensed) offer their own tours but these are usually very basic and there is no comeback if things go wrong (which they often do). Visit the Iquitos Office of Tourism and read their reports before going with an independent guide. Be sure to research apparent bargains very carefully and check references. Forged letters from 'satisfied customers' abound.

Towns and villages downstream from Iquitos
Indiana
This is a typical Amazon riverside settlement, inhabited by about 1,000 people. Founded by Franciscan missionaries, it is some 16km downriver from Iquitos on the main stream. Visits are by *colectivo* boat from Iquitos (around US$5 one way). Indiana is a mission town with schools and a small hospital where laid-back residents drape across concrete verandas, eyeing strangers in town while engaged in basketry or pottery. Several trails lead to the Napo River, the most attractive being the Pipa Trail, close to Ceiba Tops.

Francisco de Orellana
This settlement, although hardly a village, should be visited by all those travelling in Orellana's footsteps. The village is notable only for its name and the monument after which it is named, in tribute to the Spanish conquistador who made the first recorded journey down the full length of the river. He is said to have landed at this spot. Situated on the banks of the Amazon main stream, the village is close by Explorama Lodge. From here, it is easily reached on foot, or by canoe during high water. There is nowhere for travellers to stay overnight.

Pevas
Pevas (or Pebas), at the mouth of the Ampiyacú River, about a third of the way from Iquitos to Leticia, is said to be the oldest European settlement in the western Amazon. The earliest date associated with the town is 1542 and it is easy to believe that Pevas has changed little since its founding. Its population remains small, around 2,000, but it's a popular stop with the tourist riverboats because of its proximity to native Indian settlements.

The riverfront path is lined with houses built on stilts that sit in the water when it is high. On a sunny day, townsfolk spread gutted fish on bamboo platforms to dry. This effectively preserves the fish as ultraviolet from the sun naturally irradiates the food. The taste seems unaffected – much of the fish served at restaurants in the Amazon is preserved this way.

From the riverfront, you need to climb up a long, long flight of steps to reach the town square. Facing on to the plaza, a large Catholic church dominates the rise above the Ampiyacú. Built of wood, plaster and corrugated tin, the church's simplicity is appealing. Inside there are posters depicting Jesus as an Amazon Indian growing up in the jungle.

Around the corner from the main plaza is a small souvenir shop where you can buy soda or beer and, of course, blowguns and palm-fibre hammocks. Inside the store, in the kitchen and cooking area, are a green parrot and spider monkey and occasionally more exotic animals.

Behind the church is a single-storey schoolhouse, painted yellow. Facilities are typical: a blackboard, a few wooden desks and stools. The teachers welcome donated books or writing materials. The main school holiday is between April and July because of the difficulty of getting to school during flood season.

Along the riverfront path you come to a gate for the studio house of the famous artist, Señor **Francisco Grippa**, who offers any visitor a gracious welcome. With lovely views of the river, his gallery and its fine paintings are the major attraction for visitors to Pevas. Aged 54 and of Peruvian-Hungarian parents, Grippa trained in Paris, London and New York and exhibits in the US. You can see his pictures

YAGUA SETTLEMENT

You can walk here from Pevas, about half a mile along a moderate trail (steep, mud) beyond Grippa's residence. Most visitors arrive here to coincide with the pre-arranged dance/barter sessions included by a tourist riverboat on its standard itinerary.

Communal huts are the traditional mode of dwelling for the forest Indian. Several families would live in each, dividing up living space. Now there are individual houses for each family, an arrangement which arises from the European model. Yagua means red and comes from the tribe's practice of face-painting. Dramatically daubed with bright red pigment from seedpods of achiote (*Bixa* sp) to ward off evil spirits, the men, women and children join in a traditional dance. During simple, roughly-executed moves, they variously chant, beat drums or blow on bamboo flutes and panpipes, with varying degrees of skill and enthusiasm. The Yagua usually wear 'grass' skirts (really made from split palm fibres), over Western dress.

Native dress is worn only for the performance and, although somewhat artificial, the dances provide the Indians with an income and a reason to keep up old traditions, which would quite possibly die out otherwise.

Most Yagua people live by hunting and fishing, and cultivating a few crops. Their economy of exchange is based on barter. Recently, in areas visited by tourists, the sale of handicrafts, such as seed necklaces, blow-guns and ritual masks, has become important to their economy.

A Yagua settlement similar to the one near Pevas is visited by guests of Explorama Lodge who follow a trail to the Yagua Reserve.

online at www.junglephotos.com. Testament to success, his house has expanded to cover most of the hill on which it stands, and must be among the largest native-built buildings in the region. A central tower stands 32m high and is perfect for views and photographs of the town and river below.

Besides board and conventional canvas, he paints on a cloth, unique among established artists, made of bark from the fig tree *chuchuara*, (*Ficus yoponensis*), working in oils and acrylics. His goal is to interpret Amazonian life in art and his style has elements of early impressionists combined with techniques of Jackson Pollock. But as he says, 'Grippa is Grippa, and no-one else...'

Francisco makes guests welcome without an appointment, whether or not they buy a painting. There is something here for everyone. Tapes of specially composed music, postcards and prints range from US$1 to US$100. Original paintings in various colourful media are priced from US$500-5,000, about half of what they sell for in US galleries.

The only acceptable accommodation is the **Casa de la Loma** about five minutes' walk from the main plaza. It offers basic comforts for reasonable cost. Ask at Grippa's for Abelardo Campos who runs the lodge and excursions based from there. He is a reliable, honest guide. Ask about prices and availability through Amazon Tours and Cruises in Iquitos, or email: scottpevas@hotmail.com. The few fleapits in town are cheap but not very secure.

The best way to get to Pevas is by express river taxi or tourist riverboat. Tourist riverboats stop in Pevas for day-visits before visiting nearby Witoto-Bora and Yagua settlements. You could take the tourist riverboat then catch it on the return journey to Iquitos three days later. Alternatively you have the unpredictable but frequent local cargo boats.

WITOTO AND BORA SETTLEMENT

A few miles down the Ampiyacu River, the Witoto and Bora Indian village settlements can be reached by *colectivo* (motorised canoe) from Pevas (US$5). Several boats a day make the trip.

From their ancestral homelands originally in Colombia along the upper Putumayo, the Witoto and Bora Indians were forced by the government to move to the area in the 1930s following border changes made in 1922. Distinctions between the two tribes are being lost, as they have lived together and been subject to continuous outside influence for most of the last century.

There are some differences, such as the style of face-painting and clothing. Notably, during their dances for tourists, Bora women go bare-breasted whereas Witoto cover themselves. Pre-European native costumes made from wood-bark, chambira palm fibre and various animal parts are used as adornments. During set dances Indians play a type of slit drum, also found in Africa and among Pacific Islanders. The drums represent human or animal bodies. The Witoto's traditional slit-drum has a woman's head at one end and a caiman's tail at the other.

You can trade Western goods for souvenirs such as blowguns, paddles, bark paintings, carved gourds and seed necklaces. The ecopurist may decry the practice of trading, and it is true that selfish exchanges can damage relationships between visitors and Indians and have a negative impact on some people in the village. On the other hand, the local Indians do have the right to choose whether or not to barter for our goods. Should we take the moral high ground and withhold the possibility because we are somehow afraid of tainting them?

From legal and ethical standpoints, it is advisable not to buy items with significant amounts of feathers, teeth or skin or any animal products in general.

Secondary rainforest in various stages of regeneration surrounds the town, although there are some pristine areas close by. The main attraction is a small lake amid spiny palm swamp along a tributary of the Río Ampiyacua about 20 minutes' boat ride upstream from Pevas. Giant water lily pads spread across the lake waters inhabited by jacanas.

Pijuayal

Just downriver from Pevas is Pijuayal (pee-hyoo-ah-yahl). Pijuayal is an army garrison and checkpoint, where all river traffic must stop to submit papers. Should a boat pass the checkpoint and fail to stop it is, as local guide Daniel Rios put it, 'Blown out of the water'. This somewhat drastic policy is to prevent drug-running down the river.

As the garrison is behind the high riverbank you cannot see much of the installation: a couple of brightly camouflaged wooden pillboxes and a walkway, with perhaps one or two armed guards. It is unwise to point a camera in their direction, however cheerful they may seem or unimportant the facilities may appear.

San Pablo

This town of about 2,500 inhabitants is around two-thirds of the distance from Iquitos to Leticia, on the southern bank of the Amazon River. Tourist riverboats stop for a short two or three hour excursion. Otherwise you can reach here from towns up or downstream on cargo riverboats or by river taxi.

At the Witoto village is a shaman, Gabriel, who always has a wad of coca powder in his gum. He is a rich source of knowledge on herbal remedies from rainforest plants, with a cure for practically anything.

Of course, the efficacy of Gabriel's treatments is not guaranteed but it is certain that some of his medicines work. He contributed significantly to the researches of Richard Evans Schultes, founder of the science of ethnobotany. If you are suffering from an ailment or fever, Gabriel will be happy to prescribe and create a remedy for US$10.

At some time during your visit to the villages you may be offered coca leaf to chew, locally called *ipadú*. The raw ingredient for cocaine, only the leaf is used by natives. In the highlands it is chewed raw or served as a tea but in the Amazon coca is prepared differently. It is ground to a dust and then added to cercropia leaf, which is similarly powdered and contains alkaloids to enhance the active ingredient.

The greenish-brown powder is taken with a suitable leaf or piece of card, about a thimbleful at a time, and poured into the space between the cheek and the teeth. Despite a gritty texture and earthy taste it's not unpleasant and makes your teeth a little numb. The wad is kept in the mouth and encourages saliva which is spat out, along with some of the powder. Only men use it and swear that it enhances performance in hunting expeditions or during their work in the fields. Apparently, they use it for twenty years or more without ill-effect or addiction.

Numerous other drugs available from the rainforest are used for intoxication, in particular hallucinogens, such as ayahuasca, taken as an infusion, and snuffs made from the virola vine. Hallucinogens play a significant role in the religious life of rainforest tribes, even today.

The basic accommodation will suit only hardy travellers and you can get local food at several small bars.

San Pablo is touted as a 'leper colony'. In fact by far the majority of people in the town have never suffered from the disease. Sufferers who have no family or money were sent to this Amazon outpost, but no new patients have been received for several years. The basic hospital with a dozen patients in the latter stages of Hansen's Disease – as leprosy is properly called – is run by a couple of Canadian nuns.

The most noticeable legacy of the patients is a thriving industry of wood-carvers – Antonio is the best known. Vividly coloured, varnished or unpainted, his simple carvings are of rainforest animals such as anteaters, parrots and fish. The carvings are sometimes so newly finished, the varnish is still sticky. They sell for outrageously low prices of US$3–15.

Look around and you can always discover something of interest: an exquisite tropical flower, a postcard view across the Amazon, bright yellow corn drying on the pavement, kids squabbling over the pen a tourist gave them, silent pain in the eyes of a leprosy patient, or a caiman skin drying in the sun.

Caballococha

Caballococha is the last town downstream from Iquitos visited by boats before Leticia. Most visitors come here on a pre-arranged tour. Tour boats stop here for just an hour or two and moor while their passengers go off in motorised canoes to explore the nearby lake. If you're stuck here, there's a very basic hotel, a handful of shops and bars, but not much else to do.

This small town (population 2,500) has little to distinguish it except the fact that it is of strategic importance. Caballococha is the main town in Peru on the stretch of river which borders Colombia and only 80km from Leticia, and the town is bolstered with official funds to deter Colombian military adventurism. Most households receive cash handouts from the Peruvian government.

Besides having more streetlights than any town between Iquitos and Leticia, Caballococha also has a gigantic satellite dish, with global communication ability. Here in the middle of the Amazon, with the right timing, you can watch the Olympics, World Cup and other global events live on satellite TV. Close by the hospital is an ENTEL office with public phones. There's also a small military airfield that was involved in monitoring air traffic during the headline-grabbing incident when a missionary plane was mistakenly shot down in 2001.

The centre of activity is the main plaza, one side of which is the riverfront. Men sit around in the shade of a mango tree, chatting and drinking beer; a gang of urchins run around; dogs squabble over a scrap on a trash heap, joined by a platoon of indignant black vultures.

Caballococha Lake just south of town is home to pink dolphins and a wide variety of fish. This body of water is fed by the Río Marichi before it flows into the main stream of the Amazon. The lake area is important ecologically and a backdrop for spectacular sunsets.

On the edges of the lake you can go piranha fishing with varying chances of success. Rivers leading away from the lake are choked with floating vegetation, ideal habitat for caiman, easily spotted at night with the use of a torch, as you listen to the sounds of amphibians, night monkeys and the chorus of innumerable insects.

Chimbote

This is another checkpoint at which tourist riverboats and other mainstream river traffic must stop before proceeding on to Leticia. Chimbote checkpoint, with shades of Checkpoint Charlie, is on the southern bank of the main stream, close by the Colombian border. Passengers are not permitted ashore. Watch where you point your camera.

Santa Rosa

Across from Leticia is Santa Rosa, the final point for riverboats from Peru. Peruvian entry and exit border control is based here. Santa Rosa is a small settlement on an island in the middle of the Amazon River, opposite Leticia. It is the easternmost point of Peru. With views overlooking the river toward Leticia is a small bar. Behind the bar lies the village itself, which has no amenities for visitors.

Upstream from Iquitos
Nauta

On the north bank of the Rio Marañon, Nauta is a rough jungle town more important to local fishermen and farmers than to tourists. Most outsiders visit here as part of a tour to the Pacaya-Samiria National Reserve. There are no tour operators or guides so Iquitos is a better place to arrange a trip into the reserve. You can get here by river taxi for U$10-15 from the Masusa port area of Iquitos. Some may stop on a downriver voyage from the Andes to the lower Amazon. In any case, there's not much except for typical life in a typical river town. A short walk along the riverfront takes you past thatched huts to more permanent brick and concrete buildings lining streets littered with wrappings, bottle tops, crushed cigarette packets and less identifiable detritus. Along the 'main' street are market stalls selling cheap manufactured products. There's a fresh food market for stocking up if you are travelling by local riverboat. Nauta offers scant facilities for travellers – a few very basic *hospedajes* and a scattering of bars. Enough to keep you alive but not enough to put on a postcard.

Pucallpa

Capital of the Ucayali department, Pucallpa lies on the Ucayali River. Although large, with a population of some 170,000, it still retains the atmosphere of a frontier town. Indeed, though founded early in the colonial era, the town remained isolated until 1945, when the 846km railway from Lima was completed. However, Pucallpa is easiest to reach by air (it has an airport) or road. It is also accessible by river from Iquitos, and travellers trying to journey along as much as possible of the Amazon's navigable length may start or end their voyages here (pages 285).

Like many Amazon towns, Pucallpa has electricity, but most streets are unpaved and sewers are inadequate. Industries include rosewood oil processing, lumber and oil refining. An oil refinery is connected by a 76km-long pipeline to the Ganso Azul oilfields. Missionary activity is ongoing in Pucallpa and other groups have their headquarters there, such as organisations involved in settling the area.

Jungle lodges

Several companies operate lodges in the Peruvian Amazon and have more or less the same protocols for tours. Usually included in your trip price are: being met at Iquitos airport by local staff; transfer for you and your baggage to a town hotel or to the dock and then on to the lodge; and a bilingual, English-speaking, local guide who accompanies you throughout your trip and on each excursion.

Stays at jungle lodges in Peru vary from US$45 to US$150 per night, out of the range of budget travellers. 'Lodges' much cheaper than this are likely to be granny's hut, lacking basic amenities. Be prepared for a rough time: sleeping on the floor, local food, questionable water, unreliable transport, washing in the river and going to the toilet in the forest. Fine if that's what you want, but beware of claims you are going to see jaguars, anacondas and the like. Such embellishments should be a red flag.

Most rainforest lodges and camps are constructed the same way as native houses. Roofs are made of palm-thatch – remarkably watertight and insect resistant. Frames, walls and walkways are built from palm wood and other lumber. The structure sits on stilts raised above the highest flood level. Beds are simple cots or even mattresses on the wooden floor, and usually with mosquito nets.

Explorama Lodges

Several of the top lodges are run by Explorama (see page 282), Iquitos' longest-running and biggest tour operator, in business since 1964. Reliable US companies have been using them for years. VENT, Field Guides (pages 41–2) and Explorations (page 280) offer trips led by expert birders, while Explorations also have trips accompanied by more broadly-based scientists. Several established tour operators also have regular trips without tour leaders to Explorama lodges including International Expeditions, Nature Expeditions International or Southwind Adventures (see pages 41–2 for contact details).

Explorama has five facilities: Ceiba Tops, Explorama Lodge, Explornapo Lodge, the Amazon Canopy Walkway and Explortambos Camp. Each provides a different rainforest experience. The company was also instrumental in realising its vision of the canopy walkway, now one of Peru's foremost nature tourist attractions.

Explorama Lodge

Explorama Lodge is the company's main facility, with 75 rooms. It was one of the first established lodges in the Iquitos area, constructed in 1965. Through regular maintenance Explorama ensures clients are comfortable and safe yet still have an experience as close as possible to nature. The lodge is up a small tributary, close to the Amazon main stream about 80km downriver from Iquitos. The Bushmaster Reserve belonging to Explorama protects around 195ha of forest around the lodge. Nearby visitors are taken to visit a small settlement of Yagua Indians.

The area close to the lodge has been cleared and you are free to stroll and admire resident birds and animals, plus orchids and bromeliads collected from the forest and put on display. There is direct access to a number of nature trails radiating into the nearby forest. However, the company won't take responsibility for guests who wander beyond the lodge grounds unaccompanied. Well-trained English-speaking Explorama staff lead excursions on the trails and add immeasurably to your experience, as they point out birds and plants which you could easily miss.

Morning nature walks are excellent for birds and invertebrates, such as insects, spiders and snails. With some luck squirrel monkeys or tamarins may be seen. You can take for granted a mind-boggling variety of vegetation.

Around Explorama the forest comprises seasonally flooded *várzea* and upland *terra firme* forest. Most is fully-grown secondary forest with some primary rainforest that has never been logged. Without a bit of practice you'll struggle to tell the difference. This is certainly an authentic jungle experience.

The downstream journey from Iquitos takes just over two hours by company-owned *colectivo*. These long, covered motorised canoes are built in the traditional form with palm-thatch roofs. The return journey against the current is somewhat longer, four to five hours.

At high water, access to the lodge is directly by launch which leaves the main stream going up the Yanamono and pulls up to a floating platform a short way from the lodge. At low water it may be necessary to disembark from the *colectivo* on the Amazon River and climb up steps cut into the riverbank. From here you walk for 15 to 30 minutes to the lodge. Some of this is along a wooden walkway – essential to avoid tramping through a swamp – while the second portion of the walk is along forest trails.

Close by the low-water disembarkation point is the small village of Sapo Playa, home to lodge staff and their families. On the main riverbank is a still for the distillation of the sugarcane used to make the local rum (*ron*). A primitive horse-driven mangle squeezes out the juice which is poured straight into a long wooden canoe and left to ferment. The liquor is extracted and distilled through a 2m-high bulbous copper still. Adjacent to the still shed you can sample the fiery product at the ramshackle bar decorated with calendars featuring scantily-clad beauties.

On the walk to Explorama Lodge you pass cultivated areas planted with maize, manioc (locally called *yucca*), bananas and sugarcane. A large pond with wallowing water buffalo is reminiscent of a scene in southeast Asia, from where these bovids were imported after World War II.

Surrounded by forest, the lodge sleeps 150 guests in half a dozen thatched buildings. Each cabin has two single beds with mosquito nets. Adjacent to the lower cabins is a hammock area where you can relax after jungle walks.

Water is provided, along with a washbowl, as there is no in-house plumbing. Washing water is piped into your cabin and the showers are filtered but not safe to drink. Showers and toilets are a short walk from the cabins and the water is unheated, though this is rather welcome given the temperatures! If unheated shower-water bothers you, it is warmest late afternoon.

The communal latrines are simple non-flush toilets. There is no electricity here. Lighting is by paraffin lamp so keep a flashlight handy for night excursions to the toilet.

On the whole, Explorama food is tasty and healthy, though not gourmet. Filtered water is available, along with hot water for tea or coffee throughout the day. A typical breakfast includes cereal with milk and yogurt with a choice of french toast or pancakes or an egg dish. Fruit (unpeeled) includes local curiosities such as *chirimoya* or *sapodilla*, or more familiar types: mango, apples or grapes. The choice depends on seasonal availability. Lunch and supper entrées are based on chicken, beef or fish. A range of vegetable dishes and safely prepared salads will satisfy vegetarians. Between meals or after nature activities you can visit the bar. The ice is made from purified water. Local handicrafts for sale in the bar include masks, flutes, blow-guns and paddles.

The price is on a par with similar lodges, at US$285pp for two on a three-night package, and US$85 for additional nights (includes transport from Iquitos). Book through Explorama in Iquitos or through SACA, their US representatives. A number of US tour operators can also make bookings for you.

Explornapo Lodge

Tucked away on the Sucusari River, a tributary of the Napo, Explornapo Lodge is the base for trips to the ACTS Field Station and canopy walkway.

Half-day motorboat trips up the Sucusari include piranha fishing, birdwatching and dolphin-spotting. But look closely around you and, as always in the rainforest, you can find something unusual – flocks of sulphur-yellow butterflies dancing around a patch of mud, or a ball of bristling ants collecting at the top of a young cercropia stem as the waters rise and flood their home. Because of Explornapo's remote location, the forest here is less disturbed than around Explorama Lodge and extensive primary forest remains.

At high water, your boat ties up right next to the main facility. At low water, the boat ties up further away and you walk along a walkway to reach the main reception area.

Explornapo Lodge is smaller but has similar standard accommodation and meals in comparison to Explorama Lodge. Here is a real 'away-from-it-all' experience. In the lounge area hang dozens of plaques left by previous groups or individual travellers – a far more interesting record than a visitor's book! Beyond this section is a separate hammock area where you can peacefully relax, watching for birds and animals who venture into the grounds. Leading from the lodge is a 1.5km trail leading to the Ethnobotanical Medicinal Plant Garden. This was planted by one of the areas best-known shamans, Antonio Montero. Today Guiermo and Mauro, authentic shamans from two different tribes, maintain the garden. You can meet with them and discuss at length the Amazon's herbal lore, medical or marital problems, for either of which they can prescribe a natural remedy.

Most visitors stay at Explornapo Lodge en route to the canopy walkway (see below). Price and booking information is the same as for Explorama Lodge.

Ceiba Tops

This newest addition to Explorama's properties is perfect for families and those who want to sample the Amazon in comfort. By company *colectivo* it's 45 minutes east of Iquitos on the main stream of the Amazon. The lodge is on a 200ha private reserve of which 40ha is primary rainforest. It is the closest lodge to Iquitos with primary *terra firme* forest.

The emphasis is on hospitality. Sip on your welcome drink on arrival and enjoy many comfortable amenities. International cuisine is served at the buffet restaurant, where you can get self-service coffee any time.

Excursions include guided rainforest walks along trails 20 minutes to two hours in duration, birdwatching, canoe rides, piranha fishing, boat rides in search of pink dolphins, or visits to a local village and indigenous community.

You can take a full-day excursion to the Amazon Canopy Walkway (see below) in the ExplorNapo Reserve, 75 miles by river for US$150pp (minimum two persons), or combine Ceiba Tops with any of the other Explorama Lodges. From Iquitos, the all-inclusive two-day Ceiba Tops programme is US$400 double or US$225 single. Additional nights are US$85 pp. Enquire for changes in prices as promotional programs may be offered. See above sections for booking.

Explortambos Camp

Tambo is a Quechua term meaning resthouse, and in the Amazon it applies to a simply built hut. Here, Explorama have extended the concept to their new facilities, opened mid-1997 for the more adventurous. A 3km hike from Explornapo Lodge takes you through primary rainforest to the *tambos*. These comprise a 'primitive' camp for a maximum of 16 people, sleeping in individual shelters with mosquito-netted beds (shelters for couples are also available). Meals are cooked on an open fireplace. Due to the isolation, wildlife opportunities are excellent. Biologists and enthusiastic nature lovers use the tambos. In the vicinity guests have observed many different primates: red titi monkeys, yellow-handed titi monkeys, tamarins, squirrel monkeys, monk sakis, pygmy marmosets and howler monkeys. Also in the area are ocelots, tayras, arboreal anteaters, and other mammals. The basic five-day programme with two nights at Explorama Lodge and one each at ExplorNapo and ExplorTambos costs US$902pp for two people.

ACTS (Amazon Conservatory of Tropical Studies)

This is undoubtedly the best way to get a feel for what life in the canopy is like. Forty-six metres above the forest floor you come face-to-face with life's diversity at its most extreme.

The site, 140km from Iquitos, is within the privately owned and managed Explornapo Reserve, set up by a joint effort of scientists, officials and tour operators. The walkway and ACTS facility is reached by a 3km hike from Explornapo Lodge. The walk is easy for the moderately fit person.

Accommodation, bathroom facilities and food are on a par with Explorama Lodge, but don't expect to be pampered. Everyone is interested in nature and discovering things. If you're weighing up whether to visit here, any shortcomings are more than compensated for by the outstanding birdwatching, the variety of insect life and the diversity of plants.

Explorama handle all arrangements in Peru. International Expeditions, Explorations and several other tour operators offer all-inclusive trips from Miami. The cost of a typical seven-day programme is about US$2,000 with airfare and hotel in Lima. This package includes two or three days at the walkway lodge, with the rest of the time spent at other Explorama facilities.

Because of the relatively high cost of transport and accommodation, it won't be much more expensive than arranging the trip yourself and you might not have so much fun. If you arrange a trip here from Iquitos, it costs US$395 for a three-day package (including transport). However you get here, the canopy walkway is the highlight of any visit.

Canopy walkway

You can literally walk among the treetops right in the middle of the rainforest canopy, the site of the highest biodiversity in the world, strolling among the leafy branches and enjoying the 'high life'.

The walkway is among *terra firme* forest, atop a ridge. Wooden steps take you around and up trunks and branches – through the lush vegetation, to the tops of immense trees. Built on a slope, from the walkway's higher points you can see over the trees: a rolling ocean of multi-hued green, unbroken forest stretching as far as the eye can see. It is an awe-inspiring sight.

At dawn you can watch the sun rise over the treetops, as wisps and tendrils of mist waft up like ethereal smoke above the breathing trees. You are in the domain of epiphytes, such as orchids and bromeliads, and animals that never touch the ground. High above the ground, you are cooled by refreshing breezes as you leisurely inspect plants and animals you would otherwise never see. Take time to watch for wildlife, look at the rare plants or just ponder the wonder of it all.

The walkway is an engineering marvel around 500m long and 35m up in the trees. Every effort was made to minimise harm to the surrounding forest. For the US$10 million project scientists and engineers teamed up to give visitors the ultimate rainforest experience. You need no specialised climbing equipment – the facility is designed and built with safe, easy access as a priority.

NOTE You are permitted to use the canopy walkway only with a guide but you can arrange for walkway tours at any time of day.

Amazon Camp

A group of palm-thatched dwellings on stilts, Amazon Camp is about half an hour's boat ride from Punta Bellavista, the southernmost point of Iquitos. This spot is a pleasant and peaceful retreat on the banks of the Momón River, a tributary of the Nanay that feeds into the main stream. At the mouth of the Nanay is a 'meeting of waters' where the Nanay's black water flows into the Amazon's brown, not mixing for some distance. Where the two waters blend, the surface has the appearance of black-brown marble.

The lodge buildings and facilities are laid out neatly along the riverbank. There is an easy landing platform and steps up to the lodge. Accommodation comprises twin beds in mosquito-proofed cabins and en-suite wash basins and flush toilets. Water is unheated, the showers are communal and lighting is by paraffin lamp. The landing platform is a safe place from which to dive in.

Amazon Camp has a well-prepared healthy menu. A trail through *terra firme* forest leads to a Bora settlement where villagers perform for visitors. The area around the camp has little wildlife but has diverse plant life and abundant insects.

Book direct through Amazon Tours and Cruises (page 280). Tara tours offer an eight-day tour Machu Picchu-Amazon Camp combination from US$2,196.

Sinchicuy Lodge

Downriver from Iquitos, the 29km trip to this pleasant lodge takes around two hours. Plantings of orchids and other tropical plants in a small garden allow close-up inspection of species otherwise out of reach. Nearby nature spots include a lake and forest trail. Your stay includes a nocturnal canoe ride to listen to the sounds of the night.

On the banks of the Sinchicuy River the dwellings are built in the native fashion. Rooms have private bathrooms (sharing showers) while cool breezes waft through the screened dining and bar areas. Lighting is with kerosene lamps.

Due to its proximity to Iquitos this lodge is popular with tour operators but still offers excellent cultural and nature experiences. Prices start around from US$131 for a two-day/one-night package including transfers from Iquitos. You can book in the US through through Green Tracks or Sol International (pages 41–2).

Tambo Amazonico Lodge

Located beside the Yarapa River 210km upstream from Iquitos, Tambo Amazonico Lodge is among the most economical options. Accommodations are in dormitories. Beds have mosquito nets. Showers and latrines are communal and water is river temperature. The dining area is bug-proofed so you can enjoy the food without waving your hand over your food every five seconds. Lighting is by paraffin lamp. The programme includes a 'camp-out' where participants build a shelter to spend the night. Outings include the usual array of visits to local tribes, canoe rides, piranha fishing, birdwatching and jungle hikes. Book through tour operators in Iquitos for US$133 (double) for a four-day package, including transport. In the US, book through Sol International (page 42). Kontiki (page 333) offer a five day package from US$1,044.

Tahuayo Lodge

This is the only lodge with access to the Tamshiyacu-Tahuayo Reserve. It is 85km from Iquitos to the Tahuayo River and then another 70km to the lodge, a total of four hours by speedboat.

Accommodation is in 15 cabins for 45 guests. All areas within the lodge are screened. A laboratory area with an educational library is for use by visiting scientists. Rooms have private baths and toilets and lighting is by oil lamp. A small generator provides power for emergency radio and recharging camera batteries. Food is prepared for Western tastes and served buffet style.

Beyond the lodge is a rope slide that allows guests to 'fly' through the canopy. The all-inclusive cost from Iquitos is US$1,295pp for a seven-day programme, booked in the US through Amazonia Expeditions (page 280).

Amazon Ecological Lodge (Amazon Rainforest Lodge)

Built in 1992, this lodge is 45 minutes by speedboat up the Momon River from Iquitos. It is situated in a giant pasture and most of the surrounding forest is swampy. It has 13 bungalows accommodating a total 50 people. Facilities include a restaurant, bar, mini-zoo, lookout tower and swimming pool. The lodge is geared to shamanic ceremonies. Discounts are offered for students and groups of 12 persons or more. Book for US$60 per day through the office in Iquitos (Jiron Putumayo 159, Iquitos; tel: 094 233100; fax: 094 242231; email: schneide@amauta.rcp.net.pe; web: www.amazon-lodge.com).

Note This is not to be confused with Amazon Rainforest Lodge run by Andres Peña Guerra, who has convictions for several robberies and attacks on tourists. Avoid his operation.

Heliconia Amazon River Lodge

The lodge, 80km along the Nanay River north of Iquitos, built in native style, features 21 double and triple rooms with private bathrooms and hot water. Raised walkways connect the lobby, restaurant, bar and hammock room. Electric power is available during early evening. After dark the lodge is lit by kerosene lamps. Activities include forest treks, birdwatching, piranha fishing, dolphin spotting and an excursion to see giant water lilies. Most Lima or Iquitos tour operators can arrange stays here. Peru Traces' (page 282) two-day package is US$220pp (double) from Iquitos.

La Posada

This first-class lodge is on the banks of the Rio Marañon about 40km upstream of its confluence with the Ucuyali.

Ten air-conditioned rooms are screened and have private bathroom and hot-water showers. The rooms are on the first floor while the second floor comprises a large dining room, a bar and a reading room.

From the lodge several trails lead into primary forest. One goes to a lake, and another 7.5km to a native-style cabin next to a huge kapok tree. You spend an optional night here. Another trail leads to a canopy walkway half an hour's walk from the lodge.

Visits to the lodge are tied in with river cruises on Jungle Expeditions (page 282) vessels. Alternatively, for US$120 per day, three-day minimum lodge-based programmes can be arranged separately from cruises.

Muyuna Amazon Lodge

This remote lodge is located on the Yanayacu River adjacent to the Pacaya-Samiria Reserve, about 135km southwest of Iquitos – three hours by speedboat. There are eight bungalows, each with two to six beds, private bathroom with shower and a terrace with a hammock. Rooms are fully screened against mosquitoes. Lighting is by kerosene lamps – there is no electricity.

Simple, healthy dishes served buffet-style include a variety of local (*inchicapi*, *tacacho*, *chonta*, etc) and Peruvian dishes. Activities include a medicinal plant trail, piranha fishing, night boat-ride, and exploring the area's complex of lakes and streams. Near the lodge is the village of San Juan de Yanayacu where visitors can meet the local mestizo people. Wildlife opportunities are excellent due to the remote location.

A four-day trip from Iquitos costs from US$360pp single, US$310 double, through Class Adventure Travel (page 282). Lama Tours four- to six-day birding tours start from US$430pp (double). Alternatively book through their office in Iquitos (Putumayo 163; tel: 5134 242858; email: amazonas@muyuna.com; web: www.muyuna.com). Advance reservations are essential to ensure you are met in Iquitos.

Amazon Adventure Lodge

About two hours upriver from Iquitos, this lodge (open July 2002) is located along the San Jose River in a 170ha private reserve. It's among flooded forest, surrounded by montrichardia and spiny palm marshland.

Peruvian-owned, it comprises 15 double or triple cabins. Each fully-screened cabin has a private bathroom with filtered water. An additional large dormitory-style cabin accommodates up to 30 budget travellers who must provide their own bedding and mosquito nets. Walkways connect the cabins with the dining and reception areas and a hammock house. The spacious layout ensures guests do not disturb each other. Lighting is by kerosene lamps while a generator runs lights for the kitchen. Food is standard lodge fare, based on local and Peruvian dishes.

A trail behind the lodge runs alongside unspoiled wetland that has high numbers of squirrel monkeys. The birdlife will keep birdwatchers happy for many days.

The cost is US$50 per day with an English-speaking naturalist guide. Prices are lower for longer stays and for the budget accommodation. Book through the Doral Inn in Iquitos (page 293).

Other jungle lodges
Other jungle lodges in the Iquitos area offer better or worse facilities than those described here. Given the volatility of the tourism industry, lodges open or close from time to time. Use the internet or the tour operators listed in this book to check for new opportunities.

Air expeditions
This totally different type of trip for the adventurous takes you to remote areas more rapidly than you can reach them by river. At Iquitos you board a small plane for a flight far into the forest, landing by a remote tributary. By pre-arrangement, your canoe is waiting with all the basics provided. You sleep in hammocks, small camp beds or temporary sleeping quarters, either tents or huts with a thatched roof. The seven-night Tacha Curaray air expedition from Amazon Tours and Cruises (page 280) takes guests to remote parts of the Curary River, some 200km northwest of Iquitos. Enquire with them for rates.

Trails and nature walks
Here we describe a sample of popular trails and nature walks found on or near the main stream and easily accessible from Iquitos. All the lodges have trails similar to those described here, and there are far too many trails around the lodges to describe them all. If possible try to include a variety of trails to get a feel for the different habitats. At a minimum, include trails through flooded forest (*várzea*) and high ground forest (*terra firme*). Do the same trail at night for a totally different experience.

Ampiyacu Water Lily Trail
This walk passes among undisturbed lowland *várzea* forest, close by a tributary of the Ampiyacu River, about 30 minutes upstream from Pevas and not far from the Witoto-Bora village. The trail varies in length depending on the flood level but doesn't exceed 500m. Approaching by small boat, the ride to the site is through narrow channels, bordered by overhanging vegetation and thick epiphytic growth. At low water this stream is sometimes blocked off by vegetation and water weeds. At high water the trail is completely under water.

The trail opens to a small lake, surrounded by spiny palm forest. Spiny palm are equipped with vicious spines arranged in parallel circlets up the trunk.

Fed by whitewater rivers, nutrient levels are high. The lily pads grow two metres or more across. If the plants are in flower, you will see the spectacular blooms. Depending on the season, there is also a chance to see the horned screamer, hoatzin and more common waterbirds such as jacana and striated heron.

Amazon Camp Trail
Access to this trail is from Amazon Camp by the Momón River. The start is just behind the lodge dining area, through a small grassy clearing in which grows tufts of lemon-grass. The walk is about 3.5km in length, easy to moderate, but some parts may be muddy.

This secondary rainforest is in an advanced state of regeneration, and there is lots to see, with a wide variety of vegetation and fungi. Wildlife consists mostly of birds and invertebrates, including the splendid morpho butterflies. You can take night walks from Amazon Camp.

You have to negotiate a couple of muddy slopes and a rickety wooden walkway on the final part of the trail before a clearing in which stands a communal native hut. Here the walk ends with a dance by Bora Indians. Dances are based on traditional forms, to honour such animals as jaguar and caiman, and spirits of the forest.

From the village, a boat takes visitors back to Amazon Camp. At low water, a 1–2km walk may be necessary to reach the river.

Medicine Walk Trail

This trail through *terra firme* forest is close to Explorama's ACTS facility and easy to find.

On the walk visitors can find some of the vast number of plants used by natives for medicinal and other purposes. The easy walk, 1.5 km or so on a well-marked path, takes about an hour, or more if you linger. This is where the diversity of the plant life really hits home. Besides everyday uses, there seems to be some plant cure for every ailment you can think of.

Plants are marked so you can identify them easily, and ACTS provides a printed guide to the numbered plants, so you can discover more about a species' particular uses.

Yagua Reserve Trail

This is the trail taken by most visitors to Explorama Lodge. From the lodge you walk through beautiful rainforest for about 1.5km. It's an easy walk, without steep rises, though muddy and slippery in places. It leads to a clearing with a traditional Yagua dwelling, built in a round shape of bamboo and palm thatch. The place is used only for holding dances to entertain tourist groups.

Tourist riverboats

A popular way to see the Amazon is on a riverboat operated with Western tastes in mind. The larger boats have the charm of old river-steamers without the paddle wheels. These vessels offer quiet, comfortable cabins, tasty food, clean water, and reasonable prices (around US$175 per day). Most have airconditioning and private bathrooms. They tow a motorised canoe for excursions up small tributaries. The ship's onboard guide leads canoe excursions (birdwatching, caiman 'hunts' and piranha fishing) and land trips (trail hikes and visits to villages).

In Iquitos, two main companies (pages 280–2) run this type of vessel. Amazon Tours and Cruises is the longest established and has scheduled departures. Run by American Paul Wright, this company operates a fleet of 12 vessels, from the 42-passenger *Rio Amazonas* to six-passenger expedition boats. Theirs are the most popular riverboat trips in the region.

Jungle Expeditions runs six elegant, luxurious vessels built in a 19th-century style. Their cruises focus on regions to the west of Iquitos. Their ships (except one) are wooden-hulled over which there is disagreement on safety compared with steel hulls.

If you're in Iquitos it is cheapest to book direct, but you have no guarantee of a berth. Group tours with tour operators in *Chapter 2* offer a guaranteed cabin, one-payment convenience and added extras such as scientist tour leaders.

In this case, you have the choice of a dozen or more tour operators, who offer various trips each with a different focus. These are covered by the write-up for each vessel.

On any riverboat, noisy engines take some getting used to. The best cabins from this point of view are far from the engine-room, on upper decks, toward the bow. If you're in a cabin toward the engine on a smaller boat, take along earplugs to help you sleep. But after a couple of nights you'll barely notice the soothing chug of the engine.

These boats are very safe. Since beginning operations in the 1970s, there have been no sinkings and no ship-related fatalities. In 1998, pirates boarded a ship and robbed the passengers. This was an isolated incident as Peruvian naval vessels patrol the rivers. Generally security aboard is far better than on local riverboats.

El Arca

Built locally in 1988 and refurbished in 1995, the M/V *El Arca* measures 30m in length and weighs 208 metric tonnes. In 2000 a glass-enclosed air-conditioned small laboratory for guide and passenger use was installed. With its full complement of 32 passengers, the air-conditioned dining area may seem cramped, especially at meal-times. Food is tasty and nutritious but not gourmet.

Each air-conditioned cabin, with private toilet and shower, holds two passengers in bunk beds. Cabins are simple but adequate, but the windows are too small to enjoy the view from inside. However, there is plenty of room to enjoy the scenery from fore or aft observation decks. The bridge is equipped with ship-to-shore radio for use in case of emergency.

El Arca's scheduled itinerary takes it on a six-day cruise to the Pacaya-Samiria National Reserve west of Iquitos. This package costs from US$1,195pp (double occupancy) direct from Amazon Tours and Cruises. Book online via their offices in Iquitos or Miami or with various tour operators in Lima (eg: Peru Traces) or the US (Explorations). Check well in advance for availability. It is also available for special interest groups on a charter basis.

Río Amazonas

The *Río Amazonas* is spacious and comfortable by Amazon standards. Its sedate pace has a charm of its own. Larger than *El Arca* at 44.5m, the *Río Amazonas* is slower, but this ship delights those not in a hurry or who prefer more room. You can choose from several nice places on the boat to relax and watch the forest as it passes by. Engine noise is less noticeable on the *Río Amazonas* because of its larger size.

The vessel holds 42 passengers in twin-bed cabins each with piped airconditioning and private bath/shower. The cabins have large windows from which you can view the scenery. On the middle deck is a bar and dining room. Food is about the same as on *El Arca* and served as a buffet. It is healthy and safely prepared. Purified water is available round the clock.

You can book a cabin on the *Río Amazonas* direct from Amazon Tours and Cruises. Usually you can get a cabin if you walk in, but in the busy season book a month or two ahead.

The base price for an upper-deck cabin on the Iquitos-Leticia round trip is US$1,395 per person sharing (US$840 one way) or US$2,420 for a single person (US$1,440 one way). The sun-deck cabins are slightly more expensive. These prices include a night in Iquitos. Several companies offer all-inclusive packages from Miami. Explorations offer the round trip accompanied by a US biologist, for US$2,395 or unaccompanied for US$2,195. Tara Tours offer the trip for US$2,293.

Río Amazonas cruise

Besides offering a comfortable way to travel from Iquitos to Leticia, the *Río Amazonas* itinerary includes daily excursions to natural areas, native villages and jungle towns. Passengers are split into manageably sized groups and led by a local guide. You roam trails through rainforest and take side trips for bird-watching and piranha fishing. There are also night rides when the engine is switched off and you drift downriver, listening to the sounds of the Amazon night. You go ashore into

Indian villages to meet tribal people and take day trips into various towns en route such as Pevas, Caballacocha and San Pablo.

Natural areas along the route of the tourist boats, while very beautiful and well worth the visit, are partly disturbed secondary rainforest. Some areas were and still are selectively logged, while most land alongside the river has been inhabited at one time or another.

As you voyage sedately on the river, the forest appears pristine, with unbroken canopy topped by large trees, while below a riot of vines and lianas fight for the easiest route up the trees. Where forest meets river, birds and butterflies dance through the air in splashes of colour. Innumerable insects and amphibians sound out nature's symphony, especially around nightfall: a cacophony of different squeaks, chirps, whistles and grunts.

In isolated spots along the riverbank are palm-thatched huts on stilts, home for the local *mestizo* people but tiny in the immensity of the landscape. *Mestizos* have adopted the way of life of their Indian predecessors, with a simple existence of fishing, farming and hunting, adapted to the inexorable cycles of nature.

Other tourist riverboats out of Iquitos

Several other vessels, smaller than the *Arca* and *Río*, operate in the area and offer a more intimate look at the rainforest, as they are able to access shallower tributaries and hence probe deeper into virgin forest.

Delfin

Operated by Amazon Tours & Cruises, the *Delfin* sails west out of Iquitos to remote areas upstream. Trips on the *Delfin* promise lots of wildlife and go to remote areas to find it. Cabin accommodation has bunks, shared shower and airconditioning. The boat is 19.8m long and carries 20 passengers. It is used by various companies on charter cruises. You can book direct with Amazon Tours and Cruises (page 280) or through a US tour operator. The non-profit Rainforest Health Project (page 281) offers volunteer positions for medical workers and Oceanic Society Expeditions (page 42) has a research project studying the pink dolphin in the Pacaya-Samiria Reserve. Fishabout (page 55) offers fishing tours during 'prime low-water weeks' in August for US$2,100 a week – with airfare from Miami. Amazon Forays use the boat to run specialist mycology tours.

Amazon Explorer

Smaller still is the *Amazon Explorer* operated by Amazon Tours and Cruises. This steel-hulled mini-cruise-ship takes 16 passengers and is available for charter. The top deck is a covered observation area. The middle deck has eight air-conditioned cabins each with private bath and shower, and all with windows facing outside. This is recommended for special interest groups who want a little more comfort than the *Delfin*.

The itinerary depends on the preference of the charter organisation. Among those recommended is a seven-day cruise to the Pacaya-Samiria Reserve. Explorations (page 280) offer an eight-day fishing trip aboard the *Explorer* for US$2,495 for eight days all-inclusive from Miami.

La Esmeralda

The 27m long, 7m wide, 24-passenger *La Esmeralda* goes to remote areas upstream of Iquitos on seven-day cruises. She's the prettiest riverboat in the area, with carved arches over the doors and comfortable cabins. Each cabin has two beds and a

RUNNING THE HEADWATERS OF THE AMAZON

Only seriously fit and experienced adventurers with adequate back-up should consider starting their trip at the Amazon's source in the Peruvian Andes (see box on page 67). This involves a major expedition, such as the one described in *Running the Amazon* (see *Further Reading*, page 457). However, the less intrepid (or masochistic) can visit the Amazon's headwaters for some whitewater kayaking, and then pick the river up again at Pucallpa and continue downstream from there. Companies to contact for safe kayaking in the headwaters are:

Amazonas Explorer PO Box 722, Cusco, Peru; tel/fax: 084 236826. email: info@amazonas-explorer.com; web: www.amazonas-explorer.com; UK tel/fax: 01437 891743. This Anglo-Peruvian-Swiss operation specialises in environmentally and safety-conscious expeditions with inflatable kayaks, primarily from overseas bookings. Trips include Amazon source and rafting the Apurimac; 'exploratory expeditions' to new locations; Tambopata and Cotahuasi rivers in Peru and Río Tuichi in Bolivia.

Apumayo Expediciones Emilio Cavencio 160, Of. 201, Lima; tel: 04 423886. The new boys on the block who seem fairly well organised, though they recently closed down their Cusco office to concentrate on overseas bookings.

Explorandes San Fernando 320 Miraflores Lima 18; tel: 04 458683. The grandfathers of rafting in Peru, somewhat reflected in the age of their equipment and guides. A very good trekking agency that sells largely overseas and fancies itself as a rafting operator. Upmarket (clients and prices) 6-day trips down the Apurimac, largely so long because their guides go so infrequently to the river that they have to spend hours inspecting and portaging a number of rapids. Used to be the best. Now should gracefully retire!

Instinct Procuradores 50, just off the Plaza de Armas, Cusco; tel: 00 51 84 233451. At the cheap end of the market, owner Benjamin Muniz was largely responsible for bringing rafting the Apurimac to the backpacker market with his big group, low-budget trips.

private bathroom, hot water, shower and airconditioning. The dining and bar area has floor-to-ceiling windows so you can admire the scenery as you eat.

For after-meal relaxation aboard, rest in deckchairs on the partially covered observation deck. This offers all-round views and, at night, the guide operates a spotlight to catch the eye-shine of nocturnal animals. The itinerary varies according to season and river conditions.

Generally the boat travels up the Ucayali and Marañon rivers to visit the Pacaya-Samiria National Reserve and La Posada Lodge (page 309). Bookings are available from Jungle Expeditions in Iquitos. Retail price for the seven-day programme is US$1,950pp (double occupancy). The short four-day cruise is US$1,080pp. US tour operators include International Expeditions (page 41).

La Turmalina and La Amatista

These are the sister ships of *La Esmeralda* and have the same quality accommodation, but are larger and have more cabins. *La Turmalina* is 33m long and carries 28 passengers. *La Amatista* is slightly bigger. They follow the same cruise itinerary. Prices and on-board facilities are on a par with *La Esmeralda*. Bookings and enquiries through Jungle Expeditions or US tour operators.

La Malaquita

Measuring 26m long, this is the smallest of the Jungle Expeditions fleet. Accommodation is for eight passengers in four double cabins. Facilities are comparable with the other vessels. It is available for charter only.

La Aquamarina

This is the largest in the Jungle Expeditions fleet at 45m long and 8.5m wide. It carries 24 passengers in 12 double cabins. Built in style of a river barge, it is the only ship of the fleet constructed with a steel hull. Amenities and performance are comparable with its sister ships. *La Aquamarina*'s configuration and size make the ship spacious and ideal for visitors who want a trip with that extra touch of luxury.

Expedition boats

For access to remote areas at a reasonable cost, the most basic vessels offered by Amazon Tours and Cruises are expedition boats. Their present line-up includes three vessels. The two-deck boats are about 10m long and are powered by diesel engines. A small motorboat allows short trips away from the expedition boats.

On-board equipment includes 115/220V generators, emergency battery lighting, searchlight, depth finder and radio telephone. Safety measures include life vests, life-rings, fire extinguishers and a well-stocked first aid kit. The lower deck is divided into a lounge and dining area toward the bow. Amidships is a screened sleeping area with six to eight bunks with mosquito net and privacy curtains. Aft are the engine room, kitchen and shared toilet and cold shower. The upper deck comprises the bridge and a partly covered observation area. The crew includes an English-speaking guide, a boat driver, cook and helper.

The expedition boats are equipped to be out for seven to ten days without re-supply. All trips are a minimum two days, and can be combined with a floatplane to extend the possibilities of visits to remote areas out of Iquitos. Enquire with Amazon Tours and Cruises for prices and itineraries.

Jungle lodges in southern Peru

Most lodges in Peru's south cater to visitors to Manu National Park and Bahuaja-Sonene National Park and Tambopata National Reserve. These protected areas are discussed in the section on national parks and reserves (page 322).

Lodges near Manú National Park

To get to the vicinity of Manú National Park by road from Cusco you pass through picturesque Andean villages until arriving at Tres Cruces (4000m). From there the descent begins by boat along the Alto Madre de Dios and Manú rivers. This route takes two full days. The quickest option is by air taxi from Cusco, a 35-45 minute flight to the Boca Manú airfield. Most tour operators offer this. Travel continues by boat for four hours. The longest route is by river, starting from Puerto Maldonado.

Visitors have a choice of accommodations within and around the park (see list below).

This destination is not for those on tight budgets. Travel here is expensive and time-consuming. Accommodations may be booked up months in advance. You can make reservations for all-inclusive tours from the US, or book through a tour operator in Lima. You may be able to get a last-minute discount from tour operators in Cusco, but ensure you are dealing with a reputable tour operator. There are some shady businesses in Cusco.

For a lodge-based three-night trip into the park, expect to pay around US$500. Typically a tour (and prices) will include lodge accommodation, meals, land and river transport, and guided excursions led by English-speaking guides. Adventure trips with jungle huts and tents cost US$25–75 a day depending on what's included, group size, and standards of accommodation, food and guides. Condor Journeys in the UK (page 42) offer scholar-escorted tours here. Inti Travel and Tours (page 41) offer an eight-day camping package in the heart of the park for US$732. Atalaya's camping tour is based within a 600ha private reserve that contains a mammal and macaw clay lick, and three oxbow lakes where giant otters can be found. The reserve is located three hours downstream from the airfield. The campsite location is moved depending on the season (rainy season or dry season). Book through Atalaya (page 281), the only operator working this area. To prevent ecological impact the company does not want to build facilities here. Details for tour operators referred to below can be found in the tour operator section (pages 281–3).

Manú Wildlife Center

This world-class lodge on the banks of the Madre de Dios River offers a premium wilderness experience in a 16,000ha reserve adjacent to the 400,000ha Amarakaeri Reserved Zone, east of Manú National Park. The lodge is two hours' canoe ride from the Boca Manú airfield.

Accommodation comprises 22 fully screened bungalows with private bathrooms and hot showers. Facilities include a screened dining room and activities building with bar and small library. Food is tasty and nutritious international-style dishes. An electric generator is available for recharging video batteries.

Surrounding the centre are 48km of forest trails, laid out so that you traverse the maximum kinds of habitats in the shortest distance. Several tree platforms and a 40m canopy tower are located near flowering or fruiting trees, so increasing the chances of encountering foraging birds and monkeys. A 5m raised blind set up near a tapir clay lick offers a chance to see these elusive animals in the wild. Monkeys, birds and giant otter are among the other wildlife in the vicinity. The highlight of a trip here is the Blanquillo macaw clay lick close by the lodge.

Four days at the lodge costs US$990pp double (US$150 single supplement). The all-inclusive price includes return flight from Cusco to Boca Manú airfield and river transportation to the centre. Book through Manú Expeditions, Tropical Nature Travel or most tour operators in Cusco or Lima. In the US World Class Travel arrange tours.

Manú Wildlife Tented Camps

This camp is in the Manú Reserved Zone, near Cocha Salvador Forest. To get here you can choose a plane or bus. You fly in to the Boca Manú landing strip and then take a six-hour canoe ride to the tented camp.

The ride by private bus takes two days, stopping off for birdwatching in pristine cloudforest and for people-watching in postcard Andean towns. From Atalaya you take a motor canoe along the Madre de Dios and, depending on the conditions, sleep in a small lodge or camp in tents. The next day you proceed up the Manú River to the tented camp.

The set-up here will be familiar to those who have enjoyed luxury tent safaris in Africa. The twin occupancy walk-in tents are screened against insects and are on solid floors. Toilets and showers are shared, in a separate facility. The dining room is also screened.

Activities include canoe rides on Cocha Salvador, trails through various types of forest, and bird or monkey watching from a 17m observation tower.

The cost per person (double occupancy) is US$790 for the four-day fly-in programme or US$990 for the six day drive-in program. Single supplement and group (five or more people) rates apply. Book through Manú Expeditions, Tropical Nature Travel or other major tour operators in Cusco or Lima. The optional three-day extension to the macaw clay lick (Manú Wildlife Center) costs US$490pp.

Casa Machiguenga

Opened 1999, in the Cocha Salvador area, this 'rustic' lodge is part of a joint project combining efforts of indigenous people, tour operators and NGOs. Simple rooms have beds and mosquito nets, wood furniture and communal dining areas. Toilet and shower facilities are shared. Stays here are usually combined with stays at less basic lodges. Book through Manú Expeditions or in the UK through Tribes Travel (page 44).

Manú Lodge

This lodge is located in the Manú Reserved Zone, part of the buffer region between the national park proper and unprotected areas. Built in 1987 of mahogany cut from logs left by floods, the main building consists of two halves linked by raised walkways. The first half contains a bar, lobby, and a dining room/lounge. Above this are two double rooms with views of the nearby lake. The top level features an observation room. The second half includes most accommodation with ten double rooms along a screened porch. The entire lodge is screened and accessible from outside through screened double doors. Kitchen, showers and latrines are located away from the main building. Book direct through Manú Nature Tours or other Peru tour operators.

Cloud Forest Lodge

This relatively new lodge is one of the few located in cloudforest, for which it is named. The site is on forest-covered slopes adjacent to a tall waterfall. This lodge is reached in six to seven hours from Cusco in the Trans-Manú bus, or by air 20 minutes from Cusco followed by a two-hour ride by minibus. Birds in the area include cock-of-the-rock, fruit-eating tanagers, golden-headed quetzal and Amazonian umbrella bird. Woolly monkey are often sighted.

The lodge can used as a base for short rafting trips along the Qosñipata, Qeros, and Tono rivers, tributaries of the Madre de Dios River. Bookings are through Manú Nature Tours.

Tambo Blanquillo Lodge

This remote and basic facility is on the south bank of the Madre de Dios River, on the edge of the Manú National Park. You first take a 45-minute flight to the Manú airfield then take a motorised canoe two hours down the Madre de Dios River.

The lodge consists of dormitories on an open platform with 26 beds with mosquito nets. A bamboo partition between beds provides some privacy. Shared bathroom facilities are within the complex. Local-style food is served in the fully screened dining room. Boiled drinking water is available at all times.

The main attraction of the lodge is the *colpa* (clay lick) located on the riverbank about 10 minutes downstream from the lodge. From 40 to 200 macaws, depending on the season and weather, regularly gather here. Book through Manú Safaris/Explorandes or other tour operators in Cusco. Silvana Tours' all-inclusive programme from Cusco costs US$964pp for a group of two to four people.

Cock-of-the-Rock Lodge

This top-class lodge is named for the world's largest known display area of the scarlet Andean cock-of-the-rock. Most days, 4 to 25 males dance and call at this spot near the lodge. The best time to visit is from August to November when display behaviour is most intense. From April to June display activity declines considerably.

Established 1997, the lodge is in a 5600ha reserve 1600m up. This cool, mosquito-free location appeals to those who want a different experience to that offered by the lowland rainforest. The lodge is 180km from Cusco, six hours' drive. It usually takes longer, as people want to stop to observe or photograph the latest view, bird, or exotic flower.

Eight twin-bed cabins each have private bathroom and hot water. A separate complex has six double-occupancy rooms with shared bath facilities. A two-day programme at the lodge costs US$540pp including transport from Cusco. Book through Tropical Nature Travel or any of the major Lima or Cusco tour operators. In the US you can book through World Class Travel.

Pantiacolla Lodge

At 550m in upland forest, Pantiacolla Lodge is on the boundary of lowland and mountain habitats on the upper Madre de Dios River. The facilities are basic, comprising 16 beds in eight cabins with communal toilets and showers. This lodge is used as part of longer programmes with Tropical Nature Travel. A six-day programme including one night here, a night at Cock-of-the-Rock Lodge and three nights at Manú Wildlife Center costs US$1,290pp double occupancy or US$1,540 for singles. Lama Tours offers a nine-day combined camping-lodge tour from Cusco that includes two nights here for US$845pp (double).

Maskoitania

Located on the edge of the park, this basic lodge comprises 12 beds with mosquito net, kitchen and dining room. A separate cabin has toilets and unheated shower. Close by is a small campsite for people planning a long stay. Atalaya's ten-day tour includes three nights here and remaining nights at other lodges for US$650pp from Cusco. Book online or at their Cusco office.

Lodges near Bahuaja-Sonene National Park and Tambopata National Reserve

Access to this protected area is through Puerto Maldonado, a rather non-descript oil town of about 25,000 on the northern edge of the protected area. Basic hotels, banks and internet cafés meet the standard needs. For jungle tours you can make arrangements in town but a pre-arranged tour is more likely to offer more peace of mind as some local guides are of dubious intent. Flights from Lima or Cusco serve the town (details on page 285). Road access from Cusco (US$15 by truck or bus) is a rough journey taking three or four days, depending on road conditions. There's a Bolivian immigration office in town if you're heading into Bolivia. Visitors to Tambopata have several choices for accommodation, summarised below. Unless otherwise stated, these lodges are built on the native pattern, have similar buffet menus, purified water and include basic amenities. Most lodges are close by the world famous macaw clay licks, featured in the January 1994 issue of *National Geographic* magazine.

Wasai Maldonado Lodge

This luxury lodge is in Puerto Maldonado (Plaza Grau No 1) a block from the main plaza, close by the town's amenities. Air-conditioned rooms include refrigerator, hot water, fans, colour television and private bathroom. The restaurant serves regional and international dishes. A bar overlooks the river, and there is a small swimming pool. The lodge is the starting and finishing point for all Wasai tours which include day and half-day tours around Puerto Maldonado. Cost is US$36pp single or US$24pp double. Book through Wasai or Atalaya, or in the UK with Peruvian Secrets.

Explorer's Inn

Established 1976, this lodge was the first established in Tambopata Reserve. About one and a half hours by speedboat from Puerto Maldonado, it comprises seven thatched cabins housing 30 screened twin-bed rooms. Each room has a private bath. Lighting is by kerosene or, in the dining room, solar-charged battery. Beyond the buildings are a medicinal plant garden, and extensive trails leading to various lakes and clay licks. Book through Peruvian Safaris (see page 282). US tour operators include Field Guides with ornithologist-led tours, Holbrook Travel or Ecoexpeditions (pages 40–1).

Tambopata Research Center

This 13-bedroom lodge is about five hours by motorised canoe from Posada Amazonas. TRC is currently headquarters for a long-term macaw research programme. Macaw nesting biology is studied October to March, and clay lick activity the rest of the year. Affiliated with world-renowned Duke University (North Carolina), the **Tambopata Macaw Project** focuses on the ecology and natural history of large macaws. Besides scientific investigations, the project aims to empower the local community with the skills to operate ecotourism facilities and hence benefit directly from the large number of visitors to the area. Volunteers can apply online (email: djb4@duke.edu; web: www.duke.edu/~djb4/index.html).

The lodge's Peruvian biologists and professional researchers provide the chance for in-depth scientific perspective of the reserve's natural history. Besides the macaw clay lick, numerous macaw nesting sites are also nearby. The basic programme with two nights at Posada Amazonas and two nights at TRC costs US$590pp. Make reservations well in advance with Rainforest Expeditions or in the US through Journeys International (page 41).

Sandoval Lake Lodge

Within the Tambopata Reserve, Sandoval Lake Lodge overlooks the lake. During the dry season, visitors are virtually guaranteed to see rare giant otters but in the rainy season the otters tend to fish in the flooded forest bordering the lake.

TREES: CONSERVING TAMBOPATA

TReeS was founded in 1986 to promote the conservation of the area on a sustainable basis in the long term. The society supports Peruvian biologists to enable them to undertake field research and applied investigations; works with the local native people to empower them to retain their traditional activities, especially with respect to health care; supports the responses of local representative organisations to explorations within the region by multi-national oil companies; and provides advice to those visiting the area from abroad. Resident naturalist programmes offer a few places annually to biology graduates, enabling them to undertake research while guiding tourists to the lodges. Further details from TReeS, c/o 64 Belsize Park, London NW3 4EH, UK, or c/o 5455 Agostina Court, Concord, CA 94521, USA.

A 40-minute boat journey from Puerto Maldonado down the Madre de Dios River is followed by a ride on a 'rainforest rickshaw' for 3km on a trail through primary rainforest. Then you are paddled in small canoes through flooded forest to the lodge.

The lodge comprises 25 double rooms with private bathrooms (including hot showers) and fans. Facilities include a dining room, a common area with hammocks, and a fully stocked bar. Electricity is available during mealtimes and at night to 23:00.

A three day stay costs US$180pp double occupancy. Book through most tour operators in Cusco, direct through Tropical Nature Travel or take Lama Tours' package from Cusco for US$270. Tara Tours (page 42) offer an extension to their Machu Picchu tour from Cusco for US$475. Also in the US, World Class Travel offer (page 281) combination stays with the comparable Heath River Wildlife Center from US$490pp for a three-day tour.

Posada Amazonas
This 24-room lodge is two hours' canoe ride from Puerto Maldonado. Rooms are large and have en-suite bathrooms with showers. Meals are served buffet-style with international, Peruvian and local food. Lodge staff are from the local Ese'eja Native Community who co-own the lodge. Hikes are led by Ese'eja and English-speaking Peruvian naturalists. Fifteen minutes' walk from the lodge, a 35m tower provides access to the forest canopy. A three-day programme costs US$190pp sharing. Book through Rainforest Expeditions.

Wasai Tambopata Lodge
This lodge is 120km from Puerto Maldonado down the Tambopata River. Four large bungalows and the central lodge building constructed from local materials are situated on the riverbank. The lodge accommodates a total of 40 people in screened double rooms with private bathrooms. Facilities include a common area with hammocks, a research centre and library, and fishing equipment. There are 20km of forest trails, a local *mestizo* community, waterfalls, and clay licks. A 12-day programme is US$680. Per diem prices start at US$56 for a single room. Budget backpackers can use the camping area next to the lodge for US$8pp (no meals). Book through Wasai at their city offices or online, or through Atalaya. Peru Secrets have packages from the UK.

Machiguenga Center for Tropical Studies
This academic research centre is located on the Urubamba River. It's a 50-minute flight from Cusco over the Vilcabamba Range to the Indian village of Timpia. Ten double-occupancy rooms have modern bathrooms and hot water. The entire complex is screened with added mosquito nets for each bed. The spacious dining and common room has a fully stocked bar and reading area.

The centre is entirely owned by the Machiguenga Indian community. They offer educational workshops on traditions such as arrow-making, weaving, medicinal plant lore and story-telling.

Within easy access of the lodge are macaw clay-lick areas that can be reached on foot or by river and can be viewed from blinds a few metres away.

Close by is the Pongo de Mainique Canyon – a 50-metre-wide, 3.5km-long break in the Andes through which flows the Urubamba River. Raft the Urumbamba for the unforgettable ride through the Pongo. The cost is US$1,150pp on a four day trip, booked through Tropical Nature Travel (page 281). In the US, contact World Class Travel for reservations.

Heath River Wildlife Center

Six hours from Puerto Maldonado down the Madre de Dios and Heath rivers this basic but comfortable lodge comprises screened bungalows with large living area, comfortable beds, and a private bath with hot-water shower. In the vicinity are macaw and mammal clay licks and miles of rainforest trails. Stays here are usually combined with other lodges such as Sandoval Lake Lodge. Book through World Class Travel or major Lima and Cusco tour operators.

NATIONAL PARKS AND WILDLIFE RESERVES
Northern Peru
Pacaya-Samiria National Reserve

Rounding a bend in the blackwater Samiria River, your riverboat chugs gently past densely packed vegetation: huge-leaved *Elaeis* palms, morning glory vines, bright green *Heliconia* and wild ginger and *Cercropia*. Everywhere the ropes, strings and cables of chaotic lianas, arums and philodendrons tie everything into an impenetrable mass. Beyond is the canopy. Giant kapok and ficus trees poke leafy crowns above the green swathe. Along the riverbanks hundreds upon hundreds of great egrets roosting in trees and shrubs take to the air as the boat disrupts their reveries. The silence of this spectacle is broken only by the occasional croaks of cormorants and the staccato calls of solitary kingfishers that resent the intrusion. Shimmering clouds of sulphur butterflies rise from shallow beaches. Oblivious to the above-water drama, pairs of foraging pink dolphins break the water surface, leaving circles of expanding ripples. The sense of awe is slightly tainted by feelings of guilt for having disturbed this immaculate habitat. This is the Pacaya-Samiria.

The reserve is the only officially protected area entirely within Peru's lowland Amazon and is the country's second largest protected area. At 2.8 million hectares it's almost the size of Belgium! The boundaries form a triangle with the Ucayali River to the south and the Marañón River to the north. The western boundary follows the border between the districts of Loreto and San Martin, marked by the Río Samiria, a tributary of the Marañón.

The nearest sizeable town is Nauta, about 110km from Iquitos but you should arrange visits to the park with tour operators in Iquitos. Most Iquitos tour agencies charge US$50 or more per day to travel here. To get the most from a visit to the park book a trip through an established tour operator, which is expensive, but also relatively hassle-free. There's no fixed accommodation within the protected area; there are a handful of temporary refuges only. Excursions are based from lodges situated along bordering rivers. A better way to experience the Pacaya is on a tourist riverboat cruise into the reserve.

During low-water season access to some areas is hindered. During high water season (April to August) you can reach remoter areas and this is also when it is easier to observe primates and other mammals. On the other hand, aquatic species such as caiman and otters are readily seen during low water, and local and migratory birds are more abundant. Whichever time of year you go, the wildlife is spectacular.

Take care when researching a trip into the Pacaya-Samiria – Iquitos tour operators are keen to offer things you're just not going to get. Independent travel can be arranged but is not recommended due to the remoteness of the area.

In Iquitos, Rumbo al Dorado (Napo 449, Iquitos; tel: 235053; email: greenlife@pacaya-samiria.com; web: www.pacaya-samiria.com) offer lodge and camping tours within the park, including a chance to interact with local communities. Amazon Tours and Cruises (page 280) offers a six-day cruise up the Samiria River to Ranger Station 3 deep within the reserve. The US-based Rainforest Health Project (page 281) has a medical team working to bring basic healthcare in areas around the park. They offer travel opportunities (eg: US$2,500 for seven nights, including airfare from Miami) combined with volunteer work. Greentracks (page 41) offers speciality tours including herpetology trips based onboard the M/V *Delfin* from US$1,869. Chancas Expeditions (page 282) offers ten-day low-impact camping trips in dug-out canoes from US$850 beginning and ending in Tarapoto.

Explornapo Reserve

This is a private reserve of 100,000ha, whose owners hope to raise money with donations and income from ecotourism to buy more land and expand to 400,000ha. At present the reserve encompasses the watersheds of the upper Apayacu and Sucusari Rivers, protecting pristine rainforest. The reserve was set up by a joint effort of scientists, officials and tour operators. The initial US$60,000 needed for its inception was raised by International Expeditions' First International Rainforest Workshop, held in 1991. The major attraction of the reserve is Explorama's canopy walkway, a direct outcome of the workshop.

Southern Peru

Tambopata National Reserve/Bahuaja National Park system and Manú National Park are the government-protected rainforest areas in southern Peru. Southwest of the upper Amazon region, these areas are relatively undisturbed and offer unrivalled opportunities for wildlife viewing and wilderness. As they are not directly connected by air or river to major cities they are time consuming and expensive to visit. Macaw activity at clay licks, the reason most people visit, is highest between August and October.

Cusco is the main gateway into the region, so most visitors combine a visit to the parks with a tour to Machu Picchu.

Manú Biosphere Reserve

This is one of the planet's last great forest wildernesses. Manú was declared a national park in 1973 and a World Biosphere Reserve and World Heritage Site in 1977. The protected area comprises 1.53 million hectares of diverse lowland and montane forest habitats around the headwaters of the Manú River. Here is the world's most diverse flora and fauna. Also in the park live indigenous groups that were not contacted until recently.

Wildlife commonly seen by visitors includes giant otter, black caiman, jaguar and ocelot. You are virtually guaranteed to see several of the 13 or more primate species. Manú is prized by ornithologists and the bird count has topped one thousand. There are several small macaw and parrot clay licks throughout the reserve.

The Biosphere Reserve comprises three zones. There is a lot of confusion among tourists about this, and some tour operators claim to take people 'inside the national park.' This is not allowed without a guide on an organised tour, and the tour operator must get the necessary permits. Otherwise, the Reserve Zone and National Park Zone are open only to indigenous people and scientists, having been closed to casual tourism since the early 90s. If you want to go on your own, you can enter the Cultural Zone without a permit.

Bahuaja-Sonene National Park and Tambopata National Reserve

In 1995 the Peruvians established the Bahuaja-Sonene National Park. In September 2000 Peruvian President Fujimori signed a decree doubling Bahuaja-Sonene's size and adding the 253,282ha Tambopata National Reserve and a 261,203ha buffer zone west of the park. This brought the total protected area to almost 4 million hectares – just smaller than Switzerland. The Madre de Dios region east of Cusco along the Brazil/Bolivia border is a Worldwide Fund for Nature World Centre of Plant Diversity. Much of this falls within the protected areas.

This is one of the hottest of biodiversity hotspots. The region holds several world records for plant and animal biodiversity. It holds the world's highest 24-hour bird species count: 331 species. In a single location, biologists counted 550 bird species and 1,200 types of butterfly. The bird species total is over 600 and mammal species number at least 160.

For tourists, Tambopata's major attraction is the region's biggest colpa or clay lick. This is one of nature's great spectacles. Hundreds of macaws and parrots gather to nibble on the clay cliffs. Birds perform this behaviour mainly from August to October, due to seasonal decline of preferred foods. Minerals in the clay help the birds digest unpalatable food and survive during a period when they might otherwise go hungry.

Sandoval is among the most important ecological areas in the park. The focal point is Sandoval Lake – an oxbow lake formed by the shifting course of the Madre de Dios River. Sandoval Lake is a mature lake environment supporting a high diversity of wildlife and flora. Blue-and-gold and red-bellied macaws inhabit flooded palm forest on the lake's west end. Primates include brown capuchin, red howler, saddle-backed tamarin, and night monkeys.

Above left Bird of paradise
flower, *Heliconia* sp (PO)

Above Lady's veil fungus (PO)

Left Passion fruit flower,
Passiflora sp (PO)

Below Cup fungi (PO)

Left Strangler fig
buttress roots (PO)

Right Giant water
lily, *Victoria
amazonica* (RH)

Below Rainbow over
Madre de Dios
River, Peru (PO)

Bolivia

11

Simón Bolívar's wave of liberation ended in Bolivia, the country
that bears his name in tribute. Bolivia is a relative newcomer to
the travelling scene having for a long time lived in the shadow of
its more ambitious and vocal neighbours – Peru and Brazil. But
the quiet one in the middle is attracting visitors who are prepared to
risk a few of life's comforts. The reward? A special experience that
leads to a strong affection for this less well-known but endearing
country.

FACTS AND FIGURES
Geography
Bolivia's northernmost extent is 9° south of the Equator, with the extreme south a
degree north of the Tropic of Capricorn. Slightly over one million square
kilometres in area, Bolivia is landlocked by five nations: Brazil to the north and
east, Paraguay and Argentina to the south, and Peru and Chile to the west.

Bolivia encompasses a broad range of biomes, as you might expect from a
country ranging in altitude from 6,500m above sea level down to just 175m. The
Andes splits in two before entering the country from Peru, creating a vast central
plateau which stretches south from Lake Titicaca for over 800km. At an average
altitude of 3,750m, the cold, windswept and remote *altiplano* is a harsh
environment.

BASIC FACTS
Official name República de Bolivia
Area 1,098,581km² (424,165 miles²)
Population 8,476,200
Capital La Paz
Largest city (population) La Paz (811,400)
Main Amazon cities Santa Cruz de la Sierra (1,115,400) and
Rurrenabaque
Official languages Spanish (60%), Quechua (25%), Aymara (15%)
Date of independence August 6 1825
Major industries mining, natural gas, petroleum, agriculture
GDP per capita US$2,600 (2001 est)
Currency boliviano (US$1=Bs7.51; £1=Bs11.45)
Major attractions Salar de Uyuni, Lake Titicaca, Madidi, Manuripi Heath
and Noel Kempff Mercado National Parks
National holidays Jan 1, Carnival (week before Lent), Easter, Aug 6,
Oct 12, Dec 25

BOLIVIA

UP IN FLAMES
One strong human influence on the climate is the *chaqueo* – the annual burning every September of land to clear and prepare it for the next year's crops which is believed to bring rain. It is difficult to know whether the chaqueo plays any role in speeding up the arrival of the rainy season, but it isn't difficult to see that the skies of Bolivia are filled with smog during the burning. The government has tried to outlaw the practice but age-old traditions rarely change as a result of government dictates. Meanwhile, forest is destroyed by out-of-control fires.

To the north and east of the Andes, the mountains quickly fall away. Rivers cut a network of steep-sided valleys, in the north called the *yungas,* and the dry barren vegetation of the *altiplano* is soon replaced by cloudforest, montane forest and eventually tropical rainforest.

As the last few hills of the Andes ripple out across the eastern and northern lowlands, tropical rainforest and savannah take over. The Amazon lowlands of Bolivia constitute 54% of the country's territory.

Rivers
Waters from three-quarters of Bolivian territory flow into the Amazon Basin, including the vast Madeira-Mamoré-Grande system. Starting as a small stream to the south of Santa Cruz, the river quickly grows to form the Grande, travelling 3,200km before joining the Amazon River downstream from Manaus. The three other major rivers in Bolivia all join this river before leaving the national territory.

The Río Iténez, starting in the lowlands close to Noel Kempff Mercado National Park, marks Bolivia's northeastern boundary with Brazil. The Beni River flows from the northern slopes of the Eastern Cordillera, descending rapidly past lowland gold-mining towns. Upon reaching lowlands it meanders leisurely through the jungle towns of Rurrenabaque and Riberalta to join the Mamoré. The Madre de Dios River begins life in Peru's Manú National Park, crossing the border into Bolivia at Puerto Heath and then travelling east to join the Beni River north of Riberalta.

Climate
The rainy season, lasting from November to April, coincides with the southern summer. As altitude decreases clouds are more likely to produce rain. Temperatures on the *altiplano* swing from one extreme to another – comfortable during the day, regularly below freezing at night.

The *yungas* are pleasantly warm year-round – in the mid-20s celsius with regular rainfall between December and March

In the northern lowlands, comfortably warm winter temperatures in the high-20s contrast with hot and oppressively humid summer months. Between December and March, tropical downpours may change the streets of Santa Cruz and other lowland towns into rivers and streams.

Flora and fauna
Bolivia is among the world's top ten countries in terms of the number of vertebrate species. It is seventh in the world for bird species richness, with more than 1,300 species.

The country is host to more than 220 species of reptiles and more than 100 species of amphibians. Over 40% of known neotropical mammals, 316 species, are found in Bolivia, with ten of them being endemic to the country. The rare short-eared dog has been sighted in both Madidi and Noel Kempff Mercado National Parks. In the less-populated parks of Bolivia, jaguars and smaller members of the cat family are still to be found, while 20 species of primate have been identified throughout the country.

Over 22,000 plant species have been recorded from Bolivia, including over 2,000 species of orchid and 90 different types of palm.

Land use

Geography and weather conditions play the greatest role in determining land use. Around one quarter of the country is so high that only the hardiest crops survive, while the steep-sided slopes going down to the lowlands make intensive farming difficult. In lowland areas with road access, farming and ranching are prevalent.

People
Population and ethnic groups

Nearly 60% of Bolivia's population of 8,476,200 lives in cities and towns which are growing at over 4% a year, while the country's population overall increases by just 2.4% annually.

Bolivia, like many South American countries, includes a culturally diverse mixture of peoples. The main groups are of *mestizo* (30%), Quechua (25%), Aymara (17%) and European (12%) descent. Urban Indians or *cholos* make up a significant proportion of the population of La Paz and many other cities.

The lowland rural indigenous population is between 180,000 and 220,000. They comprise over 40 different ethnic groups including the Chiquitano, Mojeño, Chimane, Baure and Itonama. Comprising at least 11 linguistic families, these lowland communities lack the coherence and the numbers of the highland Indians. It is within these groups that the worst provision of education and healthcare is to be found and only recently have they begun to protest at their unfair treatment within the Bolivian political system.

Languages

Spanish is the official language of Bolivia, spoken by over 60% of the population. Quechua, the language of the Inca Empire, is the *lingua franca* for some 25% of the population particularly in highland areas. A slightly smaller percentage speak Aymara, the language used throughout the Bolivian highlands before the arrival of the Spanish or the Incas.

Languages in lowland areas reflect ethnic diversity. Bolivia has lost many indigenous languages – as a result of dominance by the three major languages and extensive migration within the country.

Education

Bolivia's education system has recently undergone several changes, pushing for better and more relevant teaching. Elementary education is free and, in theory, compulsory. In reality getting to a school in remote areas is impossible. Here, lessons are broadcast on the radio to outlying areas with outreach workers travelling the country to supplement the lessons.

There are eight state-funded universities, the largest being Universidad Mayor de San Andrés (UMSA) in La Paz, and a ten private universities.

Culture

While archaeologists argue over the beginnings of South American pottery, Bolivians happily tell the world that the true home of ceramics can be found in the Bolivian Andes with the Tiahuanaco culture, which dates back to 500BC. A contentious claim is also put forward that the geometric designs of the Tiahuanaco III era – lasting from 300BC to the first century AD – were the inspiration for one of the 20th century's great painting movements. Apparently a friend of Picasso's, on returning from a trip to Bolivia, told him of geometric animals carved on ceramics near Tiahuanaco.

Weavings are also an inspiration and delight. Detailed *aguayos*, essentially square pieces of cloth woven with ornate designs used for carrying anything from babies to fruit, vegetables to firewood, are in common use throughout the country. Older *aguayos* are available on Calle Sagárnaga, some of which are centuries-old genuine antiques and priced accordingly. Modern weaving techniques have seen the introduction of mass-produced *aguayos* fashioned from an array of day-glo colours.

Music includes the haunting melodies of the panpipe and woodwind instruments, more correctly called the *quena*. The frantic strumming of the *charango* is another typical sound of the Andes. This small guitar-like instrument was, until recently, commonly made using the plates of a (dead) armadillo as the sound box.

Lowland cultures tend to take second stage to those of the highlands. To the north of Santa Cruz, attention focuses on the mission towns encompassing Chiquitania which at Easter attract large numbers of pilgrims. The main cultural expression is through fiestas.

If there is a reason to have a party Bolivians will find it. Bolivian religious festivals merge complex Andean mythology and history with Roman Catholicism. The bizarre cultural mix, colour and noise of these fiestas is unforgettable.

In the lowlands, the Fiesta del Santo Patrono de Moxos overruns the small town of San Ignacio de Moxos, between Rurrenabaque and Trinidad. Ornate costumes and feather head-dresses, accompanied by dancing and the near-compulsory drinking, attract thousands of visitors to the normally quiet town at the end of July.

The main national carnival of the year is La Diablada in Oruro on the *altiplano*. A procession paying tribute to the Socavón de la Virgen (Cave of the Virgin) winds its way up the hill to the church overlooking the town where the Virgin resides. Thousands of dancers dressed in elaborate costumes dance, drink and meander their way along the 8km route on the last weekend before Ash Wednesday.

In La Paz the procession of El Señor del Gran Poder, a similar style of carnival, fills the city's streets at the beginning of May.

Independence Day on August 6, or the weekend closest to it, is carnival time throughout the country. Very similar to other festivals, the Independence Day parade in La Paz tends to be a slightly more formal occasion with government officials and dignitaries in official attendance.

Religion

Bolivia is nominally 95% Roman Catholic. But a quick trip to the shaman or herbalist's market in La Paz will give you a pretty good idea that other forces are at work. In rural and urban areas, particularly among Indian communities, there are still strong beliefs in the power of *pachamama*. This Mother Earth figure, if duly respected, protects those who live on or in her. Several rituals paying tribute to *pachamama* throughout the year are sufficient to keep her on your side.

A brief history
Pre-conquest
The Tiahuanacans of the *altiplano* left behind astonishing monuments and clearly attained a high degree of sophistication and organisation. Their buildings, irrigation systems and intricate ceramics and textiles attest to their achievements. In the ruined city you can still see tight-fitting stonework and lintel doorways that suggest the Tiahuanacans were the Inca's antecedents. Archaeologists have found indications that environmental changes caused the empire's sudden decline around AD1100 and subsequent fragmentation into several smaller autonomous Aymara kingdoms. The less numerous Aymaras were unable to stop the advance of the well-organised and expansionist Incas around AD1350. The Inca Empire stretched throughout the Bolivian *altiplano* and as far east as Samaipata near Santa Cruz. Although the Incas introduced Quechua as the *lingua franca*, the smaller Aymara kingdoms retained much of their character as well as their Aymara language.

Post-conquest
The conquest of the Inca Empire began in 1532. The Spanish conquistadors reaped such golden rewards from Peru in such a short period of time that the hunger to continue exploration quickly brought the Spanish into the territory of Alto Peru – modern-day Bolivia.

Although the Spanish failed to find the legendary gilded city of El Dorado, they could content themselves with the riches of Cerro Rico (Rich Hill) in Potosí. The quantities of silver taken from here financed the rapid development of an administrative infrastructure within Bolivia, including the cities of La Plata, now called Sucre (1538), and La Paz (1548).

Independence
As with much of South America, the French and North American revolutions of the 18th century encouraged the descendants of Spanish immigrants – in Bolivia to push for independence. But it wasn't until the liberation wave of the Venezuelan Simón Bolívar reached Alto Peru in 1825 that the country was free to determine its own future. On independence the country was renamed República de Bolívar and Bolívar's General Antonio José de Sucre became the country's first president.

With so many newly formed countries in South America, it is hardly surprising that most tried to extend their boundaries. Between 1835 and 1935 Bolivia's neighbours acquired national territory that reduced the size of the country by half.

The rubber boom of the late 19th century that swept through Amazonia saw Bolivia, as home to some of the most productive rubber stands producing the best quality rubber, enjoy a brief flurry of prosperity. At considerable cost, a railroad was to be built from the north of the country to transport rubber down to Porto Velho in Brazil, removing the need to carry cargo over several sets of rapids along the Mamoré and Madeira rivers. In return for the railroad Bolivia ceded the rubber-rich state of Acre to Brazil. Work began in 1890 and resulted in the death of over 6,200 workers. By 1910 the rubber industry showed signs of imminent collapse. Demand diluted, the source of income for Bolivia's lowlands was thwarted, and the railroad never completed.

The 20th century
The Chaco War (1932–35) proved costly to Bolivia. An area of 243,000km^2 was lost to Paraguay and 65,000 soldiers, mainly *campesinos* or peasants, were killed in

the fighting. Indeed the war set the stage for the political developments of the 20th century.

Increasingly disgruntled by their treatment at the hands of wealthy landholders in the name of national pride, *campesinos* rallied behind the newly formed Movimiento Nacionalista Revolucionario (MNR). The 1952 revolution saw the MNR leader Víctor Paz Estenssoro take power, and nationalisation of the mining industry and agrarian and educational reform followed. The revolution changed the consciousness of the country's population. It is still easy to get grass-roots support for a city-stopping march or a roadblocking protest.

The 1970s and 1980s saw an excessive number of military coups. The low points include seven years of presidency for General Hugo Banzer Suárez, ending in 1978, whose term saw thousands of political dissidents imprisoned while he handed out favours to the agricultural *nouveaux riches* of his home department Santa Cruz. His legacy to the nation was US$1.8 billion of foreign debt.

Crippled economically, Bolivia suffered through three presidential elections and five military coups between 1978 and 1982. The government of General Luís García Meza, with the assistance of former Nazis including Klaus Barbie, ruled over a period of torture, human rights abuses and disappearances. Bolivia's image as a plaything for the ruling classes was reaffirmed as Meza and his cronies amassed huge personal fortunes through cocaine trafficking.

The 1980s saw Bolivia shift its support behind the democratic process and aim for economic stability. Annual inflation of 25,000%, over-staffed state industries and high unemployment demanded drastic austerity measures. Plans to return state industries to the private sector led to huge numbers of redundancies, industrial disputes and increased hardship, with few foreign investors interested in taking up the opportunities. The 1980s also ushered coca leaves – a central part of Andean culture – into the international cocaine trade. Attempts to eradicate non-traditional crops gave momentum to the creation and increasing strength of the *cocaleros*.

The presidency of MNR chief Gonzalo Sánchez de Lozada, beginning in 1993, introduced 'capitalisation' to the Bolivian economy. The process – akin to privatisation - moved responsibility for nationalised industries into the private sector. Although not booming, the economy experienced several years of growth with inflation at a relatively low 10%.

In August of 1997, Hugo Banzer and Paz Zamoro's coalition ticket returned Banzer to the presidency. The reformed president, elected as a committed democrat, was forced to stand down in late 2001 through illness and died in May 2002. His deputy Jorge Quiroga assumed the presidency. Elections gave Sánchez de Lozada a second term in office. A close-run election put Evo Morales, leader of the *cocaleros* and organiser of many roadblocking protests, in second place. Lozada's acceptance speech called for Bolivians to work together to fight regional and national economic depression and for the country to 'unite, because unity is strength.' Morales, as leader of the opposition in Congress, will add an interesting unknown quantity to the presidential term.

Money

The *boliviano* depreciates slowly against the dollar. Take dollars or American Express dollar travellers' cheques. Pounds and Euros are difficult to change.

If you want to change travellers' cheques or cash go to one of the exchange houses on La Paz's Avenida Camacho. If you have any problems with travellers' cheques the American Express offices are in Turismo Magri on Avenida 16 de Julio 1490, Edificio Avenida, 5th floor.

Changing cash dollars outside the main cities is usually possible if you look hard enough, but the best option is to change as much into bolivianos as you think you will need before reaching the next city. Changing travellers' cheques outside of cities is difficult.

Budget travellers can easily get by in Bolivia on US$20 per day, but may have to choose between excursions. A more realistic figure placing few limits on activities would require around US$40 per day.

Highlights

Bolivia's Amazon region has several national parks and nature reserves. Madidi National Park and Manuripi Heath Nature Reserve are north of La Paz but neither is particularly easy to access. Both can be visited on an organised tour or independently. In either case, a knowledgeable guide gives insight into the wildlife, geography and history. Some trips are land-based. These go a short distance each day, interspersed with forest or mountain treks. Alternatively, raft trips last up to three weeks and travel through the parks to give an intimate experience of riverside habitat.

To the east, near Santa Cruz, Amboró National Park is opening up to simple trekking options. North of Santa Cruz Noel Kempff Mercado National Park protects unspoiled lowland rainforest and a Precambrian sandstone plateau that rises abruptly out of the lowlands to 550m. Also in the east is the privately operated Ríos Blanco y Negro Wildlife Reserve, completely off the beaten track.

Boats travel many of Bolivia's rivers but independent travel is limited by the lack of regular services. If you have time, wait and try your luck. Travel down the larger rivers is possible although you may have to take several different boats. Bolivia's only flotel – floating hotel – plys the Mamoré River from Puerto Villaroel, south of Trinidad. This trip takes you through rivers and lagoons surrounded by rainforest and savannah.

Only recently has ecotourism caught on in Bolivia. Expect newer agencies to experience occasional teething troubles, but on the flip side, the national parks remain mostly pristine. If you can handle less comfort, the effort required to travel to the Bolivian Amazon is worthwhile.

Away from the Amazon Basin, Bolivia has dozens of travel options. You can trek in the Andes, perhaps including a visit to the world's highest navigable lake, Lake Titicaca. The pure white expanses of the salt flats of Uyuni in southern Bolivia are an unforgettable experience – but a tough overland journey. For insight of a different kind, visit the historically important mining town of Potosí.

Tour operators
In Bolivia
Academia Nacional de Ciencias de Bolivia Av 16 de Julio 1732, La Paz; tel/fax: 235 0612; email: cmiranda@ebb.rds.org.bo; web: www.comsats.org.pk/br/brhome.html; postal address: Casilla 5829, La Paz, Bolivia. Coordinates trips to Beni Biosphere Reserve.

America Tours SRL Av 16 de Julio (El Prado) 1490, Edicio Avenida, Ground Floor No 9 (at the back), across from Monje Campero Cinema; tel: 237 4204; fax: 231 0023; email: jmiranda@ceibo.entelnet.bo; web: www.america-ecotours.com. Takes bookings for Chalalan Ecolodge in Madidi National Park, pampas tours and to Noel Kempff in the eastern lowlands.

EcoBolivia Foundation Calle Colombia, Plaza San Pedro; tel/fax: 231 5974; email: ecobolivia@mail.megalink.com; postal address: Casilla 8505, La Paz. Arranges trips to Chalalan Ecolodge in Madidi National Park.

Fremen Tours Edificion Handal, Galeria Comerical Of #13; tel: 240 8200; fax: 241 7327; email: info@andes-amazonia.com; web: www.andes-amazonia.com. This family-run company, with offices in all major Bolivian cities, arranges trips to Noel Kempff, runs flotel trips down the Río Mamoré and a broad range of trips in the Bolivian Amazon and Andes. **Fundación Amigos de la Naturaleza (FAN)** Km 7 on the road to Samaipata; tel: 355 6800; fax: 354 7383; email: sduque@fan-bo.org; web: www.fan-bo.org; postal address: Casilla 2241, Santa Cruz, Bolivia. Organises trips to Noel Kempff Mercado National Park.

In Peru
Amazonas Explorer Has rafting trips down the Tuichi River through the Madidi National Park but these must be booked in advance.

In the UK
In addition to companies mentioned in *Chapter 2* (see pages 41–3), the only UK-based specialist company is **Magic of Bolivia** 182 Westbourne Grove, London W11 2RH; tel: 020 7221 7310; fax: 020 7727 8756; email: magicofbolivia@bigfoot.com; web: www.bolivia.co.uk. They offer escorted tours of Bolivia including the Amazon.

In the US
Explore Bolivia 2510 North 47th St, Ste 207, Boulder, CO 80301; tel: 877 708 8810; fax: 303 545 6239; email: info@explorebolivia.com; web: www.explorebolivia.com. Good selection of Bolivia tours including Madidi and Noel Kempff.
Kon-Tiki Tours & Travel 940 Lincoln Rd, Ste 322, Miami Beach, FL 33139; tel: 877 566 8454; fax: 877 325 7406; email: info@kontiki.org; web: www.kontiki.org. Tailored tours to Bolivia and other South American countries for sightseeing, rainforest or adventure.
Madidi.com tel: 208 720 6808; email: info@madidi.com; web: www.madidi.com. Trips and tours to Madidi, Chalalan, Beni Biological Station from one of the early visitors to the area.

GETTING THERE AND AWAY
By air
From the US
American Airlines (tel: 1 800 433 7300) and Lloyd Aero Boliviano (LAB) (tel: 1 800 327 7407) are the only airlines offering direct services between Miami and La Paz or Santa Cruz. The cost is currently around US$600 return. The service provided by American Airlines is daily, with LAB flying the route several times a week.

From Europe
There are no direct flights from Europe to Bolivia. The most direct flight is with American Airlines, who have a connecting flight from Miami and stopping at Santa Cruz en route. Argentinas Aerolíneas, Varig and AeroPerú all travel from Europe to their home countries, with connecting flights on to Bolivia. Some of the stopover times can be up to 24 hours.

Return prices from London start at £680 in low season (April to June), rising to £860 in the high season (July to September).

Overland
Overland crossings into the lowlands are from Peru or Brazil. From Brazil, you can travel from Corumba in the Brazilian Pantanal to Santa Cruz on what has been labelled the Death Train. If possible try to book your ticket a couple of days before travel from the new station on Avenida Brasil. If you need a visa to enter Brazil the Brazilian Consulate in Santa Cruz is at Av Busch 330.

Slightly to the north, a crossing links the town of San Matías to the Brazilian town of Cáceres.

On Bolivia's northern border the main crossing to Brazil is through Guayaramerin. A short speedboat journey takes you across the Río Mamoré to the Brazilian town of Guajara-Mirim. Border details in Bolivia can be sorted out in the immigration office by the ferry terminal. In Brazil border formalities are completed at the offices of the Federal Police a few blocks behind the ferry terminal on Av Pres Dutra 70.

Those finding themselves well and truly off the beaten path, or indeed any path at all, can cross at Cobija into Brasiléia. Crossing into Peru close to the Madre de Dios River is also possible but, since there are no border officials of either nationality, locals may view you with some suspicion.

Customs and immigration

When entering Bolivia, all visitors are given a 30-day visa. If you are staying longer ask for a 90-day visa. To get an extension, visit the Immigration Ministry on Av Camacho in La Paz.

Getting around

Major cities and towns are often connected by good roads but any deviation from the main routes leads to dirt roads. Much of overland travel in Bolivia can firmly be put in the adventure category.

By bus

Buses are the most commonly used mode of transport. Intercity buses are straightforward – usually air-conditioned and comfortable. There is normally a central terminal for departing and arriving buses which adhere to the posted timetable.

Buses travelling to smaller, out-of-the-way places are a different story. Journeys last for hours or in a vehicle that seems designed for children and bounces its way over potholes jarring every bone in your body. This is what travelling in Bolivia is all about. It'll bore you to tears, amaze you with new sights, smells and sounds, and stun you into disbelief. Your first Bolivian bus experience will be unforgettable. Once you've done a few, you'll feel like an old-timer, and probably want to fly.

On all but intercity buses the schedules are theoretical. Departure times are estimates, arrival times absent and seat numbers are changeable even as you sit in them. In the northern lowlands travel is even worse!

Buses stop at meal times. If you are happy eating from roadside restaurants there's the typical selection of *almuerzos* and *cenas* to choose from. Alternatively you can buy fruit or biscuits to nibble. Bottled water is available at most stops.

Hitching

One step down the comfort ladder is hitching in the back of a truck or *camioneta* – an experience that takes you through the highs and lows of Bolivian culture as many Bolivians travel this way. There is normally a small charge.

By air

For more convenience (and speed!) take advantage of the extensive network of internal flights provided by LAB, AeroSur and TAM – the military air service – and the new Amazonas. You can travel to many small towns with one or more of the airlines. Prices are low. La Paz to Rurrenabaque, for example, costs US$52 – an option that has the added bonus of panoramic views. The simplest way to buy tickets is on arrival in La Paz through one of the airline offices: LAB (Av Camacho 1456-60; tel: 80010 3001), or AeroSur (Av 16 de Julio, Edif. Petrolero Mezannine; tel: 235 4435).

TAM provides occasional passenger services on routes to the smaller towns (tel: 237 9285).

By train

Rail lines connect Bolivia to Brazil to the west and Argentina to the south from Santa Cruz. There are also services from Ororu to Argentina and Chile. There are no train services in the Bolivian Amazon.

COMMUNICATIONS
Mail

By comparison with other countries in South America, the Bolivian postal service is quite good. It takes about a week for incoming and outgoing mail to Europe and slightly less for the US. Postcards up to 20g to the US, Europe and Australia are Bs5, 6 and 8 respectively. Package rates can be costly so it's far better to try to squeeze that little bit of extra luggage in the bag and carry it home.

If you are writing to a Bolivian postal address do not forget to include the *casilla* or box number. Individuals and organisations collect mail from the post office boxes. Conversely, to visit an office you need the full address – the postal address will take you to a little metal box!

Telephones, fax and internet

The Bolivian telephone system has undergone a near revolution in recent years. Modern telephones using 'smart' phonecards are replacing the *tarjetas telefónicas* system. Phones are found in many hotels, bars and on the street. *Tarjetas* range in value from Bs10 to Bs50 and can usually be bought from someone in the vicinity of the telephone. Local calls are Bs6/hr, to the US (Bs6.50/min), to Australia (Bs11/min) and to Europe (Bs13.50/min). International calls can be made from these phones but be sure to buy the higher value cards. (Bs50 buys approximately three minutes to Europe.)

Faxes can be sent from the better hotels or from the central telephone office on Calle Ayacucho 267 near the post office.

Bolivia has been quick to catch on to the benefits of email and cybercafés are beginning to open up. **WaraNet** is in La Paz on Calle Yanacocha #372, on the ground floor of Edificio Cristal.

Mobile telephones are popular in Bolivia and are often used as contact numbers. Calls eat up money quickly so make sure you have a number of cards if you're calling a mobile.

If you need to make several calls it can be easier to head for the Entel office where there are many telephones, a fax and internet service. Reverse charge (collect) calls can be made but they are more expensive.

The international country code for Bolivia is 591.

Television and radio

Television and radio are good ways of keeping up with the news if your Spanish is up to it. All but the most basic hotels in La Paz and Santa Cruz have cable, providing international news from CNN and BBC World.

Newspapers

A range of broadsheet and tabloid papers are available. It's worth picking one up if you want to improve your Spanish. If you have a bilingual dictionary they aren't that difficult to understand.

The English-language newspaper The *Bolivian Times* is reported to have closed down in late 2002. Look out for a replacement paper providing a mix of travel information, news and cultural pieces covering the country.

LA PAZ

La Paz is nestled in the canyon created by the Río Choqueyapu; the city is overshadowed by the beautiful snow-topped mountain of Illimani (6,439m). La Paz possesses a cosmopolitan air with flashing neon signs, a stark reminder of Westernisation. But away from the main streets urban Quechua Indians, still in traditional dress, make up 40% of the city's population.

At an altitude of 3,600m, most visitors arriving directly by plane experience altitude sickness. The effects of *soroche* include tiredness, loss of appetite, headaches, nausea and vomiting. Symptoms can take a few hours to appear and the best remedy is to rest and have a cup of coca tea. Fortunately, the steep hills of La Paz discourage too much activity.

Orientation is relatively easy as is the city being divided into three levels. At the top is the urban sprawl of El Alto, the poorest section, from where there are spectacular views of the city below. Descending some 400m in altitude is the heart of the city. The main street, the Prado, runs through the middle. Most things of interest to the visitor are close to the Prado. Dropping another step is Zona Sur, the wealthiest part of the city, with a slightly milder climate and certainly the worst views. Bolivia is often difficult to fully comprehend.

At the airport

It is a 30-minute drive to La Paz. A taxi to the centre costs about US$8 and gives you the option of stopping to take pictures of the city. Buses leave the airport for the centre of town every ten minutes or so and cost US$0.60. They wait just outside the arrivals building until full and drop you in the centre of town along the Prado. Airport departure tax is US$20.

City transport

Radio taxis are efficient and can be hailed in the street or booked by telephone. Contact numbers are posted in hotels and on the side of vehicles. Short trips cost Bs5, longer trips Bs10 to Bs15. In La Paz shared taxis called *trufis* flying green pennants run along set routes – a slightly quicker option than the buses but more expensive at Bs3. Minibuses travel likewise but are more crowded. City buses crawl along charging Bs1.40 for travel throughout the city. Destinations are signposted in the windscreen.

Where to stay

There are plenty of hotels in La Paz. Those below are close to the centre of town.

First class

El Rey Palace Av 20 de Octubre; tel: 241 8541; fax: 241 8521; email: info@hotel-rey-palace-bolivia.com; web: www.hotel-rey-palace-bolivia.com. Off the main street, this is a very good hotel popular with tour groups. Single US$70, double US$80.

Hotel Plaza Av 16 de Julio; tel: 237 8311; fax: 237 8318. A 5-star hotel providing all the comforts you'd expect and seemingly a world away from the city outside. Fantastic views from the top floor restaurant. Single US$130, double US$150.

LA PAZ: CENTRE

Key
Places of interest

1 Museo Nacional de Arte
2 Witches Market

Facilities
3 Hotel Gloria
4 Hotel Torino
5 Hotel Galería
6 Hostala República
7 Lloyd Aero Boliviano (LAB) offices
8 Hotel Plaza

Middle range

Hotel Galería Horizontes Andes 4th floor, Calle Santa Cruz 583; tel: 246 1015; fax: 246 1253; email: hgaleria@horizontandino.com.bo; web: www.horizontandino.com.bo. Thirty rooms with private bathrooms and TV. Comfortable option with good view from restaurant, internet service and helpful staff. US$35 a double.

Hostal La Republica Calle Comercio 1455 esq Bueno; tel: 220 2742; fax: 220 2782; email: marynela@ceibo.entelnet.bo. A former presidential home, close to the centre but away from the busy parts of town. Small café and travel agency. Doubles from US$24 with bathroom, US$16 without.

Hostal Naira Calle Sagárnaga 161; tel: 235 5645; fax: 232 7262. Beautiful hotel right on the main tourist thoroughfare. Double US$32.

Budget

Hostal Austria Yanachocha 531; tel: 235 1140. Popular with travellers and often full, it has a kitchen and lounge. (US$6 per person.)

El Carretero Calle Catacora #1056, between Yanacocha y Junín; tel: 228 5271. The laid-back hangout for travellers on the gringo trail. One report said you either love the place or you don't. Hot showers, kitchen available. US$3 per person.

Hotel Happy Days Sagárnaga #229; Casilla 13586; tel: 231 4759; fax: 235 5079; email: happydays@zuper.net Two dozen spotless rooms, the better beds are in rooms with shared bath, but rooms with private bath are still excellent value at US$8 per person. Very clean, run by the friendly Leonor Arocha – justifiably the budget travellers' first choice.

Where to eat

At midday, small restaurants serve a set meal or *almuerzo*. Usually three courses, the meal ranges from the unforgettable to the undesirable. An evening set meal is harder to find so you may have to visit a larger restaurant.

Hotel Gloria near to San Francisco Plaza has a vegetarian restaurant on the ground floor, a good restaurant upstairs and an excellent coffee shop on the way out. The **Hotel Plaza** restaurant on the hotel's top floor provides a good mix of European and Bolivian dishes, is reasonably priced at US$15pp and has stunning views. Arguably the best restaurant in La Paz, **Restaurant Vienna** (Federico Zuazo 1905) serves European cuisine and is popular with expatriates.

Andromeda (Av Arce and Aspiazu) serves good food with vegetarian options – very popular for *almuerzo* US$3. One road north of the Hotel Plaza is **La Bodeguita Cubana** (Federico Zuezo 1653), serving Cuban dishes while the music and cocktails keep flowing.

An essential part of the Bolivian way of life includes the mid-morning snacking of *salteñas*. Readily available on the street, the best in La Paz are from **Snack Valerie's** (Av 6 de Agosto No 2187), a few blocks down from Plaza Estudiante.

La Paz has a range of entertainment options. Also popular are the peñas with traditional dishes and dances. Try **Los Escudos** (in the basement of the building opposite the post office on Av Mariscal Santa Cruz; tel: 231 2133) or **Peña Huari** (Calle Sagárnaga #339; tel: 231 6225).

If you're looking for a drink in the evening **Mongo's** on Hermano's Manchega is a popular choice, especially on Friday and Saturday nights. A wide selection of bars are found close to Plaza Avaroa. Try **Café en Azul** for clear headed drink and chat, **Cambrinus** for a quiet sit down drink or **Diesel Nacional** for post-industrial mayhem and you've got a good overview of where the nightlife in this once quiet city is heading. The more sober-headed might want to listen to some excellent and thriving local jazz at **Thelonius** (20 de Octubre between Fernando Guachalla and Rosendo Gutierrez). In the district of Calacoto in Zona Sur on the main road is the popular British pub **The Britannia** (corner of Calle 16 and Av Ballivian). Next door is the **Abracadabra Restaurant** which will happily send a pizza or hamburger over to the Britannia. A short walk towards the heart of San Miguel leads to an area which buzzes with life. **La Terraza** is the place to be seen for a drink. If you're looking for one special meal try **Maphrao On** (Calle Claudio Aliaga #1182; tel: 279 3070) for excellent Thai cuisine.

What to see

Most things of interest to the passing tourist are in the centre of the city within a couple of blocks of El Prado, the main street. Architecturally the area around **Plaza Murillo** is of greatest interest, and is home to the **Cathedral** and **National**

Congress. The restored colonial street of **Calle Jaén** is home to four different museums looking at Bolivian history and art.

The **post office** is a rather impressive building in the style of Frank Lloyd Wright on the Prado. A few blocks behind this is the colourful **Mercado Rodriguez**, selling dry goods, fruit, vegetables, fish and meat. It's a wonderfully chaotic mixture of sounds, smells and colours, and is best on a Saturday as there are more stalls.

Up the hill from the post office is **Plaza San Francisco** with the 16th-century church of the same name. The plaza in front fills with hawkers and pedlars selling all sorts of remedies to the world's illnesses. Beside the church is the colourful street market of **Calle Sagárnaga**. There is the interesting **Coca Museum** showing the history of coca through the years, just off Calle Sagárnaga on Calle Linares, open 10.00 to 18.00, Bs8. City buses will also take you to visit the strangely eroded **Valley of the Moon** to the south of the city.

Shopping

A visit to Calle Sagárnaga beside San Francisco church, to buy clothes, textiles, jewellery and ceramics, is a must. Bartering is common. Traditional *aguayos* are sold alongside more modern goods. Most types of clothing can be bought including waistcoats, jumpers, trousers and hats; along with jewellery, rugs and blankets. The list is endless and the prices are ridiculously low.

Off Sagárnaga is the *Mercado de los Brujas* selling all manner of items, some of which would certainly be confiscated by customs on your way home.

On the same street there are several travel agents who can arrange city tours, local excursions and trips to the Amazon if you wish to organise these from La Paz.

Excursions from La Paz

Easily arranged and needing no more than a day is a short trip to the pre-Inca site of **Tiahuanaco**. An impressive display of Tiahuanacan architecture and designs occupies the site itself. A museum shows how the site might have looked at the height of the Tiahuanacan Empire. If you have a couple of days visit **Lake Titicaca**, the world's highest navigable lake, best seen at sunset from the town of Copacobana. An overnight visit on public transport will cost about US$15.

Leaving town

The daily buses to Rurrenabaque (US$13) and beyond leave La Paz around midday from the Villa Fatima district. They are often full so buy your ticket the day before if you can. The journey takes around 20 hours if there are no roadworks en route. Buses for Riberalta and Guayaramerín leave from La Paz and can take up to two days although 36 hours is the scheduled time.

Buses to Trinidad and Santa Cruz leave from the main bus terminal at Plaza Antofagasta.

THE BOLIVIAN AMAZON

While no single town can justifiably claim to be the centre of the Bolivian Amazon for visitors, **Rurrenabaque** is the most popular and the easiest spot to visit in the rainforest. Several agencies have offices in the town making it a simple and economical base for planning a trip. Most trips organised in La Paz use Rurrenabaque as a starting point.

An alternative entry point to the Amazon, with direct international access, is **Santa Cruz**, which is used as a base for organised excursions.

Large lowland towns buzz with the activity of the tropics but little of this is directed to tourism.

Rurrenabaque: gateway to the north

On the east bank of the River Beni lies the small jungle town of Rurrenabaque, with around 9,400 inhabitants. The river squeezes through a ravine upstream before spreading out to drift past 'Rurre', as locals call it.

Originally a trading and transit point for river traffic, the town developed into a supply post for surrounding communities, the logging industry and, more recently, oil company exploration notably by the French company Total. Logging is small-scale, but this is bound to change.

Despite the activity the sense that the jungle is just around the corner never leaves. Travelling salesmen occasionally set up stalls selling 'all-powerful' medicinal concoctions.

Rurre has grown in recent years and the rainforest's salvation could be the arrival of tourism. You need at least a week to enjoy the area without feeling too rushed. The centre of town is so small you'll struggle to get lost. Although lots of travellers use Rurre as a base for rainforest trips, most people are out of town for several days so the place keeps a sleepy feel.

Getting there

The daily La Paz–Rurre bus stops right in the centre of town. The journey goes through stunning scenery along a terrible road which sadly you can't see as much of the journey is at night. Not surprisingly, the internal air flights are becoming more popular, with the added bonus of spectacular scenery as you fly down to the lowlands through gaps between the mountains. TAM flies between Rurrenabaque and La Paz three or four times a week; US$50 one way. The flight is often booked up two or three days in advance so book early if you want to fly. The airport is a dirt landing strip just outside town. Trucks and taxis meet the plane when it comes in to land.

Where to stay

There are plenty of casual places to stay. **Hotel Tuichi** (US$5) is very popular, often full and the longest running and best cheap hotel. The **Hostal Beni** (US$8) on the riverfront is slightly more expensive but very clean with a patio for relaxing. The **Hotel Oriental** on the plaza is a popular choice (US$5 with private shower). A little north of town is the **Safari**, best hotel in town at US$20 for comfortable rooms and a swimming pool for relaxing. There is also the **Hotel Berlin** (US$6) one of the oldest hotels in town for those wanting to stay in part of Rurre's history.

Where to eat

Eating is often more function than flavour in this jungle town. Having said that, spectacular fish dishes like *dorado* or *surubí* may surprise you on any of the riverfront restaurants. The **Club Social** – which always looks closed – on Calle Comercio is popular with regular visitors to the town providing big portions of traditional Bolivian dishes from US$3.50.

Camila's is targeting the traveller market with 'good gringo food'. It's a bit pricey compared to other spots in town but you can't get pancakes and maple syrup in every jungle town. They also have internet, which will give you some contact with the outside world. **Heladería Bambi** provides excellent ice-cream, perfect at any time of day. If you fancy a drink, the **Mosquito Bar** is the happening place to be with cocktails and a happy hour to draw you in.

Excursions from Rurrenabaque

Climb the small hill behind the town, after leaving the main plaza heading east away from the river, for a sweeping panorama of surrounding forest, the river and the town below. Boats cross over the river to San Buenaventura. There's nothing of specific interest, but soaking up the atmosphere, whiling away some time and enjoying strange encounters can easily fill the day.

After a few days of sweating it out in the jungle cool off at the swimming pool, Balneario El Ambaiba. It costs US$2 for the day and you can come and go as you please.

If you have a little longer you could venture upstream to the frontier-style gold-mining town of Guanay. The eight-hour boat trip to Guanay costs around US$15–20 per person.

Jungle tours

Several agencies provide guided trips into the jungle up the Tuichi River, a tributary of the Beni River. The most popular trip is four days and three nights, leaving early in the morning and returning in the afternoon of the fourth day. Jungle trips need a minimum of four people. Heading upstream for four hours or so, you set up camp in the lowland tropical forest just off the beaches of the Tuichi River. A night under canvas, in reality little more than a tarpaulin, tests out the mosquito nets. The following three days and nights will take you on hikes along primary rainforest trails exploring remoter areas. Agencies ensure groups follow a different path on each trip, but you should see several animals including waterbirds, toucans, macaws, and with luck monkeys, caiman, snakes and capybara.

Included in the trips are camping, fishing and bushcraft skills, learning about edible and medicinal plants from the rainforest, canoeing to remote channels for bird and animal watching, and night treks.

Agencies will tailor trips to your needs and interests so, if you have a particular interest such as birdwatching, discuss it with the agent.

Increased tourism pressure has resulted in tours further up the Tuichi River and its tributaries. Jungle trips are beginning to include circular routes which enter one tributary, trek across to another and rejoin the canoe before heading towards Laguna Santa Rosa. The lagoon is an excellent spot to see snakes and caiman and to fish for piranha.

Pampas tours

For a change from sticky, humid jungle consider a trip to the pampas grasslands close to the town of Santa Rosa. A network of river channels is home to abundant

RURRENABAQUE NOW AND THEN
Cynthia Thompson

In 1975, no roads led to Rurrenabaque and the only way to reach the village was by river. Mario Sarabia and I travelled from La Paz through the Yungas down to Puerto Linares where we finally found a boat willing to take us to Rurre. It took six days to reach the village. We arrived sunburnt and exhausted having travelled the last day downriver through a series of difficult rapids. Just before the village of Rurrenabaque, the mountains rose tall and narrow like stage sets, then fell steeply. From the village onward nothing could be seen but the muddy Beni River disappearing into a flat green plane of steaming jungle.

The Hotel Berlin stood on the bank just up from the river – the first and, at the time, only hotel in town. Doña Aury greeted us warmly. Foreign travellers passing through were rare then and we caused a stir of interest and curiosity. Everyone knew each other in the village and the strong sense of community among the people was apparent. The houses were constructed of bamboo with thatched roofs, and only a few were made of wooden planks. The doors were never locked.

To reach San Buenaventura on the opposite shore, you had to search for someone with a canoe and ask for a ride. There were no telephones and electricity was available for only a few hours after dusk. Since no road entered the area, neither did motorised vehicles and most people travelled by horse or ox-drawn cart. Rurrenabaque's streets were worn footpaths through the grass. The Beni River was its highway and means of communication with the rest of the world.

At night, the darkness was filled with a deafening chorus of frogs and insects, and fish could be heard leaping in the river. In the early morning, the pandemonium of birdcalls, dominated by the raucous cry of macaws flying across the sky in resplendent pairs, woke the village and set the day in motion.

Twenty years later, the trip from La Paz to Rurrenabaque takes just one day by bus or one hour by plane. I took the bus down and hardly recognised the village when we pulled in that morning. Motorbikes, trucks, buses and jeeps raised clouds of dust as they drove through the town.

A large group of tourists sat at an outdoor café with a menu board written in English and Hebrew. More than a dozen new hotels had sprung up and still others were being constructed. I looked for the Hotel Berlin. That old haven of hospitality to river travellers was still standing, looking worn and crowded in between new buildings. Doña Aury, the original owner, was making plans to renovate it in order to keep pace with the times and the competition.

Ferry boats crossed the river to San Buenaventura every fifteen minutes. Discos and karaoke bars offered night-time diversion, competing with the night-time chorus of frogs and insects. The village has a telephone office now, a beautiful, clean, public swimming pool, numerous restaurants, and several ecotourism offices catering to tourists who want to see the jungle wildlife and travel the rivers of the region.

Cynthia Thompson travelled down the Beni River on a raft in 1975. Twenty years later she returned to repeat the trip.

water birds, river turtles, pink dolphins, capybara and many other animals. For wildlife, the open pampas grasslands is often more rewarding than the forest. Without the dense vegetation of the rainforest it's a lot easier to see or hear the wildlife. As with the jungle trips, it is possible to arrange tours of any duration but three days is long enough to experience most of what's on offer. Most people try to combine the jungle and pampas tour.

Choosing an agency and guide

Until recently tourism development has been unrestricted along the course of the River Tuichi and its growth has been based on demand. Madidi National Park to the west of Rurrenabaque was created to preserve the region's high biodiversity, reflecting a greater awareness of the value of conservation.

Competition has led to price cuts, and concern for the ecological systems that attract visitors seems, at times, to have floated down the river. Agencies offer the same kind of deal so competition is based on price. Trips currently cost as little as US$20/day, although agencies are trying to secure an industry minimum. Co-operation between agencies may lead to higher prices, but it gives the rainforest and animals a better chance of surviving if the extra money is used carefully.

When choosing an agency try not to focus on price alone. Think about what it is you would like to see and whether the impact of your visit will significantly reduce the prospect of following visitors seeing the same things. Make sure all rubbish is carried out. Ideal group sizes are between four and eight people.

Some of the guides can speak a little English but it is far better to have someone in your group with at least some knowledge of Spanish.

Tour operators and agencies

You can book tours in advance from La Paz, or just turn up in Rurre and organise a trip to leave pretty much immediately if you can get together a group. There are several operators. However tempting, try not to go for the cheapest and do your best to get all the trash bought out from the jungle.

Fluvial Tours (tel: 892 2372) is one block from the bus company Flota Yungueña. As one of the original tour guides in the area Tico Tudela continues to set the standard. He is popular with travellers, and recommendations are consistently good. The husband-and-wife team run a hotel, which makes it easy to sort out accommodation for your return from the jungle.

Other operators include **Aguila Tours**, reported to have friendly and informative guides, **Amazonica Tours** and **Donato's**.

NATIONAL PARKS OF THE NORTH
Madidi National Park

Created in 1995 Madidi National Park is hailed as one of the world's most diverse national parks. It is now just opening up to ecotourism.

The park's biodiversity is very high. Geographically the park borders Bolivia's western frontier with Peru stretching southward from Puerto Heath in the Amazon Basin to join the Ulla Ulla National Reserve on the Bolivian *altiplano* – a highland reserve created in 1972 to protect the shrinking vicuña population. The 1.9 million hectare park encompasses the Tuichi River basin which flows out through Rurrenabaque. The park ranges in altitude from 6,000m above sea level down to just 250m.

Conservation International carried out a Rapid Assessment Programme (RAP) of the park in 1990. The park is home to more than 50% of all neotropical bird species. Nearly 1,000 bird species can be found in Madidi National Park, 11% of all bird

BOLIVIAN LOWLANDS

species on earth, as well as 44% of all neotropical mammals and 38% of all neotropical amphibians. Madidi's floristic richness is also very high and the region is a major centre for plant endemism. The park encompasses diverse habitats including montane cloudforest, rare tropical dry forest, savannah and lowland tropical forest.

The low population density of this part of Bolivia has directly contributed to lower pressure on land than elsewhere, thus providing refuge for animals in the region.

Getting there and where to stay

If out-of-the-way is what you are looking for, stay at **Chalalan Ecolodge**. After travelling to Rurrenabaque, where you will probably need to spend at least one night, it's a five-hour journey upriver. Once dropped off, a 30-minute walk takes you to the lodge.

Several agencies arrange trips to Chalalan. It is probably best to book in advance from La Paz. One agency, **EcoBolivia Foundation**, played a vital role in raising awareness of the region and lobbied the government hard for Madidi's status as a National Park. **Fremen Tours** is a family-run Bolivian company that focuses on ecotourism. **America Tours SRL** also provides a reliable booking service for those wanting to visit Chalalan (contact information on page 332).

Trips are tailored for each group and prices reflect the length of stay and the number in the group. Four people visiting the lodge for a four or five-day trips cost approximately US$280pp, including transport to and from the lodge and all meals. Transport to Rurrenabaque from other parts of Bolivia is not included in the price and neither is accommodation while in Rurrenabaque.

Chalalan Ecolodge has three palm-roofed, wooden lodges with accommodation for up to 24 persons. The sleeping quarters are mosquito-proof and decorated with local crafts. Showers and bathrooms are provided. It's basic, but clean and comfortable. Meals provide a selection of foods from the forest including brazil nuts, coffee and chocolate. Organic vegetables are grown in the grounds of the lodge. The dining room has a view of the lake and an area to relax, complete with hammocks.

Travel opportunities

All the tour operators taking tourists to the park are keen to avoid ecosystem destruction. The 500 Quechua-Tacana Indians living in the village of San José de Uchupiamonas have lived in the Tuichi valley for over 200 years with little impact on the local habitat. Consequently the involvement of the community at every level has been important to the success of the project.

From the lodge there are excursions to nearby Lake Chalalan, the Tuichi River and Eslabón River. Travelling by dugout canoe you can pass through the spectacular Bala Gorge. In the immediate area there are ten jungle trails, totalling 20km in length, incorporating several different ecosystems. The trails are signposted and information is posted en route about flora, fauna and the distance travelled. The longest trail takes you to the Eslabón River, close to a site frequented by several species of monkey.

In addition to providing a visit to pristine rainforest, Chalalan aims to improve the socio-economic conditions in San José. Conservation-based initiatives encourage the village to grow food for the lodge and train local people as guides.

For the more adventurous

If you are fit, the best way to take in the park's natural beauty is by raft. **Amazonas Explorer** (page 281) in Peru arranges the trips. From La Paz, first by jeep and then on foot you arrive at Virgin del Rosario – a small community at the Tuichi's headwaters. From here the river flows to Rurrenabaque. It's a free ride downriver through cloudforest before you have to paddle through mixed tropical dry forest and primary rainforest. At night you camp on river beaches. As you paddle during the days, you try to convince yourself that the world around you, in all its beauty, is real. Trips are organised in advance. They cost around US$1,900, excluding international flights.

Manuripi Heath National Reserve

Close to the northern border with Brazil is Manuripi Heath Nature Reserve. Formed in 1973, the park comprises lowland tropical rainforest. The boundary of the 1.8 million hectare park is contained by the Peruvian border to the west. The Manuripi River marks the northern border, with the southern border roughly following the Madre de Dios River to its confluence with the Beni River near Riberalta.

At just 200 metres above sea level, climatic variations are minimal with the annual temperature range a mere two degrees: fluctuating between 25° and 27°C. Annual rainfall is around 1,650mm, with the dry season between June and August receiving sporadic rainfall.

Although research carried out in the park is not comprehensive, approximate species counts yield 800 types of birds, including the harpy eagle. Mammals include tapir, capybara, giant anteaters, at least six species of primate and various types of lowland cat including the elusive jaguar.

Human impact on the park is minimal, principal activities being brazil-nut and rubber extraction. Pressure from logging is increasing with the improvement of roads from Cobija to the north.

Getting there

The nearest town of significance is Cobija. Bordering Brazil along the Acre River and with a population of 15,000, this capital of the Department of Pando has nothing to differentiate it from any other Bolivian frontier town.

Oppressively hot in the summer months and with regular afternoon showers, the climate may tempt you to take a refreshing swim across the Acre River to Brazil. There are no border controls along the stretch of river in the town to stop you, but stripping for the swim attracts swarms of vicious sandflies.

Overland routes to Cobija are feasible but only for the masochist. It's a 12-hour, bone-shaking bus journey from Riberalta in the dry season – even longer in the wet season. Air travel is the only real option unless you have a strange fascination with bus travel via Riberalta. AeroSur and LAB fly to Cobija from La Paz several times a week. The cost is US$160 return.

Where to stay and eat

Accommodation options are limited with the two best options being close to the main plaza. **Hostal Sucre** provides clean rooms and efficient service for US$8, and the **Residencial Cocodrillo** US$5 has basic rooms.

Travel opportunities

A foray into the virgin jungle of Manuripi Heath offers many opportunities for the independent traveller. Either of the two main rivers would be interesting routes to consider for a boat trip if looking for a challenging expedition river. They have the added bonus of ending up near Riberalta, a convenient transit point with regular planes and buses to and from La Paz. Logistically, however, a trip to Manuripi Heath is difficult to organise and would require extensive planning.

Santa Cruz: gateway to the east

Santa Cruz is the natural access point to the eastern lowlands of Bolivia, with direct flights from Miami. Having grown rapidly in just a couple of decades, this city of over 1.1 million has become Bolivia's largest city if you don't merge La Paz and El Alto's figures together.

Its rapid growth is officially explained by the development of oil reserves in the region. While oil is important to Santa Cruz it isn't *that* important so it would be fair to assume that some of the profits from the coca-producing Chapare region have been invested in property! Agribusiness in the area has increased rapidly, with soya and other products grown for export to Brazil and Argentina.

Travel opportunities

Santa Cruz is the logical starting point for visitors interested in travelling to Noel Kempff Mercado National Park, Amboro National Park or Ríos Blanco y Negro Wildlife Reserve.

Organised trips to any these large biological reserves can be organised by Fremen Tours (see page 332) or most established tour operators in Santa Cruz.

For independent travellers the easiest trip is to Amboro with trips lasting a couple of days easily arranged through agents in town. Most tour agents can arrange trips; try **Neblina Forest** (Calle Beni #15, tel/fax: 03 333 2813; email: neblinaflorest@cotas.com.bo; web: www.neblinaforest.com). Trips to Noel Kempff are more difficult for independent travellers to organise but can be planned through Fundación Amigos de la Naturaleza (FAN) – the conservation organisation in charge of the administration and management of Noel Kempff (Km. 7, Carretera Antigua a Cochabamba; tel: 03 355 6800; fax: 03 354 7383; web: www.fan-bo.org). FAN has an information packet for independent travellers interested in visiting the park, but you shouldn't consider it unless you have more than a week to dedicate to the trip.

Boat trips down the Río Ichilo from Puerto Villaroel are one option for the independent traveller, as is exploring the savannah region between Trinidad and Rurrenabaque.

Other places to visit in the region include the beautifully restored Jesuit Missions and the pre-Inca site of Samaipata close to the town of the same name.

At the airport

Viru Viru airport, serving national and international destinations, is 16km north of the city. Buses and taxis (US$5) provide transport for the 30-minute journey to the city centre throughout the day.

City transport

Taxis are priced in a similar way to those in La Paz; short trips cost Bs6 (about US$0.70) and longer trips Bs12. Maps of the city are available from most bookshops.

Where to stay

As with any large city there is no shortage of hotels.

First class

Las Américas 21 de Mayo esq Seoane; tel: 03 336 8778; fax: 03 333 6083. Close to the centre of town. Comfortable, central and half the price of Los Tajibos. US$60 per person.
Los Tajibos Hotel Av Santa Marta #455; tel: 03 342 1000; fax: 03 342 6994; email: santacruz@lostajiboshotel.com; web: www.lostajiboshotel.com. A luxury 5-star hotel with

SANTA CRUZ: CENTRE

swimming pool and virtually every indulgence you can think of. Single US$159, double US$179.

Middle range
Hotel Bibosi Junín 218; tel: 03 334 8548; fax: 03 334 8887. In the centre of town. Single US$16, double US$25.
Hotel Copacabana Junín 217; tel: 03 336 2770; fax: 03 333 0757. Good, clean rooms from US$15 for a single.

Hotel Viru Viru Junín 338; tel: 03 333 5298. Comfortable and with a swimming pool. Single US$19, double US$29.

Budget
There is lots of budget accommodation of varying standards.

Residencial Bolívar Calle Sucre 131; tel: 03 334 2500. A couple of blocks off the main plaza. Single US$8, double US$12.
Residencial Ballivián Ballivián #71. A popular budget choice with similar prices and services to the Bolívar.

Where to eat
You can trust the locals or *cruceños* to know where the best places are. Recommendations include **Castalñuelas** on Calle Velasco 308 esq Pari (tel: 03 333 4679) which is a popular Spanish restaurant.

Victorio is on Calle Junín esq 21 de Mayo (tel: 03 332 2935). Centrally located in the Casco Viejo on the first floor, this Italian coffee shop has excellent cappuccino and cakes and is an ideal place to hang out during the day. Very central.

La Casa del Camba is slightly out of town on the second *anillo* (ring-road) on the corner with Avenida Alemana at Cristobal de Mendoza 539 (tel: 03 342 7864). They serve delicious traditional meat dishes. Almost next-door is another meat place: **La Buena Mesa** (tel: 03 342 1284).

Leonardo (Avenida Warnes 666; tel: 03 333 8282) has good Italian food but is a little pricey.

Tapekua (Calle Ballivian and La Paz) is a Swiss-owned restaurant with live music. There is a small cover charge when bands are playing but the food and atmosphere are worth the extra. Open Wed–Sun.

Going out
Cultural centres include the **Instituto de Cooperacion Iberoamericana**, known as the ICI (Calle Arenales 583); it has exhibitions and free movies. The **Casa de la Cultura** on the main square has classical concerts, theatre and other events. **Cine Arte Videas** (Calle Andres Manso 1095) has recently opened on and sometimes shows Bolivian films.

The **Irish Pub** on the east of the main plaza, on the first floor (get there through the shopping mall) is very popular with gringos and a great place to hang out.

What to see
The trees in the main plaza are reported to be home to a few sloths, but some say they have been removed for their own good. **Parque el Arenal** five blocks north of the main plaza centres on a manmade lake with several stalls around the lake selling souvenirs and the **Museo Etno-Folklorico**, a small Indian museum on the island in the middle.

The **Museo de Historia Natural** (Av Irala 565, Edif UAGRIM), close to the bus terminal, houses a dusty display of creepy crawlies. Open 09.00–18.00, closed for lunch. The **zoo** is northwest of the centre and a good trip. If you want to visit you'll get a good overview of the animals in this diverse country.

Leaving town
Buses leave from the new bus terminal alongside the train terminal to the east of town. The old terminal is a hub for local buses.

Excursions from Santa Cruz
Amboró National Park

Created in 1984, Amboró National Park is beginning to emerge as an option for the Amazon visitor. Covering an area of 630,000ha the park covers three distinct ecosystems: the foothills of the Andes, the northern Chaco and the lowland rainforest. The park hosts a great variety of flora and fauna, with over 780 birds recorded and most Amazon mammals including several species of monkey, peccaries, tapir, capybara, jaguar and other jungle cats.

Three hours northwest of Santa Cruz by bus on the road to Cochabamba, Amboró is most easily accessed through the small town of Buena Vista. There you will find a selection of hotels and services, from where you can join an organised trip to the national park or hire guides to hike on your own.

One of the most popular tours is three days with a couple of nights camping. While some will find a couple of nights in the Amazon appealing, the service level is still very basic, sleeping in huts or camping in tents. In general you carry your own equipment and walking in the high humidity is quickly tiring. Don't take on more than you can handle if this is your first foray into the Amazon.

The best time to visit in the dry season is between May and October as a trip often involves fording rivers.

Tours can easily be booked with many agents in Santa Cruz or organised in Buena Vista where you will be better positioned to explore the possibilities and opportunities. There are several good basic hotels in the town, among them the **Quimori**.

El Puente Jungle Hotel

Villa Tunari is 300km west of Santa Cruz and is the nearest town to the **Hotel El Puente**, a comfortable establishment that makes a pleasant start or end to a trip in the Bolivian Amazon.

Much of the surrounding area has been affected by logging, but the hotel is among 40ha of preserved jungle. The area is rich in birds and butterflies and has several viewing towers, jungle trails and a number of swimming holes. In addition to being an ideal place to relax, day trips to the nearby waterfalls and Inca ruins can be arranged. Trips to Carrasco National Park take you to the southernmost point of the Amazon Basin.

The hotel has a restaurant, bar and lounge and a hammock room for relaxing. All rooms have private bathrooms. Prices start from US$22 for a single and US$28 for a double. Bookings and two- to four-day trips can be organised through Fremen Tours (see page 332).

Organised boat travel

Fremen Tours provide Bolivia's only floating hotel, the *Flotel Reina de Enin*. Comfortable but simple, the *Reina de Enin* travels a circular route along the Mamoré and Ibare rivers taking in evergreen riverside forest, the Moxos savannah and palm-tree savannah, intermingled with swamps and rainforest-covered islands. Caiman, river dolphins, river turtles, monkeys and capybara are common in the area, and studies have documented over 2,000 varieties of plants, many mammals and more than 400 species of birds.

Activities include jungle walks, horseback riding, canoeing, swimming and fishing for piranha. Fremen have embraced ecotourism by supporting and encouraging the involvement of local indigenous groups in the company's activities. Groups visiting riverside communities have local guides who explain the way of life for such communities in the Bolivian savannah.

Alice Walter travelled aboard the Flotel and strongly recommends the trip.

> The Flotel had seemed an enticing prospect if only for its clever name, but we had not expected so many enchanted moments watching technicolor sunsets from deckchairs, spending lazy afternoons at the helm looking for sloths among the massive trees, or inspecting the beautiful baku bought off local fishermen for our gargantuan dinners.
>
> Life on the *Reina de Enin* takes on another dimension: swimming with pink dolphins and the odd piranha; taking off, in our pyjamas, for a spur-of-the-moment birdwatching trip downstream in one of the dugouts, swinging in hammocks with a well-deserved cool beer in hand after riding fiery horses through marshland, or most amazingly coming face to face with an adult puma valiantly swimming across a mile-wide lagoon.
>
> Not even the clouds of merciless mosquitoes or the rather cramped cabins – I recommend the ones on the lower deck - could spoil the magic of this intoxicating, unmissable experience.

Tours last up to six days at a cost of US$620. The price includes all food, accommodation and transport from Trinidad. Fremen can also arrange your transport to and within Bolivia.

Independent boat travel

One option for independent travel in the region receives contradictory reports ranging from 'best time of my life' through to 'I waited four days for a boat'. To

---

PUERTO VILLARROEL TO TRINIDAD – 1973
Hilary Bradt

Bradt Publications was born on the Río Mamoré between Puerto Villarroel and Trinidad. No wonder I have fond memories of that journey. George and I had nothing to do except sit in our hammocks writing alternate chapters of *Backpacking along Ancient Ways in Peru and Bolivia* and birdwatch. The birdlife was the best I've seen on any major river trip, maybe because at the end of the dry season the boat went so slowly and hit so many sandbars that we had more time to watch. The most exciting species was jabiru, but there were numerous kingfishers and other colourful birds.

The journey took five days, and each day was centred round the quest for food. Apart from bananas and rice, the cook had brought nothing with him. Once the crew and all the passengers went ashore to collect turtle eggs. These days I would have had a conscience about eating them, but in 1973 I was anxious to try a new taste. Strange things… the white never properly hardens whilst the yolk is like stale sponge cake. We also ate turtle meat and the enormous (and tasty) eggs of the rhea.

We arrived in Trinidad which, in those days, had no road connection with the outside world. There were smaller planes out, but these were fully booked for many days ahead. We had to stay ten days. The town boasted a typing school, and each evening after the students had gone home, the proprietor allowed George to type up our book while I stayed in the hotel working on the maps and illustrations. When it was finished we mailed the typescript to George's mother and took a motorbike taxi to the airport.

hedge your bets consider taking a cargo boat from Puerto Villarroel downstream towards Trinidad. If you're up to it you can go as far north as Guayaramerín on the Brazil border. To get there find a bus from Santa Cruz which passes the junction and ask the driver to drop you at the turn-off. The journey to the junction takes about four hours so make sure you leave early in order to complete the trip before night. From the junction you can hitch a ride with a truck.

This trip gives you the best opportunity of any in Bolivia for travelling on the river while you relax in a hammock. Buy a hammock up in Santa Cruz or you may be able to get one in Puerto Villarroel. Information about sailings can be obtained from the captain's office on the riverfront or from Transportes Fluviales just off the river. Boats are normally regular but you may have to wait for a few days if you're unlucky. The trip to Trinidad, including food, costs about US$20. Take along a few extra things to eat because, as with all non-tourist riverboat travel in the Amazon, the menu's variety leaves much to be desired.

Travelling by river has a calming and therapeutic element. With so little to do on board, life develops into a series of gentle routines. Gazing at the water and the jungle as you drift by, you see macaws and waterbirds. Pink dolphins, caiman, capybara may all make brief appearances. But even if none of these animals shows up, the gentle movement of the boat, the companionship of similarly ensconced passengers and a supply of books to read while resting in a hammock are relaxing enough.

If you want to stop in Trinidad, then jump ship at Puerto Barador and catch a truck or bus. Long-distance buses regularly make the journey from Trinidad eastwards to Santa Cruz, or westwards to La Paz. Less frequently, three or so a week, are buses heading to Rurrenabaque.

Boat enthusiasts can continue the journey downstream through to Guayaramerín on the Bolivian/Brazilian border. The trip takes up to a week and costs around US$20. Make a short bus trip to Abuña or Porto Velho in Brazil, and you can complete your journey all the way to Manaus and the mouth of the Amazon River in Belém.

Trinidad

This town of almost 80,000 is a dusty, jungle sprawl. A selection of hotels and restaurants can be found around the centre if you're planning to stay. The town is a good base to explore the *Llanos de Moxos* to the south of Trinidad.

Archaeologists have found large numbers of anthropomorphic figures and ceramics in artificial mounds or *lomas*. Built close to the rivers, the mounds were constructed to allow cultivation on the elevated land at times of flooding.

There are around 20,000 *lomas* in the region, dotted amongst 100km of canals dating back to the Enin Empire that flourished in the region over 4,000 years ago. Despite the wealth of knowledge hidden within the *lomas* there is very little information available about them and limited opportunities for travellers. One exception is a trip to Santuario Chuchini, 14km out of town. This site comprises an 8ha artificially raised mound and a small museum displaying excavated artefacts and sculptures. There are small bungalows costing US$70pp if you want to stay on the site. Details from Loreno Hinojoso (Calle 25 de Noviembre 199) in Trinidad.

Well away from any towns, Chuchini is an ideal base for walks through the rainforest to nearby lagoons. There is no regular transport to Chuchini so you will have to hitch (Sundays are best) or take a taxi.

Heading west from Trinidad
San Ignacio de Moxos

Buses travel the road heading west to the small town of San Ignacio de Moxos, a small town where just enough roads – four – converge to create the all-important plaza. On the square the Jesuit mission, built in 1689, has now been fully restored at a cost of US$75,000.

The region is the traditional territory of Mojeño Indians and the town has a substantial indigenous population. Most Indians have adopted small-scale farming and fishing, or labour on nearby ranches, as an alternative to the traditional lifestyle.

Just out of town (a 20-minute walk) is Laguna Isirere – ideal for swimming. Legend has it that a small child was abducted by a spirit in the lake, and at certain times can still be heard crying within the waters of the lake.

The town comes alive every year on the last day of July for the Fiesta del Santo Patrono de Moxos, probably the most colourful celebration in the Bolivian lowlands. The fiesta is an event for flamboyance and feathers. Costumed dancers parade the streets in extravagant masks and the town fills with people gathering to see the passing parade, or just keen to partake in the dancing and copious amounts of alcohol that are an essential ingredient of Bolivian carnivals.

Beni Biological Station Reserve

Still further west towards Rurrenabaque by bus or truck along a steadily deteriorating pot-holed dirt road is the Beni Biological Station Reserve in the Department of Beni. Its 135,000ha of protected land include tropical rainforest, pantanal and open savannah offering a broad range of ecosystems for the visitor. There are over 100 species of mammal in the reserve including jaguars, more than 470 different species of bird, 45 species of amphibian and over 2,000 recorded plant species.

In addition to having a scientific research station, the reserve acts as a buffer zone to the Chimane Indigenous Area to the north, aiming to reduce the impact of outside influences on the Chimane Indians.

The station has accommodations for groups who wish to visit the area and the surrounding forests. The station building is in the south of the reserve just off the road from San Ignacio de Moxos. Spending at least four days in the reserve will get you to the pristine forests in the north of the park; seven days would provide enough time to explore much of what the reserve has to offer. Travel is by foot and accommodation is camping. It's basic and simple. But a great way to get close to nature.

Trips can be organised through the **Academia Nacional de Ciencias de Bolivia** based in La Paz (Av 16 de Julio 1732; tel/fax: 02 235 0612; email: cmiranda@ebb.rds.org.bo; postal address: Casilla 5829, La Paz). Prices depend on the number in a group and the length of a trip. It's also possible to stay at the El Porvenir Lodge on the Curiraba River for a small fee. Kontiki have five- day trips for US$760 per person.

NATIONAL PARKS OF THE EASTERN LOWLANDS
Noel Kempff Mercado National Park

Competing with Madidi National Park in Bolivia's ecotourism market is Noel Kempff Mercado National Park with over 1.5 million hectares under protection. Tucked away in the far northeastern corner of Bolivia, Noel Kempff is one of the country's largest protected areas and is home to a combination of dramatic scenery and exotic wildlife – a large percentage of which is rare or endangered. Given Noel Kempff's remote location, its natural beauty, and the absence of a well-developed infrastructure providing relatively easy access, Noel Kempff offers an excellent opportunity for a unique travel experience. It also offers the chance to participate in an ecotourism project truly dedicated to the

NOEL KEMPFF MERCADO NATIONAL PARK

Tim Miller, formerly with Fundacíon Amigos de la Naturaleza, Santa Cruz

Noel Kempff Mercado National Park, named after a scientist murdered in the area by drug barons, is a biological reserve located in the extreme northeastern corner of Bolivia in the Department of Santa Cruz; it shares an international border on the north and east with Brazil. The park is situated in an ecological transition zone that bridges the rich, wet Amazon Basin from the north and the drier ecological communities of the Gran Chaco and cerrado to the south and west respectively, with the Andean highlands found further to the west. As a result of it's remote and unique geographic location, the relatively unstudied 1.5 million hectares of Noel Kempff are believed to contain some of the highest levels of biological diversity found in the world.

The most outstanding physical feature of the park is the Huanchaca Plateau, a Precambrian (750 million years old) sandstone escarpment which represents the southernmost limit of the Amazon rainforest. The plateau rises abruptly from the dense, wet rainforests approximately 550m to an elevated plain of grasslands and dry cerrado forests, which are similar in appearance and structure to the savannahs found in Africa. The Huanchaca Plateau is drained by numerous perennial rivers which flow over the plateau, giving rise to more than 20 spectacular waterfalls. In combination with its waterfalls, this unique formation framed by the rugged backdrop of mesas, rivers, and dense forests has blessed Noel Kempff with some of the most awe-inspiring scenery found in Latin America. The impressive size and landscape of Noel Kempff is matched only by the flora and fauna found within its borders.

The wide range of habitats and geologic formations found in Noel Kempff has resulted in an extremely high diversity of bird species residing within the park. To date a total of 613 have been identified. However, experts estimate that once a comprehensive bird study of the entire park is completed, more than 700 species of resident and migratory birds will be recorded. The

conservation and sustainable development of one of the largest protected areas in Latin America.

Getting there and where to stay

There are two main lodges in Noel Kempff: Flor de Oro and Los Fierros. Since its inception, Flor de Oro was designed to become the centre for ecotourism, scientific research and park protection in Noel Kempff and has been developed accordingly. Located in the northern section of the park, the comfortable lodge provides access to a range of habitats: large expanses of *cerrado* vegetation, periodically inundated savannahs, *terra firme* and *igapo* rainforests, oxbow lakes, semi-deciduous woodlands and the Arco Iris and Ahlfeld waterfalls found on the Paucerna River. The only reasonable access to Flor de Oro is by plane, US$1300 for up to five people. There are four trails close to the lodge passing through a variety of habitats. A short boat ride takes you to excellent spots for observing wildlife, a 90-minute trip upriver takes you to Las Torres – rocky outcrops from where there are incredible views. At every turn you'll be inspired by sights seen by only a few privileged visitors. Los Fierros, on the other hand, is located in the heart of the park and is accessible by land (450km and 11 hours from Santa Cruz) or air. Los Fierros is a converted and upgraded ranger station and provides easy access to avifauna is one of the park's main attractions. With little effort, one can spot and hear many species: from small hummingbirds to harpy eagles, toucans, macaws, over 20 species of parrots, multicoloured tanagers, and at least seven species of cracids, a group with many threatened species throughout the neotropics.

There is also an incredibly rich fauna found within the park's borders which is indicated by the frequent sighting of large mammals during hikes into the park's savannahs and forests or while travelling along the extensive river and lagoon systems. An extensive species list of over 150 mammals includes such notable species as the South American tapir, capybara, jaguar, black spider monkey, black howler monkey, silvery marmoset, bush dog, giant armadillo, the rare maned wolf, and a number of cat species including the margay, jaguarundi and ocelot.

The rivers are equally rich, with common sightings of freshwater dolphins (pink and grey), giant otters, and both spectacled and the endangered black caiman.

Profits from tour operators that work in Noel Kempff Mercado National Park go directly to the ecotourism department of Noel Kempff (FAN), a private, non-profit Bolivian organisation founded in 1988 to help conserve the biodiversity of Bolivia. Under agreements with the government of Bolivia, FAN is responsible for the management and protection of more than 2.6 million hectares in two national parks and a large biological reserve, including Noel Kempff Mercado National Park which is currently the focus of FAN's ecotourism department.

The mission of the ecotourism department is to provide eco-travellers with the best possible opportunity to visit and learn about the unique natural history of Noel Kempff Mercado National Park. The primary goals of the ecotourism programme are to create a high conservation awareness among visitors, keep physical impacts on the park's natural resources to a minimum, and provide direct economic and educational benefits to members of the local communities that surround the park.

similar habitats to those in the north and the savannahs found on top of the Huanchaca Plateau. It is possible to hike up the side of the Huanchaca Plateau and visit the El Encanto Waterfall via Los Fierros. As with Flor de Oro, the region is barely visited due to its remote location. Light aircraft access is US$1,020 for up to five people.

The park's ecotourism programme includes trips ranging in duration from three to ten days, and priced from roughly US$100 per day in Flor de Oro, US$60 in Los Fierros. It is possible to camp in Los Fierros and also at Huanchach II and El Encanto for US$2 per person per day. All accommodation must be booked through FAN in Santa Cruz. Those interested in visiting the park should get in touch with the ecotourism department of FAN for more information. They will coordinate your trip within Noel Kempff and provide you with a list of local tour operators who can help with logistics outside the park.

Perseverancia – Ríos Blanco y Negro Wildlife Reserve

The Perseverancia Centre for Tourism and Scientific Research lies in the centre of the Ríos Blanco y Negro Wildlife Reserve. Some 350km from Santa Cruz, Perseverancia is only accessible by light aircraft from Santa Cruz.

COCA AND BOLIVIA

The most lucrative crop grown in Bolivia is coca – the raw material used in the manufacture of cocaine. There are two different species of coca, creating a confusing status for the plant in Bolivia. One plant is a vital part of the nation's heritage with a wide range of cultural and medicinal uses. In the yungas the plant is grown legally, producing coca leaves for chewing or to make a tea; either of which alleviates altitude sickness and fatigue.

In the Chapare region between Cochabamba and Santa Cruz a different species of coca grows too well, in fact like a weed. Its cultivation requires no training yet it produces crops valued at US$7,000 per hectare – the nearest legal crop yields US$1,400 per hectare. The Chapare provides significant inputs of illegal raw materials into the international cocaine trade and these allegedly account for the sudden and rapid growth of Santa Cruz.

Eradication of the crop is an important part of government policy, and continues to be strongly supported by the international community.

The wildlife reserve covers some 1.4 million hectares including flooded *várzea* and *terra firme* forest, permanent marshes and a number of oxbow lakes. Over 300 bird species have been sighted in the reserve including the harpy eagle, red-and-green macaw, southern screamer and hoatzin.

Mammals are also well represented in the area. Giant river otter, tapir, capybara and jaguar have all been sighted.

Activities in the park are varied. Over 50km of trails are available, including designated birdwatching trails. Travel along the rivers is in dugout canoes or with low-impact electric-powered motors. Horse riding is also available.

Private or shared accommodation is available. Water heating systems are solar-powered. The food is good quality and snacks and refreshments are available throughout the day.

Amazonas Adventure Tours (3er Anillo Equipetrol frente a la Normal Enrique Finot #756; tel: 03 342 2760; fax: 03 342 2748; postal address: Casilla 2527, Santa Cruz, Bolivia) are the sole operators within the Blanco y Negro Reserve.

Trips are tailored for each group so prices vary. Make sure that you state your requirements in advance as getting supplies to the park at short notice can be difficult. As with other jungle trips, larger groups on longer trips benefit from the economies of scale.

Brazil

It's as big as the continental US and thirty-five times the size of Britain. It encompasses three-quarters of the Amazon Basin. From poverty-ridden slums to beach paradises, from idyllic river cruises to bone-rattling road journeys, from relaxing on packed beaches to exploring the unknown, Brazil's passion, rhythm and drama have inspired generations of adventurous travellers. Visit there and you'll feel every emotion a traveller can experience.

FACTS AND FIGURES
Geography

Brazil's huge size is as much a burden as a blessing. Difficulties in governing such a vast territory, much of it inaccessible with modern vehicles, have hampered development. Brazil borders all Amazon countries except Ecuador. Brazil's largest state of Amazonas (1.6 million km²) touches Venezuela, Colombia and Peru. The northwestern Amazon state of Roraima borders Venezuela. To the east is the state of Pará stretching north to the border with French Guiana and Guyana, with Mato Grosso to the southeast and Rondônia to the south bordering Bolivia. Acre to the southwest has a frontier with Peru and Bolivia.

The capital of Amazonas is Manaus, where the Rio Negro meets the Amazon's main stream. It is the biggest lowland Amazon city, with over a million inhabitants. Other major conurbations in the region include Boa Vista, the capital of Roraima, and Barcelos on the Negro River. South of Manaus is the city of Porto Velho and at the Amazon's mouth is Belém.

BASIC FACTS
Official name República Federativa do Brasil
Area 8,511,965km² (3,286,488 miles²)
Population 174.6 million
Capital Brasilia
Largest city (population) São Paulo (20 million)
Main Amazon city Manaus
Official language Portuguese
Date of independence September 7 1822 (Portugal)
Major industries mining, coffee, forestry, manufacturing
GDP per capita US$6,500
Currency real (US$1=R$2.75; £1=R$3.95)
Major attractions Iguassu Falls, Rio carnival, the Pantanal
National holidays Jan 1, Apr 21, May 1, Sep 7, Oct 12, Nov 2, Nov 15, Dec 25. Carnival is the week before Ash Wednesday.

Compared with smaller South American countries, Brazil has boring topography. The Amazon watershed within Brazil is generally less than 250m in altitude while none of western Brazil exceeds 90m above sea level, except for the extreme northern borders, where Neblina Peak rises to Brazil's highest elevation just over 3,000m.

Only to the south and north of the country are significant rises encountered. From the Amazon River's northern bank, mostly intact forest stretches for 1,000km until hills and valleys rise to form the vast Guyanan Shield, among the world's oldest rock formations. South of the main stream the Brazilian Shield forms the Amazon watershed's eastern limit. These two rock formations are rich in gold deposits. Sediments washed down during millennia into Amazon watersheds underlie much of today's present lowland rainforest. Rich alluvial deposits have resulted in some of the most frenetic gold rushes in recent history. Almost every Brazilian Amazon town owes its expansion over the last thirty years to the lure of gold.

Rivers

Of course the Amazon main stream is the region's dominant waterway. Major Amazon tributaries in western Brazil are the south-flowing Içá/Putumayo and Japurá/Caquetá, both running through Colombia, and the Negro, originating in the Guyanan highlands.

Flowing north are the Javari, Juruá, Purus, Madeira and Tapajós rivers. The south-flowing 2,100km Negro, in terms of volume, is the biggest main stream tributary and also carries most river traffic, while the Japura and Içá are important arteries for traffic to Peru and Colombia. South of Tabatinga, the Javari forms the northern half of the Brazil-Peru border.

Climate

Weather in northwest Brazil is dominated by a moist tropical climate, with little variation throughout the region or from season to season. In the Amazon, days are warm and humid from December to June, accompanied by high rainfall. Day temperatures virtually never fall below 22°C, and night-time lows are 18°C or so. During certain years, the cold *friagem* blows from the Patagonian steppes. On such occasions, usually associated with El Niño events, day temperatures dip as low as 15°C, severely stressing rainforest flora and fauna. July to November are the hottest months when shade temperatures can rise to over 38°C, but 26°C is average. Highlands toward the north and the southern basin are cool and pleasant, at 10–25°C.

Rainforest rainfall rarely exceeds 3,500mm annually, but some wetter places along Brazil's Atlantic coast record as much as 5,000mm (over 16ft!) in a year. The Amazon interior is considerably drier, not the constant deluge we typically have in mind. Along the upper main stream around Manaus, around 1,500–2,500mm of rain falls over twelve months. The rainy season lasts from December to May, with daily rain likely. June to November are drier months, with dry spells often lingering for several days. In recent decades deforestation in Brazil has caused shorter and less intense rainy seasons.

Flora and fauna

Ever since reports emerged from early expeditions, Brazil's flora and fauna have awed and mystified laymen and professional naturalists alike. Yet even today, these biological riches are among the most unexplored in the world, relative to their diversity. The Amazon's size and inaccessibility, and lack of expertise, seriously hinder efforts to assay the country's biological wealth. Primary ecosystems are *igapo*, *várzea* and *terra firme* forest. To the extreme north and west of Amazonas, as the land rises, dominant vegetation changes to dry tropical forest and to savannah, dotted with patches of montane rainforest. These areas are remote and good for seeing large animals but the tourist infrastructure is sparse.

All South America's tropical vertebrate groups are represented and invertebrates are exceptionally diverse. Brazil is home to 68 primate species, more than any other country in the world. Discovered in 1993 was the Río Maués marmoset (*Callithrix mauesi*), dressed in a faded striped coat and with tufted ears. Barely big enough to sit in your hand, it weighs less than 250g. Since then, three more species have been discovered, bringing the total to seven since 1990.

Land use
Most of Amazonas remains pristine tropical rainforest, sparsely inhabited by a few indigenous Indians, settlers and missionaries. Rural activities occupy little land. Most crops consist of soybeans, maize, sugarcane, manioc and bananas. Primarily, crop production is along rivers in cleared areas of flooded forest where the land is regularly fertilised with silt deposited by annual floods.

Outside of Amazonas large portions of lowland rainforest have been set aside for development projects. Most notorious were government assistance programmes for cattle-ranchers, whose tenure was marked by laying waste to large areas of forest in exchange for two or three years of good pasture. These devastated large parts of Mato Grosso, Acre and Roraima. The land-grant practice ceased in 1995, but other plans allocated large chunks to road-building and urban expansion, or hydro-electric schemes, while mining and lumber operations continue with few controls.

The people
Population and ethnic groups
In Brazil as a whole, whites of direct European descent comprise around 55% of the population, whereas 35% are *caboclos* – descendants of mixed Indian and European or African blood. Ten per cent are black, descended directly from Brazil's West African slaves. The remainder are indigenous Indians or immigrants from Europe – especially Germany – and Asia.

Despite Brazil being South America's most populous country, rural areas are largely empty, so the average population density of 17 per km^2 is much less in jungle areas. Indeed, much of Amazonas is uninhabited, being the country's most thinly populated state.

Population composition is somewhat different in the Amazon where proportions of *caboclos* and Indians are higher than average. Of indigenous peoples, a number of fairly intact cultures are in Brazil's far northwest, while in the east and along the main stream, virtually every tribe is being rapidly assimilated into the dominant way of life.

For visitors interested in visiting less culturally contaminated tribes, the most important group are the Yanomami along the upper Negro to Brazil's northern border with Venezuela. The nearly extinct Omagua live south, along the Juruá River. Other tribes include Tikuna, from the Colombian border area, and Waiwai, Arawete, Kayapo, Carajá and Xavante.

Languages
Portuguese is the official language, a legacy of Brazil's unique colonial history. Attempts to speak Portuguese, no matter how amusing, are much appreciated.

BRAZIL'S INDIGENOUS INDIANS

Depending on whose figures you believe, Brazil's Indian population is currently between one tenth and one fiftieth of the original population when Columbus arrived. Today some 150–200,000 Brazilian Amerindians survive. While many have adopted the *caboclo* or *rivereño* culture of subsistence farming and fishing, others remain unacculturated, still very isolated from the Brazilian way of life.

The wholesale extermination of indigenous peoples during the 19th century continued in Brazil until very recently and still does in more subtle ways. Even those responsible for carrying out Indian welfare programmes appear positively bent on the destruction of their country's cultural and natural heritage.

There is very little that is funny about FUNAI (Fundação Nacional dos Indios), the government organisation charged with looking after the welfare of Brazil's indigenous Indians. The history of FUNAI officials includes reports of ineptitude, corruption and even violence against the Indians, the very people they are sworn to protect. The worst outrages, documented by official public enquiry, include 'donations' of disease-ridden blankets, exploiting the vulnerability of Indians to Western diseases. Settlers were thus rid of a big obstacle to their land claims. Recent shake-ups in the organisation have put an end to such atrocities, but the same myopic mentality prevails and resources are few.

A few tribes with relatively intact cultures remain in Brazil, as in remote parts of other Amazon countries. In August 2000, the Naua tribe, believed to have been extinct since the 1920s, emerged from hiding to protest the creation of a national park in their homelands in the state of Acre bordering Peru. Then, in April 2001, the Tsohon-djapa, a tribe previously unknown to the outside world, was discovered in the Javari River region. Reservations are off-limits without hard-to-obtain permission from FUNAI (Joaquim Nabucu 473, Manaus; tel: 092 234 7632; web: www.funai.com.br).

Some 200 indigenous dialects are currently spoken; mostly among tribes virtually assimilated into dominant Brazilian society. Linguistic fragments brought over by African slaves have found their way into common usage and in some regions are the basis for local dialects. Nevertheless, the present linguistic diversity of Brazil is but a shadow of what once was.

Education

Theoretically education is free and compulsory from ages six to 16, but the ideal of education for all has not yet even been approached. Some 15–25% of 13 million school-age children have no schooling at all. Availability of schooling in urban areas is limited by lack of teachers, while in outlying areas insufficient funds are available to build even a few badly needed schools. The University of Amazonas is one Brazilian educational success story, as the region's most prestigious higher education establishment. Likewise, the internationally respected INPA researches important questions in tropical biology (page 379).

Culture

Brazil is a country of music. From salsa to rumba, Brazilian dance music is heard around the world. The country has also produced its share of talented classical musicians, while in rural areas, simple rhythms of working people provide raw material for constant innovations to the Brazilian music scene.

Also defining Brazilian culture is the obsession with football. South America as a whole is fanatical about the sport, but the Brazilians' passion makes the interest of others seem like a mere hobby. As with music, football crosses all cultural boundaries, creating one of the few unifying forces in Brazilian culture. When Brazil wins the World Cup, the whole nation celebrates as they did in July 2002.

Religion
It's the world's largest Catholic nation but numbers of Protestants are rising and currently make up 15% of the population. Afro-Brazilian religions such as *candomblé* and *umbanda,* which are also popular, have their origins in western Africa.

Fiestas
Most people have heard of the Rio carnival: the world's biggest song-and-dance festival. Thousands of dancers in glittering costumes and varying states of undress gyrate, wriggle and twirl to the hypnotic beat of countless drums. The festival's date varies from late February to early March, and if you don't mind large crowds, it's a spectacle not to be missed.

A brief history
Unwritten history
In the late 1990s, archaeologists working around the Xingu River region discovered stone tools that date the time of human presence in the Amazon to at least 10,000 years ago. However, we can only speculate on events between then and the European discovery of Brazil. Dominant tribes encountered by Portuguese explorers on the coast were Tupi-Guarani and Gê. Further inland Arawak, Carib and others were encountered by other early explorers. Two to five million indigenous people comprised the pre-European population.

Following a semi-nomadic, hunter-gatherer lifestyle, these tribes are known to have had sophisticated cultures, with their own language, religion, diets and mode of dress. We have little hard evidence but can infer the foods they ate by study of extant tribes. In charming watercolours by early artists we have glimpses of clothing; from nothing at all to elaborate adornments of rainforest bird feathers and animal teeth. From such glimpses, and written accounts of early traders, we presume there were trading links between some of these tribes and hostility between others.

The Europeans
In the year 1500, the Portuguese captain Pedro Cabal landed on Brazil's northern Atlantic coast and claimed the territory for Portugal. Others, notably Amerigo Vespucci, navigated further down the coast and were the first Europeans at the Amazon's mouth. Neither knowing nor believing it was a river, they called it Rio Mar – 'River Sea.'

The conquest of Brazil and the Amazon was not achieved through direct warfare as throughout much of South America. The colonisers trickled in, at first unsure of how to live in the new surroundings and relying on coastal Indians for labour and assistance.

Of the region's inhabitants, Francisco de Orellana knew nothing when he left Quito for his first navigation of the river in 1541–42. His exploits and those of other post-conquest explorers did little to belie the legends and superstition that so impressed Western minds: tales of female 'Amazon' warriors, lost cities and other bizarre entities.

Aside from a few missionaries, and the Portuguese explorer Teixeira who travelled upriver, for the world at large the Amazon's interior remained a mystery. It was the age of explorer-scientists, who described the place in realistic and plain language, that revealed a potential bonanza of natural resources.

For its hardwoods the region became renowned and the country took its name from the reddish *pau do brasil* hardwood. By the mid-1800s, around Manaus and further upstream the development of rainforest commerce was based first on *chicle,* then on rubber.

Independence

Brazil's struggle for self-rule was virtually over in a day and night and was totally bloodless, unlike the massacre-laden independence movements in Spanish colonies. When Napoleon captured Lisbon in 1807, King of Portugal Don João VI fled to his biggest and least-tamed colony and declared himself emperor. Returning to Portugal in 1821, he left behind his son Pedro as prince regent. Dom Pedro I became emperor of an independent Brazil in 1822 before abdicating in favour of his five-year-old son Pedro in 1831.

Taking command in 1840, Dom Pedro II took his new title seriously but went too far when in 1888 he declared slavery was to be abolished, or he would abdicate. His ploy worked, but the political price was high and Dom Pedro II was forced to flee to Paris. Brazil was declared a republic in 1889.

Scientific developments in the Amazon began with La Condamine, who noted how Indians used sap from the *Hevea brasiliensis* tree to make waterproof shoes, bouncing balls and syringe-type instruments. Following hot on the heels of geographic knowledge, Victorian scientists scrambled into the jungle's depths in search of new and usable plant and animal species. The French botanist d'Orbigny and English scientists Alfred Wallace and Henry Bates visited Manaus in the mid-18th century. By this time, the sugar trade's collapse had weakened Brazil's ruling classes and rubber had come to dominate the country's external trade. For the first time real power was centred in the Amazon and Manaus flourished in the spotlight, while labourers and Indians slaved away tapping the vast Amazon forest for rubber.

The 20th century

Brazil's 20th century will be remembered as one of change and growth, chaos and environmental degradation. From a half-forgotten ex-colony, during the late 19th century Brazil grew, assisted by the boom in the rubber trade, to become an industrial power to be reckoned with a century later.

Coffee grown in the southern state of São Paulo supplanted rubber as Brazil's main income earner early in the 20th century. The wealth from coffee financed early industrialisation in southern Brazil, creating powerful coffee barons. Despite attempts by the military to take control, the coffee-producing oligarchies of the south obstructed any change. Unrest amongst the working classes and dissatisfaction with the coffee producers brought the military dictator Getúlio Vargas to power in the 1930s on a wave of populist support. Vargas introduced a minimum wage, improved working conditions and set Brazil on the path to full modernisation while systematically removing opposition and torturing political prisoners.

World War II cut Europe off from its Asian rubber plantations, and European overtures saw Brazil recruit 30,000 tappers to harvest latex from the Amazon, thus temporarily reviving the flailing industry. World War II also saw the US begin the

THE BALBINA PROJECT

The gates of the Balbina hydro-electric dam 200km north of Manaus were sealed in October 1987 damming the Uatumá River. The project flooded 236,000ha of tropical forest and displaced one third of the remaining indigenous Waimiri Atroari Indians. The cost of the project was put at US$750 million, while the value of timber flooded was around US$400 million. Nearly 300,000 animals had to be rescued from the unnatural inundation, and even the fish have survival problems as the decay of forest biomass has turned the water fetid, acid and low in oxygen.

The benefits of the project? Eighty megawatts of power, just 32% of the installed capacity, produced at a financial price that is four times the amount considered to be reasonably competitive.

development of the Brazilian steel industry. The rapidly industrialising country continued down the road of modernisation but when Vargas, now the elected president, created the large state oil company Petrobras in the early 1950s the military and international community saw this as a step too far towards communism. Media pressure grew and Vargas, feeling increasingly isolated, was forced to stand down in 1954 and committed suicide shortly after.

Juscelino Kubitschek took power in 1955 and began an intense period of expansion. Brasilia, the new planned capital, was built in three years and was connected by road to Belém, creating the first overland link to central Amazonia. Kubitschek's legacy of spiralling inflation only increased demands from the burgeoning working classes to adopt leftist policies. Pressure for land reform in the northwest and populist movements in the south worried conservatives and the military alike, with the almost inevitable outcome of a military coup. The US considered Brazil under military rule to be an important ally in the Cold War of the 1960s. The military regime gave rise to the first Amazon colonisation plans, as agricultural labourers displaced by mechanisation in the south and drought in the north demanded action. The social costs of the regime were heavy, with over 20,000 Brazilians imprisoned, tortured and 'disappeared', while thousands more sought exile abroad. An 'economic miracle' transformed Brazil to such an extent that, when power was handed back to a civilian government in 1985, the economy had grown to be the tenth largest in the world.

Despite Brazil's return to democracy, the 1980s offered little hope as hyperinflation gripped the economy and foreign debt rose to a staggering US$120 billion. The election of Fernando Collor de Melo on an anti-corruption ticket was seen by many as a way out of the intractable economic problems. His currency stabilisation programme would hurt, but the Brazil that emerged would fully live up to the motto of 'order and progress' proudly displayed on the national flag. Notwithstanding his anti-corruption rhetoric, Collor was impeached for a scam that cost the treasury billions of dollars. Yet, in a country where corruption is a part of daily life, few were surprised.

The finance minister, Fernando Henrique Cardoso, was the mastermind behind the stabilisation programme and used its success as a platform for his election to the presidency in 1995. While Cardoso's 'Real Plan', pegging the Brazilian *real* to the US dollar, hurt the poorest sections of society, his presidency saw the economy grow, as state industries were privatised and regional trade organisation continued to remove trade barriers between South American countries.

Elections in October 1998 returned Cardoso to power, and the country has since enjoyed relative prosperity. However, grassroots support for the Worker's Party suggests socialist policies influence Brazil's political and economic future.

In January 1999, the government announced that the *real* would no longer be pegged to the US dollar. Although this move devalued the currency it helped moderate the downturn in economic growth that year. Indeed, the economy did well in 2000. Inflation kept within single digits and direct foreign investment was over US$30 billion.

In late 1999 Cardoso signed the country's first environmental crime bill. This defined deforestation and pollution as crimes punishable by jail and fines. Although enforcement has been patchy, this milestone marks official recognition for Brazil's ecological heritage. In 2002, revelations of illegal mahogany exports prompted the government to increase the penalties for unauthorized logging and totally ban export of this species.

On January 1 2003 'Lula' Luiz Inácio da Silva was inaugurated as president at the fourth time of trying. Analysts have speculated as to whether Brazil would experience complete economic meltdown akin to that endured by neighbouring Argentina. The global economic slowdown, Argentina's collapse and a credit squeeze on Wall Street helped strangle growth, expected to reach 1.5 per cent during 2002. Only time will tell whether Lula can walk the difficult line between keeping the international lending organisations on side and providing the much-needed sense of social justice demanded by his supporters.

Government

Brazil's system of government is a representative democracy headed by the president with a four-year term, requiring at least 51% of electoral support to secure office. If first-round voting does not establish a clear majority, a second round of voting with fewer candidates takes place. Congress is composed of a 513-member Chamber of Deputies and an 81-member Senate. Voting is compulsory for eligible adults aged 18–70, voluntary for the over-70s.

Economy

Although when travelling in the Amazon it is sometimes difficult to believe, the Brazilian economy is an industrial powerhouse that produces over 1.5 million cars annually, exports nearly 400,000 of them, builds aircraft and tanks, and in the mid-1980s stopped just short of becoming a nuclear power.

For the future, minerals are destined to become Brazil's economic mainstay as it makes the most of its significant deposits of bauxite and around a third of the world's iron ore reserves. Carajás, south of Belém on the Tocantins River, is one of the world's largest mine complexes producing significant exports of iron ore and several other minerals for Brazil.

In the Amazon, mining projects are less ambitious, although a major gold-producing area south of Roraima flanks the Rio Branco, its exploitation facilitated by the Caracas–Manaus highway, soon to be completely paved. In the far west of Amazonas, along the frontier with Venezuela, lie further gold bearing formations and the world's richest deposits of niobium (a metal used by the aerospace industry).

The region's exports are funnelled through Manaus from where most products end up in Brazil's industrial centres for processing and export. Considerable quantities of raw materials are exported direct to North America, Japan and Europe.

Money

Brazil's currency problems are a case-study in classic economics. With sky-punching inflation rates reaching 1,000% annually during the 1970s and mid-80s, Brazilian banknotes became literally worthless. The *real*, Brazil's present currency, is doing better than its predecessors. Cardoso's 'Real Plan' has introduced a degree of stability to the currency and foreign exchange reserves are at an all-time high.

Brazil is currently one of the most expensive Amazon countries to travel in. Acceptable budget accommodation starts at around US$15 and the cost of travel, although good value, tends to be high due to the great distances involved. Budget travellers can probably get by comfortably on a minimum of US$40–50 a day. If you're looking to do the occasional excursion and stay in more comfortable hotels, then spending over US$100 a day is easy.

Dollars are accepted in places aimed at tourists but as soon as you leave the set itinerary you will have to use reals. The best places to change money are at branches of Banco do Brasil and foreign exchange houses. In Manaus, Banco do Brasil has branches at Rua Marechal Deodoro in the centre and at the airport where you can cash travellers' cheques and change currency. Cortez (corner of Av Getulio Vargas and Rua 7 Setembro) offers a good exchange rate. If you're coming through Rio, change money there, as the exchange rate in Manaus is lower than elsewhere in Brazil.

Travellers' cheques and major credit cards are accepted at all banks and large hotels. The easiest way to get money is from ATMs (Automatic Teller Machines) that are sprouting out of walls in some of the most surprising places. With your Visa or MasterCard you can withdraw up to R$1,000 from ATMs. However, they do not always work and sometimes the machines will not accept non-Brazilian cards.

If heading off into the jungle for several days, change as much money as you think you'll need. In smaller towns you may have problems changing travellers' cheques or using your credit card over the counter. In the very smallest towns and villages you will have to work hard to convince people that the piece of paper called a dollar that you are holding is worth anything.

Highlights

Even today, as globalisation puts adventure travel within reach of the masses, the Brazilian Amazon's potential for nature tourism is largely untapped. Most visitors go to Manaus, where the Rio Negro joins the Amazon. Here is the **Meeting of Waters** where the Negro's black waters intermingle with the Amazon's brown. In the immediate vicinity and eastward along the main stream, deforestation has ruined vast tracts of rainforest. Much of the logging, mining and urban and industrial development is along major rivers in eastern Brazil.

The most unspoiled areas in the Brazilian Amazon are west of Manaus toward the Colombia-Peru border, or up the Rio Negro towards the pristine **Pico de Neblina National Park** on the Venezuela border. Up the Negro, a few hours boat ride from Manaus, is the **Anavilhanas Archipelago**, a vast labyrinth of islands, which change from day to day due to shifting currents and water levels. This wildlife haven is among Brazil's top birding locations. The area is also popular among serious sports anglers for record-breaking sizes of peacock bass and other species. For them, and for a price, top-notch facilities are available through specialist companies. If you are in eastern Brazil, the mouth of the Amazon River is the world's largest river delta, and includes the island of

Marajo, site of early Amazon settlements and today a refuge for numerous water bird species.

Wherever you go large animals are absent from rainforest around towns and villages due to excessive hunting. Even so, near Manaus, the forest supports numerous bird species, caiman, sloths and monkeys. For the best wildlife you need to visit protected areas, of which the Pico de Neblina National Park is the best known. **Iguassu Falls**, although outside the Amazon watershed, is perhaps the most scenically spectacular of Brazil's attractions. Also outside the Amazon watershed, in the southwest of Brazil, the **Pantanal** is a vast area of mixed savannah and wetlands with exceedingly rich wildlife. Package tours often combine a visit to these with tours to lodges near Manaus.

Tour operators

Several overseas tour operators organise trips along the Amazon and take bookings for the lodges found throughout the area (see *Chapter 2*). In other areas you have to go direct to operators in Brazil.

In the US

Adventures Abroad (page 40) has a wide range of tours encompassing Manaus and other Brazilian attractions.

Brazil Network 2125 Biscayne Blvd #350, Miami, FL 33137; tel: 800 218 8390; fax: 305 468 6499; email: info@brazil.com; web: www.brazil.com. Manages an array of websites dedicated to offering discounted web fares to Brazil, from the US, Canada and UK. Offers a variety of creative and affordable vacation packages to the Amazon, Buenos Aires and many other destinations in South America.

Brazil Nuts 1854 Trade Center Way Ste #101A, Naples, FL 34109; tel: 800 553 9959; fax: 239 593 0267; email: info@brazilnuts.com; web: www.brazilnuts.com. Leading US tour operator specializing in Brazil, with special expertise in the Amazon, offering a variety of lodges, riverboats and jungle expeditions.

Brazil On-line 1110 Brickell Avenue, Ste 502, Miami, FL 33131; tel: 888 527 2745; fax: 305 379 9397; email: info@brol.com; web: www.brol.com. Comprehensive online discount booking and reservation system for virtually any tour, lodge or airline in Brazil.

Ecotour Expeditions PO Box 128, Jamestown, RI 02835; tel: 800 688 1822; fax: 401 423 9630; email: info@naturetours.com; web: www.naturetours.com. Camping trips and Rio Negro cruise.

Lifelong Learning 101 Columbia, Ste 150, Aliso Viejo, CA 92656; tel: 800 854 4080; fax: 949 362 2075; email: travel@lifelong-xpo.com; web: www.lifelong-xpo.com. Cruises aboard luxury liners from Manaus to multiple destinations down-river and beyond.

Maxim Tours Ltd 50 Cutler Street, Morristown, NJ 07960; tel: 973 984 9068/800 655 0222; fax: 973 984 5383; email: maximtours@earthlink.net; web: www.maximtours.com. Have a number of different options available for the Brazilian Amazon including cruises and lodge accommodation.

Rod & Reel Adventures 2294 Oakmont Way, Eugene, OR 97401; tel: 541 349 0777/800 356 6982; fax: 541 242 0742; email: info@rodreeladventures.com; web: www.rodreeladventures.com. Premium peacock-bass fishing adventures out of Manaus aboard 'the most modern vessel serving the fishing/ecotourism industry in Amazonia'.

Stockler Expeditions 10266 NW 4 Court Plantation, FL 33324; tel: 800 591 2955; fax: 954 472 7579; email: stocklers@usa.net. Arrange a wide variety of programmes in Brazil: fishing, birdwatching, Jewish heritage, African heritage, diving, Carnival and more. Represent Guanavenas Lodge.

Tours International 12750 Briar Forest Dr, Ste 720, Houston, TX 77077; tel: 281 293 0809/800 247 7965; fax: 281 589 0870; email: toursintl@aol.com; web:

www.astanet.com/get/toursintl. Take bookings for jungle lodges along the Amazon main stream.

Luxury cruise lines with Amazon cruises to Manaus

Fred Olsen Cruise Lines White House Rd, Ipswich, Suffolk IP1 5LL; tel 01473 292 222; fax: 01473 292 345. Occasional luxury cruises travelling the Amazon leaving from England, usually via Miami.

Radisson Seven Seas Cruises 600 Corporate Drive, Ste 410, Ft Lauderdale, FL 33334; tel: 800 477 7500; web: www.rssc.com. Cruises to Manaus in the *Navigator* and *Song of Flower*. Receives many plaudits.

Royal Olympic Cruises 805 Third Avenue, New York, NY 10022; tel: 800 872 6400; fax: 888 662 6237; email: rocruises@rocusa.com; web: www.royalolympiccruises.com. Cruise between Belém and Manaus aboard the *Olympic Explorer*.

Silversea Cruises 110 East Broward Boulevard, Ft Lauderdale, FL 33301; tel: 800 722 9955; fax: 954 522 4499; web: www.silversea.com. Amazon cruise to Manaus aboard the *Silver Cloud*.

In the UK

Journey Latin America, **Scott Dunn** and **Worldwide Journeys** offer a variety of itineraries in the Manaus area and elsewhere in the Brazilian Amazon.

Kumuka Expeditions 40 Earls Court Rd, London W8 6EJ; tel: 0800 068 8855; fax: 020 7937 6664; email: enquiries@kumuka.com; web: www.kumuka.com. Expeditions that include boat trips down the Amazon.

When to go

Those averse to heat should avoid October to January; the heat sometimes lingers into February. The dry season is the time of lowest water, when fishing is better, but high water (April–July) gives you the chance to take a boat through the flooded forest.

During Brazilian holidays from December to March, coastal resorts are busy and Manaus gets crowded. Foreign tourists are most numerous during times of holidays in the northern hemisphere, ie: in the middle of summer (June–July). Therefore the best times to visit are May and August, as September is Brazilian holiday season. A bad time is from September onwards for a couple of months when farmers and loggers put large areas of rainforest to the torch. Fishing is best during low water (September–March), but the Victoria water-lilies die down during this season.

Health

Technically Brazil requires the yellow-fever vaccination if you have travelled through other endemic countries such as Peru or Colombia. The immigration authorities don't usually check but for peace of mind, get vaccinated, and keep the yellow World Health Organisation card with your passport.

Security

Crime is an increasingly serious problem facing Brazil. It is less severe in the Amazon area than in notorious conurbations like Rio de Janeiro and São Paulo, but visitors are well advised to keep up their guard. The murder of World Cup yachtsman Sir Peter Blake in December 2001 brought the bad side of Manaus to world attention. Avoid touts for jungle trips or city accommodations – there are reports of people being hustled off to be robbed. Certainly in Brazil a 'big city' mentality is essential to avoid being targeted.

GETTING THERE AND AWAY
By air
From the US
The easiest and most popular way to reach the Brazilian Amazon is to fly from Miami to Manaus. Varig, Brazil's national airline, flies the route once a week on Saturdays. It's an afternoon flight taking five hours to Manaus with another two for Belém. Check your luggage is labelled correctly. TAM, Brazil's second airline, offers fares to Manaus via Sao Paulo or Brasilia.

There are also good international connections to Manaus with flights from Los Angeles and New York.

From Europe and elsewhere
Several airlines including Varig, British Airways, Air France, Iberia and TAM fly to Brazil from Europe once or twice a week destination Rio or São Paulo. The cost from London starts at £370. Flying to Rio with Varig you can get a connecting flight to Manaus or Belém for another £70 or so.

Varig have direct flights from Caracas, and good connections to Buenos Aires, Havana, Lima, Maracaibo and Santiago.

By ship
It is possible to travel up the Amazon by cargo ship but it's expensive relative to the experience. Although almost 2,000km inland by river, Manaus is accessible by ocean-going vessels and several luxury cruise ships or foreign-registered expedition vessels regularly make the journey.

The triple frontier where Brazil, Colombia and Peru meet is one access point by ship although you have to change if you are travelling on national vessels.

Overland
The only reliable way to get to Amazonas by road is from Venezuela. The border crossing is at Santa Elena, some 200km north of Boa Vista. There is a road from Guyana into Boa Vista but it is reported to be terrible. This route and others are only sporadically available. To the south there are several road connections with Bolivia, the most commonly used being Porto Velho to Guajará-Mirim on the border (four hours by bus, US$16).

Frontier crossings by river in all other places apart from the triple frontier are not commonly used and any passport formalities, such as exit and entrance stamps, will have to be dealt with before you arrive at the frontier or the next large town after crossing the border.

Customs and immigration
Brazil's strict reciprocal visa policy requires **visas** of citizens from countries who require Brazilians to have a visa. US citizens need a visa to travel in Brazil (unless on a day trip), but European nationals in general do not. (See *Preparations and planning,* page 30).

All visitors who stay over 90 days require a visa. You have to apply in person at your nearest consulate or use a visa service agency. Getting the visa in your home country is the easiest option but you can get one from Brazilian embassies and consulates in neighbouring countries.

When entering Brazil complete the **disembarkation card** issued on your flight or vessel and keep the copy that has to be handed in when you leave. In Manaus the immigration offices are at the airport or, if you are disembarking from a ship, at the floating dock next to the tourist information office.

If you are crossing a land border, **customs formalities** are at the border crossing or, in some cases, at the nearest police station. If entering or leaving Leticia, Colombia, you need to get your passport stamped in Tabatinga.

If you need to stay longer than allowed by your entry visa, you must extend it at the offices of the Policia Federal 15 days before it expires. Overstays on a visa will cost US$1 per day for up to 75 days.

GETTING AROUND
By bus

Bus services are the only sensible way to travel by road in Amazonia. The *rodoviária* (bus station) for long-distance buses in Manaus is at the junction of Rua Recife and Avenida Constantino Nery, some 6km from the town centre (US$10 by taxi). Bus services into Manaus come from Boa Vista in Roraima, but the unpaved road is notoriously unreliable, especially during the rainy season. The 15-hour journey (US$40 one way) has to be among the most gruelling in the annals of travel. No less tough is the theoretical road to Manaus from Porto Velho to the south, invariably impassable due to flooding. Some of it is newly paved, and when complete should provide more rapid, but less tale-worthy, transit between the two cities. Santarém and Manacapuru are other towns with irregular and unreliable bus services to Manaus.

The trans-Amazonian highway was supposed to open up the Amazon to motorised land transport. But the dream has been denied by weather, terrain, remoteness and absence of money for regular maintenance. Travelling the highway is possible but the road is served only by very occasional transport and you need to use river transport for the section immediately west of Itaituba. Venturing off main roads with any kind of motorised vehicle is only for the serious expeditioner.

By air

Internal flights in Brazil are efficient and inexpensive; with the air-taxi system you pay fares of US$100 or less between many cities on regular flights. Flights with Varig can be planned in advance at www.varig.com.br. If you are planning to visit a number of different places, the Brazilian airlines Varig and VASP have airpasses (both US$530 plus US$40 service fee) that link up several of the larger cities in the Amazon, but you have to book them outside of Brazil. Domestic routes cover most cities.

By boat

ENASA (Empresa de Navegação de Amazonia), the state shipping line, offers regular passenger services between Belém and Manaus and throughout the Amazon. However, their vessels are not particularly recommended as they are large, crowded and impersonal. They are a useful source of information for finding a local riverboat for passage up the main rivers, with schedules of locally registered vessels.

From Guyana or Venezuela, one can travel overland to Boa Vista then transfer to Caracaraí on the Rio Branco to take a riverboat down to Manaus. It's relatively easy to make this river trip solo. For the two- to three-day voyage, several boats daily depart the Boa Vista docks for Manaus (US$50–75 one way, sleeping in a hammock).

From Iquitos, via Leticia, luxury ships come downriver and cross into Brazil at Tabatinga, and their passengers simply have to admire the scenery and attend the evening cocktail, with no worry about immigration formalities. Those on local boats will need to change at Tabatinga or Benjamin Constant as most local riverboats only travel as far as the borders. Dozens of boats depart on this route daily so you should find it easy to get a berth. From Tabatinga, Manaus is around a five-day cruise on the local riverboat and costs US$75.

From Porto Velho the journey downstream to Manaus costs around US$70 and takes four days when the conditions are right, far longer when things go wrong.

Travelling the Amazon on a luxury cruise is one option, and the trip has to be organised from outside Brazil. Your first tough decision is whether to do the 'full monty' and travel the full length of the Amazon from Belém to Iquitos or whether to head downstream. Up is better, because you travel from developed land near the mouth of the river towards pristine forest upriver. As the currents are slower closer to the riverbank, that's where you tend to travel. Cost is from around US$4,000pp and up depending on the quality of your cabin. If your funds don't stretch that far you can do a half-length cruise from Manaus to Iquitos, which is the best for wildlife and sightseeing, or Manaus to Belém which is not especially recommended. Your cruise agency will let you know details of dress code and ship cuisine.

COMMUNICATIONS
Mail
All towns and many smaller villages have post offices (*correios*) but the post is generally slow and prone to disappearing in either direction. Be prepared to pay two or three times more for postage than you would back home. Even airmail letters or postcards cost upwards of US$1, taking five days for US destinations and about ten for Europe.

General delivery is reported to be unreliable so to receive mail use your hotel address. American Express members can use the local Amex office. The main post office in Manaus is on Rua Marechal Deodoro. The post office is open weekdays 08.00–17.00 and on Saturdays in the morning.

Telephone and fax
Phoning is most convenient and most expensive from the hotels. If you don't mind the long queues at the TeleAmazon office it's much cheaper (eg: US$5 for a three-minute call; UK £1.50/minute). International operators at Embratel speak English if you are having problems.

Fax is the most popular and convenient way to communicate with Amazon businesses, although a few are adopting computer-based communications systems. But to send an international fax *from* Manaus can be horrendously expensive: US$10–15 per page with a commercial fax service. TeleAmazon offices are cheaper, around US$1 per page. The international phone code for Brazil is 55.

Internet
The electronic age is slowly but surely reaching the Brazilian Amazon. Most cities have internet cafés that allow you to communicate within the country and the outside world. In Manaus, try **Discover Internet**, near Praça da Policia (Rua Marcilio Dias 320, L7, Centro; tel: 092 233 0121; fax: 092 232 9443; email: discoverinternet@hotmail.com). It's open 08.30 to 18.30, US$1.25 per hour.

Email messages for remote jungle lodges are likely to be relayed to their ultimate destination by fax so don't expect a speedy response.

TV and radio
Brazilian broadcast media are largely unintelligible to the non-Portuguese speaker. There are over 250 TV stations throughout the country and almost 3,000 radio

stations. TV is no more exciting than anywhere else but Brazilians are blessed with the gloriously melodramatic soap *A Indomada* – essential viewing throughout Brazil.

For media addicts posher city hotels have English-speaking programmes including BBC World, CNN and ESPN, available via satellite.

Newspapers

Highest-circulation Río papers are *Globo* and *Jornal do Brasil*, copies of which you will see in Manaus and other large Amazon cities. At international airports and big city hotels, English-language newspapers and magazines from the US, or more rarely the UK, are available a day or three out of date.

PASSING THROUGH RIO

The three main international points in Brazil – Rio de Janeiro, Brasilia and São Paulo – are a long way from the Amazon River. If the main focus of your trip is the river itself fly directly from the US to Belém or Manaus. From Europe, connecting with a flight in Miami opens up the same possibility. Most direct flights from Europe go to Rio de Janeiro. All Brazilian international airlines connect with most regional cities and the extra cost on your ticket and the extra time saved travelling make the option worth considering.

Galeão International Airport is on Governor's Island around 15km north of the centre of the city. If you need to change money Banco do Brasil on the third floor is open 24 hours. It's also worth picking up maps of the city and other tourist information from the registered Riotur or Embratur information desks. Other desks, although providing useful information, are working for a particular chain of hotels.

As at other South American international airports, a crowd of taxi drivers gathers around the exits to cajole you into their vehicles. However, you can also take a bus or use the taxi cooperatives – both are cheaper than a private taxi.

Executive buses operated by Real Auto Onibus make the journey to the centre of town every 30 minutes until midnight, leaving from outside the terminal and charging US$5. The bus weaves its way through most city districts of interest to the visitor including the centre, where most historic sites are located, the hotel districts of Glória, Flamengo and Botafogo south of the centre, and the more expensive areas of Copacabana and Ipanema.

If you are in a group, buy a taxi ticket from Transcoopass or Coopertramo who have several desks in the airport. They sell pre-paid journeys to different parts of the city. A taxi carrying up to four people to the centre costs around US$20, slightly more to Copacabana.

For getting back to the airport your hotel will help you book a taxi through Transcoopass or Coopertramo. Hotel staff will also be able to direct you to the nearest pick-up point for the airport bus.

Where to stay

As you would expect with an international city of Rio's status, accommodation is available at all levels and prices. City guides and various other books provide hotel listings. With places of historical interest in the centre and the must-visit beaches of Copacabana and Ipanema to the south, Glória, Flamengo and Botafogo are perfectly positioned districts along the efficient and quick metro line. These districts are full of economically priced hotels, restaurants and bars. Down in Copacabana and Ipanema the hotels are more expensive.

Turístico (Ladeira da Glória 30; tel: 2557 7698) is close to the Glória metro. It's one of Rio's most popular budget hotels and often full (US$25). If you are looking for a little self-indulgence at the beginning or end of your trip, **Hotel Glória** (Rua do Russel 632 in the Flamengo district; tel: 2555 7272; fax: 2555 7282; web: www.hotelgloriario.brazil.com.br) is one of the best hotels in Rio (US$140). If you are travelling from the airport by bus ask the driver to drop you at the nearest point, or get off at Cinelândia metro stop and travel south one stop to the Glória.

Down in Copacabana there are plenty of hotels, most of them quite expensive. **Hotel Martinique** (Rua Sá Ferreira 30; tel: 521 4552) comes recommended at US$40 for a good room.

What to see

If you have time to stop in Rio you'll find it worthwhile. Most hotels can arrange trips up Corcovado Hill from where Christ the Redeemer has stood, arms outstretched, preaching his silent sermon on the mount for nearly seventy years since first taking up residence on this dramatic spot. Excursions to Sugar Loaf Mountain can also be arranged. You can walk or climb up either of these hills; or there are transport systems that will take the strain if you'd prefer.

Then it's off to the beach to hum the tunes of Manilow and Sinatra as the sun sets over Copacabana.

If you need tourist information, **Riotur** are in the centre at Rua da Assembléia 10, ninth floor, and have a multilingual telephone service (tel: 00 55 21 2542 8080).

MANAUS: GATEWAY TO THE AMAZON

Most people going to the Brazilian Amazon travel into Manaus and strike out from there. Bona fide capital of Amazonia, Manaus is so far west (1,200km) of Brazil's coast that it is in a different time zone (one hour behind). Manaus is the only city in the central Amazon with over a million inhabitants. Located at the confluence of the Negro and main stream, it is a focus for regional trade, tourism and administration. Although 1,320km from the river's mouth, Manaus lies only 32m above sea level. Today it has a rough-and-tumble atmosphere, somewhat unsettling for first-time visitors or those just returning from a two-week jungle trip.

The city began life as Barra, a fort built by the Portuguese in 1669. Its fortune waxed and waned with those of *pau do brasil*, quinine and other easy-come, easy-go products. When the French botanist d'Orbigny visited in 1830 he saw a bedraggled settlement of 3,000 inhabitants. This changed practically overnight in the 1850s, with the discovery of new ways of using rubber latex and its subsequent application in the inventions of rapidly industrialising countries.

By 1870, 3,000 tons of rubber were being exported annually, and the population had mushroomed to 50,000. By the century's end, annual rubber exports totalled 20,000 tons and the astounding wealth financed Manaus' explosive growth.

Manaus' excesses of luxury became a byword for extravagance. Never did the phrase 'from rags to riches' ring so true. Tatters were exchanged for clothes tailored in Paris and London. According to Anthony Smith, the worst spendthrifts even sent their wardrobes back to Europe just to be laundered!

Gold was the accepted medium of exchange, with business transacted in spacious, luxuriously furnished offices, toasted with champagne and cognac served by bartenders brought over from Europe. Indeed, servants were not the only immigrants: bankers, musicians, artists and eligible ladies along with women of lesser repute were among the passengers of cargo ships returning from Liverpool or New York for another load of rubber.

There was no apparent attempt to seek cost-saving solutions. Portuguese stone was imported to pave marshy areas, along with work-crews to lay the slabs. In 1896, an opera house to rival those in Europe or America was erected, equipped

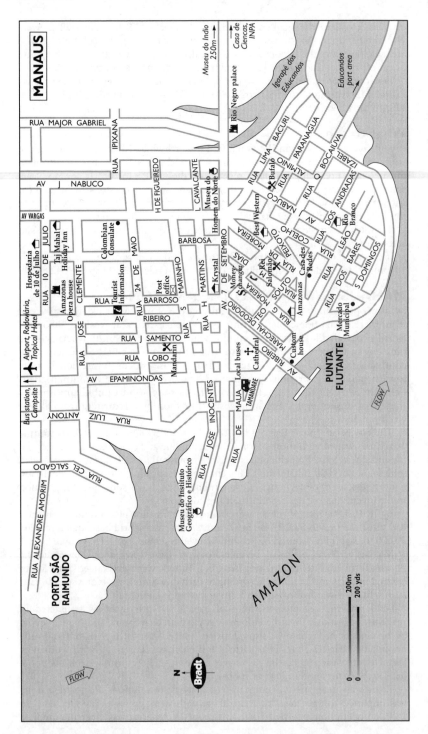

MANAUS

RUA MAJOR GABRIEL

AV J NABUCO

AV VARGAS

Museu do Índio 250m

Casa de Ciencias, INPA

Rio Negro palace

Igarapé dos Educandos

Educandos port area

Airport, Rodoviária, Tropical Hotel

Bus station, Campsite

RUA ALEXANDRE AMORIM

RUA CEL SALGADO

PORTO SÃO RAIMUNDO

AMAZON

200m
200 yds

with orchestra, full company, and guest performances by world-renowned singers. Whatever the truth behind the claim of Caruso's appearance at Teatro Amazonas, it is certain that electric trolley-cars were rattling through the streets in 1897. In the same year the latest-technology telephone exchange was installed, to serve the city's 300-plus telephones. Together with a huge floating dock, in 1902 the British built a customs house on the waterfront in a solid classical style, entirely of stone imported from England. It is still in use today. Intact also is the Municipal Market, constructed mostly of glass and wrought iron, copied from Les Halles in Paris.

In 1908–10, over 80,000 tons of rubber were exported, the income from which covered two fifths of Brazil's balance of payments. Yet the human price was steep, as thousands of indigenous Indians were virtually enslaved, and Chinese work gangs were imported. Demand for Amazon rubber slumped through competition on the international market and in 1912 one business after another fell into bankruptcy. By 1923, the collapse was complete, and Manaus seemed destined to become a ghost town.

It was not until the middle of the 20th century that prospects perked up. Amazon rubber's high quality sustained a small market and prevented the industry's total disappearance. During World War II, attrition by Japanese forces of Malaysian plantations led to a rapid rise in demand as the Amazon became the Allies' only reliable source of rubber, essential to the war effort. The town emerged from its generation-long depression.

Manaus' tax-free status, established in 1967, and more recently growth in tourism, have boosted local fortunes, while the dock facilities promise a role for Manaus in the area's commerce and travel industry for a long time to come.

Most visitors to Brazil's Amazon go to Manaus; whether you love or hate it, the city is an essential part of any visit to the heart of the Amazon. First-time travellers should study carefully to see if a trip here will suit their interests and wallet. For those lacking confidence about travel in the Amazon, Manaus is a great place to put a toe in the water. The city is fine to scope out tours, buy equipment or to relax after a jungle trip.

At the airport

Eduardo Gomez International is 18km from the city. Of the two terminals, international flights are normally served by Terminal One – but check.

You pay about US$15–20 for the 20-minute taxi ride into town. Don't take a hotel bus unless on a pre-booked tour. To avoid taxi rip-offs you can buy a set-price ticket for your destination from a booth in the airport close by the exit. On the way back get a ticket at your hotel. Never leave luggage in a taxi alone with the driver.

There is an hourly airport bus service to and from the centre of town between 07.00 and 23.00. Buses heading for the airport are marked Aeropuerto Internacional and leave from R Tamandaré near the cathedral.

Whether or not you have a tour arranged, ignore the touts at the airport and in town. Use the list in this book to select a tour operator and then visit their office. In any case choose only from state-registered (Embratur) agencies.

City transport

Transport in Manaus can be a nightmare if you want to do a lot of sightseeing. The best way of getting around is taxi. Make sure the taxi goes where you want. The taxis are expensive. Buses are frequent, inexpensive and easy enough; just use enough sign-language and say in Portuguese where you want to go. On the downside, most are crowded, old and smelly with erratic schedules.

Where to stay

Lodgings in Manaus are increasingly oriented to the tourist. There's a wide range of price and quality. Hotels tend to fill at busy times of year so try and reserve in advance. You can book any of dozens of hotels through www.viverde.com. A list of hotels is available through the **Zfnet** online city guide (www.zfnet.com/manaus/p0000.htm).

Luxury

Tropical Hotel da Ponta Negra, CEP 69037-060, Manaus; tel: 092 658 5000/0800 701 2670; fax: 092 658 5026; email: ghathm@tropicalhotel.com.br; web: www.tropicalhotel.com.br. This is Manaus' most prestigious and biggest hotel. Palatial rooms are decked with antique furniture and bathroom fittings with modern conveniences. Every conceivable amenity is available and the hotel's Taruma restaurant is one of the city's best. There's a small and rather primitive zoo! Prices begin at US$70 single, US$90 double. Airport pick-ups for advanced bookings. The hotel is 5km from the airport and about 40 minutes' drive from the city centre (US$10-15, US$5 with hotel shuttle).

First class

International chains include **Taj Mahal Holiday Inn** (Av Getulio Vargas 741, Centro; tel: 092 633 1399; fax: 092 633 1010; email: tajmahal@internext.com.br), from US$100 pp single; and **Best Western Manaus** (Rua Marcílio Dias 217/225; tel: 092 622 2844; fax: 092 622 2576; email: bwmanaus@internext.com.br), from US$55 single, US$90 double.

Other first-class hotels:

Hotel Amazonas Praça Adelberto Vale 215; tel: 092 622 2562. A couple of minutes' walk from the main dock, 182 large air-conditioned rooms, with private bathroom, hot water and TV. Facilities include a swimming pool and inexpensive but unimaginative buffet. Costs from US$85pp single.
Da Vinci Hotel Rua Belo Horizonte 240A, Adrianópolis; tel: 092 663 1213; fax: 092 611 3721. Away from town centre.

Middle range

You can choose from dozens of medium price range (US$20–50) hotels in Manaus. A morning stroll around Manaus' main commercial area between 7 de Setembro and Dos Andrades, east of the dock, will cover many options. The following are examples of what's available rather than specific recommendations.

Hotel Krystal Rua Barroso 54; tel: 092 233 7535; fax 092 633-3393. A three-star hotel, dingy on the outside, quite nice inside.
Mango Guesthouse Rua Flavio Espirito Santo #1, Kissia II; tel: 092 238 4349; email: mango@naturesafaris.com. A new hotel in the upper class Kissia II neighbourhood, away from the traffic noise of downtown Manaus and with a swimming pool. About ten minutes' drive from the airport and city centre. Bus services are also available nearby. Rates are US$40 for a single, US$50 for a double.
Rei Salomão Rua Dr. Moreira 119, Centro; tel: 092 234 7374; fax: 092 232 8479. Cool, clean, apartment-size rooms with private bathroom and phone. US$25.
Hospedaria 10 de Julho Rua 10 de Julho; tel: 092 232 6280; email: htdj@internext.com.br. 'Tourist standard' with comfortable rooms at US$28.

Budget

Hotel Río Branco Dos Andrades 484; tel: 092 233 4019. Centrally located and a favourite among gringo backpackers. It's safe and clean. Even if you don't stay here it's a great place

to meet fellow travellers and pick up titbits of information (US$7.50 per night, including breakfast).
Youth Hostel Rua Silva Ramos 685; tel: 092 234 6796. Members US$11. Non-members are welcome but pay around US$2 extra per night.

For those on a minimalist budget, other cheap hotels are concentrated around the dock area.

Camping

If you're camping to save money, you are better off staying in jungle shelters with a hammock. Ask tour operators and make sure you have a good guide.

The best place reasonably close to Manaus is **Praia da Ponte Negro**, some US$15 by taxi from town near the Tropical Hotel. Here there is a nice beach with toilet and washing facilities, a restaurant and boats for hire. Swimming is relatively safe and enjoyable except at weekends and during high season when the site is heavily used by locals. Hang on to belongings at all times. There is no charge for slinging a hammock or pitching a tent.

Where and what to eat

Restaurants, clean and inexpensive, offer a wide range of international dishes and of course, fresh fish is the regional speciality, but prepared with little imagination in most cases.

Less frequently nowadays *tambaqui* is on the menu – hardly surprising since the species has been seriously overfished, alarming some conservationists. Proposals to farm *tambaqui* are currently in the pipeline and could be the salvation of this flavourful fish.

Staples are rice, beef, chicken and beans. Try some Brazilian specialities. *Feijoada* consists of cuts of salted or smoked meats with seasoned vegetables, eaten with dried manioc (*farinha*) and grated kale and orange slices as a relish. It is most often served as the main meal for Saturday lunch. The Amazon version is called *maniçoba*. Another traditional meat dish is *churrasco*, a grilled steak and other meats with roasted manioc. Downriver, *empanhidas de camarão* are popular: shrimpburgers with heart of palm and olives. Another shrimp dish is *tacacá* – shrimp with manioc and hot sauce. *Mixira* is meat from the endangered manatee and *pirarucu* is a heavily overfished species. Both could do with a break from the menu listings.

Un-aged sugarcane rum, *aguardiente,* is the traditional alcoholic refreshment, called *cachaça* or in polite company *pinga*. A surprising choice of wines is available to accompany a meal. Brazilian wines are not wonderful, but not bad either. Choose carefully as a good bottle costs US$25–30.

A popular non-alcoholic rainforest fruit beverage is *cupuaçu* juice, while *guarána* has enough caffeine (7%) to top up even the most dedicated coffee drinker. Other fruit juices are cashew, guava, passion fruit and the lesser-known chirimoya and sapote.

The Hotel Tropical's **Tarumã Restaurant**, serves world-class international and local dishes. The desserts are excellent. A speciality is crêpes stuffed with tropical fruits and flambéed bananas. The hotel's pool bar serves drinks and a range of snacks. If it is really hot, you can always opt to have your drink served in the pool. Outdoor barbecues are held pool-side as an alternative to the restaurant.

If you get tired of hotel restaurants head for **La Barca** (Rua Recife 684), with fine upmarket international dining and excellent fish. Other good fish restaurants are **São Francisco** (Blvd Rio Negro 195), **Panorama** (Blvd Rio Negro 199; tel: 624 4626) by the river, or the most expensive: **Caçarola** (Av Rio Maués 188; tel:

233 3021). **Bufalo** (Av Joaquim Nabuco 628; tel: 633 3773) specialises in meat dishes. **Miako** (San Luis 230) serves good Japanese dishes, and for Chinese try the **Mandarin** (Av Eduardo Ribeiro 650). For non-carnivores, the **Vegetariano** (Av 7 de Setembro 752) is recommended, while good vegetarian food is served at the Indian restaurant **Chapaty** (Rua Costa Azevedo 105). Many eateries close late Sunday and all day Monday, or all weekend.

For cheap food to eat on the move, the fish market has fish and meat cooked on skewers, or various savoury or sweet snacks cooked al fresco over wood burners. They are tasty and safe enough when eaten straight from the fire and thoroughly cooked. Fresh fruit provides endless amusement as you figure out how to deal with the various alien species; it should be peeled before you eat it.

Nightlife
If the heat of the jungle makes you doubt Brazil's reputation for vitality and love of music and dancing, visit Manaus' nightclubs. Most open around 21.00 for longer than you'll be able to party. The Tropical Hotel's **Coração Blue** (Estrada da Ponta Negra) has a variety of music from pop to modern jazz. **Hype** (Estrada da Jonasa, 100 Ponta Negra, tel: 658 3502) is popular among younger Brazilians for its techno-pop. **Tukannu's** (Estrada do Turismo 121) is packed with dancers bopping, wriggling and swaying on the dance floor.

What to see
The majority of interesting sights are within 15–25 minutes' walk of the central area. This busy, bustling part of town is fascinating, with lots of shops, a couple of museums, the fish market and the floating dock. The area is quite safe to walk around during daytime, if you keep a close eye on the unstoppable traffic. After dark, sensible caution is required: walk around only with companions, dress casually, and conceal any valuables, purses and so on. Going any distance is best done by taxi.

Formerly a dingy backwater trading post, Manaus owes much of its success and status to the huge **floating docks**, completed in 1902 by the British to accommodate ocean-going ships during the rubber boom. The Porto Flutante – or more formally the Punta Escadoria dos Remedios – was essential to increasing trade through the port of Manaus.

Today, despite nearing its centennial and having suffered ship collisions and fire, the ageing edifice continues to perform sterling service on behalf of the city's shipping. Construction began in Glasgow before pieces were shipped to Manaus and assembled *in situ*. The docks are 150m long and designed to rise and fall with the annual flooding of the river, accommodating a change in water level up to 12m. It remains an engineering marvel and, even if you are not interested in tonnage capacity or shipping schedules, is worth a visit just to observe the press of human life. Riverboats and cargo ships, cruise ships and canoes, *caboclos* and foreign crews, tourists and tribespeople, hawkers and hookers, all flock to the riverfront. The docks are central to Manaus, physically and spiritually: the city's true heart. If your ship or riverboat doesn't actually berth there and you come into town by bus or plane, any local can tell you where the dock is located.

Parisian-inspired, the airy, high-vaulted design of **Manaus fish market** deserves a mention in guidebooks, but it's a great biology tutor too. The grandly titled Mercado Municipal is an education, where you can major in ichthyology, minor in Brazilian economics and take in some post-renaissance French architecture at the same time. On any given day you will spot dozens of different types of fish. Look for popular species: *tambaqui*, *dourado*, peacock bass and armoured catfish. Depending on the season, other water animals are on display; caiman and river turtle in variously advanced states of dismemberment. Hopefully you won't see parts of the endangered manatee. Besides fish and meat, numerous different types of vegetables and fruits are sold, some more familiar than others; squashes, maize, beans, manioc, avocado and dozens of herbs and nuts, primarily cashews and Brazil. You'll recognise bananas although there are several different varieties; also plantain, citrus fruits, pineapple and, when in season, mango. Less familiar are *chirimoya*, *sapote*, *guarána* and *cupuaçu*, all used in delicious juices. It's easy to spend lots of time speculating about a fruit... just buy it and try it. Vendors in the market sell fruit juices, but take care as they do not use purified water to make them.

A resplendent monument to past glory, the **Amazonas Opera House** (Praça São Sebastiao) is surely among the most splendid edifices in the Amazon. Today, just over 100 years after it opened, the building, situated atop a small bluff, dominates its surroundings. Its luxurious features were paid for with wealth earned by the slaves who enriched rubber barons. Its pink-and-white-wedding-cake style is surely testament to its sponsors' confidence and arrogance, if not taste.

Over the four years it took to erect, the Opera House so beloved of its builders was adorned with no expense spared: marble from Italy, a massive four-storey dome covered with glass tiles imported from Alsace in France, and gold plating elsewhere. The inside is decorated with English china and baroque French furniture. Enthusiastic guides will tell you the Opera House, which opened in 1896, hosted the world's greatest artistes at the time, such as Pavlova and the legendary Caruso.

Built as it was with the profits made from rubber, the Opera House was an early victim as the rubber barons' empires crumbled. The price of rubber collapsed in 1910 and in 1912 the doors of the Opera House closed, 16 years after they had so proudly opened. The building itself remained, but without a company or performances, mute testimony to a bygone age and in imminent danger of sinking into the Amazon. Restoration began in 1974 and in March 1990 the Opera House reopened, but holds only a couple of performances each year. Tours of the theatre are 09.00–15.00; Tue–Sun; admission US$5. You can walk there from the floating dock, a short but hair-raising, high-traffic-density stroll. From the dock's main gates head straight up the hill past the post office and across Av 7 de Setempro, then along Av Eduardo Ribeiro a couple of blocks and the theatre, on Praça São Sebastiao, is right in front of you: unmissable in both senses of the word.

The headquarters of the **Instituto Nacional de Pequisas da Amazonas** (INPA – National Institute for Amazon Research – Alameda Cosme Ferreira/Estrada do Aleixo 1756) is the centre for much of Brazil's rainforest research. There are pleasant botanical gardens and a visitor facility with labelled trees. Wildlife to enjoy are manatees, otters, caiman and lots of birds. It has fewer but better-kept animals than the zoo. Stroll along the well-constructed, modern walkway through the tree-tops. The **Casa de Ciencas** (Science House) showcases INPA's world-class research on Amazon ecology with projects on practical applications. Especially interesting are displays on effects of development – notably dams and mining.

Of particular interest to entomologists is their world-famous insect collection (Colecáo Sistemática de Entomologia). A visit here will give you some idea of how much you are missing if you don't think much of insects. It is near Est de Aleixo (take any bus to Aleixo), near the Natural Sciences Museum.

The **Jardim Botânico** (Botanical Garden), Av André Araujo, is a small garden dedicated to Chico Mendez, the murdered rubber tapper and trade union leader.

It's a pleasant retreat from Manaus' bustle, with a fine selection of Amazon plants containing many species which home gardeners will recognise. Open 08.00–12.00 and 14.00–17.00 daily.

Parque Zoologico do Centro de Instruçao de Guerra en Selva (CIGS Zoological Park) is at Est Punta Negra 750. This modest establishment is run by the Brazilian Army to show soldiers rainforest animals, because the reality is that most Brazilians have not seen even a wild monkey, let alone a jaguar or anaconda. So the zoo's a good place to see the animals you won't encounter on an average jungle tour.

However, many of the cages are small and the animals receive poor diets. The occupants vary but monkeys, parrots, snakes, armadillos, tapir and jaguar are usually present. Conditions are poor compared with those of our modern zoos and some visitors find the place depressing. From town take a taxi for around US$4 or a bus ('Punta Negra' or 'São Jorge') to Est Punta Negra 750, some way beyond the Hotel Tropical. Open Tue–Sun 09.30–16.30.

Museums

Before venturing into the jungle, first-time visitors should take a day to tour the main museums dotted around the city centre, as these will broaden your perspective of the region's wildlife and culture. They close weekends (or Sun–Mon) and most charge a small fee.

Museu do Instituto Geográfico e Histórico (Geographical and Historical Institute Museum). From the floating dock, turn left (if facing away from the water) along Rua M de Santa then left again all the way to the west end of Av 7 de Setembro on the waterfront. The contents of this historic building feature displays of mounted animals, ancient artefacts and fossils. It has a library, most of which is in Portuguese. Open Mon–Fri 08.00–12.00.

Museu de Ciêncas Naturais da Amazônia (Amazonian Natural Sciences Museum). To get there from the town centre direct, take a taxi (US$3–4) along Estrada Belém. A visit to this museum will give you some idea of rainforest biodiversity, with displays of butterflies and a huge variety of beetles and ants. A large *pirarucu* is on show at the aquarium. Post-tour, you can head for the museum shop to buy handicrafts. It's best combined with a trip to INPA (see page 379) by bus, after which you can continue to the museum by taxi. It's worth the effort. Open Tue–Sun 09.00–17.00.

Museu de Minerais e Rochas (Museum of Minerals and Rocks) Est do Aleixo 2150. This geological museum is worth a visit for a better understanding of what is under your feet. Open Mon–Fri 08.00–12.00 and 14.00–18.00.

Museu do Indio (Indian Museum) Rua Duque de Caxias near Av 7 Setembro. Run by the Salesian Mission, this ethnic museum is one of Manaus' most popular repositories of memorabilia including pottery, woven goods, traditional dress and art objects. Best represented are the Tikuna and Waiwai tribes, with some material from the Yanomami along the upper Negro. A small gift shop sells postcards and crafts. Open Mon–Fri 08.00–12.00 and 14.00–17.00; Sat 08.00–12.00. Additional information at www.museudoindio.com.br.

Museu do Homem do Norte (Museum of Northern Man) Av 7 de Setembro 1385. A general museum, especially focused on depicting the *caboclo* way of life, culture and history, with perspectives on local economy and social structure. Among the exhibits are photographs, models, pottery, clothing, utensils and weapons. Mon–Fri 09.00–12.00 and 13.00–17.00; Sat 13.00–17.00.

Other sites of interest

One of the city's most impressive buildings, dating from the late 19th century, the **Rio Negro Palace** was one-time home of Waldemar Scholtz, a wealthy rubber baron, and is the place to go if you have trouble believing the stories of Brazil's rubber wealth. Those days are now long gone, but the building lives on as the home for the administrators of Amazonas' state government. The palace is located on the east side of town at the end of Avenida 7 de Setembro where it meets Rua Major Gabriel. It is not open to the public but is worth a look from the outside.

The **British Customs House** is a fine example of 19th-century British architecture, showing the solid confident style typical of contemporary government buildings. Built square-shaped of English sandstone, the Customs House serves in much the same function for which it was originally intended; as an office for Manaus' inspector of port taxes. It's not open to casual visitors, although it is used today for port business, as it has been since its construction which coincided with that of the floating dock, whose traffic it was built to administer. The customs house is unmistakable and easy to find: just inside the entrance to the floating dock, left as you go through the gate.

In the **Port of Manaus Museum** (Rio Vivaldo Lima 61) you can have all your questions on the minutiae of the construction and running of the port facilities answered. The displays include photographs, maps, instruments and log-books. The museum will fascinate anyone interested in the story of the Manaus dock construction. Open Mon–Sat 07.00–11.00 and 13.00–17.00; Sun 12.00–17.00.

Excursions from Manaus

Along the confluence of the Amazon and Negro is the so-called **Meeting of the Waters** (Encontro das Aguas), some 12km from Manaus. The Rio Negro is, as its name suggests, black, or at least very dark brown, the colour of *café noir* and classified as a blackwater river. The Amazon main stream is classified as whitewater, somewhat misleadingly, being the colour of *café au lait*. Anyway, where the rivers join up, and for several kilometres downstream, the two differently coloured waters remain distinctly separate, intermingling in all sorts of interesting circular, spiral and wavy whorls and eddies.

Most tour agencies will arrange trips to see the Meeting of the Waters. The most economical option is to go by a taxi or bus (#617 'Vila Buriti') to the Careiro ferry dock and take the car ferry across the river.

About 8km outside Manaus (20 minutes by taxi, US$15), the **Salvadore Reserve** protects a lake of the same name which is a haven for numerous aquatic and forest birds, plus reptiles, amphibians and the odd lucky monkey or two (they are heavily hunted outside reserve areas). You have a good chance of seeing all of these, as the wildlife can be readily viewed from a floating deck, to which the birds especially seem quite accustomed. The reserve is best experienced early morning or around dusk but there is no accommodation so you need to coordinate transport to get you there and back. Any of the Manaus tour agencies (page 370–6) will be able to provide more information or can book tours to the reserve.

The **Amazon Ecopark** is a private nature reserve with a visitors' centre and a variety of animals. Their Brazilian ranger leads a course on jungle survival offering you the best way to learn how people 'live off the land' in the jungle. Figure on US$30–35 for a day trip (no accommodation here), including the 30-minute launch trip from Manaus. To make a booking enquire at the Ecopark office at Praça Auxiliadora 04, third floor, in the city centre. Separate from, but adjacent to, the Ecopark is the **Monkey Jungle**. This small wildlife centre run by the Living Forest Foundation is dedicated to the care of confiscated and abandoned animals. Most people come here as part of their visit to the Ecopark. Book at the Ecopark office.

Turislandia is a sort of arboretum, sure to enthral students of tropical agriculture who want to see plantation crops such as those you will encounter on a typical three- or four-day jungle trip. There's a few large jungle trees, unusual herb or epiphyte species and foreign flora. On a one- or two-hour tour, you have a good chance of seeing some plants and birds hard to find in the jungle. Guided visits can be arranged at most Manaus tour agencies (US$15–20) but you can do it a lot cheaper yourself (US$0.75 by bus, US$1 admission). You'll need a half day to visit the arboretum, located approximately 25 minutes' drive from the city centre, in the Aleixo neighbourhood.

Shopping

Brazil manufactures world-class aircraft and mass-produces VW Beetles by the million...but tourists are usually after more practical souvenirs. For those whose bank balance can meet the challenge, Brazil is renowned for its range and quality of precious gems. Top of the range are precious stones and exotic minerals.

Street hawkers and curio shops sell wood and soapstone carvings, basketry and pottery and little paste sculptures used to make figurines and all sorts of imaginative small objects. Leather goods are a more practical buy. Of less desirable acquisitions, preserved piranha heads, shoddy carvings and craftwork, snakeskin and cat furs are widely available. Trade in pelts and skins is illegal as are products with feathers or teeth so don't waste your money.

For one-stop souvenir shopping try the **Casa da Arte Indigena** on dos Andrades between Marcilio Dias and Dr Moreira. This sells most types of folk art and handicrafts you are likely to see in the region. The shop, close to Hotel Amazonas, is run by FUNAI and profits are said to help Indians maintain their traditional way of life. Try **Casa de Beija Flor** (Rua Quintino Bocaiuva 224) for native handicrafts such as blow-guns, masks and pottery and tropical fish.

If you are going to the Indian Museum their craft shop sells a few handicrafts, wood carvings and Indian hammocks. More practical cloth hammocks can be bought from a shop in front of Hotel Amazonas. Among several other places to buy handicrafts, try **Central Artesano** on Rua Recife. **Casa des Redes** conveniently located on Rua dos Andradas (corner of Rocha dos Santos) is a good place to pick up general items for a jungle trip: hammocks, eating utensils, rubber boots and so on.

The Tropical shopping arcade has a branch of **H Stern** with the best – but not cheapest – selection of gemstones and semi-precious stones. The Stern chain is Brazil's biggest and best known jeweller and a visit to their shop at the Hotel Tropical is an education in itself, with most items way beyond the pocket of mere mortals.

Leaving Manaus

Getting out of Manaus into the jungle on your own by boat or road using local transport is a very different ball-game from booking a day trip or lodge at a tour agency. Bus, boat or aeroplane are the main options. There's not much to Manaus' bus connections so we'll deal with those first.

By bus

The bus station for long-distance travel is at the *rodoviária* 6km outside the city. To get there, you can catch a 507 bus (US$0.50) from the town centre or take a taxi (US$5). Buses leave Manaus for Boa Vista along the BR174; the best bus company is União Cascavel. Otherwise there are few options for exploring the area this way. Recently, the Porto Velho–Manaus bus route has been cut from schedules.

By boat

For long journeys on the river you can choose anything from a luxury passenger liner to a rusty old banana boat. The latter are charmingly called *gaiolas* by locals. Here we refer to them as local riverboats to distinguish them from luxury liners or live-aboard tour boats.

On local riverboats your concerns will be survival-based. Most of these vessels are extremely basic. They certainly make you appreciate the simple things of life such as a solid bed, decent food and clean water. There are cabins on some boats – 20–50% more expensive than travel in a hammock – available for passengers. But most people sling a hammock. Taking your own food and water is a good idea if you don't want to risk eating and drinking the boat's fare which is almost certainly going to result in stomach upsets. Security on these vessels can be a concern but most problems occur when you are in port or stopping over for a few hours. While the boat is actually travelling a thief can't go far with a complete bag. A small lock should prevent any opportunistic dipping.

Four docks operate in Manaus. Which one you use depends on your vessel, destination and flood level. The floating dock (Porto Flutante) is used throughout the year for destinations along the Amazon main stream: Tefé and Benjamin Constant to the west or Santarém and Belém to the east. For boats up the Rio Negro during high water the main port is Ponte São Raimundo on the west side of town along Igarapé de São Raimundo (from town centre US$0.50 by bus, US$5 by taxi). During low water boats for the Rio Negro depart from the similarly named Bairro São Raimundo (about 2.5km). For trips down the Madeira to Porto Velho, use Bairro Educandos, at the end of Rua Quintino Bocaiuva in the southwest of Manaus, about 1km from the floating dock. If you are uncertain as to which dock you need, head to the floating dock and ask; someone will point you in the right direction.

Up the main stream, several local riverboats depart from Manaus' floating dock for Tabatinga leaving a couple of times a week, usually Wednesdays and Saturdays, taking six to ten days for the trip. Departure times and schedules change often. These boats are more expensive than you might expect – Tabatinga costs around US$70–100 for one-way hammock travel. If roughing it is not your thing and you can't afford a luxury cruise ship (eg: Iquitos to Manaus US$3,250), slightly less expensive expedition cruise ships and cargo vessels operate during high water. Maybe you could hitch a lift.

For boats up the Rio Negro, go to the port at São Raimundo. Most vessels depart Wednesdays and Thursdays. By local riverboat to São Gabriel this worthwhile trip costs US$60–75 with hammock. Santa Isabel, Barcelos, Carvoeiro, Moura and Novo Airão are stops along the way.

ENASA is the government shipping line, based out of the floating dock. It operates vessels carrying up to 600 passengers between major Amazon cities. Boats depart when ready and have no fixed schedule. If you're considering a trip on one of these vessels, think again. They look horrible and are unpleasant inside, with crowded, unsanitary conditions and inedible food. It is the cheapest way to travel on the river in Brazil but for a few dollars extra you will have a much better time mentally and physically aboard a *gaiola*.

Once you're ready to travel, check the ENASA bulletin board at the floating dock (for destinations along the main stream) or at São Raimundo (to the town of São Gabriel and up the Rio Branco) for sailing and arrival times. Try to get to the ship after it has unloaded or arrive early the next day. If you can't find details relating to your destination just ask someone.

Get to the boat as early as possible to give yourself the best chance of getting a good hammock spot. But as you will quickly find, multi-level hammock hanging is the norm and the boat may not leave until the deck is packed with hammocks filling every space. If your boat doesn't leave until the next day you are normally allowed to stay on board overnight but don't leave luggage unattended.

Most passenger boats take cargo, so expect to be accompanied by bananas, dried fish, exotic fruits and fuel. Fellow travellers, invariably locals, bring along their entire household including dogs, chickens, pet monkeys and anything else that might make their journey a little more amusing or painless.

Cabins are more expensive, hot and insulating, and can be claustrophobic, offering marginally better security which in reality is just psychological. Most have fans but no air conditioning.

By air
Amazon towns and cities are well-connected by domestic air services, in particular the air-taxi system connecting Manaus with Brazil's main cities and São Gabriel, Belém, Boa Vista and Tabatinga. Various air-taxi companies (eg: Taba) operate out of Manaus. Air travel gets you to remoter parts quicker, and for equable cost, but misses the fun and romance of boat travel for a week and the education of going from a city to arable areas through recently cleared forest and into untouched primary forest.

On domestic flights airport departure tax is US$2–3; for international flights US$20.

TRAVELLING THE BRAZILIAN MAIN STREAM
From the dynamic city of Belém at the river's mouth, along the main stream through tropical rainforest in variously ravaged states, passing the towns of Santarém and Alter do Chao and then the teeming metropolis of Manaus, you perceive how people live, the extent of habitat destruction and the conflict between Brazilian and Western values. Peasants cut down forest in order to sell wood, and land is cleared for ranching or plantations. Expanding populations have created serious problems of litter and sanitation which threaten to pollute the main stream, as does the danger of contamination from mine waste and industry. Cattle run unchecked through wetland habitat, disturbing nesting birds and contaminating water. The river's riches are forced from it by nets stretched across the mouths of tributary streams, dynamite fishing and the killing of dolphins for their believed aphrodisiac properties. It's not a pretty picture, but it is real and is as much part of the Amazon as the rainforest. Workable solutions have to be found to these problems.

As you voyage further westwards and beyond Manaus the population thins, towns become less frequent, villages are smaller, the pollution decreases and the rainforest reasserts itself. People are less reliant on manufactured goods and still use the forest and river in more traditional ways, with sustainable hunting and gathering and cultivation of small plots using multi-species methods. The trend continues up to and beyond the Colombia–Peru border, where the main stream – now named Solimões in Brazil – narrows and, beyond Iquitos, splits up into feeder tributaries. For practical details, see page 66.

JUNGLE TOURS AND LODGES
Choosing a jungle tour
First, do as much research as possible before you go. When you get to Manaus get some tourist information from **Embratur** who have offices at the airport, the floating harbour and in town. Their staff speak some English and they offer advice on getting around Manaus, as well as the harder job of navigating through Manaus' jungle of tour operators.

If you are hoping to arrive, stay for a day and be straight on your way to the jungle, prepare for a let-down. It is possible but, if you book with the first representative you see, there is a good chance of getting a bad tour. If you want a run for your money it could take three or four days of sifting through, checking and comparing tour agencies. Ask and shop around for the best deal.

The tour operators mentioned in the next section provide good service and are generally ecologically friendly but are still expensive for budget travellers. Expect to spend a minimum of US$100 per day for a nice boat trip, or from US$60 for hotels and US$100–150 for lodges. The cheapest accommodation is BYOH (bring your own hammock), travelling by riverboat or staying at primitive lodges, for US$15–50 a day. Motorised canoes take you to riverside accommodation, sometimes no more than a hut. Enquire beforehand what supplies you need to bring. Solo travel is most expensive, group travel on a pre-booked tour is cheapest. Pair up with a fellow tourist just to share rooms or take a jungle trip together and the savings quickly add up.

Manaus offers a wide choice of day trips or overnighters, many seemingly overpriced for what you get. Tours range from luxurious to cheap, but price is no guarantee of enjoyment. Generally the more expensive tours have better boats, more educated and environmentally aware guides, better food and, if overnight, better accommodation.

The feeling among tour operators and knowledgeable travellers is that Manaus and the immediate surrounds are rapidly being spoilt as nature travel destinations. Aside from a few responsible companies, the evocative logos and eco-names of local tour operators are largely just lip-service.

The only sensible way to experience the Amazon in this part of Brazil is to take an inexpensive, well-organised three- or four-day trip (minimum) heading to the northwest. Aim to spend at least five or six days in the Amazon with two or three nights in a remote jungle lodge. Anything else is not worth the airfare. In Manaus, look hard and you can find good tours to remote lodges. It will be worth the extra effort.

Planning a tour

Know what you want, know your physical and financial limits, know what to expect, and even then still expect the unexpected. Decide before you go what sort of jungle trip you want and what you can afford, ie: will you want to focus on birdlife, or flora, or perhaps fishing? If you are culturally oriented make sure you visit a couple of Indian villages (where indigenous tribespeople live, perhaps with a semblance of their original lifestyle). Visits to *caboclo* settlements provide a different insight as to how people eke a living out of the rainforest by subsistence farming, ranching on marginal land and clearing forest. The cultural experience is often disappointing for visitors as visits to Indian villages are normally oriented towards the tourist market and can seem false. If you want contact with 'authentic' unacculturated Indians you need to go far beyond Manaus to remote hinterlands, such as along the upper Negro around São Gabriel. Whatever your intentions, research carefully trips that claim you will meet 'native Indians'.

Other details you need to check are the type of accommodation and whether you need to take a hammock, as well as the quality of food and water, and whether the guide speaks English. (Meeting the guide before departure and having him explain the itinerary is an ideal way of judging his quality and linguistic ability.) What sort of trails are involved for walking in the jungle, and are these included as standard? Whether you take a day trip or a week-long river journey, spend as much time as you can in the rainforest because, no matter what sort of adventures you have, once you leave you will want to go back.

On a day tour beyond Manaus you should visit the tree-lined *igarapé* creeks. You won't see big animals but the birdlife and plantlife are rich. Ask about scenic spots. Lago Janauário and the *igarapé* lagoons have better birdlife and more diverse plant life than along big rivers. During the rainy season, several waterfalls beyond the city (Cachoeira do Tarumã, 30 minutes and US$0.75 by bus, US$15 by taxi) offer a relaxing opportunity to spot more unusual plant life, although the falls themselves are worth visiting only during the rainy season.

Trips to the São Gabriel region can be made independently or through a Manaus tour operator, or booked in advance through an overseas tour operator. Birders can book through Field Guides, Inc (page 353) who offer fully inclusive trips to various locations west of Manaus. Other options for exploring the area include four or five days up the Negro or, better still, the Caqueta or Iça. These trips are available only through local tour operators.

Selvatur (Hotel Amazonas, Praça Adalberto Vale, Centro; tel: 092 622 1191; fax: 092 622 2177; email: selvatur@manaus.br; web: www.selvatur.com.br) have four- to five-day tours along the Rio Negro in a floating hotel, the grandly named *Jungle Palace* (US$195pp double; web: www.junglepalace.com.br). **Viverde** (Rua dos Cardeiros, 26 Cj. Acariquara, Coroado III; PO Box 2224, Manaus 69061-970; tel/fax: 55 92 248 9988; email: amazon@viverde.com.br; web www.viverde.com.br) operate exclusively online as a reservation service for a variety of hotels, lodges and cruises in Amazonas state. Besides operating Amazon Lodge and Amazon Village (pages 389 and 390), **Nature Safari** (Rua Flávio Espírito Santo 1, Kíssia II) tel: 092 656 6033; fax: 092 656 6101; email: marketing@naturesafaris.com; web: www.naturesafaris.com) offers well-organised trips aimed at medium-budget travellers. Their trips along the Rio Negro last from three to four days and cost from US$125 a day. They also run and operate the Flotel Piranha, a floating hotel operating near Manacapuru.

Amazon Nut Safaris (Conjunto Manauense, Q/G, c/1 Bairro N S das Graças; tel/fax: 092 234 5860; email: amazonnut@buriti.com.br; web: www.amazon-safaris.com) run outstanding tours to the Anavilhanas Archipelago, several hours journey by boat from Manaus, for US$100 a day. This haven for birdlife is a complex of hundreds of islands formed by a series of convoluted streams connected with the Rio Negro.

Tours in the Novo Airão area along the Rio Negro are offered aboard the *Amazon Clipper* and *Selly Clipper* tourist-standard riverboats. The vessels cruise up the Pagodo River, a tributary of the Negro, and via Acu Creek to Anavilhanas and Novo Airão – where the *Clippers* were built. Trips on these vessels leave from the Tropical Hotel on Wednesdays and Mondays. As these boats are often booked months in advance it is best to make reservations from your home country. You can review the options online (www.amazonclipper.com.br); direct booking was not available at time of going to press but most tour operators in Manaus and the US (page 367) will make arrangements. Examples of tour prices (per person sharing, three days, two nights): Viverde US$395; Brazil.com US$409; Adventure Associates US$425. US tour operators offering combination tours include Ladatco, Southwind Adventures, Gorptravel and others.

Heliconia Amazônia Turismo (Rua José Clemente 500, Room 214, Centro; tel: 092 234 5915; fax: 092 633 7094; email: heliconia@internext.com.br; web: www.heliconia-amazon.com) offers a variety of riverboat tours from US$70 per day, including hammock-only and canoe expeditions. They can also book local lodges for you. They also organise tours to Mamirauá Reserve.

Established 1992, **Swallows and Amazons** (Rua Quintino Bocaiuva 189, Suite 13, Manaus, Amazonas, Brazil 69005-110; tel/fax: 092 622 1246; email: swallows@internext.com.br; web: www.swallowsandamazonstours.com) has an excellent reputation for reasonably priced and environmentally responsible adventure tours. A small riverboat travels on the Amazon and Rio Negro and into the Anavilhanas Archipelago. Facilities are basic but clean and comfortable. Longer Rio Negro tours feature Jaú National Park, the Rio Branco, Barcelos and climbing trips to Pico de Neblina National Park. They also operate a simple eight-bedroom lodge on the lower Negro 60km from Manaus and a six cabin air-conditioned houseboat. Other tours emphasise birding, sport fishing and indigenous tribes.

Earthwatch Institute (page 40) offers a research expedition out of Manaus in which you work with a US scientist to study seed dispersal ecology in the Mamori region. Other opportunities to participate include archaeological research on Marajo Island at the Amazon's mouth and a turtle study on the Javaes River in Tocantins State.

Smaller operators

As soon as you start walking the streets of Manaus you will be approached by someone who wants to sell you a trip on this or that boat. Heed the cautions already given and use common sense if you choose to buy from a smaller operator. The plus side is that they offer lower prices and, if you choose well, more personal service. Recommended is **Moaçir Fortes** (R Miguel Ribas 1339, tel: 092 232 7492) who operates the 12-passenger *MV Cichla Ocellaris* – named after his favourite fish – from the floating dock. Moaçir cruises along the Rio Negro to places rarely visited by other tour operators. His speciality is small fishing trips. The *Cichla* is well-kept with pleasant amenities, fresh food and cold drinks, and Moaçir is among the most sought-after guides in Manaus, fluent in English and German. Trips on the *Cichla Ocellaris* can be booked direct in Manaus. **New York Botanical Garden** (Southern Blvd. & 200th St, Bronx, NY 10458; tel: 718 817 8647; fax: 718-817-8648; email: cgracie@nybg.org; web: www.nybg.org/bsci/NYBG_excursions.html) offers expert-led natural history tours on the *Cichla Ocellaris* or another of Mo's two similar boats, the *Harpy Eagle* and the *Victoria Amazonica*, depending on group size.

Another vessel popular with overseas tour operators is the *Tucano* which plies the Rio Negro to the Anavilhanas islands and also travels the Rio Branco, spending two or three nights on this remote and beautiful river. Six- to ten-day trips are available at US$175–250 per day. In the US, book through Ecotour Expeditions, Maxim Tours (page 367), Forum Travel or Journeys International (page 40).

A number of vessels are dedicated to meeting the needs of serious anglers. The *Amazon Queen* is a three-deck, fully air-conditioned ship with clean cabins and private bath. Five-star meals are served on linen tablecloths in a spacious dining room. Fishing days start early and anglers are whisked around in tournament-style Nitro Bass boats, specially designed for jungle fishing conditions. Several different rivers are covered in a trip. The result is impressive numbers of large trophy peacock bass. An *Amazon Queen* angler holds the current world record for peacock bass (12.3kg). A seven-day fishing cruise is US$3,950 from Manaus including all transfers and applicable charter flights. Book in the US through **Fishabout** (page 55) or enquire through recommended Manaus tour operators. **Rod and Reel Adventures** (page 54) offer a similar package aboard the *Amazon Castaway* for US$3,500.

Angling safaris

Angling tours enable guests to get close to the remotest fishing areas. Locations far from inhabited areas are reached by floatplane. This maximises chances for catching record-breaking sizes. Accommodation is in tents on floating platforms that can moved to follow the best angling opportunities. Facilities are luxurious by camping standards, with comfortable beds, fresh sheets and towels and daily laundry service. The locations are selected according to season. Prices for a week's programme vary from US$2,250 in the low season (Madeira) to US$3,500 high season (Rio Negro). Book through Fishabout (page 55).

Jungle lodges
New jungle lodges and small hotels far beyond Manaus are springing up along some very remote rivers; in other words, where you want to go. For the lodges west and north of Manaus, prices are generally higher than downriver, partly determined by proximity to the city and the cost of moving food, equipment and staff. Prices given below are minimum per person sharing on a three-day package, with meals and bottled water; bar drinks extra. To get the 'Amazon experience' you should take at least a jungle walk or two (include one at night), a piranha-fishing expedition and a couple of birdwatching canoe rides. Transport from Manaus is extra in most packages. Unless otherwise noted, accommodation mentioned below can be booked only through Manaus tour operators. In many cases bookings will be part of a package that includes transfers to/from Manaus, guides and meals.

Amazon Lodge
This relatively small luxury lodge is situated on the Parana do Mamori River system, among mature secondary forest 80km downstream from Manaus – five or six hours in a launch. On the Lago Juma, the dwellings (comprising 14 rooms in small cabins) float on platforms, offering unique chances to observe Amazon aquatic life up close. Rooms are screened for mosquitoes and there are communal cold-water showers and toilets. Power is from batteries and light from hurricane lamps. A generator is used for a few hours in the evening. Beyond the lake several trails go into the surrounding forest, while canoe rides, piranha fishing and caiman hunting are included in the standard package. Situated a couple of minutes' canoe ride from the lodge is a canopy tower. At 55m high, this must be the tallest forest tower in the Amazon. Set aside US$165 per day for a three-day excursion if booked locally through Nature Safaris (page 387). Maxim Tours and Travel Innovations (pages 367 and 42) offers three-day packages, with transfers from Manaus, for US$381 per person (double) to US$529 (single).

Acajatuba Jungle Lodge
On the shore of the large blackwater Lago Acajatuba, several hours by boat east of Manaus, not far from Irandula, the Acajatuba Lodge is amidst beautiful mature secondary forest. This pleasant lodge has cabin-style accommodation with fan, private bathroom and mosquito nets and is good value at US$80 per day. In Manaus, book at Anaconda Turismo (Rua Dr Alminio, #36, Centro; tel: 092 233 7642; fax: 092 622 5072; email: acajatub@internext.com.br; web: www.acajatuba.com.br). Book in the US through Travel Innovations (page 42), with prices from US$279pp double for three days.

Ariaú Jungle Tower
A nature-lover's delight, the main feature is a raised walkway through trees and across a swampy area connecting a succession of platforms and ending with a 50m-high observation tower. The walkway is great for birdwatching especially in the morning.

The complex is situated by Lago de Ariaú in the Arquipélago das Anavilhanas. From Manaus, the journey of 35km takes about three hours. A whole day (two nights) is the minimum needed to take in the area around the tower. Accommodation is US$140 per day booked through River Jungle Hotel (Rua Leonardo Malcher 699, Centro; tel: 092 234 7308; fax: 092 233 5615; email: treetop@internext.com.br; web: www.ariau.tur.br). In the US, you can book two- to four-day packages (starting at US$280 for two days) from Forum Travel (page 41). Travel Innovations (page 42) offer an overnight package for US$280.

Tropical Lodge

This well-run lodge is the Hotel Tropical's country cousin. The facilities are located by Lago do Salvador, in the Igarapés dos Guedes. It's about 30km from Manaus, and the trip there takes around an hour by launch. Here is where to stay if comfort and ease are your main priorities. It has a good restaurant and nice rooms, but not much wildlife so nature enthusiasts may question the price: about US$120 per day. Most guests come here through the Hotel Tropical where you book with Selvaturs in the hotel lobby.

Amazon Village

Situated on the banks of the Lago Puraquequara, Amazon Village is a luxury lodge some 30km up the Rio Puraquequara. From Manaus the journey takes three to four hours by boat.

A central lodge area is surrounded by 16 twin-bedded cabins with private bath and patio, with a ready-hung hammock for dozing during siesta time. There is no generator (as there is at most lodges in Brazil) and energy is supplied by solar panels. Meals are at the lodge restaurant, with refreshments for quaffing at the well-stocked bar. Standard activities include a variety of jungle treks, canoe trips, piranha fishing, caiman-spotting and visits to *caboclo* villages.

It gets crowded during the high season, being popular with foreign tourists, within easy reach of Manaus and somewhat less expensive than average. Reservations are recommended. Book direct through Grand Amazon Turismo (Rua Ramos Ferreira 189, s403; tel: 092 633 1444; fax: 092 633 3217; email: avillage@internext.com.br; web: www.internext.com.br/avillage). Cost is US$110 per night.

From the US you can book through Maxim Tours; US$326 per person double, US$381 single. Tours International in the US offer three nights at Amazon Village as part of a twelve-day round-Brazil tour (see page 367).

Amazon Ecopark

This 20-cabin lodge located on Tarumã-Açu Creek, a tributary of the Negro, is about one hour by powerboat west of Manaus. Each unit has three air-conditioned screened rooms each with private bathroom and hot shower. Facilities include a thatched-roof open-air restaurant, a private beach with natural 'swimming pool' and 10km of trails. Nearby is the Primate Rehabilitation Center. The centre takes in monkeys captured for the illegal wildlife trade then returns them to the wild. At the centre you can photograph a variety of rare monkeys. Other activities include observing the rubber-tapping process, and instruction on jungle survival and medicinal plants. The most popular package is 3 days/2 nights for US$280pp double. It's US$75 for additional nights (special rates for children). Transfers are free at the guest's convenience day or night. Book direct through their office in Rio de Janeiro (tel/fax: 55 21 2275 6544; email: info@ecopark.com; web: www.amazonecopark.com).

Aldeia dos Lagos Resort

Aldeia dos Lagos Resort is part of Silves, a locally managed ecotourism project with technical support and sponsorship of the Worldwide Fund for Nature. Profits are used to preserve the lake system, and to improve the quality of life for the Silves community. (More information is at the WFN Brazil website: wwf.org.br.)

The first section of the three-hour drive is along a 'surfaced' road, the AM010 to Itacoatiara. From here you take a 90-minute boat ride to Silves Island. Luggage is limited to 15kg per person. During the dry season, the river section might only be possible by dirt road, 120km by bus or taxi.

The resort comprises two main buildings with 12 apartment rooms. Each has private bathroom, screened window, fan and veranda. Other facilities include a gift shop, the restaurant and a lookout. Phone is available. Prices begin at US$385pp for four days. Bookings are through Viverde.com (web.www.viverde.com). In the US you can book through Forum Travel International (page 40).

Apurissawa Jungle Lodge

This forest hotel is located on the Cuieiras River, a tributary of the Negro River, 80km from Manaus in a scenic area near the Anavilhanas archipelago. The small floating lodge accommodates 14 in two suites and five rooms (shared bathroom). Another four can stay in each room of a two-room cabaña (private bathroom) on the riverbank. Facilities are basic but acceptable. A wide range of activities is available. Prices start from US$290pp for a three-day trip for three persons. Book through Amazon Nut Safaris (page 387) in Manaus.

Guanavenas Jungle Lodge

This is a luxury lodge named in honour of a now-extinct Indian tribe. Here 'you are the guest and nature is the show.' Built in 1980, it's located on an island near Silves, about 300km east of Manaus. To get there, you travel three hours by bus and another hour by powerboat down the Urubú River.

The facility comprises twenty circular cabañas with 52 rooms, all with air conditioning, private bathroom with hot shower, mini-refrigerator and private verandas. Facilities include a buffet dining room, two swimming pools, game room, lawns and a 30m observation tower. Long-distance telephone and fax are also available.

You can book direct in Manaus (Constantino Nery Av 2486, Flores 69050; tel: 092 656 3656; fax: 092 238 1211; email: reservas@guanavenas.com.br; web: www.guanavenas.com.br). They're represented in the US by Stockler Expeditions. Maxim Tours (page 367) offer a two-night package (including transfers) at US$305pp sharing.

Rio Negro Lodge

Opened in October 1998 this lodge is on the south bank of the Rio Negro is 100km upriver from Barcelos. Accommodation is in eight spacious cabins, each with air conditioning, two double beds and private bath. The large dining room overlooks the Rio Negro, while the international food with local specialities is excellent. Other amenities include an open bar, daily laundry service and satellite phone. Guests can buy satellite calling cards and use the lodge phone number for home or business use. The lodge caters to serious fishing enthusiasts and has top of the line boats that cover a large area of water daily. The cost from Manaus for a nine-day programme (six fishing days) is US$3,950. Book through Fishabout (page 55) in the US.

NATIONAL PARKS AND WILDLIFE RESERVES

Historically, Brazil has not cared much for the notion of national parks and even today government officials seem barely ecoconscious – there is little in the way of information for protected areas. Given the size of the territory, much of it still pristine and undeveloped, Brazil has allocated a minute amount of land for conservation. However, the protected areas are remarkable wildernesses, as yet untouched by man. The effort to travel there will be great, but then so will the reward. Of the 42 National Parks, nine are in the Amazon Basin. They are Amazônia (864,047 ha), Cabo Orange (619,000 ha), Jaú (2.2 million ha), Monte Roraima (116,000 ha), Pacaás Novos (764,801 ha), Pico da Neblina (2.2 million ha), Serra da Mocidade (350,960 ha), Serra do Divisor (846,633 ha) and Viruá (227,011 ha). Not all accept or welcome visitors either for reasons of protection or due to lack of access.

Jaú National Park

This is the only fully protected area of tropical lowland rainforest in the state of Amazonas. Covering a total 22,720km² it is basically an unofficial reserve for Yanomami still living a relatively traditional way of life. Indeed it is the closest place to Manaus where you can see Indians in a natural setting – otherwise you have to go north up to the remote area near the Venezuela border. Covering a large area west of Manaus, between the rivers Solimões and Negro, the easiest way to get there is to proceed to Novo Airão (via boat from Manaus), from where you can hire a boat to take you to the park area. A guide is essential for any visits to the park.

Rio Negro Forest Reserve

This government reserve covers a huge and very remote triangular area from the headwaters of the Negro down to the Rio Uaupés on the Colombia border. The reserve is about half a day's travel, by motorised canoe (US$35) upriver from the small town of São Gabriel. In town you can hire a guide for about US$20 per day. Camping is the only option for accommodation, with you bringing bedding and all necessary utensils. As the area develops, permanent accommodation may become available so check in Manaus for the latest opportunities.

Pico de Neblina National Park

This relatively small park protects the mountainous area in the far northwest of Amazonas on the Venezuelan border. The area includes Neblina Peak, Brazil's highest point at 3,014m above sea level, which only experienced climbers should attempt. The Neblina Peak is highly inaccessible, with no roads or navigable rivers close by, and reaching the foothills takes several days' hike through dense jungle. From Manaus, the national park is remote and hard to reach, but all efforts will be amply worthwhile. São Gabriel is the closest town to the park. Once there, a couple of tour operator offices can arrange a guide for camping trips into the park. You must supply bedding, food and utensils for yourself and usually for the guide as well. Alternatively, book your trip to the park through one of Manaus' tour operators, such as Swallows and Amazons (page 388). In the US, Inti Travel offers a 15-day camping tour for US$3,250 per person. These are more expensive but all-inclusive. For details see page 41.

Amazon National Park

With almost one million hectares close to the town of Itaituba (page 414), south of Santarém, Amazon National Park is relatively easy to reach yet completely off any beaten track.

The park is primarily *terra firme* forest but also includes *várzea* forest encompassing a number of different watersheds. It has high biodiversity. Park authorities have recorded over 40 species of tree per hectare and large numbers of orchids and bromeliads. The park is home to spider, howler and cebid monkeys, four different species of marmoset, collared and white-lipped peccaries, giant river otters, anteaters, tapirs, caiman and jaguar. Seeing these depends on luck and on how long you can spend in the park.

There is a 25-person lodge at the park entrance in Uruá with basic cooking facilities and beds, or you can camp. Whichever option you choose you have to provide your own food so bring it canned or dried from Itaituba. You can explore the park on your own but getting lost is a very real possibility. Alternatively talking to the park staff will reveal the best places to go and you can ask them to guide you for a small fee.

What you get out of a trip to the park depends on what you put in. A couple of days gives you a feel of the place but spending up to a week gets you to some of the least disturbed areas.

Permission needs to be obtained from Ibama's offices on the outskirts of Itaituba (Av. Marechal Rondon, tel: 091 518 1530; fax: 091 5181530) – get a taxi to take you there from town. Charges to visit the park are US$20 per day, plus US$20 administration fee, which is payable at Banco do Brasil in town. Transport to Uruá can be arranged through Transportes Itaituba. Their jeeps pass the entrance, 50km out of Itaituba, on the way to Buboré.

Mamirauá

The Sustainable Development Reserve of Mamirauá, covering 1,124,000 ha is the largest protected floodplain (*várzea*) area in Brazil. The reserve is in the Tefé province, at the confluence of the Solimões, Japurá and Auati-Paraná rivers. The project was initiated in 1992 to conserve biodiversity and for sustainable development of existing communities and in early 2002 opened for ecotourism. Profits are put into community projects and scientific research. The Uakari Lodge is comfortable and uses solar energy and an adequate sewage system to minimize the environmental impacts. From Manaus you can reach there by air via the Tefé airport (staff will meet you). Prices for the lodge begin at US$160pp sharing for two nights. Alternatively, you can travel a couple of hours by motorised canoe. Book through Forum Travel International (page 40) or in Manaus through Heliconia Amazônia Turismo (page 387).

TOWNS AND VILLAGES WEST OF MANAUS
Along the Solimões

Immediately upstream from Manaus, the landscape differs little from that downriver: patches of secondary rainforest among sprawling, dirty villages, their attendant planted areas, grazing fields and newly hacked-down forest. Not a pretty sight, but it is less severe than east of Manaus and does not continue for long. As you get further west beyond the conurbation, the vegetation reasserts itself and begins to crowd in on the river. Only every now and then are the tall, dense woods broken by shacks and huts, usually atop stilts. Some of these merge into *bona fide* towns, most of them visited by riverboats at least once or twice a week. Some of the hamlets listed below are on the itinerary of international cruise or expedition ships.

Manacapuru

This typical Amazon river port is usually missed by the cruise ships, being less than a few hours' sail from Manaus. The smaller riverboats stop here to trade goods or make repairs – a frequent event; after all the town is 85km upriver from Manaus!

Manacapuru is remarkable only for its obvious poverty. Although you may not come here for nature or beauty, you should visit it for insight into the living conditions of the vast majority of Brazilians who dwell in the Amazon Basin away from major settlements. There is not a lot for the visitor to see or do, except take in the atmosphere; a bit smelly near the river, where a lot of sewage is dumped straight down the bank.

The town itself has two or three hotels suitable for the less fussy traveller who can put up with sharing a room with the unseen critters scurrying around at night. One establishment with a below-average density of cockroaches is **Hotel Coqueiro**, where local dishes are served. Not gourmet, but good value.

Manacapuru is about US$12–15 by launch or riverboat, or can be reached by ferry from São Raimundo docks and then a bus, though a boat is better. Going upstream from the town, some riverboats stop at Anon and Codajas. Further upstream is Coari, a village at the confluence of the Rio Coari and lying on the shore of the surprisingly named Lago Coari.

Tefé

After Manacapuru, Tefé is the next sizeable town up the Solimões, 600km from Manaus; it is actually the biggest town between Manaus and Tabatinga and marks the halfway point of the main stream between Manaus and the Colombia-Peru border.

This town is a good starting point for jungle tours, available from three to seven days in duration. A minimalist camping or jungle-shelter trip using hammocks costs US$40–50 per day. During the high-water season, every week or so, foreign-registered cruise ships stop here, during which time 70 or 80 tourists descend, to mingle with somewhat bemused locals. There is no permanent dock so the cruise ships moor some distance offshore and send in their passengers by inflatable Zodiac dinghies.

As tourists are here only twice a month, you'll enjoy the beach on the riverfront and the Monday morning market. At a Franciscan convent, nuns sell small crafts and embroidered cloths. Of the two or three decent hotels, **Anicelis** (Santa Teresa 294) has air-conditioned rooms, and is clean and inexpensive. If it is full try the **Panorama Hotel**.

It's a fairly boring journey, as most of it is along the broad river, and after a while the forest begins to look much the same mile after mile and you ache to get off and explore. Still, some nice boats run between Tefé and Manaus. One-way the voyage costs around US$50 for first class on a better riverboat, with nice clean cabins and safe if not gourmet food. Varig has flights between Tefé and Manaus which can be booked at their Tefé office on the airport road (Est do Aeropuerto 269; tel: 97 343 2466), US$220 return. Rico also have flights.

Fonta Boa

Nothing sets this typical jungle town apart; it's just a stop for local riverboats to trade goods and stock up before the final leg to Benjamin Constant. It takes some time by boat, after you leave Tefé, to make the 180km to Fonta Boa. The route upriver takes you past major tributaries, notably the Jutai and the Içá. From Fonta Boa, boats arrive and depart up the Rio Juruá, eventually to Cruzeiro do Sul, in the Andes foothills, on Brazil's southern border with Peru.

Benjamin Constant

This town is the end-point for all upriver travel through Brazil and the starting point for trips downriver. There's not much to distinguish the place; some shops, travel agencies, a bank and a few hotels. Visit the rubber plantation nearby to see rubber tappers at work. Benjamin Constant is the departure point for trips down the Javari River, which offers excellent nature experiences among pristine lowland rainforest. This journey is highly recommended for birdwatching and wildlife (tourist boats heading down the Javari also originate in Iquitos). For most people, the main reason to be here is just to be passing through upriver to Leticia or down to Manaus. You can pick up a boat down to Manaus, but if you are coming from Leticia, you might as well sail from Tabatinga.

Tabatinga

Just inside the Brazil–Colombia border is Tabatinga, Siamese twin to Colombia's Leticia, but more sprawling and unkempt. The two towns are one; indeed the whole area, including Santa Rosa across the Solimões in Peru, is a free-trade zone. Tabatinga is Brazil's westernmost town along the Amazon River, and a far-flung outpost it is indeed.

Raw, shabby and virtually ignored by tourists, Tabatinga's citizens collectively suffer an inferiority complex, derived from having busier and wealthier Leticians as their immediate neighbours. Tabatinga's couple of hotels and handful of restaurants are OK, but you can find much better food, accommodation and generally friendlier people just next door with a quick taxi ride into Leticia, Colombia, with no border formalities in between. If you must stay in Tabatinga, the **Hotel Martíns** (1220 Av da Amizade; tel: 412 2128) is acceptable for the foreign traveller: basic but clean and comfortable.

To change money in Tabatinga, go to Avenida Internacional, just past the border, where you have a choice of two *casas de cambio*, although the rates are invariably better in Leticia (see page 226). If entering or leaving Brazil, get your passport stamped at the Policia Federal at Avenida da Amizade (the airport road). It's open daily, 08.00–12.00 and 14.00–18.00.

From within Brazil, Tabatinga is easily reached, with three flights a week from Manaus with Varig (US$170, one way). To continue to Iquitos, you can fly from Tabatinga for US$125 (one way) with two flights per week. Irregular military flights depart for Iquitos from Santa Rosa in Peru. To continue on local boats you have to book further passage in Leticia. A choice of vessels from tourist riverboats, river taxis and local riverboats ply the Iquitos–Leticia route. From Manaus, boats leave on Saturdays and Wednesdays costing US$150–190 with a hammock, or US$200-plus per person for a double cabin on a seven- to ten-day journey.

Most westbound Brazilian-registered vessels turn around at Benjamin Constant. To continue west in this case you must disembark and pick up a river-taxi ride (US$10, one hour) from Benjamin Constant to Tabatinga. Alternatively, make sure your boat is going through to Tabatinga. If you're heading into Colombia and staying there for more than 24 hours, be sure to stop at the immigration post in Tabatinga before proceeding into Leticia.

To return to Manaus from Tabatinga you can take a local riverboat and do the reverse trip. Most of these leave Tabatinga on Wednesday or Saturday mornings, passing through Benjamin Constant in the same afternoon.

If you're looking for something to do in or around Tabatinga don't get your hopes up. There isn't much. No tours are operated from the town as all this business is in Leticia. Likewise for accommodation, virtually every visitor heads over the border for the better choice and quality.

Most day trips to Leticia involve a bus ride to Tabatinga's only tourist attraction... **the market**. On the riverfront, multiple plastic-covered shacks sit around a tiny square.

If you can get over the flea-bitten, scrawny and down-trodden mongrels, the market proves to be a lively, colourful, bustling place, and a good spot to observe local life. The shopping is nothing remarkable but the activity levels are great and at their highest early in the morning.

A gathering of shacks and stalls sells the ubiquitous plastic goods, fishing equipment and straw hats. If you're peckish, local goods include Brazil nuts, passion fruit, mango and wild-harvested berries. Further up the hill a couple of newer concrete buildings have stalls that sell a variety of fruit, meat and fish in what are supposedly more sanitary conditions than before.

For non-vegetarians, hot snacks are cooked on open fires; catfish sliced open and plonked on a grill or small, skewer-roasted squares of meat. If curiosity can overcome repulsion, you may want to look at what it is you might be eating, displayed without consideration for the squeamish. On the slab is turtle meat or capybara; hanging 2m down from rafters are salted *pirarucu* fillets; in enamel bowls lie a dozen or so armour-plated catfish or cuts of wild peccary meat.

Along the Rio Negro

Northwestern Brazil is among the wildest, least inhabited parts of the Amazon. The main route into the area is up the Rio Negro, the biggest Amazon tributary and a great river in its own right. The Negro is a blackwater river, with *igapo* flooded-forest vegetation along its banks. Due to the water chemistry, the flora is distinct from vegetation along the whitewater main stream.

Numerous Manaus tour operators offer boat trips up the Negro. Especially popular are fishing trips for peacock bass (*Cichla ocellaris*). This species is prized for its fighting abilities and excellent flavour. Along the Negro, record sizes are caught. The Negro fulfils the aesthetic as well as the sporting instinct, for in its dark, tea-coloured waters swim highly sought-after aquarium fish. Short day trips are possible but these do not get far enough beyond Manaus to see the interesting wildlife in the region.

A hundred kilometres or six hours by motorised canoe upriver from Manaus you reach Anavilhanas, the world's largest freshwater archipelago, comprising some 400 islands. The area offers some of the best birding sites in the Amazon and is relatively easy to reach. Tours can be booked from Manaus, with the best time for trips at low water being between August and December.

Another option, two days upriver from Manaus, is Jaú National Park, accessed through Novo Airão. As you travel up the Negro, far beyond the outreaches of Manaus, the population thins out and the riverside becomes largely uninhabited. Only a few villages with a handful of huts here and there hug the shore. Across a vast flat plain, barely above sea-level, the flora is relatively intact, pristine in many places or at most lightly logged in the more accessible areas. Birds and animals are abundant, with good chances to see sloth, caiman, river dolphin and monkeys.

You can take an adventure trip in a local riverboat up the Negro as far as São Gabriel. This town gives access to Pico Neblina National Park on the Venezuelan border. From São Gabriel you can venture into Venezuela to navigate the Casiquiere Canal that links the Orinoco and Amazon river systems (see pages 205–6).

On local riverboats you must provide your own hammock and should take your own food. If you don't speak Portuguese, you'll need a good phrasebook to help you explore this remote river. If you are not on a pre-arranged tour you can usually hire a local guide (around US$20–30 per day) to take you on jungle trails. A definite plus for the area is the acidity of the Rio Negro which deters mosquitoes from breeding, thus allowing you to camp on beaches without getting attacked. There are still a few, though, and malaria is present so keep up with your malaria pills and anti-insect protection.

Novo Airão

Situated on the Negro's western bank, this small town of some 2,500 inhabitants is two days by launch from Manaus and has little to recommend it except as stopover for destinations further upriver. Consisting of typical nondescript shanty dwellings, it is worth wandering around for a bit, especially if you will not have another chance to visit any other small Amazon towns. Riverboats on their way to Boa Vista or Barcelos often visit here as a first stop after Manaus.

Novo Airão's main industry is boat construction. Along the main street are small shops where you can buy bread and biscuits and there is a market selling fish and vegetables. The town has unreliable international telephone facilities. For Amazon adventurers, the main reason to visit here is as a launch point for a visit to Jaú National Park, accessed via the mouth of the Rio Jaú, a tributary of the Negro.

Moura

You won't ordinarily visit this nondescript settlement of a couple of hundred military personnel three days upstream from Manaus. However, should any problems arise for travellers, the camp has telephone links, medical facilities and an airfield for emergency evacuation… but don't have an accident at high water, as the airfield is only operational at low water.

Carvoeiro

The first major town after Novo Airão is Carvoeiro opposite the mouth of the Rio Branco, three or four days upriver from Manaus. There are not many reasons to stop here: except as a break from travelling by riverboat en route to São Gabriel, or to catch a boat up the Rio Branco to Boa Vista if your boat is heading for São Gabriel. The town has a hotel (US$7.50) where you can stay before catching a boat up to Caracaraí for Boa Vista. If you're going there during August you might want to time your arrival to coincide with the town's annual festival.

Barcelos

Biggest town on the Negro between Manaus and São Gabriel, Barcelos takes three to four days by riverboat from Manaus. The trip costs US$20 and up. Boats departing upriver from Barcelos to São Gabriel (US$15–25) leave Saturdays: a four-day journey in the rainy season, double that during the dry season. If you are travelling to São Gabriel, you just pass through Barcelos, after which your boat continues up the Negro, passing Tapurucuara, Içana and a handful of other settlements.

Barcelos is the first sizeable town beyond Manaus around which you can take tours into the surrounding forest, which remains intact in most places. You are more likely to see animals such as caiman and pink dolphin here than downriver. The Nara family operates jungle tours from Barcelos (including meals and cabin-style accommodation), but you must book in Manaus before making the trip. (Dr Anita Nara, c/o Unidad Mista, Barcelos, Amazonas 69700; tel: 092 721 1165.)

Aracá River Camp is a jungle camp about 300km by river north of Barcelos. Although oriented toward fishing tours, it has lots to interest birdwatchers and photographers. Accommodation is safari-style permanent tents (private bathroom/shower) on wooden platforms. With only five tents, each with two beds, the camp provides an intimacy absent from large lodges. The facility is linked together by raised wooden walkways. Electric power comes from a 24-hour generator which cannot be heard. High-power fishing boats are state-of-the-art. Seven days all-inclusive with flight from Manaus is US$2,800. You can book locally in Brazil through Andetur (Av Eng. Roberto Freire, 576 SL 19, Centro Sul Ponta Negra) or in the US (Andetur, PO Box 52, 105 Old Oak Drive, Montegut, LA 70377; tel: 985 594 0147; fax: 603 250 5298; email: dreid@andetur.com web: www.andetur.com).

São Gabriel da Cachoeira (Uaupés)

Banks edged in overflowing green with butter-yellow beaches in places are the typical scenery along the Rio Negro around São Gabriel. A closer inspection reveals the riverbanks marked only with the trident feet of wading birds or perhaps the tracks of a *jacaré* (caiman) or river turtle. In the dry season, long white sandy beaches are visible along the banks, giving the place a tropical-island atmosphere. Towards the east, three peaks are visible, forming the Curicurairi Mountains, locally known as the 'Twin Sleeping Beauties.' The town has all the services required to explore the surrounding area and has developed rapidly in recent years. It's the best base for climbing Pico de Neblina and the nearby 'Six Lakes', included on most Pico trips, is well worth the effort.

The 900km journey to São Gabriel is a five-day run by boat from Manaus

PICO DE NEBLINA
Riaan Vorster

Towering 3,014m above sea level, Pico de Neblina forms the highest peak in South America, east of the Andes. Pico – as locals call it – lies in a remote corner of the Pico de Neblina National Park, in northwestern Brazil, tight against the Venezuelan border.

You travel up remote tributaries by motorized canoe surrounded by untouched jungle and distant mist-shrouded peaks. Meeting Yanomami Indians en route, you trek for days through rainforest and witness how it transforms into an otherworldly landscape as you climb higher. Then, out of the mists appears the ghostly massif of Pico – so out of place, you stand frozen in your tracks, mesmerized by its sheer size and rugged beauty. You scramble up her moss-grown, rocky slopes as your explorer instincts drive you ever upwards towards the peak...

A reasonably fit and healthy person will successfully make the summit. You're wet everyday – if not from rain, then from walking 4 to 6 hours a day with a loaded backpack through humid tropical jungle (there is a small trail). Insects will plague you day and night and you will face exhaustion every day. Drink lots of water and don't feel obliged to keep up with the guides' pace. The last day of about eight, from base camp to the summit, is through alpine habitat and a delightful lack of insects. The climb does not involve the use of any specialised mountaineering equipment and no climbing experience is required.

Pico is much more accessible from Brazil than Venezuela. The route, trails and access are significantly better, there are fewer restrictions on travel, greater availability of knowledgeable guides and easier access to funds at São Gabriel de Cachoeira in Brazil.

leaving on Fridays from Port de Raimundo. Boats return to Manaus on Fridays, taking 3–4 days. Cost is about US$45. Flights to Manaus with Rico Airlines take three hours and cost US$120. São Gabriel is Brazil's biggest town near the Venezuela-Colombia border, located close to Pico de Neblina National Park. About 25km upstream the Negro meets the Rio Uaupés, which heads west, past Taraqua and the Colombian border. This route offers the prospect, with another day's journey, heading along the border to the Colombian town of Mitú. There are no tours on this route, so logistically this trip is tough going – you must organise all the transport, paperwork and supplies.

São Gabriel is the place to come to escape. There are a couple of hotels, the Hotel Roraima (in the centre of town) or the Hotel Walpes (Uapes) overlooking the Negro River. The latter is popular due to its stunning location and cheaper rates. Rooms are clean and safe with private bathrooms; prices start at US$15 a night with a fan, breakfast included. A dozen or so small shops sell a few staples and daily essentials. Banco de Brasil has an ATM machine accepting Visa, MasterCard and Cirrus. There's also an internet café just round the corner from the post office.

For independent travellers, excursions from the town are organised by a couple of tour operators with independent guides who offer the chance to visit the Yanomami people. Many of these people remain in remote, far-off villages but a few come from their lands around the headwaters of the Orinoco down to the Brazil-Venezuela border and into São Gabriel, the biggest settlement for

Most trips to Pico leave from São Gabriel. Currently, there are a couple of operators with regular trips. A popular choice is Agencia de Turismo. They occasionally make use of an English speaking freelance guide by the name of Valdes (pronounced Wal-gee) de Silva. He is just about the only English speaking person in São Gabriel and helps when negotiating price, buying supplies and discussing the itinerary and general conditions of the trip.

Be gently assertive on the itinerary, costs and make sure that they stick to that agreement. It's a good idea to pay two-thirds before you depart and the remaining third once you return.

The cost depends on your negotiating skills and the size of the group. A solo trip with Agencia de Turismo is about US$900. With more people you should be able to split the cost. The price should include boat, engine, permission to enter the park from IBAMA, all transport and fuel costs and food (purchased from a local shop with your guide). Be sure to take warm clothing.

Pico de Neblina means 'Peak of Mist' – a very appropriate name considering the fact that it is covered in a thick fog most of the time. Those expecting to enjoy a spectacular view when reaching the top *will* be disappointed. You have to be extremely lucky just to get a partial view from the summit! There is, however, a way by which you can increase your chances considerably: by staying overnight on the summit. The reason for this is because the misty veil lifts briefly in the early mornings. You will need a tent, foam mattress and a warm sleeping bag. If you do this, convince your guide to stay also, since it is easy to lose your way back down to base camp (4 to 6 hours up and 3 to 5 hours down). Also, the weather can trap you on the summit when rain (guaranteed) turns small streams into raging torrents within minutes.

hundreds of miles. Politically the area is tense, due to conflict between gold-mining *garimpeiros*, who are illegally settling the Yanomami's protected land in their search for gold.

Overland to Venezuela – Rio Negro route

The route from São Gabriel to Venezuela up the Rio Negro offers adventurous travellers prepared to rough it a uniquely rewarding experience. The main feature of this trip is a climb up Cucui Rock (550m), just across the Venezuelan border. Don't let its size fool you – it's a tough climb, but offers spectacular views. It involves some scrambles up steep granite slabs, but no specialist equipment is required. Don't do the climb when it's raining – you slide down the granite like a bar of soap into a bathtub!

Take a bus from São Gabriel (Hotel Walpes, 09.00, US$5, tickets from the shop next door) to Cucui. Buses depart Wednesdays and Saturdays, and return Thursdays and Sundays. It is an excruciating six-hour ride on a bad gravel road. Cucui lies about 3 km south of the Venezuelan border. It's a sleepy frontier town crawling with military personnel. There are no banks or telephones. You can stay over at Lilies, a small hotel on the main road as you enter town.

Cargo boats also ply the river between São Gabriel and Cucui. The journey takes a day upriver, 12 hours downriver and costs around US$25 one way. On average, two boats per week depart for Cucui, outside the dry season. River traffic comes to a virtual standstill during the dry season (November to March) when the Negro's water level is too low to navigate safely. Ask around the dock area in São Gabriel for boat arrivals and departure times.

Ask around for a guide (about US$15 per person). It is much cheaper to get a guide in Cucui than in São Gabriel.

The trek begins with a one-hour canoe ride up the Rio Negro, from where you start a two-hour hike through the jungle. You start the steep ascent up the rock face, using lianas in some places to pull you up. The route goes through a small cave with bats, past a human skeleton (!) and thick undergrowth to eventually reach the top two hours later. On a clear day, you can see as far as Pico de Neblina. It's a demanding hike, but worth the effort.

The border guards usually allow the climb without immigration formalities. There is no passport control in Cucui or at the border.

Continuing north from Cucui into Venezuela can only be done by boat. There is no regular passenger service to San Carlos, the first town in Venezuela. Small riverboats often take on passengers in Cucui before heading to San Carlos. Ask around at the grocery stores and look out for new boats arriving at the riverside.

(Details for this section contributed by Riaan Vorster, who spent several months in the region.)

Along the Branco

This Rio Negro tributary is a whitewater river creating a meeting of waters at the confluence. This area has more insects than around the Negro, so stock up on repellent before you set off. But by way of compensation, the birdlife is richer, wildlife is more abundant and fishing is better compared with those of blackwater rivers. The river's watershed is mostly uninhabited and a journey up to Boa Vista is highly rewarding for naturalists. For this reason don't use the bus service to Boa Vista unless you are short of time; take the boat instead. For those not strapped for cash, the best way to visit this area is aboard the tourist riverboat *Tucano* (see page 388). With its wildlife and unspoiled scenery, and being off main tourist routes, this trip gives you the chance to feel that you really are exploring!

Santa Maria

Two days by riverboat up the Rio Branco gets you to Santa Maria, a small settlement of four or five hundred, mostly army personnel manning an airfield. Although not often used, the facility maintains regular radio contact with Manaus. Other residents scratch out a meagre existence from increasingly infertile plots of recently cleared rainforest. A few general stores, rarely open, and a couple of small churches are among the village's other attractions.

TOWNS AND VILLAGES NORTH OF MANAUS
Boa Vista

Largest town on the Rio Branco, Boa Vista is the capital of Roraima state. The BR174 from Manaus is partly paved but still difficult and unreliable in the rainy season. As state capital, Boa Vista is home to many civil servants. The city's founding fathers approved an amazing town plan, laying the city out in impressively wide avenues following neat geometric arrangements. It must have been fun to draw up the blueprints of such aesthetically pleasing patterns, but it is less than fun for the pedestrian. Unless you can afford wheeled transport, you are doomed to wander the airy, expansive streets for many hours. Boa Vista struggles with its isolation from the rest of Brazil. The well-ordered layout of the city is surrounded by poverty and there's not much of interest except to students of architecture and town planning.

Getting there and away

Boa Vista's main importance for Amazon travellers is as the northern gateway to Venezuela. It is the largest city between the Amazon main stream and the frontiers with Venezuela and Guyana, whose overland routes into Brazil merge here. The road from the Venezuelan border to Boa Vista is fully surfaced and offers easy eventual access to the Caribbean. Buses run to Bonfim (Guyana) but the road is often reported impassable. It is easier to fly into Georgetown from Boa Vista. Heading south, it's a short drive to Caracaraí from where you can take a boat down the Rio Branco for the river trip to Manaus. Heading south, you can travel to Manaus first by bus via Caracaraí and then by boat for the seven- to ten-day trip down the Rio Branco. This is the most relaxing option should you have the time.

Boa Vista's international airport is 4km from the city centre, US$10 by taxi or you can take a bus ('Aeropuerto') for US$1. Varig (Rua Araújo Filho 91 – Centro; tel: 095 224 2269) has daily flights to Manaus (US$130 one way) or take an air taxi (MMTA at airport), with three departures a week. The cheapest way to/from Manaus is by bus. Buses leave Manaus at 6.00am and 8.00pm, and take 11 hours, US$30.

Where to stay and eat

Visitors can get help from the **Tourist Information Office** (Rua Coronel Pinto 241; tel: 095 224 9977). Ask there about hotels and restaurants (of which there is a pretty good choice), foreign exchange, banking and postal facilities. They can direct you to the city cultural centre, park and beaches, and provide limited information on the better local tour operators. Hotels in the top range begin with **Hotel Aipana Plaza** (Praça Centro Civico 53; tel: 095 224 4800) with sumptuous rooms from US$60 per night. For US$30 per night the **Hotel Eusebio** (Rua Cecilia Brasil 1107; tel: 095 224 0300) is popular with all sorts of travellers. For lodgings under US$10 per night the **Hotel Ideal** (Rua Aranjo Filho 467; tel: 095 224 6342) has good rooms and OK breakfast. If it's full try the **Hotel Monte Libano** (Av Benjamin Constant 319; tel: 095 2224 7521).

Excursions from Boa Vista

Beyond the city are plenty of nature opportunities. On the fringe of the Amazon Basin, three habitats come together: tropical rainforest, savannah grasslands and *tepuis* – flat-topped mountains rising from the surrounding terrain. There is lots of unspoiled jungle to the north and west; the south is a major gold-prospecting area.

Jungle trips from Boa Vista are worthwhile on account of much unspoiled habitat. A typical tour consists of a two-hour boat or bus ride to a scenic site, such as a tree-covered island, followed by walking for a couple of hours along a forest trail. Another place to visit is the archaeological site at **Pedra Pintada**, located between Santa Elena and Boa Vista, where you can see huge carved rocks (petroglyphs). Also worthwhile is a day trip (about $US95) to **Lago Caracaraña** which is fringed by lovely white beaches, good for swimming and shaded by stands of cashew trees. Several hours from town by bad road is the ecological research station at **Ilha de Mara**; and nearby is the **Fazenda São Marcos** Brazilian-style ranch which has accommodation (US$75). Two hours by boat from town is **Forte São Joaquim** (day trips cost US$35), the ruins of a Portuguese colonial fort, constructed in the 1700s.

River trips along the Rio Branco are highly recommended, as are trips into the **Serra Grande uplands** for patches of rainforest, good wildlife-viewing and lots of birds.

Tour operators

Recommended tour operators in Boa Vista include **Anaconda Tours** (Av Silvio Botelho 12; tel: 095 224 4132) and **Monte Roraima Tours** (Rua Floriano Peixoto 374; tel: 095 224 9523).

TOWNS AND VILLAGES DOWNSTREAM OF MANAUS
Santarém

With a population of 300,000, Santarém is a town that has experienced extraordinary growth in the last fifteen years due to gold prospecting and timber. Positioned at the confluence with the Tapajós River, halfway between Manaus and Belém (daily boats from Manaus, departing late afternoons for the two-day journey), it's the fourth largest town in Brazilian Amazonia, and is a good spot to rest for a couple of days or to equip an expedition. But despite its size, money changing is difficult, and impossible for travellers' cheques. The staff at the Varig office might change cash.

Steve Alexander at **Amazon Tours** (Trav Turiano Meira 1084, Santarém; tel: 091 552 2620; fax: 091 552 1098; email: amazontours@amazonriver.com;

INDIAN RAIN RITUAL STOPS FOREST FIRES

Exceptionally dry weather, believed to be caused by El Niño, meant that seasonal fires from slash-and-burn agriculture went wildly out of control in early 1998, burning an area of over 33,000km² in the state of Roraima. The fires, burning for over two months, destroyed the small farms of thousands of families and threatened to burn through the forest reservation of the Yanomami Indians.

Despite attempts by the federal government to put out the fires, it was rain that finally quenched them. Two Indian Kaiapo shamans from the Xingu reservation in Mato Grosso and known throughout the Amazon for their rain-making skills, performed an ancient rain ritual on a dried-up river. Rainfall came just two hours later.

web: www.amazonriver.com) belongs to a consortium of independent tour operators along the Amazon main stream. He offers a wide variety of tours throughout the lower Amazon region from Manaus to Belem, including Marajo Island and Caxiuanã National Forest. He can also be contacted through Swallows and Amazons in Manaus or in Iquitos, Peru, through Amazon Tours and Cruises.

The road south to Cuiabá (1,777km) is not paved and makes for an arduous bus journey, especially in the rainy season. Yellow fever inoculations are insisted upon if you travel this road. A good excursion is to Alter do Chao, very peaceful during the week, which is a weekend retreat for the inhabitants of Santarém, with good swimming in the Tapajós. Extensive beaches appear from August to January. The failed rubber plantation of Henry Ford at Fordlândia is also worth a visit.

Belém

Named after the biblical village of Bethlehem, with which it has little in common, this noisy, bustling port serves as the gateway for all Brazil's international Amazon boat traffic – as it has for some 400 years since its founding in 1616. Beneath accumulated centuries of grime glimmer a few remnants of this colonial legacy, crammed between shimmering skyscrapers and blotchy grey tenements, adorned with hanging clothes and forests of television aerials.

On the mouth of the Amazon, Belém is the second largest city on the river and the only other in lowland Amazonia with a population over one million. Now state capital of Pará, Belém grew fast with the rubber boom during the late 19th and early 20th centuries, its expansion attributed to its location and good international travel connections.

Because of the better nature opportunities upstream, most people arrive in Belém en route to Manaus for the start or end of an Amazon cruise.

Getting there and away

International flights to Belém arrive via Rio or São Paulo. The Varig office is at Avenida Presidente Vargas 768; tel: 091 3084 8484, with daily flights to Manaus (US$370 return).

Most people who leave or arrive at Belém by sea do so via *gaiola* riverboat or, at the other end of the comfort and cost scale, by luxury cruise ship, including expedition vessels like the *Explorer*. Travel to Santarém (two/three days) or Manaus (four/five days) by riverboat with hammock accommodation is straightforward though hardly comfortable. Buy tickets at the Agenasa (Agencia de Navegaçao a Serviçio da Amazonia; tel: 091 246 1085) office at the *rodoviária*, on the east side of town, 1km from the town centre along Avenida José Malcher. The trip to Santarém costs around US$75 for hammock space (US$100 per person in a four-berth cabin) or about US$105 to Manaus (US$150 for a cabin). Meals are not included. Agenasa also provide transport from the bus station to the dock. Boats depart Monday, Tuesday, Wednesday and Friday.

Where to stay

Being a port Belém has plenty of accommodation, mostly inexpensive. For convenience, stick to the central area which is quite safe for the most part. However, especially after dark you should not go out alone and always be on your guard against pickpockets, bag snatchers and so forth. The area around the waterfront market – Mercado Ver O Peso at the southern end of Vilha Castilho França – is dodgy, but the sights, sounds and smells make a visit worth the minor risk.

The plushest hotel is the **Hilton** (Av President Vargas 882; tel: 091 217 7000; fax 091 225 2942), with all the luxuries (US$110 per room per night) and little soul, as you'd expect. Close by is the rival **Excelsior Grão Pará** (Av President Vargas 718; tel: 091 242 9044), with nice views and very nice rooms at US$75pp. For medium-priced lodgings try **Manacá Hotel** (Travessa Quintinio Bocaiuva 1645; tel: 091 223 3335) for US$35 a night in rooms with fans. It's a little way from the city centre but still within walking distance. The best value in this price bracket is **Vidonho's Hotel** (Rua O de Almeida 476; tel: 091 225 1444), in the city centre with clean spacious rooms including fridge and TV for US$25 for a single room, US$35 for a double. If you're penny-pinching, the **Hotel Fortaleza** (Travessa Frutuoso Guimarães 276; tel: 091 241 5005) is slap-bang in the middle of the city centre and one of the better cheap 'n' cheerfuls for US$10 per night.

What to see
If you're in Belém for a couple of days, take time for sightseeing. A city tour typically includes the **Teatro de Paz** (Praça de Republica; tel: 091 224 7355), which is Belém's version of the Manaus Opera House and almost as splendid. The **Emílio Goeldi Museum** (Avenida Magalhães Barata 376; tel: 091 249 0163) is a

combination of park, zoo, aquarium and collect ion of Amazon Indian artefacts and mineral specimens. The **zoo** is one of South America's best and a visit is well worth every penny of the admission fee (US$4). Open Tue–Thur 09.00–12.00 and 14.00–17.00; weekends 09.00–17.00. City tours are available from travel agents from about US$25 per person. Try **Mururé Turismo** (Avenida Presidente Vargas 134; tel: 091 241 0891; fax: 091 241 2082) or shop around for the best deal.

Of course, what's of interest to some travellers is what is not included in the tour. These are places – such as the **market** – where you see the daily life of the people of Belém. In the heart of the city, opposite the Hilton hotel, is **Praça de Republica**, a small park – focus for local musicians, tradespeople, craftsmen and bohemians. It's a fun place to wander and watch the local life go by.

Excursions from Belém

There aren't a whole lot of reasons to stay in Belém on its own account, at least not if you're interested in visiting pristine rainforest. The best excursion is a trip to **Marajó Island** in the river's mouth. About the size of Belgium, this is the world's largest river delta island. Although overrun by Asian water buffalo, the island offers excellent birding opportunities. Expedition and cruise ships going from the main stream to Belém take a short cut along the east of the island through the Breves Channel. You can catch a boat from the Belém docks (near Porto do Sal) costing US$5 for the five-hour trip. On the island is a small settlement with simple lodgings at the basic **Hotel Ponta de Pedras** (US$12 per night). In the village you can hire a bicycle to explore the island on numerous tracks and trails. Allow at least a full day (two nights) to make the journey worthwhile.

SOUTH FROM MANAUS

To go south of the main stream you'll need to arrange your own travel. Passenger and cargo boats travel up the Rio Madeira to Porto Velho. Jump ship in Humaitá if you want to go east along the Transamazônica Highway. If you reach Porto Velho you can head east through Rondônia or south and west to Bolivia and Peru. Given the dearth of tourist facilities it's not easy to travel to remote areas. The few towns of any size are mere reference points between empty expanses where you only have your wits and intuition to rely on.

Boats up the Madeira

Riverboats leave from the main dock in Manaus on Fridays and Mondays taking around five days upstream at a cost of US$80 including food. Water is provided for the journey but probably comes from the river so sterilise it or take along your own.

You'll need your hammock and a few books to while away the hours. The boats regularly take longer than scheduled. This is meant to be a five-day trip upstream, four days downstream; the downstream journey took one traveller 11 days.

The food on the boats is basic. Breakfast is typically crackers and coffee. Lunch and supper is fish or chicken with rice, beans and, on good days, noodles. Sprinkled with the ubiquitous *farinha* this is tasty and nutritious. But this diet gets a little trying after a few days, so take some food with you. Buy fruit and biscuits from traders on the dockside

Up the Madeira

The journey first takes you from Manaus down the Amazon before heading south up the Madeira. The boat stops at towns including Borba along the river depending on the destination of cargo, passengers and the mood of the captain. A couple of days from Manaus the town of Manicoré is a regular stop for picking up and dropping off cargo. If the blandness of the food is getting to you there is a small market just off the main square. Other towns along the journey are little more than mission outposts; or a bar with a pharmacy round the back or a palm frond-thatched hut in the middle of nowhere to which pilgrims trek from the surrounding area to sit and gaze at the flickering light emerging from within: a television.

The next main town of significance is Humaitá, another stopping point for boarding and disembarking passengers. The square overlooking the high riverbank is empty and lifeless since the road from Porto Velho dragged the centre of town to the bus station.

If you want to experience the ongoing battle between colonisers of the Amazon and the rainforest, get off the boat at Humaitá (or return there from Porto Velho) and head east along the Transamazônica Highway for roughly 1,000km towards Haituba, and on to Santarém. (See page 412.)

Travel on this size of boat is unlikely to put you in touch with nature. The river is too wide and the river traffic too busy. Tugs push huge barges loaded with over 25 lorries between Manaus and Porto Velho. Any animal seeking a peaceful life would move up one of the smaller, less-used tributaries.

Life on a riverboat is a fascinating display of Amazon culture. On all but the very smallest boats there is usually a top deck where people gather and while away the hours talking, playing cards, drinking and dancing to music; none of the sobriety of simply getting from one place to another. As the boats move so slowly up the river there seems little reason not to stretch the longest yarns to near breaking point. It's a great exhibition of story telling. Tempers rise and fall, friendships wax and wane. Having spent such an intimate time with so many people, it can seem a little strange, once back on land, to be amongst a throng of nameless faces.

Porto Velho

Capital of the state of Rondônia, Porto Velho has grown at a staggering pace from a small Amazon outpost to a city with over 350,000 inhabitants in just twenty years. As you arrive by boat the small sleepy district close to the port obscures the bustling energy of the city.

At the turn of the century the city was set to become an important centre for the movement of rubber from Bolivia further downstream to Manaus. After many decades the Madeira-Mamoré rail line linking Bolivia with Porto Velho was completed in 1912. The toil of six thousand labourers who died in the four-year construction was wasted – by then the rubber boom was over. In the 1970s gold was discovered in the area. This, combined with government colonisation programmes, resulted in huge numbers immigrating into the area. Even without the railroad, the city's role as a distribution centre has flourished. Trucks commute along the BR364, the main artery to the south of Brazil, while to the south and west smaller but equally significant roads stretch out to Bolivia and towards Peru.

The centre of the city – if there is such a thing – is Avenida 7 de Setembro. It's a busy street with hundreds of over-staffed shops selling all sorts of things that nobody even knew they wanted. There are several bars and *lanchonetas* or snack bars along the street, also a cinema. Towards the port is the post office which is the best place from which to send a letter and also has an ATM cash machine for Visa cards. If the ATM's not working, the Banco do Brasil on Avenida José de Alencar changes travellers' cheques and foreign currency, and gives cash advances.

Visit the **Museu Estadual de Rondônia** (corner of Av Farqhuar and Av Sete

PORTO VELHO

Rodoviária (1km)

Buses to Rodoviária

AV NAÇOES UNIDAS

AV BRASILIA

Vila Rica

AV JOAQUIM NABUCO

PENA

MARECHAL   DEODORO

AFONSO

Nunes

Cuiabano

250m
250 yds

0
0

RUA CARLOS GOMES

RUA DAO PEDRO II

RUA

GONCALVES   DIAS

Banco do
Brasil

AV SETE DE SETEMBRO

RUA ALMIRANTE

N

Bradt

RUA JOSE DE ALENCAR

Post office

AVENIDA

R   WEBER

AV   FARQHUAR

Museu Estadual
de Rondônia

Estrado de Ferro
Madeira-Mamoré
(Railway Museum)
and riverfront cafés

Boats
downstream
to Mánaus

Madeira

FLOW

de Setembro) for extensive displays of ceramics, pickled creatures and animal skins. Other exhibits include musical instruments, feather headdresses, arrows and fighting sticks. Language tables explain relationships between the area's indigenous groups.

Only a handful of Indian groups still live in Rondônia, once home to 40 different tribes. Traditional lands were barely considered during the building of the BR364, which displaced numerous Indian populations. On the riverfront the **Estrado de Ferro Madeira-Mamoré** is a tribute to the arduous task of building a railway through the Amazon lowlands. The railway was built to avoid carrying rubber around 18 sets of rapids between northern Bolivia and Porto Velho.

The museum itself is uninspiring. Even today the display inside looks completely out of place. If you're enamoured with the romance of steam remember that 6,000 people died during the railroad's construction. Trains and railroads are heavy industry, and the difficult conditions imposed by the Amazon's environment were certain to doom such efforts, especially in 1912.

The museum is filled with renovated engines and railway equipment. Victorian leather-upholstered chairs sit at worn tables, bureaux bear ink stains over a century old and cabinets hold trinkets and glasses that could not look more out of place. There are several photographs of the managers and workers who gave all or part of their lives to the railroad.

The railroad remains the passion of dedicated enthusiasts who restored part of the line and a couple of engines. Internationally the Maderia-Mamore Railway Society is slowly promoting interest and awareness (web: www.geocities.com/martincooper_2000/Index.htm). Outside the museum is a terraced area where several stalls serve juices, coconuts and pizzas.

Getting there and away

Travel out of Porto Velho is either by boat down to Manaus, or by road. Humaitá is four hours to the north by bus and the trip costs US$8. Cuiabá is a gruelling 1,965km journey to the southeast along the BR364. Unless you have the stamina, don't do the trip without stopping overnight. Buses heading west to Rio Branco (US$12, seven hours) leave along a good road. Going in the same direction, buses turn south off the road to Guarajá-Mirim (US$10, four hours) on the border with Bolivia.

Local buses to town run from outside the *rodoviária* (bus station). Buses to the terminal leave from 7 de Setembro. Internal flights to most Brazilian cities leave from Ter Guaporé airport 7km out of town.

Where to stay

Accommodation in Porto Velho is either grubby or over-priced. Finding something affordable and reasonable is quite difficult. The best in the centre of town is **Hotel Vila Rica** at Rua Carlos Gomes 1616 and Av Joaquim Nabuco (tel/fax: 069 224 3433; web: www.hotelvilarica.com.br), easy to find as it is the tallest building in the city (US$45). **Hotel Nunes** (tel: 069 221 1389) and **Hotel Cuiabano** (US$15) are both considerably cheaper places on 7 de Setembro. If you're arriving at the *rodoviária* late at night or leaving early there are several options around the terminal. **Novo Hotel** (Av Carlos Gomes 2776, two blocks west of the station; tel: 069 224 6555), is clean and tidy (US$36). **Guajará Palace Hotel** (Rua Miguel Chaquian 1468; tel: 069 225 3227) claims to have the best service in Porto Velho (US$32). Budget accommodation along Av Carlos Gomes includes **Hotel Ouro Fino** at #2844 (US$10) and **Hotel Amazonas** which is slightly better at #2838 (US$10). South of the station are a few cheapies, the best of which is **Hotel São Cristoval** (US$7).

Where to eat

Porto Velho has a rather limited choice of places to eat. The floating restaurant outside the rail museum serves good fish...when it is open. One recommendation is the **Remanso do Tucunaré** (Av Brasília) in the Senhora das Graças district. There are several restaurants close to the Hotel Vila Rica including the **Chinese Oriente** (Av Amazonas 1280). Several stalls offer street food close to Av 7 de Setembro. Near the bus station there are a few *parrilladas* selling meat by the carcass. For beer and drinks take a stroll down Av 7 de Setembro.

Excursions from Porto Velho

There are few sightseeing or shopping opportunities around Porto Velho. At weekends boats cruise up the Madeira with mostly local passengers dancing, listening to music and generally having a good time.

An alternative excursion, although still in its embryonic stage as yet, is to visit Parque Nacional de Pacaás Novos. Covering over 750,000ha and home to several indigenous groups including the Uru-eu-wau-wau, this national park is 200km south of Porto Velho. The park is primarily tropical forest with transitional zones and savannah. Access is along the BR364, turning off at Ariquemes. There is no public transport to the park, although it is possible to hitch.

For details contact Carlos Rangel; IBAMA-Rondônia; tel: 069 223 3597; fax: 069 223 3599; Av Jorge Teixiera 3559 (buses from the bus station heading north), CEP-78904-320, Porto Velho, Rondônia, Brasil.

TO GUAJARÁ-MIRIM AND BOLIVIA

Buses from Porto Velho to Guajará-Mirim on the Bolivian border leave almost hourly. The road still has a frontier feel with small towns dotted along it and pockets of rainforest between the cleared farmland. The quiet, orderly town of Guajará-Mirim is on the northern bank of the Mamoré. The *rodoviária* is several kilometres out of town; from there you can walk to the centre or catch a bus or taxi. There's a selection of hotels including the **Mini Estrela** and **Fenix Palace** along Av 15 de Novembro, but if you're on a tight budget the hotels on the Bolivian side are cheaper.

If you're crossing to Bolivia for more than a day you'll need an exit stamp from the Brazilian Federal Police on Av Presidente Dutra. A passenger boat buzzes back and forth across the river and costs next to nothing. On the Bolivian side, immigration is next to the ferry terminal. Most accommodation is close to the main plaza a few blocks straight up behind the ferry terminal.

The Rio Guaporé feeds into the Mamoré upstream from the town and marks the border between Brazil and Bolivia. The river is remote and unspoiled, and if you can find transport, would be a rewarding trip. Three days upstream by boat is the border post Forte Príncipe da Beira built by the Portuguese in the 1770s to mark the boundary between Portuguese and Spanish territory. Due to the expansion of roads, river transport is less available. If you really want to make the trip you may have to wait, but with luck you'll find a boat heading upstream. An alternative upriver destination is Trinidad (see page 352).

West of Porto Velho to Rio Branco

Travelling west towards Rio Branco through cleared forest along a good road, opportunities for stopping are limited and there seems little reason to do so. The town of Abunã is close to the Rio Madeira. Barges take all transport across the river and beyond.

Rio Branco, capital of Acre state, is some 550km from Porto Velho. The town itself is bustling with energy. The meandering traveller is barely noticed, let alone acknowledged. The days start early because of the heat so if you arrive at midday you may find yourself wondering where the city's 200,000 inhabitants have gone.

Rio Branco is sliced in two by the Rio Acre. The centre of town, with most of the hotels and places of interest, is on the north bank. The bus station and airport are several kilometres south of the river.

Two museums in the town are worth a visit. The **Museu da Borracha** or Rubber Musuem is on Av Ceará and has a range of ethnological, archaeological and historical exhibits on display. The **Casa do Seringueiro** gives some insight into the realities of the rubber tapper's life, with particular reference to Chico Mendes who was assassinated in Acre in 1988.

Getting there and away
The *rodoviária* is about 2km out of town and is served by regular local buses. If you are just passing through there are plenty of hotels around the station that are fine for a night.

The airport is another kilometre or so out from the centre of town. Buses run from the end of the airport road. There are regular flights to Manaus and Porto Velho but locations further west can be reached only by air taxi.

Money
Banco do Brasil on the plaza has an ATM and changes travellers' cheques and dollars. If you're heading further west this is probably the last chance for a while so stock up with all the money you need.

Where to stay and eat
In the centre of town at the top end of the range is the **Hotel Pinheiro Palace** (Rui Barbosa 91; tel: 068 223 7191; email: pinheiro@irmaospinheiro.com.br; web: www.irmaospinheiro.com.br) from US$80 with swimming pool and AC. Considerably cheaper, the **Hotel Rio Branco** along the same road (#193, tel: 068 224 1785) is also comfortable. The area around the bus station has several hotels including the **Hotel Rodoviária** (tel: 068 221 4434) and **Hotel Nacional** both charging US$12 for a single and US$16 for a double. A little more upmarket is the **Hotel Flor da Mata** at US$22 and US$28.

Casarão (Av Brazil 110), near the bottom of the plaza, is the most popular restaurant in town, serving good fish dishes with live music at weekends. **Pizzeria Bolota** is opposite the Hotel Pinheiro Palace. Near the old bridge there is a small food market and a few bars.

Excursions from Rio Branco
Short trips to visit rubber tappers and nearby forest can be arranged with **Acretur** next to Hotel Rio Branco at Rui Barbosa 193, as can trips one of the many nearby religious sects including Colonia Cinco Mil.

Boca da Acre to the north of Rio Branco is a good spot for swimming and fishing. The trip downriver to Lábrea takes two days and travels through quiet stretches of *várzea* forest. There is a reasonable amount of river transport but if you're trying to go a long distance you may have to use several different boats. From Lábrea it is possible to travel east by road to Humaitá or you can continue further downriver which eventually will lead you to Manaus.

South from Rio Branco
From Rio Branco the dirt road splits. The southern fork takes you to Brasiléia, which links to the Bolivian town of Cobija and on to Assis Brasil on the border

with Peru. Both crossings leave you in frontier town territory where by and large you have to make your own travel arrangements. Heading west takes you along the last section of the BR364 to Cruzeiro do Sul from where you can cross the border into Peru, and after a jungle trek of a day or two, arrive in Pucallpa.

Both roads are dirt tracks and can be impassable in the rainy season between November and March.

To Brasiléia and Assis Brasil
The advance of settlers in this part of Brazil is steady. A few years ago moving around the area proved difficult, but now four buses a day make the journey from Rio Branco to Brasiléia (on the border with Bolivia; US$10, three hours).

Ghost towns and thriving settlements line the road. Some are quite picturesque, others ugly. The scenery is a striking insight into the rainforest destruction we hear about. Once uniform rainforest, the area is now an expanse of cattle pasture dotted with woodland patches. Near the Bolivian frontier intact forest remains, as this part of Bolivia has, for the moment at least, not yet been stripped bare.

While the ranchers and peasants who work on the land seem to be trapped in or very close to poverty, it is likely that their circumstances would have been better if the rainforest had been left standing.

Halfway between Rio Branco and Cobija is the turn-off to Xapuri where the rubber tapper Chico Mendes was assassinated. There are a couple of hotels and a small exhibition in tribute to the murdered eco-martyr.

If you're going to Bolivia you'll need to have your passport stamped at the Federal Police offices in Brasiléia near the entrance to town. You can get a Bolivian entrance stamp from the Bolivian Consulate on Rua Major Salinas 205. The bridge that crosses the river into Bolivia is quite a long way through the town, and down the hill.

Accommodation in Brasiléia is limited but if you need to stay the **Hotel Kador** (tel: 068 546 3752) is on the way into town and the **Pousada las Palmeiras** (tel: 068 546 3284) is in the centre.

To Assis Brasil and beyond
Like Brasiléia, Assis Brasil has little to interest a visitor. Its main role is being the place to stop before crossing to Peru. That said, if you were headed from Peru and want an adventure, then you could canoe downstream, passing through Brasiléia.

Transport from Brasiléia is by bus in the dry season – the road is bad. Once in Assis you can spend the night in the **Hotel Aquino** or get an exit stamp from the Federal Police and walk the 2km to the Peruvian town of Iñapari, from which trucks leave for the Peruvian jungle town of Puerto Maldonado.

To Cruzeiro do Sul and beyond
From Rio Branco the BR364 continues, in name at least, to Cruzeiro do Sul (population 60,000) some 600km to the west. The road is frequently assailed by the elements and there is no bus service at present, although you can fly from Rio Branco (US$50 one-way, one hour). It may be possible to hitch. The *Quatro Rodas* road map of Brazil says that 4WD is necessary but it's likely that regular buses will be travelling the road soon.

There are a few cheap hotels, with the **Sandrais** probably being the best, then the **Flor de Maio**, with **Hotel Novo Acre** bringing up the rear.

A visit to Cruzeiro can be rewarding if only because you will be one of the few visitors to the area. You'll have to negotiate trips to see rubber tappers but you may get insights that are hard to come by in more accessible places.

If you're looking for an easier route there are flights from the airport, 7km out of town.

Cruzeiro do Sul is about 100km from the border with Peru at Brazil's westernmost point. The town of Pucallpa is a similar distance from the border on the Peruvian side. A land crossing is possible but take care if you choose to travel with locals – there are reports of extensive smuggling activity in this area. Having gained an exit stamp from the Federal Police in Cruzeiro you can continue along the road to the border. From there you will need to make your way through the jungle to a river heading down to Pucallpa. Don't attempt the journey without a guide because you'll probably get lost.

THE TRANSAMAZÔNICA HIGHWAY

Laidback boat travel, with its eccentricities and benevolent chaos, epitomises the Amazon's romantic nostalgia. In contrast, travel along the Transamazônica Highway gives a profound sense of the colonist's indomitable frontier spirit. The road may not be romantic, but it is an important part of the Amazon story – central to the settlement of the interior. Some parts are so ghastly, you might think people are forced to live there. Yet settlers freely choose to move here believing that the opportunities are better than elsewhere.

After the government built the road, migrants moved in and cleared large areas for crops and grazing – leading to widespread deforestation. Along the highway, the trailblazing culture promotes habitat destruction. We can admire the colonist's spirit since we know rewards come to those who help themselves. Yet their actions destroy the rainforest. Such contradictions are central to the conservation dilemma and pose a serious problem for environmental organisations.

The road's original blueprint connected Brazil's Atlantic coast at Belém to the westernmost point near Cruzeiro do Sul. At present the road stops in Lábrea, over 1,000km short of its destination. Travel along the road by bus or truck is hard and often frustrating. Sections of the road are often impassable so river transport is an easier option. Travel in the rainy season between November and March is likely to be difficult but there is always a way if you have the time! There's not much natural beauty along the way. The rewards of travelling this route are in meeting people and learning about a different way of life.

Apart from the towns of Itaituba and Marabá, there are few opportunities to change currency or get cash so stock up before you travel. Accommodation and food are available in all the towns, but are basic.

In the past few years, this area has greatly increased malaria incidence so take prevention. Heed this advice because medical facilities are absent and emergency evacuation is next to impossible.

Humaitá

A sizable jungle town of several thousand, Humaitá makes its living supplying nearby ranches and logging. The bus station has become the new centre of town making the plaza alongside the river quiet most of the time.

Regular buses leave Porto Velho for Humaitá (US$8, four hours). Boats also stop off in Humaitá. The road passes through completely cleared rainforest. In the burning season, September and October, the landscape looks like Armageddon – the final battle between good and evil.

On the edge of town is the **Hotel Macedonia** charging US$25 for a double, tel: 092 373 1230. The **Hotel Brasil** charges US$25 for a single and US$45 for a double. It has a restaurant and bar. These two hotels are surprisingly smart, no doubt waiting for a sudden increase in demand for good-quality hotels in the middle of the Amazon.

The best of the rest is **Hotel Maia** charging US$8 for a single. It is family run and serves food in ridiculously large portions. **Soveteria Tropical** serves very welcome ice-cream.

Apart from watching the gentle flow of life there is little to do in Humaitá. The church is rather ostentatious. Towards the ferry crossing there is a saw-mill which you can look round once you've obtained permission from the site manager in the office at the gate. Trees of the rainforest are cut and shaped for distribution to Brazilian and international markets, while the workers operate heavy machinery in flip-flops. Blades that easily slice through trees three metres thick don't have problems with human limbs, a risk the workers take for US$300 a month. (The management don't like you taking photographs.)

Beyond Humaitá

From Humaitá the twice-weekly bus service to Apuí takes 12 hours. A more interesting way to travel is to hitch from the riverfront where a ferry transports vehicles across every other hour. An early start increases your chance of making any real dent on the 1,000km to Itaituba.

The road quickly deteriorates. Solitary huts sit patiently alongside it optimistically waiting for an economic or tourist boom. The road travels through the northern extremity of the Tenharim-Transamazônica Indigenous Area. It then arrives at a town named Kilometre 180. A popular spot, it has two restaurants, a few wooden buildings and a hut with a mattress on the floor. A sign points out that this is 'accommodation.'

Another 300km down the road is the town of **Apuí**; its appearance preceded by billboards promoting the 'amazing' sounds of Radio Apuí.

Paved road surfaces and a number of shops distinguish the town from the rest of the Transamazônica. The population of around 5,000 lives on ranches and agricultural plots close to the town. Hardworking and industrious, Apuí is a supply town for the region, providing everything from food and clothes through to fishing nets, guns and machetes. At weekends everything and everyone stops, and indulges in the Brazilian passion for football, with teams travelling from hundreds of kilometres away to play. The pitch is a couple of blocks behind the main street, next to the corral which has occasional rodeo festivals.

Accommodation is plentiful and desperate. Most is on or close to the main road. Charging US$30 are **Hotel Route 66** and **Hotel Silverado**, both with air conditioning. At the bottom end – and they really are deep down – are **Hotel Goiana** and **Hotel Al Vorada**. There are several restaurants and bars, none of which stands out.

From Apuí, transport thins out even further with a weekly bus travelling to Jacareacanga. Alternatively you can try to hitch from the eastern end of town. There is also a twice-weekly cooperative bus that makes the journey to **Sucunduri**, roughly halfway along the road.

Spend any time in one of these towns, and you eventually ask yourself how they came into being. Sucunduri has, more or less, a valid reason. As Apuí grew too big, a group of settlers decided to push eastwards, attracted by free plots of land. When they reached the Sucunduri River the group of 800 could go no further – the river posed too great an obstacle – and decided it was as good a place as any to create a new settlement.

A chat with the people of the town might get you on a fishing trip or a short trip upriver in the afternoon. If you're feeling truly adventurous an eight-day paddle upstream takes you to the waterfall of Monte Cristo. You can't really get lost, but you might want to take a guide for the logistics of meals and lodging. Travelling downstream on the Rio Sucunduri, eventually joining the Rio Madeira just south of the Amazon main stream, is another option, but involves travelling through the Coata Laranjal Indigenous Area which is off limits unless you have a permit from FUNAI.

A hut at the river end of town is **Sucunduri's** only hotel. Astoundingly, a government official has assessed the log bed and cardboard mattress as suitable accommodation. The same place serves meat, rice, pasta and beans.

Travelling onwards requires patience or luck. A weekly bus goes to **Jacareacanga**, 150km (six hours) down the road, or you may get a ride in a truck. The jungle is fighting hard to reclaim this section of the road and may, without more traffic, eventually succeed.

Jacareacanga is a sleepy frontier town stuck in the haze of a Saturday morning lie-in. Living out the last few years of a gold-prospecting boom, in just a few years the town could be empty. There are a couple of hotels and a few restaurants. Air taxis can also connect you to Itaituba (US$90) and Santarém (US$150).

The road between Jacareacanga and Itaituba is often closed. Cargo boats connect the towns regularly, making the two-day trip down the Tapajós River from the port outside the town. The journey costs around US$30 including food. Hammocks can be bought in Jacareacanga. The cargo boats are smaller than those found on the larger Amazon tributaries and are generally cleaner and healthier.

The boats drop off cargo and pick up passengers mid-stream, and stop off at gold-mining settlements. There are several sets of rapids which in the dry season can cause problems. If the water is too low the boat stops in Buboré from where a truck takes you the last couple of hours to Itaituba.

The road to Itaituba passes the entrance to Parque Nacional da Amazônica (Amazon National Park). Entrance permits to use the park are obtainable from IBAMA in Itaituba.

Itaituba

The gold rush that attracted *garimpeiros* and gave this town a rough reputation has been tailing off for several years as the easily obtained gold has mostly been extracted. What remains is a melancholic atmosphere as the workers patiently wait for the better times ahead.

The state of Pará has extensive deposits of 'greenstone', which is among the richest gold-bearing rocks. Globally, greenstone rock produces about 70% of the world's gold. Multinationals are concentrating on concessions within the Tapajós watershed and several companies expect to announce major operations within the next couple of years. There are also plans to dredge over 1,000km of the river to allow year-round navigation by large ships. In addition to changing the course of the Amazon basin's largest clearwater river, the accompanying road at the upper limits of the river would damage the relatively undamaged Teles Pires tributary.

People in the town have time to talk and are friendly. The waterfront has a colourful market and food stalls. Around the town there are several clean and professionally organised shops buying and selling gold.

Hotels include **Juliana Park Hotel** (Travessa Joãa Pesoa 31A; tel: 091 518 2358; fax: 091 518 1706), which is smart, tidy, clean and close to the waterfront. Doubles are US$25. A couple of blocks back is the **Central Plaza Hotel** (Trav 13 de Maio 194; tel/fax: 091 518 1841) with doubles at US$44, and across the road is the slightly cheaper **Santa Rita Palace Hotel** (tel: 091 518 1724).

The best of the cheapies is the **Hotel Riozinto** (doubles US$15), right on the waterfront just in front of the market. It appears rough but is family-run. The evening barbecue is a feast but you could be put off if you saw how the meat is stored!

The waterfront has several restaurants of different quality. The telephone office is along the waterfront upstream. Banco do Brasil, opposite Santa Rosa Palace Hotel, has an ATM cash machine for Visa cards. The general response to travellers' cheques and cash in all the banks is 'Eh... en Santarém.'

Protecting over 1000km², the Amazon National Park is the best reason to visit Itaituba. Some 50km outside Itaituba and relatively easy to reach, the park is accessible yet remote and unspoiled. (See page 392.)

From Itaituba, boats and buses head north to Santarém; or you can continue along the Transamazônica to Altamira. The boat for Santarém departs from the dockside and the trip takes a couple of days but with the completion of the road to Santarém most Brazilians now travel there by bus, from Miritituba on the east bank of the Tapajós. Miritituba, reached by an hourly ferry service free to foot passengers, is also the place to catch buses travelling further along the Transamazônica to Altamira (US$35) and Marabá (US$60). Adventurous travellers may want to travel the road south to Cuiabá heading first to the town of Novo Progresso (US$25), from where you can catch another bus on to Cuiabá.

Alta Floresta

Totally off any natural route or circuit, about halfway between Cuiabá and Santarém, is the town of Alta Floresta (population 70,000). As with many other towns in the Amazon, Alta Floresta experienced a gold boom that has now faded.

Alta Floresta has two ecotourism opportunities that set it apart from other small towns: **Cristalino Jungle Lodge** and **Thaimaçu Lodge**. Neither option is cheap, independent travel is not an option and ideally you should book before arriving in Alta Floresta.

Getting there

There are regular flights to Alta Floresta from Cuiabá with Trip regional airlines; the return fare is US$245. From Cuiabá there are good links on the Varig airpass with Rio de Janeiro, São Paulo and Manaus.

From Cuiabá in the south buses run to Alta Floresta several times a day, costing US$75 and taking 12 hours. If you're coming from the north, buses make the ten-hour journey on very rough roads from Novo Progresso. The buses go to Sinop – 160km past the Alta Floresta turn-off – but ask the driver to drop you off at the junction for Alta Floresta and then hitch a lift.

Getting into town

Taxis serve the centre of town from the airport, 2km west of town, and the *rodoviária* (bus station), 2km to the south. Two parallel roads make up the main boulevard with most restaurants, bars and hotels found close by.

Where to stay

The best is **Floresta Amazônica Hotel** (Av Perimetral Oeste 2001, Alta Floresta; tel: 066 521 3601; fax: 066 521 2221; web: www.cristalinolodge.com.br). There is a pool, sauna, excellent air-conditioned rooms and beautifully prepared food. It's close to the airport and rooms start at US$50 for a single. A small nature reserve of 15ha at the bottom of the garden is home to monkeys, toucans and parrots, so you can walk out of the four-star hotel straight into the rainforest at any time of day or night. The Floresta also operates the Cristalino Jungle Lodge and is the base for trips. Other local visits can be arranged here – ask Vitoria.

On the airport road closer to town is **Pirâmide Palace Hotel** (Av Aeroporto 445; tel/fax: 065 521 2400). Rooms are tidy, with AC and TV as options. Doubles from US$40. On the main road is **Estoril Hotel** (Av Lucovico da Riva 2950; tel: 065 521 3298); its rooms are basic but the staff are friendly and the hotel restaurant is very good and handy (doubles US$25).

Close to the *rodoviária*, which is too far away from the centre of town for convenience, are a few cheapies. The best is probably **Londres Hotel** (Av Ludovico da Riva Neto; tel: 065 521 2858), in front of the bus terminal, at US$20 for a double.

Where to eat

On the plaza is the **Nova Lanchete da Praça** serving hamburgers, beers and refreshments. On the other side of the main street is **Choparia e Pizzaria Feitico** which is popular and has a pleasant atmosphere. The restaurant next to the Hotel Estoril is a good *churrascaria*, as is the one opposite Pirâmide Palace Hotel on Av Aeroporto.

Excursions from Alta Floresta

Ecotourism is developing slowly and a few facilities may appeal to natural-history lovers.

Projeto Vivero de Mudas de Plantas is a small project researching and promoting the traditional use of medicinal plants from the area. Close to this is the town's zoo which has a short jungle path with named plant specimens. The zoo's primitive conditions can be disturbing, but it does promote awareness of the region's wildlife. There is also a fisheries and craft project in town.

Jungle lodges
Cristalino Jungle Lodge

The lodge sits in pristine rainforest on the banks of the Rio Cristalino, a small blackwater tributary of the Rio Teles Peres which flows down to the Rio Tapajós. A one-hour jeep ride from Alta Floresta followed by a 40-minute boat trip takes you to the lodge. There are eight bungalows with private toilets and sun-heated showers, each sleeping two or three, and a couple of dormitory-style buildings divided into smaller rooms. There are several hammocks. The restaurant serves local dishes.

Eight trails have been laid out through the forest near the lodge and others are a short boat trip away. The trails are easy but quickly immerse you in the rainforest. The Brazil Nut Trail takes you to see these magnificent forest giants draped in lianas, vines and epiphytes. The Sierra Trail takes you up through tall trees to scrubby, semi-deciduous vegetation. You then arrive at the granite summit for a panorama over the rainforest canopy. Other trails take you through bamboo forest, home to antbirds, and sightings of hoatzins are common.

The shortest trip to the lodge is four days. If you have longer, a ten-day expedition upriver leads you to Cristalino Waterfall: a dramatic cascade of water.

Book Cristalino Lodge with Floresta Tours at the Floresta Amazônica Hotel. (page 415)

A week at Cristalino for two costs US$900pp. The price includes airport transfers, accommodation in Alta Floresta and Cristalino and all meals. English-speaking guides are also included in the price. From the US you can book a stay here through Travel Innovations (page 42). Maxim Tours (page 367) has a three-night package (one night in Alta Floresta) for US$298pp in the low season, US$370pp high season.

Thaimaçu Pousada-Lodge

On the Rio São Benedito, this fishing lodge is situated a few metres from where the 150m-wide river creates a small but dramatic waterfall. The comfortable air-conditioned cabins accommodate 20 people. The food, grown in the surrounding area, is excellent and beautifully presented. There is also a bar in which to tell those fisherman's tales of the one that got away. The lodge is family-run and is the passion of Carlos Muñhoz, an extremely affable and knowledgeable man who speaks a wonderful blend of Portuñol (Portuguese and Español) and is happiest when chatting with guests about the river, fish and Brazil.

From Alta Floresta it's a short 40-minute flight to the private landing strip at Thaimaçu Lodge. Flights can be organised when booking through Carlos. Above the waterfall crystal-clear pools are inhabited by tiny iridescent fish. You might see the Amazon kingfisher dive into the water or a pair of razor-billed curassows grubbing among forest leaf litter. Along the river, dense woods give way to open gallery forest. Here flocks of hoatzin scramble awkwardly through the trees. Monkeys, tapirs and caiman may also be in the vicinity.

Around the cabins macaws nest in the trunks of dying trees. A tapir wandering around at night was adopted as a youngster after its mother had been killed by a jaguar.

As you would expect from a fishing lodge, angling is excellent; some would say world class. Catch-and-release is practised to prevent over-fishing. Dominant species are peacock bass and payara, while the more focused angler can try deeper spots for giant catfish or a 40kg *jaú* or *pirara*, or even the 100kg *piraíba*.

Six nights at the lodge, including the flight from Alta Floresta and all meals, cost US$1,280. The lodge is closed between mid-December and the end of January. For details and booking contact: Carlos Muñhoz, Thaimaçu Pousada-Lodge, Rua C2 #228, Caixa Postal 04, Alta Floresta, Mato Grosso, CEP 78.580-000; tel/fax: 065 521 3587; email: pescaesportiva@thaimacu.com.br; web: www.thaimacu.com.br.

Guyana, French Guiana and Suriname

In this chapter we cover three of South America's smallest countries. Despite their size, the diversity of wildlife is on a par with those of other Amazon countries. Strictly speaking, only Guyana claims part of the Amazon River watershed. However, similarities in natural history and proximity to the Amazon ecosystem justify their inclusion in this book.

GUYANA

> ### BASIC FACTS
> **Official name** The Cooperative Republic of Guyana (formerly British Guiana)
> **Area** 214,969km² (83,000 miles²)
> **Population** 780,000
> **Capital** Georgetown
> **Largest city** (population) Georgetown (175,000)
> **Official language** English
> **Date of independence** May 26 1966
> **Major industries** minerals, agriculture, fisheries
> **GDP per capita** US$4,800
> **Currency** Guyanan dollar G$ (US$=G$180; £1=G$284)
> **National holidays** Jan 2, Feb 23, Easter, May 1, Dec 25–26

Facts and figures
Geography, rivers and climate
Meaning 'land of many waters', the name Guyana originally referred to the triangle of territory between the three great rivers of northern South America – the Amazon, Orinoco and Negro. The national territory is bordered to the south by Brazil. Venezuela lies to the west and Suriname to the east, and persistent frontier disputes with both countries continue.

With the Atlantic to the north, the country encompasses a wide range of ecological habitats, from coastal mangrove to montane tropical forest in the wild hinterland. The northeastern half comprises a relatively flat coastal strip, 15–60km wide, covered with dense tropical rainforest or mangrove along the narrow tidal belt.

In the central western region the Pakaraima Mountains, forming part of the Guianan Shield, rise to over 2,750m. To the south are the Kanuku, Wassari and Acarai ranges; effective barriers between Guyana and north-central Brazil.

The five major rivers are the Cuyuni, Demerara, Essequibo, Berbice and Amacuro.

Most densely populated of Guyana's administrative districts is East Demerara. Situated in its northwest corner is the country's capital Georgetown, at the Demerara River's mouth. The largest district is Rupununi, a rolling savannah covering the rugged southern hinterland to the Pakaraima foothills.

Kaieteur Falls is one of the country's major tourist attractions. Along the Potaro River, a tributary of the Essequibo, it has a sheer drop of 222m, nearly five times that of Niagara Falls. Yet it is only one of several splendid waterfalls, including Orinduik Falls, on the Ireng River.

Georgetown's average annual temperature is 27°C. The coast experiences two wet seasons, from April to August and November to January. The south of Guyana has only one wet season, from April to August. Rainfall is heavy on the coast. The high interior grasslands receive less, typically 1,780mm per year.

People and languages

Guyana's small population gives it the second lowest population density in South America after French Guiana. The population is concentrated along the coast and in Georgetown.

About half the inhabitants are of East Indian origin while Africans comprise about a third. Mulattoes, Creoles, Amerindians, Chinese, Portuguese and Lebanese make up the remainder. Amerindian tribes still inhabit remote hinterlands. Main ethnic groups include Carib, Arawak, Arrau, Makuxi, Waiwai and Kawaio.

English is the official language. Ethnically, over 80% are African or East Indian but most people speak 'talkie-talkie' or Creole English, while Hindi and Urdu are spoken among the Indian community.

Education is of relatively good quality, with about 95% literacy. All children must attend school (free of charge) from 6 to 14 years of age.

History

Of pre-European history, it is known that peaceful Warrau Indians colonised the Guianan Highlands in the first millennium BC, but were later supplanted by the more warlike Arawaks and Caribs.

Spain largely ignored the area known as the Wild Coast between the Orinoco and Amazon deltas. Europeans first settled there in the early 17th century, when the Dutch established trading posts inland, dating from 1621, and imported slaves from West Africa to farm sugarcane.

In 1796 the British took over the Dutch town of Stabroek, changing the name to Georgetown, and purchased territories along the Essequibo, Berbice and Demerara rivers in 1814.

Large numbers of slaves were imported by the Dutch West India Company to plant sugarcane. When slavery was abolished in 1834 many of the 100,000 freed slaves left the coastal zones for the hinterland, leading to a wave of immigration from Portugal, China and India.

In 1962 Venezuela renewed its claim to portions of Guyana, a dispute that went to the United Nations in 1982 and remains unresolved.

Independence was not attained without difficulty. After a decade of civil unrest, proportional representation was introduced in 1964, and the country opted for full independence in 1966 under the leadership of Forbes Burnham. During the 1970s, Burnham consolidated his position and in 1980 declared that his government would follow socialist doctrine.

In 1978 Guyana was the site of a mass suicide committed by 913 members of a religious cult led by the Reverend Jim Jones.

Following the collapse of the Soviet Union in the late 1980s, the Guyanan government adopted free-market policies. An about-turn in the country's fortunes in 1991 led to the highest growth rates seen in decades. Severe drought and political turmoil led to a negative growth of -1.8% in 1998. Growth was modestly positive in 1999 and 2000, mostly in the agriculture and mining sectors, helped by a more favorable atmosphere for business and continued support by international organizations. President Jagdeo, the former finance minister, is reforming the economy by restructuring the inefficient and unresponsive public sector. Problems include a shortage of skilled labor and a deficient infrastructure. Early 2002, a severe crime wave led later in the year to calls for the government to declare a state of emergency, underscoring the problems of violence in the country.

The public sector is dominant, following socialist policies of public ownership through nationalisation; but private economic activity is increasingly important. Despite rich mineral and natural resources, Guyana's GNP has actually declined from the mid-1980s and its per-capita income is currently South America's lowest.

Money
Guyana dollars are not available outside the country but US dollars are widely used. It is easy to change travellers' cheques or get credit card advances. Overseas visitors must use hard currency to pay hotel bills and locally purchased air-tickets. Georgetown has several foreign exchange houses with better rates than the banks.

Highlights
The government resisted tourism until the 1990s. Following the general policy reversal, a Ministry of Tourism was created, and efforts began to improve the tourist infrastructure.

Visiting the only South American country in which English is the official language will surely appeal to Anglophiles. This makes Guyana potentially easy for independent travellers from the UK and US.

With the low cost of living and favourable exchange rates, travel in Guyana is cheap; but not simple. Tourist facilities are under-developed, but the country is working to develop the infrastructure to meet the needs of independent travellers.

Few tour operators offer group travel, but numerous opportunities are available to independent travellers. Guyana is hardly the world's best known holiday hotspot so few tour operators offer organised tours. Inland trips are a real adventure as travel away from the coastal strip is not easy. But the effort is highly rewarding, with rugged, unspoiled scenery, quiet accommodation and the occasional 'discovery' of some unpublicised waterfall or natural area.

When to go
If you can take the heat, the best time to go to Guyana is during the dry season from September through November, although this coincides with the hottest period. Most days, though, temperatures are not high enough to be oppressive. Rainfall in the Rupununi region to the south is low enough that the short rainy season does not provide problems for travellers.

Tour operators
In Guyana
Earth Tours 106 Lamaha St, North Cummingsburg, Georgetown; tel: 22 54020; fax: 22 65340; email: earthtours@hotmail.com; web: www.etl-gy.com. Rainforest, resort, fishing and adventure tours to destinations throughout Guyana.

Essequibo Adventure Tours 42 Second Av, Bartica, Essequibo; tel: 05 2441; fax: 05 2956.
Evergreen Adventure Tours 158 Charlotte St, Lacytown, Georgetown; tel: 22 60605;
fax: 22 51171; email: evergreen.adventures@webworksgy.com; web: www.evergreen-
adventures.com. Various nature and leisure tours throughout Guyana. Agents for the
upmarket Rockview Lodge.
Hinterlander Tours 76 First Av, Subryanville, Georgetown; tel: 22 64025; fax: 22 64025.
Iwokrama International Centre for Rain Forest Conservation and Development
67 Bel Air, Georgetown; tel: 22 51504; fax: 22 59199; web: www.iwokrama.com. Non-
profit conservation organisation with a variety of canoeing, hiking and birding tours to
remote areas in the Iwokrama Forest.
Nature Tours 238 BB Eccles East Bank, Demerara; tel/fax: 233 2454; email:
naturetours60@hotmail.com. Trips to Kaieteur and all interior resorts as well as city tours.
Rainforest Tours 33 Barrack Street, Kingston, Georgetown; tel: 22 72013; fax: 22 75632;
email: rainforesttours@solutions2000.net. Specialists in overland rainforest hikes.
Shell Beach Adventures Le Meridien Pegasus Hotel Kingston, Georgetown; tel: 22
54483; fax: 22 60532; email: info@sbadventures.com; web: www.sbadventures.com.
Award-winning ecotourism company with various itineraries to resorts and natural areas.
Torong Guyana 56 Coralita Ave, Bel Air Park, Georgetown; tel: 22 58101; fax: 22 50749;
email: toronggy@networksgy.com. Specialise in Kaieteur and Orinduik, Rupununi, city
tours and resort visits. Custom designed itineraries for individuals and groups.
Wilderness Explorers Cara Suites, 176 Middle St, Georgetown; tel: 22 77698; fax: 22
62085; email: info@wilderness-explorers.com; web: www.wilderness-explorers.com.
Guyana's leading tour operator offers ecologically sensitive, professional tours to a variety
of destinations in Guyana and neighbouring countries. Kaieteur and Orinduik Falls,
Rupununi, interior resorts, Essequibo and Mazaruni. Birdwatching, turtle nesting,
individual, groups and custom designed itineraries.
Wonderland Tours 158 C Waterloo St, North Cumingsburg, Georgetown; tel: 22 59795;
fax: 22 59795. Day and overnight trips to Essequibo River. Day trips to Kamuni and Santa
Mission, Kaieteur and Orinduik Falls and city tours.

In the US
Dreamweaver Travel, **Field Guides** and the **Oceanic Society** all offer tours – see pages
40–2 for contact details.
Latin American Escapes 712 Bancroft Av, Walnut Creek, CA 94598; tel: 800 510 5999;
fax: 925 945 0154; email: travel@latinamericanescapes.com. Broad selection of Guyana
tours.

In the UK
Condor Journeys and Adventures, **Discovery Initiatives** and **Trips Worldwide** all
offer tours – see pages 42–4 for contact details.

Getting there and away
Getting there
By air
International flights arrive and depart at Timehri International Airport. 40km
outside Georgetown. Several airlines serve the airport including Guyana Airways,
BWIA, Carib Express, LIAT and Suriname Airways. BWIA flies daily direct from
Miami and New York. **North American Airlines** have five flights a week direct
from JFK, beginning at US$600 return in the low season. Their office is at 126
Carmichael Street, South Cummingsburg, Georgetown; tel: 227 5805; fax: 227
4164; in the US at 127-18 Liberty Ave, 2nd floor, Richmond Hill, NY 11419; tel:
800 371-6297; fax: 718 322 7572; email: acooper@northamericanair.com; web:

www.northamair.com. Other direct flights originating in North America are from Atlanta, Miami and Toronto.

As there are no direct flights from Europe, you must fly to North America first or take another route with a connecting flight. The best and least expensive route is London–Miami–Georgetown. Another easy alternative is London–Barbados–Georgetown, although you will have to overnight in Barbados.

By ship
Georgetown is a major seaport and a passenger terminal for cruise ships and river ferries. Luxury liners sometimes stop here on the way to or from cruises along the Amazon or around South America.

By road
The only way to approach by bus or private vehicle from Brazil is via Boa Vista to Bonfim and then across the border at Lethem, on a difficult road.

There are no road links with Venezuela and just a pedestrian ferry connection with Suriname.

Customs and immigration
In 1994 Guyana relaxed its previously stringent visa requirements to encourage tourism. Citizens of the US, UK and most European countries do not require visas.

There is a US$8 departure tax from Guyana.

Getting around
Guyana's roads are generally poor, unsurfaced or with tar sprayed on a graded track. Repairs on flood-damaged main highways invariably take several days. Few roads penetrate the interior so the only sensible way to get around is by river transport or aeroplane.

For domestic flights, Guyana Airways has routes to large towns. Most internal traffic is carried by smaller airlines that offer a variety of services: charters, scheduled flights, travel services, excursions, and medical evacuation. Due to the poor road system, these are the main ways to travel between Georgetown and the country's interior. Most internal flights leave from Georgetown's Ogle Airport where you can book charter flights directly.

Air Services Ogle Aerodrome, Ogle, East Coast Demerara, PO Box 10176, Georgetown; tel: 592 222 4357/4368; fax: 592 222 2005; email: ASL@solutions2000.net
Roraima Airways 101 Cummings St, Bourda, Georgetown; tel: 22 59648; fax: 22 59646; email: ral@roraimaairways.com; web: www.roraimaairways.com.
Trans Guyana Airways 159 Charlotte St, Lacytown, Georgetown; tel: 022 2525; fax: 022 5462; web: www.transguyana.com

Canals throughout the coastal region connect estates and villages and are served by passenger services.

Communications
The general post office in Georgetown is on North Road. The service is expensive and unreliable so any important mail is best sent registered or by private courier.

The government exerts practically complete control over its own media: one radio station and a daily newspaper *The Chronicle*. *The Mirror* represents opposition views, while the highly regarded *Catholic Standard* is considered neutral.

Guyana's first television station opened 1988, also under government control, but now two independent channels show US satellite television.

Telecommunications are generally good, with global direct dialling and relatively low rates. The large hotels have international dialling facilities. Calls are cheaper from the Guyana Telephone & Telegraph (GTT) office in the Bank of Guyana building (North Street). For those in a hurry service is quicker but more expensive at the Tower Hotel. Several internet cafés have sprung up recently. One of the most popular is **Byte 'N' Surf** (288 Middle St, Georgetown; email: romonacb@hotmail.com).

The country code for Guyana is 592.

Georgetown

Awash in moth-eaten colonialism, Georgetown's schizoid personality arises from a bygone era hauling itself into the 21st century. Victorian buildings of imposing, confident architecture still line many city streets.

The town has the air of a rough-and-tumble port peopled by a combination of hurried business people and laid-back stall traders, tourists and street people. Even during the day there's a latent energy capable of tensing all who feel it. Maybe it's an absence of security, given that Georgetown is among the most dangerous cities in South America for theft, muggings and violence.

But somehow, when this background fades, an evening ocean breeze rustles the palm leaves and a spicy aroma wafts across the air, Georgetown can be heaven.

Transport

From Timehri International Airport to Georgetown – a trip that should only be done during the day – expect to pay US$20 for a taxi into town. A fleet of minibuses also make the journey, charging US$1.50.

In Georgetown the visitor finds it relatively easy to get around in taxis and buses. Fares are very low, about US$0.25 for minibus rides anywhere in town. Go to Stabroek Market to catch long-distance minibuses to Linden (US$12) and Parika (US$8). For destinations outside Georgetown buses leave from the station, located between Stabroek Market and Avenue of the Republic.

Where to stay

Accommodation in Georgetown is relatively expensive compared with other Amazon countries. Most hotels are in the western part of the city around the main commercial district. Note that 10% room tax is charged on all accommodation.

Luxury

Cara Lodge Taitt House, Quamina St, Georgetown; tel: 22 55301; fax: 22 55310; email: caralodge@carahotels.com; web: www.carahotels.com. Guyana's first Heritage House Hotel, built in 1840, originally consisted of two houses. All rooms have private bathroom, AC, international direct dial, television, ceiling fans, and refrigerator. Rates start at US$95 per night.

Le Meridien Pegasus Hotel Seawall Rd; tel: 800 225 5843; fax: 22 53703; web: www.LeMeridien-pegasus.com. Along the seafront: the best and most expensive hotel in town (US$175), and their El Dorado restaurant is considered Georgetown's finest dining. Views over the Demerara River, the city and the Atlantic Ocean.

Main Street Plaza 45 Main St, Cummingsburg, Georgetown; tel: 22 70313; fax: 22 57666; email: mainstplaza@solutions2000.net; web: www.mainstplaza.com. Guyana's newest luxury hotel. Purpose-built with restaurant, café, pool, conference/ballroom, 24-hour room service.

Mid-range

Friends Hotel 82 Robb Street, Lacytown, Georgetown; tel: 22 72383; fax: 22 70193; email: jwalco@solutions2000.net; web: www.friendshotel.com. Several different room types cater either to the overnight guest or the long-term resident. Rooms from US$25. Clean and friendly.

Woodbine International 41–42 New Market St; tel: 22 59430. Friendly and modern but near a rough part of town (US$40-50).

Budget

New Tropicana 177 Waterloo St. Cheapest in town. Single rooms with private bathroom are US$12. Sometimes noisy due to bar, restaurant, disco.

Rima Guest House 92 Middle St; tel: 02 57401. Family-run and safe, in the heart of town. Single rooms with shared bathrooms for US$20.

Where to eat

Most restaurants and cafés are located along Main Street. There is a reasonable choice of places to eat out in Georgetown including European, Caribbean, East Indian and South American influences. For an upmarket meal (US$10–20) the better establishments are **Del Casa** (232 Middle Street) and **Caribbean** (175 Middle Street). Also recommended as one of the best in Georgetown is the **Cabazon** (74 Main Street; tel: 02 72011) in the Tower Hotel.

What to see

The **railway station**, an interesting example of mid-Victorian architecture, is at the north end of Carmichael Street. **St George's Anglican Cathedral** has a towering spire 43.3m high – among the tallest in South America. National cultural institutions centre on Georgetown, notably the **Parliament Building** (a block west of Stabroek Market) and the **Presidential Residence** at the southwest corner of the botanical gardens. City tours can be arranged for around US$30.

Encompassing a large park area in the southeast of Georgetown the **Botanic Gardens** (admission US$0.10) provide the setting for the city zoo. The zoo is quite impressive considering the limited finances. Birders will appreciate the bird collection, including a hyacinth macaw. Many specimens of tropical South American animals are represented so you can see a number of species from Amazon areas which you may have missed during jungle tours.

In the commercial centre of Georgetown is the very good **Guyanan Museum**. Much of the museum, inside and out, is ageing, and the contents have hardly changed since British colonial times. However, the place is not moth-eaten, rather growing old gracefully. Overall the displays and collections tell a full story of the country's past and natural history.

Shopping

Avid souvenir hunters have much to occupy their attention in Georgetown. Handicrafts are of a quality and price not seen along the more tourist-beaten path. The Amerindian Handicrafts Centre (1 Water St) has a wide selection of weapons, native costumes and adornments. Stabroek Market (on the Demerara riverfront) has some handicrafts, including baskets and hammocks, plus more prosaic machetes and rubber boots, along with a wide variety of local agricultural produce.

More information

Once you're in the country, the best source of information is the industry-funded **Tourism and Hospitality Association of Guyana** (157 Waterloo Street,

Georgetown; tel: 02 50807; fax: 02 50817; email: thag@networksgy.com; web: www.exploreguyana.com). They publish a travel guide which has a map and information on upmarket hotels and lodges throughout the country. There are some informative websites on the country and travel facilities. Among the best are **www.guyana.org** with photos, news, history, government information and **www.lasalle.edu/~daniels/guyexp/bgintro.htm**, which offers a personalised perspective on just about every topic of interest to prospective visitors. Also worth a visit is **www.guyanatours.com**, an online travel guide. Check *Appendix 3* for more online resources.

Warning Parts of Georgetown are very dangerous and must be avoided even during daylight. Especially notorious is the Tiger Bay district.

Beyond Georgetown

Close to Georgetown, one option is a trip to the mining town of Linden (population 75,000), the second biggest town in Guyana. It has a few decent hotels (US$10–25) which cater to the traveller of reasonably modest expectations.

Several Georgetown tour operators offer a variety of options to explore the wild Guyanan hinterlands already described. Another option is to explore the coastal region which has the advantage of relatively easy access. However, this area is hot and humid so many people prefer to go further inland.

River rafters will love four days of river rafting on the Cuyuni River. Rapids along the Nekuima Canyon, requiring seven days, are among the most spectacular scenery in the area, and provide thrills, in between relaxing at accommodation in riverside jungle camps and lodges.

Guyana's 'Amazon'

Most of Guyana is rainforest and the interior is practically uninhabited. Where extractive operations are absent, the forest is pristine and the wildlife abundant.

Guyana's back-country has few towns or villages that could be considered 'gateways', as most are isolated from road traffic, and accessed usually by small plane or, nearer the coast, by launch or dugout canoe. The few establishments that do exist are top-notch and, if you can afford the price, well worth the effort to travel beyond the coastal plain. In turn this region offers excellent opportunities for birding and exploring tropical rainforest.

Jungle towns and villages
Lethem

This is the main town for trips to the central Rupununi savannah region, notable for expansive rolling grasslands, ideal for birdwatching and horse riding. The town is set within a valley formed by the Pakaraima Range to the north and a huge arc of high peaks of the Serra Acari Range to the west and south.

Lethem is a modest market town with buildings varying from quaint to horrible and streets with a smattering of shops supplying the basics needed for life in what is still very much frontier country: maize meal, machetes, sugar, tea and hammocks. In Lethem itself the climate is cool at night and warm during the day. Shorts and T-shirt are usually fine from mid-morning to early evening but you'll need jeans and sweatshirt to keep the evening chill at bay. Because of the cooler temperatures, biting insects are not bothersome. With the valley and mountain landscapes and variety of savannah and tropical forest habitat, the nature is outstanding.

The twice-weekly, hour-long flight to Lethem from Georgetown with Guyana Airways costs US$65 one way.

Tours are arranged through Georgetown tour operators who offer swimming, angling and horseback excursions. Birdwatching in the extensive grasslands surrounding the town is excellent and the open grasslands make a nice contrast with the lowland tropical jungle to the north where vegetation obscures much of the birdlife.

Close to Lethem is Guyana's earliest established Amerindian village of Annai. The Waiwai and Macushi tribes are largely acculturated but still retain some traditional handicrafts such as the use of colourful feathers in ceremonial costumes. Ask in the village for a guide (US$10) to take you on a 20-minute walk from the village to Mocomoco Falls, a beautiful cascade surrounded by thick vegetation.

Another pleasant trip several hours' drive from Lethem is Lake Pan, located in the lower Rupununi Valley. The place is popular with locals for its temperate clean waters, lacking in significant currents and offering most enjoyable swimming and snorkelling. The lake's fish life is diverse, including the Amazon's biggest freshwater fish, *arapaima,* and a local species, *lukunani,* said to make good eating. With greater technical skill than required of hook and rod, natives shoot *arapaima* fish with a simple bow and arrow.

A trip to Mocomoco Falls or Lake Pan costs around US$150 per day, with a minimum three or four days needed to make the most of the nature and culture opportunities. In remoter areas, accommodation is a combination of camping and simple forest cabins with transport from Lethem costing US$35–100.

Imbaimadai

In the west of Guyana, this town is the gateway to the Pakaraima Range. Visitors can enjoy clear rivers running down valleys with sheltered patches of montane elfin forest among expansive grasslands. Although Imbaimadai is not far from the Venezuelan border, there is no way to cross officially from the town. It is, however, a popular starting point for trips to the Pakaraima Range and Kaieteur Falls National Park.

There is little to see or do in this frontier mining town along the Mazaruni River, apart from watching a gold-rush in action as gold and diamonds are dug from the alluvial sediments of the riverbanks.

Ask your tour operator to arrange Indian (Kawaio) guides to the nearby Maipuri Falls. Sometimes tour operators include this in the itinerary with Kaieteur Falls. Further on are 700-year-old Indian cliff drawings, a 30-minute hike from the falls. It is very difficult, if not impossible, to make it here on your own from town.

Bartica

This is an old gold-mining camp, gaining importance as a stopover before and after jungle trips. Though not far from Georgetown, it lies on the coastal plain's innermost portion on a promontory at the confluence of the Essequibo, Mazaruni and Cuyuni rivers. Between the Essequibo and Mazaruni rivers, the Hinterland Road heads south with various routes taking you to several small jungle towns. There is little to do in Bartica but if you have to overnight here there are a handful of very basic hotels from US$10 per night. Among the better is **Zen's Plaza** (43 Second Av, Bartica; tel: 05 2441; fax: 05 2956; web: www.geocities.com/zensplaza), clean and comfortable with private shower. Prices begin at US$11 for a single, to US$16 for a room with TV and balcony.

Jungle lodges

No stilt-borne, palm-thatched, solar-panelled 'luxury eco-lodges' grace Guyana's wilderness, but the prepared traveller will enjoy the simple camps, and small but very pleasant hotels, ranging from modest to sumptuous. Popular places to stay have all the amenities expected of tourist-standard lodges and accommodations.

Comfortable, ranch-style accommodation overlooking the Essequibo River is provided is provided at **Shanklands**. This fine lodge on the northern edge of the Rupununi savannah is surrounded by an area incredibly rich in birdlife. Built in an elaborate Victorian style, Shanklands is a converted villa set among attractive gardens. The veranda and balconies of the comfortable rooms overlook vast grassy plains with beautiful views. Activities include birding, horse-riding and trekking along remote open trails. Prices begin at US$60pp. You can book direct at Cara Suites Hotel (176 Middle Street, Georgetown; tel: 22 61612; fax: 22 68907; email: info@shanklands.com; web: www.shanklands.com), or with Georgetown tour operators. Opened 1998, **Rock View** is also on the Essequibo, located at Annai in the North Rupununi. It has similar standards and prices to Shanklands. They also run the **Surama Guest House** – simple timber and brick accommodation with hammocks and outside bathroom. The most basic option is **Burro-Burro Camp**, by the river with a separate kitchen, latrine and showers. This costs US$30 with breakfast and dinner or US$10 without. Activities at Rock View include pony trekking, nature and adventure tours, and sports fishing. Food is Brazilian and Creole cuisine. Rates for meals and accommodation at Rockview start from US$60pp. Book through Evergreen Adventures (page 422; email: info@rockviewlodge.com; web: www.rockviewlodge.com). A three-day package is US$445 including two-way Georgetown airfare. From the UK, Journey Latin America has a tour including Shanklands and Rockview on a ten-day itinerary costing £2,095pp in the low season.

Among the best facilities in the hinterlands is **Timberhead**, located on the Pokerero Creek in the Amerindian Reservation of Santa Mission, about two and a half hours from Georgetown. For the luxury-minded traveller, this place offers comfortable jungle accommodation at US$105 for an overnight stay with meals and transport included. Book through Le Meridien Pegasus (see page 424). The least expensive stay in lowland rainforest within easy reach of Georgetown is the **Rainbow River Safari** – a camping facility about four hours by speedboat from Georgetown. On the banks of the Mazaruni River, close by Marshall Falls, the camp caters to backpackers, and offers basic facilities and simple food. You can sleep on raised camp beds under tarps or bring your own hammock. Cost is US$44 for the first night, US$33 thereafter, including transfers. Book direct at 234 Almond Street, Georgetown; tel: 22 69874; fax: 22 56959; email: tedsabat@aol.com; web: http:/hometown.aol.com/tedsabat/rainbowrivermarshallfallsguyana.html.

Amazonian Cacique Manabaru and **Amazonian Cacique Madewini** are twin lodges that opened in 1998. Each is comprised of 12 well-equipped cabins. Paths and walkways connect the buildings. Facilities include a canopy walkway, aquarium, trails, creeks for swimming and sunbathing. Each tour includes a day to fly over the waterfalls of the Ireng River on Guyana's Brazil border and a trip to Kaieteur Falls for lunch overlooking the gorge. Book through Tower Hotel in Georgetown.

As with lodges in the interior it is best to arrange transport and reserve accommodation through tour operators in Georgetown. New businesses open and close with high frequency, so contact the Tourism and Hospitality Association of Guyana for recommended companies, hotels and lodges.

National parks and wildlife reserves

The most important government-protected area is **Kaieteur National Park**, established to protect the watershed of the Potaro River, down which tumbles

Kaieteur Falls. The park is a vast area of pristine tropical vegetation supporting a wide variety of tropical fauna. Accessible by road from Bartica, the nearest town to the falls is Mahdia from where you will have to try to catch a lift. There is no accommodation in the park so take your own camping equipment.

On the Ireng River, a tributary of the Negro and part of the Amazon proper, Orinduik Falls is a spectacular waterfall, ranking with Niagara Falls for majesty and beating it hands down in terms of unspoiled natural beauty. On package tours a visit to Orinduik Falls and the nearby Patamona Indians is usually included with a trip to Kaieteur Falls (US$175–200 from Georgetown for three days).

On the northern edge of the northern Rupununi savannah is the recently established **Iwokrama Forest Reserve** measuring 371,000 hectares. Here the birdlife is among the richest in the country, with expanses of primary rainforest which are home to a number of typical Amazon species including scarlet macaws, curassows, parrots and numerous antbird species. New accommodation is now available for short stays in the reserve (see Iwokrama International Centre, page 422).

FRENCH GUIANA

> **BASIC FACTS**
> **Official name** Département de La Guyane
> **Area** 91,000km² (35,135 miles²)
> **Population** 175,000
> **Capital** Cayenne
> **Largest city** (population) Cayenne (42,000)
> **Official language** French
> **Status** Overseas Department of France
> **Major industries** fisheries, forest products, gold
> **GDP per capita** US$6,000
> **Currency** Euro (US$1 = €6; £1 = €10)
> **Major attractions** Îles du Salut, Kourou Space Centre, Kaieteur Falls, Rupununi savannah
> **National holidays** Jan 1, Easter, May 1, July 14, Aug 15, Nov 1, 2, & 11, Dec 25

A small enclave on the northeast coast of South America, French Guiana is the smallest country in South America, dwarfed by giant Brazil on the south and east and big brother Suriname to the west. Nevertheless it remains an anachronistic testament to colonialism.

Facts and figures
Geography, rivers and climate
Over the aeons rivers have eroded the underlying crystalline rock of the Guiana Highlands leaving a coastal terrain that is flat for the most part. To the northwest, ancient riverbeds underlie a savannah-type habitat. East of Cayenne, more recent alluvial deposits form swampy plains, ending in mangrove flats on the coast. Occupying the country's south towards Brazil, the Tumuc-Humac Mountains (Massif des Tumuc-Humac) form rolling hills, up to elevations of 850m, covered with tropical evergreen woodlands.

Running northwards from the highlands are five major rivers of which Fleuve Oyapock's 500km length defines the eastern boundary with Brazil. The 725km-long Fleuve Maroni forms the border with Suriname to the west. Recent proposals to dam the central Mana, Oyapock and Sinnamary rivers for hydro-power were met with strong protests by environmentalists.

With no high mountains and a humid, warm climate, dominated by heavy rain, much of French Guiana is covered with dense tropical rainforest, habitat for a rich variety of typical Amazon birdlife and large animals including cats, tapirs, manatees, turtles, caiman, but not pink dolphin. Due to low population and lack of access about 90% of this forest remains pristine.

This is among the wettest places in South America. Rainfall averages 3,800mm annually and is heaviest around Cayenne, especially from December to July. Warm all year round, average temperatures at Cayenne are 25–27°C.

People and languages

Like its independent English-speaking twin, French Guiana has a low population density. The majority of Guianans outside cities and towns are subsistence or part-time farmers.

The population is 90% Roman Catholic, whereas East Indians and Southeast Asians practise Buddhism and Islam.

Diverse ethnic communities form the basis for French Guiana's varied cultural life. Black people and native Indians, primarily in rural areas, take their heritage from African and indigenous influences. In urban areas, the main culture is mixed-Creole. Amerindians mostly constitute the rural population especially away from the coast. Among the important groups are Arawak, Wayana, Oyampi, Galibi, Emerillons and Palikors.

French is the national tongue. A crash course or at least a bilingual dictionary is indispensable for non-French-speaking independent travellers.

History

French Guiana is among the earliest settled parts of South America, with Spaniards recorded as exploring the region as early as 1500. French presence in the area was established by merchants who set up a trading post in 1624 at Sinnamary.

Getting the country off to a good start, the community for freed slaves at Mana set an example of humanitarianism rarely equalled at the time. However, in 1846 the community was closed and Guiana became the main French penal colony. In 1852, Napoleon III decreed that convicts with sentences over seven years were to serve time in French Guiana, a policy that remained until the prison stopped admissions in 1945. It finally closed in 1953. The year 1877 saw representation of free Guianans in the French Parliament and in 1946 the colony became a *département* of France. Major post-war developments were the rocket launch facility at Kourou (1968) and the Green Plan (Plan Vert), a 1970s project to increase agricultural production and timber harvests.

French Guiana attains distinction as the only territory on the continent that is not an independent nation, and indeed the continent's smallest 'country'. It is ruled by the French government, subject to the French constitution and with the president of France as head of state.

As a business concern, France's colony fights a losing battle. Its trade deficit continues to grow, imports outweighing exports by ten to one. Inflation is often rampant and unemployment rates are usually in double figures. Yet, bolstered by regular injections of cash and industrial aid from France, French Guiana has one of the highest per-capita GNPs in South America.

Money

French Guiana's medium of exchange is the euro. If you are changing oreign currency (eg: pounds or dollars), you normally get a better exchange rate in your home country than in French Guiana. If you have a credit card you can get euros from ATMs throughout Cayenne and in larger towns.

Expenses in French Guiana are higher than in France and most South American countries so budget accordingly. The frugal traveller will spend US$50/day. Lodgings start at around US$20. Budget around US$3 or US$4 for each meal. Tours and travel services are correspondingly expensive.

Highlights

French Guiana is still relatively under-used by major tour operators – delightful for travellers looking for the unbeaten path. Organised tours are few and far between and the tourist infrastructure is undeveloped, making French Guiana well-suited to the independent, flexible traveller. Getting up remote rivers – there are no significant roads into the interior – takes some perseverance, but is worth the effort.

Nature opportunities abound. Over 80% of the country's forest cover remains intact. Wildlife includes all the major Amazonian mammals, reptiles and hundreds of bird species. Watered by seasonal rains, rivers rise and fall in the lowlands of French Guiana, as they do in the Amazon proper, resulting in flooded and *terra firme* forest.

Most people start in the coastal region, where travel is relatively cheap and accommodation is easily available. Wildlife and nature thrive on the nutrient-rich mud that is deposited by tides and rivers dropping their loads as they flow into the ocean, supporting a diverse mix of sea, shore and forest birds. Leatherback turtles nest on several beaches, notably at Aouara from April to July.

To get to really remote rainforest, your best bet is to book a canoe trip through a tour operator in Cayenne. If you're travelling independently, your only option is to fly to one of the isolated towns of the interior. Saül is almost slap-bang in the middle of the country, on the Inini River and within a day's journey of Montagne Machoulou and Pic Coudreau, French Guiana's two highest mountains. Maripasoula is even closer (about 10km) to Montagne Machoulou and provides easier access than Saül. Maripasoula is a small jungle town on the Maroni River, which forms the border with Suriname, and offers among the best nature and adventure travel opportunities in the interior.

Especially recommended for the adventurous is the jungle trip to Mount Rorata in the Montagne de Mahury Range, occupying the southern half of the country. After a long, leisurely motorised canoe trip 100km up the Sinnamary River, you take long rewarding walks (moderate to difficult) through mountainous landscape dotted with groves of elfin forest, abounding in orchids, butterflies and tree-ferns. The hike eventually takes you to three lakes of Mount Rorata. Also in the area are a number of river trips, with nights spent in hammocks at jungle shelters.

When to go

If rain is not a bother, any time of year is good, given the uniformity of temperatures from month to month. The rainy season from December to July really ought to be avoided, unless you have a specific desire to get wet. During a mid-February weekend, locals celebrate carnival. Revellers dress up in bizarre colourful costumes to dance, gyrate and bop to the country's favourite music: zouk, béguine and samba.

Tour operators
In Cayenne
Atmosphère d'Amazonie tel/fax: 346697; email : Contact@atmosphere-amazonie.com; web: www.atmosphere-amazonie.com. Specialist fishing tours to remote hinterlands.
Espace-Amazonie/Takari Tour in Kourou at CV 7, 1, RDC, Simarouba; tel: 323430; fax: 325702; email: espamaz@nplus.gf; web: www.espace-amazonie.com, in France at 8 Rue du Capitaine Bernard; tel: 311960; fax: 315470; email: takari.tour@wanadoo.fr. Established tour operator with several tours including a two-week round-country tour from US$1,600.
JAL Voyages 26 Av General de Gaulle; tel: 316820; fax: 301101; email: jal@jal-voyages.com; web: www.jal-voyages.com. Nature and birding tours around the country using dugout, riverboat and hydroplane.

In the US
New York Botanical Gardens (email: smori@nybg.org; web: www.nybg.org/bsci/french_guiana/tour.html). Scientist-led botany tours to the Saül area.
Radisson Seven Sea Cruises include French Guiana on their Amazon itinerary aboard SS *Bremen*.

In the UK
Journey Latin America

Getting there and away
By air
French Guiana's La Rochambeau International Airport is about 19km outside Cayenne. Flights arrive from the US, and from several South American and Caribbean countries. Air France is the main airline with four flights weekly from Miami. Air France departs three times a week for Cayenne from Paris, and weekly from Lima. The Brazilian airline Cruzeiro del Sol has two flights a week from Belém.

By ship
Some ships call in to French Guiana before or after Amazon cruises, sailing northwest to Îles du Salut, where cruise passengers disembark and go to Cayenne for the return flight home.

By road
By the coastal road, access to French Guiana is from either Brazil to the southeast or Suriname to the west, although there is no car ferry from Suriname. No viable roads penetrate French Guiana's back-country from Brazil.

Customs and immigration
Citizens of the EU, the US, Canada and Japan do not need visas to enter the country.

Departure tax is US$20 except for flights to France which have no departure tax.

Getting around
Paved roads are very good in most places but deteriorating in areas which are less travelled. Most roads outside the coastal zone are unpaved and a 4WD vehicle is essential to get around on your own.

The public transport system is inadequate, with too few vehicles and routes. Fares tend to be expensive, so if you intend to travel along the coast, consider hiring a car in Cayenne. Alternatively have a tour operator make your local travel arrangements between jungle sites and towns. If either is beyond your budget, or inclination, you can make do with communal taxis (*collectifs*) for road transport between towns and motorised launches or hand-paddled canoes (*pirogues*) for travel to the Guianan interior.

Internal flights are available but few routes are served, flights are often fully booked days in advance and fares are high.

Communications

Postal services are efficient, with letters taking about a week to reach international destinations. French stamps and rates are used. The main post office (Poste Centrale) in Cayenne is at Route de Baduel about 20 minutes' walk from the town centre.

As you might expect in a country which has South America's only space-port, French Guiana's telephone system works well and is available in most towns. The best way to make a phone call is to use a phonecard. The Carte Téléphonique Prépayé is a prepaid long-distance or overseas phonecard, and is cheaper than the France Télécom card. Faxes can be sent from most hotels and there are several internet shops in Cayenne.

The international country code for French Guiana is 594.

La Presse de Guyane is the principle newspaper. English publications are not widely available.

Cayenne

Almost exactly on the fifth parallel above the Equator, Cayenne is by far the French colony's most important urban development.

On the site of present-day Cayenne, in 1643, the settlement of La Ravardière was founded by merchants from Rouen and Paris. In 1777 the Dutch renamed the town Cayenne after a local Indian tribe that also gave its name to a hot red pepper from the region. Since then, Cayenne has remained the country's administrative and economic centre. Home to around 50,000 people, Cayenne's events and culture dominate the country.

Tourism facilities in Cayenne are expanding fast in response to increasing numbers of travellers who are attracted by the surrounding unspoiled nature, and the outstanding hotels and restaurants.

Getting around

Taxis and rental cars are available in the city and at the airport. Taxis from the airport cost US$20 (no bus). To get to the airport you can get a *collectif* taxi for about US$2.50 which leaves from Gare Routière.

Collectif taxis and minibuses, run between major coastal towns. Though inexpensive, they are often full and run an erratic schedule.

Transport problems mean plane or motor-launch and *pirogue* are the only way to travel sensibly around the interior.

Where to stay

Accommodation in Cayenne is among the most expensive in South America. **Novotel** (Rue de Montabo; tel: 303888; fax: 317898; email: h0677@accor-hotels.com; web: www.novotel.com), 3km out of town, has a swimming pool, restaurant and bar. Rooms start at US$90. Centrally located on the main shopping avenue, **Hotel Amazonia** (28 Avenue General De Gaulle, Cayenne; tel: 288300; fax: 319441; web: www.bestwestern.com/prop_93468) belongs to the Best Western chain; rooms from US$65. **Central Hotel** (on the corner of Rues Becker and

Molé; tel: 256565; fax: 311296; web: www.centralhotel-cayenne.fr) is near the seafront and costs US$45 single, US$55 double. About 2km from the centre, **Ajoupa** (Rue Cabassou; tel: 303308; fax: 301282; email: Hotel-ajoupa@wanadoo.fr) is relatively quiet with a restaurant, bar and swimming pool and good value from US$40. Cheaper accommodation includes **Neptima** (21 Rue F Eboué; tel: 301115; fax: 301478; email: hotel-neptima@wanadoo.fr), which is rather run-down but has air-conditioned rooms and private bath; singles from US$25. About the same price but better value is **La Bodega** (42 Avenue General De Gaulle; tel: 302513; fax: 294284; email: karlb@wanadoo.fr; web: www.labodega.fr), also with air-conditioned rooms. Close to the airport, about 26km from Cayenne, is **Emerald Jungle Village** (tel: 280089; fax: 300682). Run by biologist Joep Moonen, this lodge is used mostly by Dutch and American clients. Cost is about US$15 per night and US$5.00 for a continental breakfast. For the price, it offers the best value nature experience within easy reach of Cayenne.

What and where to eat
Given the great culinary tradition of France, it is perhaps not surprising that French Guiana has plenty to offer the gourmet. From upmarket restaurants to cheap and cheerful streetside cafés, the range of countries and food types represented is truly global.

Novotel's restaurant, the **Angelique**, is among the best and most expensive. Fine French dining is to be had at **La Belle Epoque** (88 Rue Lalouette) but you'll pay less at **Le Saloon** (21 Rue Christophe Colomb). For Creole food, **Le Paradis des Amis** (5 Rue Mole) or **Restaurant Le Tatou** are both good. For Asian food at good value, **Le Chateau de Asie** (21 Rue Lieutenant Brasse) or **La Rivière des Parfums** (10 Rue Justin Catayée) are suggested.

What to see
Cayenne's city sights offer interesting perspectives on its past and present ties with France. The city's compact enough to walk around but, to see most or all the sights mentioned below, you should take a city tour (US$25). The **Hall of Prefecture** was the **Governor's Palace** during early colonial times. Dating from 1750, built by Jesuits, it faces on to **Place Grenoble**, near the port area in the western end of the city. In the same square is **Montravel Fountain**. The oldest remaining evidence of early colonial settlement is found at **Ceperou Fort**, built 1643 by Charles Poncet de Brétigny. Heading west towards the sea, from the Place Grenoble in the northwest of town along the seafront, take a small alleyway to the fort. Members of the French Foreign Legion are based there to this day. If you're in town, a good place to people-watch or do some shopping is **Place des Palmistes** in the city's far northwest corner.

Also included on city tours is Cayenne open market, first held in 1910 on the **Place du Coq**. It's a bustling mass of people, mostly locals doing their weekly shopping for fish, fruit and vegetables.

The **Pasteur Institute** is an important research centre that employs about 100 scientists specialising in tropical diseases. Their highly regarded work includes investigating cures for malaria and screening rainforest biota for medically useful properties.

In the town centre, the **Franconie Museum** (Av de Gaulle) named after deputy Alexandre Franconie, is housed in a building dating from 1901. Collections of historic papers and pamphlets documenting Amerindian lifestyle and arts are interesting. Near Place des Palmistes is the **Musée Departemental** (Rue de Remire) with models of Cayenne and the Îles du Salut to give a sense of perspective.

More information

For the latest travel, lodgings and restaurant information and details on new tour operators, as well as free city maps and brochures, contact the **Tourist Office** at 12 Rue Lalouette (tel: 300900), open Mon–Fri 08.00–12.00 and 15.00–18.00, with English-speaking staff. You can also try the **Comité du Tourisme de Guyane** (tel: 266500; fax: 309315; email: fotsig@nplus.gf; web: www.guyanetourisme.com).

Beyond Cayenne

Most towns of any note in French Guiana are situated along or near the coast, and are therefore easy to reach by vehicle. However, a number of towns a short way inland offer ready access by motorised canoe into deep forest. To the untrained eye this habitat is virtually identical to the steamy, dark jungle typical of much of lowland Amazonia, and much of it is pristine. All this wilderness does not come easy and if you take a tour into the backlands don't expect luxury treatment. These trips use temporary jungle shelters for accommodation, with simple food.

Kourou

There can be few sights as incongruous as a space rocket blasting off from the middle of the jungle. Yet at Kourou the lucky visitor (or those who planned ahead) can sometimes arrange to observe this awesome spectacle.

Kourou was chosen as the launch site for the European Space Agency's Ariane due to its equatorial location. You can tour the **Space Centre** (Centre Spatial Guyanais), but the guide only speaks French. Ask at the tourist office (Av des Roches in Kourou) to reserve a place on the tour. Book several days in advance, from Cayenne if necessary. Entrance to the Space Centre is free; open Mon–Thur 08.00–12.00 and 14.00–17.00, closed Wednesday afternoon.

Travellers have a choice of international-standard hotels and auberges from US$25. **Mercure Kourou Ariatel** (Lac Bois Diable, tel: 328900; fax: 326160; email: mercure@ariatel.com; web: www.ariatel.com) has a full range of facilities from US$130 for a single room. **L'Hotel des Roches** costs about US$90 and offers a similar service. **Gros Bec** offers apartment-style rooms at about US$50. Besides hotel restaurants, which are rather good, you could try **Le Lotus** for Vietnamese cuisine or **N'Jifa** for African food. To the west of Cayenne, Kourou is easily accessible on a good surfaced road after a 20km drive.

A good road takes you from Kourou 210km west along the coast to the town of St Laurent de Maroni – point of departure for trips up the Maroni River to Maripasoula. Espace-Amazonie/Takari Tours (tel: 323430; fax: 325702) have offices in town.

Roura

Some 20km southeast of Cayenne via the town of Matoury on the airport road, Roura is located about 18km inland up the Mahury River estuary. This small town provides access to the Montagne de Kaw region, a beautiful formation rising a couple of hundred metres above extensive coastal forests, swamps and marshes lying between the Mahury and Approuague estuaries. This area is rich in waterbirds, amphibians and reptiles. A paddled canoe ride, included in a standard US$100-a-day tour, is a memorable experience. You are serenely propelled through broad marshes, fringed here and there with thick tropical jungle. Ask tour operators in Cayenne about these trips.

South from Cayenne the road to Roura first goes through Matoury and then about 10km out of town is the turn-off to Stoupan. This settlement marks the point on the Mahury River from which a ferry crosses to Roura (US$1 passengers,

US$5 vehicles). In Roura there are a couple of basic hotels: **Auberge des Orpailleurs** (tel: 376297) and **Le Relais du Galion** (tel: 270879). Southeast from Roura, about 40km along a variously tarred and dirt road, pretty bad in places, is the country village of Kaw. Day trips from Cayenne cost US$75 or more but time spent here is highly rewarding as the village, on the banks of the Kaw River, is sure to reward photographers, birdwatchers and nature-lovers. Primates, sloths and dozens of forest birds inhabit the high canopy, while the waters are infested with caiman. Tours in this area are available from Cayenne tour operators but they are expensive. JAL Voyages (page 432) offer overnight birdwatching tours for US$220. **Entomotech Lodge** (email: informations@entomotech-lodge.com; web: www.entomotech-lodge.com) is located in primary forest in Kaw Nature Reserve and run by scientists. The lodge comprises two cabins with TV and private bathroom. Facilities include a laboratory with refrigerator. Pricing is based on use of scientific collecting equipment (optional) and includes all transfers and accommodation from US$1,500 to US$2,250 for the collector expedition. They also have tours designed to suit people with reduced mobility, from US$4,800. Meals are extra. Independent travellers should enquire at tourist information offices for budget camping and cabin accommodation.

St Georges d'Oyapock
This small town, 152km southwest of Cayenne in the low-lying valley of the River Oyapock, serves as the main transit point for overland traffic between the Guianan and Brazilian frontiers. Travellers heading for Brazil should get visa-related paperwork completed in Cayenne. A couple of basic hotels and restaurants provide accommodation and meals, along with some duty-free shops.

Mana
This small town, graced by quaint colonial buildings, is situated on the coast at the mouth of the Mana River, 200km by road northwest of Cayenne. Mana's relaxed atmosphere makes it a pleasant diversion just to relax and enjoy the ambience. Jungle tours visit Acarouany, inhabited by villagers from the Vietnamese Hmong tribe.

Mana attracts travellers who want a break on the way between Suriname and Cayenne. The Suriname border crossing is at St Laurent de Maroni, 40km to the south along the river. Surrounded by mixed mangrove and tropical rainforest, the area around Mana offers plenty of birding, wildlife and natural history opportunities. Night rides in canoes looking for caiman are always successful, while night birds, frogs and insects have so many different calls that it is difficult to tell whether a chirp or whistle comes from a tiny hyalid frog or a small tropical owl.

Aouara
This small Indian village is situated some 22km northwest of Mana along the coastal road. If you're not here on a package tour, your best bet is to hitch a ride from Mana. Aouara offers the nature-lover get-away-from-it-all jungle living, with the bonus of beautiful beaches and friendly tribal people. Once in Aouara ask for directions to the beach hut where you can stay for a paltry US$5. Facilities at the beach include covered beach shelters of palm and bamboo sleeping ten people. You must bring full camping equipment, mosquito nets and fresh water. Bathrooms and toilets and some simple foodstuffs are available at the site.

Aside from a rich birdlife and abundance of shore animals, the beach is a nesting site for turtles that lay their eggs in the nesting season between April and June.

St Laurent de Maroni

With a population over 5,000, this town on the Suriname border remains a tranquil colonial backwater. Somewhat rundown, its fascinating past connects it with French Guiana's history as a penal colony. Today the town serves as a border crossing for overland travel into Suriname and also as the main departure point for package trips and commercial traffic up the Maroni.

The few hotels and restaurants are good, but no less expensive than those of other towns in French Guiana. For mid-range accommodation try the **Star Hotel** (109 Rue Thiers; tel: 341084), costing from US$25 per person. For US$60 there is the **Relais des Tres Lacs** (19-21 Domaine du Lac Bleu; tel: 340505; fax: 340276). A couple of cafés provide cheap eats while the Indonesian outdoor stalls cook all sorts of spicy delights, with a satisfying meal of noodles and fish stew costing US$5.

If you have some time in town, be sure to visit the original prison site and centre for convicts, the **Camp de la Transportation**, with buildings dating from 1857. Collective taxis and buses provide public transport to and from Cayenne, 250km southeast, costing from US$15 one way, and leaving from the ferry pier at the southern end of Avenue General de Gaulle.

The ferry pier is also, logically enough, the departure and arrival point for overland travellers to and from Suriname. Customs and immigration procedures for the crossing into Suriname are very security-conscious.

Leaving from the pier, river trips along the Maroni take you south deep into primordial jungle through some 400km of sparsely settled, dense rainforest to the jungle town of Maripasoula. On package tours, bilingual naturalist-guides point out the natural history of the river as you proceed past the small village of Apatou, 60km downstream from St Laurent. Guides accompany you along two or three trails a day. Numerous forest birds and waterbirds inhabit the river's edge: anis, kiskadees, kingfishers, herons and the jabiru stork. Transport is in comfortable motor launches. Booked through Espace-Amazonie/Takari Tour in Cayenne (see page 432) a six-day voyage up the river in a safe comfortable launch will cost about US$600 per person, excluding airfare back to Cayenne (US$125 one way).

Maripasoula

Located in the hinterlands on the Suriname border, Maripasoula is accessible via a daily flight from Cayenne. Most people fly from the town back to Cayenne, having arrived on a riverboat cruise. If you're not on a package tour, you may be able to scrounge a ride on one of several small cargo boats leaving for St Laurent daily from the pier. Passage is difficult to arrange as vessels are usually fully loaded, but with perseverance and a couple of days to spare you may get lucky. Cost for the trip is US$75–100.

Travel further upriver requires written permission from the police in Cayenne.

Jungle lodges

Association Yawo Ya Délé tel: 343253. In Awala – arranges stays with local Amerindian communities.

Chez Maryse 59 Rte de St Maurice; tel: 342855. In Saut Sabbat by the Mana River. Hammock space from US$6 per night, or US$75 for a weekend in cabins.

CISAME Typical thatched cabins in Approuague, from US$50 per night. Book through JAL Voyages (page 432).

Maripas Km 17.5 Degrad Saramaca; tel: 320541; fax: 223102; email: maripas@guyanespace.com. Typical Amerindian cabins on the banks of the Kourou River for groups and individuals. Hammock accommodation for US$10 (US$5 for hammock

rental), with shared bathrooms. Book direct or through Espace-Amazonie/Takari Tour.
Quimbé Kio tel: 270122; fax: 270148. Small lodge with room or hammock (from US$7.50) accommodation in Cacao.
Lodge Tolenga 29 Rue Lieutenant Becker; tel: 294894; fax: 294894; email: lodge.tolenga@wanadoo.fr. Thatched cabins on the Inini River (a tributary of the Maroni) just south of Maripasoula, with private bathrooms. Rooms from US$100, hammock US$75, including transport from Cayenne.

Places of interest

One is surely forgiven for wondering why the Islands of Salvation are so-called when their purpose was the incarceration and inhuman treatment of people. Indeed the name given to one of them, Devil's Island, seems more appropriate. They were named originally because their freedom from malaria and other tropical diseases made them an ideal spot for convalescing colonials.

Located about 12km off the Guianan coast, the Îles du Salut group comprises three islands. Île Royale is the most interesting island as it was used for the main incarceration facility. The autobiography of Henri Charrière, *Papillon,* who spent ten years (four of them in solitary confinement) on the islands, is now familiar to millions throughout the world.

Mere statistics fail to convey the impression of this place. Of 50–70,000 convicts, the only ones to leave alive were the 5,000 there when the prison closed.

The Îles du Salut are not the most accessible or joyous holiday destination. To spend a night there could be trying on one's psyche, to say the least. However, the visit is an education. The islands' palpable atmosphere and notorious past are sure to leave a lasting impression.

The **Hotel Auberge Îles du Salut** (tel: 321100; fax: 324223; web: www.ilesdusalut.com) has air-conditioned rooms, with private bathroom and wooden storm shutters on the window, for US$105/150 (single/double). Sea-view rooms are US$60 or you can use the hammock area for US$10. Trips can be booked with tour operators in Cayenne or you can make your own way there by boat from Kourou (US$30).

SURINAME

BASIC FACTS
Official name Republiek Suriname (Republic of Suriname)
Area 163,820km² (63,251 miles²)
Population 440,000 (2002 est)
Capital Paramaribo
Largest city (population) Paramaribo (201,000)
Main 'Amazon' city Paramaribo
Official language Dutch
Date of independence Nov 25 1975 (The Netherlands)
Major industries bauxite, food processing, wood products
GDP per capita US$3,400 (1999 est)
Currency Suriname Guilder, Sf (US$1 = Sf2,200; £1 = Sf3,500)
Major attractions Dutch colonial architecture, national parks and nature reserves
National holidays Jan 1, Holi Phagwa (Mar), Easter, May 1, July 1, Nov 25, Christmas

Located on the central eastern coast of northern South America, Suriname's western border is with Guyana, while to the east is French Guiana and south is Brazil. Suriname is the smallest independent state in South America.

Facts and figures
Geography and climate

Topographically, the country's north comprises a narrow coastal plain, about 365km long from east to west. This is formed of mudflats and sandbanks deposited by equatorial currents from the Amazon's mouth. Developed areas in the low-lying coastal zone lie below river flood levels and require extensive drainage. Inland to the south lies extensive dense forest, covering hills and low mountains, for about 80% of Suriname's territory. To the southwest lies a region of upland savannah. Of the original forest cover over 90% remains intact – the greatest proportion of any country. Most deforestation is in the coastal region and river valleys.

Flowing northwards, all the country's major rivers discharge into the Atlantic, their upland stretches characterised by numerous falls and rapids. Major rivers are the Corantijn, marking the border with Guyana, the Coppename, the Suriname and the Maroni, which marks the border with French Guiana.

Suriname's climate is equatorial maritime: humid year-round but with refreshing northeast breezes. Rainfall is relatively high but occurs mostly in the mountains. These receive an average 3,000mm per year. The coast is somewhat drier, getting 1,900mm over a year. In the northern populated regions, four seasons of alternating wet and dry periods are recognised. Heaviest rains are from April to August, with a minor rainy season from November to February, the months between being relatively dry. In the south there is no distinctive wet or dry season.

Annual mean temperatures hover around 27°C, varying little throughout the year.

Flora and fauna

Suriname's flora is highly diverse, with over 4,000 fern and higher plant species from the coastal zone. Four-fifths of the land remains covered with its original tropical rainforest from which at least a thousand tree species are known.

Suriname's vertebrate fauna is typically neotropical with 150 recorded mammal species. The rare black-tailed hairy porcupine (*Coendou melanurus*) is found in Suriname. Five species of marine turtles, protected by law, breed on coastal beaches along the coast and estuaries. Around 650 bird species are recorded from Suriname and 350 or so kinds of fish are known from coastal and fresh waters.

People and languages

Second least populous country in South America, Suriname's population actually declined during the 1970s and 1980s by a third because of migration, mostly to Holland. Four-fifths of the population live in Paramaribo and the surrounding areas.

Minority ethnic groups include Amerindians, blacks, Dutch and Chinese. Major groups are East Indians, Creoles and Javanese. The Bush Negroes (Boesch Negers) have returned to a West African way of life, adopting its customs, religion and slash-and-burn agriculture, together with hunting and fishing.

Dutch is the official language though English is widely spoken, along with Sranan or Taki-Taki – a Creole dialect – and a variety of Asian, African and Amerindian languages. Sarnami is spoken by East Indians. Trio and Wayana are two important linguistic groups.

All the world's major religions are practised. Around two thirds of the people are Christian; East Indians are generally Hindu, although a few are Muslim, as are most Javanese. The Chinese practise Confucianism. Judaism has been practised in Suriname since the 16th century. Native Indian and African religions thrive among indigenous peoples and Bush Negroes.

History

Suriname's earliest inhabitants were the indigenous Surinen, after whom the country is named. In 1593 the Spanish claimed Suriname but the Dutch were the first (in 1602) to set up a trading post and fort. In 1682 the Dutch West India Company introduced coffee and sugarcane, along with African slaves to cultivate the crops. Brutally treated, many slaves escaped to the interior where they remained free, were eventually recognised as such and were awarded lands.

Apart from two brief spells under British colonial rule at the beginning of the 19th century, Suriname remained a Dutch colony. In 1863, a slave revolt lasting two years led to the abolition of slavery. To overcome labour shortages, indentured workers were hired from China, Java and India.

Constitutional reforms in 1948–51 led to the creation of two-party self-government in 1954. When Suriname declared its intention to separate from Holland in 1973, the skilled and professional Dutch classes emigrated en masse.

A military coup in 1980 led by Colonel Dési Bouterse established martial law in Suriname. The execution of 15 opposition leaders in 1982 was followed with raids by the National Army on forest villages, resulting in the death or detention of many Bush Negroes. Almost 15,000 sought refuge in French Guiana. Rebel activity around Albina closed the economically important border with French Guiana in 1986.

A new constitution, approved by the electorate in 1987, forced Bouterse to take a back seat. Following the military-led bloodless coup in 1990, Johan Kraag was made president. The French Guiana border reopened in 1991 and violence subsided. In May 1991, peaceful elections were held, with the New Front coalition, led by Ronald Venetiaan, winning 30 seats. Peace accords between rebel guerrillas and the government were successfully negotiated in August 1992. In May 1996, national elections resulted in NDP vice-chairman Jules Wijdenbosch assuming the presidency. However, realignment of coalition members in 1997 and early 1998 weakened the government mandate and slowed legislative action. By the end of 1997, the Dutch froze development funds as relations with the Netherlands deteriorated. Growth slowed in 1998 and spiralling expenditures, poor tax collection, a bloated civil service, and reduced foreign aid in 1999 contributed to the fiscal deficit, estimated at 11% of GDP. Protests in July 1999 resulted in cautions from the US State Department. Crime is increasing in the major cities, and somewhat less in the interior. However, the country remains among the safest of any in South America.

Relatively high standards of living compared with the South American norm are enjoyed by Surinamese. People are generally well-off and poverty is scarce.

The economy is based on private and public sector development, with bauxite, alumina and aluminium production dominating the industrial sector. One in five workers are occupied in agriculture.

Money

Suriname guilders are the main currency, divided up into 100 cents, although a guilder is worth about a one twentieth of a US cent. The black market rate from exchange houses is 5–10% better than the official rate given by banks and hotels.

Costs in Suriname are reasonable; it's far less expensive than French Guiana and not much pricier than Guyana. Some payments must be made in US dollars.

Budget travellers can figure on US$5 per night for decent accommodation and about the same for food when eating out.

Highlights

Up until recently, Suriname was absent from the itineraries of most travel agents and tour operators. In 1993, the Suriname government welcomed tourists for the first time in ten years.

Paramaribo offers insight into the legacy of Dutch colonialism, the only such opportunity in the Americas. The most obvious Dutch influence is in the architecture and language. Streets are lined with four- or five-storey houses, fronted with the curved, feminine gables typical of colonial Dutch buildings. As a beach resort, the city offers more to nature enthusiasts than to leisure seekers; nearby rivers and tidal conditions conspire to keep the beaches muddy and the ocean water murky, and mosquitoes often reach unbearable numbers.

Beyond the city, the tropical flora and fauna remain largely intact, partly because the interior is so inaccessible, with just a few hotels and restaurants beyond Paramaribo. Conditions are difficult for independent travellers. Full board is rarely available, accommodation is basic, and even the better-off will have to take a hammock, mosquito net, and quite often their own food.

The rainy season (April to August) is unpleasant for rainforest excursions. Prices are higher and lodgings harder to find during the high seasons: mid-March to mid-May, July to September and then the year-end holiday.

Tour operators

Amar Ecotours Estabrielstraat 16, Zorg en Hoop, Paramaribo; tel: 400372; email: ahkco@yahoo.com; web: www.parbo.com/weekly/amar_index.html. Personalized low budget one- or two-day hiking and swimming tours to four-day jungle adventures to Joden, Blakkawatra, Brownsberg and Raleigh Vallen.

Ara Cari Kwattaweg 252, Paramaribo; tel: 434888; fax: 497308; email: henkgum@sr.net; web: www1.sr.net/~t100908. Specialise in tours to Arapahu and Tafelberg.

Cardy Adventures Cornelis Jongbawstraat 31, Paramaribo; tel: 422518; email: info@cardytours.com; web: www.cardytours.com. Full-range of adventure tours throughout Suriname.

METS (Movement for Ecotourism in Suriname) Anton Dragtenweg 7, Paramaribo; tel: 472387; fax: 424811; email: resinpbo@sr.net; web: www.metsresorts.com. Tours to three interior resorts from US$325 for five days.

STINASU (Foundation for Nature Conservation in Suriname) Cornelis Jongbawstraat 14, Paramaribo; tel: 427102; fax: 421850; email: research@stinasu.sr; web: www.stinasu.sr. Organizes ecotours to Brownsberg, Galibi and Raleighvallen. Guests have the option to take an all-inclusive guided tour or venture out on their own and simply rent a lodge.

Sun & Forest Tours Gravenstraat 155 Paramaribo; tel/fax: 597 478383; email: sunforest@sr.net; web: www.surinamesunforest.nl. A variety of tours to interior resorts.

In the US

Oceanic Society – see page 42. Suriname programmes include a participation in a project to assess conservation status of giant otters and beach-based work on monitoring sea turtle populations. You work with field biologists to collect data and log information.

Getting there and away
By air

Paramaribo's Johan Pengel International Airport, better known as Zanderij is served by several international airlines. Flight prices vary dramatically. The minimum return airfare from Miami is US$500 while the regular fare is US$750 and up.

Suriname Airways (SLM) has two flights a week from Miami and one a week from New York, Amsterdam and Curaçao. Dutch airline KLM has one flight a week from Amsterdam. Air France flies from Cayenne once weekly providing the cheapest way of reaching Suriname from Europe.

Departure tax is US$25 payable in dollars.

By ship
Paramaribo is Suriname's main port-of-call for cruise ships navigating up or down the coast, on their way from the Caribbean wintering grounds to the Amazon or the South Atlantic.

By road
From French Guiana, it is possible to drive by road to Suriname, but not into it, as the ferry from French Guiana across the Maroni has no facilities for vehicles. Around one-third of the country's 2,750km of road are paved along the coast. No major roads enter the interior. To cross to Corriverton in Guyana you can take the ferry across the Corantijn from the terminal just outside Niuew Nickerie.

Customs and immigration
Because of internal conflict and serious border disputes, Suriname is wary of visitors and is only now getting used to the idea. A **passport** valid for six months is required and **visas** are needed for citizens of most countries. It costs about US$35 (prices vary depending on your nationality). You can download an application form from www.surinam.net. When you enter you'll also need passport photos for the Alien Registration Bureau, return ticket and if coming from neighbouring countries, proof of yellow-fever vaccination.

Getting around
Internal air transport is efficient and usually the best way to reach remote back-country areas. Road transport is under-developed and limited to the coastal region. An east–west highway runs along the coast connecting the borders of French Guiana and Suriname.

Wide rivers along the coast admit ocean-going vessels, chiefly to Paramaribo. River navigation along interior waterways is hampered by rapids and falls in upland regions.

Communications
The main post office in Paramaribo is on the corner of Wagenwegstraat. Mail is reliable and inexpensive (US$0.50 for a postcard within the Americas), though slow. Telephone, telegram and fax services are available but costly. Several internet cafés have opened recently. Among the better is **Zeelandia** at the south end of Klein Waterstraat, next to the popular Café/Bar 't Vat.

The international country code for Suriname is 597.

Two daily Dutch-language newspapers and one Chinese publication are available in Paramaribo and larger towns. Of the two television stations, the official channel is STS. There are six radio stations, two of them government controlled.

Paramaribo
Imagine a 1950s Amsterdam (minus canals), transport it to tropical jungle and allow it to decay for thirty or forty years. Paramaribo is a city whose dominant

feeling is one of decadent, worn-out post-colonialism. Yet grandeur remains. Rows of houses, fronted with typically colonial Dutch gables, lend an exotic air to the city.

Paramaribo (often called 'Parbo') has its attractions: fine architecture, rich history and a highly diverse, cosmopolitan culture. The major sights are within a small area in the centre, located in a triangle bounded by Waterkant to the south, Rust en Vredstraat to the northwest and Gravenstraat-Soldatenstraat to the northeast.

Transport

Most international flights use Zanderij International Airport, 45km south of Paramaribo (US$10–15 by taxi). Some domestic flights and others to nearby countries depart or arrive at Zorg en Hoop Airfield just outside the city (US$1 by taxi). Domestic destinations are served by SLM and Gum Air.

Generally, transport is inexpensive but choice is limited. Around Paramaribo taxi prices are US$1–2 for a ride across the city. During the day you can get taxis from a number of locations. The main ones are in front of the Krasnapolsky and Torarica hotels, Waterkant by the jetty, near the Heiligenweg (bus station), opposite Telesur, and on the corner of Sophie Redmondstraat and Waaldijkstraat. Wilde Busses (wild buses) are minibuses that service regular routes. This is a fun and cheap way to see the city, but the buses are often full. Make sure you have small change to pay the exact fare – US$0.50 in town and US$1.00 for outlying areas. Shout 'Halt Chef!' when you reach your stop. Long-distance buses heading east from Paramaribo leave from the ferry terminal near Waterkant, and westbound buses depart from the corner of Hostraat and Dr Sophie Redmondstraat.

Where to stay

Combi Inn Kleine Waterstraat 9, Paramaribo; tel: 426001; fax: 426005; email: combi-inn@paramaribo.net. Rooms with private bathroom, fridge, TV and phone. Expect to pay about US$45 for a double.

Ecoresort Inn Cornelis Jongbawstraat 16, Paramaribo; tel: 425522; fax: 425510; email: info@ecores.com; web: www.ecores.com. Fully equipped air-conditioned rooms with balconies from US$65/70 single/double. Facilities at the Torarica are available to guests.

Guesthouse Fanna Prinsessestraat 31; Paramaribo; tel: 476789. Rather dingy but cheap small hotel with 14 rooms from US$16-27.

Residence Inn Anton Dragtenweg 7. Forty tasteful, well-appointed suites located in the former Russian Embassy. The spacious hotel grounds are in a peaceful location, within 15 minutes' walking distance from the centre of Paramaribo. From US$50pp (single) including breakfast – book through METS (page 441).

Torarica Rietbergplein 1, tel: 471500; fax: 411682; email:info@torarica.com; web: www.torarica.com. Upscale four-star resort hotel along the Suriname River, within walking distance of the Palmentuin, Fort Zeelandia and the city centre. Rooms include all modern facilities.

YWCA Heerenstraat 14-16; tel: 472089; fax: 472072. Ask for the 'Whykuh' and you'll end up at this white wooden building in the city centre. Accommodations are simple and clean from US$15.

Where and what to eat

Food here is tasty, varied and wallet-friendly. One of the best upmarket restaurants is **Sarinah** (Verlengde Gemenelansweg 187; tel: 430661), about 20 minutes' ride from the city centre (US$1 by taxi). They serve really hot Indonesian food, the way it should be – you have been warned. A good international restaurant is **La Bastille** (Kleine Waterstraat 3; tel: 473991), easy to walk to from downtown, near Waterkant, behind Palmentuin. They serve outstanding food: under US$5 for a full meal. Other restaurants include **Chi Min** (Cornelis Jongbawstraat 83; tel: 412155) for authentic Chinese and **Sunshine** (Wilhelminastraat 23) with inexpensive and tasty Creole food. For the best breakfast in town try the **Plantation Room** in the Torarica.

What to see

To get a rush of sights, sounds, colours and smells in one location, visit **Waterkant Market** on the riverfront– a great place for shopping and people-watching. The **People's Palace** on Gravenstraat, built in typical Dutch colonial style, dates from the mid-1700s. It's in the main city centre park, the **Palmentuin** (next to Waterkant). In front of the Palace is **Unity Square**, the heart of the city centre and a good place to begin orienting yourself around Paramaribo.

Paramaribo's religious buildings hold some interest. The **Roman Catholic cathedral**, on Gravensraat (close by Wulfingstraat), is said to be the largest wooden building in the western hemisphere and remains closed waiting to be restored.

For a perspective on Suriname's heritage, visit the **Surinaams Museum** (Commewijnstraat 18, Zorg en Hoop) on the outskirts of town. Displays feature Amerindian relics and artefacts and the latest exhibition. Open 07.30–14.00 weekdays, except Friday and weekends 17.00–20.00; admission US$0.10.

History buffs will enjoy a visit to **Fort Zeelandia** in Niuew Amsterdam. This is a ruined fort built to guard the confluence of the Commewijne and Suriname rivers. It's easy to reach from Paramaribo. Catch a #4 bus from the city centre to Leonsberg. The museum describing the area's history and efforts to restore the ruins is worth the US$1.50 admission.

Shopping

Local handicrafts are of good quality and not too touristy. In simple stalls erected along the airport road, Bush Africans sell carvings and basketwork. Of course, in the towns are the usual array of curio shops selling handicrafts and local art. The main native handicrafts are drums, baskets and wooden carvings.

More information

Recovering from the damaging civil war and now encouraging tourists, Suriname is changing fast and new accommodation, restaurants and tour operators are setting up all the time. Up-to-date tourist information is available from the **Tourist Department** office (Cornelius Jonbawstraat 2; tel: 471163). Another excellent source for information on travel beyond Paramaribo is **Stinasu** (page 441), a local conservation organisation which can take bookings for all the places mentioned below. For information and advice on booking a tour visit the **Suriname Tourism Foundation** (Abraham Crijnssenweg 1; email: stsur@sr.net). Suriname is well-represented on the web. For details on accommodation, tours, and general travel information, **www.surinfo.org** is easy to navigate and comprehensive – perhaps the best online resource if you are researching for a visit. They sell *The Guide to Suriname*, the first travel guide in English, now in its second edition (1996, US$15). For general information start with **www.surinam.net** which is a comprehensive online travel and information guide to Suriname. For off-beat virtual tours of various countries including Suriname visit **www.runningmanonline.com**.

Beyond Paramaribo
Albina
This small town, 140km east of Paramaribo, exists primarily to serve border traffic crossing between Suriname and French Guiana. Almost deserted in the late 1980s on account of rebel activity around the town, Albina has recovered somewhat since 1991 when the border with French Guiana was re-opened. The town is easily reached from Paramaribo on fairly good roads with regular buses (four to five hours, from US$5 one way). Basic accommodation is available at the nearby town of Moenga (US$2 by taxi).

The main reason to come to Albina is to visit the nearby **Galibi Nature Reserve**. STINASU and other Paramaribo tour operators can make arrangements for you. Alternatively, for motorised canoe trips up the Marowijne, you can hire an independent guide (US$10–15 per day) for day trips or overnights at temporary jungle shelters. You'll need to take camping gear. On the river beyond inhabited areas you head deep into the interior. Here is pristine rainforest with a variety of plants and animals on a par with anywhere in the Amazon.

Stoelmanseiland
This small settlement on the Lawa River, a tributary of the Maroni, is set in a beautiful landscape of rivers and forested rolling hills, some 150km downriver from Albina. Lodgings are provided at the pleasant **Stoelmanseiland Guest House**, with bedding and meals provided (US$15 per night). Make reservations for the lodge and transport (US$28 one way from Paramaribo) with tour operators, who offer four- to seven-day packages from US$25 per day. By motorised canoe it takes about two days to get here from Albina.

Apoera
About 120km inland on the Corantijn River, Apoera is a small port town accessible to ocean-going ships. No buses ease the effort of getting there but you can try to hitch along the Paramaribo–Apoera road (about 325km).

En route is Marie Blanche Falls, formed by the River Nickerie. Nearby you can stay at the **Dubois** guest house (US$25). Opportunities for nature activities are very good, with chances for outstanding birdwatching, easy-to-moderate trekking and swimming in clear forest rivers. The Dubois can be booked in Paramaribo through any of the listed tour operators.

To reach Guyana you need to catch a river taxi to Nieuw Nickerie from the Apoera wharf.

Nieuw Nickerie
This town of 8,250 on the border with Guyana is 5km inland on the Nickerie River, and is of most interest to travellers as a point to cross the border into Guyana. The town has half a dozen hotels ranging in price from moderate to cheap. One of the best in town is **Ameerali** (GG Maynardstraat 32; tel: 231642; email: hotelame@sr.net; web: www1.sr.net/~t101223/), with clean, air-conditioned rooms from US$25. Cheapest in town is the **Luxor** (St. Jozefstraat 22; tel: 231365) from US$3-6.

Jungle lodges
The choice of jungle lodges in Suriname is improving, as tourists have yet to discover. The facilities will suit those who want a wilderness experience – for whom luxury is less important than wildlife and scenery. Consult local tour operators to get into the country's interior. Lodge stays can be combined with

canoe safaris through tropical forest accompanied by a guide to point out animals, birds and plants. Budget travellers will readily find affordable packages.

Brokopondo

About 120km inland south from Paramaribo, Brokopondo is a small settlement on the edge of the Brownsberg National Reserve. The drive takes about two hours along a surfaced road but no buses come this far. The village is most often visited on package tours to the nearby reserve from Paramaribo. Book through most Paramaribo tour operators.

Inexpensive (US$10 per night) accommodation is at a government resthouse, spartan but clean, with bedding and simple utensils provided. The facility is self-catering so take food. The main reason to be here is to take excursions into the park, including walks along easy-to-moderate trails. For a guide you must book a package tour in Paramaribo. The huge **Afobaka Dam** can be reached a few kilometres down the Brokopondo Dam Road and is the main point to begin exploring the WJ van Blommestein Meer – one of the world's most extensive manmade bodies of freshwater (area about 1,500km^2), created by the dam.

Brownsberg Chalets

Situated in the high rolling hills of the Brownsberg area of the **Central Suriname Nature Reserve** 100km south of Paramaribo, a handful of small, simple chalets offers visitors comfortable lodgings, surrounded by wilderness. Each dwelling sleeps 8–10, with cooking facilities, shower and beds, for US$10 per person per night. STINASU, Cardy Adventures and other Paramaribo tour operators arrange all-inclusive guided packages from US$40 per day. You can get there by bus (US$5) from Paramaribo. Set among a grove of trees with well-kept gardens, the chalets are a good base to explore surrounding montane rainforest for birds and wildlife, notably by the WJ Blommestein Meer that marks the park's eastern boundary.

Matapica Beach

Situated on the boundary of the Wiawia Nature Reserve, some 50km east along the coast from Paramaribo, Matapica Beach offers basic lodgings for visitors to the reserve. These are simple beach huts and definitely not for the comfort-lover, although nature-lovers will be in heaven. You must provide your own bedding and food, but it's inexpensive; around US$5 per night. Book stays and arrange transport through STINASU, whose package includes an English-speaking guide to take you along the reserve's trails through a variety of swampy lowland habitats from tropical rainforest to coastal mangrove and tidal estuaries.

National parks and wildlife reserves

Suriname's impressive system of reserves and parks protects a variety of different ecosystems, from mangrove swamp to upland rainforest, comprising 11 reserves and one national park. Most have guides written about them (in Dutch). Simple accommodation is usually available either inside the boundaries or close by.

The 6,000ha **Brownsberg Nature Park** is the most accessible inland reserve – only two hours' drive on tarred road south of Paramaribo, via the village of Brownsweg. The reserve protects montane forest habitat, rich in epiphytic plants such as orchids, ferns and bromeliads. Fauna includes several monkey species, sloths, anteaters and spotted cats. A guide to the park and the reserve's birds is available from STINASU (US$2.50) and a guide to trails can be bought from the park headquarters in the park (US$1).

About 53km from Paramaribo, **Wiawia Nature Reserve** encompasses 36,000ha of beach along a narrow coastal strip. The undisturbed area protects nesting sea turtles that come ashore to lay eggs. Commonest of the five recorded species are green turtle, leatherback and Ridley's. Birdwatchers will enjoy large flocks of flamingo, scarlet ibis and storks. Simple accommodation is available at Matapica Beach.

Galibi Nature Reserve is another small shore area set aside for marine turtles. Along the Marowijne Estuary, the reserve can be reached from Albina. Take a river taxi from town to the reserve for a day of birdwatching and walking easy trails. There is no accommodation in the park.

Half-an-hour's drive (35km) west of Paramaribo along a good road, **Coppename Estuary National Park** protects the lower Coppename River. Along the river are a couple of jungle camps and a thatched restaurant. Ask Paramaribo tour operators for details on accommodation or package trips up the Coppename. Canoe rides along the river and its wetlands are rewarding for flora and fauna. Shore and water birds are abundant and diverse.

About 150km southwest of Paramaribo is the northern boundary of the **Central Suriname Nature Reserve**, a UNESCO World Heritage Site, and an inspiring example of conservation. Established 1998, it combined three other reserves to encompass 16,000km^2, about a tenth of the country. The reserve is home to eight species of primates and most kinds of large South American mammals, an estimated four hundred bird species and uncounted insect species. Over 6,000 kinds of higher plants have been collected from the region. Lowland tropical rainforest is the main habitat. A unique ecosystem in the reserve is the Roraima sandstone savannah, the only one of its type in Suriname. The most accessible areas include Mount Voltsberg (for hard but exhilarating hikes) and Foengoe Island on the Coppename River, which has a basic tourist lodge. The closest town is Witagron, located where the road crosses the Coppename.

Nine-banded armadillo

Appendix

EMBASSIES AND CONSULATES
In Venezuela

Australia Av Francisco de Miranda with Av Sur, Altamira, Piso 1, Caracas; tel: 58 212 263 4033; fax: 58 212 261 3448; email: caracas@dfat.gov.au

Canada Av Francisco de Miranda with Av Sur, Altamira, Caracas 1062; tel: 58 212 264 0833; email: crcas@dfait-maeci.gc.ca

Netherlands Edificio San Juan, Piso 9, Av San Juan Bosco and Transversal 2, Altamira, Caracas; tel: 58 212 263 3622; fax: 58 212 263 0462; email: nlgovcar@internet.ve

UK Edif Torre Las Mercedes, Piso 3, Av La Estancia, Chuao; tel: 58 212 993 4111; fax: 58 212 993 9989; email: britishembassy@internet.ve

USA Calle S y Calle Suapure, Colinas de Valle Arriba, Caracas; PO Box 2291; tel: 58 2 977 2011

In Colombia

Australia Carrera 18, #90-38, Bogotá; tel: 57 1 218 0942; fax: 57 1 610 9790

Canada Carrera 7, #115-33, Bogotá; tel: 57 1 657 9800; fax: 57 1 657 9912; email: consular@bgota01.x400.gc.ca

Netherlands Carrera 13, #93-40, Piso 5, Bogotá; tel: 57 1 611 5080; fax: 57 1 623 3020; email: nlgovbog@colomsat.net.co

UK Edif ING Barings, Carrera 9, #76-49, piso 9, Bogotá; tel: 57 1 317 6690; fax: 57 1 317 6265; email: britain@cable.net.co

USA Calle 22D No 47-51, Bogotá; tel: 57 1 315 0811

In Ecuador

Australia Kennedy Norte, Edif Teciseguros, Calle San Roque and Av Francisco de Orellana; Guayaquil; tel: 593 4 680 823; fax: 593 4 682 008; email: presid@gye.satnet.net

Canada Edificio Josueth González, Av. 6 de Diciembre 2816 y Paul Rivet, piso 4, Quito; tel: 593 2 223 2114; fax: 593 2 250 3108; email: quito@dfait-maeci.gc.ca

Netherlands Netherlands Edif World Trade Center, Torre A, 1er piso, Av 12 de Octubre 1942 y Cordero; tel: 593 2 222 9229; fax: 593 2 2567917; email: nlgovqui@attglobal.net

UK Edif Citiplaza Building, piso 14, Av Naciones Unidas and Republica de El Salvador, Quito; tel: 593 2 297 0800; fax: 593 2 297 0809; email: britembq@impsat.net.ec

USA Av 12 de Octobre y Av Patria, Quito; tel: 593 2 562 890; fax: 593 2 250 2052

In Peru

Australia Av Victor Andres Belaunde #147, Via Principal #155, Edif Real Tres, Oficina 1301, San Isidro, Lima; tel: 51 1 222 8281; fax: 51 1 221 4996; email: infoperu@austrade.gov.au

Canada Calle Frederico Gerdes 130, before Libertad 130, Miraflores; tel: 51 1 444 4015; fax: 51 1 242 4050; email: lima@dfait-maeci.gc.ca

Netherlands Av Principal 190, piso 4, San Borja; tel: 51 1 476 1069; fax: 51 1 4756536; email: nlgovlim@terra.com.pe

UK Torre Parque Mar, piso 22, Av Jose Larco, 1301 Miraflores; tel: 51 1 617 3000; fax: 51 1 617 3100; email: britconsulate@terra.com.pe

USA Av La Encaldada cdra 17 s/n, Surco, Lima 33; tel: 51 1 434 3000; fax: 51 1 434 3037

In Bolivia

Australia Honorary Consul, Carlos Fernández, tel: 591 2 244 0459; fax: 591 2 244 0801; email: chf@wara.bolnet.bo

Netherlands Edif Hilda, piso 7, Av 6 de Agosto, La Paz; tel: 591 2 244 4040; fax: 591 2 244 3804; email: lap@minbuza.nl

UK Av Arce 2732, La Paz; tel: 591 2 243 3424; fax: 591 2 243 1073; email: ppa@mail.megalink.com

USA Av Arce 2780, La Paz; tel: 591 2 350120

In Brazil

Australia Ronaldo Veirano, Honorary Consul, Veirano and Associates, Av Presidente Wilson # 231, 23 floor, Rio de Janeiro; tel: 55 21 3824 4624; fax: 55 21 262 4247; email: honconau@terra.com.br

Canada Av Atlântica, 1130 - 5° andar, Atlântica Business Center, Copacabana, Rio de Janeiro: tel: tel: 55 21 2543 3004; fax: 55 21 2275 2195; email: rio@dfait-maeci.gc.ca

Netherlands Rua Miranda Leão 41, Manaus; tel: 55 92 622 1366; fax: 55 92 622 1354; email: ilko@bemol.com.br

UK Honorary Consul, Swedish Match da Amazônia; Rua Poraquê, 240; Distrito Industrial Manaus; tel: 55 92 613 1819; fax: 55 92 613 1420; email: vincent@internext.com.br

USA Av Nacoes, Lote 3, Brasilia; tel: 55 61 312 7000; web: www.embaixada-americana.org.br

In Guyana

Canada High and Young Streets, Georgetown, tel: 592 227 2081; fax: 592 225 8380; email: grgtn@dfait-maeci.gc.ca

UK 44 Main St, Georgetown; tel: 592 226 5881; fax: 592 225 3555; email: bhcguyana@solutions2000.net

USA 100 Young and Duke Streets; tel 592 225 4900; fax: 592 225 8497

In Suriname

Netherlands (serves Suriname, (French) Guiana and Guyana) van Roseveltkade 5, Paramaribo; tel: 597 477 211; fax: 597 477 792; email: nlgovprm@sr.net

UK c/o VSH United Buildings, Van't Hogerhuystraat 9-11, PO Box 1860, Paramaribo; tel: 597 402 558; fax: 597 403 515; email: united@sr.net

Appendix 2

LANGUAGE
English-Spanish glossary

A brief list of commonly used words and phrases with Spanish equivalents, including weekdays, months and numbers. Phonetic pronunciation is given for each word. The list gives a visitor with no knowledge of Spanish enough to get around, find luggage, ask the time, look for food and communicate other basic needs.

English	Español	Pronunciation (accent on underlined syllable)
hello	ola	<u>oh</u>-la
goodbye	adiós	ah-dee-<u>oss</u>
how are you?	¿como está usted?	<u>coh</u>-moh eh-<u>stah</u> ew-<u>stayd</u>
see you later	hasta luego	<u>a</u>stah lew-<u>ay</u>goh
good day	buenos días	boo-<u>ey</u>nohss <u>dee</u>-ahs
good afternoon	buenos tardes	boo-<u>ey</u>nohss <u>tarr</u>-dayz
good evening	buenos noches	boo-<u>ey</u>nohss <u>noh</u>-chayz
morning	mañana	man-<u>nya</u>-na
afternoon	tardes	<u>tarr</u>-dayz
evening	noches	<u>noh</u>-chayz
very good	muy bien	mwee bee-<u>en</u>
thank you	gracias	<u>grah</u>-see-ahs
please	por favor	pohr fah-<u>vor</u>
excuse me	perdóneme	pehr-<u>dohn</u>-ay-may
many thanks	muchas gracias	<u>moo</u>-chas <u>grah</u>-cee-yahs
yes	sí	see
no	no	noh
what is your name?	¿como se llama?	<u>koh</u>-moh say <u>jah</u>-mah
my name is…	mi nombre es…	mee <u>nohm</u>-bray ays
I don't understand	no comprendo	noh cohm-<u>prayn</u>-doh
do you speak…	Habla…	<u>a</u>-blah…
…English	…Inglés	…en-<u>glays</u>
I'm hungry	tengo hambre	<u>ten</u>-goh <u>am</u>-bray
how much?	¿quantos?	<u>kwahn</u>-tohss
that's expensive!	¡está caro!	eh-<u>stah</u> kar-oh
that's too much!	¡está todo mucho!	eh-<u>stah</u> toh-doh moo-cho
I want	quiero	kee-<u>eh</u>-ro
I don't want	no quiero	noh kee-<u>eh</u>-ro
I would like	quisiera	kee-see-<u>eh</u>-ra
I am lost	estoy puerde	eh-<u>stoy</u> <u>pwehr</u>-day
to the right	a la derecha	ah lah day-<u>ray</u>-chah
to the left	a la izquierda	ah lah eez-kwee-<u>ehr</u>-dah

where is...	¿donde está...?	dohn-day eh-stah...
restaurant	el restaurante	el reh-staw-rahn-tay
bathroom	el baño	el bahn-yo
hotel	el hotel	el oh-tehl
bedroom	la habitación	la ab-ih-tas-yon
towel	la ropa	la roh-pah
soap	el jabón	el zhah-bohn
telephone	el teléfono	el tay-lay-foh-noh
currency exchange	la casa de cambio	la kasah deh cahm-bee-oh
bank	el banco	el bahn-coh
river	el río	el ree-oh
forest	la selva	la sehl-bah
airport	el aeropuerto	el ahy-roh-pwahr-toh
Indian village	el pueblo de los Indios	el poo-weh-bloh day loss een-dee-oss
boat	la barca	la bar-kah
bus station	stación del autobús	stah-see-ohn dehl ow-too-boos
street	la avenida	la ah-vehn-eedah
house	la casa	la cah-sah
guide	el guía	el gee-yah
luggage	equipaje	eh-kee-pah-hey
what time is it?	¿que hora es?	kay orah ays
what time is...	¿que hora...	kay orah...
the meal	la comida	la koh-midh-ah
breakfast	desayuno	day-say-ooh-noh
lunch	almuerzo	ahl-moo-ehrt-soh
dinner	cena	say-nah
what is your...	que es su...	kay ays soo...
phone number?	número de teléfono?	nume-eh-row day tay-lay-foh-noh
address	dirección	dee-rek-shee-yon

Weekdays — **Días laborables**

Sunday	domingo	doh-min-goh
Monday	lunes	loo-ness
Tuesday	martes	mahr-tess
Wednesday	miércoles	mee-ehr-coh-less
Thursday	jueves	hoo-ay-bess
Friday	viernes	bee-err-ness
Saturday	sábado	sah-bah-doh

Months — **Meses**

January	Enero	ay-nay-rho
February	Febrero	fay-bray-roh
March	Marzo	mahrso
April	Abril	ab-reel
May	Mayo	my-oh
June	Junio	hoo-nee-oh
July	Julio	hoo-lee-oh
August	Agosto	ow-go-stoh
September	Septiembre	sayp-tee-aym-bray
October	Octubre	ock-too-bray
November	Noviembre	noh-bee-aym-bray
December	Diciembre	day-see-aym-bray

Numbers	**Números**	
zero	*cero*	zay-roh
one	*uno*	<u>oo</u>-noh
two	*dos*	dohs
three	*tres*	trayss
four	*cuatro*	<u>kwat</u>-roh
five	*cinco*	<u>seen</u>-koh
six	*seis*	says
seven	*siete*	see-<u>aytay</u>
eight	*ocho*	<u>oh</u>-cho
nine	*nueve*	noo-<u>ay</u>-bay
ten	*diez*	<u>dee</u>-ayz
eleven	*once*	<u>ohn</u>-say
twelve	*doce*	<u>doh</u>-say
thirteen	*trece*	<u>tray</u>-say
fourteen	*catorce*	kaht-<u>ohr</u>-zay
fifteen	*quince*	<u>keen</u>-zay
sixteen	*diez-y-seis*	<u>dee</u>-ayz ee <u>says</u>
seventeen	*diez-y-siete*	<u>dee</u>-ayz ee see-<u>aytay</u>
eighteen	*diez-y-ocho*	<u>dee</u>-ayz ee <u>oh</u>-cho
nineteen	*diez-y-nueve*	<u>dee</u>-ayz ee <u>noo-ay</u>-bay
twenty	*veinte*	bay-<u>ihn</u>-tay
twenty-one	*veinte-y-uno*	bay-<u>ihn</u>-tay ee <u>oon</u>-o
thirty	*treinta*	<u>trayn</u>-ta
forty	*cuarenta*	kwahr-<u>ehn</u>-ta
fifty	*cincuenta*	seen-<u>kwen</u>-tay
sixty	*sesenta*	says-<u>ehn</u>-ta
seventy	*setenta*	say-<u>tehn</u>-ta
eighty	*ochenta*	oh-<u>chen</u>-ta
ninety	*noventa*	noh-<u>ben</u>-ta
one hundred	*cien*	<u>see</u>-ehn
two hundred	*doscientos*	dhos see-<u>ehn</u>-toss
one thousand	*mil*	meehl
one million	*millón*	meeh-jee-<u>ohn</u>

English-Portuguese glossary

A brief list of commonly used words and phrases with Brazilian Portuguese equivalents, including weekdays, months and numbers. Phonetic pronunciation is given for each word. The list gives a visitor with no knowledge of Portuguese enough to get around, find luggage, ask the time, look for food and communicate other basic needs.

Stress

If a word ends in a vowel with a tilde (~), stress the last syllable, unless another vowel in the word is accented.

If a vowel has an acute (´) or circumflex (^) accent, stress that vowel no matter where in the word it comes.

If a word ends in r, stress the last syllable, unless there's an accented vowel somewhere else.

Otherwise, in words of two or more syllables, stress the penultimate vowel.

English	**Português**	**Pronunciation**
hello	*olá!*	ol-<u>lah</u>
goodbye	*adeus!*	er-deoosh

cheerio	*tchau!*	chow
how are you?	*como vai?*	comb-oh v-eye
see you later	*até breve!*	er-teh-brev
good day	*bom dia!*	bom <u>dee</u>-er
good afternoon	*boa tarde!*	<u>bow</u>-ah <u>tar</u>dee
good evening	*boa noite!*	bow-ah noy-chee
morning	*manhã*	mer-nyah
afternoon	*tarde*	targee
evening	*noite*	noy-chee
very good	*muito bem*	mween-too bem
thank you	*obrigado/a*	oh-bree-gah-do/dah
please	*por favor*	poor fah-vor
excuse me	*desculpe*	dish-koolp
many thanks	*muito obrigado/a*	mween-too obri-ga-doo/er
yes	*sim*	seem
no	*não*	nawm
what is your name?	*¿como se chama?*	koo-moo set sha-mmer
my name is...	*chamo-me...*	sha-moo mer
I don't understand	*não entendo*	nawm ayn-tay-doa
do you speak...	*fala...*	fa-ler
...English	*...Inglês*	een-glaysh
I'm hungry	*estou com fome*	e-stoo com fom
how much?	*¿quanto custa?*	kwan-too cush-ter
that's expensive!	*e caro*	eh ka-roo
that's too much!	*muito caro*	mween-too karoo
I want...	*queria...*	ker-ree-er
I don't want...	*no queria...*	No ker-ree-er
I am lost	*estou perdido/a*	ish-toh per-dee-doo/er
to the right	*á direita*	a dee-ray-ter
to the left	*á esquerda*	a ishkairder
where is the...	*onde é...*	ond eh.....
restaurant	*o restaurante*	o rish-tow-rawnt
bathroom	*a banho*	a ba-nyoo
toilet	*a banheiro*	a bah-nyay-ro
the hotel	*o hotel*	o ot-tehl
bedroom	*o quarto da dormir*	o kwar-too der door-meer
towel	*a toalha*	a too-al-yer
soap	*o sabonete*	o ser-boo-nayt
the telephone	*o telefone*	o ter-ler-fon
currency exchange	*o câmbio*	o kawm-byoo
bank	*o banco*	o bawn-koo
river	*o rio*	o ree-oo
forest	*a mata/a floresta*	a floo-resh-ter
village	*a aldeia*	a al-dag-ea
airport	*o aeroporto*	o eh-ro-poartoo
boat	*o barco*	o bar-koo
bus station	*a rodoviária*	a hodo-vyar-rhea
street	*a rua*	a rhu-a
house	*a casa*	a ka-saa
guide	*a guia*	a gee-er
luggage	*a bagagem*	a ber-gaz-haym
can you tell me the time?	*dizia-me as horas*	dee-zee-er mer er zor-ush

a meal	*comida*	co-mee-dah
breakfast	*café da manhã*	ka-feh dah man-yah
lunch	*almoço*	al-moa-soo
dinner	*jantar*	yan-tar
can I have your…	*pode dar-me o seu…*	pod dar-mer oo se-oo
phone number?	*número de telefone?*	noo-me-roo der ter-ler-fon
address?	*endereço?*	arn-der ray-soo

Weekdays / Dias

Sunday	*domingo*	doo-meen-goo
Monday	*segunda-feira*	ser-goon-der fay-rer
Tuesday	*terça-feira*	tart-ser fay-rer
Wednesday	*quarta-feira*	kwar-ter fay-rer
Thursday	*quinta-feira*	keen-ter fay-rer
Friday	*sexta-feira*	says-ter fay-rer
Saturday	*sábada*	sa-ber doo

Months / Meses

January	*janeiro*	zher nayroo
February	*fevereiro*	fer ver ray-roo
March	*março*	mar-soo
April	*abril*	er-brill
May	*maio*	mig-hoo
June	*junho*	zhoo-nyoo
July	*julho*	zhoo-lyoo
August	*agosto*	er-goash-too
September	*setembro*	staym-dro
October	*outubro*	oh-too-broo
November	*novembro*	noo-vaymbroo
December	*dezembro*	der-zaym-broo

Numbers / Números

zero	*zero*	ze-hroo
one	*um/uma*	oom/er
two	*dois/duas*	doysh
three	*três*	traysh
four	*quatro*	ka-troo
five	*cinco*	seen-koh
six	*seis*	saysh
seven	*sete*	set
eight	*oito*	oy-too
nine	*nove*	nov
ten	*dez*	desh
eleven	*onze*	onz
twelve	*doze*	doaz
thirteen	*treze*	trays
fourteen	*catorze*	ker-toarz
fifteen	*quinze*	keenz
sixteen	*dezesseis*	dzer-saysh
seventeen	*dezessete*	dzer-set
eighteen	*dezoito*	dzoy-too
nineteen	*dezenove*	dzer-nov

twenty	*vinte*	veent
twenty-one	*vinte e um/uma*	veen-tee oom/er
thirty	*trinta*	treen-ter
forty	*quarenta*	kwer-rayn-ter
fifty	*cinqüenta*	seenkwayn-ter
sixty	*sessenta*	ser sayn-ter
seventy	*setenta*	ser tayn-ter
eighty	*oitenta*	oy tayn-ter
ninety	*noventa*	noo vayn-ter
one hundred	*cem*	saym
two hundred	*duzentos/as*	doo-zayn toosh/ush
one thousand	*mil*	meel
one million	*um milhão*	oom mee-lyawn

Appendix 3

FURTHER READING

See www.junglephotos.com/links for a complete list of over 200 Amazon-related books in print.

Travelogues

Angus, C, *Amazon Extreme: Three Ordinary Guys, One Rubber Raft, and Most Dangerous River on Earth*, Broadway Books (2002). Five-month endurance test by three inexperienced rafters shouldn't put you off rafting with established tour operators.

Clark L, *The Rivers Ran East: Travelers' Tales Classics*, Travelers' Tales Inc. (2001). Reprint of classic adventure stories by explorer looking for lost cities in the Peruvian Amazon.

Chapman S, *The Monster of the Madidi, Searching for the giant ape of the Bolivian Jungle*, Aurum Press, London (2002). A colourful personal account of experiences in Bolivia's underexplored wildernesses.

Cousteau, J Y and Richards, M, *Jaques Cousteau's Amazon Journey*, Harry N Abrams, New York (1984). A coffee table book replete with colour photos telling the story of Cousteau's 1981 Amazon expedition.

Fawcett, Col P H, *Exploration Fawcett*. Hutchinson, London (1st edn, 1953). Reprint Century, London (1988). Follows the legendary explorers travels in the lowlands of Bolivia and his ultimate disappearance in Mato Grosso.

Ghinsberg, Y, *Back from Tuichi*, Random House, New York (1993). The true story of an Israeli who went missing for three weeks in the jungles of Bolivia.

Gott, R, *Land without Evil, Utopian journeys across the South American watershed*, Verso, London, (1993). Travel and history of the eastern lowlands of Bolivia – most in-depth treatment to date.

Gordon, N, *Tarantulas, Marmosets and Other Stories: An Amazon Diary*, Metro, London (1997). A highly readable account of travelling in the rainforests of Venezuela and Brazil based on the author's wildlife filming.

Harrison, J, *Off the map*, Summersdale Travel, Chichester (2001). John Harrison was travelling on Amazon rivers when most of us were in babies. This entertaining book covers a trip down his beloved Jari with his wife Heather. Excellent for so many reasons.

Harrison, J, *Up the Creek*, Bradt Publications, London (1986). Out of print, but essential reading for anyone planning an independent canoe trip who needs a little preparation.

Jordan, Tanis and Martin, *Out of Chingford*, Frederick Muller, London (1988). Scary, awe-inspiring and hilarious, journeys by inflatable boat in Peru, Suriname and Venezuela..

Kane, Joe, *Running the Amazon*, Knopf, New York; Pan, London (1997). Classic account of the full-length voyage by kayak. Essential reading for anyone doing whitewater trips in the upper Amazon.

Kelly, B and London M, *Amazon*, Harcourt, Brace Jovanovich, New York (1983). Travelling the main stream by plane and boat during the pre-tourist boom era in the 1970s, with chapters on Iquitos and Leticia at the time.

Lutz, R L, and Lutz, D, *The Hidden Amazon: The Greatest Voyage in Natural History*, Dimi Press (1998). International Expeditions' tours on Pacaya-Samiria riverboats and to Explorama's canopy walkway.

MacCreagh, G, *White Waters and Black*, University of Chicago Press (2001). Humorous account of a 1923 scientific expedition to the upper Amazon where everything seems to go wrong.

Morrison, T, *Lizzie: A Victorian Lady's Amazon Adventure*, BBC, London (1985). Follows the journey of Lizzie Mathys who travelled with her husband up the Amazon through Peru, taking the Madre de Dios to reach Bolivia and work for the rubber baron Nicholás Suárez.

O'Hanlon, R, *In trouble again: A journey between the Orinoco and the Amazon*, Penguin, London (1997). The author's detailed account of travels in the Venezuelan rainforest.

Shoumatoff, A, *The Rivers Amazon*. Sierra Club Books, San Francisco, (1986). The author's tale covers his voyage up the full length of the Amazon from its mouth to Pucallpa, Peru.

Starkell, D, *Paddle to the Amazon: The Ultimate 12,000-Mile Canoe Adventure*, McClelland & Stewart (1999). Astonishing true story of a father and son's canoeing trip from Canada to the mouth of the Amazon.

Van Dyk, J, *The Amazon*, National Geographic 187: 2-39 (1995). The author describes a riverboat journey along the full length of the Amazon.

History

Gheerbrant, A, *The Amazon: Past, Present and Future*, Harry N Abrams, New York (1992). Well-written and beautifully illustrated book that tells the story of the Amazon from its early discovery to the present day. Has a full chronology of events in Amazonia, mostly in Brazil.

Hemming, J, *Red Gold: The Conquest of the Brazilian Indians*. Macmillan, London (1978). A detailed and highly readable historical analysis of the exploitation of the Indians of Brazil and the Amazon.

Hemming, J, *Amazon Frontier: The Defeat of the Brazilian Indians*, Macmillan, London (1987). Continuing the story set in *Red Gold* explaining the continued decimation of the Indians of the Amazon from 1755 up to 1910.

Muscutt, K, *Warriors of the Clouds: A Lost Civilization in the Upper Amazon of Peru*, University of New Mexico Press (1998). Illustrated well-written text places the Chachapoya or Cloud Forest people in the larger context of Andean prehistory.

Smith, A , *Explorers of the Amazon*, Viking/Penguin, New York (1990). The most comprehensive history of the Amazon from early discoverers to the rubber boom.

The Latin American Bureau have an *In Focus* series providing a guide to the people, politics and culture of each country bordering the Amazon Basin. International mail order available. Contact Latin America Bureau (LAB), 1 Amwell Street, London EC1R 1UL; tel 0171 278 2829.

Ethnology

Allen, R, *Amazon Dream*, City Lights, San Francisco (1993). A first-hand account of the author's travels to Pucallpa, Peru, to study the pottery of the Shipobo tribe living along the upper Marañon.

Chagnon, N, *Yanomami: The Last Days of Eden*, Harcourt Brace Jovanovich, New York (1992). A French anthropologist gives an excellent sympathetic account of this Indian tribe living in the remote forests of southern Venezuela and Brazil.

Descola, P, *The Spears of Twilight: Life and Death in the Amazon Jungle*, Flamingo, London (1997). A detailed insight into the life of the Achuar Indians of Ecuador based on the anthropologist author's two years spent living close to the banks of the Pastazo.

Plotkin, M J, *Tales of a Shaman's Apprentice: An Ethnobotanist Searches for New Medicines in the Amazon Rain Forest*, Penguin Books, New York (1994) Account of medicinal plants used by various tribes and prospects for curing major diseases.

Popescu, P, *Amazon Beaming*, Penguin, New York (1992). Describes the author's adventures among the 'Cat People' Amazon tribe of southern Venezuela.

Tidwell, M, *Amazon Stranger*, Lyons Press, New York (1997). A reporter's touching account told with wit and sensitivity of the Cofan, a small Ecuadorian Indian tribe, and their American chief's battle to save the Cuyabeno Reserve from the big oil companies.

Up de Graff, F W, *Headhunters of the Amazon: Seven Years of Exploration and Adventure*, Garden City Books, New York (1923). A fascinating account of the upper Amazon at the beginning of the 20th century, including descriptions of Iquitos at the time, as well as graphic descriptions of the now-outlawed practice of headhunting.

Wheeler, J, *The Adventurer's Guide*, David MacKay Inc, New York (1976). Describes, among other things, the author's year-long experience living with Shuar Indians of the Ecuadorian Amazon. Lots of detailed information on how he prepared for his adventure.

Conservation

Caufield, C, *In the Rainforest: Report from a Strange, Beautiful, Imperiled World*, University of Chicago Press, Chicago (1984). This book highlights the causes and consequences of rainforest destruction, with emphasis on the fate of the Amazon.

Cousteau, J Y, *The Cousteau Almanac: An Inventory of Life on Our Water Planet*. Doubleday, New York (1981). An encyclopaedic source of information on all aspects of the aquatic realm, with comparative data on the world's rivers and a useful section on Amazon conservation.

Collinson, H (ed), *Green Guerillas*, Latin American Bureau, London (1996). A study of environmental conflicts and initiatives in Latin America and the Caribbean with several chapters looking specifically at the Amazon.

Fisher, R (ed), *The Emerald Realm: Earth's Precious Rainforests*, National Geographic Society, Washington DC (1990). A general treatment of rainforests, with lots of beautiful photos to illustrate brief but informative articles by separate authors on ecology, tribes, uses and conservation of rainforest worldwide.

Hecht, S and Cockburn, A, *The Fate of the Forest: Developers, Destroyers and Defenders of the Amazon*, HarperCollins, New York (1990). Rainforest conservation is the major theme of this outstanding book in which the authors do a fine job of untangling the knotty issues and personalities.

Lewis, S, *The Rainforest Book*, Living Planet Press, Berkeley Books, New York (1990). Accessible to school-age children, this is a useful source book on rainforest conservation issues.

O'Connor, G, *Amazon Journal: Dispatches from a Vanishing Frontier*, Plume Books (1998). Unbiased documentary of consequences of modern encroachment on the Brazilian Amazon.

Slater, C, *Entangled Edens: Visions of the Amazon*, University of California Press (2001). Impassioned and well-reasoned plea to emphasise conservation of Amazon cultures as well as natural resources.

Stone, R, *Dreams of Amazonia* (2nd edn), Penguin Books, New York (1993). The author uses the theme of failed megaprojects in Amazonia to illustrate the futility of unbridled development of rainforest habitat.

White, P T, *Nature's Dwindling Treasures: Rain Forests*, National Geographic 163: 2-48 (1983). An article sounding a relatively early warning alarm of rapidly increasing destruction of tropical rainforests.

Natural history

Ayres, J M, *Scarlet Faces of the Amazon*, Natural History 3/90:33-40 (1990). An article describing research on the red uakari, an unusual and very rare monkey living only in flooded forests of western Brazil.

Bates, H W, *The Naturalist on the River Amazons*, University of California Press, Riverside (1962). A classic Victorian travelogue and natural history of the author's years spent in Brazil during the middle of the 19th century.

Campbell, J A and Lamar, W W, The venomous reptiles of the Western Hemisphere. Cornell University Press, Ithaca, New York (2003). 1,000 pages in two volumes with 1,500 colour photographs, 225 black-and-white figures and 131 distribution maps. Systematics, natural history, ecology and medical aspects for all of the venomous reptiles of the Americas - a must for any serious student of herpetology, for medical and military personnel and ecotourists.

Castner, J L, *Amazon Insects: A Photo Guide*, Feline Press (2000) Pocket guide to common insects, but not comprehensive.

Conniff, R, *Tarantulas*, National Geographic 190: 98-115 (1996). Fascinating article on physiology and ecology of giant Amazon spiders.

Duke, J A and Vasquez, R, *Amazonian Ethnobotanical Dictionary*, CRC Press, Boca Raton, FL (1994). Essential research material for those interested in native use of wild plants, containing a list of some 1,400 plant species, each with a description of ailments treated.

Emmons, L H, *Neotropical Rainforest Mammals: a Field Guide*. Chicago University Press, Chicago (1990). A must for scientists and naturalist-guides interested in Amazon mammals. Every known mammal species is fully described and illustrated in colour or black-and-white, with scientific name.

Forsyth, A and Miyata, K, *Tropical Nature: Life and Death in the Rainforests of Central and South America*, Scribner & Sons, New York (1984). Just about the most readable text on tropical rainforest ecology and evolution. The authors draw on extensive experience in Ecuadorian and Costa Rican rainforests to paint a dramatic and sometimes amusing picture of the inner workings of tropical plants and animals.

Clements, J F and Shany, N, *A Field Guide to the Birds of Peru*, Ibis Publishing (2001). Long-awaited but disappoints compared with Ecuador and Colombia bird guides. Read reviews before buying.

Gentry, A H and Forsyth A G, *A Field Guide to the Families and Genera of Woody Plants of Northwest South America*, University of Chicago Press (1996). Encyclopaedic treatment of Amazon flora by two of the foremost experts. For serious amateur botanists and scientists.

Goulding, M, *Amazon: The Flooded Forest*, Sterling Publishing Co., New York (1990). Based on a BBC documentary series, this book is written for the layman (eg: no scientific names) interested in the flooded forest habitats of the Amazon.

Goulding, M, *Floods of Fortune: Ecology & Economy along the Amazon*, University of Columbia Press (1995). Comprehensive review of the Amazon's riparian ecology and what will be lost if economic development destroys it.

Hallé, F, *A Raft Atop the Rainforest*, National Geographic 178: 128-138 (1990). A Frenchman describes his new technique for exploring the rainforest canopy in French Guiana.

Hilty, S L and Brown W L, *A Guide to the Birds of Colombia*, Princeton University Press, Princeton, NJ (1986). Although it technically covers only Colombia, this is the most comprehensive field guide (some 1,500 species described with hundreds of colour drawings) of the upper Amazon avifauna and will be useful for birdwatchers visiting Ecuador and Peru.

Kricher, J C, *A Neotropical Companion*, (2nd edn), Princeton University Press, Princeton, NJ (1997). Written for the informed layman, it offers useful insights into rainforest ecology and evolution.

Line, L, *Silence of the Songbirds*. National Geographic 183: 68-91 (1993). A sobering article on how migratory songbirds are declining in population due to deforestation in Latin American rainforests.

Marshall, E, *A deadly parasite spurs up-to-the-minute biology*, Science 267:811 (1995a). A summary report on the status of Brazilian research into Chagas' disease, transmitted by a biting insect.

Marshall, E, *Homely fish draws attention to Amazon deforestation*, Science 267:814 (1995b). This short article describes the present status of fisheries in the middle Amazon, with special reference to the highly sought fish called tambaqui.

Moffett, M W, *The High Frontier: Exploring the Tropical Rainforest Canopy*, Harvard University Press, Cambridge, MA (1993). A scientifically rigorous and excellently written text describing the latest research on the biodiversity, ecology and evolution of the rainforest canopy, with examples from the Amazon and Latin America.

Moffett, M W, *Poison-dart Frogs: Lurid and Lethal*. National Geographic 187: 98-111 (1995a).

Moffett, M W, *Gardeners of the Ant World*. National Geographic Vol. 188: 98-111 (1995b).

Montgomery, S, *Journey of the Pink Dolphins: An Amazon Quest*, Simon & Schuster, New York (2000). Naturalist and columnist's lyrical account of the myths, legends and biology of the cetaceans.

Munn, C A, *Winged Rainbows: Macaws*. National Geographic 185: 118-140 (1994). A summary of recent research into the ecology and conservation of scarlet macaws at Tambopata Reserve in Peru.

Murawski, D A, *Passion Vine Butterflies: a Taste for Poison*. National Geographic 184: 122-137 (1993). The author describes her studies into the ecology of Heliconiid butterflies and their evolutionary interaction with their host plant.

Pearson, D L, et al., *Brazil - Amazon and Pantanal (A Volume in the Ecotravellers' Wildlife Guides Series)* Academic Press (2001). Information on the most frequently seen animals, including identification, ecology, behavior, and conservation.

Prance, G T and Lovejoy, T E, *Amazonia*, Pergamon Press, New York & London (1985). An excellent photo-essay of the Amazon's floral and fauna wealth, written by two of the world's foremost tropical biologists.

Rettig, N, *Remote World of the Harpy Eagle*. National Geographic 187:40-49 (1995). Describes the ecology and conservation status of the Amazon's largest bird of prey.

Ridgely, R S and Greenfield, P J, *The Birds of Ecuador*, Comstock Publishing Association (2001). Illustrated encyclopaedic guide to Ecuador's avifauna. Rather heavy as a field guide but serious birdwatchers should consider it as an alternative to Hilty and Brown's Birds of Colombia.

Smith, A, *Science on the Amazon*. Viking, New York (2000). Thorough account of scientific research conducted in Amazonia.

Smith, N. *The Amazon River Forest: A Natural History of Plants, Animals, & People*, Oxford University Press (1999). Authoritative exploration of ecological, historical, cultural, and socioeconomic issues, with practical suggestions for developing the Amazon floodplain to enhance, rather than destroy, biodiversity.

Wheatley, N, *Where to watch birds in South America*, Princeton University Press (1995). A comprehensive guide to birds and the best birding sites throughout the Amazon and South America.

Wilson, E O, *Rain Forest Canopy: the High Frontier*, National Geographic 180: 78-107 (1991). Excellent introductory material to the structure and function of the canopy layer of rainforest.

Wilson, E O, *The Diversity of Life*, W W Norton, New York (1992). The founder of sociobiology and world's foremost ant expert takes a broad perspective to show the importance of biodiversity, with several useful examples from Amazonia.

Travel guides

If you intend staying in one country a long time and travelling beyond the Amazon, you will find a country-specific guide useful as these cover areas outside the Amazon Basin. Bradt's travel guides cover general travel information to specific countries (eg: A Bradbury, *Guide to Brazil,* and H Dunsterville Branch, *Guide to Venezuela*) or specific activities within a country (eg: R Rachowiecki, *Climbing and Hiking in Ecuador*). Footprint (Bath, England) publish the *South American Handbook,* lovingly referred to as 'The Bible' by many travellers. They have country guides giving information on virtually everything.

Most countries have been covered by Lonely Planet. These guides emphasise information on accommodation, eating out and transport and really help you stretch your travel dollar.

Insight Guides' *Amazon Wildlife*, and their country guides have lovely photographs, but the information is very selective and practical travel information is somewhat limited. Other Amazon travel guides include Pamela Bloom's *The Amazon Up Close* (1997, Hunter Publishing) and Cadogan's *The Amazon* (2000) by Robinson et al. *The Green Travel Sourcebook* (1992, D and S W Grotta, John Wiley & Sons) is for travellers who want information on environmentally conscious travel. It would benefit from an update.

WEBSITES
List of websites

Sites are in English unless otherwise noted. Broadly speaking, the general list follows the structure of the book – background-related sites are first, followed by travel planning sites, natural history sites, and then sites of miscellaneous interest.

Hint To read foreign language sites in English copy the URL and go to Google. Click on 'Language Tools' and paste the URL into the 'Translate a web page' window. Select the language you want to translate from (eg: Spanish to English), click on 'Translate' and Google will automatically translate the page for you. It's not perfect, but you'll get the idea – and the occasional laugh! (For example: In order to sail by the different pages, it uses the menu of down. Meaning: to surf this site scroll down the menu.)

General

www.worldairportguide.com Information on airport facilities worldwide.
www.MapQuest.com Printable maps of locations around the world.
www.wunderground.com Weather forecasts for virtually any city in the world.
www.latinamericapress.org Award-winning journalism on Latin America.
www.planeta.com Award winning information resources that covers environmental issues.
forests.org Worldwide forest biodiversity campaign news.
www.nativeweb.org International, nonprofit, educational organization with information about indigenous nations, peoples, and organizations.
www.Ayahuasca.com A reference site reflecting the growing global interest in ayahuasca and traditional South American shamanism.
www.junglephotos.com Amazon plants, animals, people and conservation photos and information from Roger Harris, co-author of this guide.
babelfish.altavista.com/tr Among the fastest and most accurate autotranslation websites.

Countries
Venezuela

www.venezuela.gov.ve website of the Venezuelan government - good source of official information.
www.auyantepui.com Venezuela's very own Yahoo style search engine, packed with information.

www.eluniversal.com For the most up-to-date news from one of the country's leading newspapers.

www.inparques.gov.ve Overview of national parks, national monuments and news updates to keep in touch with developments.

Colombia

www.ColombiaUpdate.com Excellent site for latest news on happenings in Colombia, with log entries from people who have visited there.

www.webcolombia.com/parks Comprehensive list of Colombia national parks with descriptions and travel information.

www.colombiaemb.org Colombian Embassy in the US, covers economy and culture, US-Colombia relations, and travel and visa information.

www.presidencia.gov.co Official government presidency site covers government, history, geography, human rights issues, and policy on drug policy.

Ecuador

www.ecuadordaily.com Latest news on happenings in Ecuador and Latin America.

www.ecuadordiscover.com Helpful details on planning minutiae for trips to Ecuador.

www.vivecuador.com Official Ministry of Tourism site. Easy to navigate. Overview and details on destinations, trails, travel updates, and directories of hotels, restaurants, tour operators, etc.

www.igm.gov.ec Official site of Instituto Geografico Militar — source of official maps and geographical information.

www.ecuador-adventure.com Encyclopedic source of information on all things Ecuadorian.

Peru

www.cusco.info Comprehensive site for travel to Peru and Cuzco. Package tours, hotel booking, Inca trail hikes, travel information.

www.peru.org.pe Official government site: useful data for travelers, travel FAQ, weather, accommodation, travel agents, restaurants and other tourist services, tourism for people with disabilities.

www.perulinks.com Peru links directory — most complete index of Peru web links. Lists around 800 Peru-related sites including over 200 travel sites.

www.peru.com/peruinfo/ingles/index.html Comprehensive information about Peru including history, geography, statistics and useful sections on each department.

www.andeantravelweb.com The most comprehensive site on travel in Peru. Excellent.

www.projectamazonas.com Non-profit research, conservation, education and humanitarian-oriented organization with operations in the upper Amazon.

Bolivia

www.boliviangeographic.com A slowly building attempt to record the many facets of Bolivian geographic life.

www.boliviaweb.com Bolivia based search engine that should help point you in the right direction.

www.boliviantimes.com Bolivia's English-language newspaper. Not packed with content but a good starting point.

www.la-razon.com National newspaper with good, broad coverage.

Brazil

www.amazonia.org.br Packed with general Amazon information, travel, conservation updates, news, economics, science, photos, videos and lots more.

brazil.start4all.com Everything from Brazil: travel, news, sport, books, culture, carnival, etc.

www.manaustur.com.br City of Manaus official website.

belem.cybercityguides.com Belem city guide and hotels.

Guyana, French Guiana and Suriname

www.guyana.com Official Site of extensive links and information.

www.cguyana.com Index of links to information about Guyana.

www.guyanainfoline.com Guyana and its people, news, business, travel, education.

www.maintour.com/frguyana/homepage.htm Preview French Guiana hotels, attractions, recreation, and special events.

www.surinfo.org On-line travel guide to Suriname.

lanic.utexas.edu/la/sa/suriname Links to Suriname-related sites.

Index

Page numbers in bold refer to major entries; those in italics indicate maps